Cape Breton & Prince Edward Island Fiddle Tunes for Clawhammer Banjo

136 Note-for-Note Authentic Banjo Arrangements in Clear Tablature

by Ken Perlman

Collected by Ken directly from master fiddlers, painstakingly adapted to banjo, and recorded by him on these four solo CDs:*

- *Devil in the Kitchen*
- *Frails & Frolics*
- *Island Boy*
- *Northern Banjo*

** Most audio illustrations for the tunes in this book are drawn directly from these recordings.*

Plus instruction on basic and advanced techniques; fingering diagrams & detailed fingering suggestions; a systematic approach to playing up-the-neck; a thorough treatment of playing triplets, grace notes, and other characteristic ornaments in clawhammer; guides on how to approach reels, hornpipes, jigs, strathspeys, marches, and other tune genres; and a framework for understanding the modes you'll encounter in fiddle music. Rounding out the volume are historical notes on the tunes and musical traditions, plus biographical information on source fiddlers.

Online Audio

For audio of Ken playing all the tunes, exercises and most musical examples in this book, go to:
www.melbay.com/31054MEB

WWW.MELBAY.COM

I0805596

Acknowledgments

Many Thanks . . .

* **For Financial Support of the Prince Edward Island Collecting Projects:** *The Canadian Museum of History; The Earthwatch Organization; the Estate of Bishop Faber MacDonald, & Robertson Library, University of P.E.I.*

* **For Material Support of the the Prince Edward Island Projects:** *Eddy Arsenault, Georges Arsenault, Peter Arsenault, Hélène Arsenault Bergeron, Kevin Chaisson, "Young Peter" Chaisson, "Fr. Charlie" Cheverie, My Earthwatch Teams, Dan Gillis, The Iona Foundation, The Institute of Island Studies, Philippe Leblanc, Richard Lepage, Allan MacDonald, Ward MacDonald, Edward MacDonald, Margaret Ross MacKinnon, George MacPhee, Leonard McDonald, Gail Mullen, The P.E.I. Fiddlers' Society, Attwood O'Connor, Denise Reiser, Alan Stanley, Archie Stewart, Amy Swenson, Teresa MacPhee Wilson, & many more. . .*

* **For Introducing me to Cape Breton Fiddle Music:** *The Canadian-American Club of Watertown, Massachusetts & The Boston Scottish Fiddle Club*

* **For Help Navigating Copyrights and Obtaining Tune Permissions:** *Paul Cranford of Cranford Publications; also Gordon Aucoin & Janine Randall*

* **For Tune Permissions:** *Peter Arsenault & the Arsenault family (for Eddy Arsenault); J.D. Cameron (for Dan R. MacDonald); Patricia Chafe; The Gordon Duncan Foundation; Lowell Frizzell (for Lillian Frizzell); Roberta Head (for Jerry Holland); Lyndon MacKenzie (for Carl MacKenzie); Howie MacDonald; & Brian Mitton (for Earl Mitton)*

* **For Photo Permissions:** *Cranford Publications; Mike Hird; & Robertson Library, University of P.E.I.*

* **Cover Photos: Ken Perlman** *by R.L. Geyer*; **Prince Edward Island North Shore** *by Ken Perlman*

* For **General Help and Support:** *Andrea Kronman*

. . . And Hearty Thanks to the Fiddlers of Prince Edward Island for Their Music, Stories, & Kindness

About Ken Perlman

Ken Perlman is a pioneer of the 5-string banjo style known as melodic clawhammer; he is considered one of the top clawhammer players in the world, known in particular for his skillful adaptations of Appalachian, Celtic, & Canadian fiddle tunes to the style. He has toured throughout most of the English-speaking world and in Western Europe, both as a soloist and – for fifteen years – in a duo with renowned Appalachian-style fiddler Alan Jabbour. An acclaimed teacher of folk-music instrumental skills, Ken has written some of the most widely respected banjo and guitar instruction books of modern times, was a regular columnist for *Banjo Newsletter* for nearly forty years, and has taught at prestigious music camps and teaching festivals around the world. Ken founded and has also served as director for several music-instruction events; he currently directs American Banjo Camp, Midwest Banjo Camp, and Suwannee Banjo Camp. Also an independent folklorist, Ken spent well over two decades collecting tunes and oral histories from traditional fiddle players on Prince Edward Island. On the basis of these experiences he published the tune collection, *The Fiddle Music of Prince Edward Island: Celtic & Acadian Tunes in Living Tradition* (Mel Bay), and the ethnography, *Couldn't Have a Wedding Without the Fiddler: The Story of Traditional Fiddling on Prince Edward Island* (University of Tennessee Press). He has also produced several anthology recordings devoted to Prince Edward Island fiddling, and served as curator for *bowingdownhome.ca,* a website based on the field recordings he collected. Ken's most recent CD is *Frails & Frolics*; his latest book is *Appalachian Fiddle Tunes for Clawhammer Banjo* (Mel Bay).

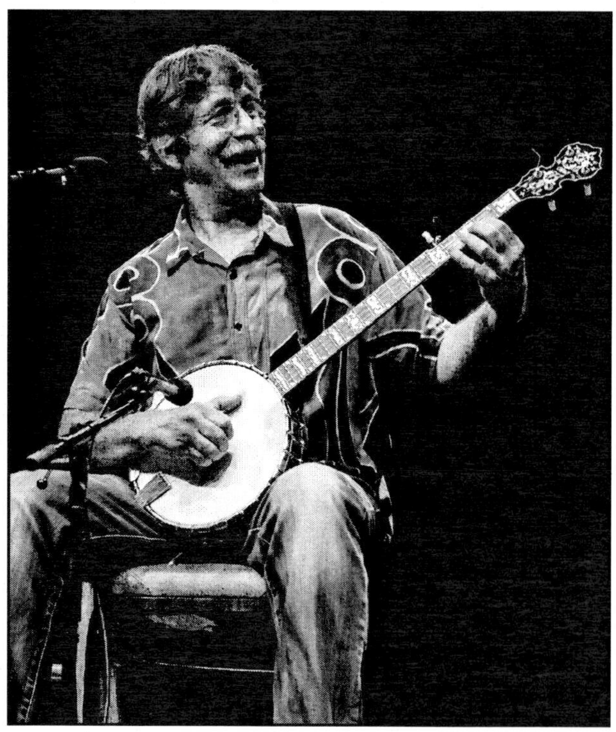

For a Complete List of Ken's Publications & Recordings, See Appendix E (pg. 184)

Table of Contents

For Alphabetical List of Tunes & Online Audio Playlist, see Appendix D

Chapter 1. Introduction

Cape Breton and Prince Edward Island (locals tend to refer to it by its initials: P.E.I.) are located directly off the Atlantic coast of Canada and form part of a region known as the Maritime Provinces, or simply the Maritimes (Figure 1-1). P.E.I. is a province unto itself, whereas similar-sized Cape Breton Island is the northeasternmost sector of the Province of Nova Scotia. The two islands are close enough so that on a clear day you can look across the Gulf of St. Lawrence from the eastern shore of P.E.I. to the western shore of Cape Breton. Both Islands have been hotbeds of fiddling virtually since they were first settled, and have distinct – yet substantially related – fiddling traditions.

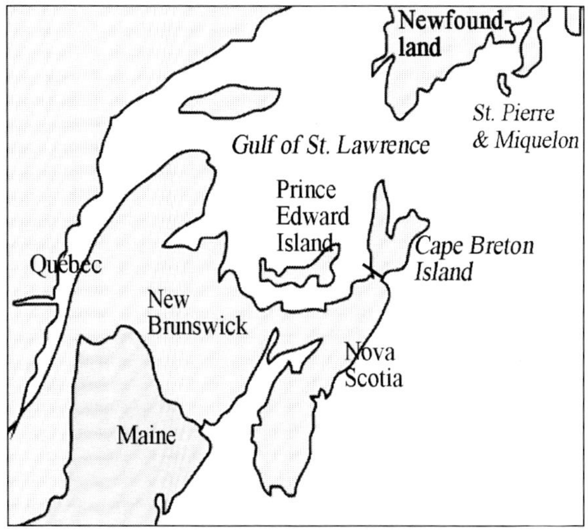

Fig. 1-1. *The Canadian Maritimes*

This book presents a collection of 136 fiddle tunes from Cape Breton and P.E.I., arranged note-for-note for clawhammer banjo with as much flavor and nuance as humanly possible. These "settings" are all eminently playable and fully benefit from my half-century of experience playing banjo, arranging for banjo, and researching fiddle music traditions.

To help you learn, this volume offers instruction on basic and advanced techniques; general tips on fingering and a systematic approach to playing up the neck; hints on understanding modes; and a thorough treatment of playing triplets, grace notes, and other characteristic ornaments in clawhammer. I also offer technical help for individual tunes in the form of fingering diagrams and detailed fingering suggestions.

With a very few exceptions, I learned the tunes in this volume directly from master fiddlers steeped in local musical traditions. I learned my first Cape Breton tunes in the late 1980s from John Campbell, Joe Cormier, and Ludger LeFort – three well-known Cape Breton fiddlers who made their homes in the Boston area; and added to that stock by hearing Buddy MacMaster, Jerry Holland and other Cape Bretoners play for dances and concerts at the Canadian-American club in nearby Watertown.

Then in the summers of 1991 and '92 – with much assistance in terms of funding and volunteer labor from the Earthwatch Organization of Massachusetts – I conducted a major music-collecting project on P.E.I. and recorded close to one hundred high quality fiddlers from dozens of communities across the Island. Most of these players were taped in their own kitchens with their families and favorite accompanists in attendance. I came away from this experience with the feeling that these artists were every bit as unique and musically intriguing as any folk-instrumentalist I had ever heard on an old 78. Even more important, these fiddlers impressed upon me what their tunes were really for – to make people exhausted from a day of hard physical labor want to get up and dance!

Prince Edward Island may have been relatively small geographically – only about 130 miles from tip to tip – but it was big enough to be home to several distinct playing styles, which can be most easily described by referring to the Island's three counties: Kings, Queens, and Prince (Figure 1-2). In northern and eastern Kings County, fiddlers' playing styles and repertoires tended to be deeply influenced by those of Scotland and Cape Breton. In Prince County on the opposite side of the Island, the Acadian French influence was paramount. The styles of many Queens County fiddlers could be considered a blend of Scottish/Cape Breton and Acadian influences. Fiddlers in southern Kings and southeastern Queens Counties tended to play older Island styles that fell largely outside the Cape Breton/Acadian continuum.

Once I had the recordings in hand I set to work and

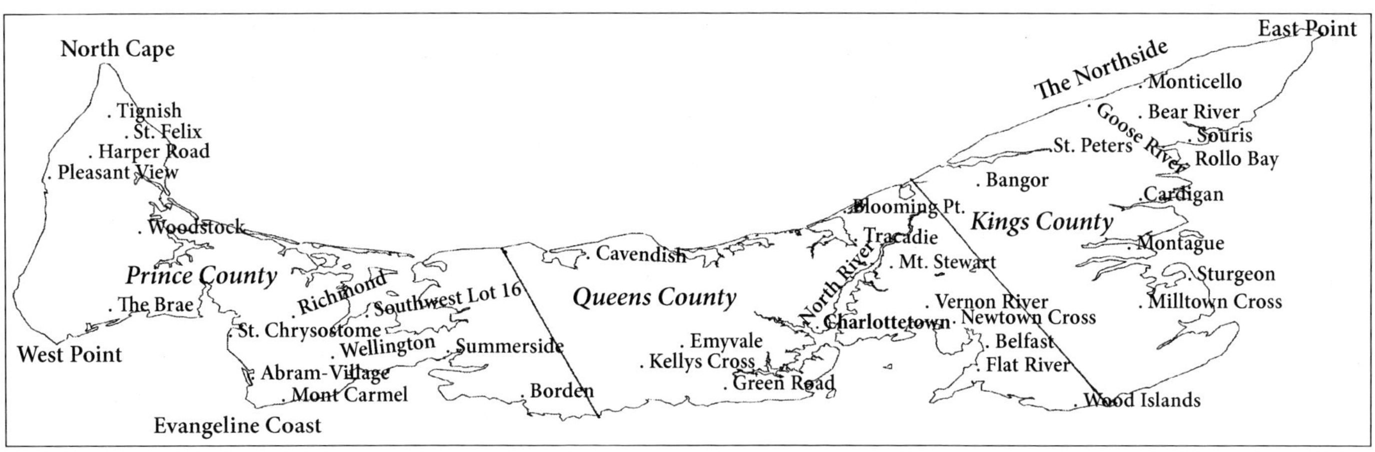

Fig. 1-2. *Prince Edward Island (with place names mentioned in the text)*

transcribed many of the tunes into standard notation. Each selection was transcribed as a particular fiddler played it with as much precision as I could muster, including such subtleties of style as ornamentation, double stops, and the melodic idiosyncrasies known in local parlance as *twists*. The result: living, breathing versions of tunes filled with the vitality of a people whose great love for their music was expressed in every bow-stroke. This first set of transcriptions was published by Mel Bay as *The Fiddle Music of Prince Edward Island: Celtic and Acadian Tunes in Living Tradition* (1994).

In 2006, I was commissioned by the Canadian Museum of History of Gatineau, Québec to conduct a follow up project on P.E.I. fiddling. I recorded an additional few dozen players and transcribed roughly an additional 150 tunes; these transcriptions, along with hundreds of recorded performances and other materials from the entire project are available on the website: *bowingdownhome.ca*.

I was certainly no neutral bystander during these recording sessions. As the fiddlers played, I was absorbing elements of rhythm and style. And after nearly every session, most fiddlers would almost demand that I get out my banjo and accompany them. P.E.I. had no banjo-playing tradition to speak of, so this process often led fiddlers to exclaim, "The banjo and the fiddle, they go together pretty good, eh!" I also had many opportunities during the course of the project to attend dances and view how closely many elements of melody and phrasing were linked to movements of the dance.

After I completed any given transcription, my first impulse was to get out the banjo and try to capture the tune's melody, rhythm, and spirit on my instrument. Ultimately, I worked out literally hundreds of banjo settings. In the years since, I've recorded many of my favorites on the four CDs whose repertoires form the heart of this volume – *Devil in the Kitchen* (1993), *Island Boy* (1996), *Northern Banjo* (2002), and *Frails & Frolics* (2017). The complete playlists of these recordings, along with credits and other related information appear in Appendix A. For the backstory on each recording, see Appendix C.

Cape Breton & Prince Edward Island: Two Capsule Musical Histories

THE MUSIC GENRE WE NOW CALL "FIDDLE TUNES" originated in Scotland in the early 18th century; by mid-century extensive fiddle tune collections were already being published in that country. Scottish settlers carried the music across the Atlantic to both P.E.I. and Cape Breton in the late 18th and early 19th centuries; this original stock of tunes was then supplemented via later-arriving Irish immigrants, and via input from the original European inhabitants of both Islands: the Acadian French. Because of a variety of historical factors – not the least of which was a long term policy by the Canadian Federal Government that promoted growth in the center and west of the country while ignoring the east – the Maritimes region was long an economic and cultural backwater. As a result continent-wide technological and cultural trends that caused fiddling to decline elsewhere relatively early in the 20th century bypassed the region almost entirely.

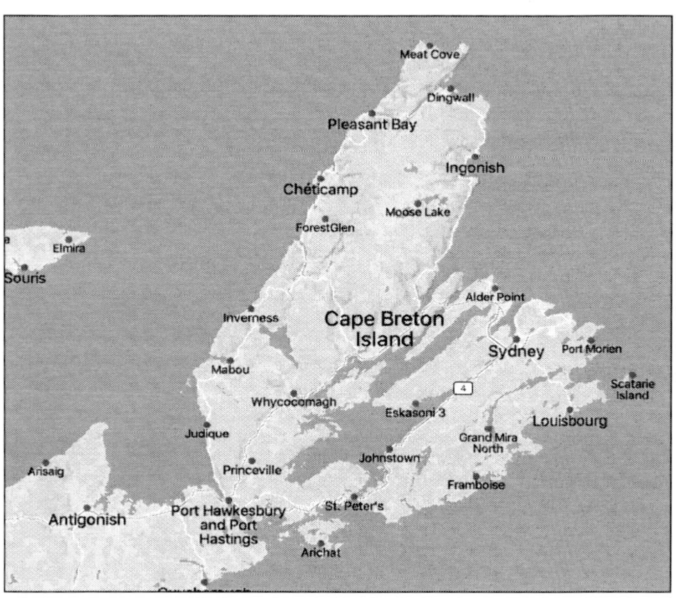

Fig. 1-3. *Cape Breton Island*

Most older fiddlers I interviewed could remember a time when virtually every community had its own stock of fiddlers who supplied the music for the dances that served as the primary form of recreation. The most common venue for these dances was the informal house party. Word would go out that the event was in the offing, a kitchen would be cleared, the fiddler would set himself up in the corner, and the neighbors would gather together for an evening of *square sets* (as the local variant of square dancing was called) interspersed with episodes solo step dancing (closer to the floor than Appalachian clogging, and with more upper body movement than Irish step dancing).

Not only did fiddling and dance provide entertainment, but they also served other important functions within the community. When money had to be raised for the up-keep of the local school house, the community held a fiddle-dance. When the local church needed support, it scheduled dances as part of church socials or parish picnic. When a wedding was decided upon, virtually the first act of the families involved was to line up the fiddler.

P.E.I. got a head start as a center of radio broadcasting in the 1920s when station CFCY, Charlottetown acquired a powerful transmitter. A few fiddlers from P.E.I. such as Lem Jay, Hector MacDonald, and George Chappelle were featured on local radio but starting in 1939 and continuing into the 1970s, the local airwaves were dominated by a fiddler from New Brunswick named Don Messer. The show featuring Messer and his ensemble, known as the Islanders, would be broadcast regularly for decades on CBC (the Canadian Broadcasting Company's radio station), making him virtually a household name throughout the country and also in those parts of the U.S. that could pick up the CBC signal.

Aside from Messer's activities, fiddling on P.E.I. was practiced primarily at the local level, and there were virtually no commercial recordings made of P.E.I. fiddlers until well into the 1990s.

Given that Messer's broadcasts were so influential, it should be no surprise that many of the tunes he introduced were absorbed into the P.E.I. repertoire. Other early media tune sources include Québecois fiddlers broadcast via CHNC on the Gaspé Peninsula; and American country fiddlers broadcast via WWVA, Wheeling West Virginia, which could be picked up on clear nights in certain parts of P.E.I.

Cape Breton (Figure 1-3) was of course a very different story. Beginning in the 1930s, a major recording and broadcasting scene devoted to fiddling developed on Cape Breton beginning with such artists as Angus Chisholm, Dan J. Campbell, and Hugh A. MacDonald; continuing in the 1950s with Winston "Scotty" Fitzgerald, Joe MacLean and others; moving into the 1970s and 80s with Joe Cormier, John Campbell, Jerry Holland, Carl MacKenzie, and Buddy MacMaster; and continuing through to the present day. It has been estimated that in just the period 1935-89 as many as 4000 recorded selections by 60 different fiddlers were released. In addition, radio stations CJFX in Antigonish on mainland Nova Scotia, and CJCB in Sydney broadcast widely disseminated fiddling shows.

One important consequence of this burgeoning recording and broadcast scene was that fiddlers seeking recognition felt the need to continually come up with new material. This motivated some fiddlers to compose their own tunes, and others to *go to the books* – search through the pages of Scottish, Irish, and American tunebooks from the 18th-, 19th- and early 20th- centuries for tunes worthy of recording or performing. Ultimately, both processes led to a vast expansion of the number of tunes in circulation.

Many of these new compositions and newly-introduced older tunes eventually found their way into the P.E.I. repertoire – both through the media and via oral transmission.

One reason for the viability of recordings featuring Cape Breton fiddling is that for generations the art has been regarded as an important cultural legacy by many Nova Scotians, and that fiddlers from that region were seen as true heirs of 18th-century Scottish musical traditions.

For more on the history of fiddle music and traditional fiddlers on P.E.I. – and on the Cape Breton influence – see my book, *Couldn't Have a Wedding Without the Fiddler: The Story of Traditional Fiddling on Prince Edward Island* (University of Tennessee Press, 2015).

The Dances & Tune Genres

FIDDLING ON CAPE BRETON AND P.E.I. has always been associated with social dancing. In the old days, these dances were done in what might be termed standard square-dance or square-set formation, with four couples lined up at right angles. The oldest fiddlers I spoke to remembered dances called *breakdowns* – the Scotch reel, the four-hand reel, and the eight-hand reel – in which participants step-danced through most maneuvers. By the 1920s, these dances had given way to others – variants of the *quadrille* – where most maneuvers could be walked through. Thereafter, step-dancing took the form of spontaneous exhibitions by solo dancers at house parties and other local dance events.

The distinctive feature of the quadrille – and its cousin the *Lancers* – is that each dance is divided into distinct segments called *figures*. Each figure has different steps, each is accompanied by a different kind of tune, and each is followed by a distinct pause to offer everyone a breather. Most fiddlers I spoke to remembered that the square sets in their respective communities had four figures. As time went on, each community evolved its own version of the quadrille which varied from those of its neighbors in terms of the order of figures, the actual steps done, and the kinds of tunes played for them.

Nowadays, at least on P.E.I., dancers no longer line up in squares, but instead perform the various figures and steps of the quadrille from a single circular formation.

Nearly all the tune genres played on Cape Breton and P.E.I. are used primarily for dance accompaniment.

TYPES OF TUNES & THE DANCES THEY ACCOMPANY

- *REELS* (AND HORNPIPES PLAYED AS REELS) accompany figures of the quadrille and step dancing.
- SET TUNES accompany figures of the quadrille.
- *JIGS* accompany figures of the quadrille.
- *STRATHSPEYS* accompany step dancing, generally serving as moderate-tempo preludes to reels.
- *WALTZ* tunes accompany waltz dances.
- *MARCHES* and *AIRS* generally serve as opening tunes in performance sets. Marches can also be played as reels; airs in 3/4 or 6/8 time can also be played as waltzes.

PERFORMANCE SETS

IN CONCERT PERFORMANCE CAPE BRETON AND P.E.I. fiddlers often play medleys, or *sets* of tunes, generally with all tunes in the same key center. These are the most common patterns.

- Two or more reels
- Two or more jigs
- One or more strathspeys followed by one or more reels
- A march or air, followed by one or more strathspeys, followed by one or more reels

Definitions and stylistic directions for the various tune genres appear at three locations in this book. For reels, hornpipes, and set tunes, see sidebar 3-1; for jigs, see Chapter 9; for marches, strathspeys, airs, and waltzes see Chapter 10.

On Translating Fiddle Tunes to Banjo

Although getting the notes right is the first job when creating a good banjo "setting" of a fiddle tune, this is only the beginning of the process. In fact, how to make a series of notes sound like an authentically played fiddle tune is one of the major challenges of progressive/melodic clawhammer. The subject is far too vast to cover in just a paragraph or two, but here are at least some of the factors involved.

• **Phrasing.** There's a 1980s folksong by Kate Wolf that describes a great divide "where the rivers change direction." Melodies also contain numerous internal divides where the flow of music stops ever so briefly, then starts up again and proceeds in a new direction. The flow of music within each pair of divides is called a *phrase*; and understanding the *phrasing* of a tune – where all these divides are and how to bring them out from a continuous stream of notes – is crucial to bringing any fiddle tune to life.

Bringing out phrasing often involves fingering choices – finding just the right spot on the banjo to locate your notes, and knowing just when to shift *fingering positions* (see Chapter 2). You have to know when to let notes ring together and when to cut them short, and choose whether to obtain certain notes via plucking-hand or fretting-hand techniques. But perhaps most important is coming up with a setting that puts your plucking hand in position to control the shape of the melody through subtle shifts of weight between downstroke and thumb, so that *upbeats* and *downbeats* are clearly delineated.

• **Obtaining strong runs of notes.** Other things being equal, the second note of an eighth-note pair sings out best and is most easily controlled when it is plucked by the thumb (as opposed to being obtained via such fretting-hand maneuvers as hammer-ons or pull-offs). With this in mind, I often employ several fingering strategies that allow for additional plucking-hand thumb use, such fretting the 5th string, using fingering forms that incorporate open or fretted 5th-string notes, and employing a strategy I call clawhammer Keith-picking (alternating open-string downstrokes with fretted up-the-neck thumb-strokes). All these techniques are discussed and illustrated in Chapter 3.

• **Range Issues.** In the normal run of things, tunes on banjo are played an octave below what is customary on the fiddle. For example, we banjoists generally treat the open third string in G tuning as if it is equivalent to G above middle C on piano, a note generally played on fiddle with the third finger on the third string. In terms of actual pitch, however, that note is equivalent to G *below* middle C on piano (the open fourth string on fiddle).

Given this convention, banjoists simply run out of notes when fiddle tunes descend far enough to go below low D in open G tuning, or below low C in double-C tuning. When this happens there are several options, depending on how the rest of the tune fits together. You can leave out some or all of the below-range notes; change the tuning so that below-range notes are available; take just the below-range notes or the brief phrase of which they are part up an octave; or take an entire part – or even an entire tune – up an octave. When applicable, I'll alert you in the tune intros as to which of these strategies were employed.

About This Book

How the Tunes Are Organized

Since the tradition among Cape Breton and P.E.I. fiddlers is for all tunes in a medley to have the same key center, it would make sense to organize all the tunes in this book by key. I had more than enough reels and hornpipes to organize those tunes by key and you'll find four such chapters here. Separate chapters are devoted to reels in G and G modal; reels in D and D-modal; and reels in A and A-modal. The final reels chapter is devoted to tunes in three keys: namely C, F, and B♭.

Chapters 9 and 10 are genre specific and feature tunes in a variety of keys. Chapter 9 is devoted to *jigs* (6/8 time fiddle tunes), while Chapter 10 covers pipe-marches, fiddle-marches, and strathspeys – tune genres that are more or less unique to the Scottish, Cape Breton, and Prince Edward Island repertoires – along with fiddle airs and a waltz.

I strongly recommend that you begin your exploration of Cape Breton & P.E.I. fiddle music tunes with the tunes in Chapter 4, aptly named, "Try These Tunes First!!" This chapter is populated by over a dozen highly playable tunes in varied keys; I arranged them with full flavor but tried to keep technical complications to a minimum. Start with these settings to get a sense of the style and many of the techniques you'll encounter, before diving into the rest of the book.

Within each chapter, the tunes are presented very roughly in order of difficulty. This said, some of these calls were unavoidably arbitrary, and layout considerations sometimes factored into this ordering. In some cases I also went out of my way to put tunes from the same recorded medley on facing pages. Once you make it through Chapter 4, therefore, I recommend that you try the arrangements in any given chapter as they strike you, rather than attempt to plow through them in the presented order.

Tune Information

When I was putting together my very first music instruction book back in the 1970s, it occurred to me that it might be a good idea to present historical information along with each tune. I asked around and was told about a fellow named Jim Morrison (no, not *that* Jim Morrison) who lived nearby and collected the kind of information I needed. I arranged a visit and was presented with a box full of hand-printed index cards; I was then permitted to copy by hand whatever information I needed.

In the 1990s, when I needed historical information for the tunes published in *Fiddle Music of P.E.I.,* I often found myself exploring musty university archives or sending off for books and unpublished dissertations through the Inter-Library Loan Program.

The situation today is vastly different. A quick internet search can lead you to sites that offer a treasure trove of information on Celtic and Canadian tunes. This information may be unvetted, but many claims can be checked either via a personal book collection or by searching for scans of original sources located elsewhere on the internet. This said, whenever I did draw information from the internet, my motto was, "Trust but verify!"

My process for researching the tune information presented here was usually as follows. I began by harvesting the information I had once gathered for *Fiddle Music of P.E.I.* For more on publishing histories, I turned to a wonderful resource called *The Scottish Tune Index* by Charles Gore (1994), which lists nearly every tune found in nearly every published Scottish tune collection c. 1750-1900. For Cape Breton recording history, I consulted an extraordinarily comprehensive unpublished Master's thesis called "Fiddling to Fortune: The Role of Commercial Recordings Made by Cape Breton Fiddlers [. . .]," by Ian Francis MacKinnon (1989); it lists and cross-references just about every recording made in the Cape Breton tradition from the 1920s through the 80s. For biographical information on Cape Breton fiddlers I was able to consult *The Cape Breton Fiddle Companion* by Liz Doherty (Cape Breton University Press, 2015). Finally, I would go onto the internet to see what else might be of interest; usually the first site on my list was *Traditional Tune Archive* (tunearch.org).

Standard Tune Headings

At the top of each tune page is a heading with several kinds of information as illustrated below. The entries on the left deal mostly with matters of provenance: composer (if known) or country/region of origin; the fiddler or other musician from whom I learned the tune; and where I recorded this banjo arrangement (when an arrangement has not yet been recorded by me, this line is left blank).

The entries on the right deal with musical issues: key; mode; and tuning and capo information. Note that if either key or mode information is complicated, additional explanation is offered in the introductory paragraph; for further explanation on keys and modes see also the section, "Demystifying Modes" in Chapter 3.

Tune-Heading Categories

Composer or Origin:	Key:
Source:	Mode:
Appears on:	Tuning:

Tune Intros

The intro paragraphs place tunes in their historical or cultural context, offer a sense of their publishing and recording histories, and make mention of alternative titles, colorful anecdotes, and more. Where relevant, complicated modal features and other musical considerations are also discussed.

Because the internet now offers so much information – and disinformation – on tunes, I needed to narrow the scope of the intros to leave enough room on the page for music. I don't necessarily mention every alternative title or title variant, cite every publication where a tune appears, or list every recording where it has ever been included. Here is the information you can expect to find.

• The tune's very first appearance in print or recording (or at least a very early one)

• The path by which the tune was carried via major tune collections from the late 18th century through the late 19th and early 20th centuries

• The first recording of the tune – or at least a highly influential one – by a fiddler from Cape Breton or elsewhere in the Canadian Maritimes

Biographical Information for Source Fiddlers & Historical Fiddlers

Capsule bios for fiddlers whose playing served as sources for the tunes that appear in this book – plus some important historical Scottish, Irish, and Cape Breton fiddlers mentioned frequently in the text – appear in *The Fiddlers' Hall of Fame* (Appendix B).

Important Tune Collections & Shortcuts Used in Tune Intros

For tune collections mentioned just once, or at most a few times in this book, editors' names and some publishing information appears in the intro paragraphs. Major collections that are mentioned again and again in the text are represented via the following shortcuts. Abbreviated titles used in this book are shown in the left column; more complete versions of titles, editors, and other publishing information are shown in the right column.

Scottish Collections

Late 18th & Early 19th Centuries

• *The Gow Collection*	Niel Gow. *A Collection of Strathspey Reels [. . .]* (Dunkeld & Edinburgh: several vols., 1784-1822)
• *The Gow Repository*	Nathaniel Gow. *The Complete Repository of [. . .] Strathspeys and Dances* (Edinburgh: four vols., 1799-1839)

Mid-19th Century

• *Lowe's Collection*	Joseph Lowe. *Lowe's Collection of Reels, Strathspeys, Jigs [. . .]* (Edinburgh: 1844)

Late 19th & Early 20th Centuries

• *Kerr's Merry Melodies*	James S. Kerr. *Kerr's Collection of Merry Melodies for the Violin* (Glasgow: 4 vols., 1870)
• *The Athole Collection*	James Stewart-Robinson. *The Athole Collection of the Dance Music of Scotland* (Edinburgh: 1884)
• *The Skye Collection*	Keith Norman MacDonald. *The Skye Collection of Best Strathspey Reels [. . .]* (Edinburgh: 1887)
• *Harp & Claymore*	James Scott Skinner. *The Harp & Claymore* (Glasgow: 1903)

American & Irish Collections

• *Ryan's Mammoth Collection*	Wm. Bradbury Ryan. *Ryan's Mammoth Collection of More Than 1050 Reel and Jigs [. . .]* (Boston: 1883); later re-published by the M. M. Cole Company as *1000 Fiddle Tunes*
• *O'Neill's Music of Ireland*	Capt. Francis O'Neill. *O'Neill's Music of Ireland: Eighteen Hundred and Fifty Melodies [. . .]* (Chicago: 1903)
• *O'Neill's Dance Music of Ireland*	Capt. Francis O'Neill. *O'Neill's Dance Music of Ireland: 1001 Gems [. . .]* (Chicago: 1907)
• *The Roche Collection*	Francis Roche. *The Roche Collection of Traditional Irish Music* (Dublin: 1912)
• *Allan's Irish Fiddler*	Hugh McDermott. *Allan's Irish Fiddler: Reels, Jigs, Hornpipes [. . .]* (Glasgow, c. 1950)

Two More Shortcuts

• *Fiddle Music of P.E.I.*	Ken Perlman. *The Fiddle Music of Prince Edward Island* (Mel Bay, 1994)
• *Everything Clawhammer*	Ken Perlman. *Everything You Wanted to Know About Clawhammer Banjo* (Mel Bay, 2005)

On Tune Titles

There's a real temptation in folk music circles to ascribe considerable importance to tune titles, and to assume that locked within them are clues to deep folkloristic insights. From everything I've observed and heard first-hand on the subject, in practice Cape Breton and Prince Edward Island fiddlers paid little attention to tune names. Instead, fiddlers would classify tunes in their minds "musically" (that is, by melody); and instead of calling for tunes by name they would simply sing or whistle a couple of bars, or quickly scratch those same bars out on an instrument. The perspective that every tune ought to have a unique name associated with it only arises after collecting, publication, and recording become major factors. Ultimately, fiddle-tune titles are more a by-product of these three phenomena, than they are an essential feature of the music.

Truth be told, the state of titles is quite chaotic all across the fiddle-tune world. Tune names often vary widely among regions, and among different players in the same region. Some tunes have different names in each of several published collections, and some have even been printed under several different names in the same collection (especially notorious in this regard is the above-mentioned American work, *Ryan's Mammoth Collection*). Many tunes appear on commercial recordings under names quite different from the ones they bear in books. Sometimes all this confusion was the result of genuine regional or personal differences. Sometimes, however, publishers and record companies created new titles to skirt copyright laws; and some collectors and recording artists simply made up names as they went along.

Chapter 2. Tablature & Techniques

ALL MODERN BANJO TABLATURE descends from a system created by Pete Seeger in the late 1940s, which itself was at least partially derived from the fretted-instrument notation used during the Renaissance and Baroque eras. By now banjo "tab" has become fairly standardized but I'll quickly go over the elements of the system used here. Where appropriate I'll offer a brief explanation of techniques. To get started at clawhammer, I recommend my book *Clawhammer Style Banjo* (Centerstream/Hal Leonard). For thorough treatments of virtually the entire spectrum of clawhammer techniques – along with illustrative exercises and banjo arrangements – see my book, *Everything You Wanted to Know About Clawhammer Banjo* (Mel Bay).

The Staff. 5-string banjo "tab" is written on a 5-line staff, with each line corresponding to a string: the top line signifies string 1 (the highest long string), the bottom line signifies string 5 (the short drone string), and so on. Numbers on the lines indicate frets: "0" means an open (unstopped) string, "1" means first fret, "5" means fifth fret, and so on.

Numbers On The 5th String. By convention, frets on the short 5th string are calculated as if that string starts at the long-string nut. So the first fret of the 5th string is always referred to in the tab as fret 6; the second fret of the 5th string is referred to as fret 7, and so on. This convention makes fret-level calculations much easier to keep track of as you move up the neck.

Time Signatures & Rhythm Notation. Time signatures are the same as in standard music notation: 2/2 or cut time (𝄵), 3/4, 4/4 (often written: 𝄴), 6/8, and so on. Time value is shown via a system that more or less parallels the one used for standard notation, as shown in Example 2-1. Illustrated from left to right are a whole note (a), half note (b), quarter note (c), a pair of eighth notes (d), two single eighth notes (e), a triplet (f) two beamed sixteenth notes and two single sixteenths (g). Also illustrated are a single grace note leading to a quarter note (h) and a double grace note leading to a pair of eighth notes (i).

Dotted Notes. A dot placed next to a note increases its value by 50%. For example, a dot placed next to a half note in 4/4 time (j) increases its value from two beats to three beats. Also shown in Example 2-1 are a dotted quarter note (k), and a dotted eighth note + sixteenth note (L).

Stacked Notes. Notes on multiple strings shown in vertical alignment are brushed at the same time (Example 2-1m).

Ties vs. Slurs. When an arc connects two identical notes – Example 2-1n – it is called a *tie* and indicates that the first note should sound through the time value of the second note. When the arc connects different notes it is called a *slur* (hammer-on, pull-off, and so on); see below for explanation.

Example 2-1

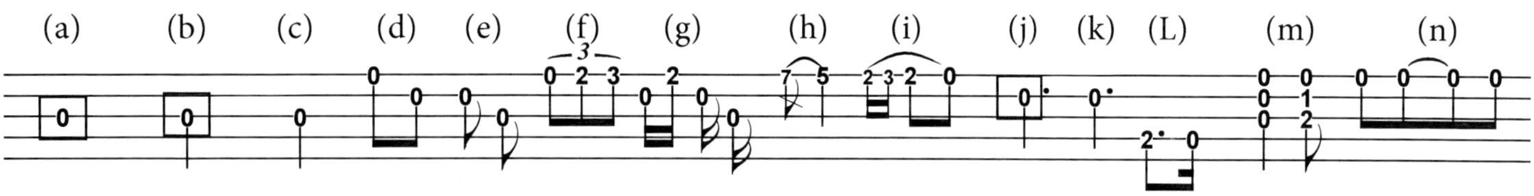

The Basic Clawhammer Stroke: Picking-Hand Indications Below the Staff

Indications below the staff show how notes are obtained, as illustrated in Example 2-2.

The fundamental clawhammer motion is accomplished via the alternation of downstroke and thumb-stroke. The downstroke (M), is driven by wrist and forearm; the player uses that motion to strike one of the long strings of the banjo with the back of either the middle or index fingernail. In the most basic form of this fundamental motion, the downstroke is followed by a thumb-stroke (T) on the short 5th string, which is often referred to as the *drone-string*.

No Indication. When the pattern described above is followed – M plucks a long string (or brushes multiple strings) on the beat, and T plucks the short 5th string between beats – there is no indication below the staff, as shown in Example 2-2a. This also applies to the widespread banjo rhythm known as the *bumm-titty,* or *bum-diddy strum* (b), consisting of a quarter-note downstroke plus two eighth-notes played via a brush and thumb-stroke on the long strings and 5th string, respectively.

Drop-Thumbing & Double-Thumbing (T). When the thumb is used on any long string, the indication "T" appears below the note, as shown in Example 2-2c.

When you'll see "M." When there is unusual downstroke usage – for example, if a downstroke is called for between

Example 2-2

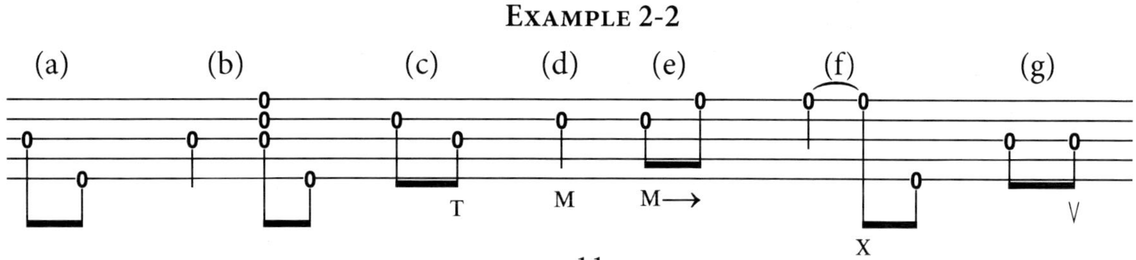

beats – or if it is not quite clear that a downstroke should be used, the indication "M" appears under the note in question (Example 2-2d)

Arpeggio-Stroke (M→). To perform an arpeggio stroke, pluck an inner long string with M, and – without a fresh wrist stroke – continue in a downward direction to pluck one or more additional strings. This is indicated in the tablature by M with a right-facing arrow (Example 2-2e).

Skip-Strokes (X). Many syncopated rhythmic figures in clawhammer grow out of a simple technique I call a skip stroke, also known in the trade as a *ghost brush* (Example 2-2f). Start with an ordinary brush-thumb motion, but brush soundlessly over the strings (avoid contacting any strings during your brush). Drag the thumb into the 5th string as in a normal brush-thumb, wait there half a beat, then pluck the string with a pop. For more on this technique, see Chapter 3.

Upstroke (V). Sometimes an upstroke (Example 2-2g) is the only way to get a second consecutive eighth note. Pluck the first note of a pair of eighth notes with M as usual; to get the second note, use the underside of your picking nail like a flatpick and simply pluck the string in an upward trajectory. For best results, keep the finger still and direct the upward movement entirely with your wrist.

More Indications Below the Staff: Fretting-Hand Maneuvers (H, P, S, and ◇)

There are several methods for obtaining additional notes with the fretting hand after a string has been plucked, called *slurs* in formal music but known to banjoists as hammer-ons (H), pull-offs (P), and slides (S). As shown in Example 2-3, an arc, or *slur sign* connects all these left-hand maneuvers to the initial plucked note.

Hammer-ons (H). To perform a hammer-on (2-3a), a finger of the fretting hand produces an additional note by coming down sharply on a sounding string (your finger must retain its "arch" throughout the maneuver). Tip: when hammering from one fretted note to another on the same string (2-3b), avoid trying to stretch your finger and hammer at the same time. Stretch first, and then hammer!

Pull-offs (P). To perform a pull-off (2-3c) strike a fretted string, then draw the fretting finger in towards your palm in such a way as to produce another note; in effect, you are plucking that string with a finger of the fretting hand. When pulling from a higher to a lower fret on the same string (2-3d), this requires anticipation. Place two fingers on the fretboard simultaneously when you pluck the string, then pull from the higher fret to the lower one.

Alternate-String Pull-Offs: All Open Strings. Pluck one long string, then pull-off another, usually higher long string (2-3e). Tip: for best results, have a finger waiting on the alternate string when you strike the initial string.

Alternate String Pull-Offs: Fretted plucked string (2-3f). Pluck one long string, and – at the same time – place two fingers on the fretboard: one finger on that string and another within reach on the higher string that will be pulled off. When it's time to play the second note, use the finger waiting on the higher string for the pull-off.

Alternate String Pull-Offs: All Fretted Strings. Example 2-3g illustrates this technique via use of a barre. Place the barre at the fifth fret and – at the same time – place a finger on string 2 above the barre. Pluck string 3 and – when it's time to play the second note – pull off the finger waiting on string 2, thereby producing a pitch at fret 5, string 2. Example 2-3h is a little more complicated; place *three* fingers at the same time: the plucked string (fret 2, string 3), the note to be sounded by the P (fret 2, string 1), and some point on string 2 higher than fret 1. When it's time to play the second note, keep fret 1 firmly pressed down and pull off from the higher location on string 2.

Example 2-3

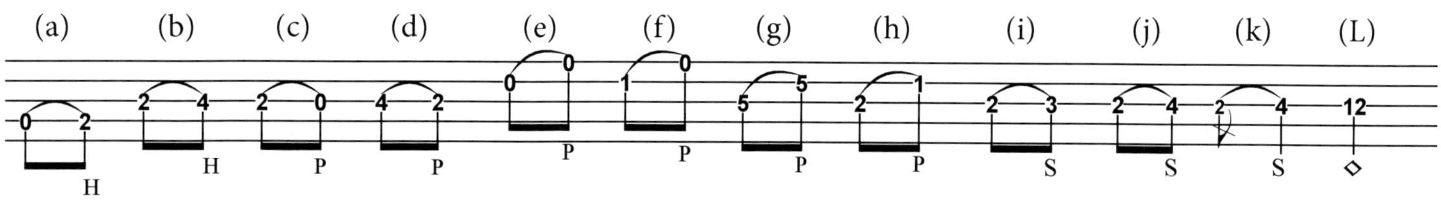

Slides (S). In an even slide (2-3i), start by plucking a stopped string. Hold that string down for its full value (quarter note, eighth note, etc.), then glide with full pressure up or down the neck to a destination fret and linger there until that second note's full time value has elapsed. Tip for multi-fret slides (2-3j): use full pressure only up to the next fretwire in your path (in this case, the one between frets 3 and 4). As you pass over that fretwire, relax pressure sufficiently to prevent the production of a discreet extra tone (but not enough to stop the string from sounding).

Quick-Slides. In an ornamental, or quick-slide (2-3k), there is no initial stopped note with a definite time value. Instead, stop the string and begin to slide at virtually the same time. The listener does not hear the initial note – only a sliding sound and the note at the destination fret. Observe that the initial attack is written as a grace note, which has no specific allotted time-value.

Harmonics (◇) are bell-like tones created by tapping into the overtone series (Example 2-3L). To obtain a harmonic, touch the string right over the fretwire at the upper end of certain strategic frets (the most common ones are frets 12, 7, and 5). When you pluck the string you'll hear the beginnings of a bell-like tone; if you then pull your finger away the tone will ring out.

Fretting Hand Fingers & Fingering Diagrams

Fingering assistance is often provided via fingering diagrams. These are fairly standard in approach, with vertical lines indicating strings (the first string is shown at the right) and horizontal spaces indicating frets. Dots on a vertical line within a horizontal space indicate where fingers are to be placed. Fingers are indicated as follows.

- index finger = 1
- middle finger = 2
- ring finger = 3
- little finger = 4

When the diagram begins up the neck, the top fret has an indication such as 5fr (5th fret), 7fr (7th fret), etc.

Diagrams are referenced via typographical symbols above the staff. The symbols appear in this order.

*, †, ‡, §, ¶, **. . .

Full & Partial-Barres. Barring with the first finger is indicated via dots on adjacent strings at the same fret, all connected along the top by a curved line, or arc.

Indications Above the Staff: Roman Numerals (II, III, V, IX . . .)

Roman numerals Above the Staff indicate fingering positions. The idea behind *position playing* is that in general one finger is assigned to duty on a given fret. If you're playing near the nut, for example, the 1st finger covers all notes on the first fret of any string, the 2nd finger covers all notes on the second fret of any string, the 3rd finger covers all notes on the third fret and (if you use it) the 4th finger covers the fourth fret. This is called *playing in 1st position* (shown by placing the Roman numeral "I" above the staff). Let's say, however, you have a tune with no notes at all on the first fret but it has lots of notes distributed between frets 2 and 5. The best way to handle this is to approach these passages in *second position* ("II" above the staff); now the 1st finger handles all notes on fret 2 (regardless of the string), the 2nd finger handles all notes on fret 3, the 3rd finger handles all notes on fret 4, and the 4th finger handles all notes on fret 5. Second position is illustrated in Example 2-4a.

Additional positions can be set up for each fret on the neck. In third position (III), the 1st finger covers all notes on the third fret, regardless of string. The 2nd finger covers the fourth fret, the 3rd finger covers the fifth fret, and so on. In fifth position (V), the 1st finger covers the fifth fret, the 2nd finger covers the sixth, and so on. In seventh position (VII), the 1st finger covers the seventh fret; in tenth position (X), the 1st finger covers the tenth fret. . . you get the idea!

Put another way, in position playing we essentially set up fingering "territories" at various locations around the neck, and think about moving from territory to territory instead of from fret to fret.

The Vertical Rule. Because of the way the fingers line up in a chord diagram when established in a given position, I like to refer to this as the *Vertical Rule* of fingering.

Two More Important Fingering "Rules"

- **The Horizontal Rule.** Simultaneous or consecutive notes that fall on the same fret of different strings can usually be dealt with via this rule: *the lower number finger plays the higher number string*, as illustrated in Example 2-4b.

- **The "Cotton-Eyed Joe" Rule.** Fingering is a purely practical matter; feel free to jettison any rule if you find a better way. The ultimate criterion is, as the song says: "Where you come from, where you go."

Example 2-4a. Second Position: ***The Vertical Rule***

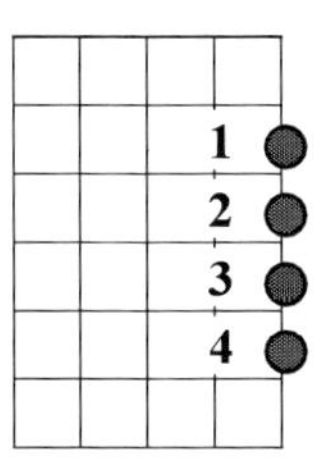

Example 2-4b. ***The Horizontal Rule***

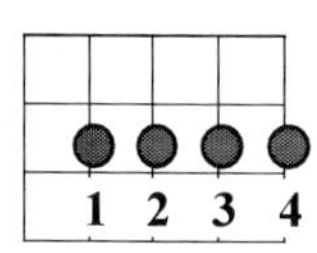

Tech Tips: Additional Technical Assistance on Fingering

When position notation *and* fingering diagrams are not enough, I offer "Tech Tips" that describe how to get between fingering shapes or from one place to another. Here is a guide to how fingering help is expressed.

- **Counting Measures.** The pickup or "upbeat" measure in any part is *NOT* counted. For example, Part A, measure 1 refers to the first *full measure* of Part A.

- **Counting beats.** Strictly speaking, reels and hornpipes are in *cut-time* (2/2), which means that there are only two beats per measure, usually with four eighth notes per beat. For the sake of more easily locating the position of notes within a measure, however, the tech tips are based on a 4/4-time format (which looks exactly the same as 2/2).

- **Cutting a note *short*.** This is a two-step process. First relax pressure on the string to stop it from sounding; then remove the finger. This technique is also referred to as a *controlled release*.

• **Glide.** Slide *without pressure* up or down a given string, using it as a guide wire (this fingering aid is *not* meant to produce sound).

• **Pivot.** One finger holds firm in place on a given fret and string; it is then used as a fulcrum while other fingers swing to spots within reach.

• **Glide & Pivot.** Slide *without pressure* up or down a given string, establish a finger at a given fret, then use it as a pivot to move other fingers into place.

• **Balance.** Concentrate the weight of your hand on a single finger, and get ready to spring into action.

More Indications Above the Staff: Chord Accompaniment

In this book, chord indications are offered primarily for the benefit of accompanists. This said, knowing the harmony helps you determine which notes to let ring together and which to cut short or, in the words of country singer Kenny Rogers, "When to hold 'em and when to fold 'em."

Chord Indications with "Capo-2" (C\D or G\A). Banjoists often play tunes in the keys of C and G that are intended to be tuned up or capoed up two frets to D and A when playing with a fiddler or band. I couldn't decide whether to make the chord indications consistent with tab notation or with fiddle pitch; ultimately I included both. For most D and A tunes, therefore, you'll see chord notations like this: C\D or G\A. In each case the chord to the left of the backslash is consistent with tab played on an open banjo; the chord on the right is consistent with fiddle pitch or the sound of the banjo capoed or tuned up.

Chords with a 5-Suffix (G5, D5, A5, E5, etc.). When accompanying "modal" tunes, omitting the middle note of major or minor chords is often an effective strategy (for more on this, see Chapter 3). For example, instead playing either an A-chord (A-C♯-E) or an A-minor chord (A-C-E), you would simply play A-E. This kind of "tone cluster" – equivalent to *power chords* in rock guitar – is sometimes referred to by musicians as *hollow fifths*, and can be indicated via the "5" suffix. See the chart below for some chords of this type commonly found in G, G-modal, and double-C tunings.

1

Chords with a 5-Suffix, or "Power Chords" for Banjo

***Dual Chord Symbols:** Chord to left of backslash goes with open banjo; chord on right is for capoed banjo or fiddle*

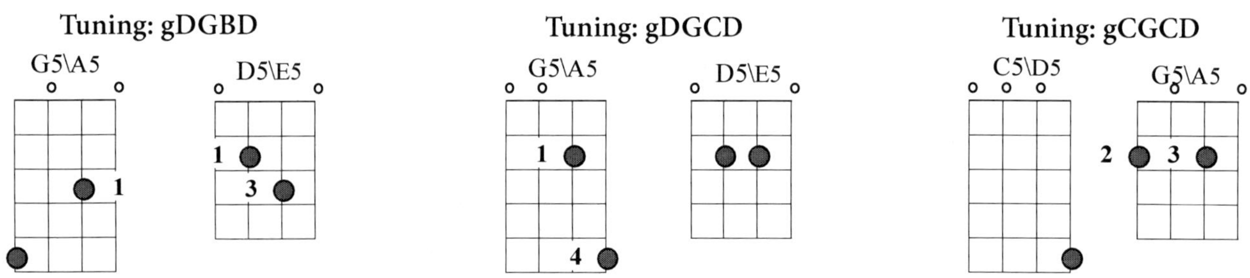

"Capo-2" and the 5th String: Tuning and Notation

The indication "Capo-2" means that if you want to play a given tune in the same key as a fiddler or band, you need to place your capo at the 2nd fret. In this case you also need to tune your 5th string up the equivalent of two frets, or place it in a 5th-string capoing device at the second 5th-string fret (equivalent to fret 7 on the long-strings).

Effect on Notation. Once you have capoed up, fret locations shown on the 5th string in this book assume that you are using a 5th-string capoing device. If instead you tune up the 5th string the equivalent of two frets, all fret locations on that string necessarily *go down* two frets.

Parts, Alternative Parts, and Alternative Measures

Most Fiddle Tunes have two Parts: one in relatively low range and one higher up. Historically these two parts have had names reflecting their musical characters, such as *low and high turns*, *coarse and fine parts*, or *tune and turn.* Nowadays, most people simply call them A Part and B Part – sometimes leading to confusion about which is which. If tunes have more than two parts they are simply labeled C, D, E, and up.

Alternative Parts. Variations or alternative versions on a given part are labeled with a "prime" character, as in A', B', and so on.

Alternative measures. Alternative ways to play specific measures sometimes appear at the end of a tune. For example, "Alt. A1-2" means, "alternative version for Part A, measures 1-2."

Playing Directions Borrowed from Standard Notation

Several common standard-notation playing directions are used in this tab system.

First and Second Endings. The first time through a section, play the material under bracket #1; the second time skip what's under #1, and play the material under bracket #2.

D.C. al Fine; D.S. al Fine. *D.C.* (da capo) means return to the beginning and keep playing until you see the notation, *Fine* (the end). *D.S.* (dal segno) means "return to the *segno,* (𝄋), and continue playing until you see the notation, *Fine.*

Coda and Proceed-to-Coda Sign (𝄌). A prescribed or suggested ending, or *coda* for a piece of music is indicated via the coda sign. If the same sign appears within a piece, it signals that on the very last time through, you should proceed from that point directly to the coda.

D.C. al Coda; D.S. al Coda. Return to the beginning or to the *segno*, (𝄋), and – the very last time through – go from the proceed-to-coda sign (𝄌) directly to the coda.

Fermata, or Musical "Eyelash": (𝄐**).** When a *fermata* appears above a note, let that note linger.

Arpeggio, or broken-chord symbol (⁏ **).** This symbol calls for a controlled brush that brings out the individual strings.

Banjo Tunings Used in This Volume

G Tuning (gDGBD)	**G-Modal Tuning (gDGCD)**	**Double C Tuning (gCGCD)**
• Tune string 3 to G below middle C • Tune open string 2 to fret 4, string 3 • Tune open string 1 to fret 3, string 2 • Tune open string 5 to fret 5, string 1 • Tune fret 5, string 4 to open string 3	(Also known as *Mountain Minor* and *Sawmill Tuning*): • Start with open G-tuning • Tune up open string 2 to match the pitch of fret 5, string 3	• Start with open G-tuning • Tune open string 2 up to match the pitch of fret 5, string 3 • Tune fret 7, string 4 down to match open string 3 (Or: tune string 4 an octave lower than string 2)

Brush Up on Your Double-Thumbing

Double-thumbing is an alternation of downstrokes and thumb-strokes in which each successive use of the thumb also alternates between one of the long strings and the 5th string. Following is an exercise that runs through most of the possible string combinations and is guaranteed to sharpen your mastery of this truly fundamental clawhammer skill. Included are:

- Regular Double-Thumbing (T on long string first)
- Reverse Double-Thumbing (T on 5th string first)
- Alternating Regular and Reverse
- Second Downstroke Returns to the Preceding Drop-Thumb String
- Clawhammer Backward "Roll" (second downstroke crosses back over the preceding drop-thumb string)
- Drop-Thumb on Non-Adjacent String

Double-Thumbing Exercise

2

Any Tuning

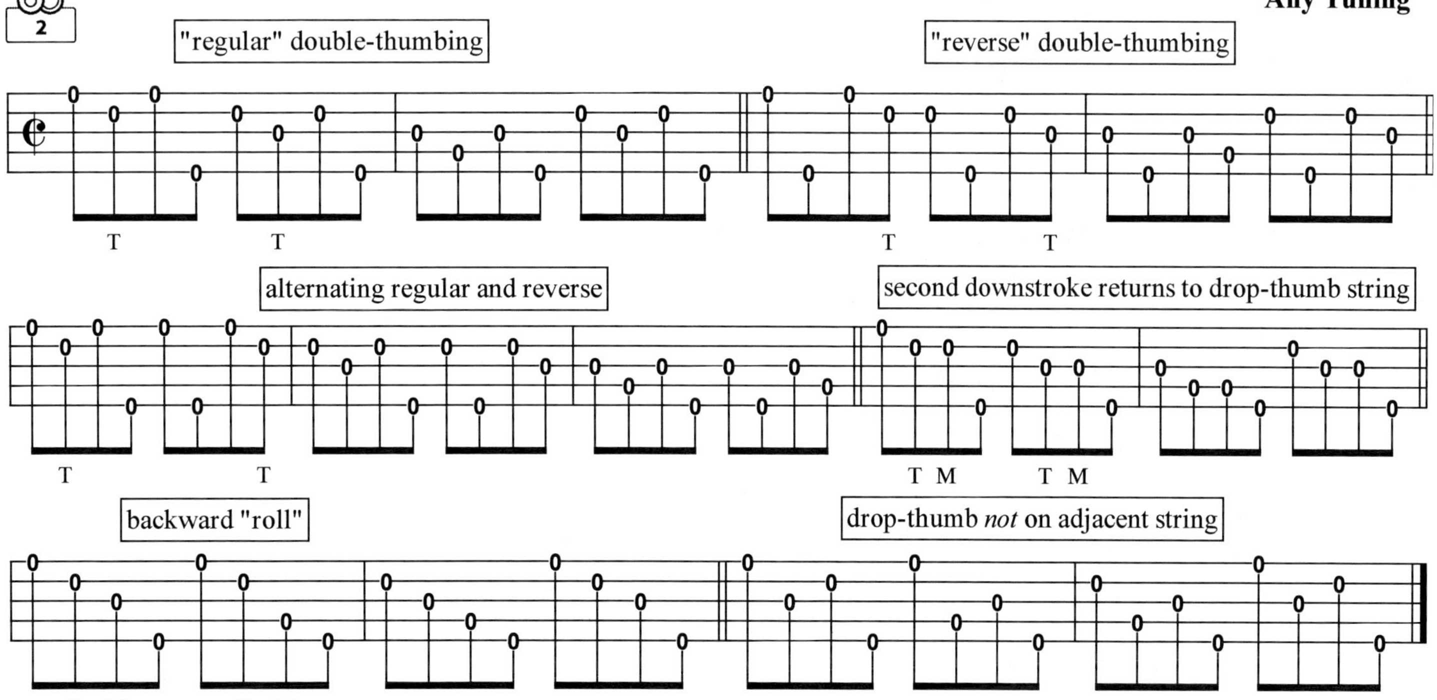

Chapter 3. Pointers on Technique & Style

Playing Ascending Runs and Projecting Melody Up the Neck

Other things being equal, you'll always get the strongest sounding notes and most control over the shape of the melody through the use of drop- and double-thumbing. Drop-thumbing does have one technical limitation, however. When the plucking hand is held in normal clawhammer configuration, the thumb is stationed so that only the long strings *lower in pitch* than the preceding downstroke are directly accessible. As illustrated in Example 3-1a, if you pluck string 2 with a downstroke, the following T-note would generally fall either on strings 3 or 4 (*not* on string 1). Similarly, if you pluck string 3 with M (Example 3-1b), the following T-note would generally fall on string 4 – *not* on strings 1 or 2). Because of this logistical quirk, it is simply much easier to play descending runs of notes in clawhammer than to play ascending runs.

Using alternate-string pull-offs is one common method for playing ascending runs in clawhammer (Example 3-1c; for explanation see p. 12). Two others – each involving fretting-hand strategies that enhance the scope of drop-and double thumbing – are *Keith-Picking* and *5th-String Fretting.*

Example 3-1

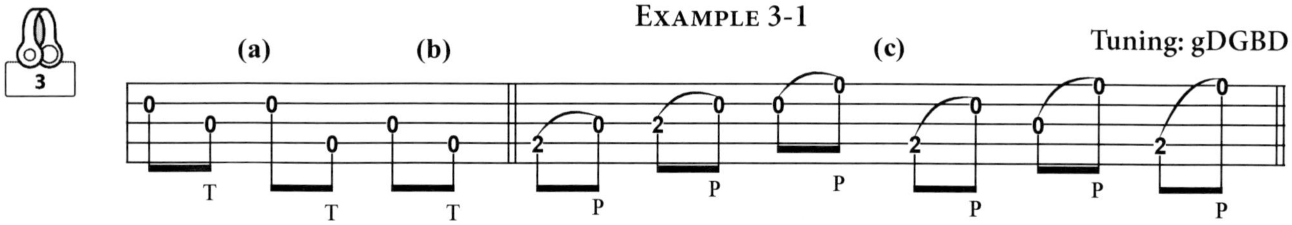

Keith-Picking

Keith-picking is an approach to fretted instrument playing borrowed from 3-finger "melodic banjo," as pioneered by Bill Keith (1939-2015). For every pair of eighth notes, the idea is to take the fretting hand far enough up the neck so that the pitch of the thumb-string is actually higher than the pitch of the open string that precedes it. Example 3-2 shows an ascending and descending G major scale played Keith-style. For the very first pair of notes (3-2a), the downstroke is open string 3 (G), but the following T-string – fret 7, string 4 – is one note higher in pitch at A. For the next pair of notes (2b), the downstroke is open string 2 (B), but the following T-string – fret 5, string 3 – is one note higher in pitch at C. When the scale is descending, observe that strings can be skipped; for example, Example 3-2c shows the downstroke at open string 1 (D), but the next note down in the scale (C) is played by the thumb two strings away at fret 5, string 3.

Example 3-2 . Keith Picking

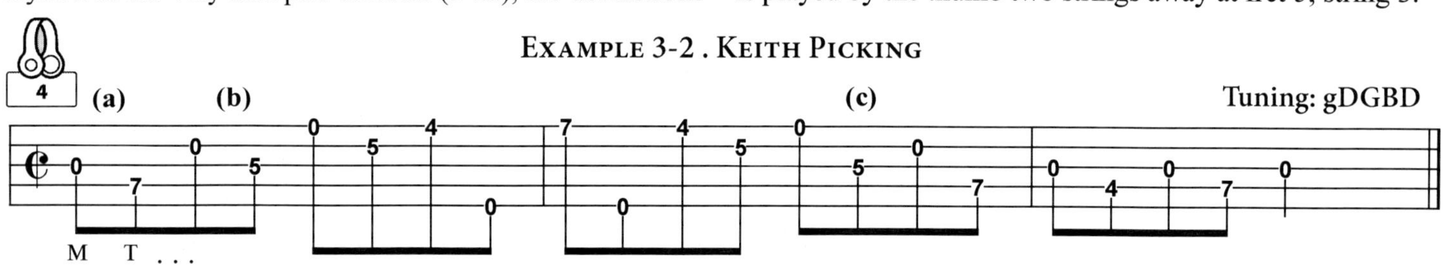

Taking the 5th: How Fretting the Drone-string Opens Up Melodic Horizons

Here's another trick borrowed from our bluegrass banjo-pickin' cousins. Somewhere along the line, somebody declared that it simply wasn't proper to fret the 5th string in old-time banjo. This never made sense to me, and indeed having the frets on this string at your disposal dramatically increases the amount of musical territory you'll be accurately able to cover. In fact, once you fully incorporate this tactic into your repertoire, playing ascending runs in clawhammer *above the fifth fret* ceases to be particularly problematic.

To make sure your fretted 5th string plays in tune, there are a few things you'll need to take into account

- **Bridge.** Position the bridge correctly; on the 5th string, the fretted note and harmonic must match at the 17th fret.
- **Pip.** The *pip* (5th-string nut) must be low enough for notes on the string to fret true.
- **5th-String Capo.** "Railroad spike" capos or similar devices must sit entirely below the level of the fretwires, or be set outside the path of the string.

Will I Run Out of Frets? Many open-back banjos built these days have *frailing scoops* that in effect do away with the instrument's top several frets. The length of these scoops has never been standardized but most of them allow you at least a few frets above the 12th fret, or *octave.* Rest assured that only a relatively small proportion of the settings in this volume go that high, and that only a very few hit the 17th fret or higher. Borderline situations may arise when the tab calls for a capo at the second fret, in which case you might simply tune the entire banjo up the equivalent of two frets instead of using a capo.

FRETTING THE 5TH STRING LENDS ITSELF to using up-the-neck *fingering forms*, or shapes – finger configurations that yield specific three- and four-note runs when the strings are plucked in succession – usually via an alternation of downstroke and thumb. Let's look at the shape in Example 3-3, which for the sake of illustration I've located at fret 7 (that is, *seventh position*). Observe that there are three possible string orders involving double thumbing, as illustrated in Example 3-4: 1-2-1-5 (a); 1-5-1-2 (b); and 2-5-1-2 (c). In addition, there are two string orders that call for two consecutive downstroke + drone sequences, also illustrated in Example 3-4, namely 2-5-1-5 (d), and 1-5-2-5 (e).

EXAMPLE 3-3

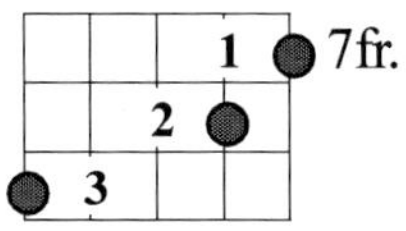

Tuning: gDGBD

EXAMPLE 3-4. FRETTING FORM PICKING OPTIONS

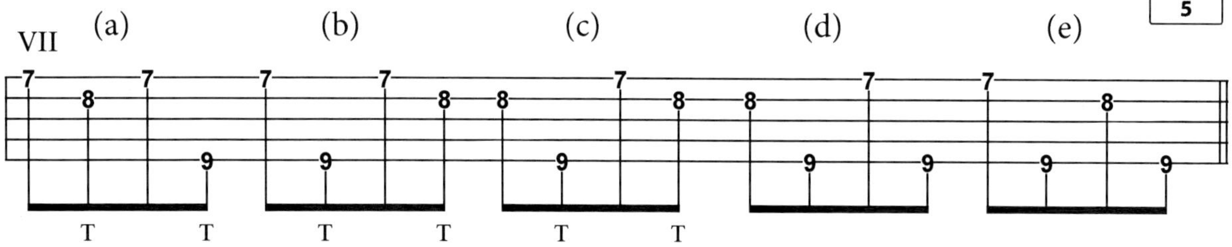

EXAMPLES 3-5 AND 3-6 SHOW SEVERAL SUCH FORMS for G tuning and Double C tuning, respectively, most of which appear fairly frequently in this book. Below each example, corresponding exercises illustrate how these shapes can be turned into series of commonly used runs via the 2-5-1-2 string sequence. Note that each chord shape is marked with a typographical symbol, which is then referenced above the corresponding passage in the exercise.

HINT FOR SERIES 1. For Series 1 sequences in both tunings, keep the 1st and 4th fingers spread out on strings 5 and 1, respectively as you glide from shape to shape, and adjust your other fingers on string 2 as called for.

HINTS FOR SERIES 2. For Series 2 sequence in G Tuning, keep the 1st and 3rd fingers spread out on strings 1 and 5, respectively, as you glide from shape to shape, and adjust your other fingers on string 2 as called for. For Series 2 in Double C Tuning, most of the forms call for maintaining a 2-string half-barre on strings 1 and 2; then – as you move among shapes – you can use either the 2nd or 3rd finger on string 5.

EXAMPLE 3-5a. G-TUNING SERIES 1

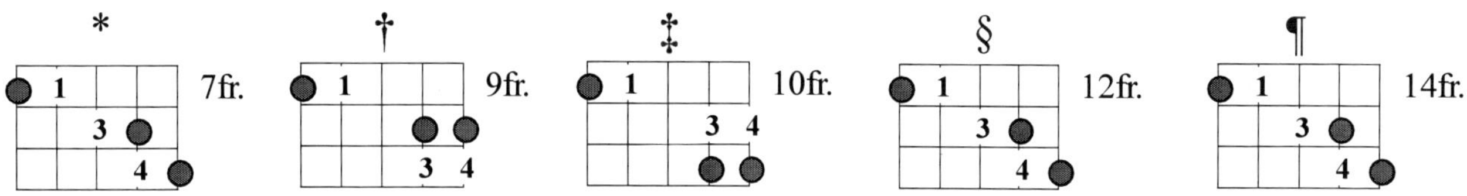

G-TUNING SERIES 1 EXERCISE

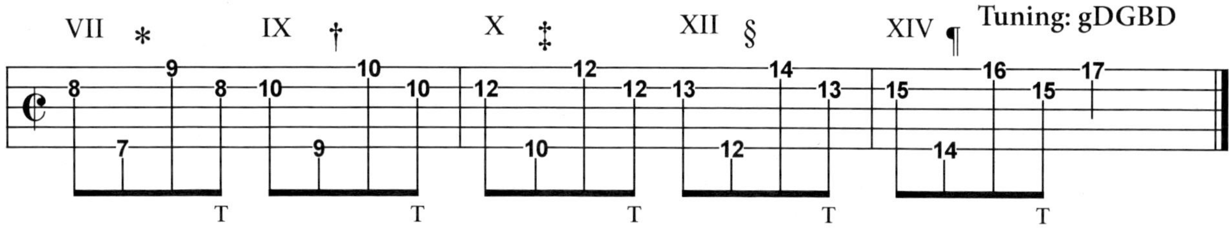

EXAMPLE 3-5b. G-TUNING SERIES 2

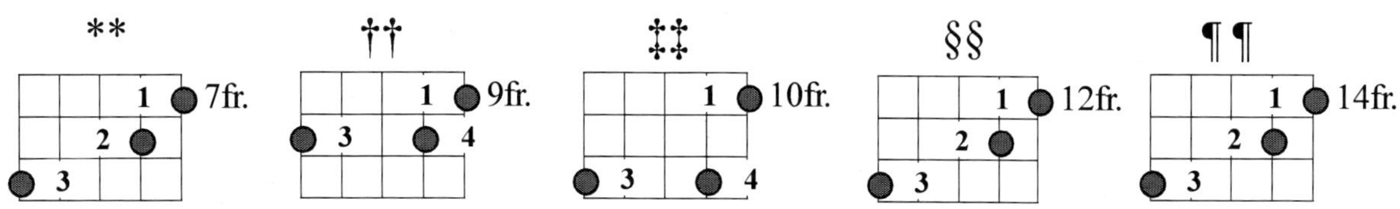

G-TUNING SERIES 2 EXERCISE

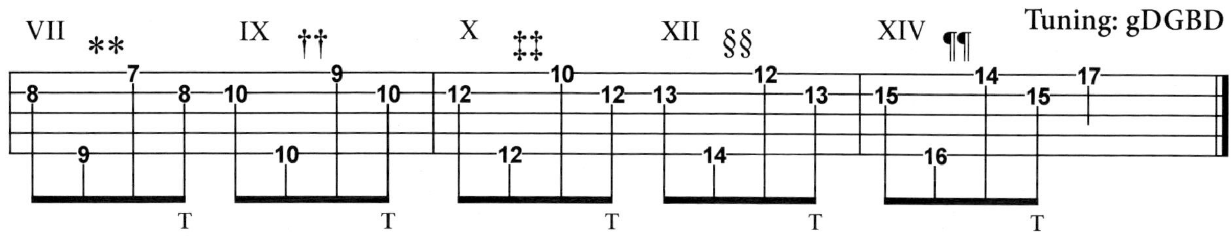

Example 3-6a. gCGCD Series 1

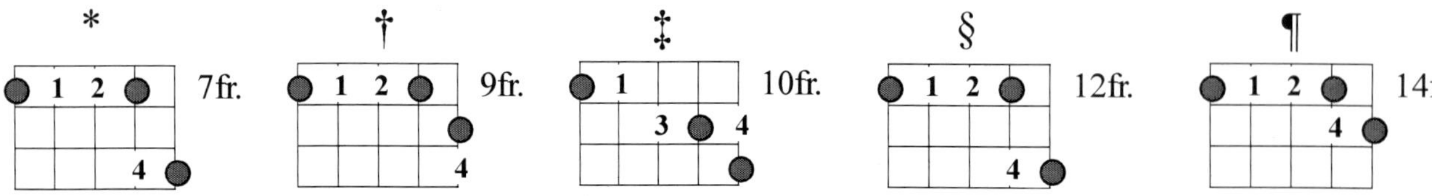

gCGCD Series 1 Exercise

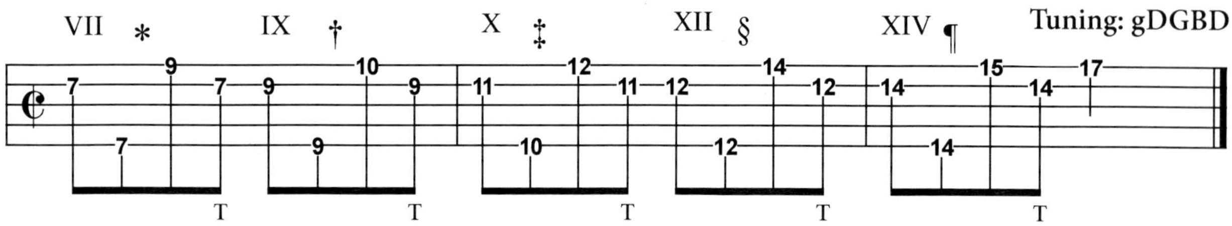

Example 3-6b. gCGCD Series 2

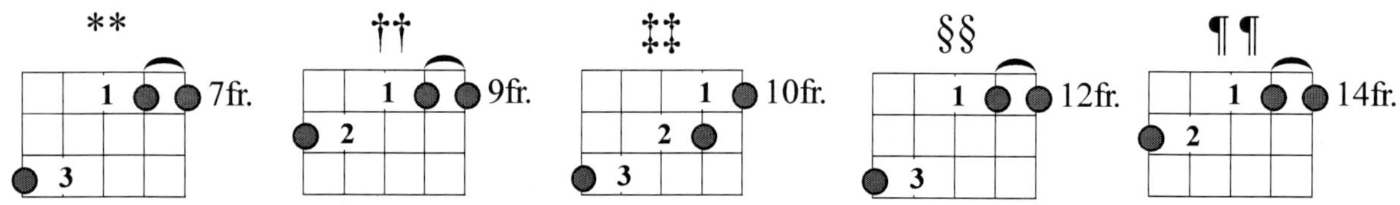

gCGCD Series 2 Exercise

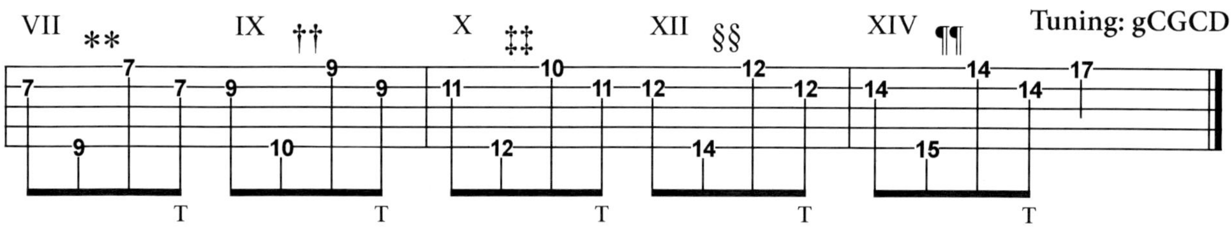

Priming

One stylistic feature that appears frequently in Cape Breton and P.E.I. fiddling is sometimes called *priming*. Fiddlers amplify the volume of an open string by simultaneously noting the same pitch on the adjacent lower string; they then bow the two strings at once. For example, a fiddler might bow the open first fiddle string (high E) and use a left-hand finger to press down the same pitch on the fiddle *second string;* he or she would then bow both first and second strings together to get the desired sound.

I often like to use the priming technique on banjo, and I'm convinced that it makes both for more resonance and a more authentic sound. Example 3-7 shows how this works for three common banjo tunings. In open G-tuning (gDGBD), for example, double the first open string (D) by pressing down fret 3, string 2 (then pluck both at once via a downstroke). Similarly, in double C-tuning (gCGCD), double the open second string (C) by pressing down fret 5, string 3 (then pluck both at once).

Example 3-7. Priming

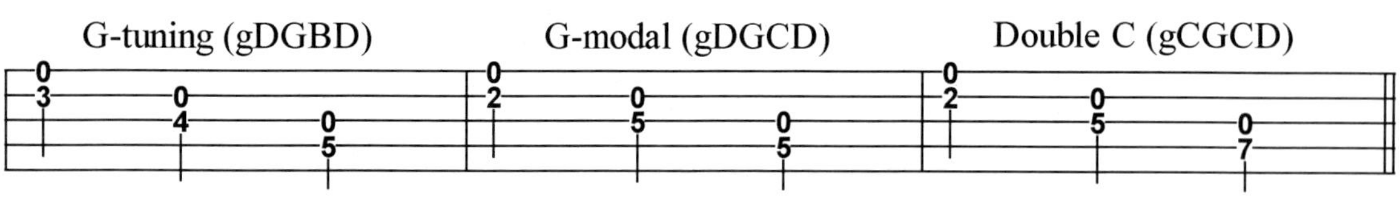

Triplets

A triplet is a group of three notes – in "duple meters" such as 4/4 and cut-time – played in the space normally occupied by a quarter note or two eight notes. Generally, they appear topped by a horizontal bracket with a centered number 3. In clawhammer, most triplets are obtained via an initial downstroke followed by some combination of hammer-ons (H) and pull-offs (P). Some common examples are illustrated in Example 3-8 and described below. The count is: 1-&-a, 2-&-a, and so on. Observe that three-note groupings in 6/8 time (jigs) are treated somewhat differently, and are discussed in the intro to Chapter 9.

• **MHH Triplets** can start on either an open or stopped string (Example 3-8a and b). If the H involves a stretch, don't try to stretch and hammer at the same time; always stretch first and then hammer.

• **MPP Triplets** can lead to either an open or stopped string (3-8c and d). The trick is to place all fingers involved on the fretboard at once, then peel them off one at a time.

• **MHP Triplets** can start on either an open or stopped string (3-8e and f). The H must be strong enough to generate the sound that supports the final P-note. If the initial note is fretted, that note must continue to sound until the hammering finger reaches the fretboard.

• **MPH Triplets** can include middle notes that are either open or fretted (3-8g and h). The final H always needs to be strong; if the middle note is fretted, make sure to keep that note sounding until the H reaches the fretboard.

• **MPT Triplets** (3-8 i and j). These triplets are essentially drop-thumb pairs with a pull-off inserted in the middle. The challenge is to make sure that the three notes are even.

11

Example 3-8. Triplets

Tuning: gDGBD

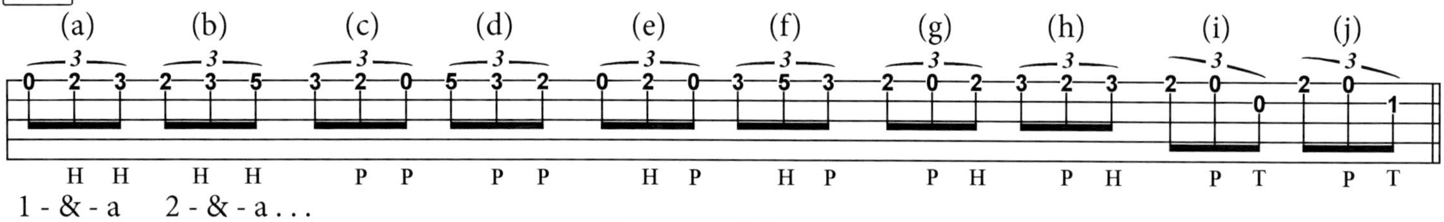

Grace Notes

As the name implies, grace notes, or *graces* are used for musical decoration. Let's look at three varieties – *slow graces, single graces,* and *double graces*. And as usual, it will help to listen to the provided audio examples.

Slow Graces

The slow grace note, also known by its formal name, *appoggiatura*, is basically an elongated lead-in to a strong note of the measure; and often comes to that note from below. For example, if the first note of a tune in the key of G is B (Example 3-9, first measure), you can decorate it by starting on A (two frets lower), then hammering from that note to B, as shown in Example 3-9, second measure. Since slow graces often appear in the tab as conventional hammer-ons (or sometimes slides), you may not even notice them unless you are on the lookout.

12

Example 3-9. Slow Grace

Tuning: gDGBD

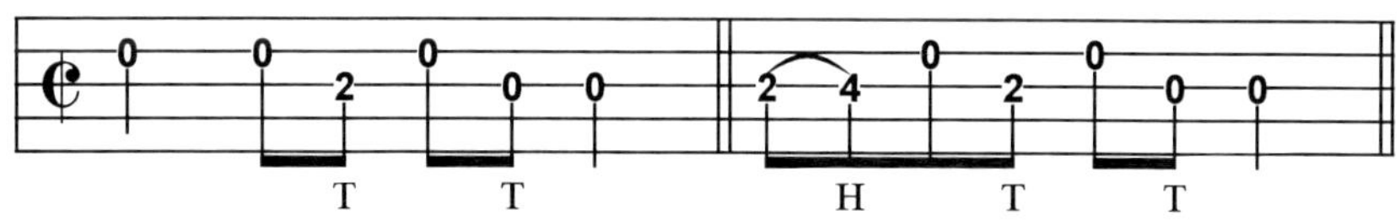

Single & Double Graces

The most important thing to remember about single- and double graces is that they theoretically occupy no time, and above all must not affect the listener's time perception of the full-fledged note(s) that follow. This is necessarily something of a balancing act because of course graces must occupy some time; to make this work a bit of "legerdemain" (sleight of hand) is required.

Single graces (Example 3-10a) are very quick notes that can be expressed as a pull-off, hammer-on, or slide. The trick is to start your H, P, or S as soon as you pluck the string, then linger on the hammered, pulled, or slide-destination note throughout the remainder of its notated value. The first measure of 10a (excerpted from "Lord Gordon") shows the passage without the grace note; the grace note – marked * – is then added at the start of the second measure. On beat 1, strike fret 2, string 2 then immediately pull that string off. At the conclusion of the P, let open-string 1 sound for the duration of its notated value (that is, half a beat). The companion audio illustrates how the grace note enhances the melody without changing the rhythmic relationship among full-fledged notes.

Double graces (Example 3-10b) are generally performed in clawhammer as a pair of super-quick hammer-ons or pull-offs, or as a combination of Hs and Ps. The trick is to play your Hs, Ps (or combinations thereof) as soon as you pluck the string, then linger on the full-fledged note that follows throughout the remainder of its notated value. The first measure of 10b (also excerpted from "Lord Gordon") shows the passage without the grace note; the double grace – marked † – appears at the start of measure 2. On beat 1,

13

Example 3-10a. Single Grace

Tuning: gCGCD

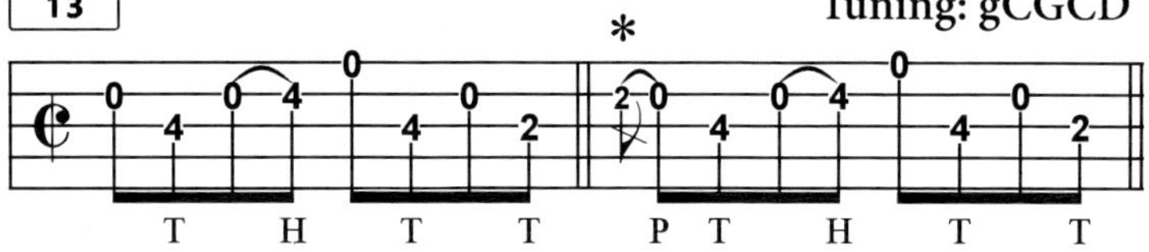

14

Example 3-10b. Double Grace

Tuning: gCGCD

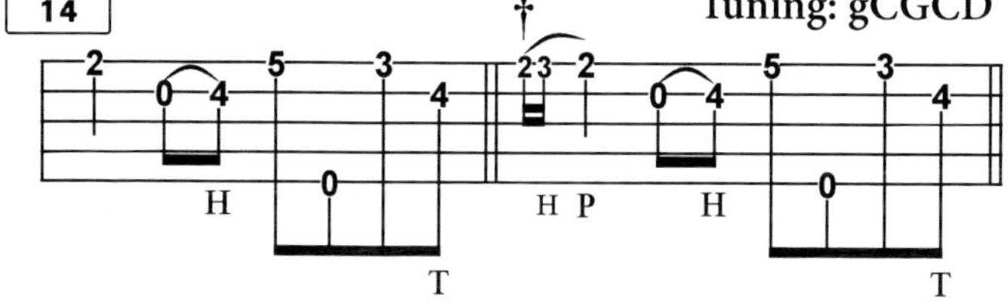

strike fret 2, string 1; hammer quickly to fret 3, string 1; then pull off just as quickly from that fret back to fret 2. At the conclusion of the P, let fret 2, string 1 sound for the duration of its notated value (that is, one beat). The companion audio illustrates how the double grace enhances the melody without changing the rhythmic relationship among the full-fledged notes.

It is extremely important that these maneuvers be performed with sufficient crispness so that the listener can plainly perceive which are the grace notes, and which are the full-fledged notes that follow. In other words, the melody should sound as clearly comprehensible after you add graces, as when you play it unadorned.

Here's one fiddler's description of the gracing process on his instrument, which I was able to apply to banjo. He described the transition from upward slur to downward slur (equivalent to transiting from a hammer-on to a pull-off on banjo) as a kind of rubbing movement on the string; he didn't really need to press down very much during the transition.

Another way of thinking about double graces is by comparing them to triplets. Observe that the *MHP Triplet* (Examples 3-8e and f) is obtained via downstroke, hammer-on, and pull-off – exactly the same maneuvers used to perform the double grace. The only difference between the triplet on the one hand, and the double-grace-followed-by-quarter-note on the other, is the time relationship between the notes involved. In the triplet, each note is even; in the double grace the first two notes are very quick, while the last note is long.

The Cape Breton "Cut," or Scottish "Birl"

To serve in place of a whole battery of complex piping ornaments, Scottish fiddlers developed a bowing technique known as the *birl*, which is known as *cuts* or *cuttings* in Cape Breton and Prince Edward Island. The Cape Breton cut most often involves two alternations in bow direction on the same pitch (usually down-up-down), yielding an uneven triplet-like figure generally written in cut time and 4/4 time as two sixteenth notes followed by an eighth, as illustrated in Example 3-11a.

Irish fiddlers came up with a somewhat different solution to the same problem. Instead of using bow strokes to emulate piping ornaments, they developed a technique called the *Irish roll* that involves slurring several graces and full-fledged notes off the same bow stroke.

Over the years, I have employed several methods for emulating cuts in clawhammer style, depending on the feel of the piece and its tempo. Sometimes I'll use modified MHP or MPH triplets (Example 3-11, b and c); and sometimes I'll use a technique I developed some years ago that essentially uses the picking fingernail as a flatpick (3-11d). Start with a conventional downstroke; follow that with a wrist-driven upstroke (V) in which you catch the string with the underside of the fingernail; then conclude the figure with one more downstroke.

Hint on Style. Quite often it is customary to lean into a cut from a preceding eighth or sixteenth note as illustrated in Example 3-11, measure 2 (excerpted from "Devil in the Kitchen"). The companion audio illustrates how this sounds.

15

Example 3-11. Cuts, or Birls

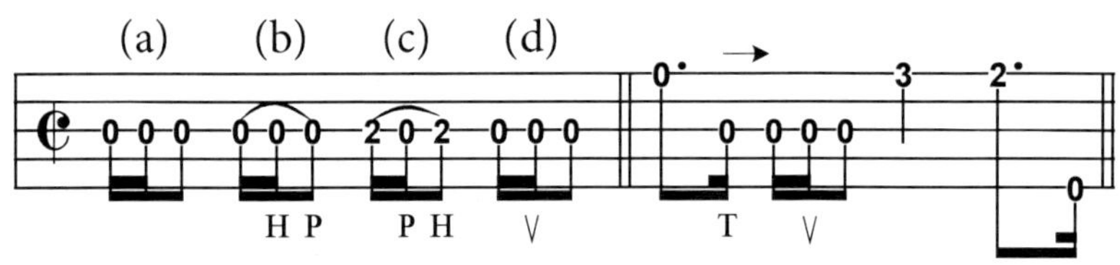

Tuning: gDGBD

Syncopation

In "music-speak," syncopation is defined as an *unexpected* musical accent. The term "unexpected" is of course relative, but as used here it means placing an accent on a "weak" beat of a measure, or – more to the point – between the beats of a measure. In 4/4 time, for example, the first beat of a measure is "expected" to be the strongest beat and the third beat is the second strongest; if instead you place a major accent on beats two or four that would be considered to be a syncopation. Alternatively, if you place a major accent on an eighth note located between any two beats, that would also be considered a syncopation.

Note: Although most reels, hornpipes set-tunes, and marches are properly written in cut-time (2/2), for ease of visualization I refer to beats in any given measure as if the time signature is 4/4.

My approach to syncopation begins with a very simple building block I call a *skip-stroke* (others call it a *ghost brush*). Here's how it goes. Play a bum-titty strum, written as a quarter note and two eighths (Example 3-12a), and get the feel of the maneuver. Now, play the same maneuver but with one important modification. The quarter note is still played by M and the brush-thumb movement is the same. What's different is that during the brush motion, M *skips* over the strings (in other words, it avoids hitting any strings at all). As the ghost-brush movement continues, T is brought into contact with the 5th string, ready to play. Finally, T plucks the 5th string in the same way it would in an ordinary brush-thumb. This appears in tablature as shown in Example 3-12b. The "tie" shows that the quarter note continues to sound through the first half of the second beat, while an "X" placed under the skipped-note tells you that a full brush motion is performed.

This technique always places a strong 5th-string, or drone note exactly half-way through the pattern's second beat. We can elaborate this maneuver by replacing the initial quarter note in the bumm-titty rhythm by two eighth notes (Example 4-1, c-g). The first of the two eighth notes is of course played by a downstroke, but there are several ways that the second eighth note can be obtained, namely via hammer-on (4-1c), pull-off (4-1d), slide (4-1e), or thumb-stroke (4-1, f-g). Throughout all these maneuvers, observe that the second eighth note is tied over through the skipped-note that follows, while the "X" placed under the skipped-note tells you that a full, but soundless brush motion is called for. The skip that follows the second eighth note creates a "space" that allows that note to sing out in its between-beat spot; in effect, this prominence immediately identifies the note as a syncopation.

For a more detailed exploration of how to obtain syncopated rhythmic figures in clawhammer, see my book, *Appalachian Fiddle Tunes for Clawhammer Banjo* (Mel Bay).

16

Example 3-12. Syncopation

Tuning: gDGBD

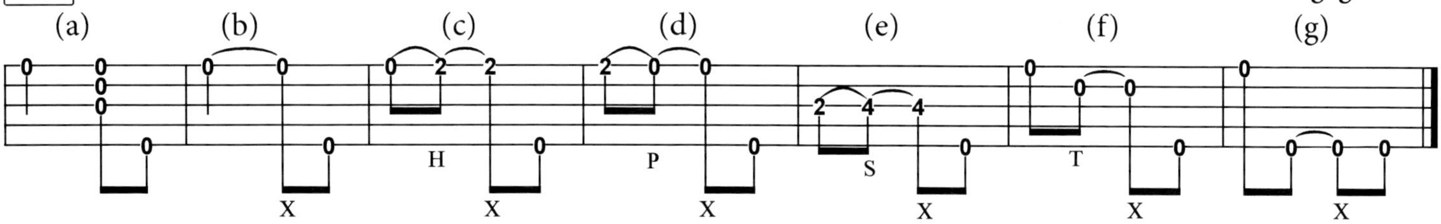

Demystifying Modes

A mode can be thought of as an ordered collection, or *gamut* of pitches plus an explicit or implied set of rules for using them. When we talk about modes – or use the term "modal" – in Celtic or Canadian music we are referring to the many non-major scales commonly found in fiddle tunes. Although I can't offer a comprehensive treatment of modes in this space, I can present a relatively simple system that will help you make sense of what you're likely to encounter.

When dealing with any particular modal tune, our main priority should be accurately hearing and reproducing the notes actually played – not trying to assign a tune to any particular category. It may have been a great step forward in the early 20th century when folk-song collector Cecil Sharp urged musicians to stop trying to change traditional melodies so they followed formal rules associated with major and minor scales. However, his suggested solution – using *church modes* such as Dorian, Mixolydian, and Aeolian for classification – eventually proved to be nearly as limiting.

Before we get started, here are some definitions.

• **Gamut.** The pitches that make up a piece or mode set in order from low to high (usually for the distance of an octave).

• **Half & Whole Tones.** Half tone = one fret; whole tone = two frets

• **Diatonic.** A seven-note scale, equivalent to the white keys of the piano, such as C-D-E-F-G-A-B-(C)

• **Pentatonic.** A five-note scale with no half tones, equivalent to the black keys of the piano; for example, C Pentatonic = C-D-E-G-A-(C)

• **Scale Inversion.** Begin on any note of a diatonic or pentatonic scale and go up an octave. The first inversion of the C diatonic scale, for example, begins on D (D-E-F-G-A-B-C-D). Similarly, the first inversion of the C pentatonic scale is D-E-G-A-C-D

•**Pentatonic Inversion Nomenclature.** Pentatonic inversions are traditionally named for French-system note names (Do-Re-Mi-Sol-La); For example, the first pentatonic inversion is also known as "Re-Pentatonic." In this book, however, I will generally refer to "Do-Pentatonic" as *major pentatonic,* and to "La-Pentatonic" as *minor pentatonic.*

• **Inflection.** Whether a given note is natural, sharp or flat (for example, G, G♯, and G♭ are all inflections of the note G)

• **Interval.** Musical distance; observe that the distance from a note to itself counts as "one" (playing two notes at the same pitch, as in priming, is called a *unison*).

• **Major 3rd vs. Minor 3rd.** A major 3rd interval = four frets; a minor 3rd interval = three frets (example: A-C♯ is a major 3rd; A-C♮ is a minor 3rd).

• **Major 7th vs. Minor 7th.** A major 7th interval = one fret less than an octave; a minor 7th interval = two frets less than an octave (example: A-G♯ is a major 7th; A-G♮ is a minor 7th).

• **Sixths.** A major 6th interval = 3 frets less than an octave; a minor 6th interval = 4 frets less than an octave (example: A-F♯ is a major 6th, but A-F♮ is a minor 6th).

• **Tonic Tone:** the key note (the note G in the key of G)

• **Tonic and Dominant Chords.** The tonic chord is the key chord, (often called the I-chord by musicians); the dominant chord is the one that generally leads back to the tonic. In the major mode, the dominant chord is based on the fifth note of the scale (often referred to by musicians as the V-chord).

Diatonic Modes

The church modes, sometimes called "Sharpian Modes" are *inversions* of the diatonic scale. We learn a lot about their similarities and differences by transposing them so that they all begin on the same tonic note. Example 3-13 shows the four church modes you are likely to encounter in Celtic and Canadian fiddling, all starting on a G tonic.

Start by **Checking the 3rd and 7th tones** of a given *gamut;* this is where most modal variation takes place. Observe that in Example 3-13, all 3rd tones are marked with an asterisk, and all 7th tones are marked with a dagger.

Major-Like vs. Minor-Like. Whether a mode is perceived as "major-like" or "minor-like" depends primarily on the third note of the scale. In the key of G, for example, if a mode features a major 3rd (B♮), we tend to hear it as major-like. If the mode features a minor 3rd (B♭), we tend to hear it as minor-like.

Major/Ionian vs. Mixolydian. The 3rd tone of the scale is major in both these modes. The difference between them is the 7th tone. The major mode features a major 7th tone (F♯ in the key of G), whereas the Mixolydian mode features a minor 7th tone (F♮ in the key of G).

Mixolydian vs. Dorian. The 7th tone is minor in both these modes (F♮ in the key of G). The difference between them is the 3rd tone. The Mixolydian mode features a major 3rd tone (B♮ in the key of G), whereas the Dorian mode features a minor 3rd tone (B♭ in the key of G).

Dorian vs. Minor/Aeolian. Both 3rd and 7th tones are minor in both these modes (B♭ and F♮, respectively in the key of G). The difference between them is in the 6th tone (marked with a double dagger); the Dorian mode has a major 6th tone (E♮ in the key of G), whereas the minor/Aeolian mode features a minor 6th tone (E♭ in the key of G).

17

Example 3-13. Diatonic Modes from the Same Tonic Note

Tuning: gDGBD

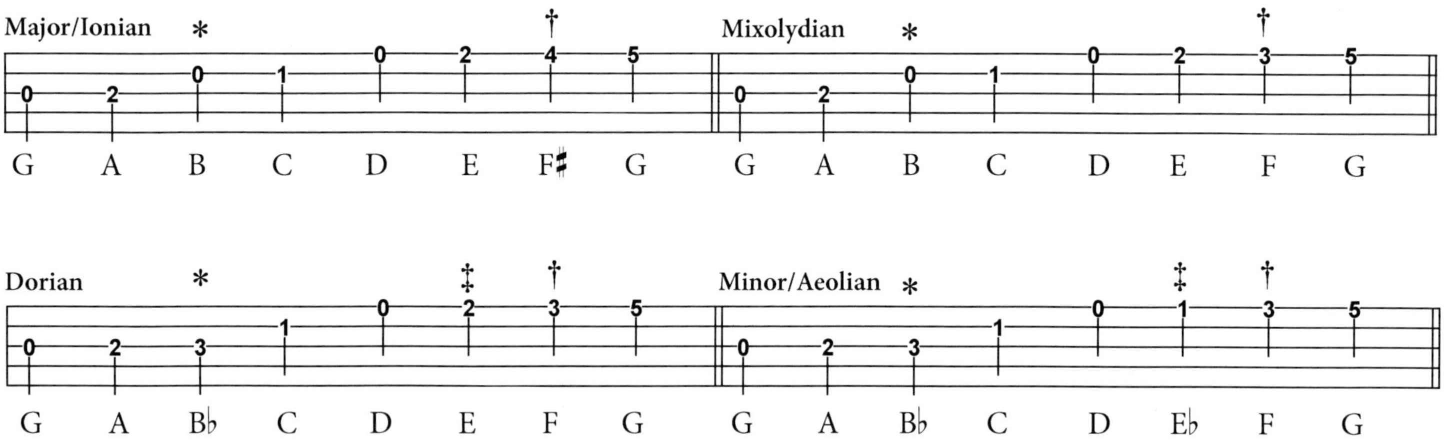

Limitations of Diatonic Mode Classification

Diatonic mode classification is all well and good in a musical laboratory. When dealing with actual "modal" fiddle tunes collected in the field, however, the melodies often do not fit into these convenient categories. Here are some of the common issues that arise.

- The 7th diatonic tone can sometimes be major and sometimes minor within the same tune; it can also be missing entirely. In a tune with a G key center, for example, the 7th tone can fluctuate between F♯ and F-natural (and sometimes there's no F at all).

- The diatonic 3rd tone can vary within the same tune among major, minor, and even *neutral* inflections (a neutral 3rd falls somewhere between major and minor values). The 3rd tone can also be entirely missing. In a tune with a G key center, for example, the 3rd tone can fluctuate between B♮ and B♭ (and sometimes there's no B at all).

- The 6th tone of the scale can be absent from a tune. In a tune with a G key center, for example, the note E can be missing entirely.

These inconsistencies often make it impossible to assign a given tune to a specific diatonic mode. For example, a major-like tune with a variable or missing 7th tone cannot be definitively categorized as either major or Mixolydian. Similarly, a minor-like tune with a missing 6th tone cannot be tagged as either Dorian or minor/Aeolian. And tunes with a consistent minor 7th tone cannot be categorized as either Mixolydian or Dorian if the 3rd tone is variable or missing.

Instead of trying to determine the church mode of a given piece, it is far more fruitful to simply observe the notes that are actually played, with the understanding that the inflection of any given note can vary between parts within the same tune or even among phrases within a given part. In this book then, you'll encounter some modal descriptions such as "major 3rd tone with variable 7th tone;" "variable 3rd and 7th tones," "Dorian gamut," and so on.

Pentatonic Modes

When tunes have consistent "gaps" (missing 3rd, 6th, 7th, or other tones) it is likely that a pentatonic scale is in play. Pentatonics are an older musical system than diatonics; by skipping over the diatonic half-steps they traverse an octave with only five tones instead of seven. Since pentatonics skip the half steps, they are referred to as *anhemitonic* scales.

Example 3-14 shows the three most common pentatonic modes you'll encounter, all starting from a G tonic. These include Do-Pentatonic (*major pentatonic*); *Re-Pentatonic;* and La-Pentatonic (*minor pentatonic*). The row of letters below the example gives the notes and the row of numbers shows diatonic-equivalent scale tones. The first point in each scale where a diatonic half-step is skipped is marked *; the second point is marked †.

Do/Major Pentatonic. This is a major-like mode with a major 3rd scale tone; it "skips" over the 4th and 7th tones of the diatonic scale.

Re-Pentatonic. Re-Pentatonic is the first inversion of the major pentatonic scale. It is somewhat minor-sounding but in fact skips over both the 3rd and 6th diatonic scale tones. If your tune has no 3rd or 6th tones, this is probably the mode you are dealing with.

La/Minor Pentatonic. This is a minor-sounding mode with a minor 3rd scale tone. It skips both 2nd and 6th diatonic scale tones. In some musical circles, this mode is referred to as *the blues scale*.

Another Thing to Keep in Mind. The intrusion of an occasional note borrowed from the diatonic universe that fills in pentatonic "gaps" is quite commonplace and does not negate a tune's overall pentatonic nature.

18

Example 3-14. Pentatonic Modes from the Same Tonic Note

Tuning: gDGBD

Do-, or Major Pentatonic — Re-Pentatonic — La-, or Minor Pentatonic

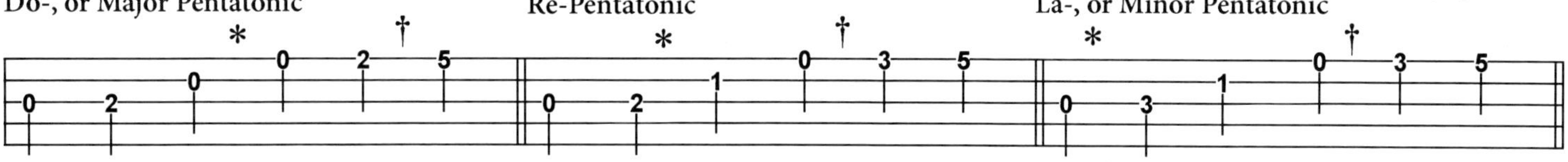

G	A	B	D	E	G	G	A	C	D	F	G	G	B♭	C	D	F	G
1	2	3	5	6	8va	1	2	4	5	7♭	8va	1	3♭	4	5	7♭	8va

Accompaniment for Modal Tunes

Coming up with effective chordal accompaniment for modal tunes is often problematic – mostly because the harmonic system we are most familiar with was created for dealing only with major and *harmonic minor* scales (see below). The main chords used to harmonize major tunes – major chords built on the first, fourth and fifth notes of the scale - are known respectively as tonic, sub-dominant, and dominant, or I-chord, IV-chord, and V-chord. In the key of C major, for example, the I, IV, and V chords are C, F, & G; in A major, the I, IV, and V chords are A, D, and E.

For minor keys, the I, IV, and V chords all start as minor chords. To make the harmonic properties of minor keys operate more like those of major keys, however, composers created *harmonic minor,* and transformed the minor V-chord into a major chord. So in the key of A harmonic minor, for example, the I, IV, and V chords are Am, Dm, and E-major.

What determines whether a three-note chord, or triad is major or minor is the inflection of the middle note. The difference between A major and A minor chords, for example, is the inflection of the middle note (C): the A major chord in root position is A-C♯-E; A minor is A-C♮-E.

This is where the 3rd and 7th tones come in. It's the third note of the diatonic scale that serves as the middle note of the tonic chord. And it's the seventh note of the diatonic scale that serves as the middle note of the dominant, or V-chord. When modes feature 3rd and 7th tones that are variable or missing, we can't determine whether major chords or minor chords should be used for accompaniment.

This is why it often makes so much musical sense to avoid using full chords as tonics and dominants for modal tunes, and to use hollow fifths/power chords instead (see "Chords with a 5-Suffix," p. 14).

The Modal Dominant. Quite often, the major chord based on the minor-7th tone (F♮ natural in the key of G; C♮ in the key of D; G♮ in the key of A) serves as an effective dominant chord for modal fiddle tunes.

On Circular Tunes

Many fiddle tunes in Celtic-based traditions were composed with what appears to be "inconclusive" endings. Instead of coming to a firm conclusion on the tonic note – or on a note that suggests the tonic chord – some tunes end on a note that suggests the dominant chord, or even the sub-dominant. The explanation is not hard to fathom.

Since fiddle tunes are intended to be played over-and-over, it is often useful to create an ending whose main purpose is to lead back to the beginning. Tunes with this format are sometimes referred to as *circular.* For those who prefer a more definitive conclusion, however, I have suggested final-sounding endings, or *codas* for most circular tunes.

Sidebar 3-1: About Reels, Hornpipes & Set Tunes

Reels

In Celtic and most North American fiddling traditions, reels are by far the most widely played type of fiddle tune. They have two beats per measure and are generally written either in cut time (2/2) or 2/4 time.

Reel Structure. Most reels have two repeated eight-measure parts; there is also an alternative short-format version consisting of one repeated four-measure part followed by a non-repeated eight-measure part. A typical measure consists of two groups of four notes, which – depending on the time signature – can be written either as eighth or sixteenth notes (Example R-1).

Example R-1: Typical Reel Measures (in Cut Time)

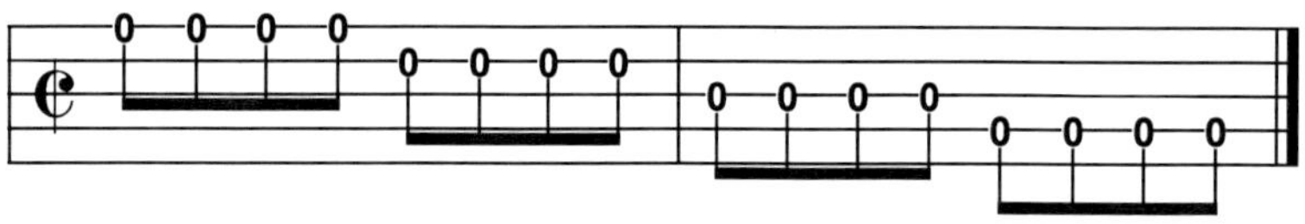

Reel Meters & Tempos. Reels should be played at tempos suitable for square dancing, contradancing, or step-dancing, namely 100-120 beats, or half-measures, per minute; in metronome-markings, that range is 𝅗𝅥=100 to 𝅗𝅥=120. At tempo, it often takes considerable energy and skill to shape all the notes in a typical reel into a coherent and danceable melody.

Reel History. The term *reel* is descended from the Anglo-Saxon word "rulla," meaning "to whirl." As a musical form, the reel originated in Scotland, probably in the last quarter of the 17th century or early 18th century. The first published collection to include examples was Robert Bremner's *A Collection of Scots Reels or Country Dances* (several volumes, 1751-61). Initially, reel tunes were employed to accompany a dance known generically as *the Scotch Reel.* Before long, they were also pressed into service as accompaniment for *country dancing,* the most popular dance form of 18th-century Britain and its colonies. There were two basic varieties: *longways* country dancing with couples aligned in two facing lines (later known in North America as *contradancing*); and square-formation country dancing, known at the time as *cotillions* but later evolving into *quadrilles* and other, less formal square dances. Throughout much of North America, dancing to reels eventually became so popular that many other tune genres were ultimately eclipsed.

Reel Phrasing

If the reel format of eight eighth notes per measure presents a special challenge to the clawhammer banjoist it is one of phrasing. To make reels come alive and make a given performance sound like dance music, each passage needs to be shaped, or "phrased" into distinct sub-melodies – each with a distinct origin and conclusion. In the most common pattern, there is an almost imperceptible break, or breath in the stream of notes prior to the last note of each four-note group; that note then leads to the first note of the next group. As shown in Example R-2, this forward-leaning from upbeat to downbeat – illustrated via a right-facing arrow – also holds true across measure lines (the comma above the staff shows the location of the "breath"; the note to the right of the comma initiates the new phrase). As for how to bring these phrases out on your instrument, I always think of this as an ever-so-slight shift in the weighting of the plucking hand that allows for a given thumb-note or downstroke to conclude one phrase or begin another.

19

Example R-2: Reel Phrasing

Source: *The Brae Reel*

Tuning: gDGCD

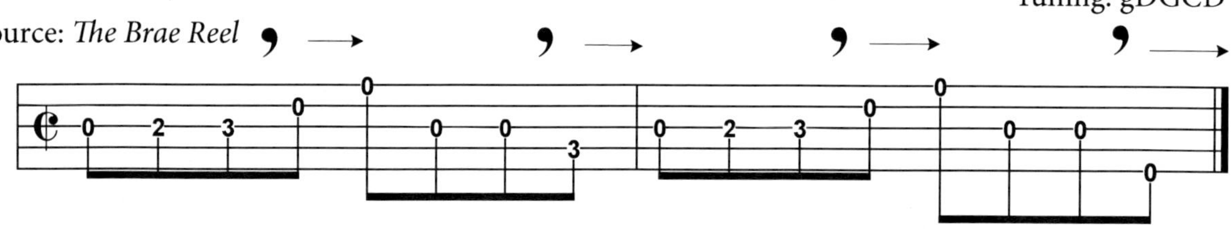

Example R-3 illustrates an alternative pattern where the breath in the stream of notes occurs prior to the third note of the second four-note group; the last two notes of the group then lead on to the first note of the next measure. Quite often a clue that the second pattern is operative is the presence of two eighth notes in the pickup measure.

20

Example R-3: Alternative Reel Phrasing

Source: *The Miramichi Fire*

Tuning: gDGCD

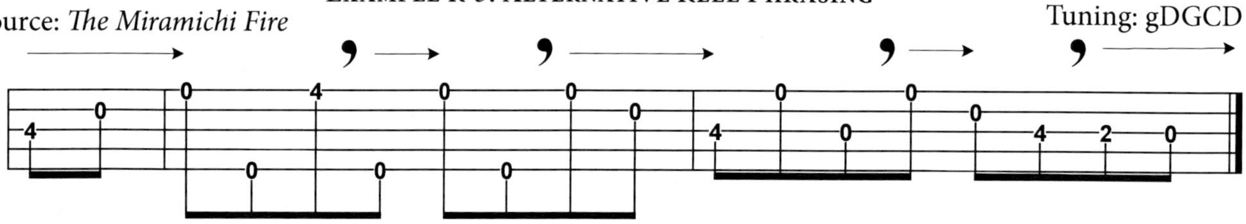

Hornpipes

Hornpipes have the same structure as "long-form" reels (that is, two repeated eight-measure parts); the same phrasing principles also apply. The modern hornpipe dates from about the third quarter of the 18th century and probably grew up in Britain as a slow to medium-tempo adaptation of the reel designed to accompany step dancing.

Hornpipe Style. In the original style of hornpipe playing – still operative in Britain and Ireland – the tunes are performed at a much slower tempo than reels, and – assuming cut time – all eighth-note pairs are played with a pronounced "dotted" rhythm. This rhythm is often notated as *dotted pairs* – alternating dotted-eighths and sixteenths (Example R-4, measure 1). Although this notation implies that the first note in each pair is three times as long as the second note, in practice the first note of each pair is only *twice* as long. It would therefore be more accurate to notate dotted pairs as triplets with the first two notes tied (measure 2). This rhythm can be expressed more "elegantly" as a quarter note plus a single eighth note under a triplet bracket (measure 3). The count, as for triplets, is 1-&-a, 2-&-a, 3-&-a, 4-&-a, etc. To get the right sound, play the dotted eighth on the "number-count" and the sixteenth on the "a-count" (the "&-count" is skipped).

The "Hornpipe Style" Label. In this volume, tunes labeled *Hornpipe Style* above the top staff should be played with the dotted rhythm as described above and at the slower tempos suggested by accompanying metronome markings.

Hornpipes Played in Reel Style. Since the late 19th century, most North American fiddlers – including those from Cape Breton and P.E.I. – have played hornpipe tunes at the same brisk tempos and with the same note-rhythms as reels. Unless otherwise indicated, this is the way that tunes with hornpipe titles in this volume should be performed.

21

Example R-4: "Dotted" Pairs in Hornpipes

Tuning: gDGBD

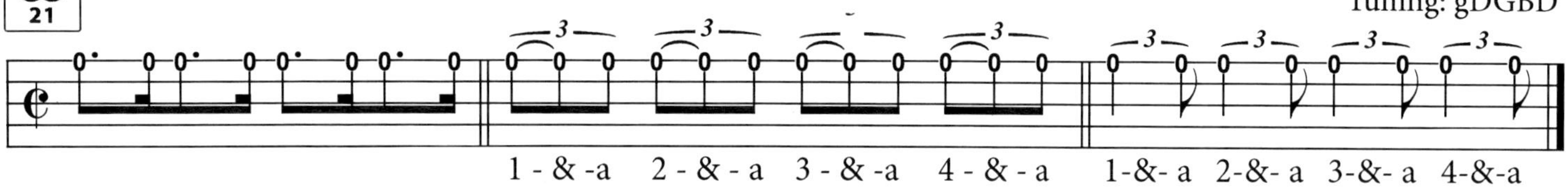

Set Tunes ("Slow Tunes")

The term *set tune* is a catch-all for cut-time melodies played at tempos suitable for square dancing and contradancing that are neither reels nor hornpipes. Many of these tunes are old folk songs or popular-song melodies that have been adapted for use as dance tunes. Such tunes are generally made up of a high proportion of quarter notes, and are therefore much less musically dense than reels. They are relatively easy to shape into phrases and often possess a bouncy, light-hearted character; but they generally lack the rhythmic drive of reels and hornpipes. On P.E.I., many fiddlers refer to this genre as *slow tunes* – presumably because with fewer notes to play per measure, the fiddler's bow moves a bit slower than it would for playing reels. Some set-tunes have sixteen bars per part instead of eight.

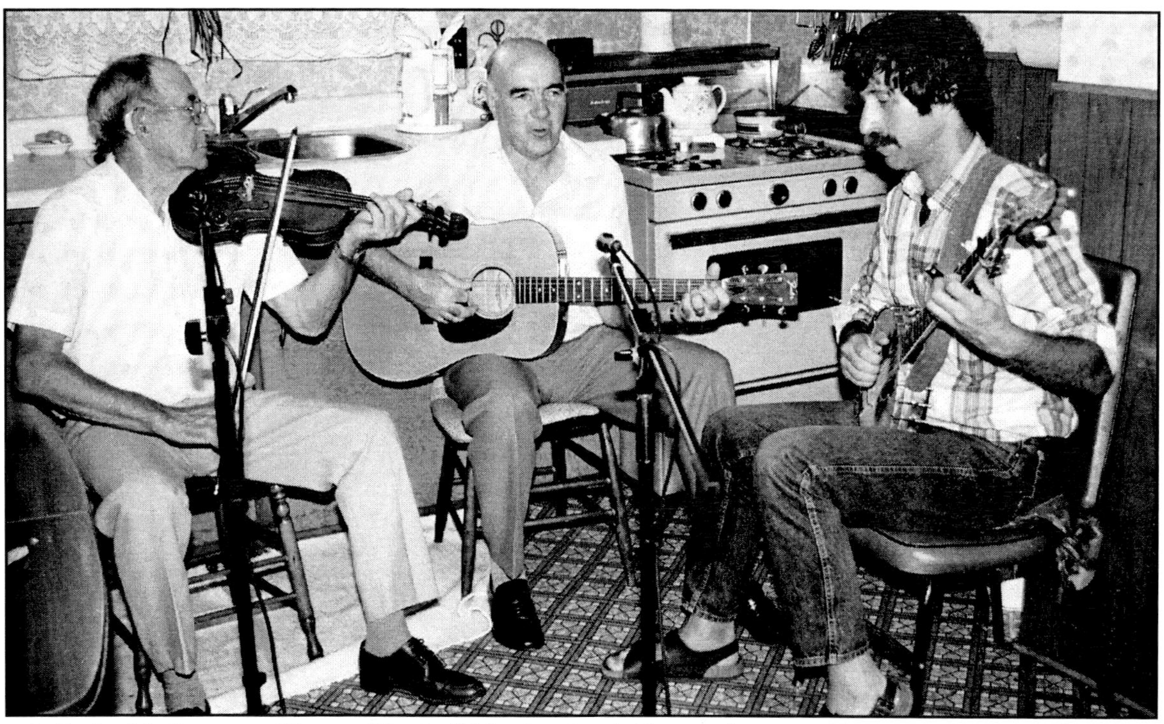

L-R: Archie Stewart, Chester "Junior" MacSwain, & Ken Perlman: Milltown Cross, P.E.I. (1991).
Photo by Earthwatch Team; courtesy Robertson Library, University of P.E.I.

Chapter 4. Try These Tunes First

HERE ARE SOME RELATIVELY STRAIGHTFORWARD TUNES to help you sharpen your playing skills and deepen your understanding of the Cape Breton and Prince Edward Island genres. Most of the elements that you'll need are here – drop-thumbing on every string, alternate-string pull-offs and a few up the neck moves – but they occur sparingly and are relatively easily managed. Before proceeding, I recommend strongly that you go over the introductory material, particularly such elements as position playing, Keith-picking, and up-the-neck fingering forms.

22

The Drunken Piper

REEL

ORIGIN: SCOTLAND
SOURCE: HILDA MACPHEE MACDONALD

KEY: A (G ON BANJO)
MODE: SEE INTRO
TUNING: gDGCD (Capo-2)

This tune probably entered the Cape Breton and Prince Edward Island repertoires via the piping tradition. It appears in David Glen's *Collection of Highland Bagpipe Music, vol. 1* (1876) and – as "Highland Rory" – in Wm. Ross' *Collection of Pipe Music* (1869). Glen credits the tune to a piper named Alexander MacLeod and offers 1862 as the year of composition. The version here starts with major 3rd and minor 7th, suggesting a Mixolydian gamut; the 3rd tone is missing from then on, however, which implies Re-Pentatonic. Standard notation for my source version is in *Fiddle Music of P.E.I.*

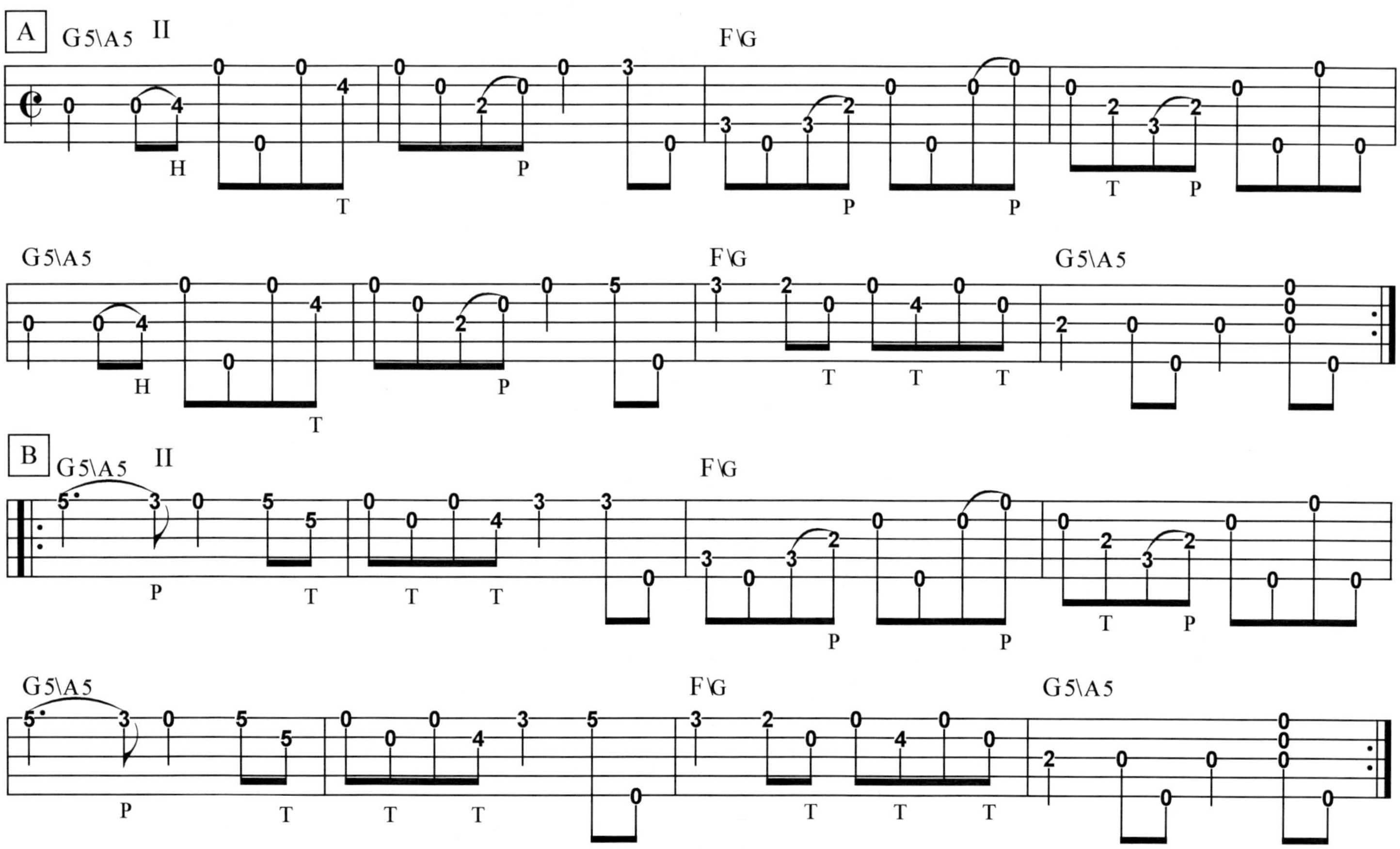

PLAYING NOTE FOR *THE DRUNKEN PIPER*

DUAL CHORD SYMBOLS: Chord to left of backslash goes with open banjo; chord on right is for capoed banjo or fiddle

23

The Meeting of Waters

SET TUNE

ORIGIN: SCOTLAND
SOURCE: WILFRED BERNARD

KEY: D (C ON BANJO)
MODE: MAJOR
TUNING: gCGCD (Capo-2)

In the Scottish country-dance scene, it has long been customary to play this tune as accompaniment for the well-known dance also known as "The Meeting of Waters." Otherwise, it is most likely to be encountered at New England contradances and in the repertoire of bagpipe bands. There is also a version of this melody in the Scottish repertoire converted to 6/8 time that goes by the title, "Adam Haugh." Standard notation for my source version is in *Fiddle Music of P.E.I.*

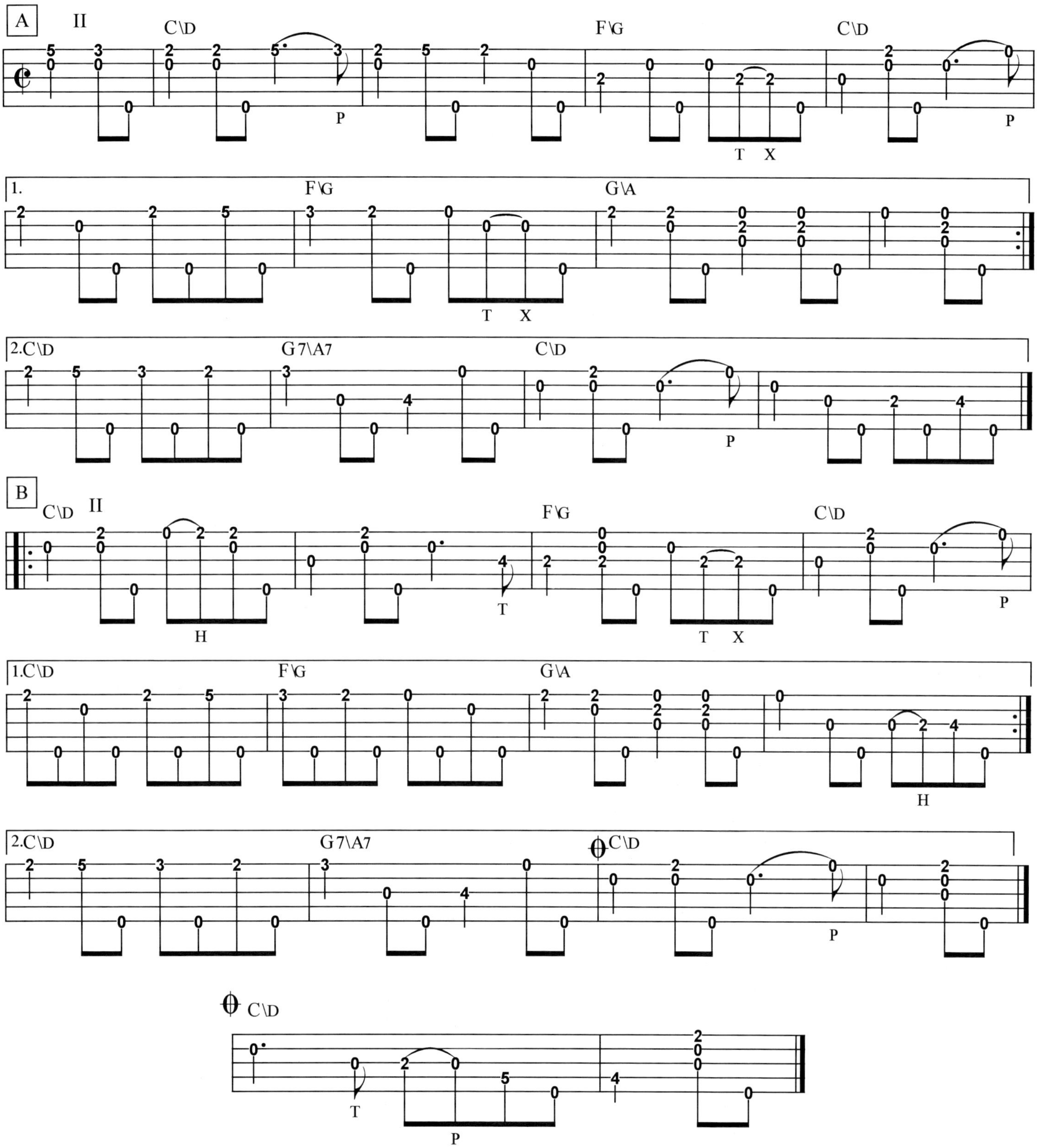

DUAL CHORD SYMBOLS: Chord to left of backslash goes with open banjo; chord on right is for capoed banjo or fiddle

24

Silver & Gold

Set Tune

Origin: Canadian
Source: Johnny Joe Chaisson

Key: D (C on Banjo)
Mode: Major
Tuning: gCGCD (Capo-2)

This is a very widely played tune on Prince Edward Island. Don Messer recorded it in 1947 as "Silver & Gold Two-Step" and included it in his collection, *Way Down East* (1948). The tune also appears – as played by Nebraska fiddler Uncle Bob Walters – in R. P. Cristeson's *Old-Time Fiddlers' Repertory* (1973); but Walters admitted to having learned it on radio and in all likelihood got it from Messer's CBC broadcasts. Standard notation for my source version is in *Fiddle Music of P.E.I.*

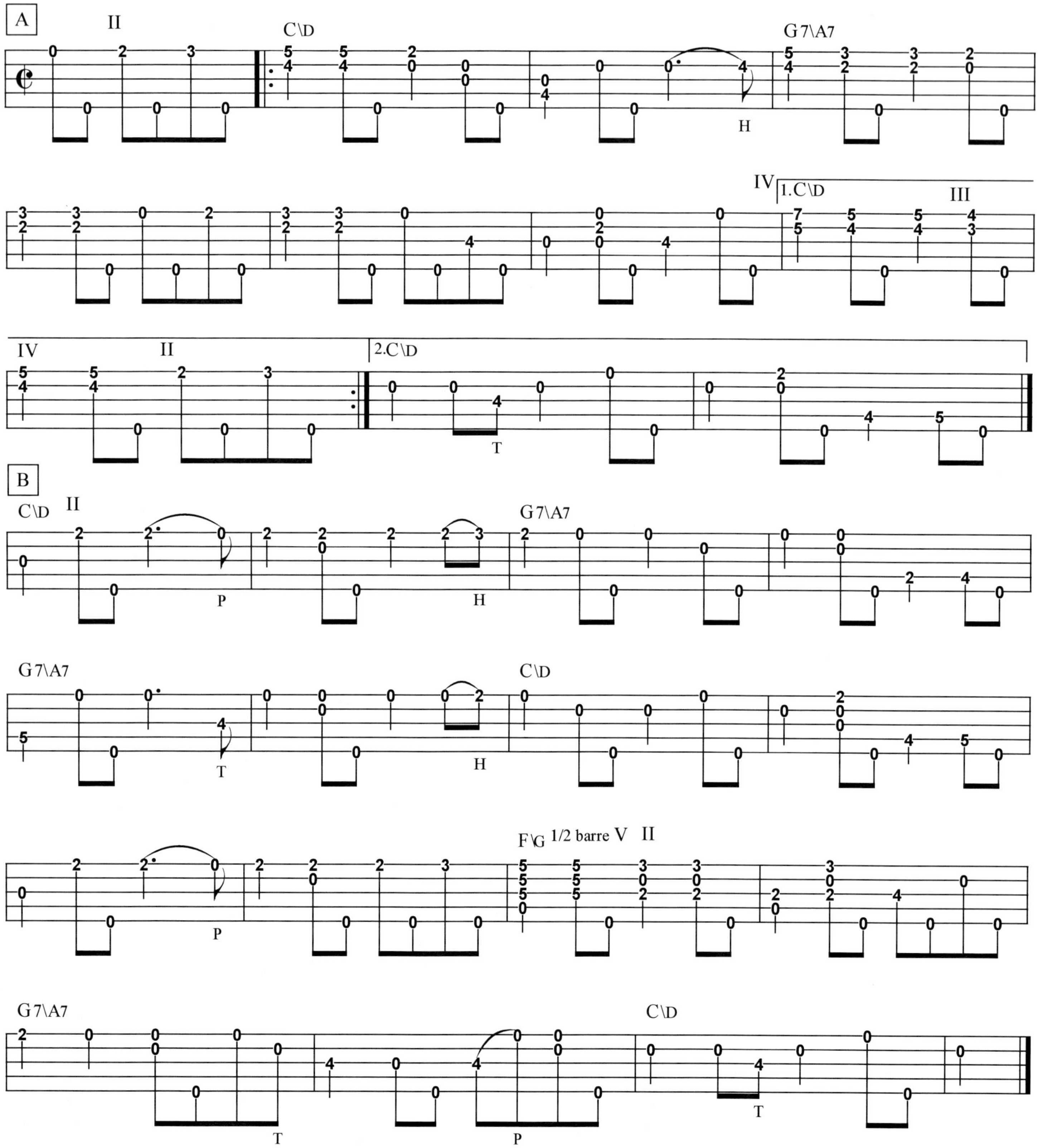

***Dual Chord Symbols:** Chord to left of backslash goes with open banjo; chord on right is for capoed banjo or fiddle*

25

The Rose in the Garden

Set Tune

Origin: Scotland
Source: Attwood O'Connor

Key: D (C on Banjo)
Mode: See Intro
Tuning: gCGCD (Capo-2)

This poignant melody almost certainly started out as a Scottish song. According to O'Connor, the tune was not much favored by local accompanists, who generally insisted that each part should end on the tonic chord, D major instead of the more natural-sounding dominant chord, A major (C and G, respectively on open banjo). Part A is fully major pentatonic, while Part B incorporates a few 4th tones – G♮ on fiddle; F♮ on open banjo – into its otherwise pentatonic gamut. Standard notation for my source version is available on *bowingdownhome.ca.*

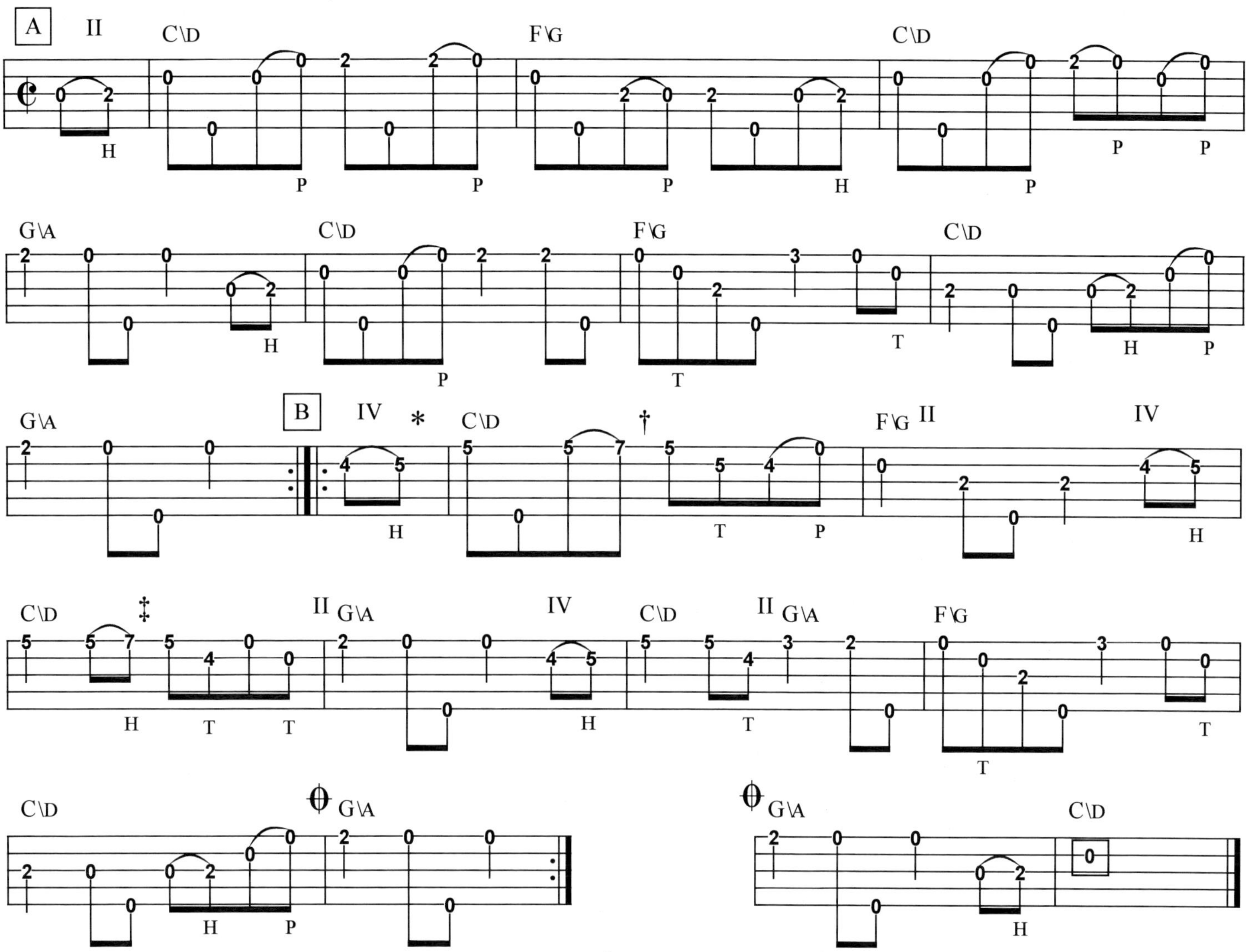

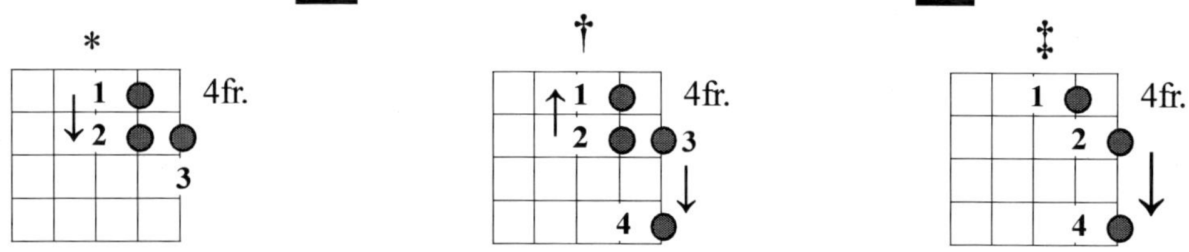

Playing Tips for *Rose in the Garden*

Dual Chord Symbols: Chord to left of backslash goes with open banjo; chord on right is for capoed banjo or fiddle

• Part B, measure 1. Halfway through beat 3, balance on the 2nd finger at fret 5, string 2 and make sure that the 1st and 3rd fingers are in the position shown in Diagram †. On beat 4, having cut fret 5 short, remove the 2nd finger and pluck fret 4, string 2 (keeping the 3rd finger in place). Then, halfway through beat 4, use that finger for the alternate-string P.

• Part B, measure 3. Start the measure with the 3rd finger on fret 5, string 1 as shown in Diagram †; but on beat 2 switch to the 2nd finger, as shown in Diagram ‡,

26

MacDonald's March "Reel"

Origin: Scotland
Source: Johnny Morrissey

Key: A (G on Banjo)
Mode: See Intro
Tuning: gDGCD (Capo-2)

This mid 19th-century pipe march is generally played as a reel today. An early appearance in print was in *Ross's Collection of Pipe Music, No. 16* (1869). Morrissey played a two-part version akin to the one in Ross's, but many fiddlers today play a three-part version similar to the one featured in *Kerr's Merry Melodies.* The setting offered here adds a commonly played version of the third part (that is, Part C) to the two parts I collected from Morrissey. The mode is complex. The Mixolydian gamut – with major 3rd and minor 7th – prevails at the opening of Parts A and B, measures 5-6 of Part A, and throughout Part C. The 3rd tone – C♯ on fiddle; B♮ on open banjo – disappears for the remainder of the tune, suggesting Re-Pentatonic.

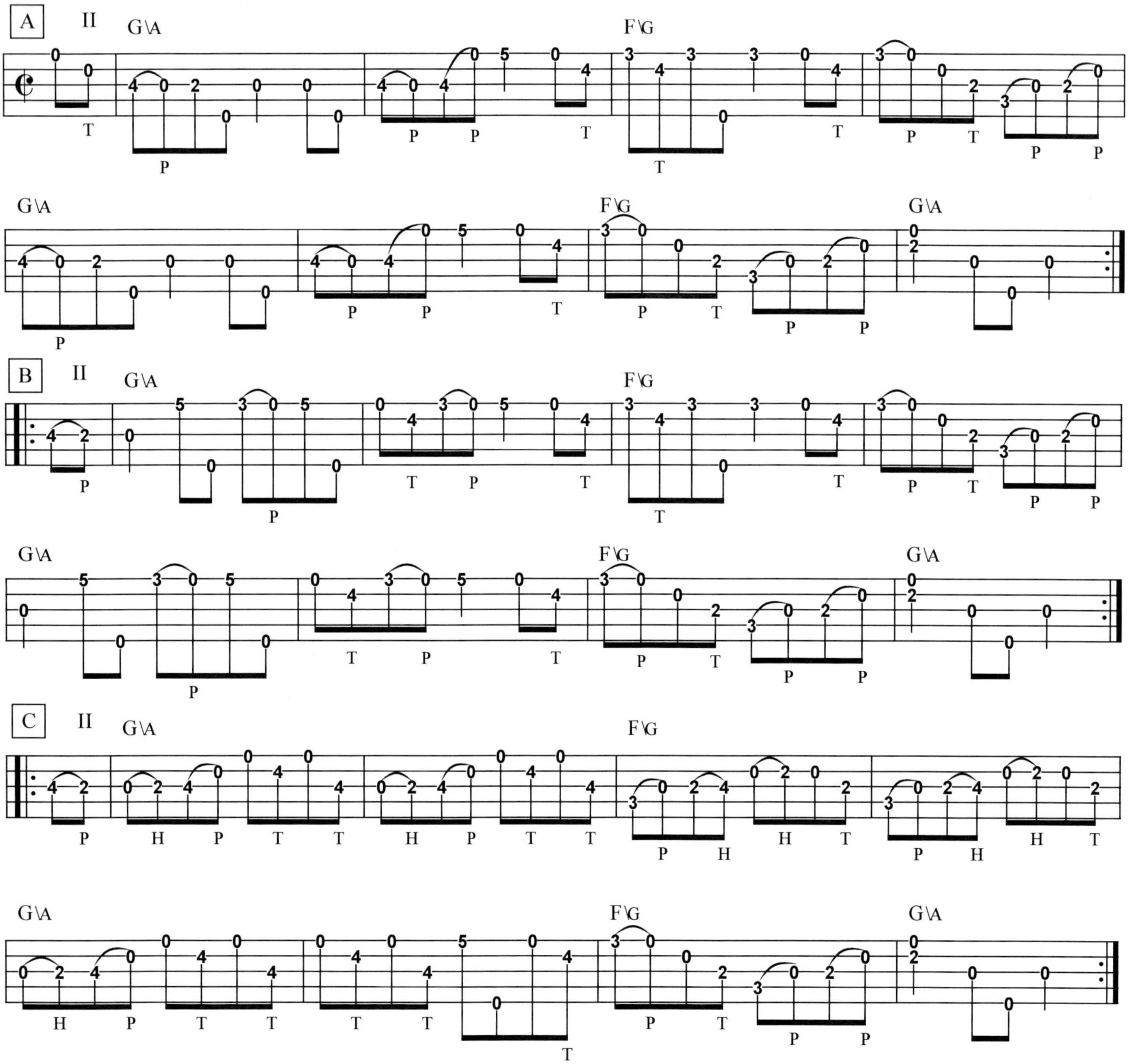

Playing Note for *MacDonald's March*

***Dual Chord Symbols:** Chord to left of backslash goes with open banjo; chord on right is for capoed banjo or fiddle*

27

St. Anne's Reel ("Original" Version)

Origin: Québec
Sources: Various
Appears on: See Intro

Key: D (C on Banjo)
Mode: Major
Tuning: gCGCD (Capo-2)

At the time of my collecting project, "St. Anne's Reel" was one of the most widely played tunes on Prince Edward Island. The version that most people know was first popularized via a 78 rpm recording entitled "Reel de Ste. Anne," played by Joseph Allard of Montreal (1873-1947) and issued by Victor in 1930. Many older fiddlers I encountered on P.E.I. learned the tune via radio broadcasts of Allard and others from station CHNC in New Carlisle, Québec. By the late 1930s, fiddler George Chappelle was playing the tune on CFCY radio in Charlottetown. Don Messer performed "St. Anne's" widely in the 1940s and 50s, and no doubt also had a role in popularizing it throughout Canada and beyond. I recorded a version very similar to the setting presented here on my LP, *Clawhammer Banjo & Fingerstyle Guitar Solos* (Folkways Records). For my banjo arrangement of an intriguing variant of "St. Anne's" from Prince County, P.E.I. see p. 73.

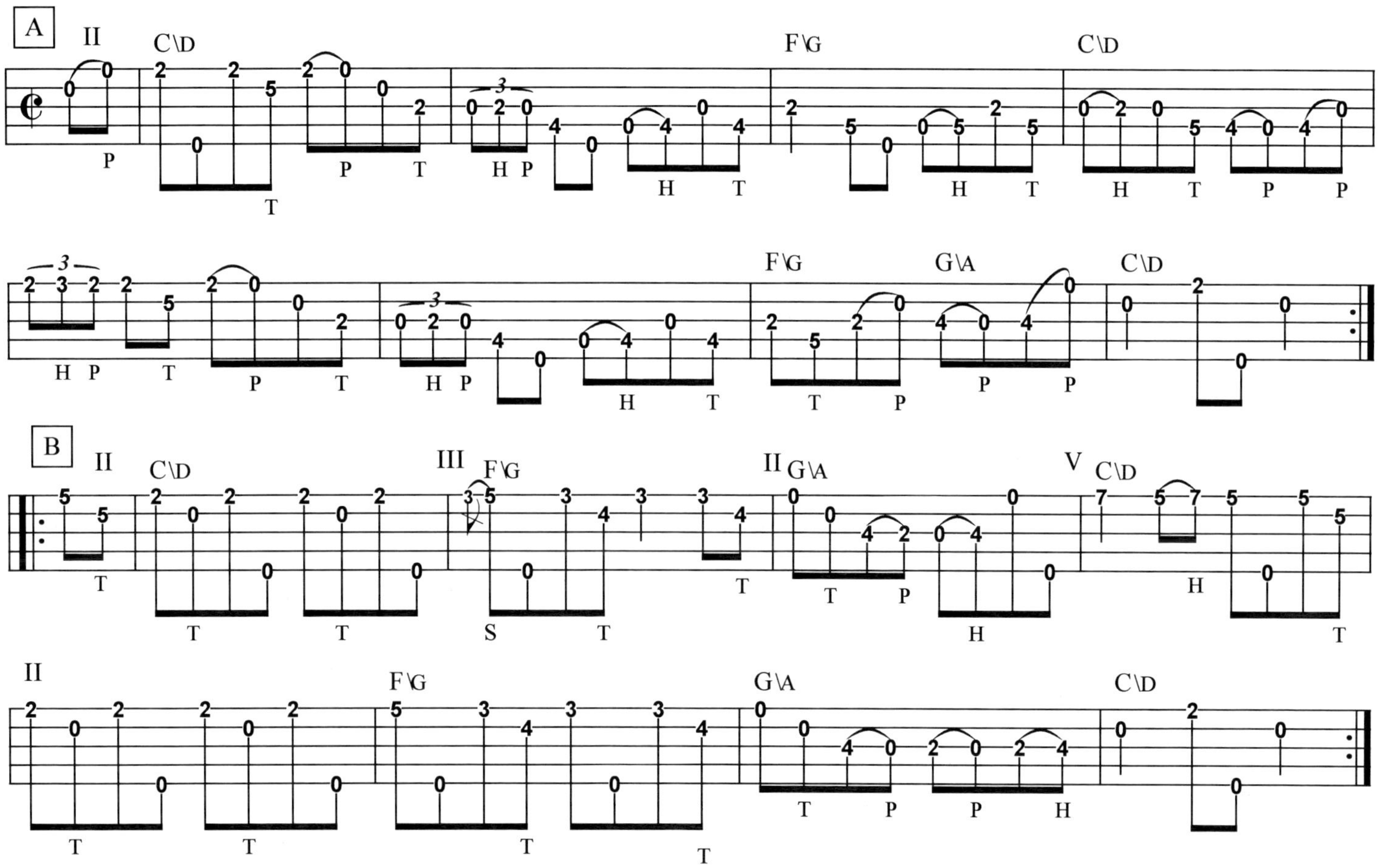

Playing Note for *St. Anne's Reel*

***Dual Chord Symbols:** Chord to left of backslash goes with open banjo; chord on right is for capoed banjo or fiddle*

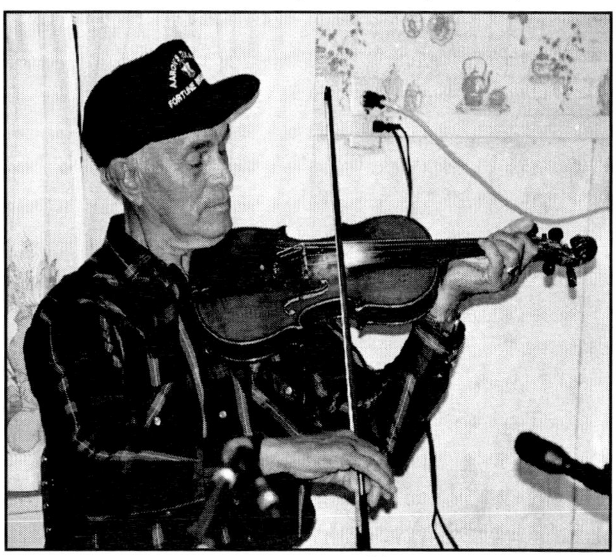

Gus Longaphie at Project Headquarters, Monticello, P.E.I. (1991). Photo by Earthwatch team; courtesy Robertson Library, University of P.E.I.

28

You Married My Daughter, & Yet You Didn't

Reel

Origin: Québec
Sources: Various
Appears on: *Devil in the Kitchen*

Key: G
Mode: Major
Tuning: gDGBD

Also known as "Cobbler's Reel" ("Reel du cordonnier"), this tune is probably based on a Québecois song called, "Tout d'un coup tu maries ma fille," ("All of a Sudden You Marry My Daughter"). The tune began circulating in New England in the 1970s, probably due to popular recordings by Louis Beaudoin and The Fennigs All-Star Band, a highly influential hammer-dulcimer based ensemble from that period.

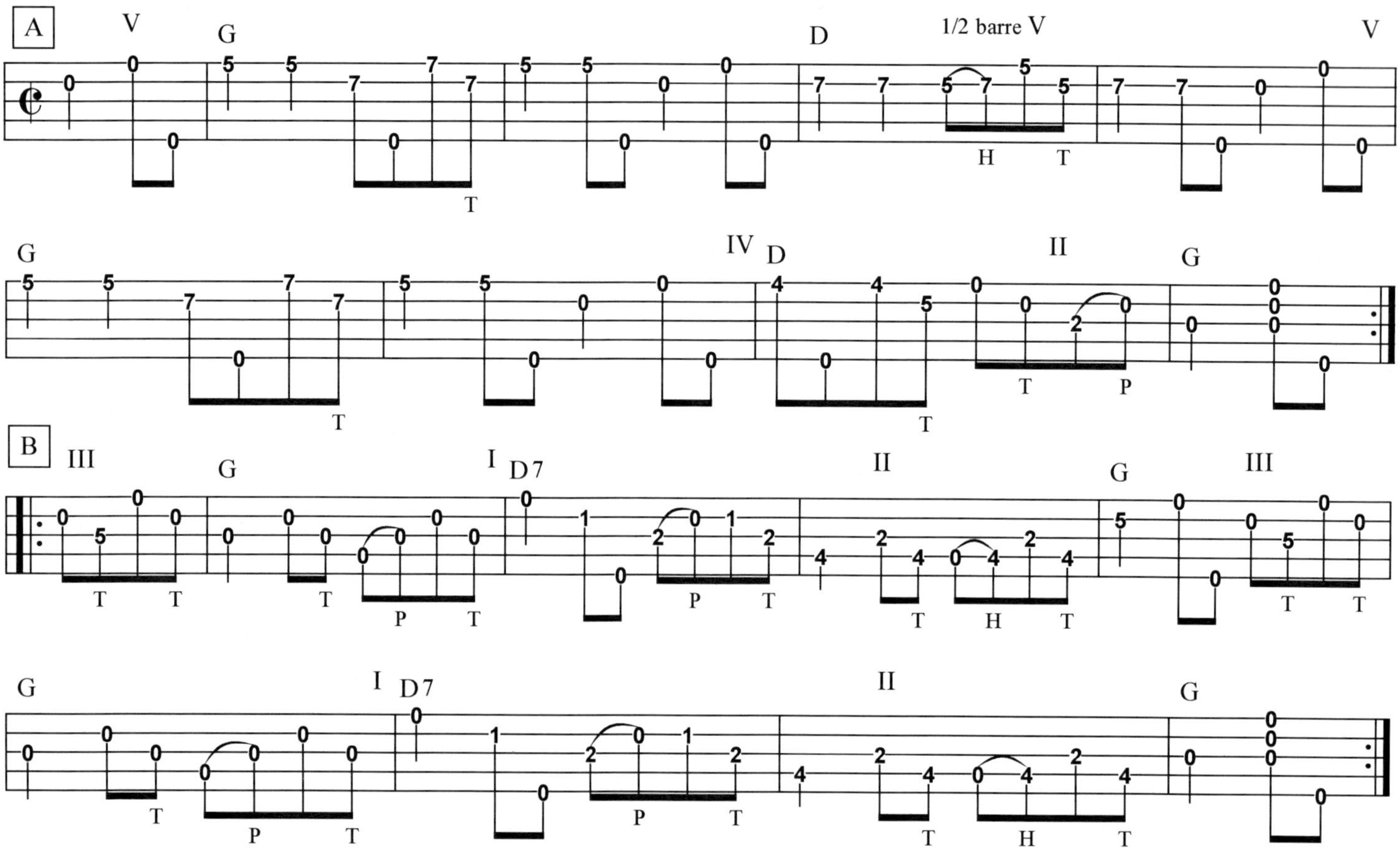

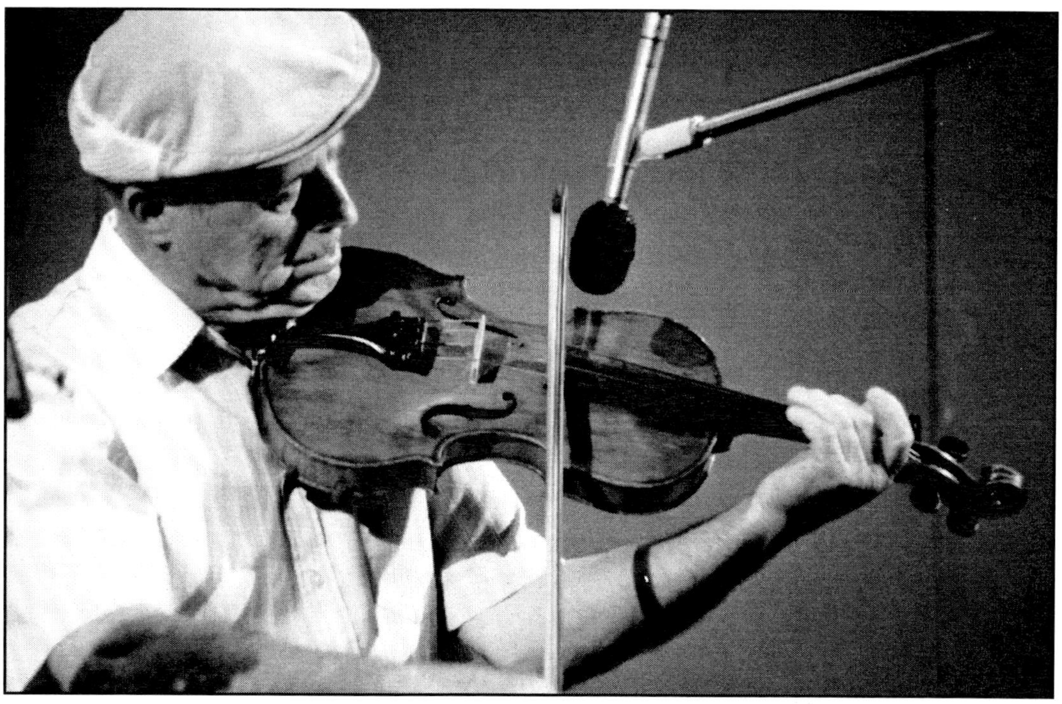

Eddy Arsenault at Atlantic Jamboree: Abram-Village, P.E.I. (1992).
Photo by Ken Perlman; courtesy Robertson Library, University of P.E.I.

29

Pigeon on the Gatepost

Reel

Origin: Local Variant of Irish Tune
Sources: Eddy Arsenault & George MacPhee

Key: A (G on Banjo)
Mode: (Mostly) Re-Pentatonic
Tuning: gDGCD (Capo-2)

This has been one of the most widely played tunes on Prince Edward Island for generations; among its many other local names are "The Twin Sisters," "Jack Tar," "Pigeon on the Pier," and "The Sturgeon Tea." It is one of two distinct widely-played P.E.I. variants of the 19th-century key-of-A Irish reel, "Pigeon on the Gate." A difference in mode seems to be the major factor that separates the two. The sister variant – called "Pride of the Ball" in this volume (p. 86) – is characterized by a straight Mixolydian gamut. The melody of "Pigeon on the Gatepost," on the other hand, operates almost entirely in the Re-Pentatonic orbit. The tune has no 3rd at all and a minor 7th throughout; Part B features the occasional major 6th (F♯ on fiddle; E on open banjo). For more on the parent tune's publishing history, see "Pride of the Ball." Standard notation for my source version is in *Fiddle Music of P.E.I.*

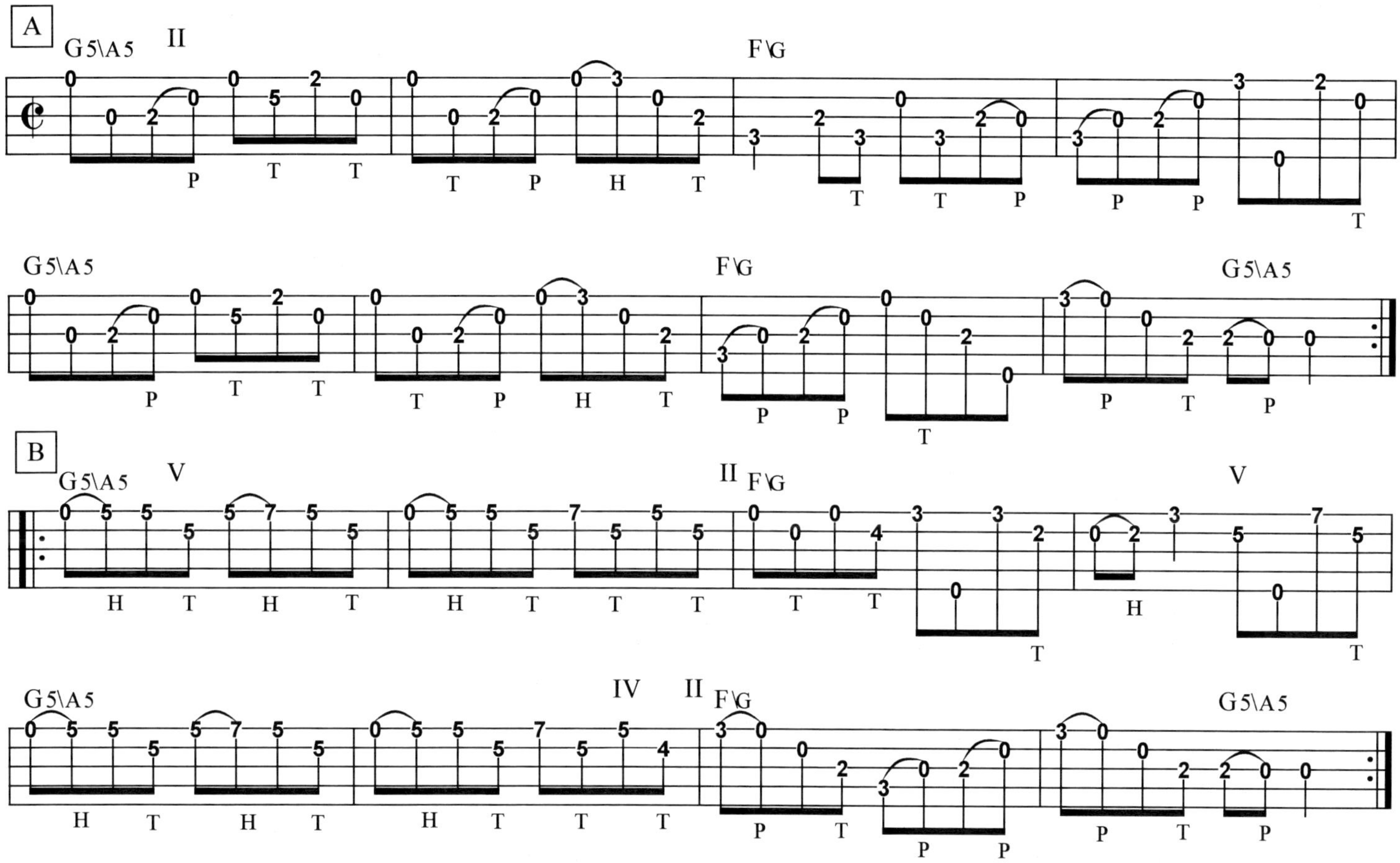

Playing Note for *Pigeon on the Gatepost*

***Dual Chord Symbols:** Chord to left of backslash goes with open banjo; chord on right is for capoed banjo or fiddle*

30

Brenda Stubbert's Reel

Composer: Jerry Holland
Sources: Carl & Jackie Webster

Key: A (G on Banjo)
Mode: (Mostly) Re-Pentatonic
Tuning: gDGCD (Capo-2)

Named for a prominent Cape Breton fiddler of Holland's generation, this is probably his best known and most widely-played composition. Part A is reminiscent of the early 20th-century piping tune, "John Morrison, Assynt House" by Pipe Major Peter MacLeod (1879-1965). The mode is Re-Pentatonic except for the very salient minor 3rd that appears at the start of measure 4 of both parts (C♮ on fiddle; B♭ on open banjo); this note creates a compelling contrast that gives the tune its distinctive character. An alternative version for Part B, measures 1 and 5 offers the option of a fancier setting. Standard notation for my source version is in *Fiddle Music of P.E.I.*

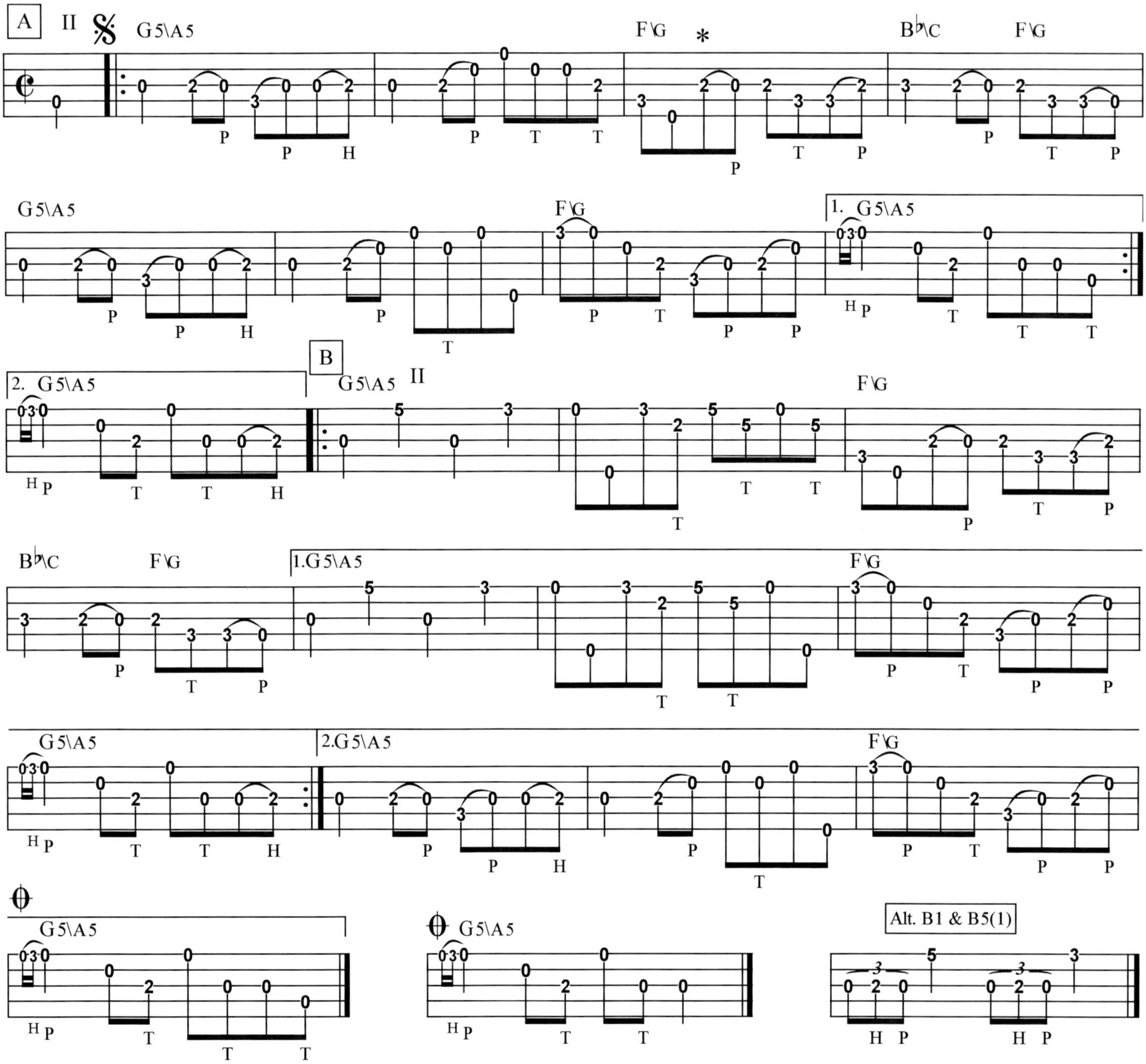

Playing Note for *Brenda Stubbert's Reel*

***Dual Chord Symbols:** Chord to left of backslash goes with open banjo; chord on right is for capoed banjo or fiddle*

31

Fay's Hornpipe

ORIGIN: SCOTLAND
SOURCE: ROLAND JAY

KEY: G
MODE: MAJOR
TUNING: gDGBD

"Fay's Hornpipe" first appeared in print in *Middleton's Selection of Strathspeys, Reels [. . .]* (1870), edited by noted fiddler-composer Peter Milne (1824-1908). A Shetland version called "Da Peerie Hoose Ahent da Burn" ("The Little House by the Stream," or "The Out-House") is played up-tempo as a reel. Standard notation for my source version is in *Fiddle Music of P.E.I.*

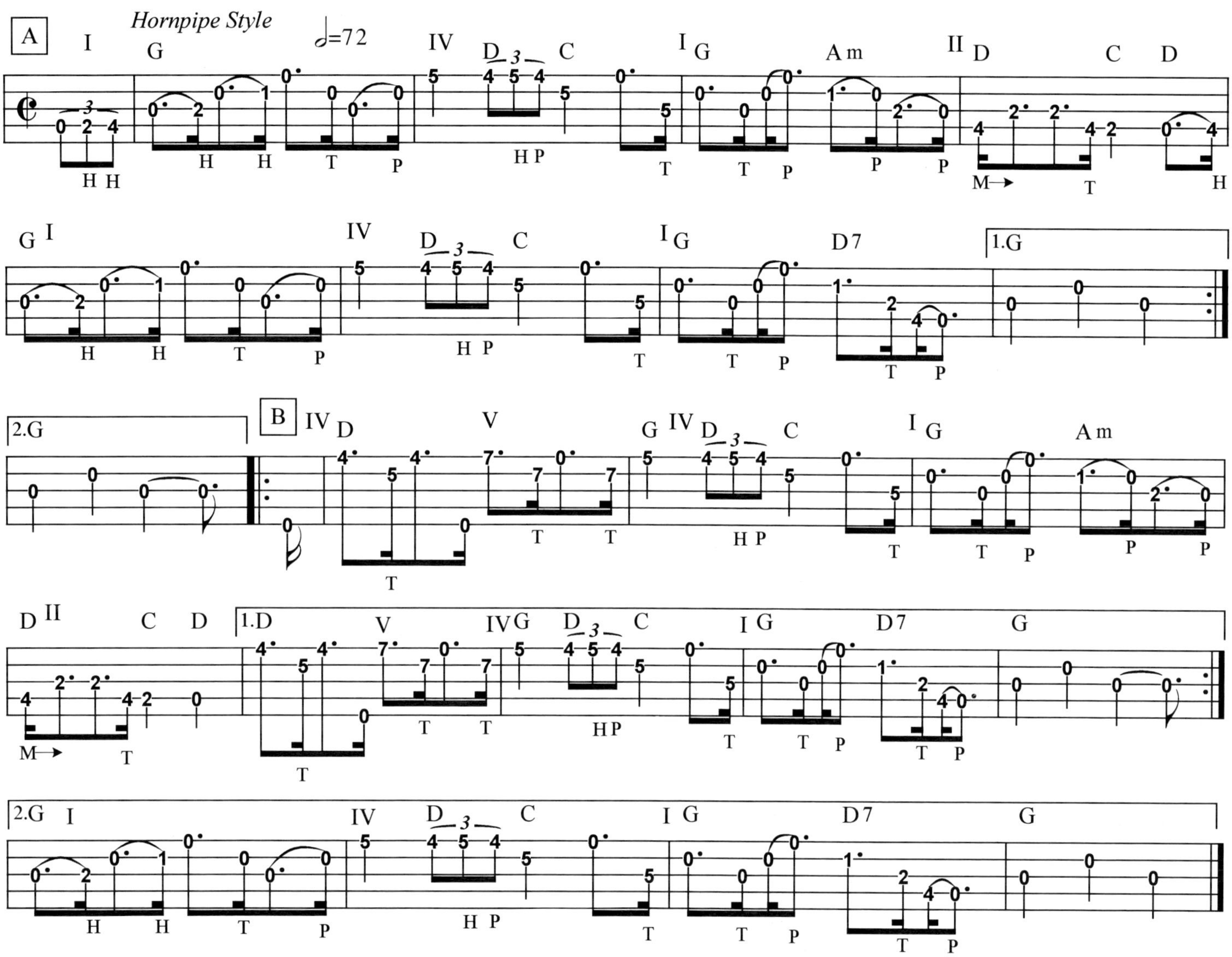

PLAYING TIPS FOR *FAY'S HORNPIPE*

***DUAL CHORD SYMBOLS:** Chord to left of backslash goes with open banjo; chord on right is for capoed banjo or fiddle*

• PARTS A AND B, MEASURES 3, 4, & 7. Each of these measures contains what appears to be a "reverse" dotted pair in which the sixteenth note is first. These are *Scotch snaps,* which are commonly employed by Scottish, Cape Breton, and Prince Edward Island style fiddlers as a form of rhythmic ornamentation in hornpipes. For more explanation, see p. 151.

32

Homeward Bound

Reel

Origin: See Intro
Source: "Young Peter" Chaisson
Appears on: *Island Boy (as Guitar Solo)*

Key: D (C on Banjo)
Mode: (Mostly) Major Pentatonic
Tuning: gCGCD (Capo-2)

This truly sweet tune is one of the most widely played tunes on P.E.I., particularly in the eastern half of the Island; it is often played in medley with "Jerome's Farewell to Gibraltar" (p. 75). Cape Breton fiddler-composer Dan R. MacDonald recorded "Homeward Bound" for Celtic Records in 1939. Although he is often credited with having composed the tune, he attributed it to "Little Rory" MacDonald, who is also listed as the composer in Gordon MacQuarrie's *Cape Breton Collection of Scottish Melodies for the Violin* (1940). The tune was probably in circulation decades before either man was musically active, however, as evidenced by two published melodies that are nearly identical to it – namely "Gem of Ireland" from *Ryan's Mammoth Collection* and "Clarkson's Reel" from *O'Neill's Dance Music of Ireland*. Standard notation for my source version is in *Fiddle Music of P.E.I.*

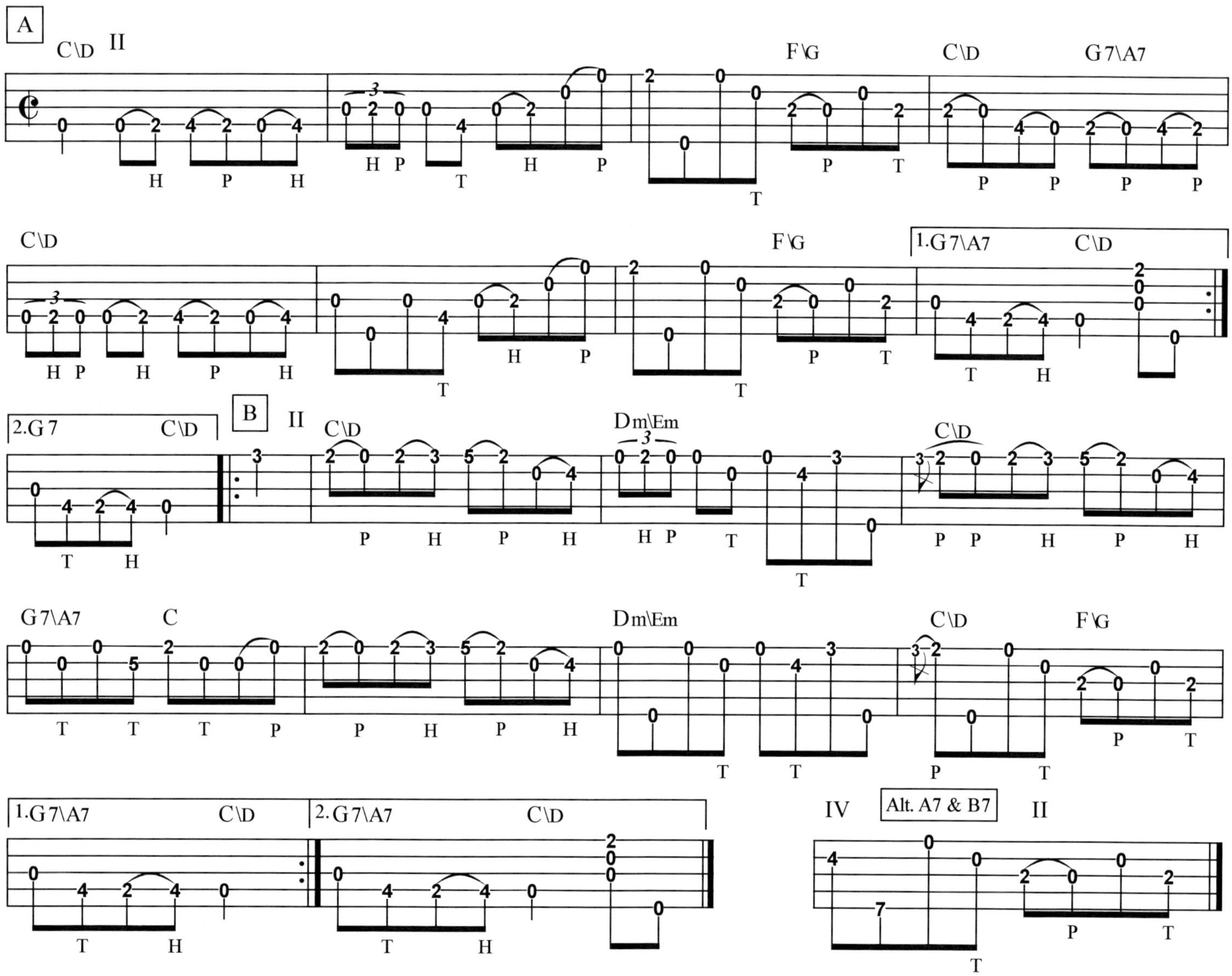

Playing Note for *Homeward Bound*

***Dual Chord Symbols:** Chord to left of backslash goes with open banjo; chord on right is for capoed banjo or fiddle*

33

Northside Tune

SET TUNE

ORIGIN: CONVERTED BRITISH OR IRISH SONG
SOURCE: STEPHEN TOOLE
APPEARS ON: *ISLAND BOY*

KEY: G
MODE: MAJOR
TUNING: gDGBD

Stephen Toole was simply a master at playing this type of tune; I was so struck by the charm of his rendition that I just had to come up with a banjo arrangement. I was told that the melody was derived from a British song called "Sexton Ring the Bell," which may be similar to the American, "Watchman Ring the Bell" (a sexton is a church official, usually a layman, who acts as caretaker of church property and – if needed – bell ringer). The "Northside" in the title refers to the north shore of Kings County – long a hotbed of fiddling. Standard notation for my source version is in *Fiddle Music of P.E.I.*

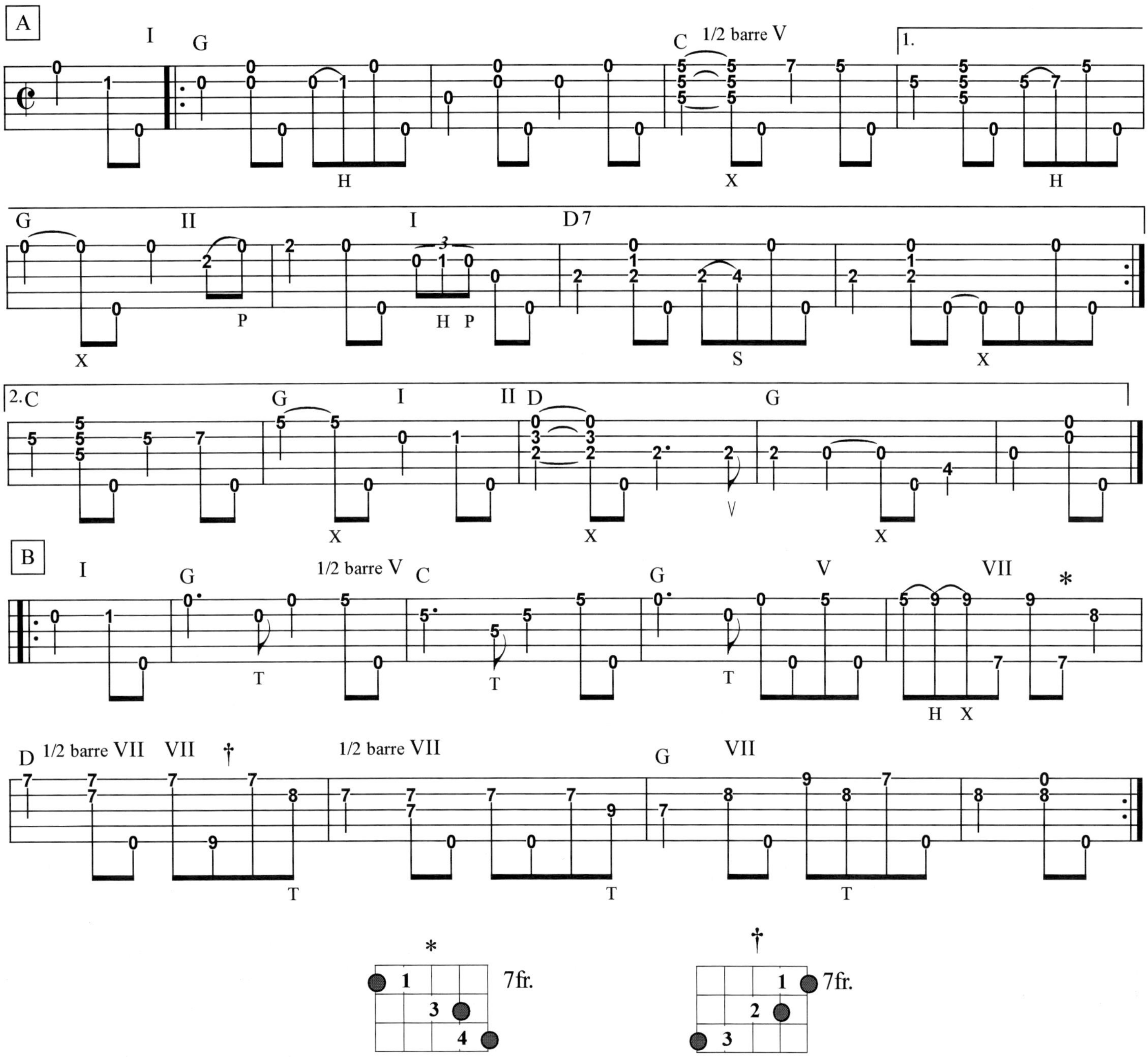

34

Southern Melody

Origin: Southern US Composite
Source: Reuben Smith

Key: D (C on Banjo)
Mode: Major
Tuning: gCGCD (Capo-2)

Noted Cape Breton fiddler Winston Fitzgerald recorded this tune in the 1950s on the LP, *Winston "Scotty" Fitzgerald & His Radio Entertainers*. Fitzgerald began playing the tune while touring around Nova Scotia and New Brunswick in the late 1930s in the backup band for Hank Snow (1914-99), a Nova-Scotia-born singer who later moved to Nashville and became a country-music star. The tune itself sounds like several fiddle rags and syncopated country songs that were popular at the time, and it's hard to say with any confidence which one(s) served as Fitzgerald's model. Fingering diagrams for this tune appear on the facing page. Standard notation for my source version is in *Fiddle Music of P.E.I.*

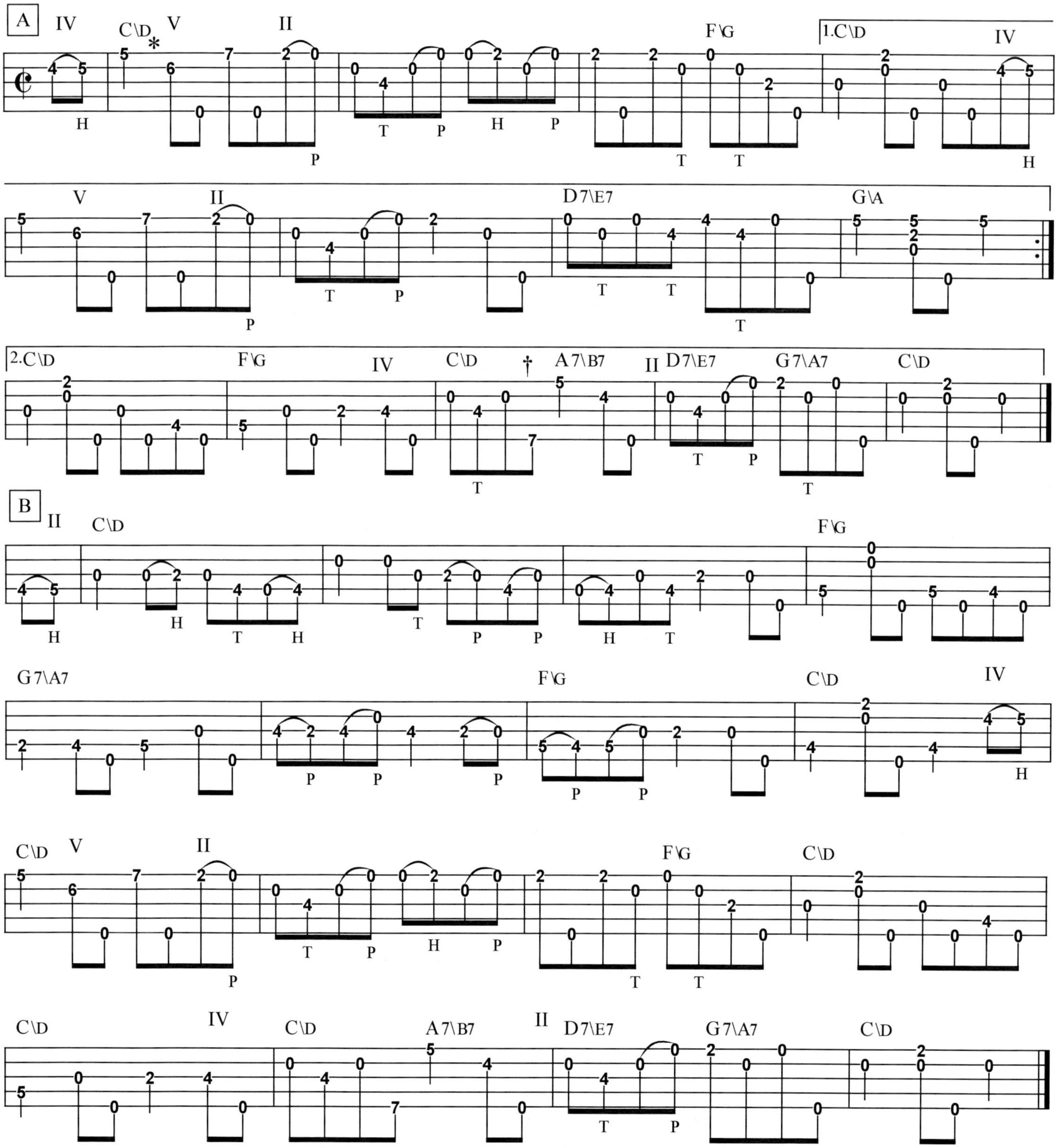

Dual Chord Symbols: Chord to left of backslash goes with open banjo; chord on right is for capoed banjo or fiddle

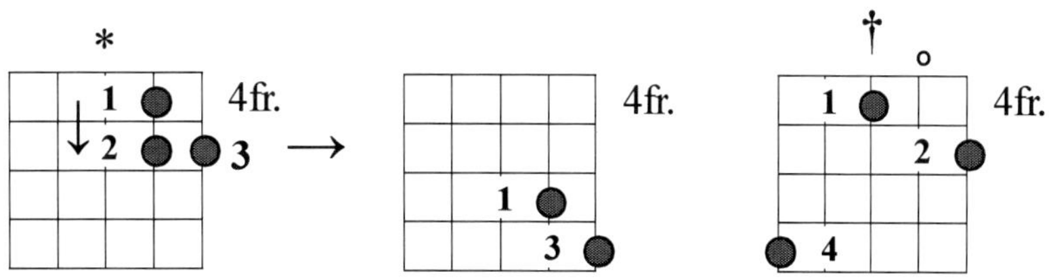

35

Bonaparte Crossing the Alps

HORNPIPE

ORIGIN: IRELAND
SOURCE: JOHNNY MORRISSEY

KEY: A (G ON BANJO)
MODE: SEE INTRO
TUNING: gDGCD (Capo-2)

Fiddler Lem Jay of Fanningbrook, P.E.I. (1882-1960) is said to have always performed "Bonaparte Crossing the Alps" on the special New Year's Eve radio program he hosted for station CFCY from 1931-58. It's not clear whether the title refers to an actual event – Bonaparte's invasion of northern Italy in May 1800 – or to the widely exhibited paintings depicting that event: "Napoleon Crossing the Alps" by Jaques-Louis David and "Bonaparte Crossing the Alps" by Paul Delarouche. The tune first shows up in several mid-19th century Irish manuscripts; it was published as "Bonaparte's Retreat" in *O'Neill's Music of Ireland* and "Bonaparte's March" in *The Roche Collection*; other titles that have circulated include "The Battle of Waterloo" and "Bonaparte Crossing the Rockies." Several songs have been set to this melody, ranging from the mournful Southern lament, "The Old Church Yard" to the rollicking Irish ditty, "Let Mr. McGuire Sit Down." A close variant, "Poor Auld Woman" appears in *Kerr's Merry Melodies*. The mode mostly features a Dorian gamut (minor 3rd and minor 7th), but at the start of Part B the major third (C♯ on fiddle; B♮ on open banjo) makes for a delightful contrast. Standard notation for my source version is in *Fiddle Music of P.E.I.*

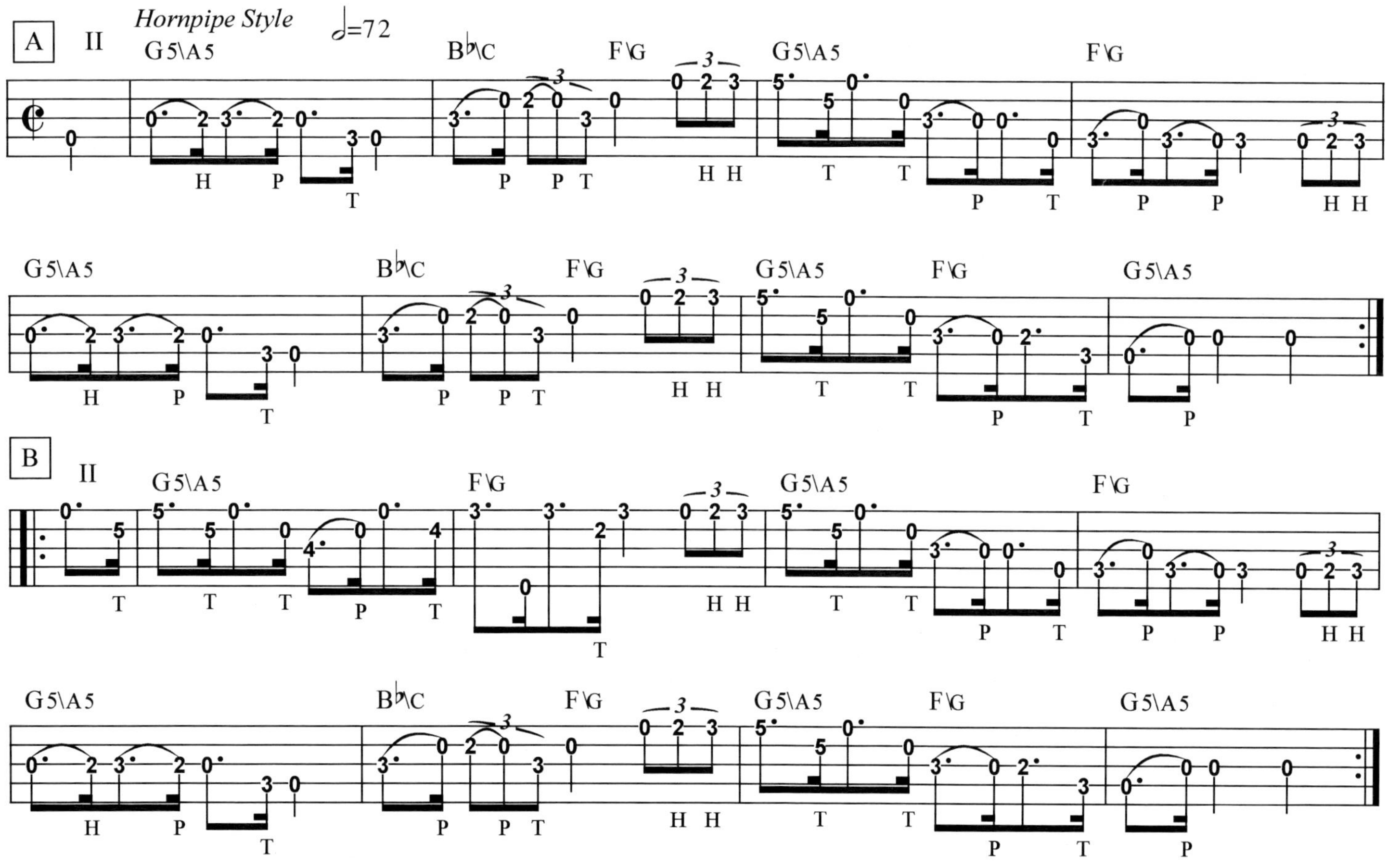

PLAYING NOTE FOR *BONAPARTE CROSSING THE ALPS*

__DUAL CHORD SYMBOLS:__ Chord to left of backslash goes with open banjo; chord on right is for capoed banjo or fiddle

Chapter 5. *Reels – & Hornpipes – in G & G-Modal*
with E-Modal

In standard violin tuning (GDAE), the two lowest strings are both part of the G-major and G-minor chords, which tends to give tunes in that key a resonant sonority. And since G-tunes can start right at the fiddle's lowest note, they often have a relatively wide range. Prince Edward Island fiddlers seem to be particularly partial to this key, and devote considerable energy to elaborating G tunes and bringing them to life with full energy. Although most G tunes in the Cape Breton and P.E.I. repertoires are in a major tonality, you'll also encounter diatonic tunes in this key that have flat or variable 3rd or 7th tones; and tunes that are pentatonic in whole or part. Most G-tunes have at least one section where the melody goes up to high-B (on banjo: fret 9, string 1); this requires banjoists to spend a portion of each repetition with their fretting hand situated at fifth position or higher. Since I also arranged several *E-Modal* tunes in open-G tuning, it made sense to also include them in this chapter.

36

Cheticamp Reel

Origin: Cape Breton
Source: Sterling Baker
Appears on: *Frails & Frolics*

Key: G
Mode: Major
Tuning: gDGBD

"Cheticamp Reel" may well have originally been a polka melody. It is named for a town in Cape Breton known both as a major center of Acadian culture and as a hotbed of fiddling (it's the hometown of such well-known players as Joe Cormier, Arthur Meuse, and Ludger LeFort). Standard notation for my source version is in *Fiddle Music of P.E.I.*

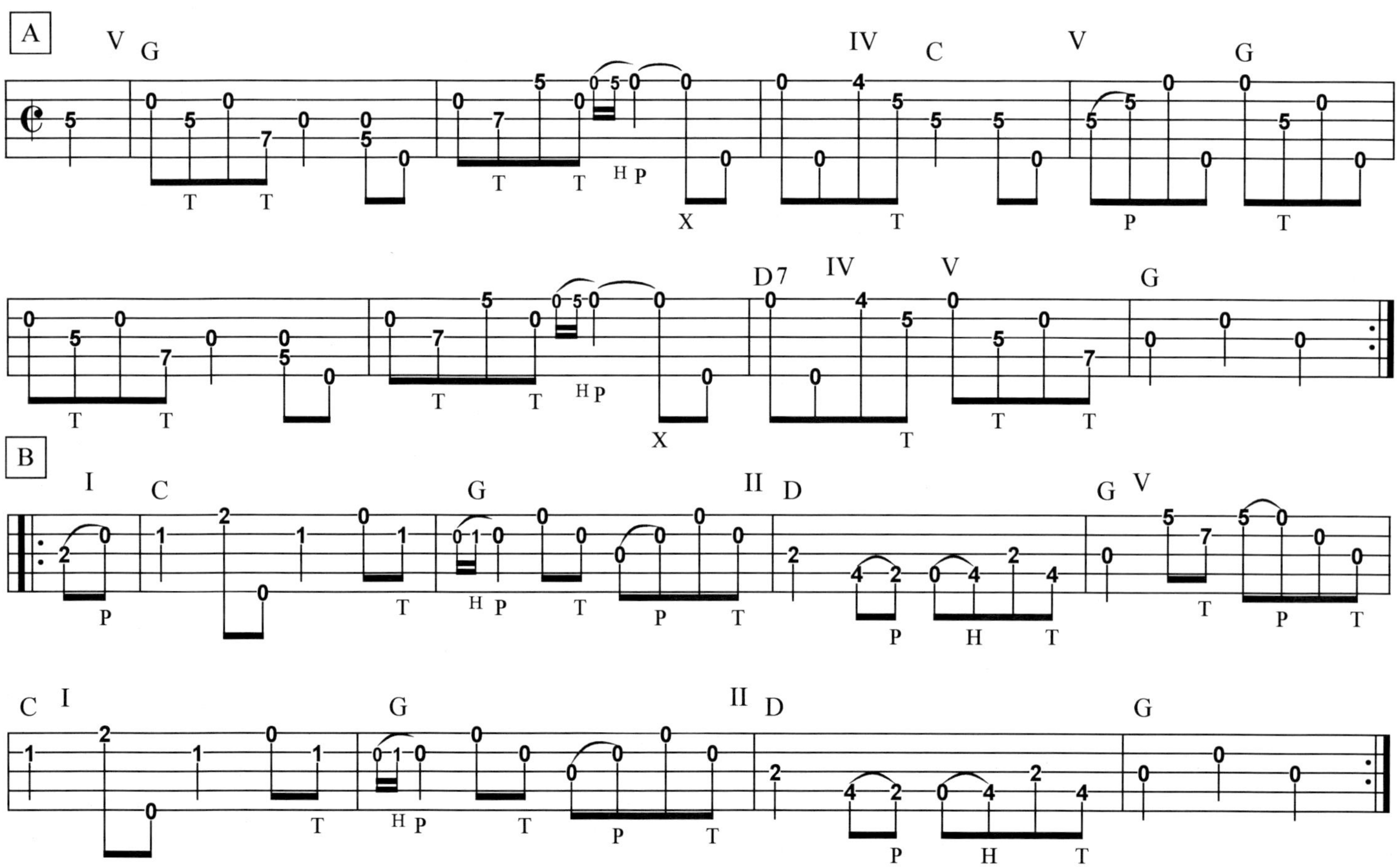

37

Emil Gaudet's Reel

Origin: Local Variant
Source: David Gaudet
Appears on: *Frails & Frolics*

Key: G
Mode: Major
Tuning: gDGBD

David Gaudet (pronounced: "Goody") told me that he learned this tune from his uncle Emil. Given its 16-bar structure, the tune probably originated as a song melody; to my ear it seems reminiscent of the American folk song, "Little Stream of Whiskey." David played the tune in D but I switched it to G to make it fit better on banjo. Note that neither part is repeated. Standard notation for my source version is available on *bowingdownhome.ca*,

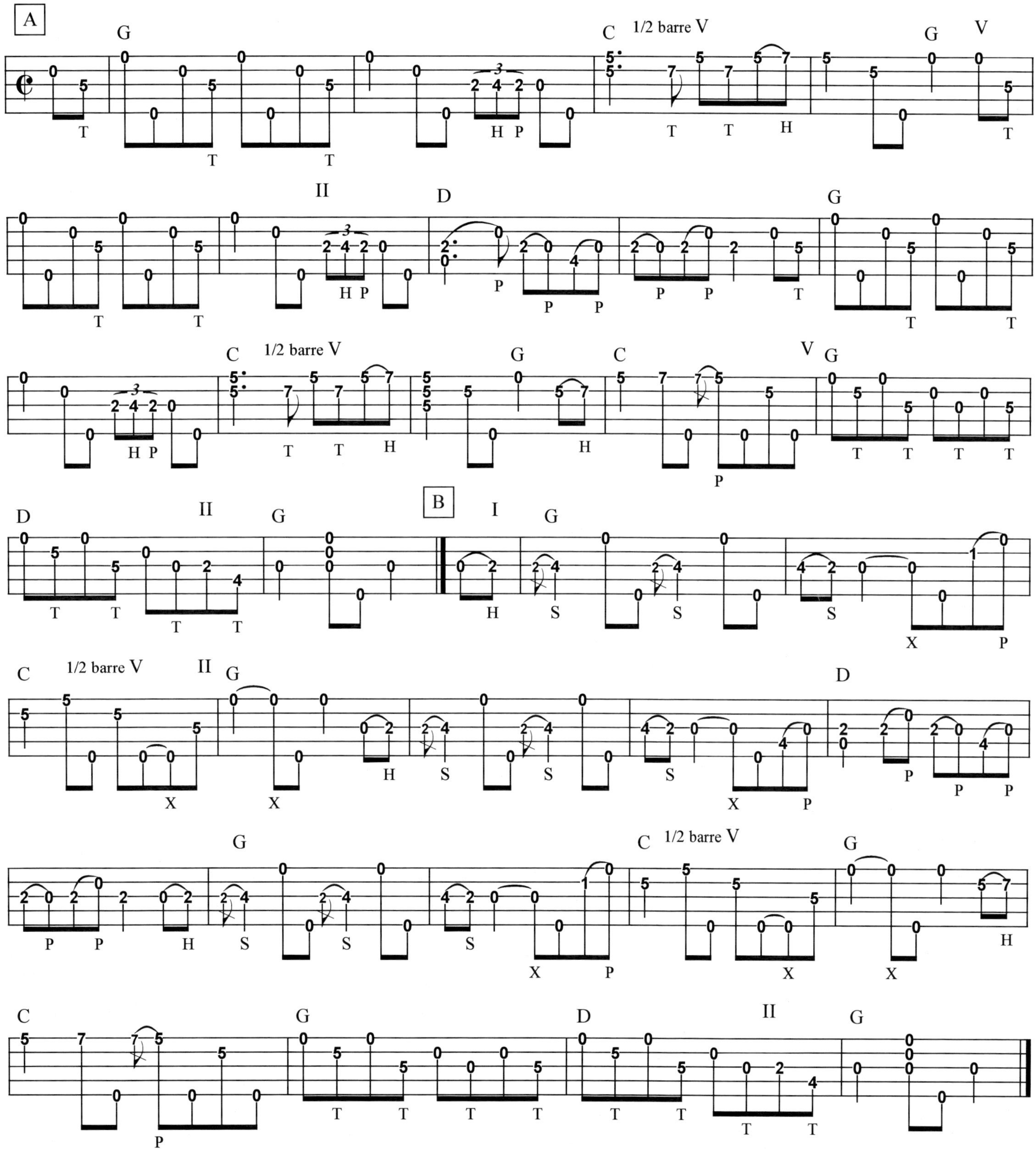

38

The Chaisson Reel

Origin: Northeastern P.E.I.
Source: "Old Peter" Chaisson
Appears on: *Northern Banjo* (as Guitar Solo)

Key: G
Mode: Major Pentatonic
Tuning: gDGBD

The title of this delightfully hypnotic tune references a prominent fiddling family from Kings County, P.E.I.; the tune is also locally known as "Northside Reel" (for their home region), and "Kennedy's Reel" (for a fiddler from times gone by to whom the tune is sometimes attributed). The melody strikes me as a version of the well-known Scottish reel, "Mrs. McLeod of Rasay" (also known as "Mrs. McCloud's Reel" and "Hop High Ladies"), in which all diatonic phrases are transformed into pentatonic ones (in other words, all 4th and 7th tones of the major scale – C and F♯ in the key of G – are skipped). The ending is circular, and I've included a final-sounding coda. Standard notation for my source version is in *Fiddle Music of P.E.I.*

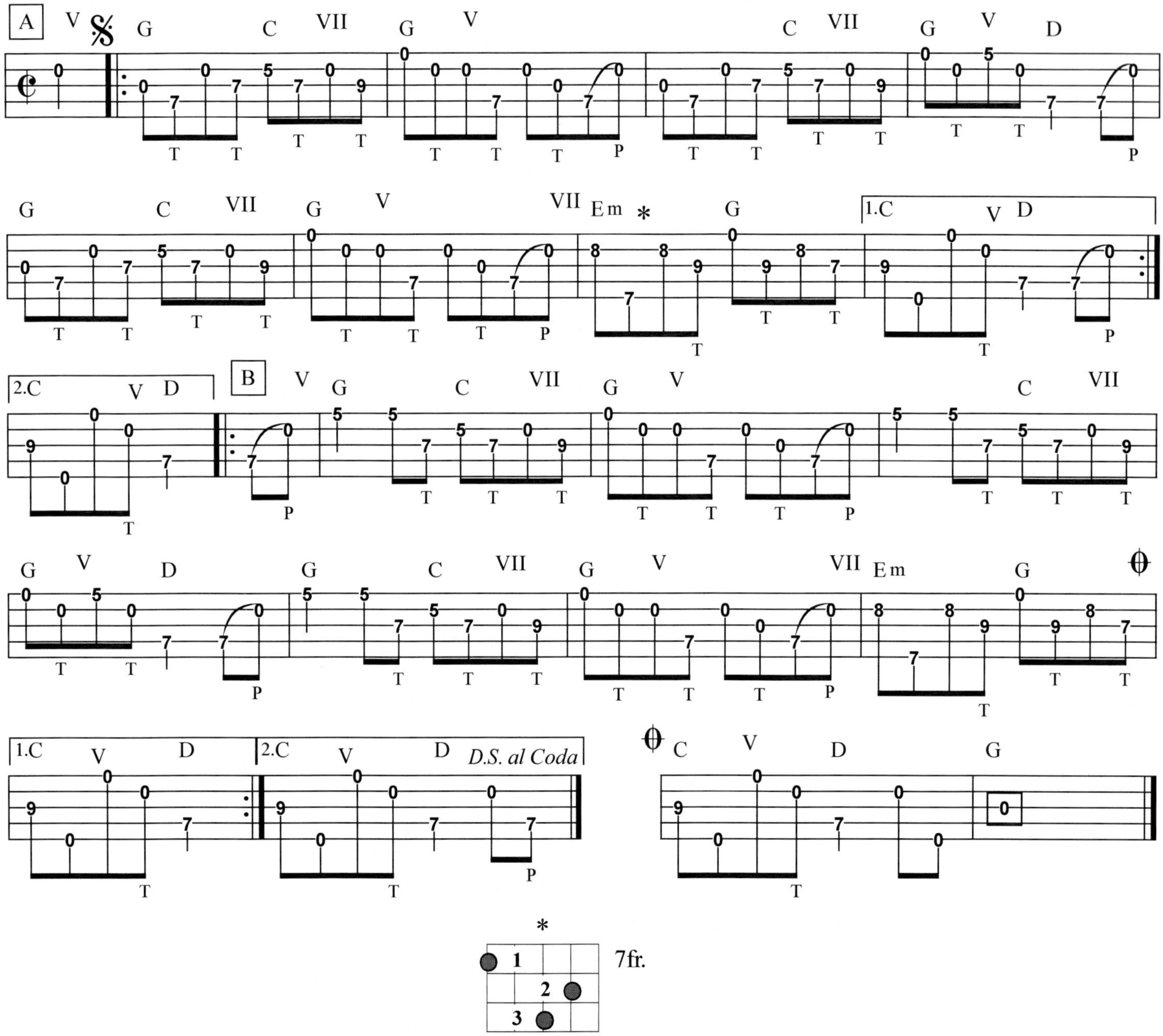

Playing Tips for *The Chaisson Reel*

• General Approach. This arrangement provides an excellent example of how to use *Keith Picking* in clawhammer to best advantage (for more explanation, see p. 16).

• Part A, measure 1. Using the open string on beat 4, move the 3rd finger up from fret 7, string 3 to fret 9 on that string; although this seems like an awkward move, it allows the fret 9 note to serve as a strong upbeat for the following phrase.

39

The Dragger's Reel

Composer: Eddy Arsenault
Source: Eddy Arsenault
Appears on: *Island Boy*

Key: G
Mode: Major
Tuning: gDGBD

Arsenault often recounted how this tune came to him while he was "dragging" (fishing with a net) near his home in St. Chrysostome, P.E.I. Although it has similarities to a tune by Johnny Wilmot of Cape Breton called "Hughie Shortie's Reel," it has its own character and feel. This is an absolutely super tune for accompanying Acadian-style step dancing. Standard notation for my source version is in *Fiddle Music of P.E.I.*

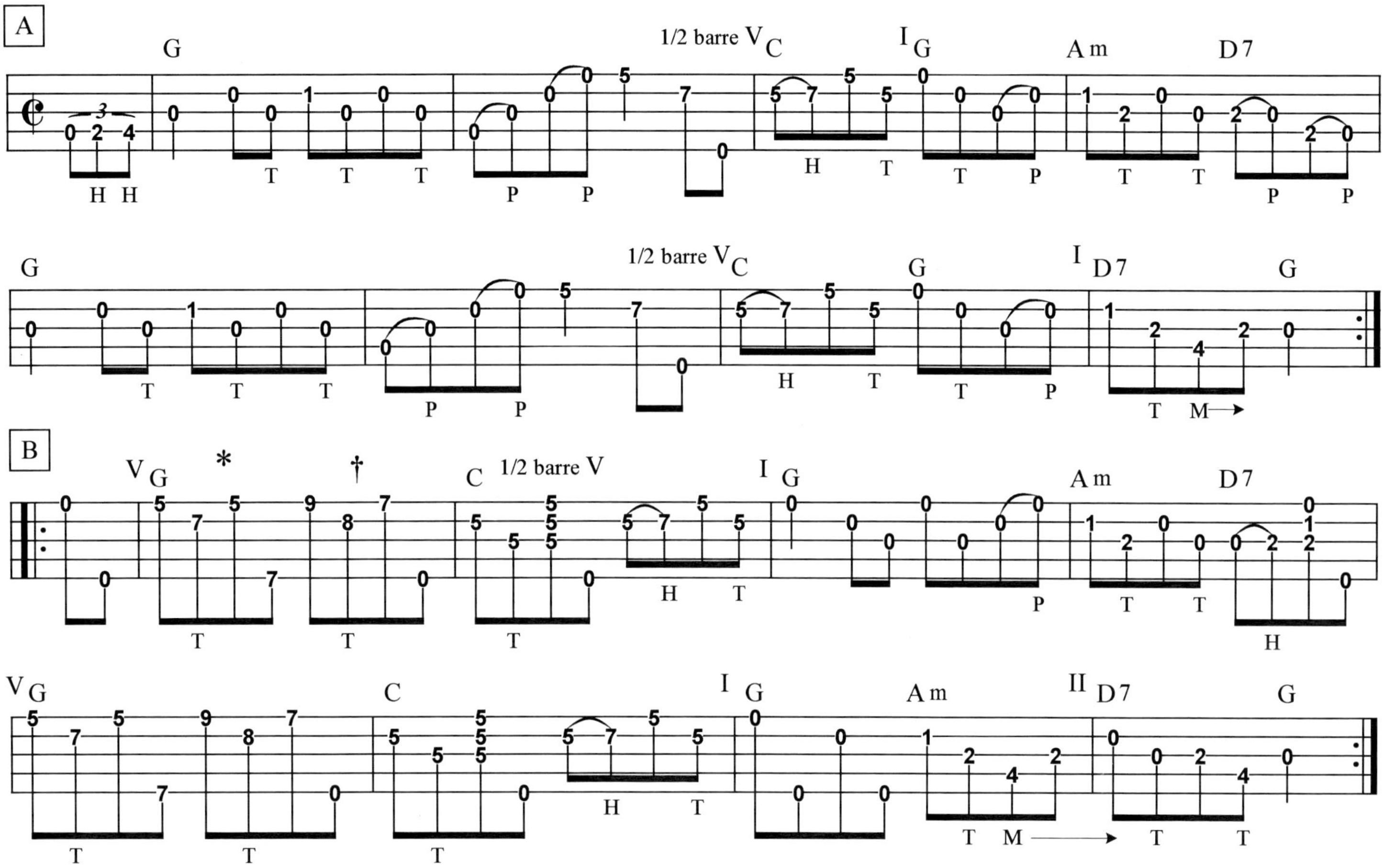

*

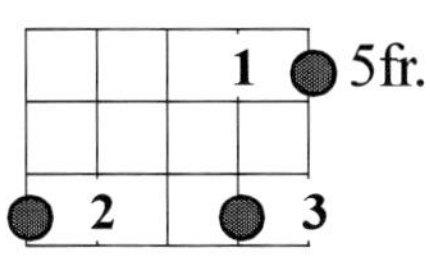

†

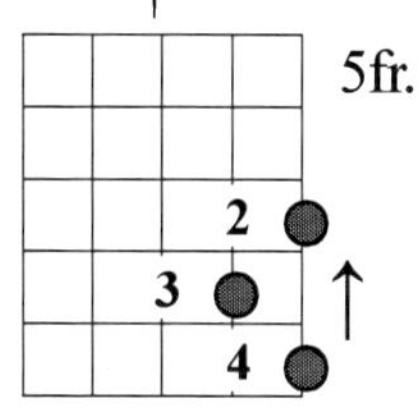

Playing Tips for *The Dragger's Reel*

• Part B, measure 1. Use the fingering shown in Diagram *, and – halfway between beats 2 and 3 – balance on the 2nd finger at fret 7, string 5. Use that finger as a pivot to reach up with the 3rd and 4th fingers to frets 8 and 9 on strings 2 and 1 respectively, as shown in Diagram †. Then on beat 4, lift up the 4th finger and bring the 2nd finger over to fret 7, string 1.

40

The Honeymoon

Origin: Probably Ireland
Source: Archie Stewart
Appears on: *Northern Banjo, Southern Summits*

Key: G
Mode: Major
Tuning: gDGBD

When I first heard Archie Stewart play this tune I was so smitten that I hummed it during the entire drive back to my lodgings, then immediately got out my banjo and started working on an arrangement. He called it "Lumberjack's Reel," but I later found it twice in *Ryan's Mammoth Collection* – once as "The Honeymoon" and separately as "The Ha' Penny." Digging further, I learned it was one of the very first fiddle tunes ever recorded in North America (untitled, as part of a medley cut in 1916 by accordionist John J. Kimmel). A somewhat deconstructed version of the tune was recorded in 1928 by Crockett's Kentucky Mountaineers; roughly a half-century later the Highwoods String Band re-recorded the Mountaineers' version as "Crockett's Honeymoon." The setting here is what I recorded on *Northern Banjo;* to get close to how Alan Jabbour and I played it on *Southern Summits,* use the alternative measure shown below. The ending of the tune is circular, and I've included the final-sounding coda used on the recordings. Standard notation for my source version is in *Fiddle Music of P.E.I.*

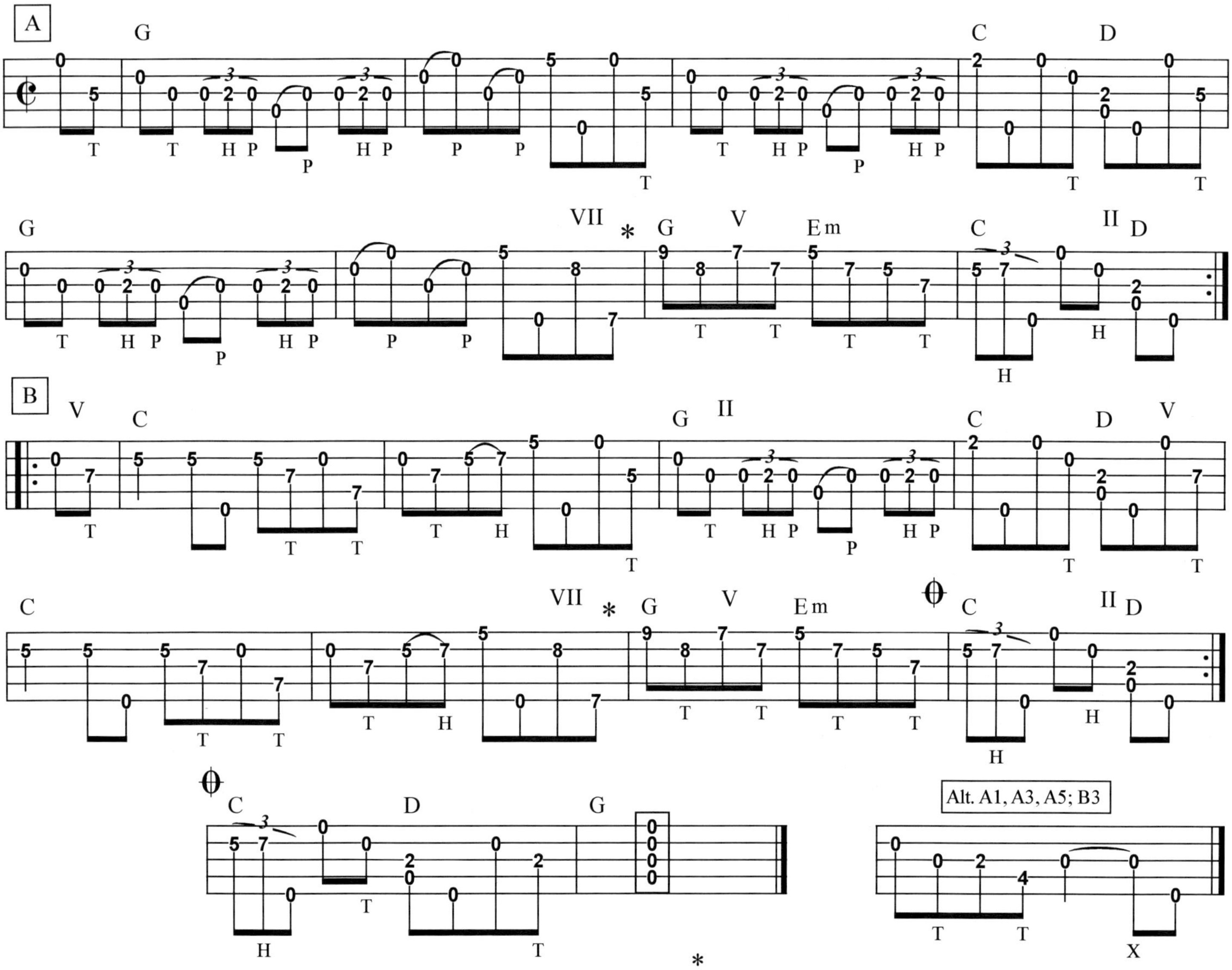

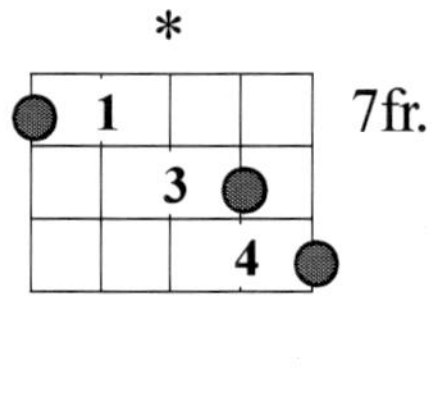

Playing Tips for *The Honeymoon*

• Part A and B, measure 7. At the end of beat 1 (Diagram *), your 3rd and 4th fingers should be on fret 8, string 2 and fret 9, string 1 respectively. On beat 2, take those fingers, and move them both down to fret 7 on those same two strings. On beat 3, balance on the 3rd finger (string 2) and catch fret 5, string 1 with the 1st finger.

Fermoy Lasses

41

Origin: Ireland
Source: Louise Arsenault
Appears on: *Island Boy*

Keys: E & G
Mode: See Intro
Tuning: gDGBD

Named for a city in south-central Ireland roughly 30 miles north of Cork, this tune appears in the classic tunebook, *O'Neill's Music of Ireland*. The E-Aeolian (E-minor) gamut dominates Part A and infuses the tune with a dark atmosphere, which is immediately dispelled when Part B opens on a strong G major chord and continues in the G major mode. The open third-string notes on the off-beats of measures B1, B3, and B5 should be treated as long-string drones that mimic the sound of a rocking bow. The ending is circular, and I've included a final-sounding coda. Standard notation for my source version is in *Fiddle Music of P.E.I.*

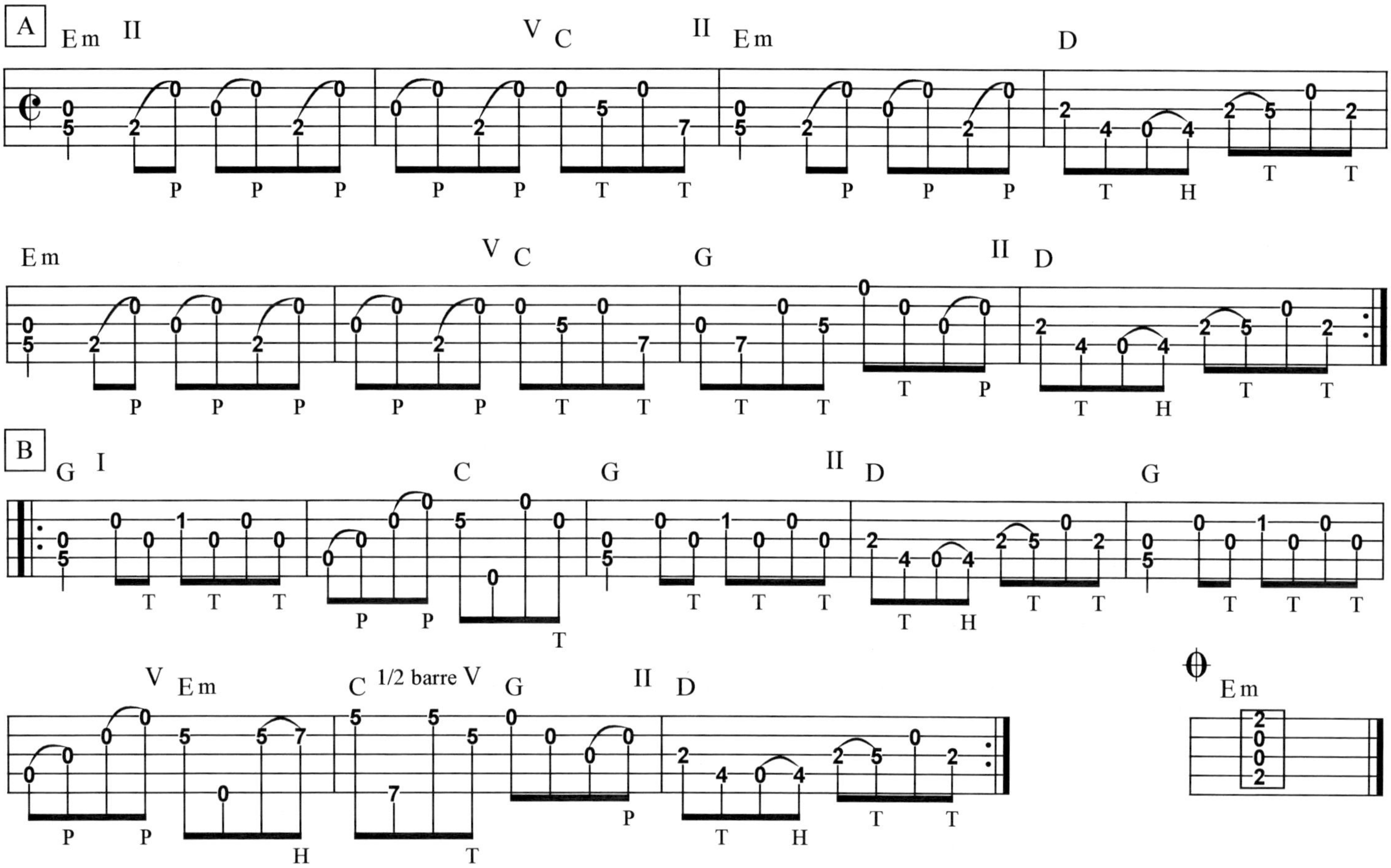

Playing Tips for *Fermoy Lasses*

• Part A, measures 1-3, 5-6. On beat 2 of each measure, use the 1st finger to press down fret 2, string 4 (and hold it); then alternate the fingers used to pull-off the open strings. I use the 3rd finger to pull off open string 2, and the 2nd finger to pull off open string 3.

• Part B, measures 6-7. For best results, start your ½-barre V on the last beat of measure 6. Then use the 4th finger to hammer from fret 5 to fret 7 on string 2; this frees the 3rd finger to reach over to get fret 7, string 5.

42

Paddy on the Turnpike (a Kings County Version)

Origin: Eastern P.E.I. Variant
Source: Francis MacDonald
Appears on: *Island Boy*

Key: G
Mode: See Intro
Tuning: gDGBD

This modal classic – diatonic with both variable 3rd and 7th scale tones – is one of the most widely played tunes on P.E.I. Despite its common title, the tune may well be Scottish in origin, appearing as "The Old Reel" in James Davies' *Caledonian Repository* (1829). Two of the first tune books to use the appellation, "Paddy on the Turnpike" were both published in Boston: Septimus Winner's *The Excelsior Collection for the Violin* (1864) and *Ryan's Mammoth Collection*; the tune also appears in *The Roche Collection* as "The Mills Are Grinding." Many Acadian fiddlers on P.E.I. call the tune "Marie à Pierre" (facing page). Standard notation for my source version is in *Fiddle Music of P.E.I.*

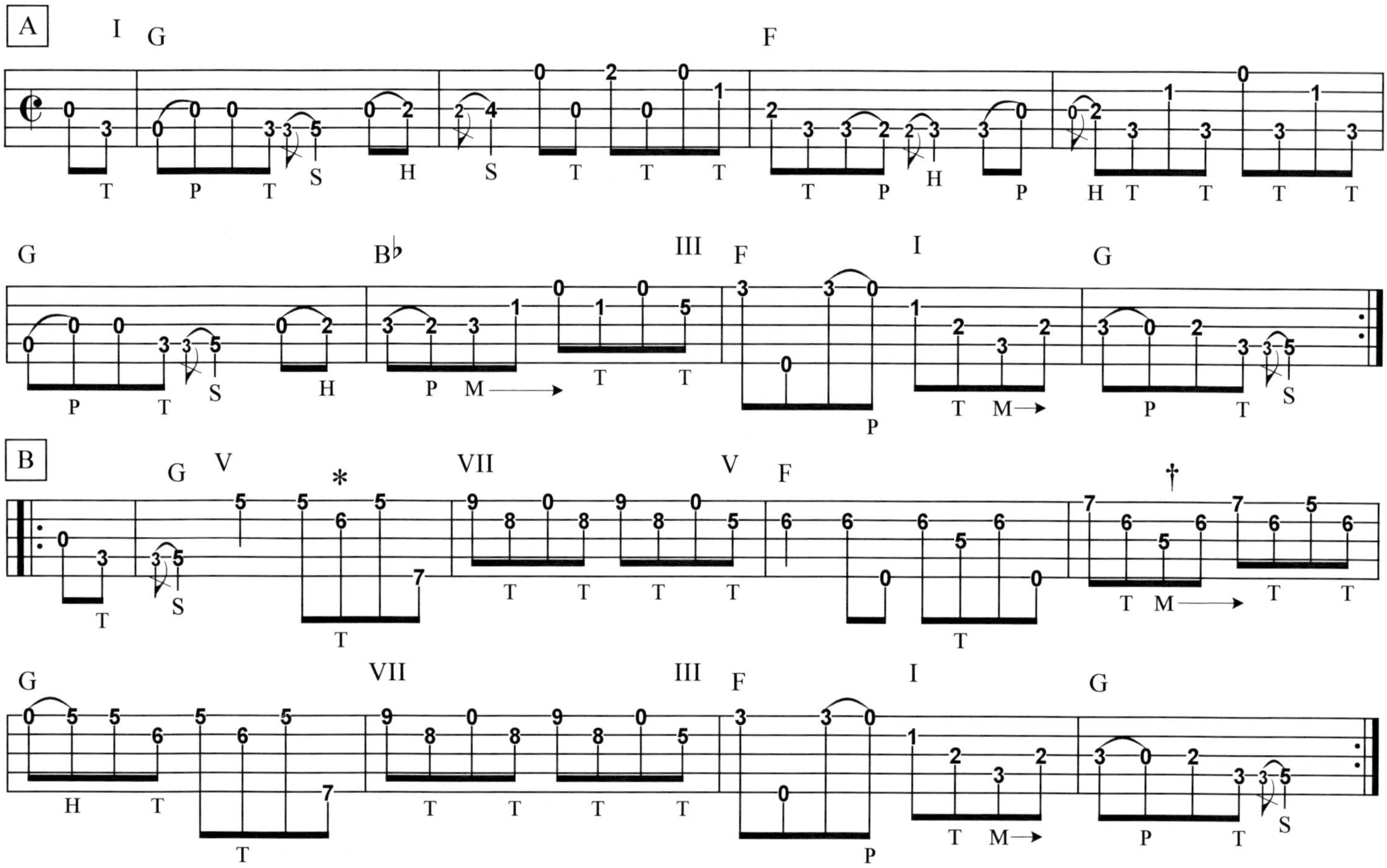

*

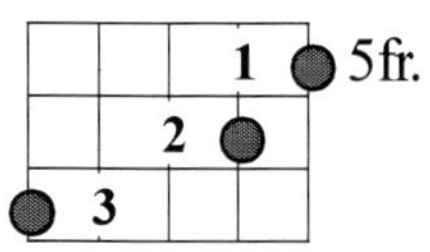

†

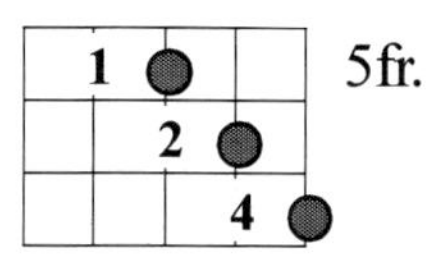

Playing Tips for *Paddy on the Turnpike*

• Part B, measures 1-2. By beat 3 of measure 1, you should be in the fingering shape shown in Diagram *. At the end of measure 1, balance with the 2nd finger on fret 6, string 2. On beat 1 of measure 2, take that finger, glide up string 2 to fret 8, and – with the 4th finger – stop fret 9, string 1.

• Part B, measure 6-7. On beat 4 of measure 6, use the open string to scoot down the neck from seventh to third position, and – with the 3rd finger – grab fret 5, string 2. At the start of measure 7, you're then in a convenient spot to stop fret 3, string 1 with the 1st finger.

43

Marie à Pierre

Origin: Western P.E.I. Variant
Source: Victor Doucette
Appears on: *Frails & Frolics*

Key: G
Mode: Variable 7th Tone
Tuning: gDGBD

"Marie à Pierre" is a lively Acadian variant of "Paddy on the Turnpike" (facing page) that retains just a hint of the tune's original modal character. When I recorded this version from Victor Doucette of Harper Road, his acrobatic foot tapping was so energetic that he seemed to almost levitate off the floor. The title roughly translates to "Marie, Pierre's Wife." Standard notation for my source version is available on *bowingdownhome.ca.*

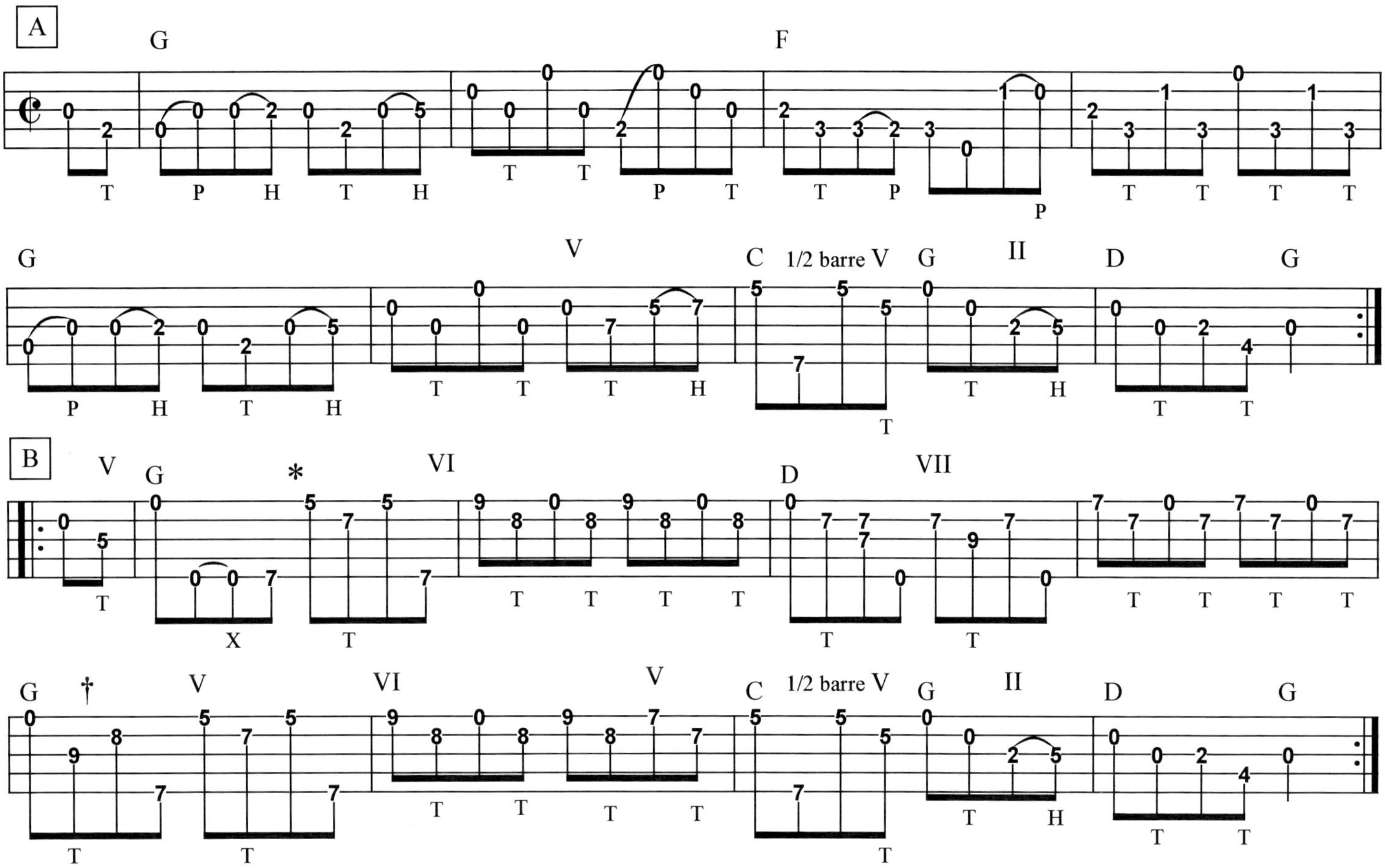

Playing Tips for *Marie à Pierre*

- Part B, measure 1-2. Halfway between beats 2 and 3 of measure 1, use the 2nd finger to stop fret 7, string 5; this puts you in position to use the fingering suggested in Diagram *. At the end of measure 1, balance on the 2nd finger; then at the start of measure 2, reach out with the 3rd and 4th fingers to grab fret 8, string 2 and fret 9, string 1, respectively.

- Part B, measure 5. At the end of beat 2 balance on the 1st finger (Diagram †) and cut short fret 7, string 5. Then scoot down to fifth position and re-assume the shape from Diagram *.

Lad O'beirne's Reel

Origin: Irish
Source: Kenny Chaisson
Appears on: *Frails & Frolics*

Key: G
Mode: Major-Like (See Intro)
Tuning: gDGBD

"Lad O'beirne's" is sometimes attributed to well-known Irish fiddler and composer Ed Reavy. It was popularized in Atlantic Canada by Cape Breton fiddler Jerry Holland. The tune is ultimately in G major, but contains several major-pentatonic passages and otherwise flirts with the E minor/Aeolian mode. Standard notation for my source version is in *Fiddle Music of P.E.I.*

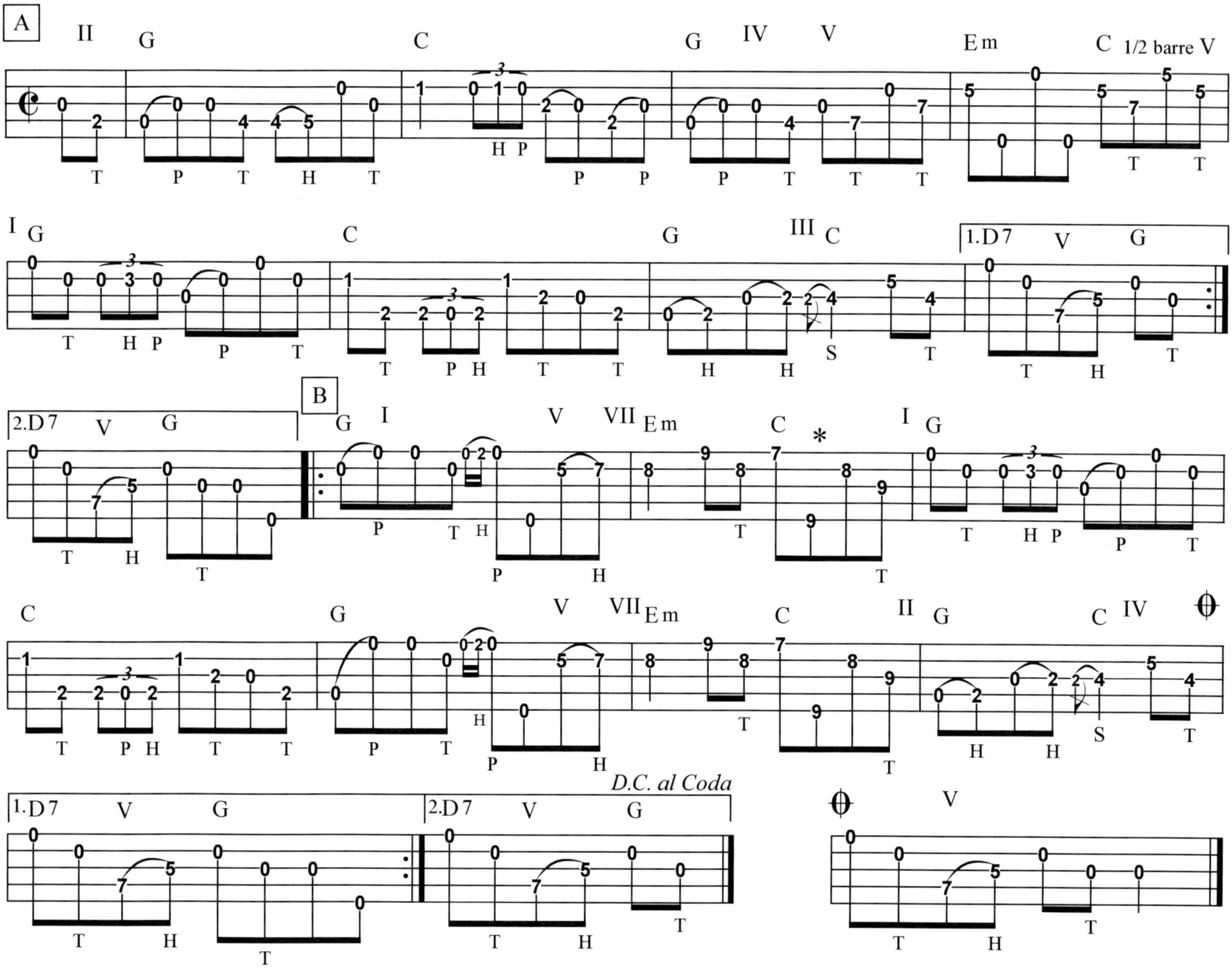

*

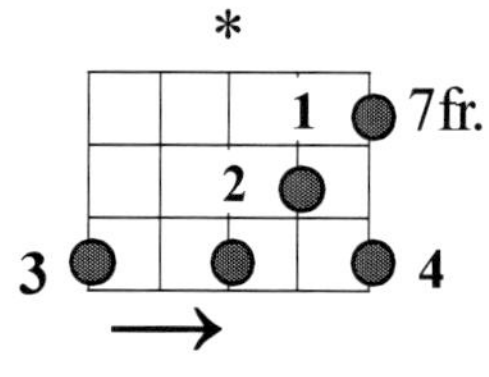

Playing Tips for *Lad O'beirne's Reel*

• Part B, measures 1-2. On beat 4 of measure 1, hammer from fret 5 to fret 7, string 2 and balance on the 3rd finger (but keep the 2nd finger lurking close behind it). At the start of measure 2, scoot up with the 2nd finger and plant it on fret 8, string 2. Use that finger as a pivot as you gradually assume the shape shown in Diagram *. On beat 2, use the 4th finger to stop fret 9, string 1; on beat 3 – keeping the 2nd finger in place and lifting the 4th – use the 1st finger to stop fret 7, string 1. Then on beat 4 (still keeping the 2nd finger in place), move the 3rd finger from fret 9, string 5 to fret 9, string 3.

45

Joe Kearney's Reel

Origin: Local Tune or Variant
Source: Joe Kearney
Appears on: *Island Boy*

Key: E
Mode: Dorian Gamut
Tuning: gDGBD

I've been unable to otherwise identify this exciting modal tune, so I named it for the fiddler I collected it from: Joe Kearney of Sturgeon, in south-central Kings County, P.E.I. Standard notation for my source version is in *Fiddle Music of P.E.I.*

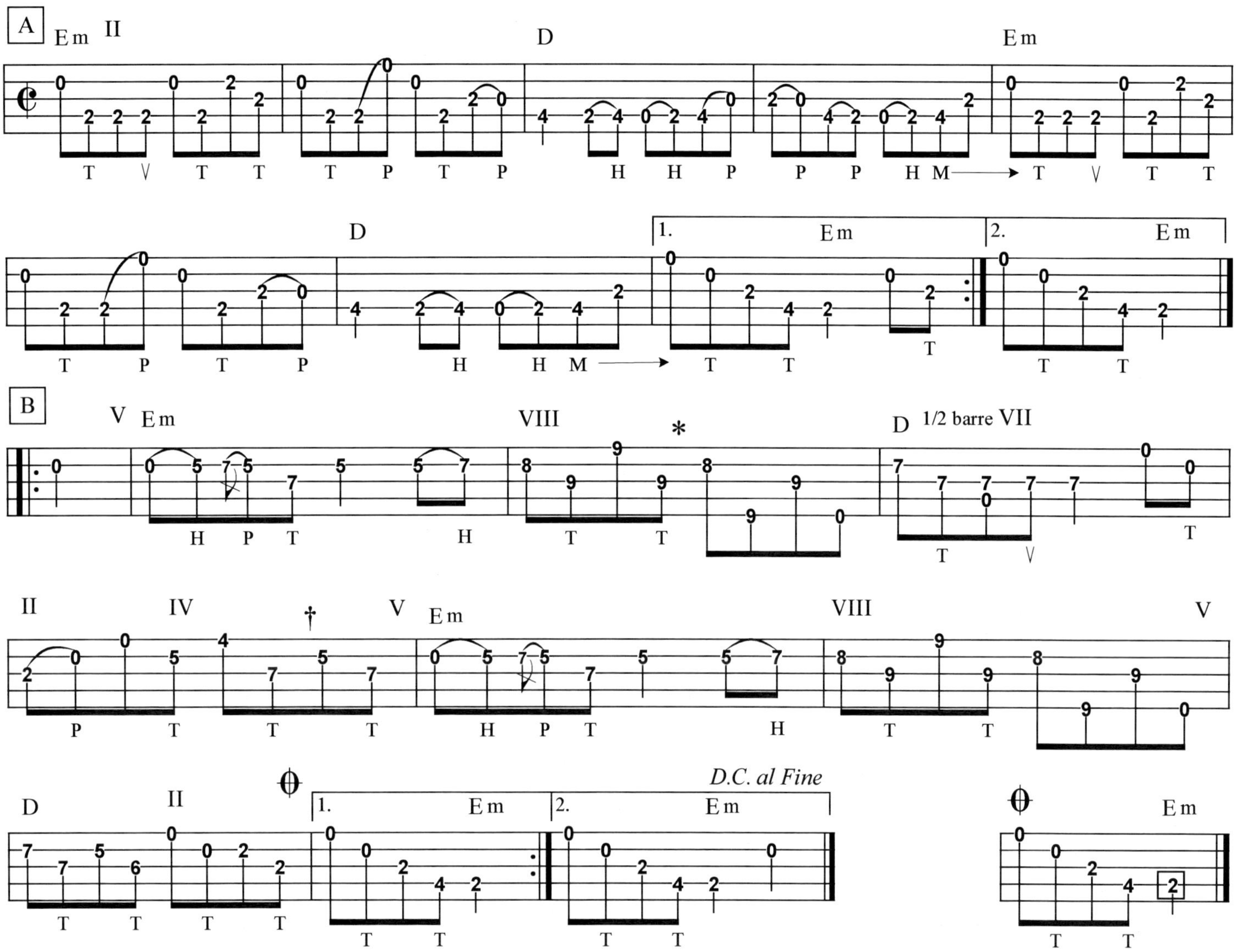

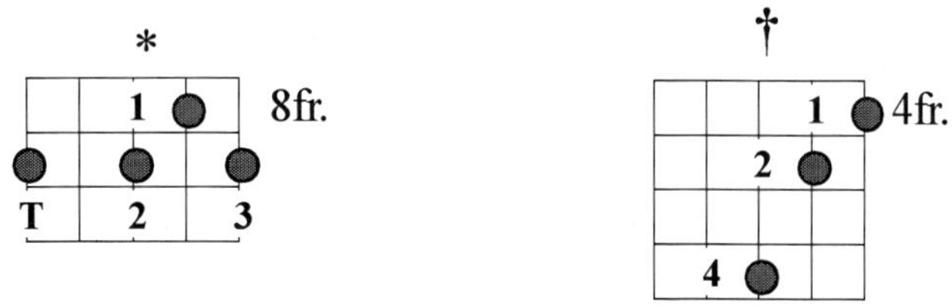

Playing Tips for *Joe Kearney's Reel*

• Part B, measure 1-2. Keep the fingering shape shown in Diagram * in mind. At the end of measure 1, balance on the 3rd finger (fret 7, string 2), and with the 1st and 2nd fingers form "in the air" that portion of the shape that falls on strings 2 and 3, respectively. At the start of measure 2, jump up with those fingers to frets 8 and 9 (on strings 2 and 3) as shown in the diagram. Then on beat 2 bring the 3rd finger to fret 9, string 1 (as shown). You don't need to place the fretting-hand thumb on fret 9, string 5 until halfway between beats 3 and 4.

46

Miss Georgina Campbell

Origin: Scotland
Source: "Old Peter" Chaisson
Appears on: *Northern Banjo*

Key: G (F on Banjo)
Mode: Major Pentatonic
Tuning: gCGCD (Capo-2)

This winsome, fully pentatonic 19th-century reel appears as "Lady Georgina Campbell" in *The Skye Collection.* I used a capoed-up double C tuning for this key-of-G tune for two reasons. First, the way the notes fell on the fretboard made for a better grasp of the phrasing. Second, I wanted to create a medley featuring tunes in three different keys using the same tuning. On *Northern Banjo*, this tune is followed by "Little Jack's Reel" in E-Dorian (facing page) and "Levantine's Barrel" in D major (p. 77). Standard notation for my source version is in *Fiddle Music of P.E.I.*

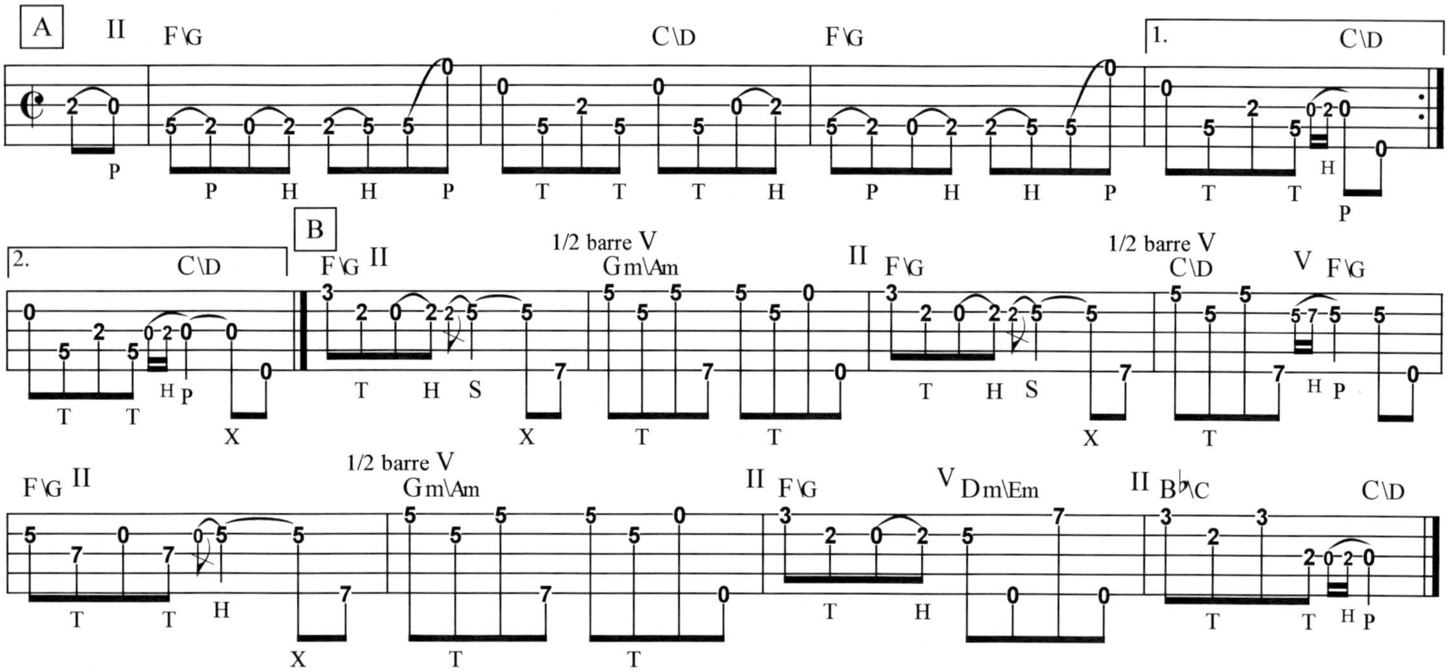

Playing Tips for *Miss Georgina Campbell*

Dual Chord Symbols: Chord to left of backslash goes with open banjo; chord on right is for capoed banjo or fiddle

• Part A, measure 1. On beat 3, hammer from fret 2 to fret 5, string 4, using the 1st and 4th fingers, then hold the 4th finger in place. At the beginning of beat 4, reach over to string 1 with the 2nd finger and place it at a reachable spot. Then halfway through beat 4, use that finger to pull off string 1.

• Part B, measures 1-2. At the end of beat 2 of measure 1, balance on fret 2, string 2 with the 1st finger. On beat 3, use that finger to perform a quick-slide to fret 5, and – halfway between beat 4 and the end of the measure – use it as a pivot to get your 3rd finger over to fret 7, string 5. At the start of measure 2, use the 3rd finger as a pivot to grab a half-barre at fret 5 (this sequence is repeated in measures 3 and 4).

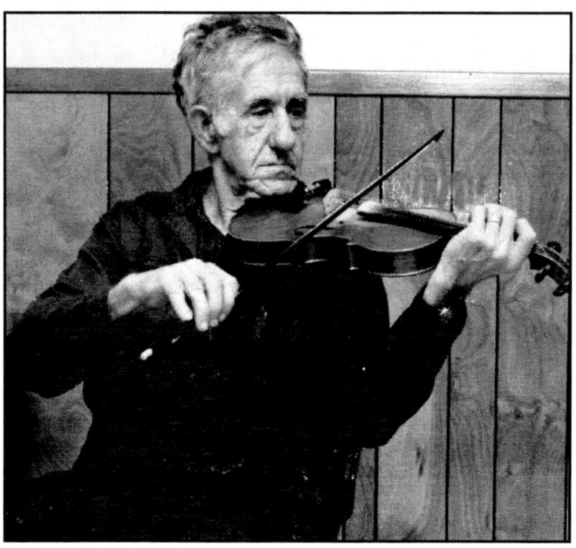

"Old Peter" Chaisson: Bear River, P.E.I. (1996). Photo by Ken Perlman; courtesy Robertson Library, University of P.E.I.

47

Little Jack's Reel

Origin: Scottish "Hybrid"
Source: Kevin Chaisson
Appears on: *Northern Banjo*

Key: E (D on Banjo)
Mode: Dorian Gamut
Tuning: gCGCD (Capo-2)

This "hybrid" tune was recorded by Little Jack MacDonald in the 1930s (Part A is from "Mrs. Ramsey's Strathspey" – as it appears, for example, in *Kerr's Merry Melodies* – but I have yet to identify a source for Part B). I liked the tune's general ambiance in a capoed C-tuning, and I wanted to create a medley featuring tunes in three different keys using the same tuning. On *Northern Banjo*, this tune is preceded by "Miss Georgina Campbell" in G (facing page) and followed by "Levantine's Barrel" in D (p 77). The ending is circular, and I've included a final-sounding coda. Standard notation for my source version is in *Fiddle Music of P.E.I.*

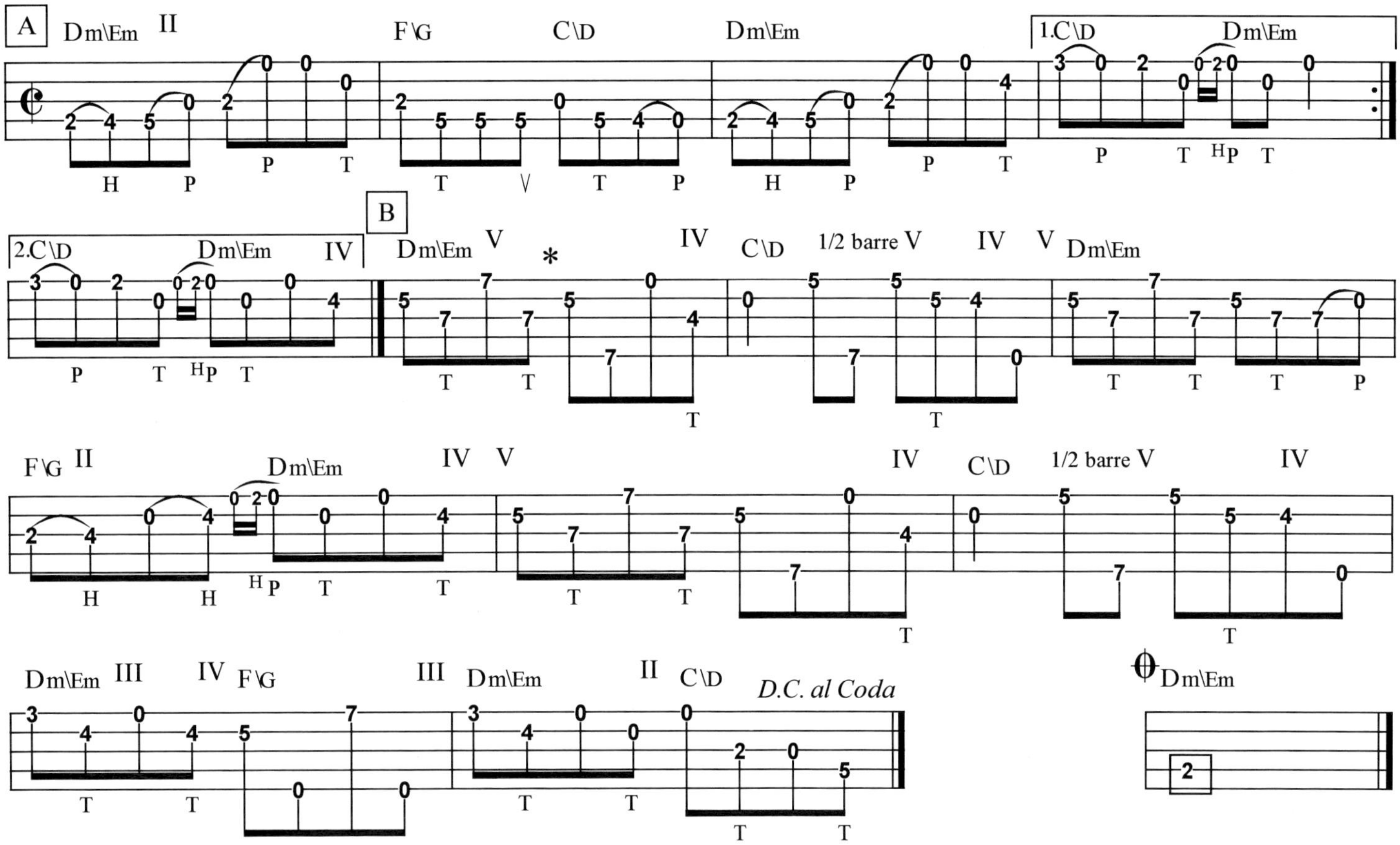

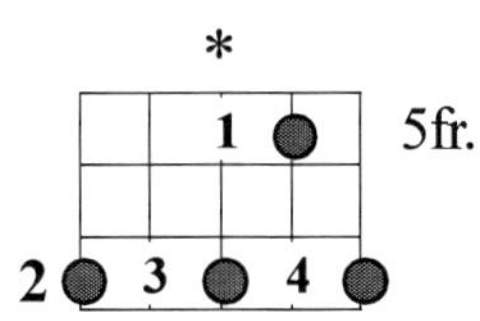

Playing Tips for *Little Jack's Reel*

***Dual Chord Symbols:** Chord to left of backslash goes with open banjo; chord on right is for capoed banjo or fiddle*

- Part B, measure 1. Refer to Diagram *, but you can wait until beat 3 before bringing your 2nd finger over to stop fret 7, string 5.

The Farmer's Reel, or The Golden Wedding

Origin: Probably New Brunswick
Source: Francis MacDonald
Appears on: *Devil in the Kitchen*

Key: G
Mode: See Intro
Tuning: gDGBD

At the time of my collecting project,"The Farmer's Reel" was one of the most widely played, and beloved tunes all across Prince Edward Island. It is known elsewhere in Canada and in New England as "The Golden Wedding Reel," and indeed fiddler Don Messer performed it under that title. In Part A, measures 3-4 the tune features the minor 7th tone characteristic of the Mixolydian mode (F♮, or fret 3, string 4); the rest of the tune is major. Part B' represents the original variation I recorded on *Devil in the Kitchen.* Standard notation for my source version is in *Fiddle Music of P.E.I.*

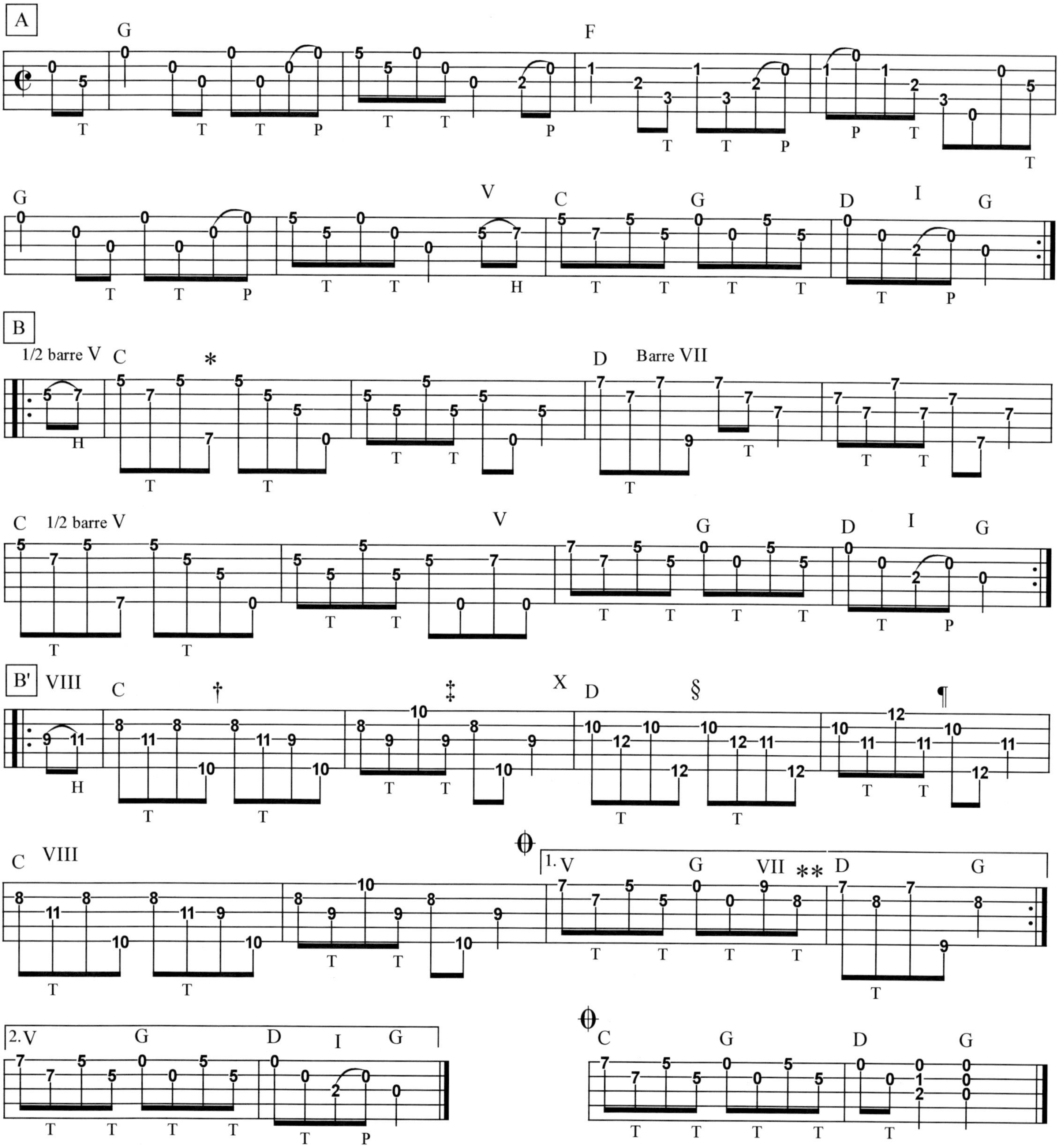

*Fingering Diagrams for *Farmer's Reel* on Facing Page*

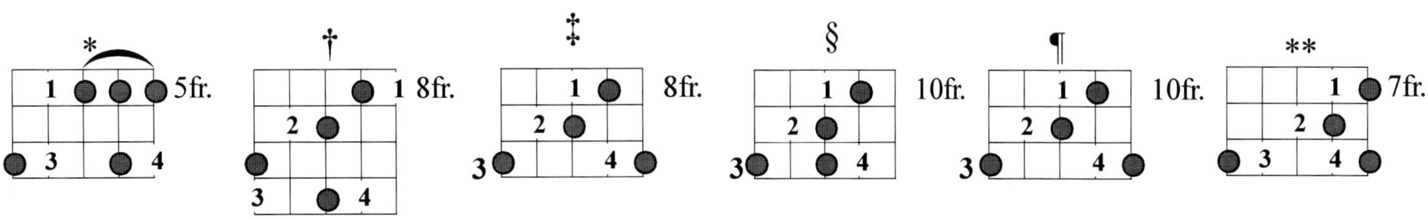

The Stack of Barley

ORIGIN: IRELAND
SOURCE: LOUISE ARSENAULT
APPEARS ON: *NORTHERN BANJO*

KEY: G
MODE: MAJOR
TUNING: gDGBD

This tune was published as "The Little Stack of Barley" in both *O'Neill's Music of Ireland* and in *The Roche Collection*. In the Irish tradition it is almost always played in hornpipe style, but on P.E.I. the tune is usually performed as a reel. An early version appears in "The Goodman Music Manuscripts," compiled in the 1860s by James Goodman, an Irish clergyman and Professor of Irish at Trinity College, Dublin. Standard notation for my source version is in *Fiddle Music of P.E.I.*

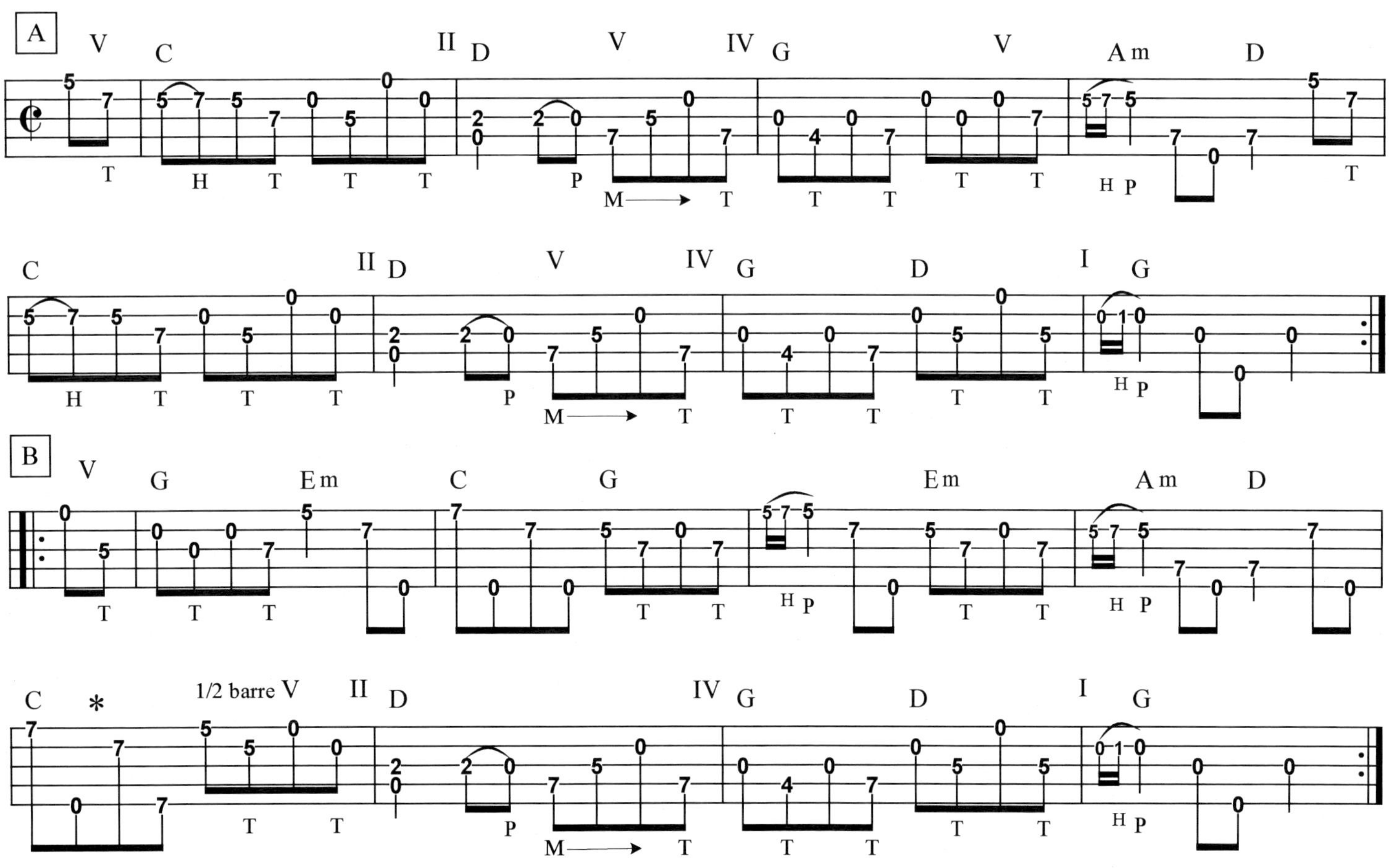

The East Neuk of Bear River (a Kings County Variant)

50

Origin: Local Variant of Scottish Tune
Source: George MacPhee
Appears on: *Northern Banjo*

Key: G
Mode: Major-Like (See Intro)
Tuning: gDGBD

This lively variant from northeastern Kings County, P.E.I. – which I named for a local district – is derived from the well-known Scottish tune, "The East Neuk of Fife." I recall an evening when MacPhee launched into the tune at the end of a long medley as the gathering cheered and the entire house was shaking from the power of the collective foot-stomping. The Scots word "neuk" means a corner or sector – analogous to the word, "nook" in English; Fife is a city in east-central Scotland. One early appearance in print for "The East Neuk of Fife" was in Wm. MacGibbon's *A Collection of Scots Tunes [. . .]* (1746); the tune was carried through the 19th century via *Kerr's Merry Melodies, The Skye Collection, The Athole Collection,* and James Scott Skinner's *Harp & Claymore.* In terms of mode, Part A of this variant is major but Part B is major pentatonic. The tune is circular, and I've offered a final-sounding ending. Standard notation for my source version is in *Fiddle Music of P.E.I.*

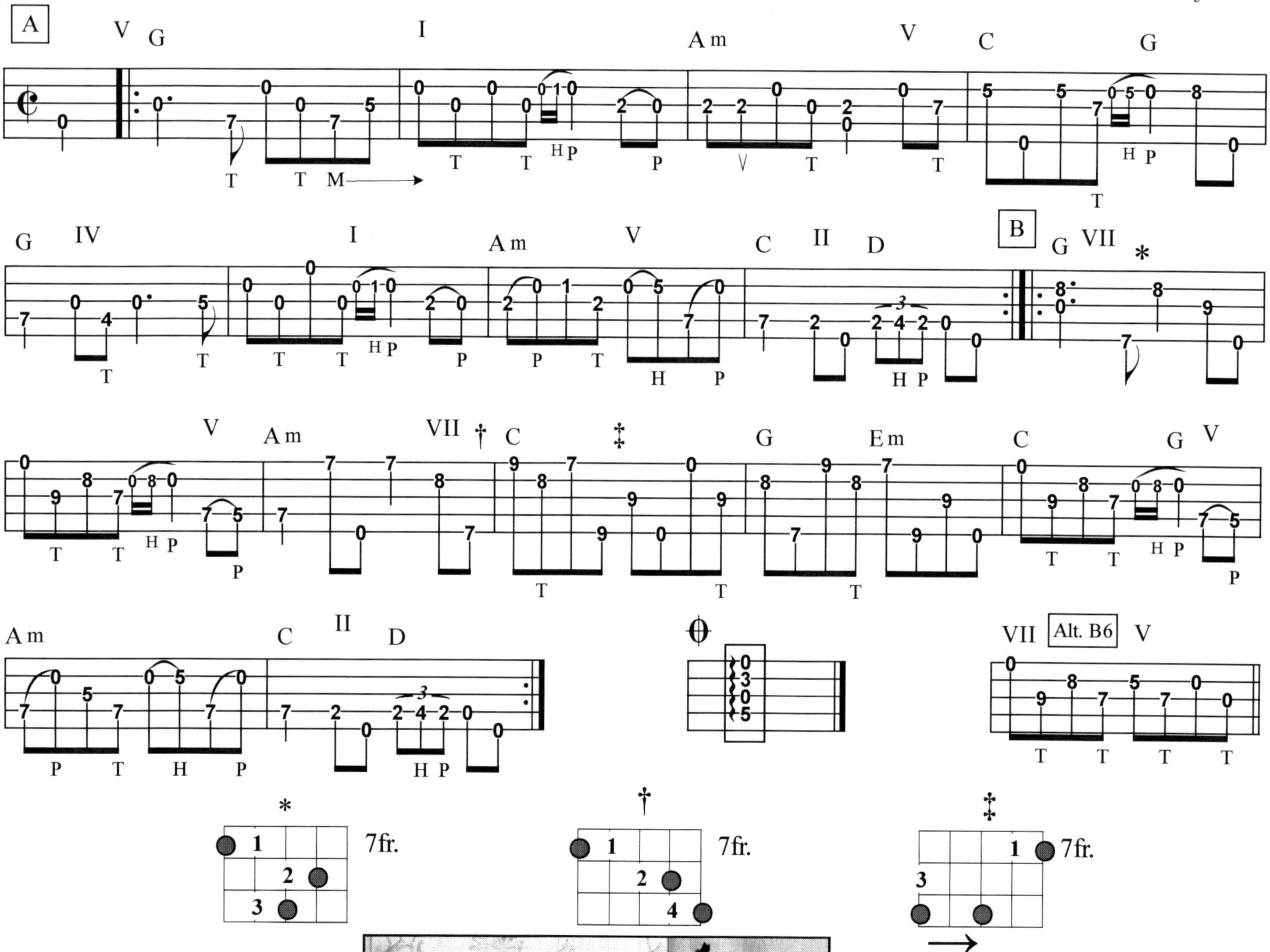

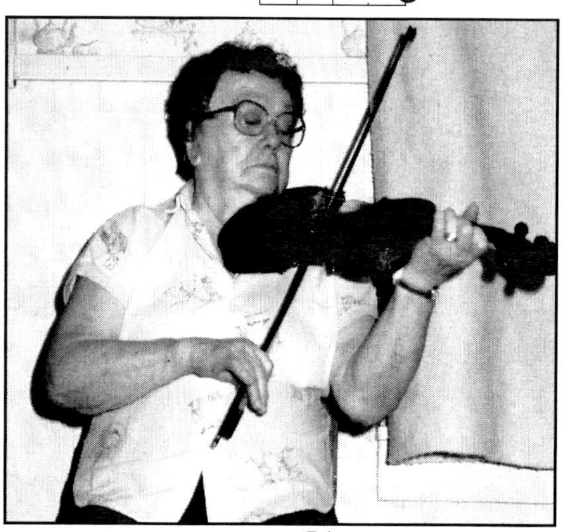

Hilda MacPhee MacDonald at Project Headquarters, Monticello P.E.I. (1991). Photo by Earthwatch team; courtesy Robertson Library, University of P.E.I.

Green Meadow Reel, or Over the Moor to Maggie

51

ORIGIN: IRELAND
SOURCE: EDDY ARSENAULT
APPEARS ON: *ISLAND BOY*

KEY: G
MODE: MAJOR
TUNING: gDGBD

This truly lovely tune has a long and varied history in the Irish and North American fiddling traditions in both two- and three-part formats. The two-part version is still widely played in Atlantic Canada and also – as "Waynesboro" – in the American old-time music tradition. One of the two-part melody's first appearances in print was R.M. Levey's *First Collection of the Dance Music of Ireland* (1858); the "Green Meadow" title may derive from *Allan's Irish Fiddler.* The three-part version was published in *O'Neill's Dance Music of Ireland* as "Over the Moor to Maggie"; this is the version you'll almost always hear played nowadays in the Irish traditional music scene. Standard notation for my source version is in *Fiddle Music of P.E.I.*

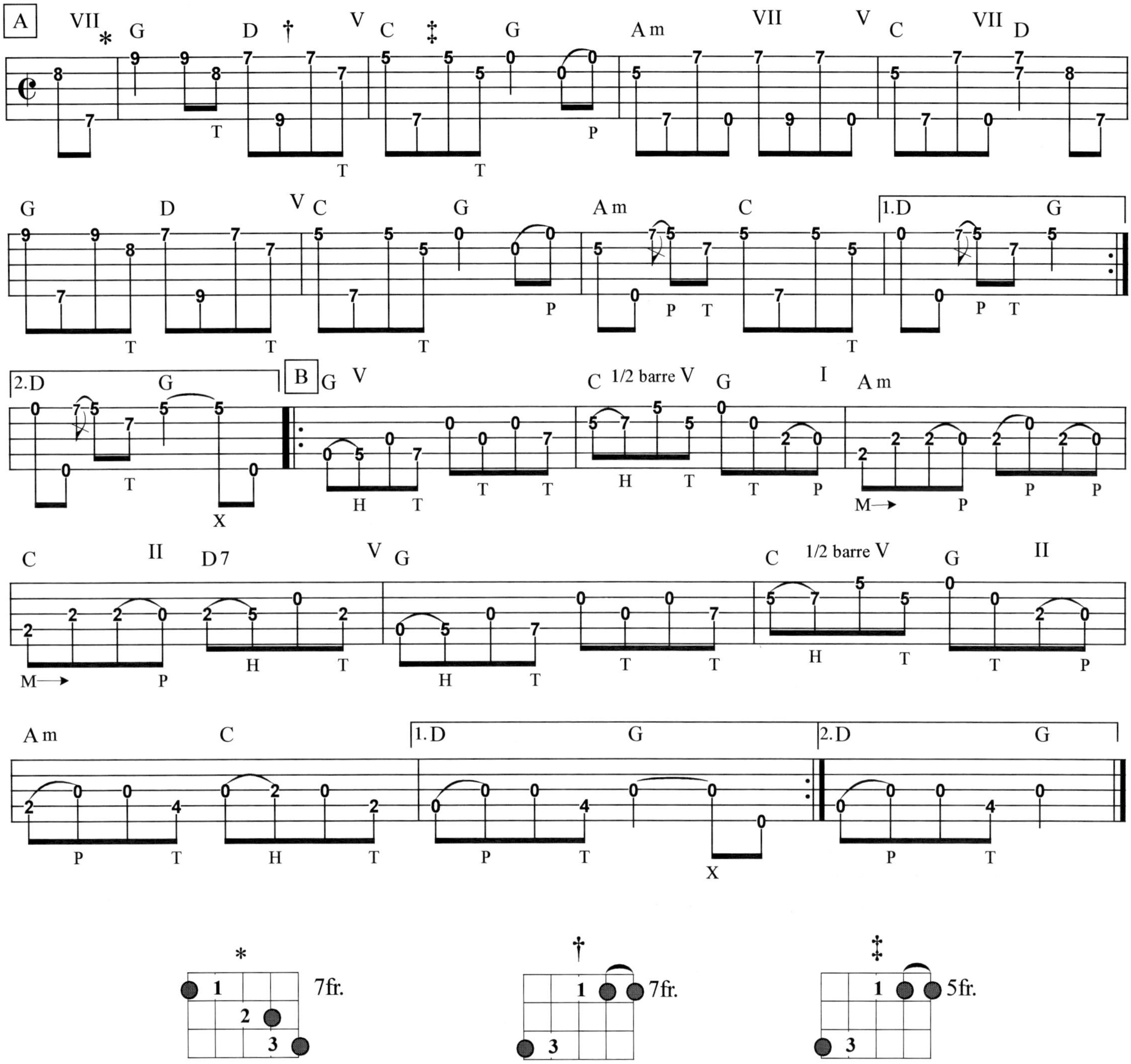

52

Darlin' Don't You Meddle Me

Origin: Local Variant of Irish Tune
Source: Allan MacDonald
Appears on: *Island Boy*

Keys: G & E
Mode: See Intro
Tuning: gDGBD

MacDonald learned this tune from his father, Hector; it appears to be a local variant of a reel from Northern Ireland called "Lark in the Morning." The melody floats between a major-like G mode and a minor-like E mode, both of which almost entirely avoid all inflections of the note C (that is, the 4th *tone* of the G major gamut and the 6th *tone* of the E minor gamut). The one exception is the ending of part A where the note C♯ is introduced (fret 2, string 2) and the melody seems to edge towards E Dorian (E-F#-G-A-B-C#-D-E). On *Island Boy*, I play the tune in medley between two others that feature strong E modal segments: "Joe Kearney's Reel" (p. 49) and "Fermoy Lasses" (p. 45). The tune is circular, and I've added a final-sounding ending. Standard notation for my source version is in *Fiddle Music of P.E.I.*

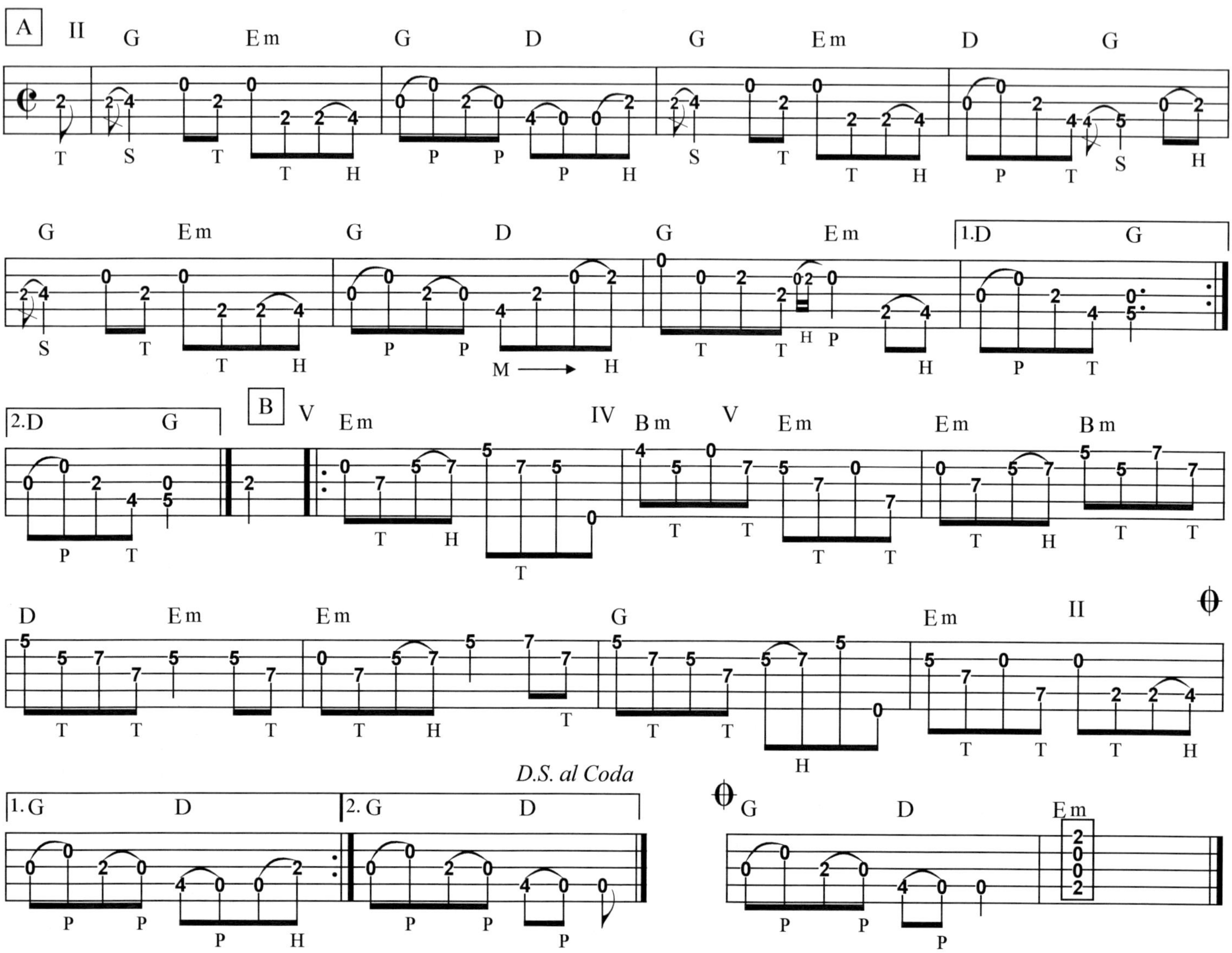

53

Dublin Porter

Origin: Ireland
Source: Kenny Chaisson
Appears on: *Island Boy*

Key: G
Mode: Major
Tuning: gDGBD

Named for a pub in the Irish capital, "Dublin Porter," or "The Dublin Porter House" can be found in *The Roche Collection*; it was introduced to the Cape Breton repertoire by fiddler Jerry Holland. The phrasing in Part B is particularly worthy of note; the melody seems to go over the edge at least twice, but neatly recovers each time and reaches a four-square conclusion. The double-sixteenth + eighth note figures in Part B emulate the sound of Cape Breton style *cuts* (see p. 20). Standard notation for my source version is in *Fiddle Music of P.E.I.*

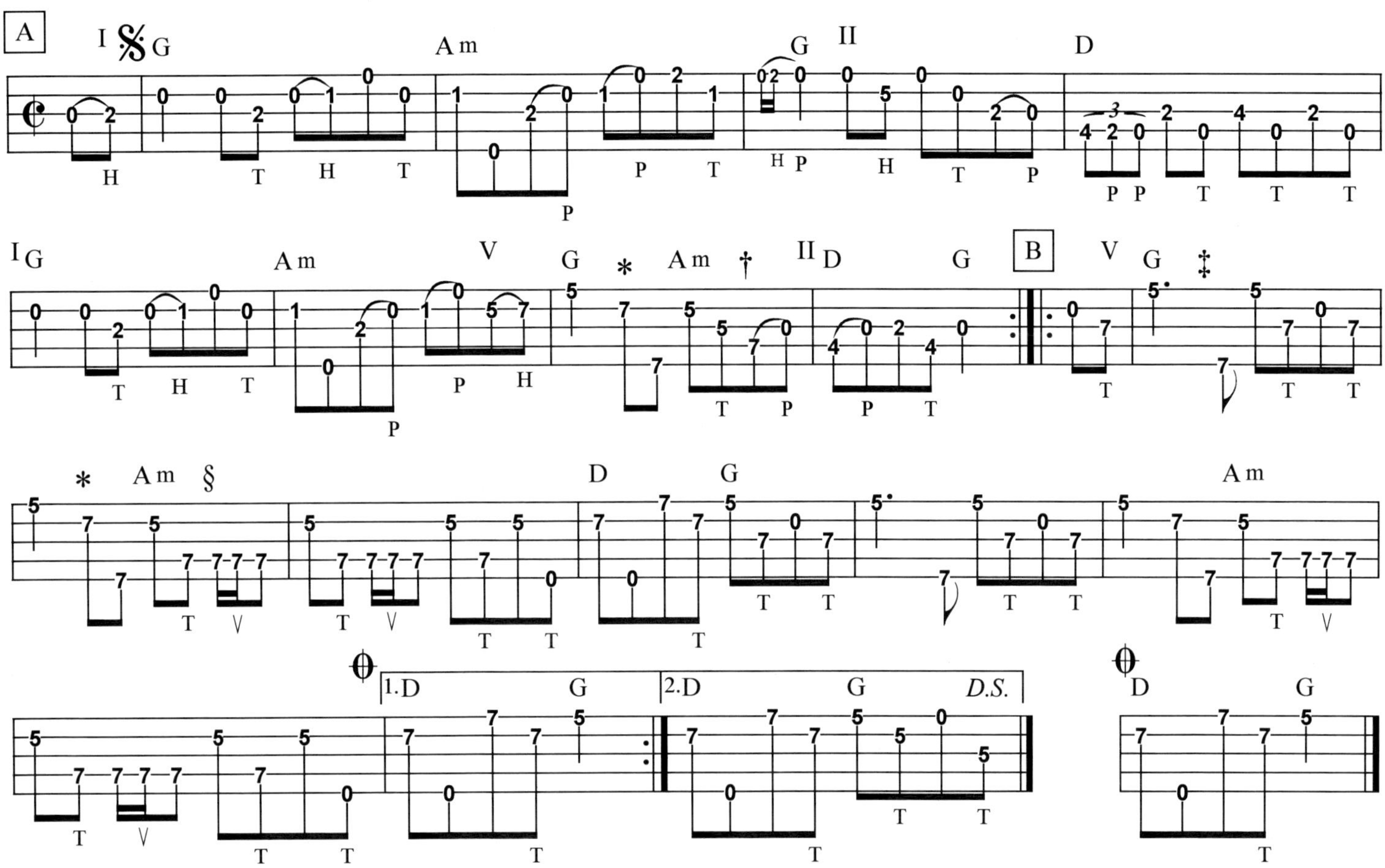

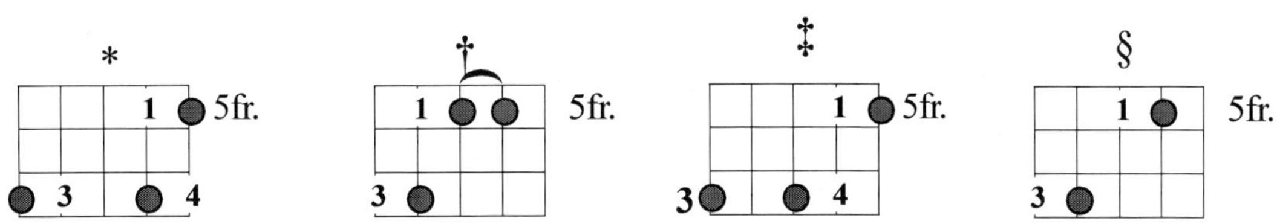

Playing Tips for *Dublin Porter*

• Part A, measures 6-7. Halfway through beat 3 of measure 6, use the time-interval provided by the open string in the alternate-string pull-off to scoot up to fifth position. Midway through beat 4, use the 4th finger for the H to fret 7, string 2. At the start of measure 7, use the 1st finger as a pivot and swing the 3rd and 4th fingers into place as shown in Diagram *. On beat 3, pivot on the 3rd finger and swivel the 1st finger into position as a half-barre on fret 5. Then on beat 4, bring in the 3rd finger to stop fret 7, string 4 as shown in Diagram †. To get the alternate-string P at the end of the measure, you'll need to first toggle the 1st finger from half-barre to arched position on string 3.

54

Lord MacDonald's Reel

Origin: Scotland
Source: "Old Peter" Chaisson
Appears on: *Island Boy & Northern Banjo*

Key: G
Mode: Major
Tuning: gDGBD

At the time of my collecting project, this four-part reel was one of the most widely played and most highly regarded tunes among Prince Edward Island fiddlers. They seemed to put everything they had into crafting a personal version, or *twist* that suited them, and no two fiddlers played the tune exactly the same way. Attributed in *The Skye Collection* to Sir Alexander Macdonald, "Lord MacDonald's Reel" has been in print since the late 18th century (an early appearance was in *The Gow Collection*). It is still widely played by Celtic and Canadian fiddlers, and a variant called "Leather Britches" – originally popularized via a 1930 recording by the Skillet Lickers – is popular among American musicians. Standard notation for my source version is in *Fiddle Music of P.E.I.*

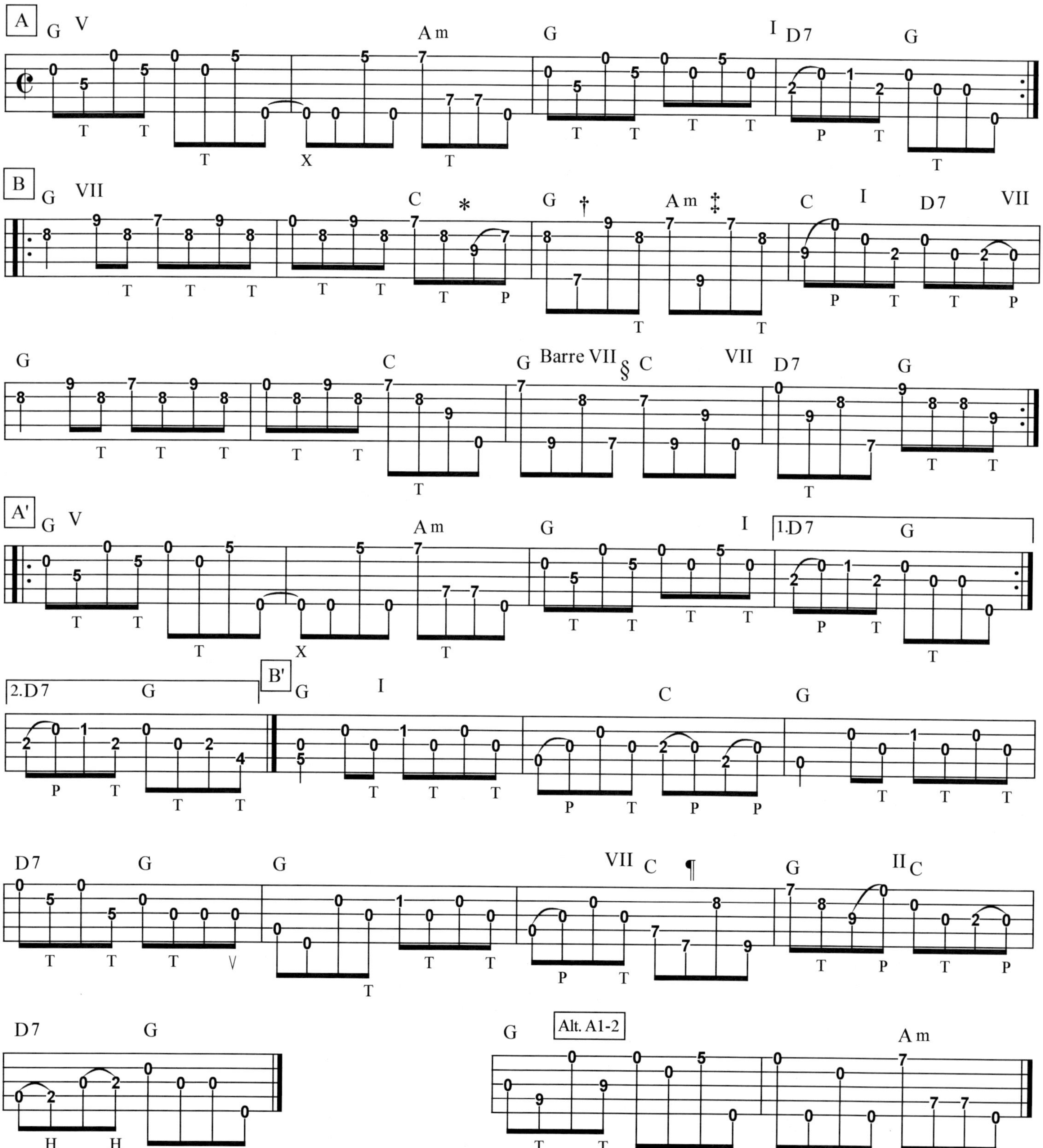

Fingering Diagrams for *Lord MacDonald's Reel*

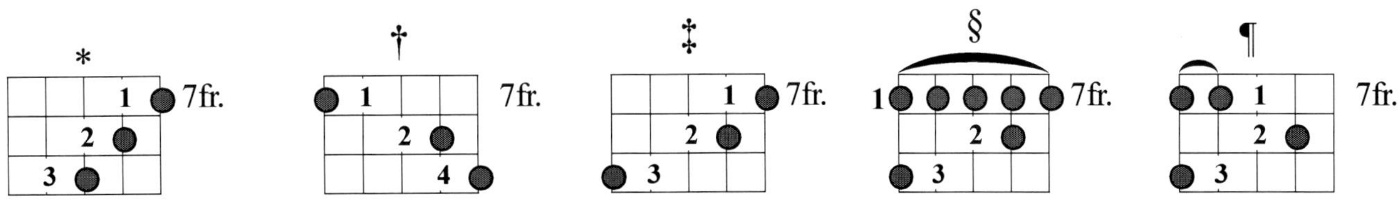

Playing Tips for *Lord MacDonald's Reel*

Part B, measures 2-3. Keep the 2nd finger firmly planted on fret 8, string 2 and pivot your other fingers as shown in the Diagrammed shapes * and †.

Part B, measures 6-7. On beat 4 of measure 6, balance with the 3rd finger on fret 9, string 3. At the start of measure 7, place a barre at fret 7 with the 1st finger and – shortly afterwards – bring the 3rd finger into contact with fret 9, string 5 – as shown in Diagram §. On beat 2, release the 3rd finger and – with the 2nd finger – press down fret 8, string 2. On beat 3, do the reverse (that is, release the 2nd finger and bring the 3rd finger back into contact with fret 9, string 5). Then on beat 4, release the barre and balance again with the 3rd finger on fret 9, string 3.

Playing Tips for *The Poppy Leaf* (tab on p. 60)

- Part A, measure 2. Use the open 5th-string note between beats 1 and 2 to get ready to spring up the neck. On beat 2, grab fret 12 on strings 5 and 2 with the 2nd and 3rd fingers respectively. On beat 3, glide down the neck on string 5 with the 2nd finger and land on fret 9 (as the 1st finger lands on fret 8, string 2). On beat 4, the 1st finger glides on string 2 up to fret 15 (and the 3rd finger lands on fret 17, string 5).

- Part A, measure 3- 4. On beat 1 of measure 3, catch fret 14, string 1 and fret 15 string 2 with the 1st and 2nd fingers, respectively. On beat 2, glide down string 1 with the 1st finger to fret 10, and catch fret 12, string 2 with the 3rd finger. On beat 4, bring the first finger over to fret 10, string 2 and – at the start of measure 4 – use that finger to pivot into the shape shown in Diagram †.

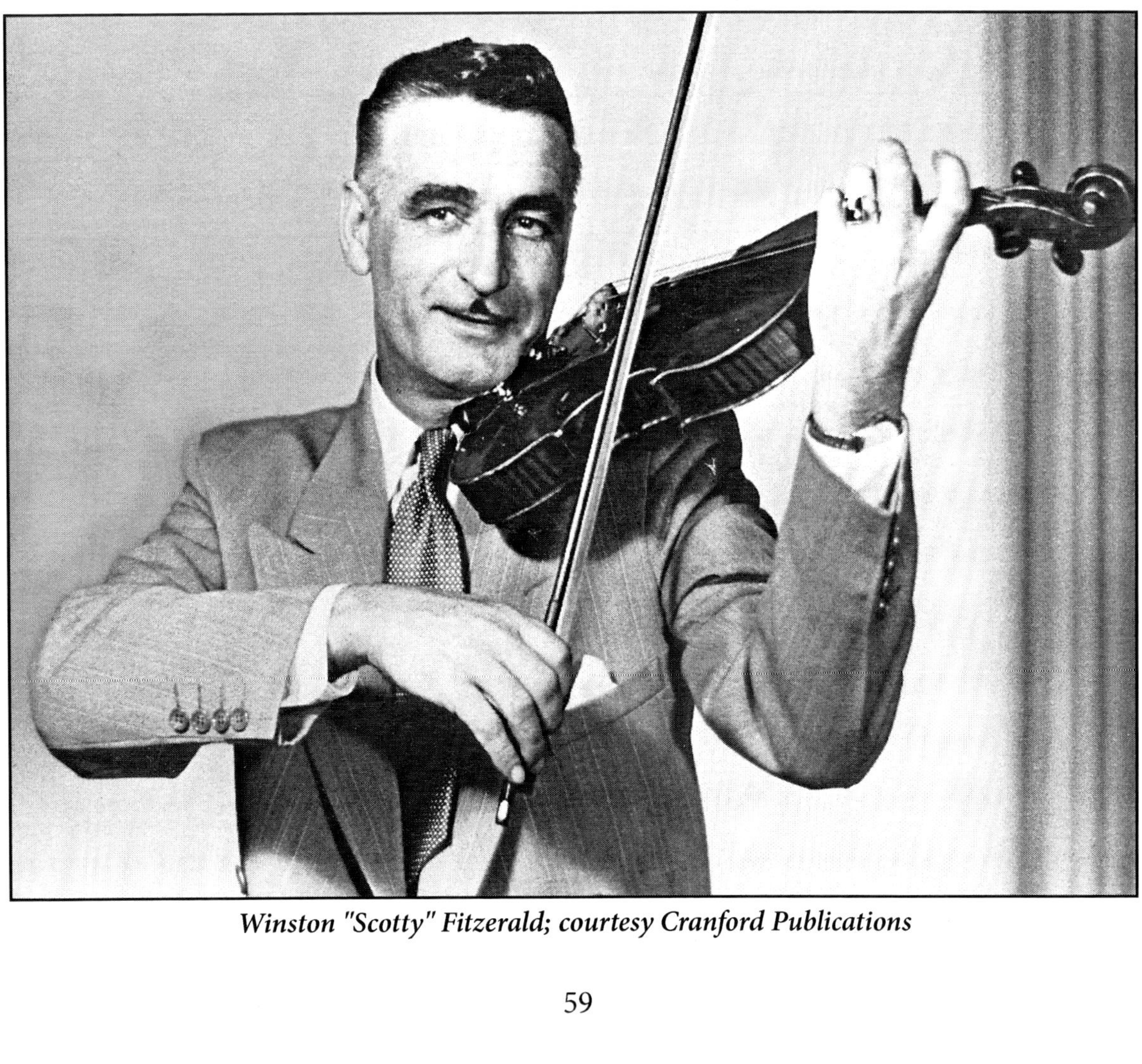

Winston "Scotty" Fitzerald; courtesy Cranford Publications

55

The Poppy Leaf

Origin: Probably New England
Source: "Young Peter" Chaisson
Appears on: *Northern Banjo*

Key: G
Mode: Major
Tuning: gDGBD

"The Poppy Leaf" is a 19th-century North American hornpipe; its earliest appearance in print was in *Ryan's Mammoth Collection.* It was popularized in Atlantic Canada via the 1950s LP, *Winston "Scotty" Fitzgerald & His Radio Entertainers.* The two-octave ascending G-chord arpeggio at the start of Part A is truly appealing, but it also proved to be one of the most challenging passages to adapt to clawhammer that I've encountered. Standard notation for my source version is in *Fiddle Music of P.E.I.*

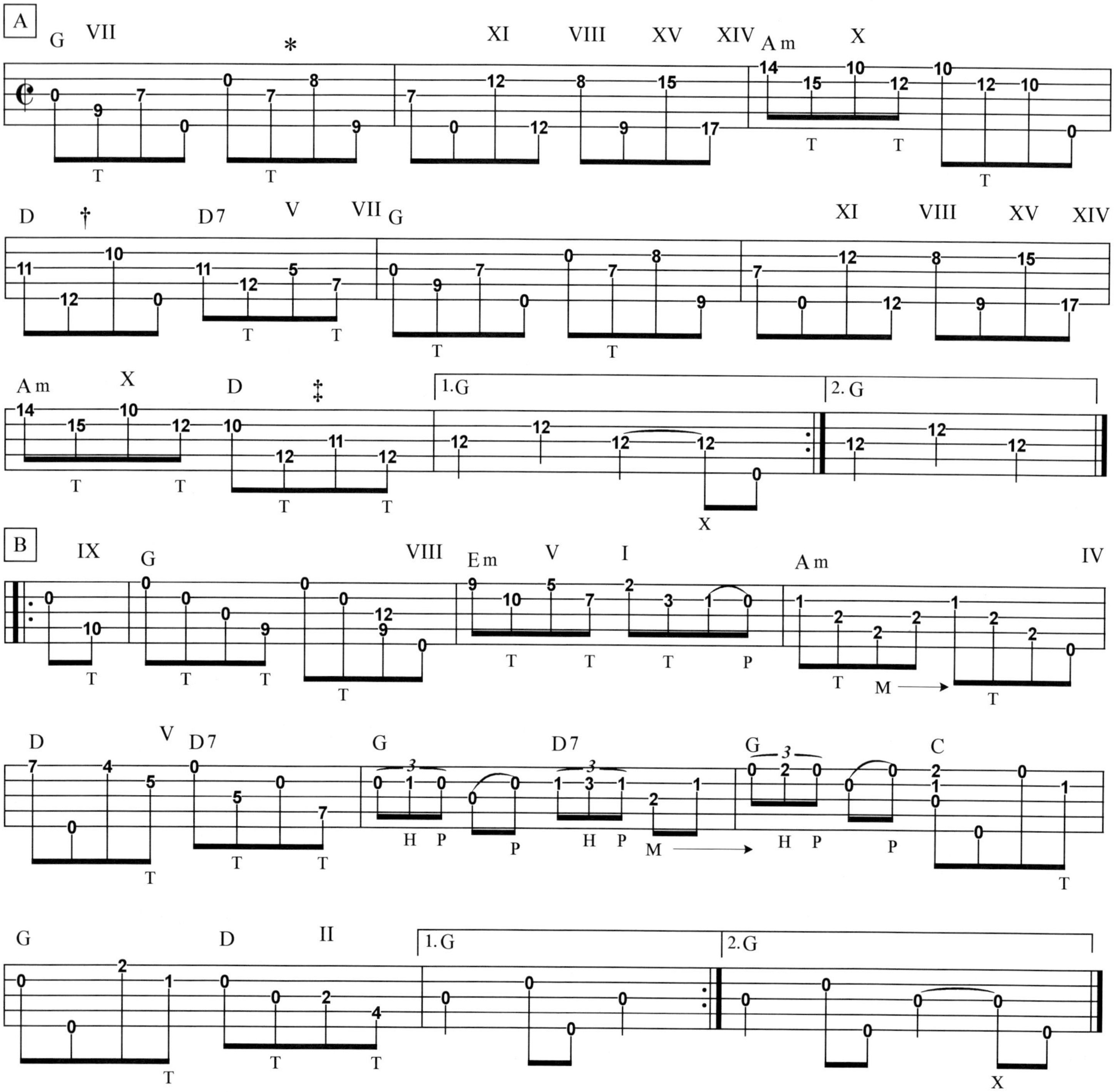

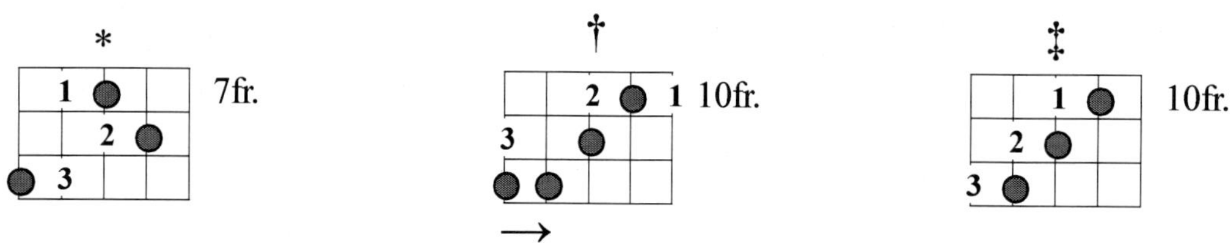

*For *Poppy Leaf* Playing Tips, See Page 59 *

56

Princess Reel

Origin: New Brunswick
Sources: Eddy Arsenault & Attwood O'Connor
Appears on: *Island Boy & Northern Banjo*

Key: G
Mode: Major
Tuning: gDGBD

"Princess Reel" is one of the most popular tunes on Prince Edward Island. O'Connor told me that the tune originally came from New Brunswick, became widespread on P.E.I. in the 1930s, and originally circulated as "Charlie's Reel" and "The Silver Wedding." Hector MacDonald of Bangor, Kings County is said to have been the first fiddler to play the tune on local radio. Note that the alternative measures for Part A offer different methods for obtaining the same notes. Standard notation for my source version is in *Fiddle Music of P.E.I.*

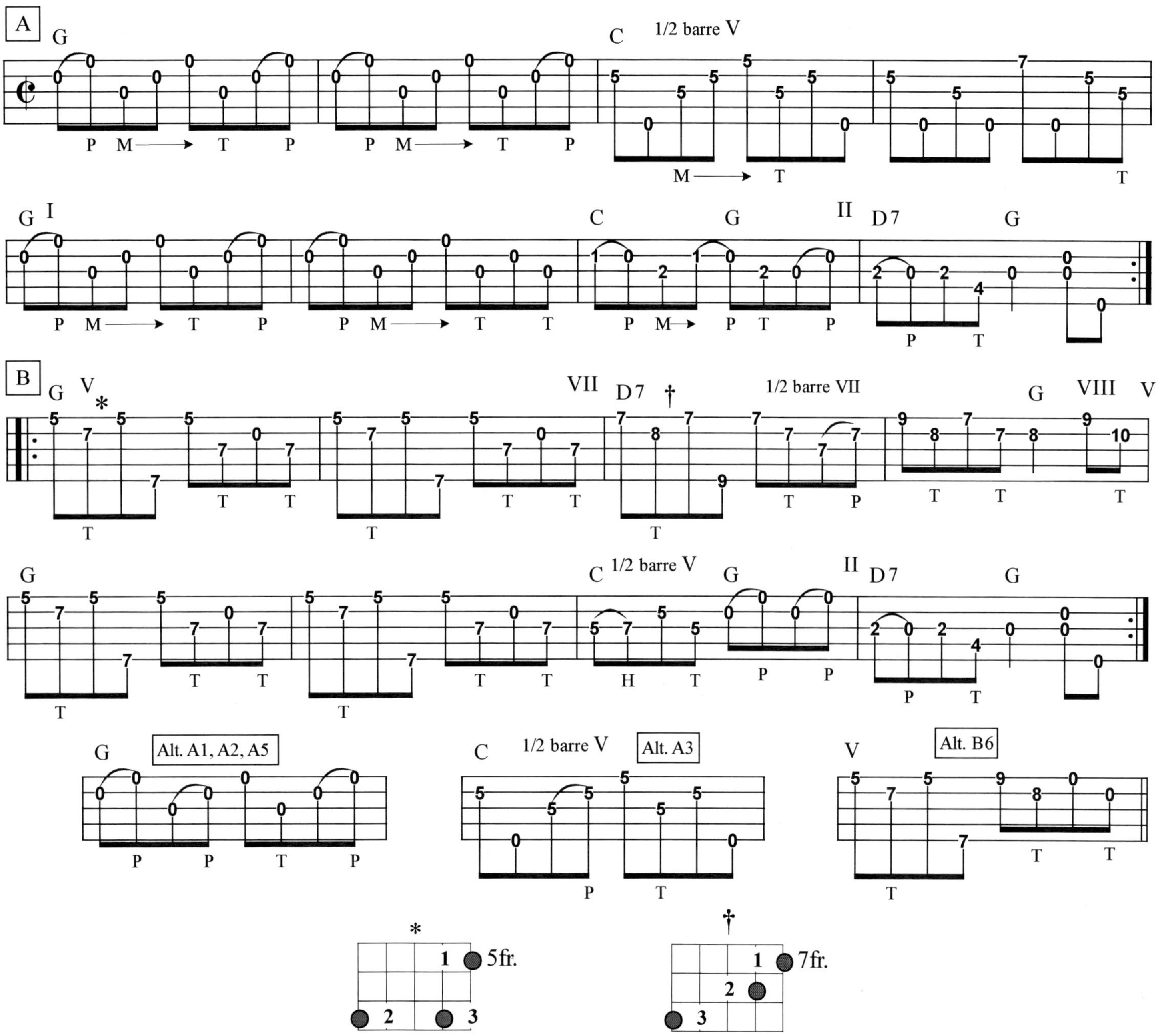

Playing Tips for *Princess Reel*

• Part B, measure 3. Halfway through beat 2, balance with the 3rd finger on fret 9, string 5 (Diagram †), and use that finger as a pivot to swing into a half-barre with the 1st finger on fret 7. On beat 4, place a finger on string 2 above fret 7; then halfway through that beat, use that finger to pull off the 2nd string; this makes the note sound at fret 7, string 2.

• Part B, measures 4-5. On beat 4 of measure 4, stop fret 9, string 1 and fret 10, string 2 with the 2nd and 3rd fingers, respectively. Then at the beginning of measure 5, glide down the neck on string 2 with the 3rd finger to fret 7. Pivot on that finger, and swing the 1st and 2nd fingers in place at fret 5, string 1 and fret 7, string 5, respectively as shown in Diagram *.

57

The Ottawa Valley Reel

Origin: Prince Edward Island
Sources: Edward P. Arsenault & Leonard McDonald
Appears on: *Frails & Frolics*

Key: G
Mode: Major
Tuning: gDGBD

Named for a hotbed of fiddling in southeastern Ontario, "The Ottawa Valley Reel" is probably local to P.E.I.; it is played with great relish throughout the Island by fiddlers of Scottish, Irish, and Acadian backgrounds. The harmony of Part B is a bit more adventuresome than that of most fiddle tunes, featuring the circle-of-fifths progression A7-D7-G. Getting the syncopation right for the opening phrases of Part A in clawhammer proved to be a real challenge and required some unusual fret- and string-sequences. Standard notation for my source version is in *Fiddle Music of P.E.I.*

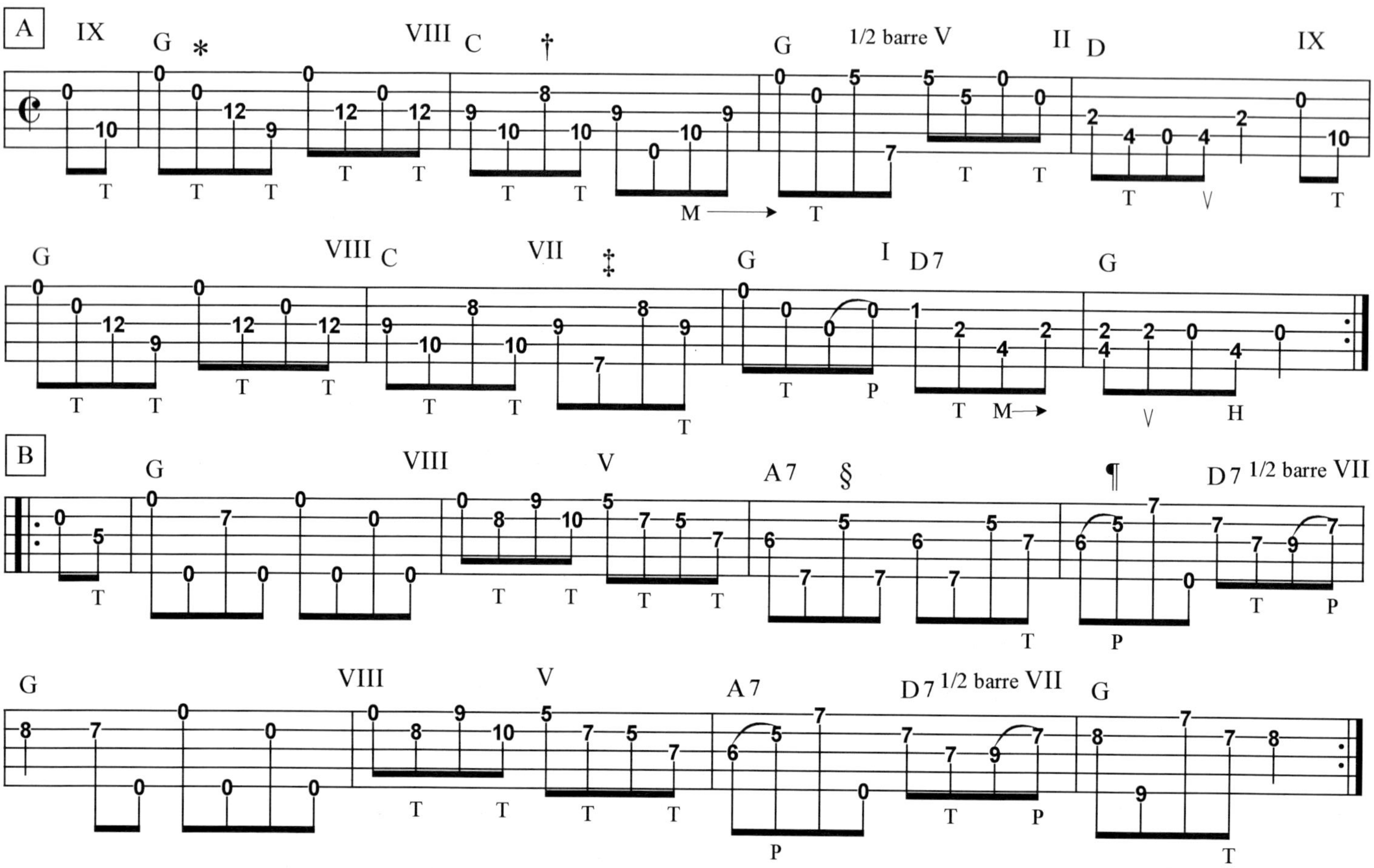

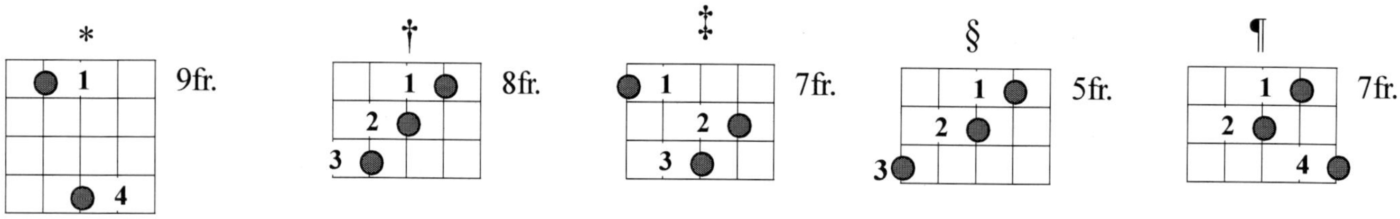

Playing Tips for *Ottawa Valley Reel*

• Part B, measure 4. Assume the shape shown in Diagram ¶. At the start of the measure, press the 2nd and 1st fingers down firmly (on frets 6, string 3 and fret 5, string 2 respectively), and – at the same time – place the 3rd finger on fret 6, string 2. Then halfway through the first beat, use the 3rd finger on string 2 to pull off at fret 6; this causes fret 5 to sound.

Chapter 6. *Reels – & Hornpipes – in D & D-Modal*

with B-Modal

BECAUSE OF THE OF THE WAY THEY SIT ON THE FIDDLE, D tunes tend to be bright-sounding and lively. Most D tunes you'll encounter in the Cape Breton and P.E.I. traditions are major, but there is a sizable contingent of diatonic tunes with a minor 7th tone (C♮), and many others that have a *variable* 7th tone (some passages feature C♮ and others C♯). You'll also find tunes that are pentatonic in whole or part. Nowadays, most clawhammerists play D tunes out of double C tuning (gCGCD) raised up two frets in pitch to the key of D, either by capoing or by tuning up all strings proportionately (when all strings are tuned up proportionately, it is now fairly common to refer to the tuning as *double-D:* aDADE). Because of the way the notes tend to fall in this tuning you'll find that you spend quite a bit of time in second position, and that from time to time you'll need to move up to fourth and fifth positions. Tunes that are *B-Modal* in whole or part also work well in capoed double-C tuning, and I've also included a couple of them in this chapter.

Important Note re Capoing & Notation on the 5th string. If you capo your banjo at fret 2, fret notations on the 5th string are correct *only* if you also capo up the 5th string via a 5th-string capo or "railroad spike." If you simply tune up the 5th string two frets, you must then subtract two from every fret indication.

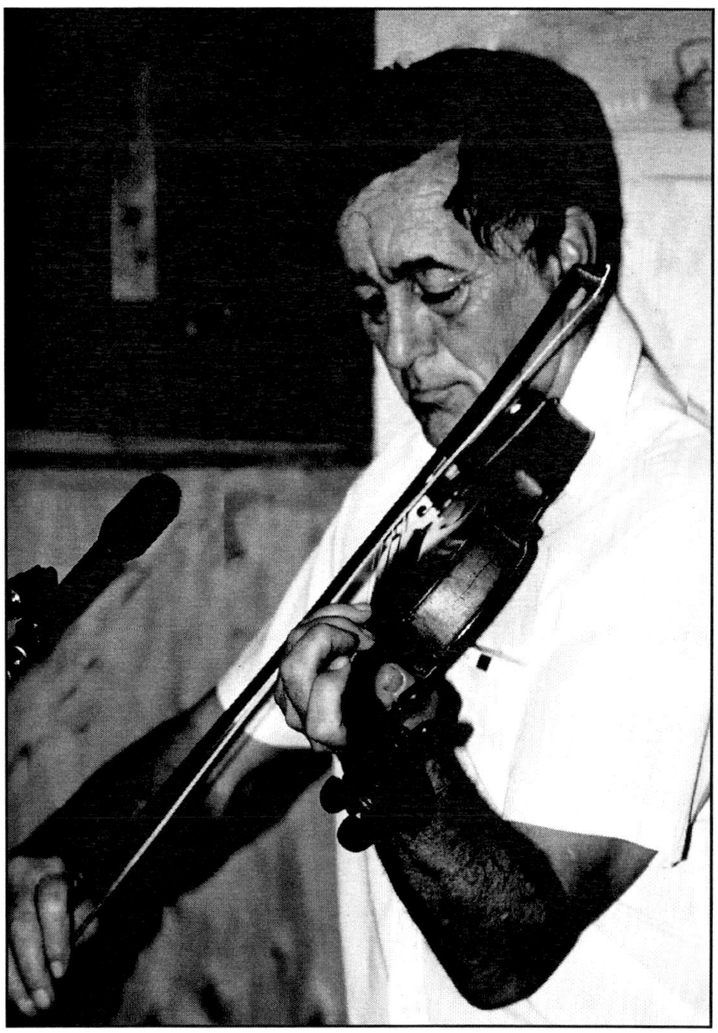

"Young Peter" Chaisson at Project Headquarters, Monticello P.E.I. (1991).
Photo by Earthwatch Team; courtesy Robertson Library, University of P.E.I.

58

Jenny Dang the Weaver

Origin: Scotland
Source: "Old Peter" Chaisson
Appears on: *Frails & Frolics*

Key: D (C on Banjo)
Mode: (Mostly) Major Pentatonic
Tuning: gCGCD (Capo-2)

"Jenny Dang the Weaver" appears in many important 18th- and 19th-century Scottish tune collections – notably *The Gow Repository, Lowe's Collection, The Athole Collection,* and *Kerr's Merry Melodies*. It was recorded in the 1930s by Angus Allan Gillis of Cape Breton. My version includes a couple of *twists* on the melody borrowed from my source fiddler. The mode in Part A is major pentatonic; Part B adds the 4th tone (G♮ on fiddle; F♮ on open banjo), but the 7th tone – C♯ on fiddle; B♮ on open banjo – is absent throughout. The measure labeled "Alt. B4(2)" transitions to the opening of "Sleeping Maggy" (p. 76), the next tune in the medley on *Frails & Frolics*. Standard notation for my source version is in *Fiddle Music of P.E.I.*

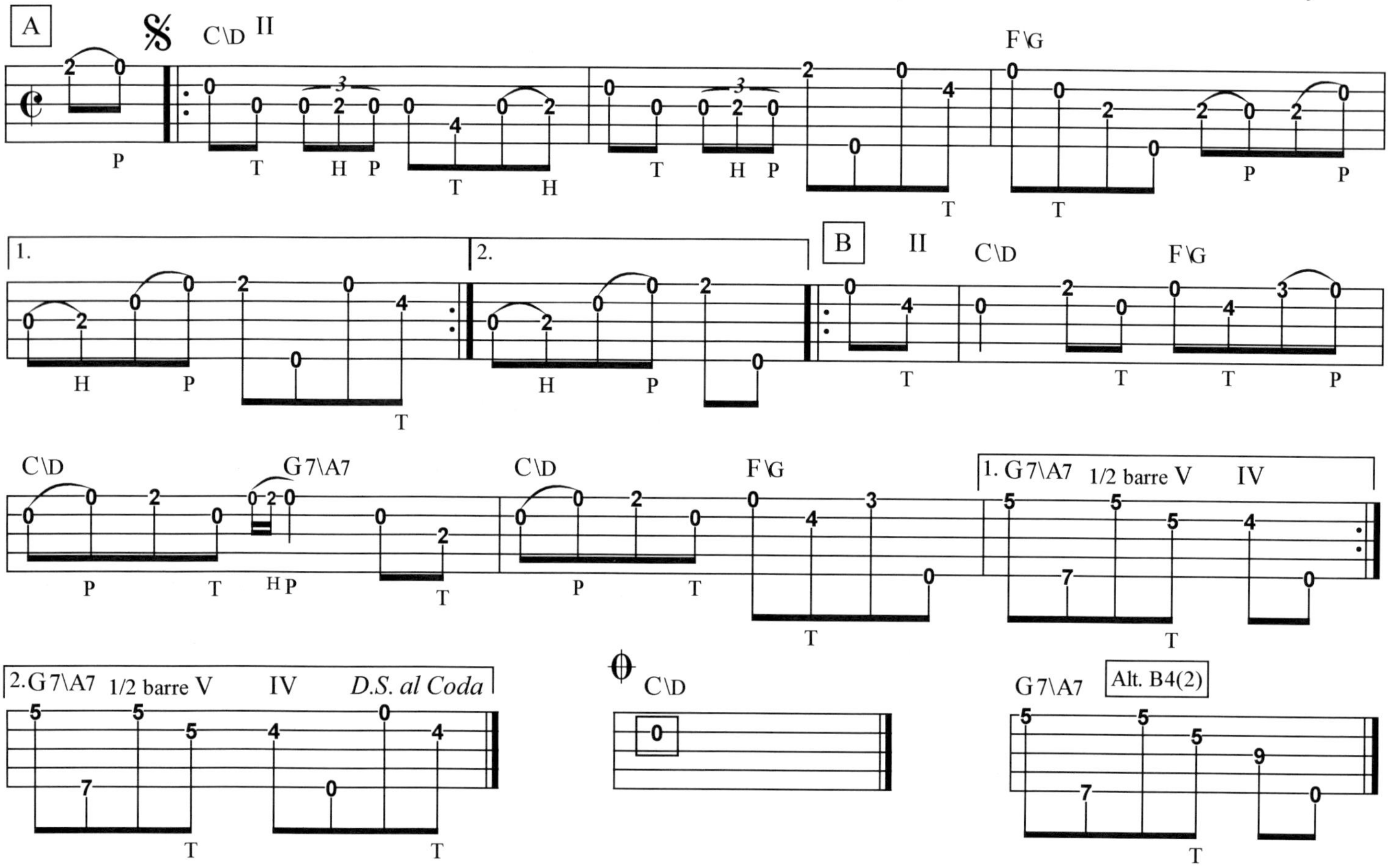

Playing Note for *Jenny Dang the Weaver*

***Dual Chord Symbols:** Chord to left of backslash goes with open banjo; chord on right is for capoed banjo or fiddle*

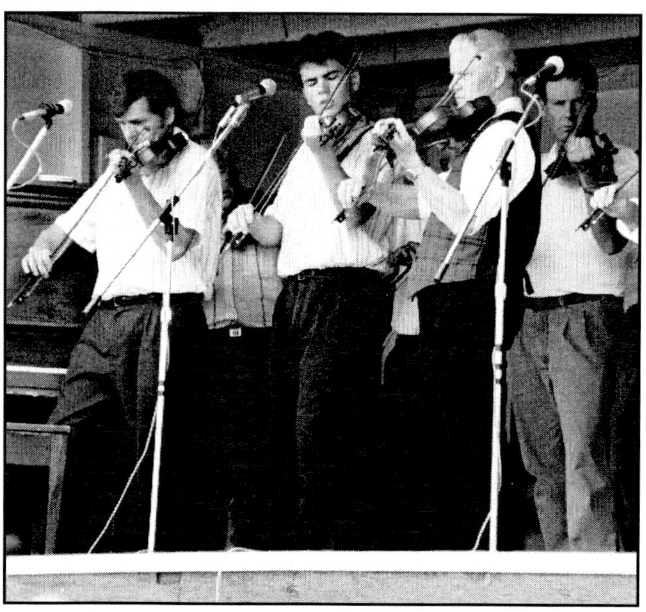

L-R: Kenny Chaisson, Paul MacDonald, "Fr. Charlie" Cheverie, & Allan Macdonald: Rollo Bay Scottish Fiddle Festival, Rollo Bay, P.E.I. (1991). Photo by Earthwatch Team; courtesy Robertson Library, University of P.E.I.

59

Robert Stubbert

Composer: Jerry Holland
Source: Eddy Arsenault
Appears on: *Island Boy*

Key: D (C on Banjo)
Mode: Major
Tuning: gCGCD (Capo-2)

Holland named this truly sweet reel for well-known fiddler Robert Stubbert of Point Aconi on the North Side of Cape Breton (1923-2008). The father of well-known Cape Breton fiddler Brenda Stubbert, he was known in particular for bringing tunes of Irish origin into the Cape Breton fiddle repertoire. Brenda Stubbert recorded this tune for the first time in 1987. Standard notation for my source version is in *Fiddle Music of P.E.I.*

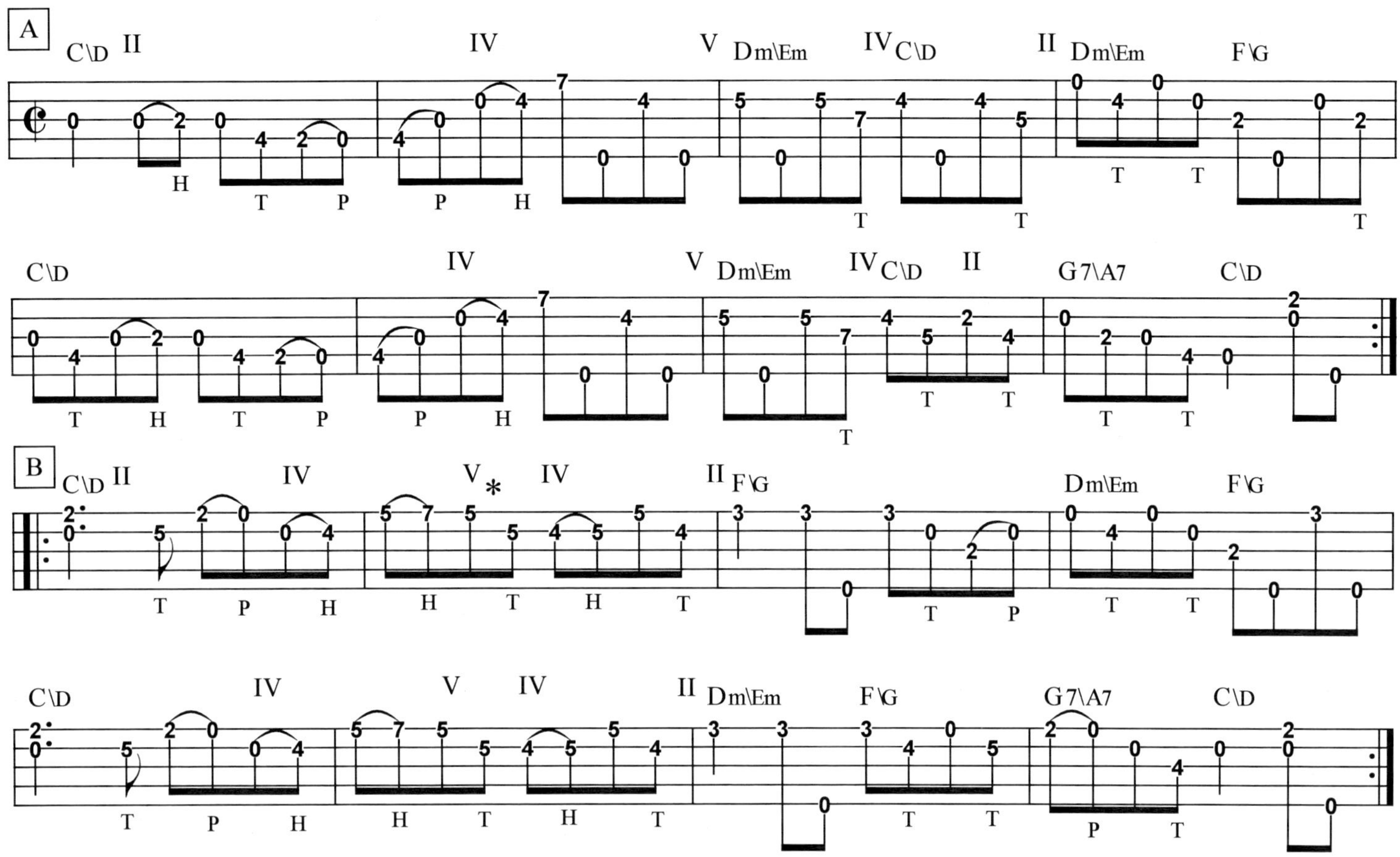

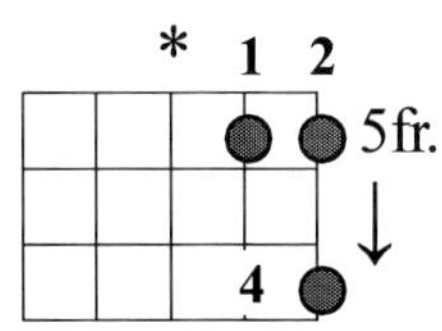

Playing Tips for *Robert Stubbert*

Dual Chord Symbols: Chord to left of backslash goes with open banjo; chord on right is for capoed banjo or fiddle

- Part B, measures 1-2. At the end of measure 1, balance on fret 4, string 2 with the 1st finger; then at the start of measure 2, sneak the 1st finger up to fret 5 (and at the same time bring in the 2nd finger to stop fret 5, string 1). This puts those two fingers into the configuration shown in Diagram *, and also puts you in position to use the 4th finger for the H to fret 7. At the end of beat 2, balance on the 1st finger at fret 5, string 2; and at the start of beat 3, glide with that finger back down string 2 to fret 4 and use it as a pivot to bring your 3rd finger over to stop fret 5, string 1. Finally, halfway between beats 3 and 4 – and making sure to hold down the 1st and 3rd fingers – perform an H on string 2 from fret 4 to fret 5.

60

Delphine's Reel

Origin: Local Variant
Source: Edward P. Arsenault

Key: D (C on Banjo)
Mode: Major 3rd; variable 7th
Tuning: gCGCD (Capo-2)

For more than a generation, Delphine Arsenault's extended family provided much of the dance music for the Evangeline Coast region, one of the major Acadian sectors on P.E.I. Her father, Joe à Bibienne Arsenault was a noted fiddler, while she and several of her sisters were among the first female dance fiddlers on the Island. This tune was collected from Delphine by folklorist Georges Arsenault, and has since been adopted whole-heartedly by the younger generation of Acadian musicians. Particularly worthy of note: it is one of the very few *crooked* (metrically irregular) tunes to have been collected on P.E.I. Standard notation for my source version is available on *bowingdownhome.ca.*

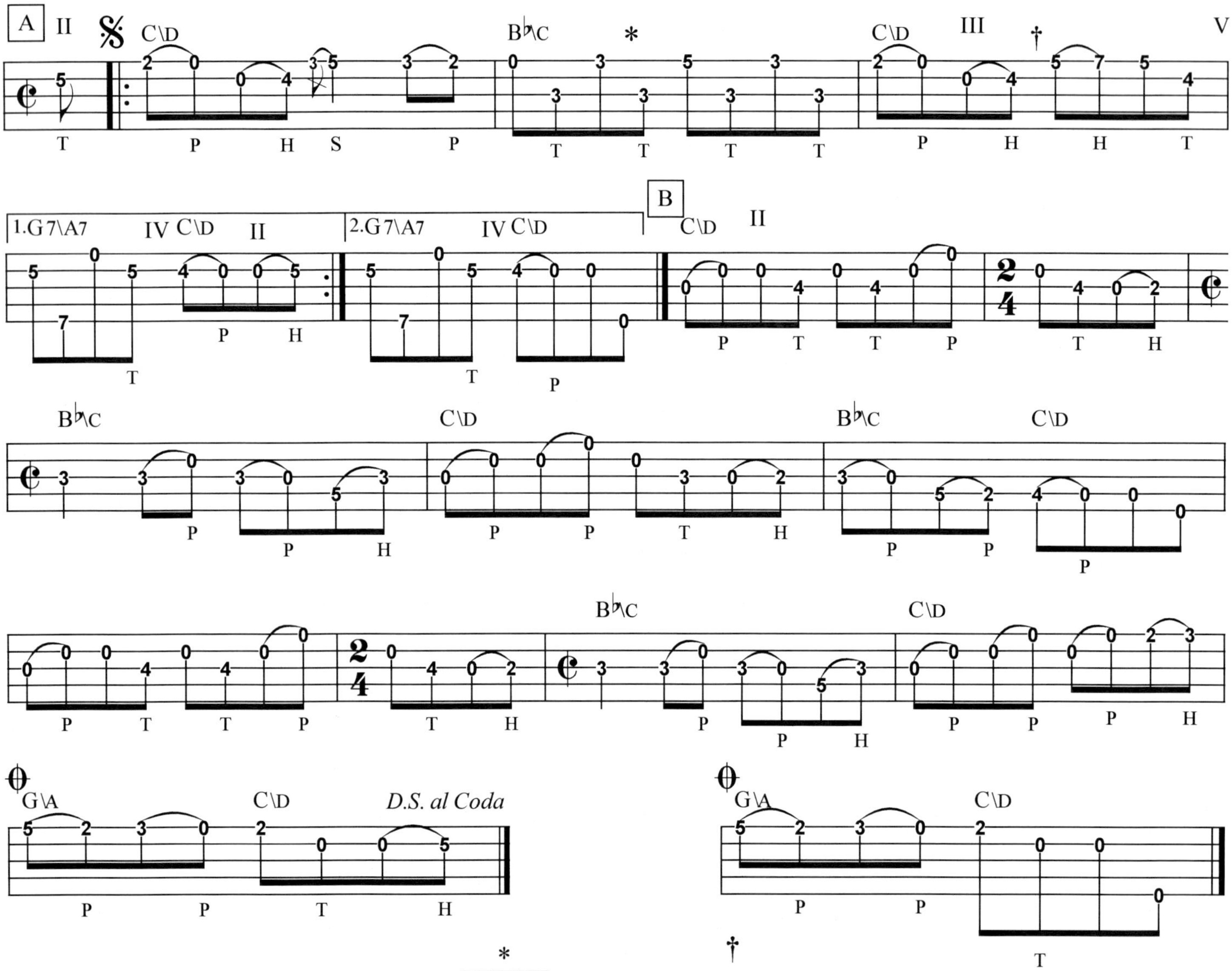

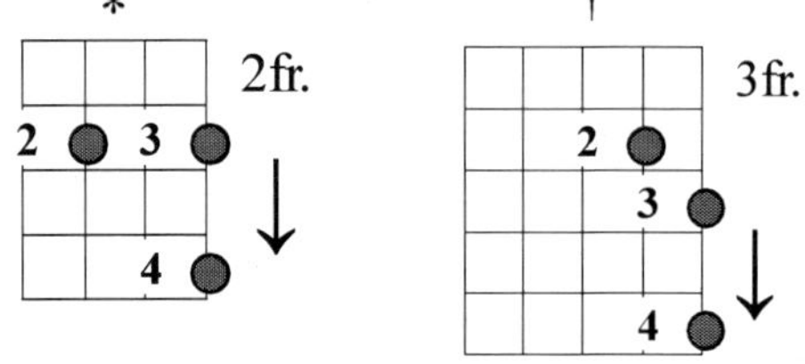

Playing Tips for *Delphine's Reel*

Dual Chord Symbols: Chord to left of backslash goes with open banjo; chord on right is for capoed banjo or fiddle

• Part A, measures 1-2. On beat 3 of measure 1, use the 2nd finger for the quick-slide from fret 3 to fret 5 on string 1. On beat 4, glide back down string 1 with that same finger to fret 3 and – after placing the 1st finger on fret 2 – use the 2nd finger to perform the pull-off from fret 3 to fret 2. Then at the start of measure 2, move the 2nd finger over to fret 3, string 3 and pivot the 3rd finger over to string 1 as shown in Diagram *.

61

The Farmer's Daughter

Origin: Scotland
Source: Winston "Scotty" Fitzgerald

Keys: D & B (C & A on Banjo)
Mode: Part A: Major; Part B: Aeolian
Tuning: gCGCD (Capo-2)

Fitzgerald's rousing performance of this old piping tune, first released in the 1950s on his LP, *Winston "Scotty" Fitzgerald & His Radio Entertainers*, became one of his signature numbers and still serves as one of the iconic representations of Cape Breton fiddling. A close variant of the tune appears in *The Skye Collection* as "Aberarder Rant." The tune is circular, and I've offered a final-sounding ending.

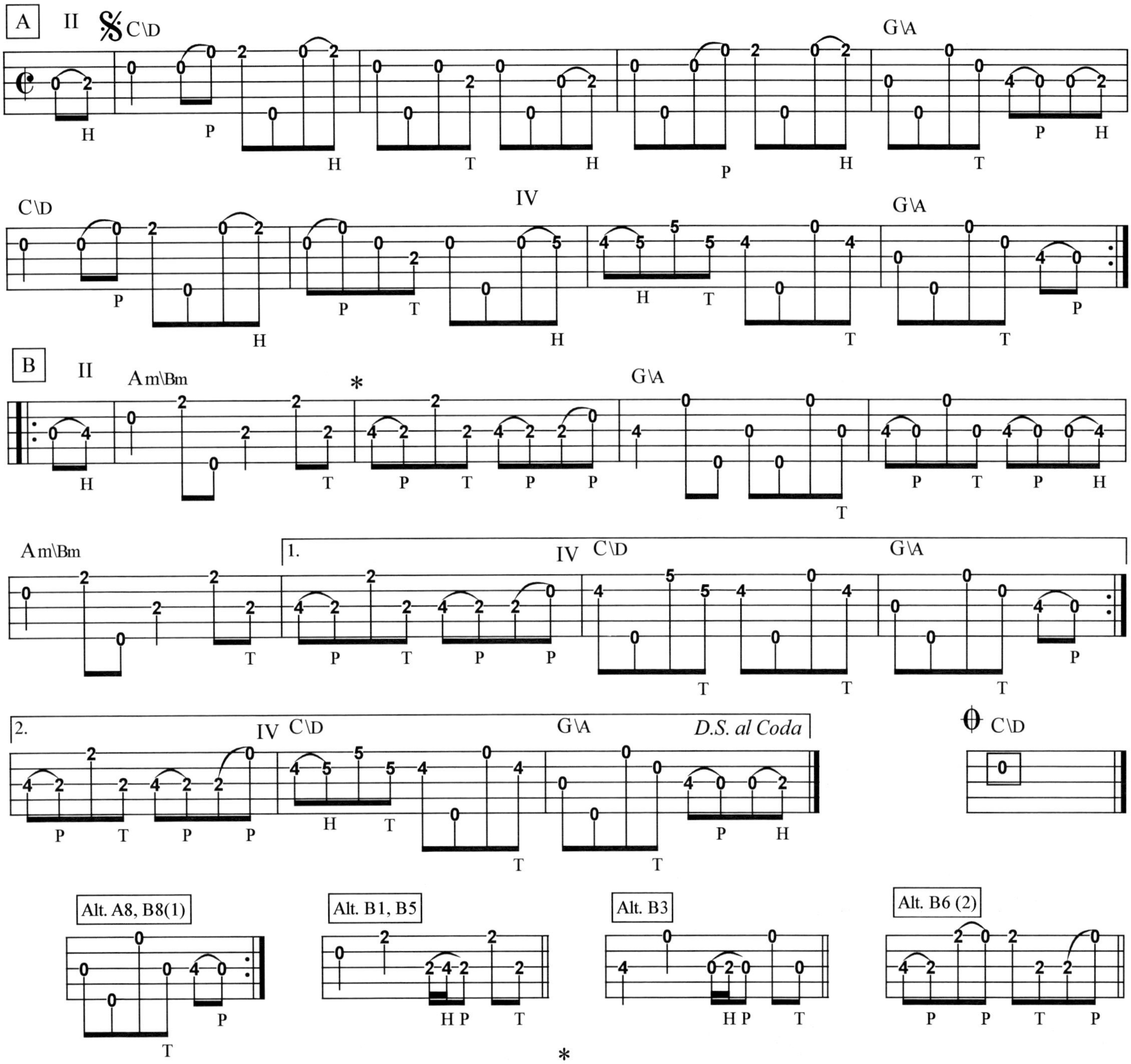

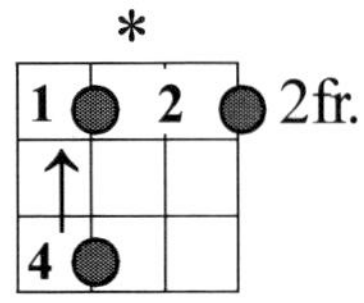

Playing Note for *The Farmer's Daughter*

***Dual Chord Symbols:** Chord to left of backslash goes with open banjo; chord on right is for capoed banjo or fiddle*

62

Hector's Fancy

Origin: Probably Eastern P.E.I.
Source: Hector MacDonald
Appears on: *Frails & Frolics*

Key: D (C on Banjo)
Mode: Major 3rd; variable 7th
Tuning: gCGCD (Capo-2)

This tune appeared untitled on a family-made tape featuring fiddler Hector MacDonald of Bangor in northern Kings County, P.E.I. MacDonald was one of the great dance fiddlers of his region during the middle third of the 20th century, and was among the first Prince Edward Island fiddlers to play on radio. I assigned the title used here as a gesture of respect to the player. Observe that both endings of Part B are "short" (half-length), making this one of the few *crooked* (metrically irregular) tunes I collected. "Hector's Fancy" is circular, and I've suggested a final-sounding ending. Standard notation for my source version is available on *bowingdownhome.ca.*

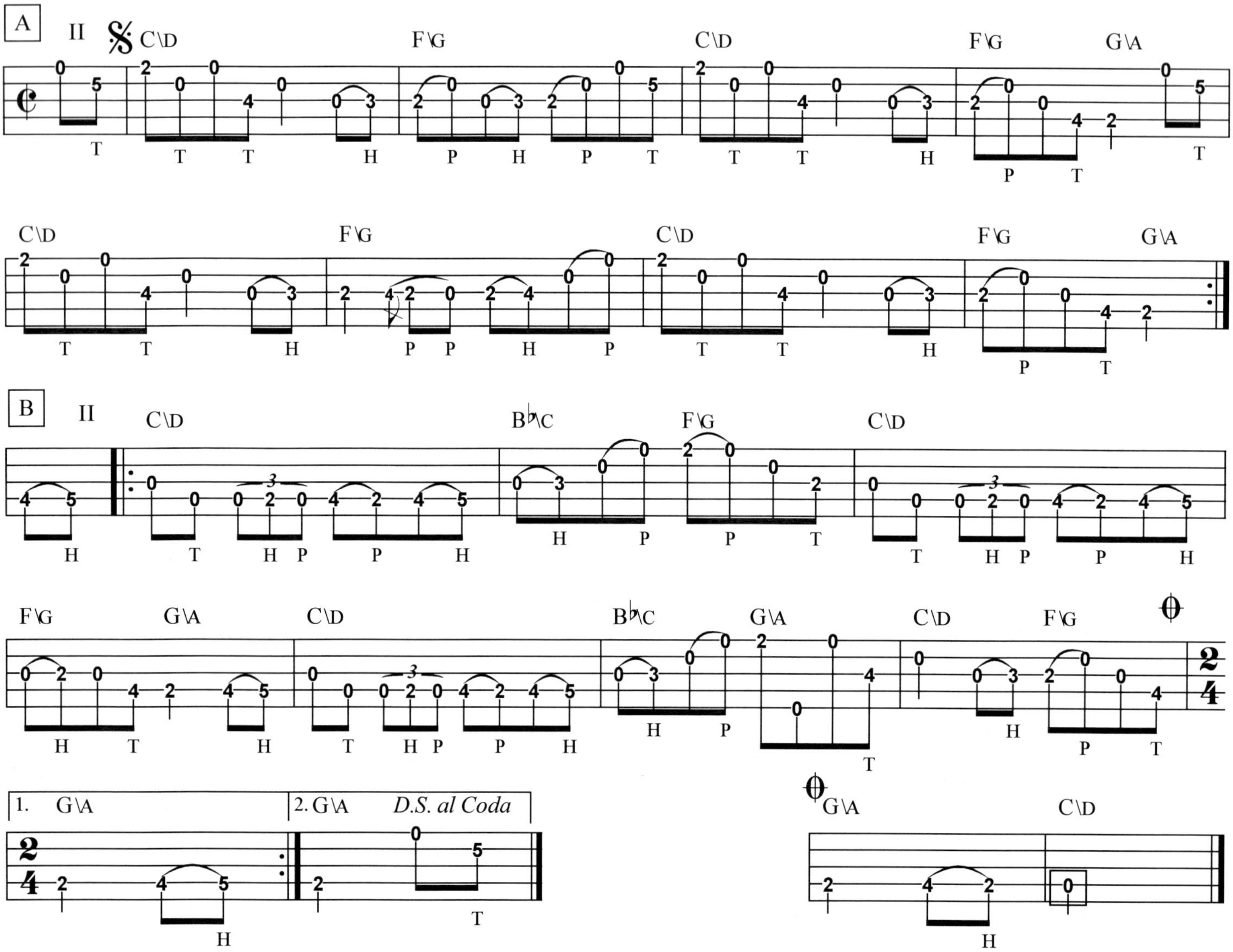

Playing Note for *Hector's Fancy*

***Dual Chord Symbols:** Chord to left of backslash goes with open banjo; chord on right is for capoed banjo or fiddle*

63

Hector's New Dance Hall

Origin: Local Variant of Irish Tune
Source: Allan MacDonald
Appears on: *Frails & Frolics*

Key: D (C on Banjo)
Mode: Major
Tuning: gCGCD (Capo-2)

This tune is a much-evolved variant of the Irish reel, "London Lasses" (see *O'Neill's Music of Ireland*). I got it from Allan MacDonald of Bangor, Prince Edward Island who learned it from his father, Hector. Allan described how he and Hector built a small dance hall on their property in the early 1960s and the two of them provided the music. This tune was a great favorite, and to build suspense Hector took to extending Part B by an extra couple of measures. When he finally got back around to the top of Part A, the dancers would go wild. Allan had no name for the tune, so to honor the story I dubbed it, "Hector's New Dance Hall." The melody is circular, and I've suggested a final-sounding ending. Standard notation for my source version is available on *bowingdownhome.ca.*

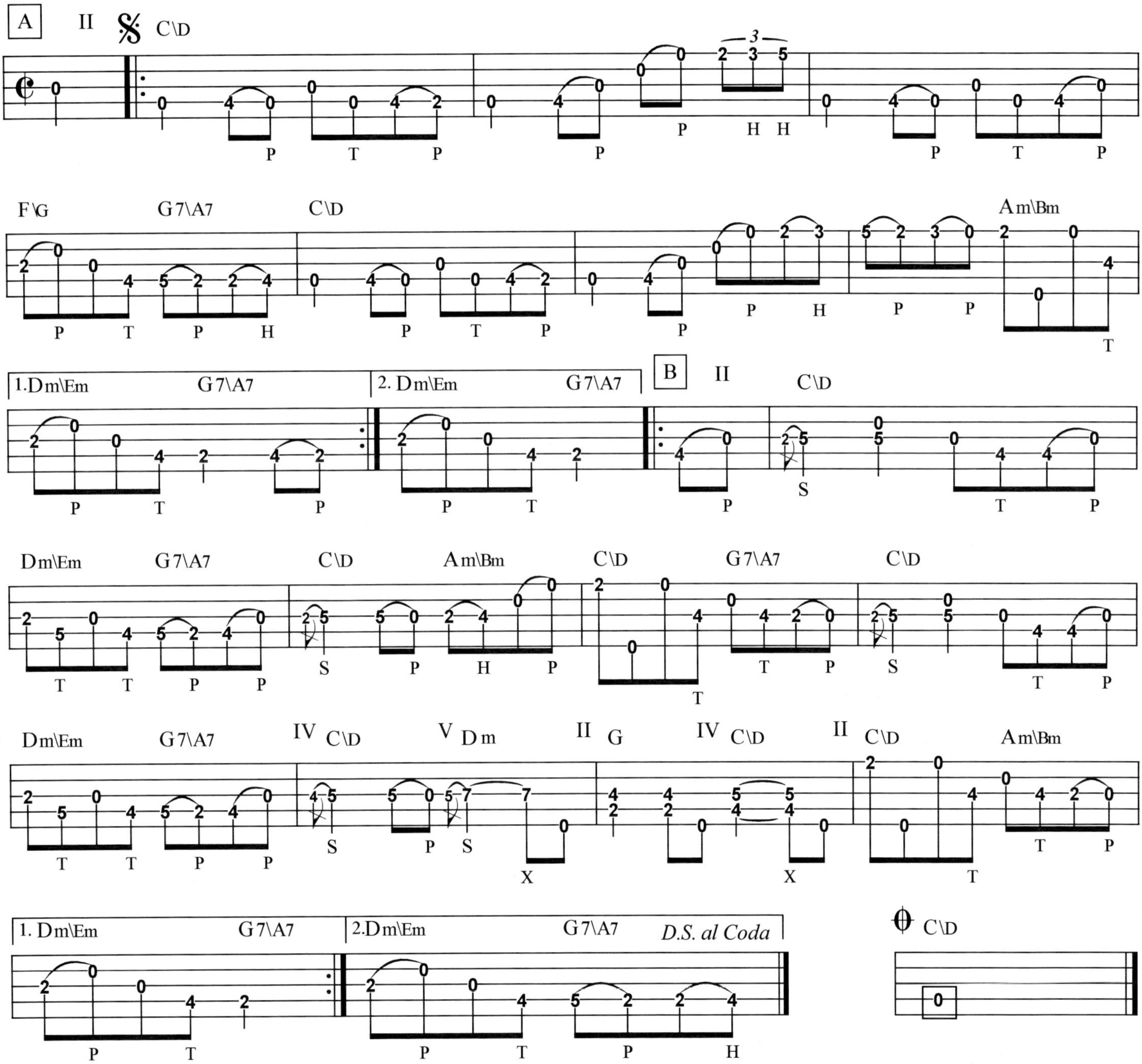

Playing Note for *Hector's New Dance Hall*

***Dual Chord Symbols:** Chord to left of backslash goes with open banjo; chord on right is for capoed banjo or fiddle*

Londonderry Hornpipe

64

Origin: Britain or Ireland
Source: Eddy Arsenault & George MacPhee
Appears on: *Frails & Frolics*

Key: D (C on Banjo)
Mode: Major
Tuning: gCGCD (Capo-2)

Named for the city of Derry in Northern Ireland, "Londonderry Hornpipe" usually appears in print as a three-part tune (see, for example, *Kerr's Merry Melodies, Allan's Irish Fiddler,* and – under the title, "Ladies Hornpipe" – *The Roche Collection*). All three parts circulate on Prince Edward Island, but most fiddlers only play two of them: either A & B or A & C. On *Frails & Frolics,* I play A and B the first time through like Eddy Arsenault, but A & C on the second rep like George MacPhee. In *O'Neill's Music of Ireland,* the tune appears in six parts. Standard notation for my source version is in *Fiddle Music of P.E.I.*

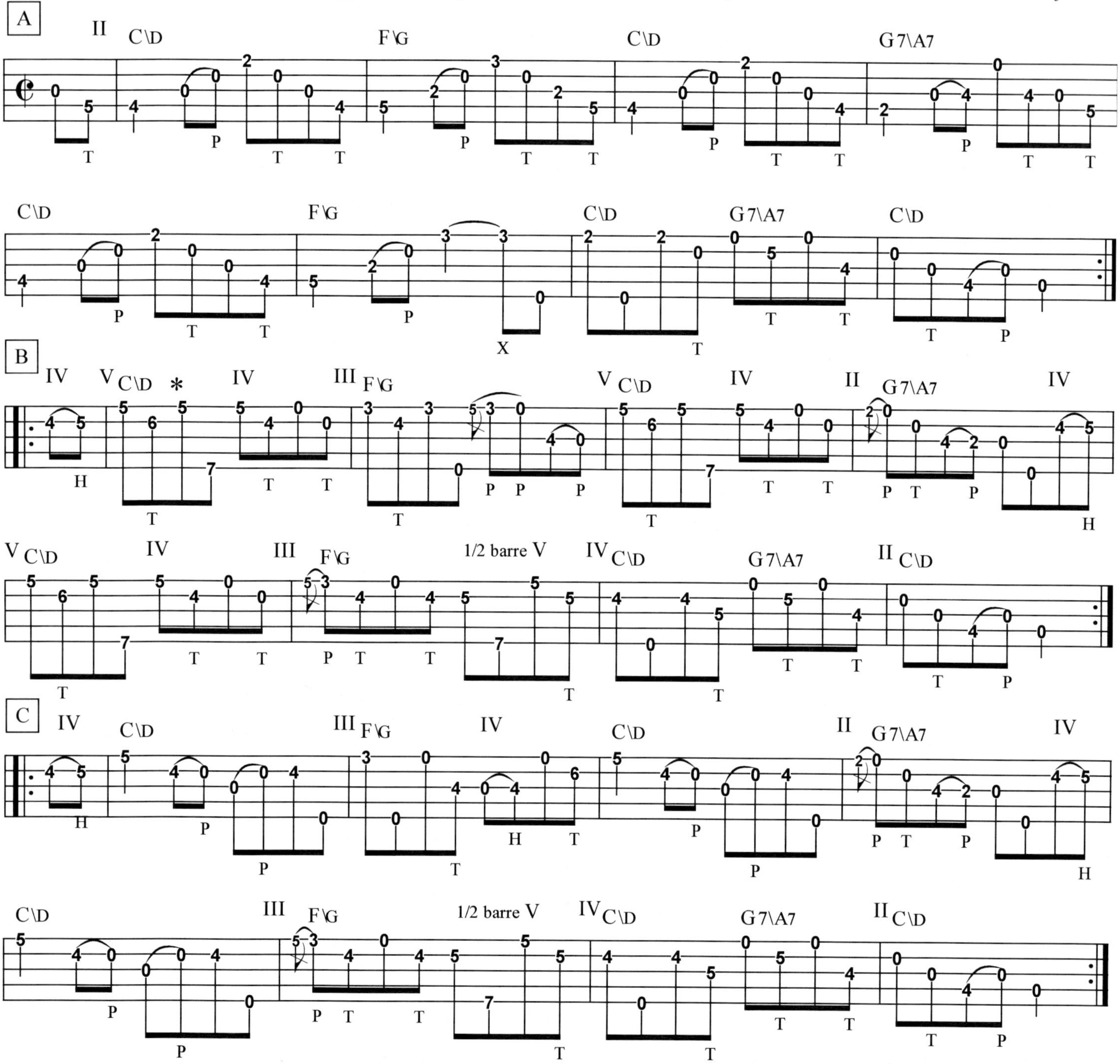

*

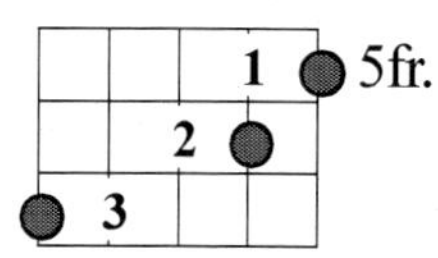

Dual Chord Symbols: Chord to left of backslash goes with open banjo; chord on right is for capoed banjo or fiddle

*For Londonderry *Hornpipe* Playing Tips, See Facing Page*

Playing Tips for *Londonderry Hornpipe*

• Part B, pickup into measure 1. At the end of the pickup, balance with the 2nd finger on fret 5, string 2. At the start of measure 1, glide up string 2 with that finger to fret 6 and use it as a pivot to get the 1st and 3rd fingers into position on strings 1 and 5 as shown in Diagram *.

• Part B, measure 1. Halfway through beat 2, balance on the 3rd finger at fret 7, string 5 and begin to stretch with the 1st and 2nd fingers towards fourth position. At the start of beat 3, the 1st and 2nd fingers should have landed on fret 4, string 2 and fret 5, string 1, respectively.

• Part B, measure 6. At the end of beat 2, balance with the 1st finger on fret 4, string 2. At the start of beat 3, glide with the 1st finger up to fret 5, flatten it into a 1/2-barre and swing the 3rd finger over to fret 7, string 5.

Island Boy

65

Origin: Local Variant of Irish Tune
Source: Ervan Sonier & Toussaint Arsenault
Appears on: *Island Boy*

Key: D (C on Banjo)
Mode: Major
Tuning: gCGCD (Capo-2)

This lively reel – the title-tune of my *Island Boy* CD – is widely played among older Acadian fiddlers in Prince County, P.E.I. It is derived from a key-of-G Irish jig called "Larry O'Gaff" (see *O'Neill's Music of Ireland*), and indeed some fiddlers on P.E.I. still call the tune "Larry O'Gaff Reel." There is a also decided resemblance here to the well-known tune, "Whiskey Before Breakfast," but this appears to be simply a case of convergent evolution. Standard notation for my source version is in *Fiddle Music of P.E.I.*

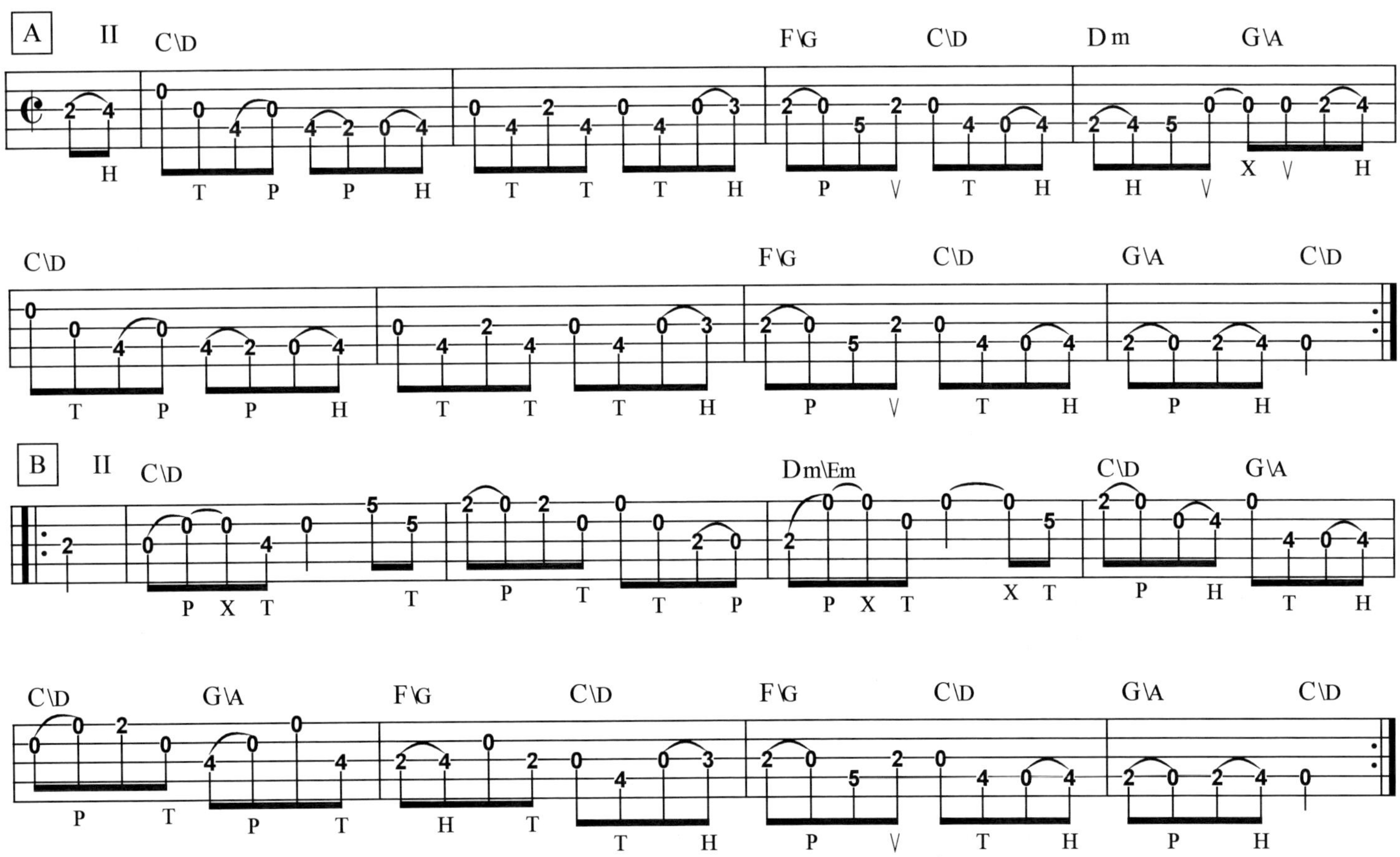

Playing Note for *Island Boy*

Dual Chord Symbols: Chord to left of backslash goes with open banjo; chord on right is for capoed banjo or fiddle

66

Lord Gordon

Origin: Scotland
Source: Winston "Scotty" Fitzgerald
Appears on: *Devil in the Kitchen*

Key: D (C on Banjo)
Mode: Major
Tuning: gCGCD (Capo-2)

For generations, the Dukes of Gordon – based in Fochabers, roughly 60 miles northwest of Aberdeen, Scotland – were great patrons of fiddling and fiddle music. This version of "Lord Gordon" is from Fitzgerald's performance on his LP, *Winston "Scotty" Fitzgerald & His Radio Entertainers*. The tune appears in print in *Ryan's Mammoth Collection* and *O'Neill's Music of Ireland*, but the Fitzgerald version is much closer to the opening of a 1930s-era recording by well-known Irish fiddler Michael Coleman (1891-1945; Coleman's recording also features several brilliant variations on the theme). "Lord Gordon" is circular (each part concludes on the IV-chord), and I've provided a final-sounding ending.

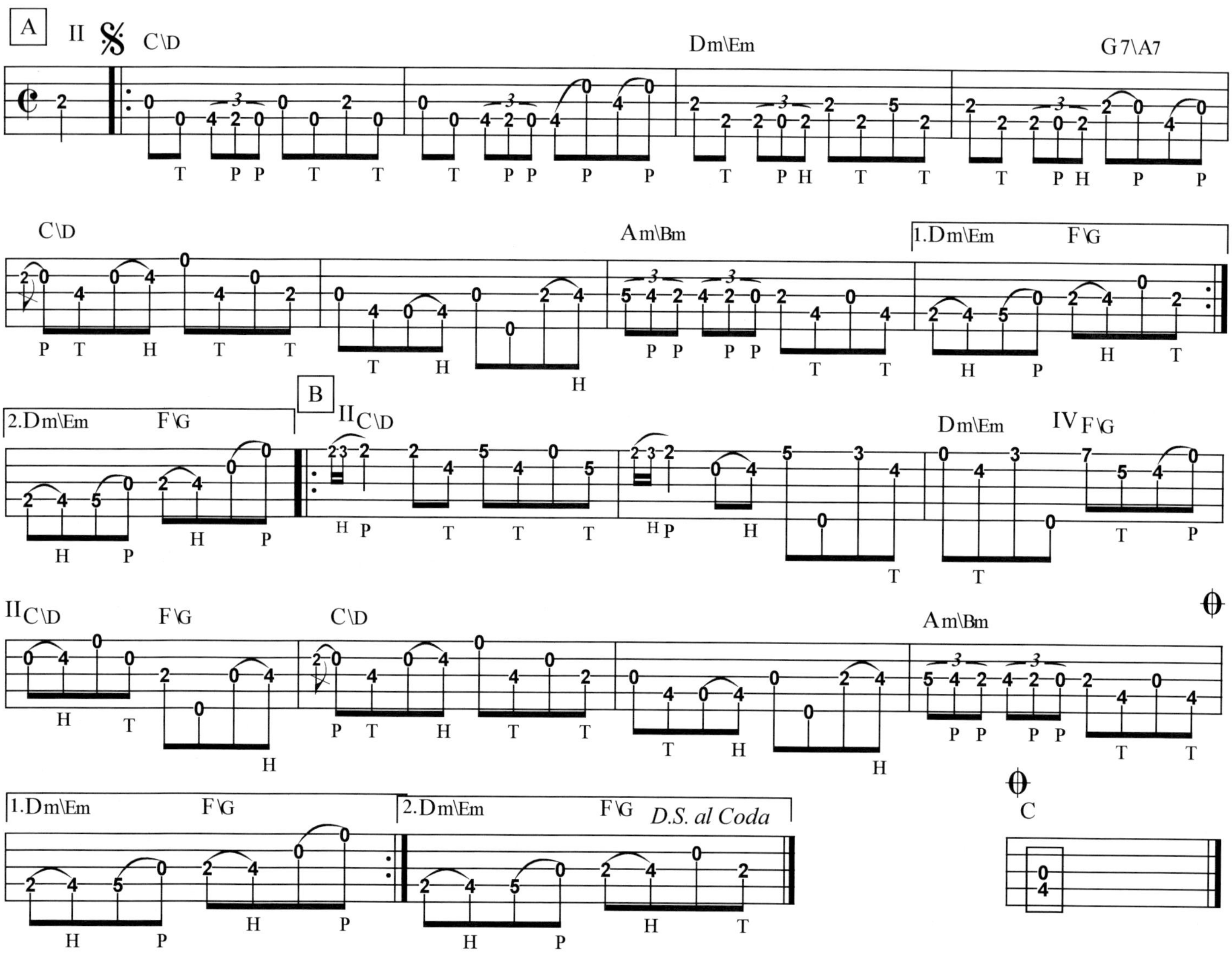

Playing Tips for *Lord Gordon*

***Dual Chord Symbols:** Chord to left of backslash goes with open banjo; chord on right is for capoed banjo or fiddle*

• Part A, measure 2. On beat 3, use the 3rd finger to stop fret 4, string 4 and the 1st finger for the ensuing alternate-string P. On beat 4 use the 4th finger to stop fret 4, string 3; then once again, use the 1st finger for the ensuing alternate-string P.

• Part B, measure 1-2. Halfway through beat 3 of measure 1, use the 3rd finger to stop fret 4, string 2. At the start of beat 4, strike open string 2, then sneak up that string with the 3rd finger to catch fret 5. Then at the start of measure 2, stretch out the 1st finger to get fret 2, string 1.

67

St. Anne's Reel (a Prince County Version)

Origin: Local Variant of Québec Tune
Source: Elmer Robinson
Appears on: *Island Boy*

Key: D (C on Banjo)
Mode: Major
Tuning: gCGCD (Capo-2)

The version of this tune that most people know was first popularized via a 78 rpm recording entitled "Reel de Ste. Anne" played by Joseph Allard of Montreal (1873-1947) and issued by Victor in 1930 (for a banjo arrangement close to the Allard version, see p. 31). The tune has been substantially transformed by fiddlers in Prince County, P.E.I. to suit the rhythms of the local brand of step-dancing; the version here – from Elmer Robinson of Woodstock – is a lively example of how the tune has changed. The transformation process was described by Andrew Jones of Pleasant View.

> *We used to play "St. Anne's Reel" the old way. That didn't go very good with step-dancing. Somebody'd get up to dance and they'd get kind of mixed up because there was slow action onto it. So among our friends we changed it to suit the stepdancer, We'd get them to dance; we'd follow the stepdancer with the bow, and we'd jig it up according to his steps.*

Standard notation for my source version is in *Fiddle Music of P.E.I.*

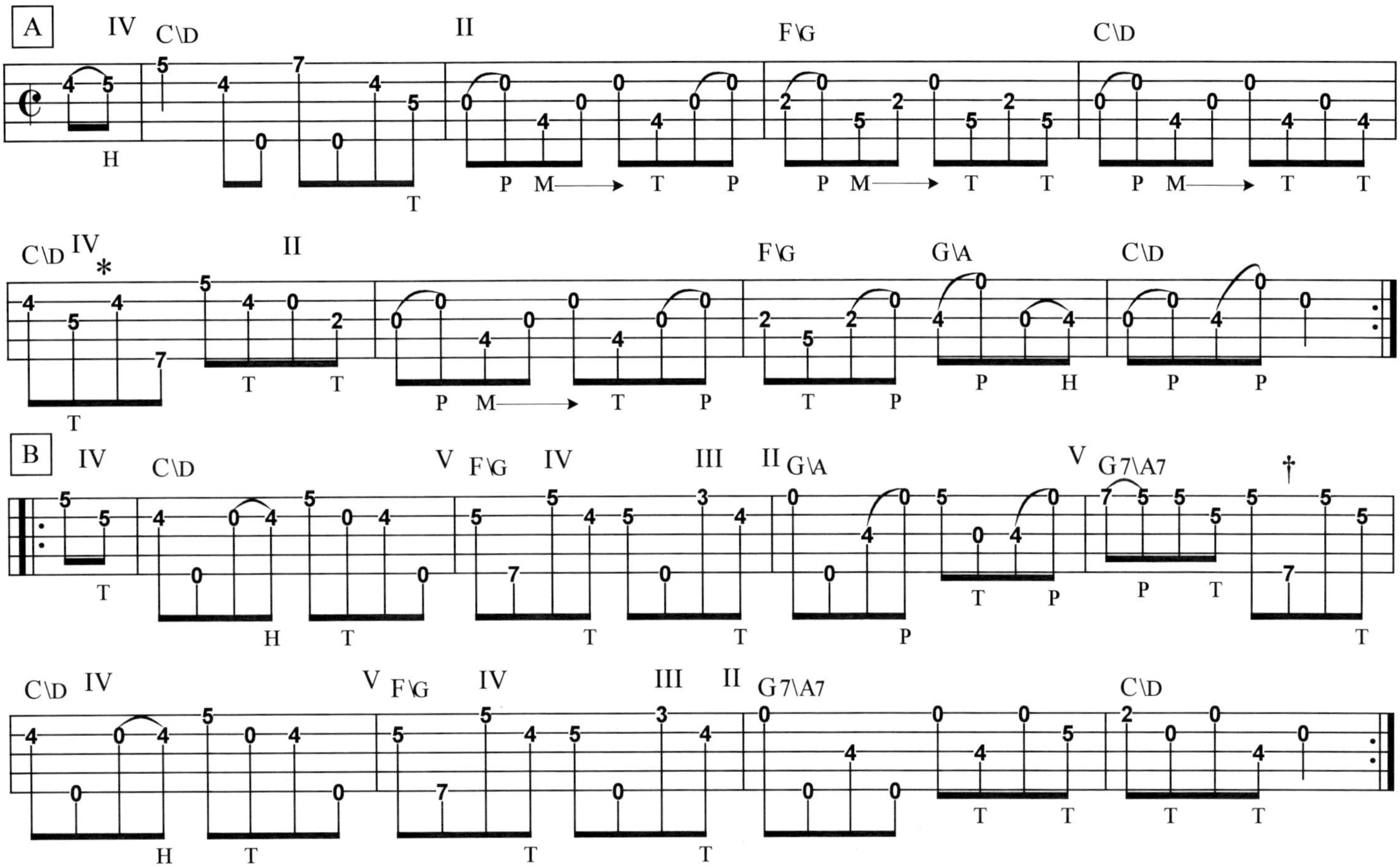

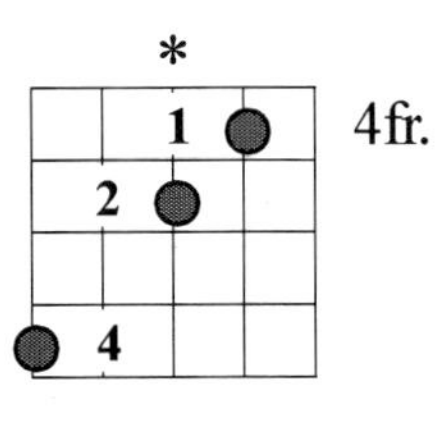

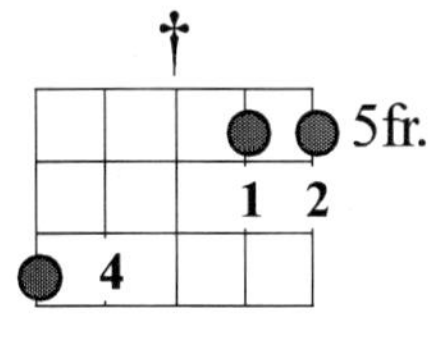

Playing Tips for *St. Anne's Reel* (Prince County Version)

Dual Chord Symbols: Chord to left of backslash goes with open banjo; chord on right is for capoed banjo or fiddle

• Part A, measure 5. At the end of beat 2, balance with the 4th finger at fret 7, string 5 and begin to stretch out the 1st and 2nd fingers. At the start of beat 3, the 1st and 2nd fingers should land at fret 4, string 2 and fret 5, string 1, respectively.

• Part A, measure 7. On beat 2, balance on the 1st finger and swing the 2nd finger under it to perch on string 2. Halfway between beats 2 and 3, use that finger to pull off string 2. On beat 3, use the 3rd finger to stop fret 4, string 3, and – halfway through that beat – use the 1st finger to get the alternate-string P on string 1.

68

The Plains of Boyle

Origin: Ireland
Source: An Itinerant Uillean Piper
Appears on: *Devil in the Kitchen*

Key: D (C on Banjo)
Mode: See Intro
Tuning: gCGCD (Capo-2)

The title refers to a region in County Roscommon, Ireland roughly 90 miles northwest of Dublin. This tune may well have originated early in the 20th Century among Irish musicians living in America. Indeed, several 78s featuring "The Plains of Boyle" were released in the 1920s by Irish musicians living in the New York City area, notably uillean piper Michael Gallagher (1887-c. 1958) and Sligo born fiddler James Morrison (1891-1947). The minor-7th tone – C♮ on fiddle; B♭ on open banjo – makes a dramatic appearance in Part A, measure 4; otherwise the tune is major.

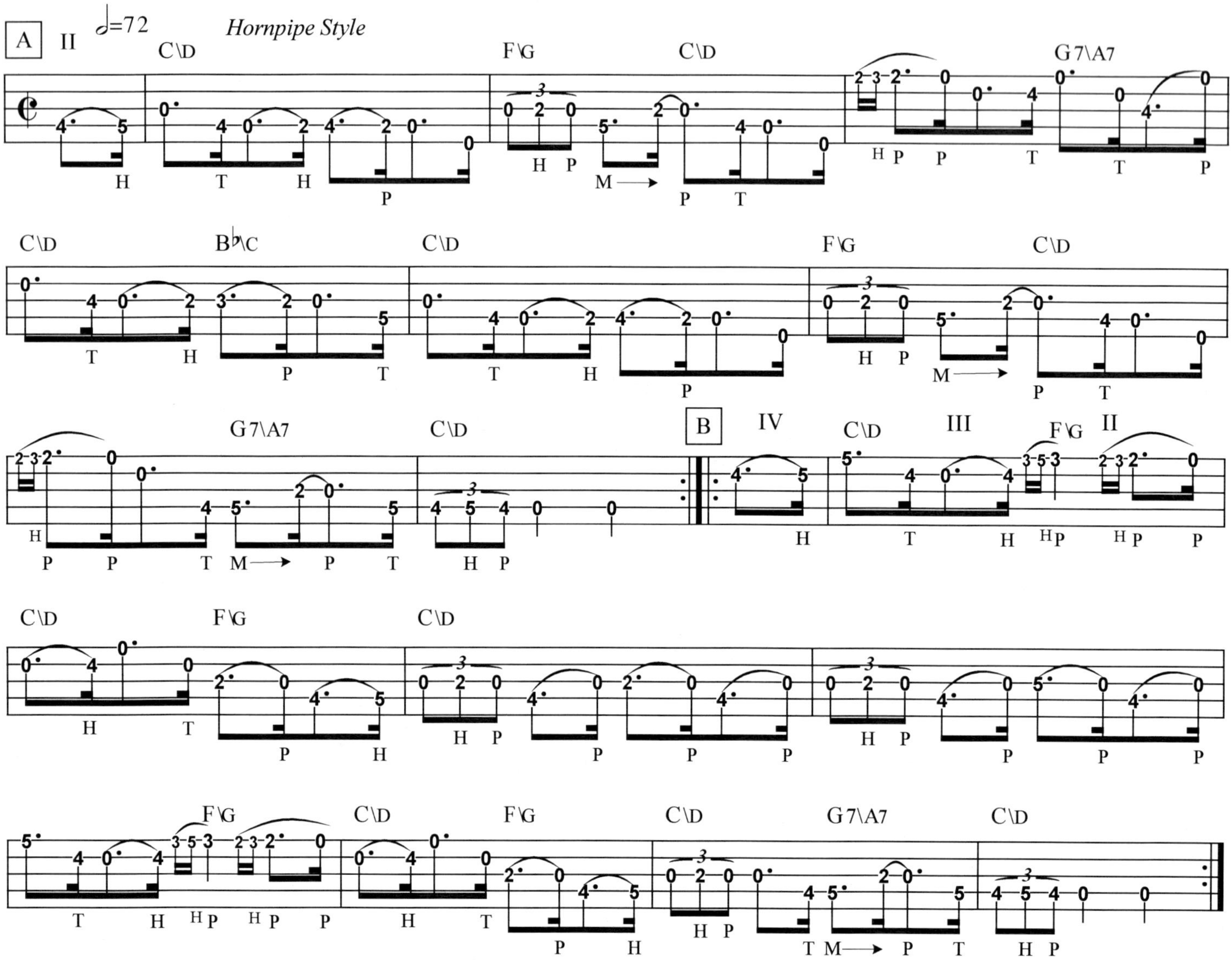

Playing Note for *Plains of Boyle*

***Dual Chord Symbols:** Chord to left of backslash goes with open banjo; chord on right is for capoed banjo or fiddle*

Jerome's Farewell to Gibraltar

69

ORIGIN: (PROBABLY) VARIANT OF IRISH TUNE
SOURCE: LEONARD MCDONALD

KEY: D (C ON BANJO)
MODE: MAJOR-LIKE BUT NO 7TH TONE
TUNING: gCGCD (Capo-2)

At the time of my collecting project, "Jerome's Farewell" was one of the most widely played tunes on P.E.I. – often played in medley with another key-of-D favorite, "Homeward Bound" (p. 36). Don Messer recorded the tune under this name and may be at least partially responsible for its local popularity. Another name I frequently encountered on P.E.I. was "Jerome's Farewell to Georges Banks." A close cousin of this tune is widely played in the Irish tradition; it appears under the title, "Boys of the Lough" in both *Allan's Irish Fiddler* and on a well-known 1920s-era recording by Sligo-style fiddler Michael Coleman (1891-1945). In *The Roche Collection,* the melody is called "Rose of Castletown." Standard notation for my source version is in *Fiddle Music of P.E.I.*

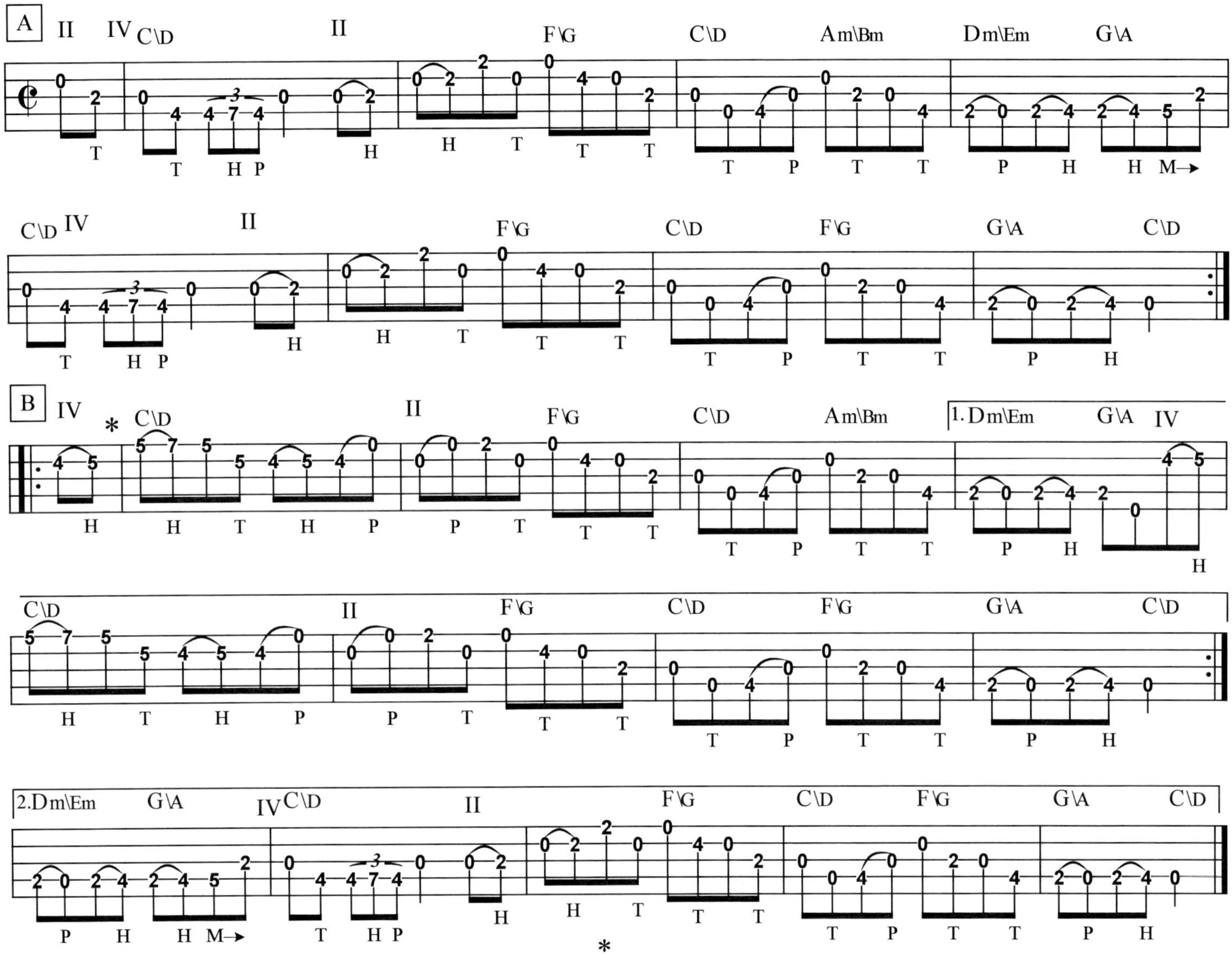

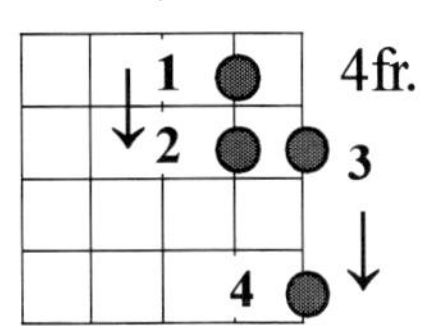

PLAYING TIPS FOR *JEROME'S FAREWELL TO GIBRALTAR*

DUAL CHORD SYMBOLS: Chord to left of backslash goes with open banjo; chord on right is for capoed banjo or fiddle

• PART B, PICKUP THROUGH MEASURE 1. Start by checking Diagram *. At the start of the pickup measure, use the 1st and 3rd fingers to press down fret 4, string 2 and fret 5, string 1, respectively. Then holding these fingers down, hammer with the 2nd finger from fret 4 to fret 5. At the start of measure 1, release the 2nd finger and – still keeping pressure on the 1st and 3rd fingers – hammer with the 4th finger from fret 5 to fret 7 on string 1.

70

Sleepy Maggie

ORIGIN: SCOTLAND
SOURCES: VARIOUS
APPEARS ON: *FRAILS & FROLICS*

KEY: B (A ON BANJO)
MODE: DORIAN GAMUT
TUNING: gCGCD (Capo-2)

"Sleepy," or "Sleeping Maggie" appears in several late-18th and early-19th century Scottish collections as well as in such later works as *The Athole Collection* and *The Skye Collection*; it is closely related to the Irish tune, "Jenny's Chickens." I often wonder if at some point the "challenge" offered by this title inspired an Irish musician to compose the classic reel, "Drowsy Maggie" (intriguingly, these two tunes appear on the very same page of *O'Neill's Music of Ireland*). There appears to be no standard version of this four-part tune, so I followed the advice of noted Cape Breton fiddler Sandy MacIntyre and selected those parts from different sources that I liked the best. Note that the melody of Part C echoes the opening theme of the well-known Appalachian tune, "Cluck Old Hen." The tune is circular; and I've included the final-sounding tag ending I used on *Frails & Frolics*.

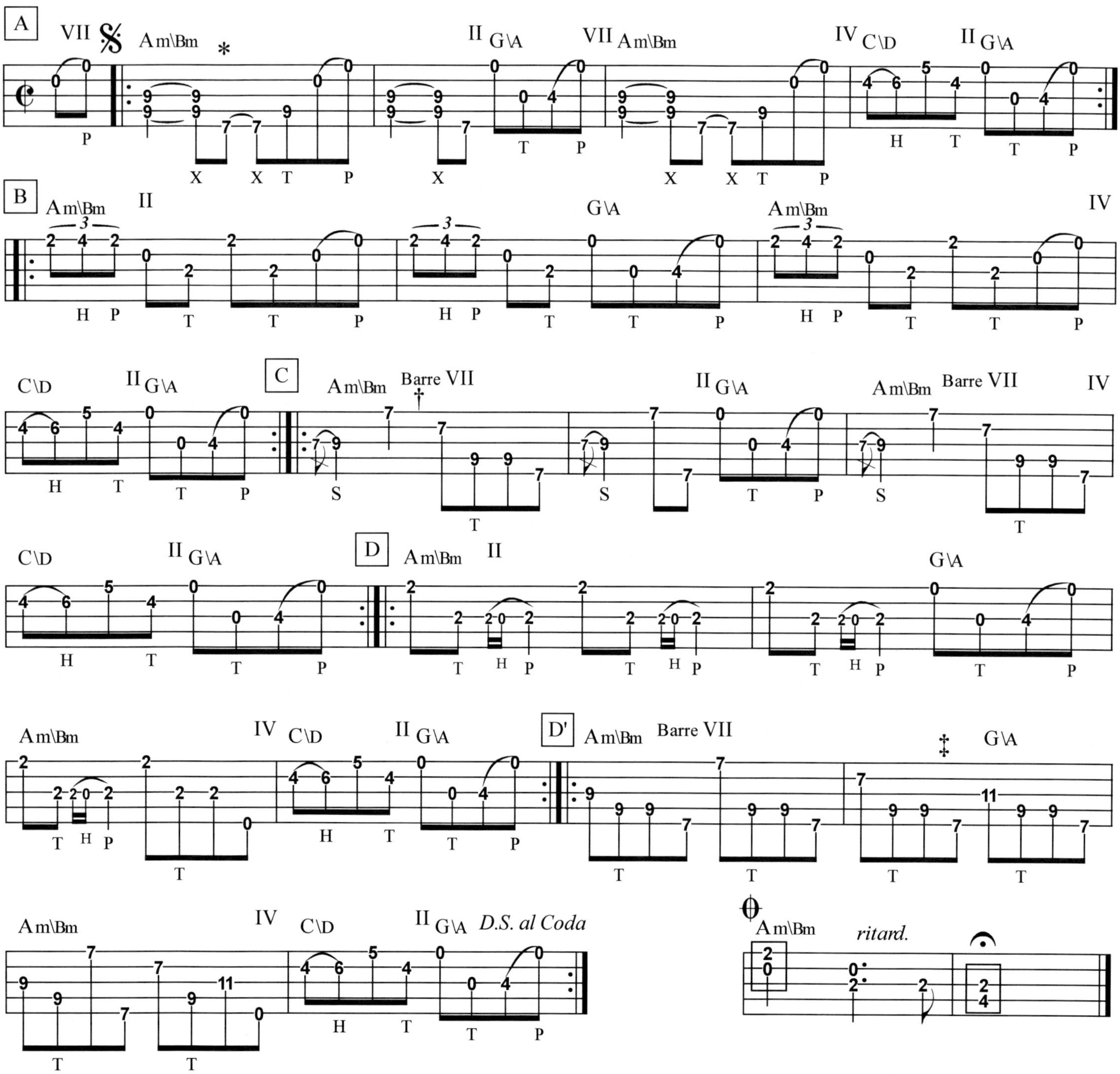

***FOR *SLEEPY MAGGIE* FINGERING DIAGRAMS & *PLAYING TIPS*, SEE FACING PAGE ***

Fingering Diagrams for *Sleepy Maggie*

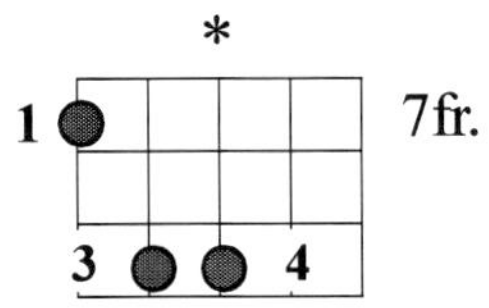

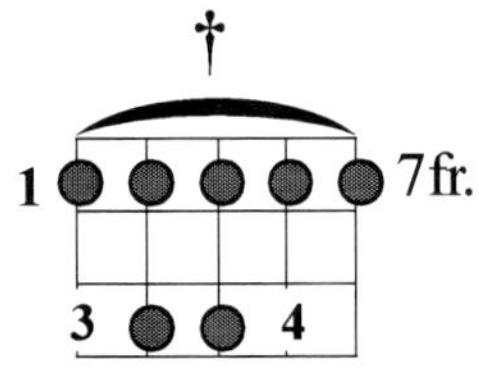

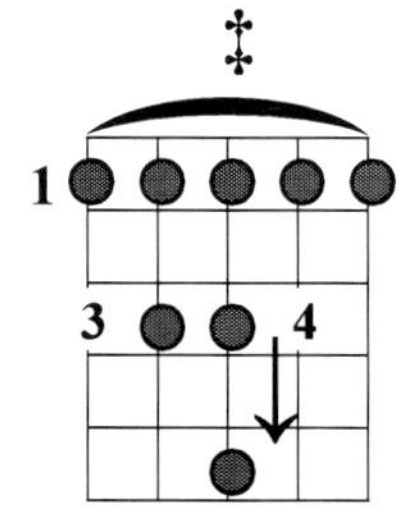

Playing Tips for *Sleepy Maggie*

Dual Chord Symbols: Chord to left of backslash goes with open banjo; chord on right is for capoed banjo or fiddle

• Part A, measure 1. My arrangement starts with a *compound skip* (see the section on Syncopation, pp. 20-21). Start with an ordinary bumm-titty strum, but skip the downstroke on beat 2, bringing T into contact with string 5. Play string 5, halfway between beats 2 and 3, then do a second skip on beat 3, but this time bring T into contact with string 4.

• Part B, measure 1. For the triplet on beat 1, use the 2nd finger to stop fret 2, string 1 and the 4th finger on fret 4. The 1st finger then stops fret 2, string 3.

• Part C, measure 1. Slide up string 3 with the 4th finger. That puts you in position to pivot into the shape in Diagram †.

71

Levantine's Barrel

Origin: Northeastern U.S.
Source: Sterling Baker
Appears on: *Northern Banjo*

Key: D (C on Banjo)
Mode: Major
Tuning: gCGCD (Capo-2)

This tune was named for a 19th-century American vaudeville performer and "equilibrist" named Fred Levantine (1851-1929) and his most famous balancing act. Levantine, a native of Maine whose birth-name was Frederick F. Proctor, would go on to establish a chain of vaudeville houses throughout New York State and New England. Printed as "Levantine's Barrel" in *Ryan's Mammoth Collection*, the melody is part of a widespread North-American tune family; just a few of its musical relatives are "Bummer's Reel" (U.S. Northeast), "Rose Division" (U.S. South) and Galop de St. Paul (Québec).

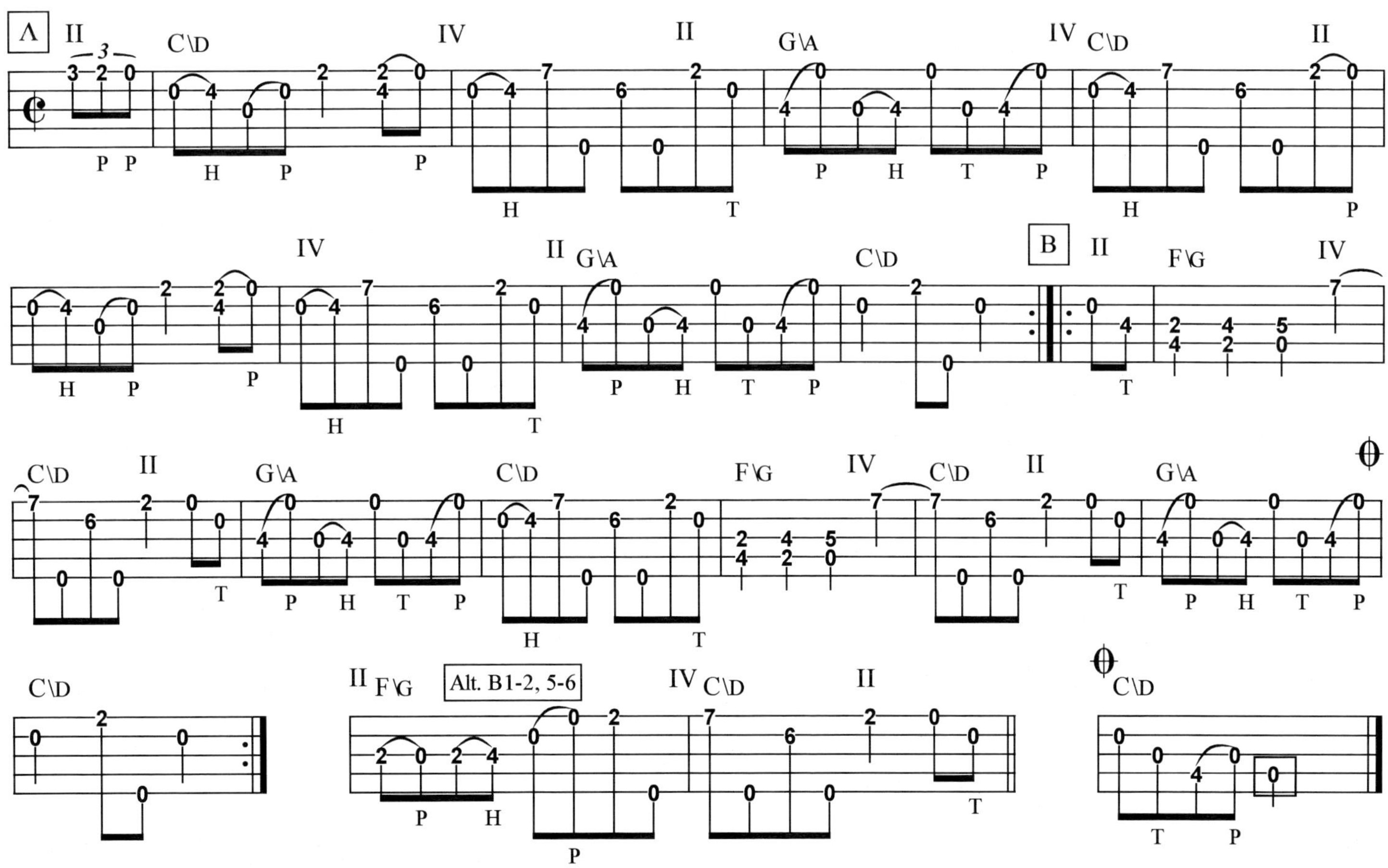

Playing Note for *Levantine's Barrel*

Dual Chord Symbols: Chord to left of backslash goes with open banjo; chord on right is for capoed banjo or fiddle

72

Durang's Hornpipe

Composer: "Mr. Hoffmaster"
Sources: Franklin George & Alan Jabbour
Appears on: *Frails & Frolics*

Key: D (C on Banjo)
Mode: Major
Tuning: gCGCD (Capo-2)

John Durang was a renowned step-dancer of the late 18th Century who rose to fame performing in the early American circus owned by Samuel Ricketts, for whom the well-known tune, "Ricketts' Hornpipe" was named. Durang wrote in his diary that he commissioned his namesake tune from a composer in New York City, identified only as "Mr. Hoffmaster." The tune is printed in *Ryan's Mammoth Collection* and elsewhere but oral transmission has not been kind; quite a number of popular variants circulate in North America in which the original melody is only faintly recognizable. I was moved to learn this version of "Durang's" after hearing it played by West Virginia fiddler Franklin George (1928-2017); Alan Jabbour then showed me the wonderful variation on Part B that George used to play, which I had to take up an octave to fit on banjo.

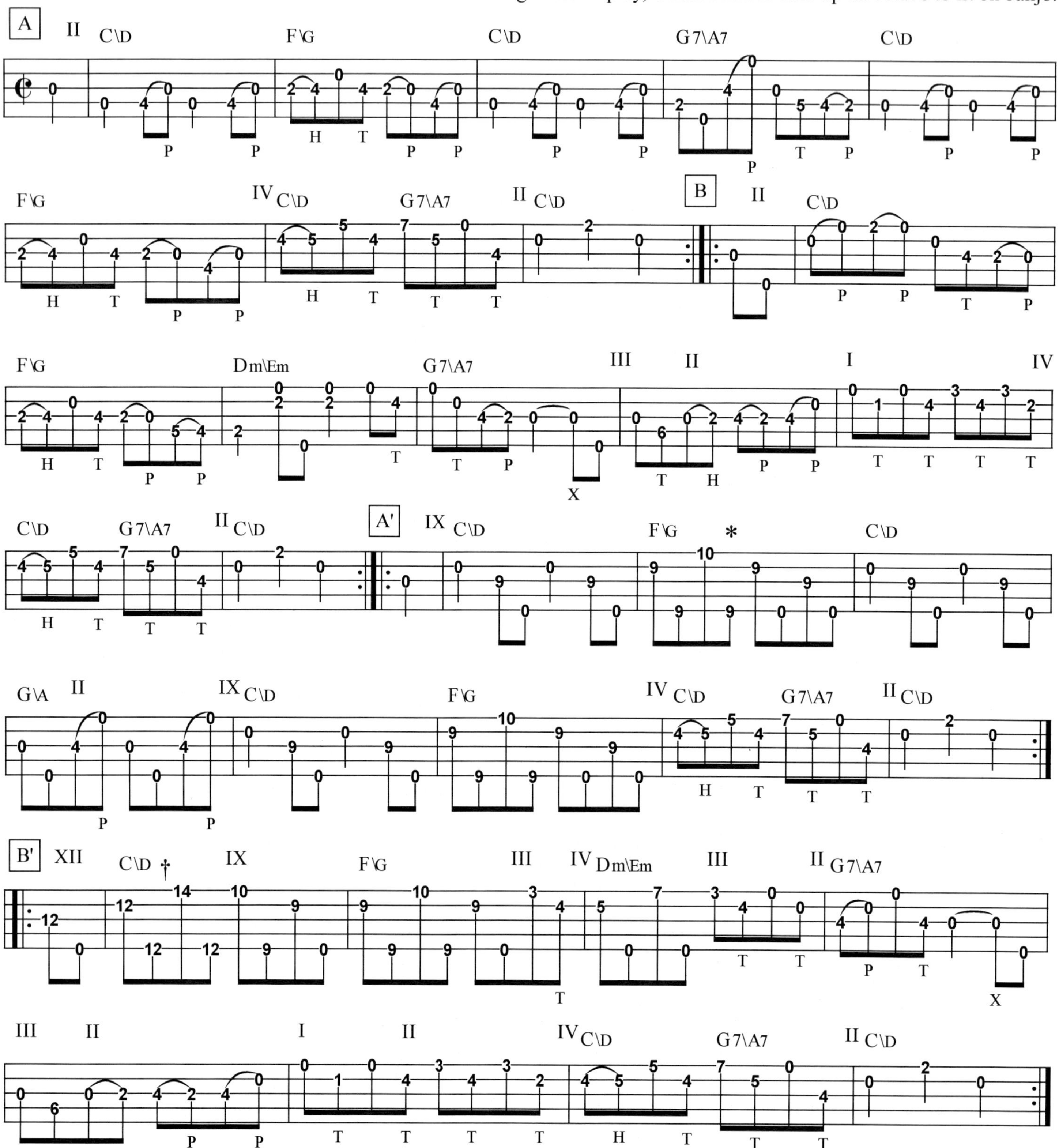

*For *Durang's Hornpipe* Fingering Diagrams & *Playing Tips*, See Facing Page *

Fingering Diagrams for *Durang's Hornpipe*

Playing Tips for *Durang's Hornpipe*

Dual Chord Symbols: Chord to left of backslash goes with open banjo; chord on right is for capoed banjo or fiddle

• Part B', measures 1-3. The trick here is "glide and adjust." In measure 1, start with the shape shown in Diagram †. On beat 3, cut all three notes short and glide with the 1st, 2nd and 4th fingers down their respective strings to perch on fret 9, string 5; fret 9, string 2; and fret 10, string 1 (same as illustrated in Diagram *). On beat 4 of measure 2, use the 2nd finger to glide down string 2 to fret 4; then pivot on that finger and bring the 1st finger into position at fret 3, string 1. Then at the start of measure 3, glide up string 2 with the 2nd finger to fret 5; then pivot on that finger and swing the 4th finger over to stop fret 7, string 1.

Fingering Diagrams for *The Belfast Hornpipe*

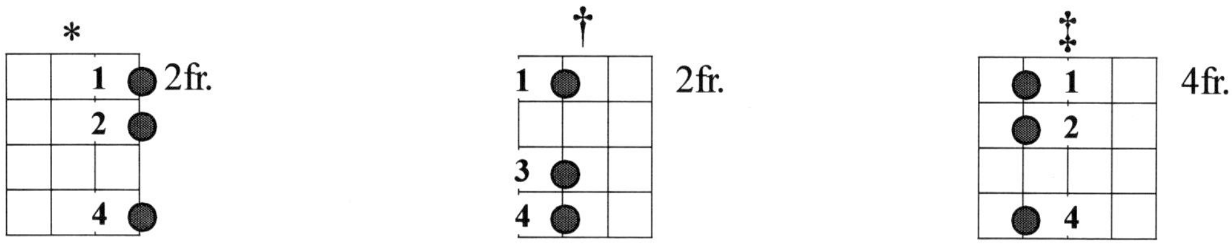

Playing Tips for *The Belfast Hornpipe* (tab on p. 80)

Dual Chord Symbols: Chord to left of backslash goes with open banjo; chord on right is for capoed banjo or fiddle

• Part A, measure 4; Parts A, B, & C, measure 7. Each measure contains what appears to be a "reverse" dotted pair in which the sixteenth note is first. These are *Scotch snaps,* which are commonly employed by Scottish, Cape Breton, and Prince Edward Island fiddlers as rhythmic ornamentation in hornpipes. For more explanation, see p. 151.

• Part C triplets. The trick here is maintaining finger balance and simultaneously placing all the fingers you need for a particular series of H's and P's on a given string.

◦ Part C, measures 1, 3, & 5. Place the 1st, 2nd, and 4th fingers on string 1 at frets 2, 3 and 5 as shown in Diagram *. Then use them in succession for a pull-off and two H-P triplets.

◦ Part C, measures 1-2 & 5-6. On the last beat of measures 1 and 5, have the 1st finger placed in waiting on string 3 at fret 2 as shown in Diagram †, then use the 3rd finger and 4th fingers for an H-P triplet on that string involving frets 4 and 5. On beat 1 of measures 2 and 6, continue to keep the 1st finger down and use the 3rd finger on string 3 for an H-P triplet. Finally, the 1st finger is readily available to perform an H-P triplet on open string 3.

◦ Part C, measure 6. On beat 3, place the 1st, 2nd, and 4th fingers on string 4 at frets 4, 5 and 7; as shown in Diagram ‡. Then use them in succession for two H-P triplets.

73

The Belfast Hornpipe

ORIGIN: PROBABLY NORTHERN ENGLAND
SOURCES: VARIOUS

KEY: D (C ON BANJO)
MODE: MAJOR
TUNING: gCGCD (Capo-2)

This is truly a tune of many names. It is called "Lancashire Clog" in Elias Howe's *Musician's Omnibus* (c. 1880); "Millicen's Favorite (or Royal Belfast) Hornpipe" in *Kerr's Merry Melodies;* "Great Western (Lancashire) Clog" in *Ryan's Mammoth Collection;* and "The Sweep's Hornpipe" in *O'Neill's Music of Ireland.* The moniker, "Belfast Hornpipe" – by far the most common name in current usage – traces to *Allan's Irish Fiddler.*

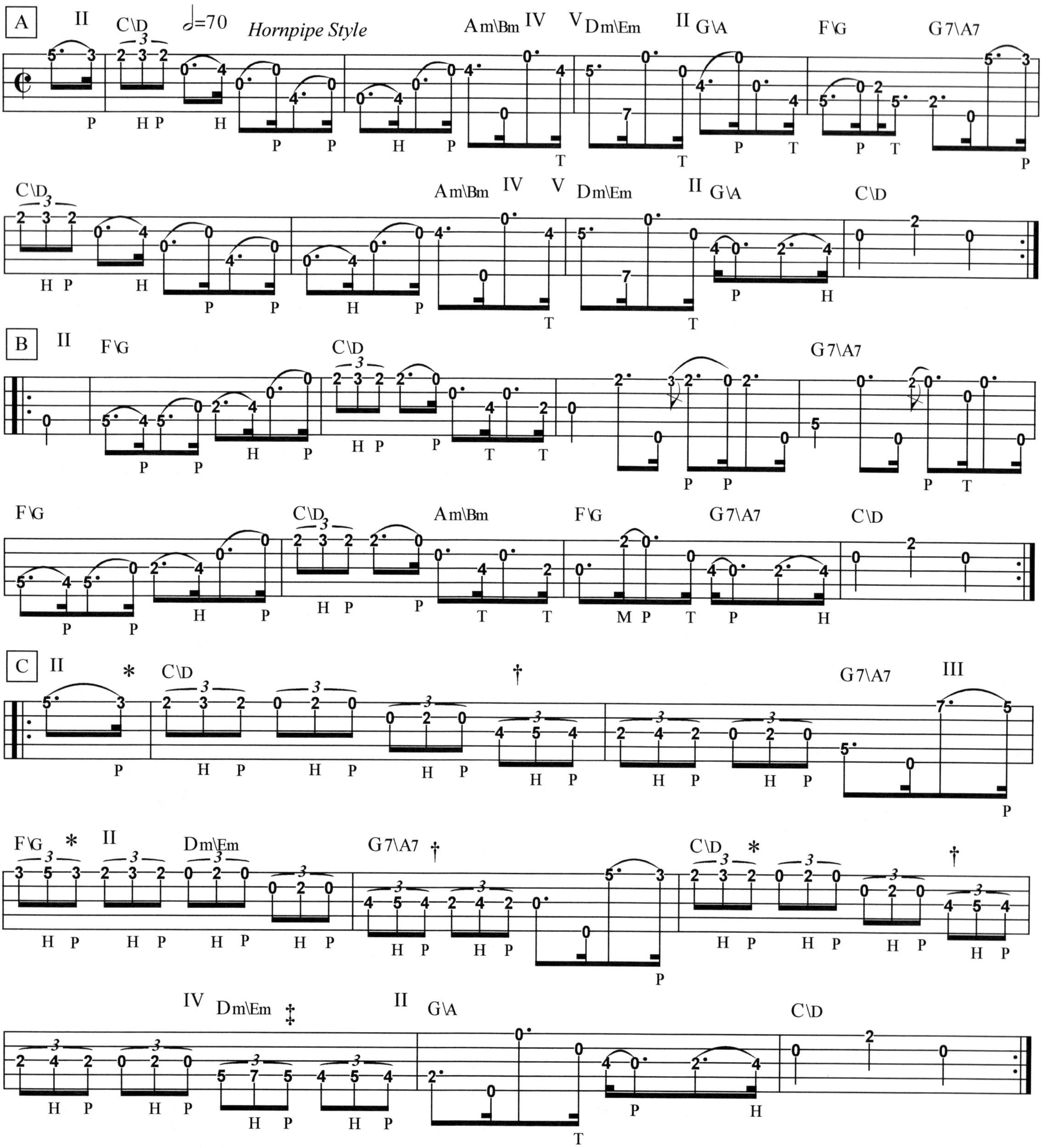

FOR *BELFAST HORNPIPE FINGERING DIAGRAMS & PLAYING TIPS*, SEE PAGE 79

Chapter 7. *Reels – & Hornpipes – in A & A-Modal*

KEY-OF-A TUNES CAN VARY CONSIDERABLY IN CHARACTER. Some have a bright tonality and very narrow range; others hover in the low end of the fiddle and are quite dark. Narrow-range key-of-A tunes can often be played on banjo without departing from first and second positions. Other key-of-A tunes have complex melodies and occupy as wide a range as you'll encounter in the fiddle-tune genre; playing tunes like this on banjo often requires taking them in whole or part up an octave.

The key of A is where most modal variation takes place in fiddle tunes (see below). Depending on modality, range, and fingering convenience, there are several tuning options available. The tunings you'll find here are gDGBD (capo-2), gDGCD (capo-2), and gCGCD (capo-2). Banjoists who prefer to tune up all strings two frets in pitch instead of capoing, may prefer to refer to these tunings as *open A* (aEAC♯E), *A modal* (aEADE), and *Double D* (aDADE).

Important Note re Capoing & Notation on the 5th string. If you capo your banjo at fret 2, fret notations on the 5th string are correct only if you also capo up the 5th string via a 5th-string capo or "railroad spike." If you simply tune up the 5th string two frets, you must then subtract two from every fret indication.

Modes In The Key Of A

MOST MODAL VARIATION IN FIDDLE TUNES INVOLVES CHANGES IN THE 3RD AND 7TH TONES of the diatonic scale. Focusing on the key of A, the 3rd tone of the scale (C) can be major (C#), minor (C♮), or missing; sometimes the third-note can be "neutral" (between major and minor values). The 7th tone of the diatonic scale can also be major (G#) or minor (G-natural). Note that modes can vary among parts within the same tune or even among phrases within a given part. Pentatonic modes with an A key center also play an important role; the three types most commonly encountered are major pentatonic (A-B-C#-E-F#-A), Re-Pentatonic (the first inversion of the G-major pentatonic scale, or A-B-D-E-G-A), and minor pentatonic (the fourth inversion of the C-major pentatonic scale, or A-C-D-E-G-A). For more on diatonic and pentatonic modes, see Chapter 3.

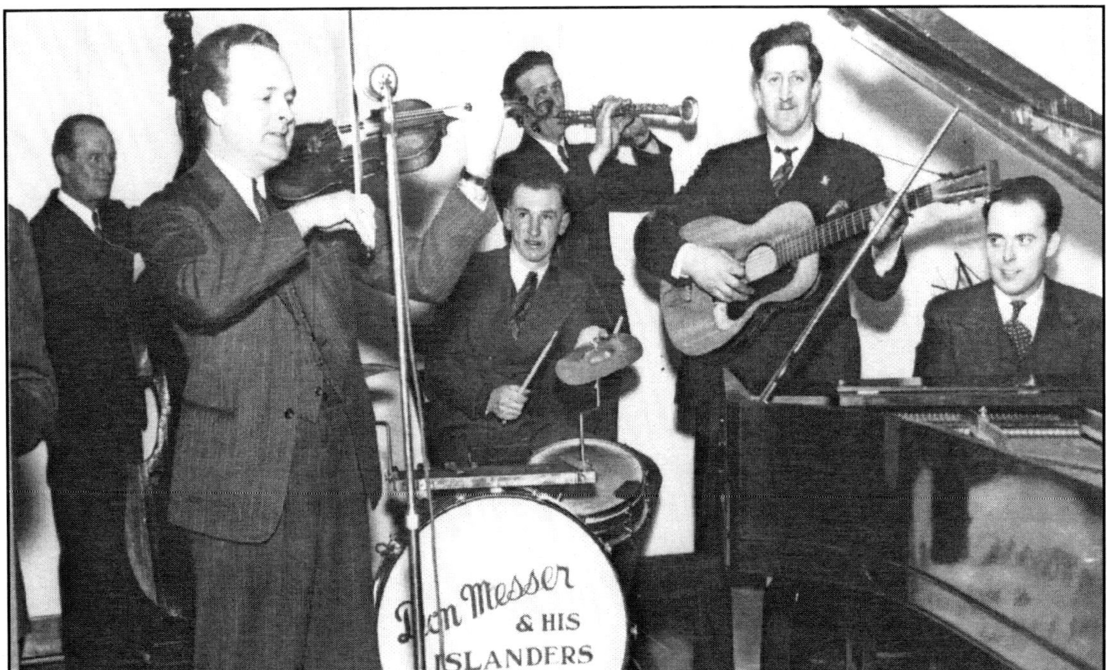

Don Messer & His Islanders, late 1940s. L-R: Duke Nielson (bass), Messer, Warren Macrae (drums), Rae Simmons (soprano sax), Charlie Chamberlain (guitar), & Jackie Doyle (piano); courtesy P.E.I Public Archives & Records Office; Accession #4268

74

Dillon Brown

ORIGIN: IRELAND
SOURCE: PAUL MACDONALD
APPEARS ON: *NORTHERN BANJO*

KEY: A (G ON BANJO)
MODE: MAJOR
TUNING: gDGBD (Capo-2)

The "Dillon Brown" melody first appears – in the key of G – in late 19th-century Irish manuscripts. In 1939, it was recorded in the key of A as "Langton's Reel" by Sligo fiddler Paddy Killoran (1903-65), who subsequently re-recorded the tune under the "Dillon Brown" title; it also appears under this name in Breandán Breathnach's *Folk Music & Dances of Ireland* (1971). Interestingly, the title "Dillon Brown" occurs in *O'Neill's Dance Music of Ireland* but it is associated with an entirely different melody. Standard notation for my source version is in *Fiddle Music of P.E.I.*

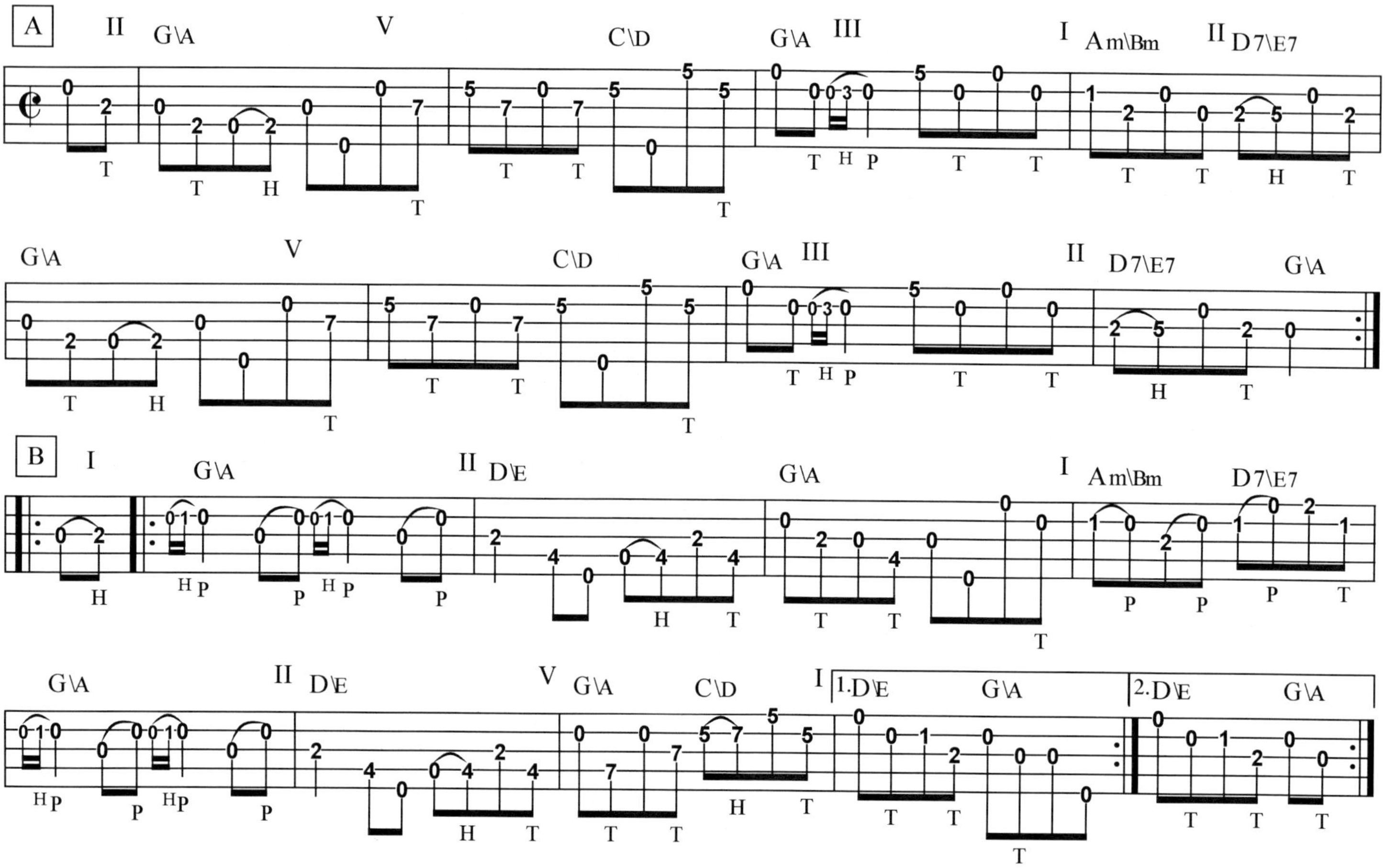

PLAYING NOTE FOR *DILLON BROWN*

***DUAL CHORD SYMBOLS:** Chord to left of backslash goes with open banjo; chord on right is for capoed banjo or fiddle*

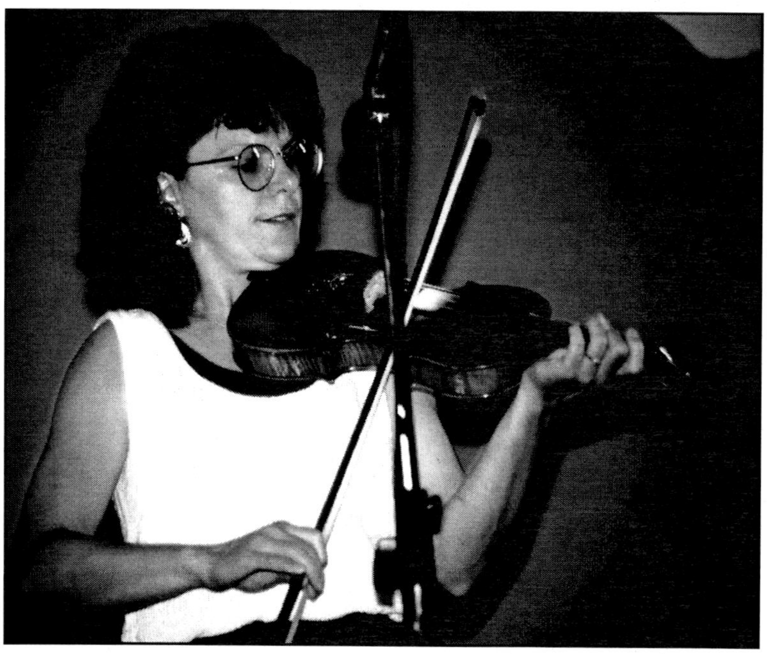

Louise Arsenault at Atlantic Jamboree: Abram-Village, P.E.I. (1992). Photo by Ken Perlman; courtesy Robertson Library, University of P.E.I.

75

Angus Campbell

Composer: James Scott Skinner
Source: Francis MacDonald
Appears on: *Northern Banjo*

Key: A (G on Banjo)
Mode: Major
Tuning: gDGBD (Capo-2)

Skinner published "Angus Campbell" in two of his well-known works: *Harp & Claymore* and *The Scottish Violinist*. It was intended to draw on the same general turns of phrase as his strathspey, "The Laird o' Drumblaire." Fiddler Don Messer recorded the tune in 1944; one of the first Cape Breton fiddlers to do so was Jimmy MacLellan (1910-88). Standard notation for my source version is in *Fiddle Music of P.E.I.*

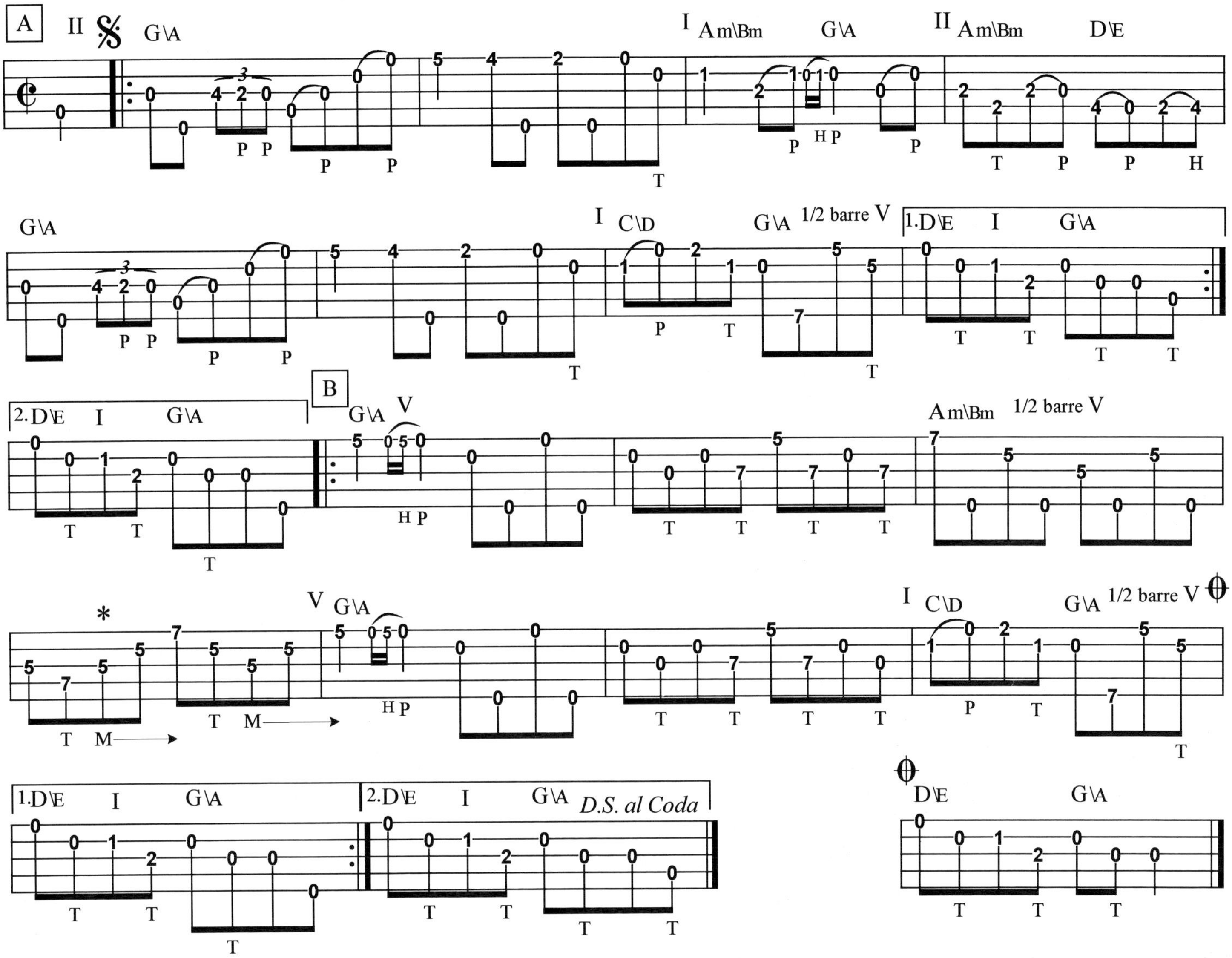

Playing Note for *Angus Campbell*

__Dual Chord Symbols:__ Chord to left of backslash goes with open banjo; chord on right is for capoed banjo or fiddle

76

The Miramichi Fire

Origin: New Brunswick
Source: Andrew Jones
Appears on: *Island Boy*

Key: A (G on Banjo)
Mode: See Intro
Tuning: gDGCD (Capo-2)

The Great Miramichi Fire of October 1825 originated in the Miramichi River Valley of New Brunswick (pronounced: "mi-ra-mi-SHEE"); it ultimately consumed roughly 6000 square miles of forest land and leveled a substantial portion of Fredericton. According to oral tradition, the fire was so bright that it was visible from the facing shore of Prince County in western P.E.I. "The Miramichi Fire" is one of the most variable tunes in the repertoire. Versions from Kings County tend to be sparse and relatively sedate, while those from Prince County – like this one – are often notey, up-tempo, and highly syncopated. The mode features a major 3rd, variable 7th, and no 6th at all (A-B-C♯-D-E-G/G♯-A on fiddle; G-A-B-C-D-F/F♯-G on open banjo). Standard notation for my source version is in *Fiddle Music of P.E.I.*

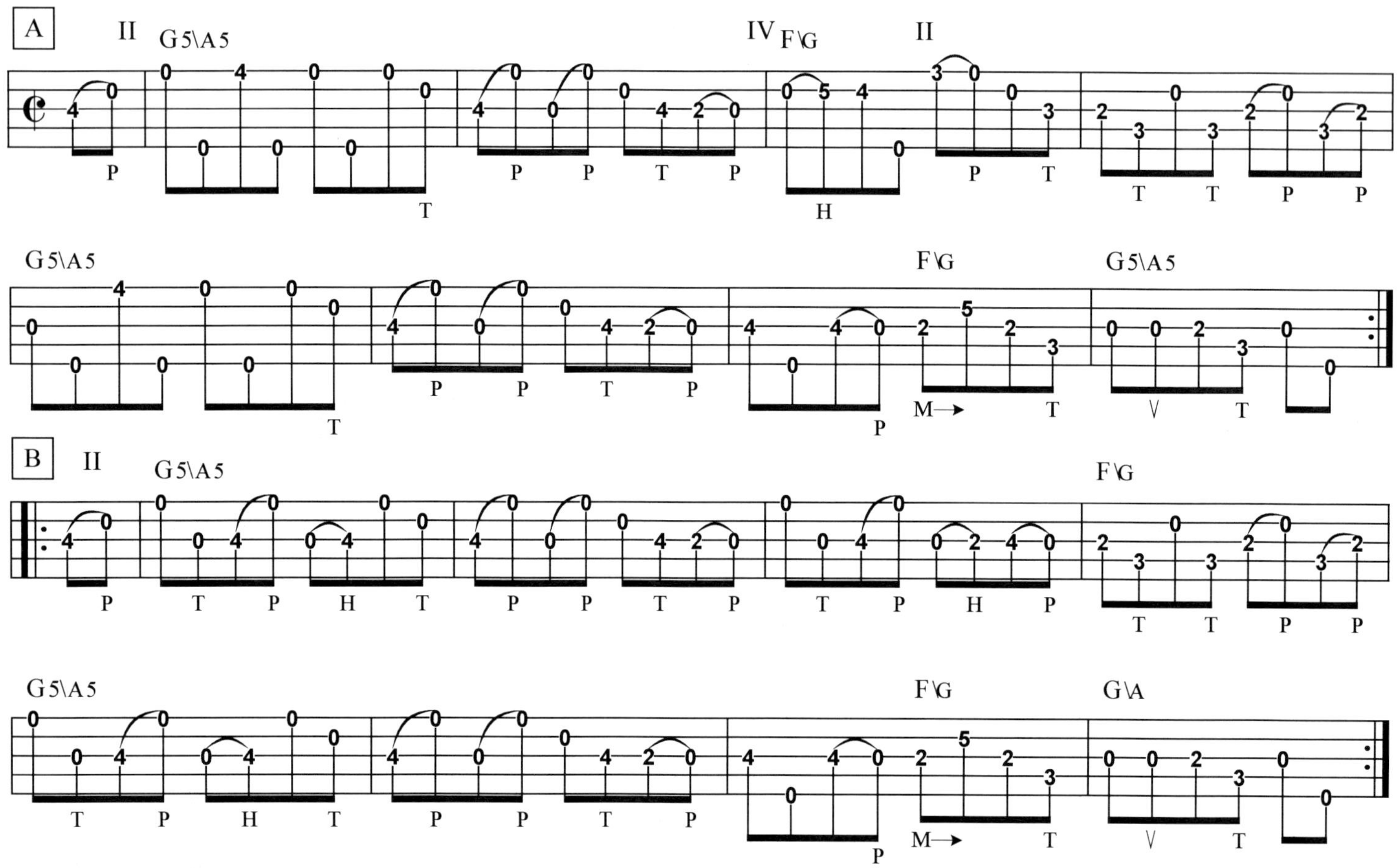

Playing Tips for *The Miramichi Fire*

Dual Chord Symbols: Chord to left of backslash goes with open banjo; chord on right is for capoed banjo or fiddle

• Part A and B, measure 7. In the second half of the measure you are asked to immediately follow an arpeggio stroke from string 3 to 2, with a drop-thumb from string 3 to 4. The trick is to avoid giving too much weight during the arpeggio-stroke so that you maintain the balance of the plucking hand.

The Brae Reel

77

ORIGIN: WESTERN P.E.I.
SOURCE: EDWARD P. ARSENAULT
APPEARS ON: *ISLAND BOY*

KEY: A (G ON BANJO)
MODE: DORIAN GAMUT
TUNING: gDGCD (Capo-2)

This haunting modal reel was popularized on Prince Edward Island – and given its name – by the great Acadian fiddler Eddy Arsenault. Arsenault described his own source as "an old fiddler from The Brae," a hamlet roughly 25 miles northwest of his home in St. Chrysostome (although the word *brae* means "hillside" in the Scots language, the land around this small village is almost completely flat). This version of the tune is from Edward P. Arsenault (a distant relation of Eddy's). I had to raise Part A up an octave to make it fit on banjo. Standard notation for my source version is in *Fiddle Music of P.E.I.*

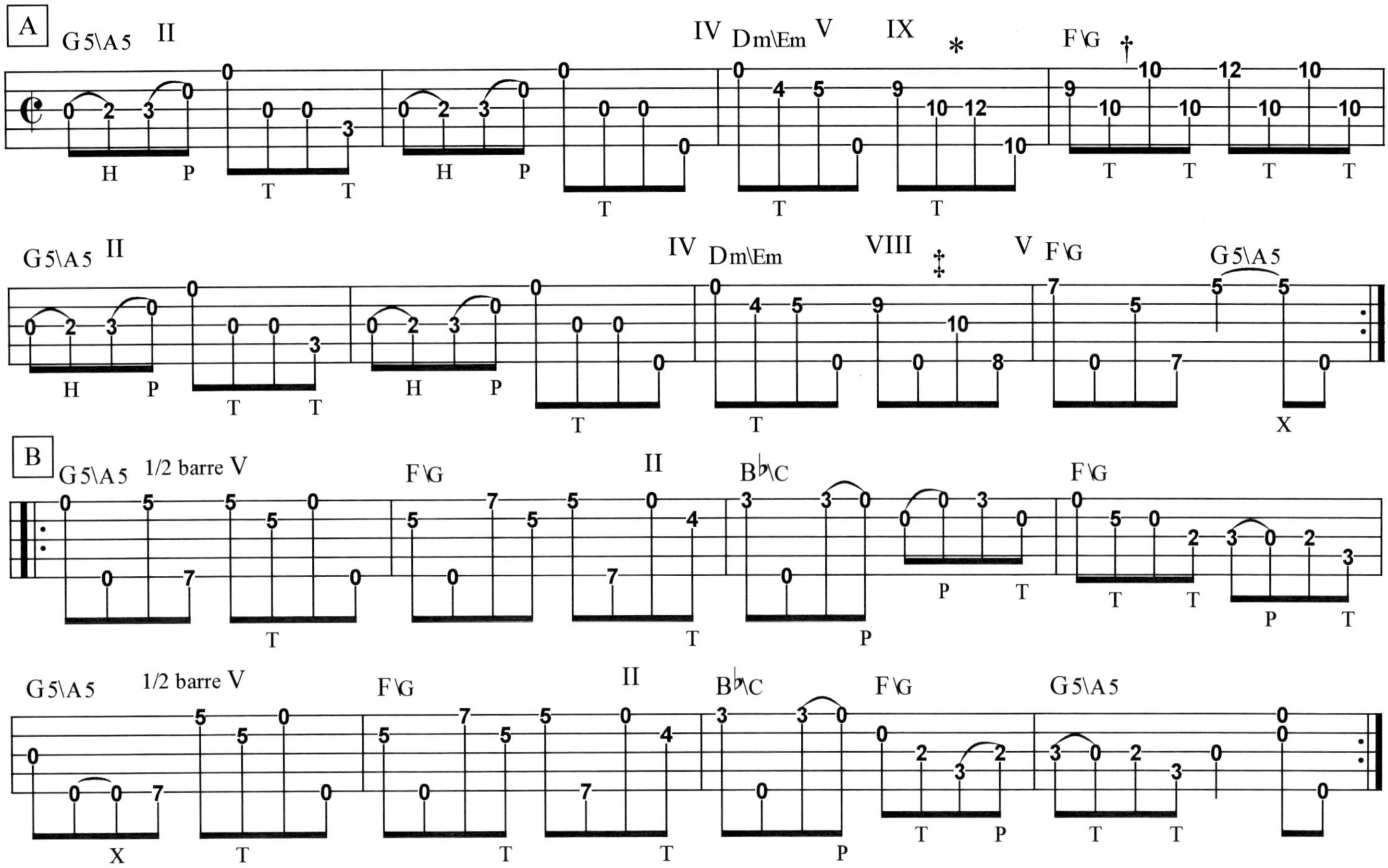

*

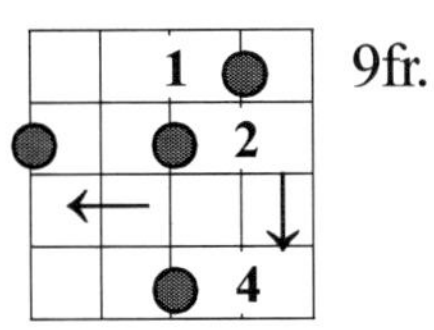

†

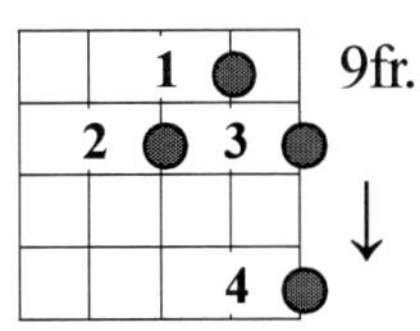

‡

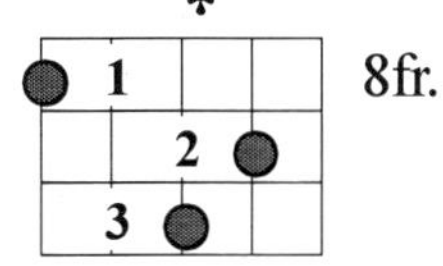

PLAYING TIPS FOR *THE BRAE REEL*

***DUAL CHORD SYMBOLS:** Chord to left of backslash goes with open banjo; chord on right is for capoed banjo or fiddle*

• PART A, MEASURE 3. At the end of beat 1, balance on the 1st finger at fret 4, string 2. At the start of beat 2, glide up on that finger to fret 5, then use the time provided by the following open string to glide up the neck to fret 9. On beat 3, use the 1st finger as a pivot to bring the 2nd finger into place on fret 10, string 3. Then in quick succession, pivot on the 2nd finger to swing the 4th finger into place on fret 12; and pivot on the 4th finger to bring the 2nd finger over to fret 10, string 5 (Diagram *).

• PART A, MEASURE 7. Start as in measure 3, but this time at beat 2 use the 2nd finger on fret 5, string 2. On beat 3, glide with that finger to fret 9, and use it as a pivot to swing the 1st and 3rd fingers into place as shown in Diagram ‡.

78

Pride of the Ball

Origin: Local Variant of Irish Tune
Source: "Young Peter" Chaisson
Appears on: *Frails & Frolics*

Key: A (G on Banjo)
Mode: Mixolydian Gamut
Tuning: gDGCD (Capo-2)

This is a P.E.I. variant of the key-of-A setting of the 19th-century Irish reel, "Pigeon on the Gate." It is known by the above title in some parts of the Island, but also by a host of other local monikers such as "The Queen's Marriage," "Roddy Joe's Reel," "Speed the Plough, and "The Twin Sisters." Versions of the tune can be found in print as "Pride of the Ball" and/or "Pigeon on the Gate" in several 19th and early 20th century collections, including *Kerr's Merry Melodies, Ryan's Mammoth Collection,* and *O'Neill's Music of Ireland*; in *Allan's Irish Fiddler* a close analog is called "Swallowtail Reel." A distinct sister variant of this melody – generally known as "Pigeon on the Gatepost" (p. 33) – also circulates widely on P.E.I. The main difference between the two variants is their modal character; "Pride of the Ball" employs a Mixolydian gamut; whereas "Pigeon on the Gatepost" – with no 3rd at all, a minor 7th, and just a hint of the 6th tone – is close to Re-Pentatonic. Standard notation for my source version is in *Fiddle Music of P.E.I.*

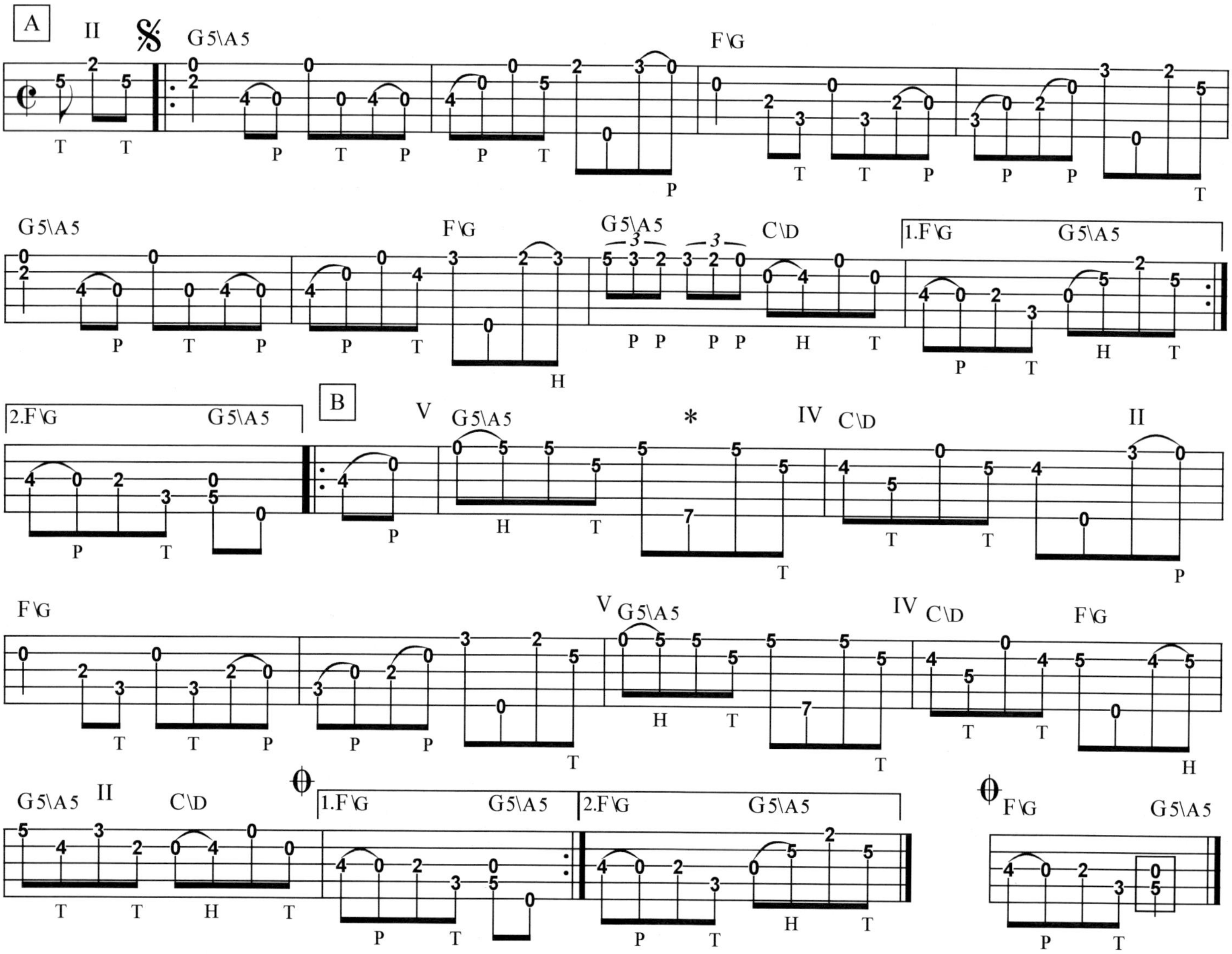

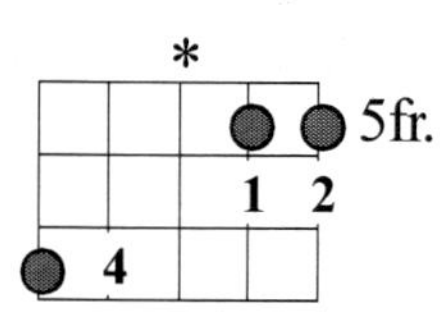

Playing Note for *Pride of the Ball*

Dual Chord Symbols: Chord to left of backslash goes with open banjo; chord on right is for capoed banjo or fiddle*

79

The Cape Breton Wedding Reel

Origin: Scotland
Source: "Old Peter" Chaisson
Appears on: *Island Boy*

Key: A (G on Banjo)
Mode: See Intro
Tuning: gCGCD (Capo-2)

This tune was once played to accompany the ceremonial step-dance that initiated wedding festivities in Cape Breton (see also "The Prince Edward Island Wedding Reel," p. 94). The melody is derived from the 18th-century Scottish strathspey, "John of Badenyon." An early print appearance for the strathspey was in Alexander MacLashan's, *A Collection of Reels [. . .]* (1786); it can also be found in *The Skye Collection*. The mode comes very close to minor pentatonic (A-C-D-E-G-A on fiddle; G-B♭-C-D-F♮-G on open banjo); it features a minor 3rd and minor 7th; fully avoids the 6th scale tone and only uses the 2nd tone – B on fiddle; A on open banjo – sparingly. I employ a C tuning because I needed the low note on open string 4 in measure 8 of both parts. Standard notation for my source version is in *Fiddle Music of P.E.I.*

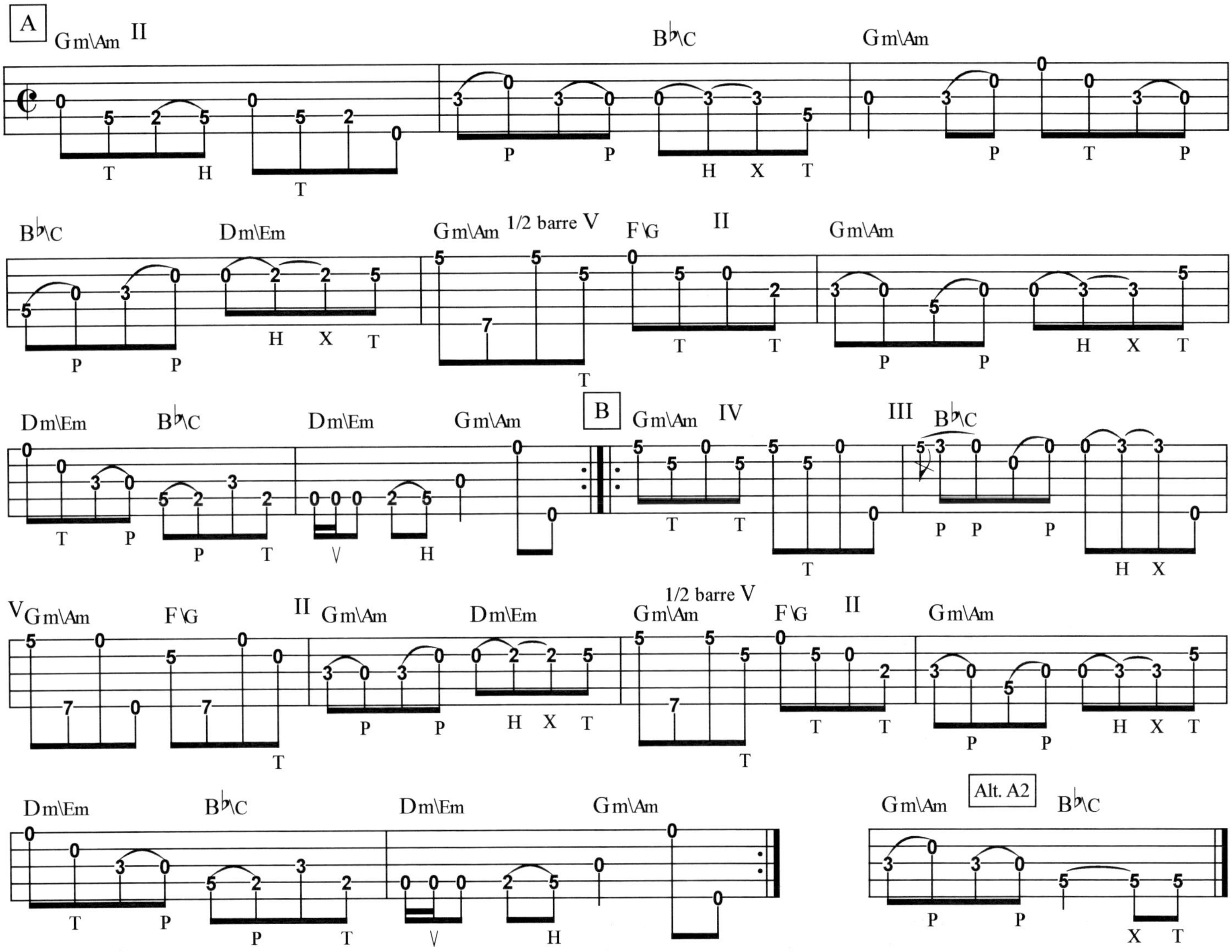

Playing Note for *Cape Breton Wedding Reel*

***Dual Chord Symbols:** Chord to left of backslash goes with open banjo; chord on right is for capoed banjo or fiddle*

80

Little Donald in the Pigpen

Origin: Probably Eastern P.E.I.
Source: "Young Peter" Chaisson
Appears on: *Frails & Frolics*

Key: A (G on Banjo)
Mode: Mixolydian Gamut
Tuning: gDGCD (Capo-2)

This title can be traced to Hector MacDonald of Bangor, P.E.I., who performed the tune on CFCY radio, Charlottetown in the late 1920s or early 30s. My source fiddler based his version on the one popularized by Cape Breton's Rankin Family. Observe that the reel is short-format, and therefore Part B is *not* repeated. The tune is circular, concluding on the sub-dominant chord (D on fiddle; C on open banjo); I've included the final-sounding tag ending that concludes the cut on *Frails & Frolics*. Standard notation for my source version is in *Fiddle Music of P.E.I.*

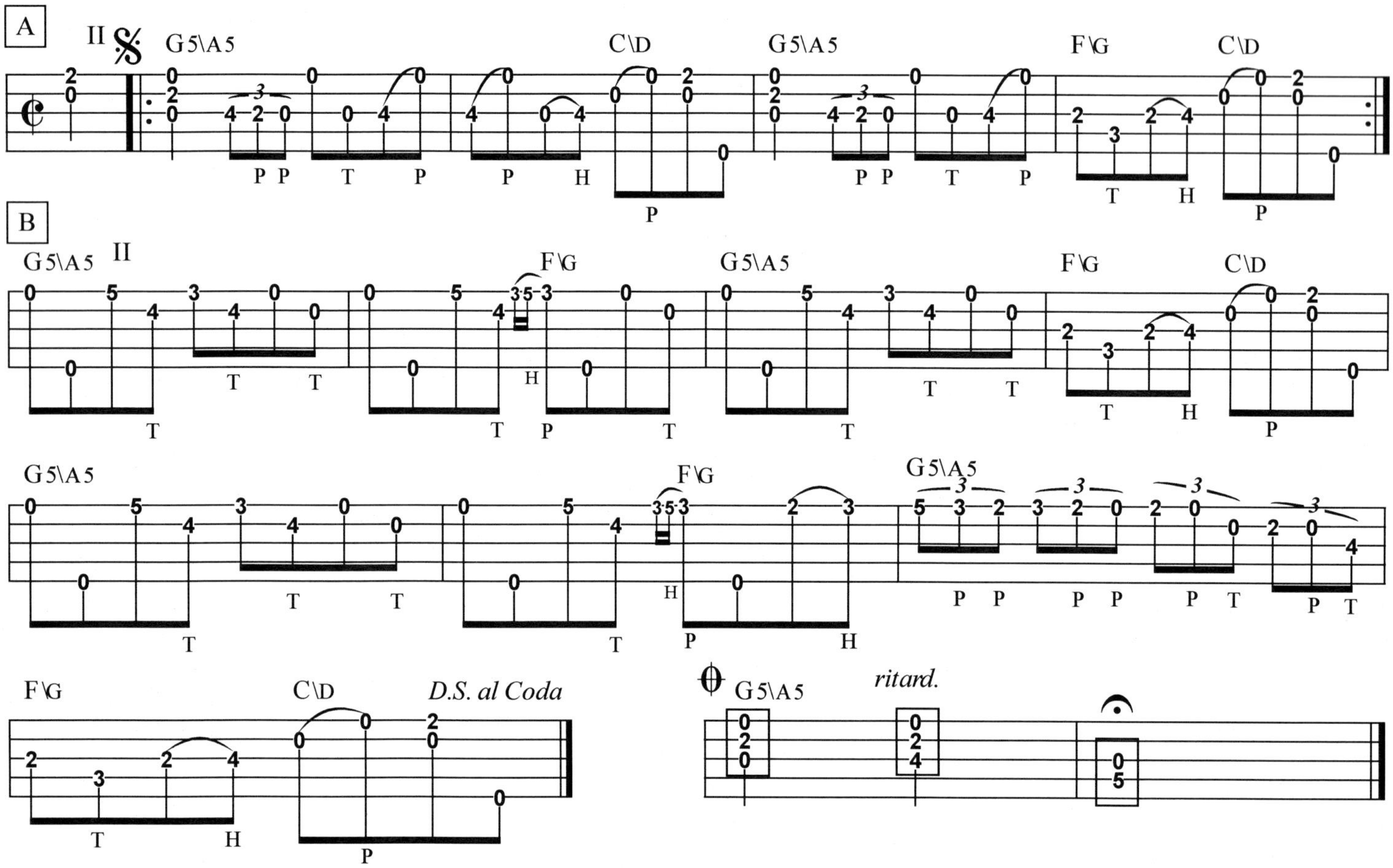

Playing Tips for *Little Donald in the Pigpen*

***Dual Chord Symbols:** Chord to left of backslash goes with open banjo; chord on right is for capoed banjo or fiddle*

• Part B, measures 6-7. At the end of measure 6 (that is, at the conclusion of the H), make sure to leave the 1st and 2nd fingers in place on string 1, frets 2 and 3, respectively. On beat 1 of measure 7, add the 4th finger (at fret 5, string 1), then peel the fingers off one at a time on string 1 to make the first triplet. To make the second triplet, hold onto the 1st finger at fret 2, and replace the 2nd finger on fret 3. At the start of beat 2, pull off from fret 3 to fret 2, and then – with the 1st finger – pull off from fret 2 to the open string.

81

St. Kilda Wedding

Origin: Scotland
Source: Francis MacDonald
Appears on: *Frails & Frolics*

Key: A (G on Banjo)
Mode: Major-Like (See Intro)
Tuning: gDGCD (Capo-2)

"St. Kilda Wedding" appears in the *Athole Collection, Kerr's Merry Melodies,* and *The Skye Collection*; and is still widely played among Scottish, Cape Breton, and P.E.I. fiddlers. The tune is named for the Scottish Island of St. Kilda, so far off the coast and difficult to supply that in 1930 the British government elected to relocate all its inhabitants to the mainland. Winston "Scotty" Fitzgerald recorded a version on his LP, *Canada's Outstanding Scottish Fiddler.* The melody is major-like with strong major 3rd and 7th tones, but the 4th tone (D on fiddle; C on open banjo) is completely avoided. The tune is circular, concluding on the dominant-chord (E on fiddle; D on open banjo); and I've included a final-sounding tag ending. Observe that the reel is short-format, and Part B is *not* repeated. Standard notation for my source version is in *Fiddle Music of P.E.I.*

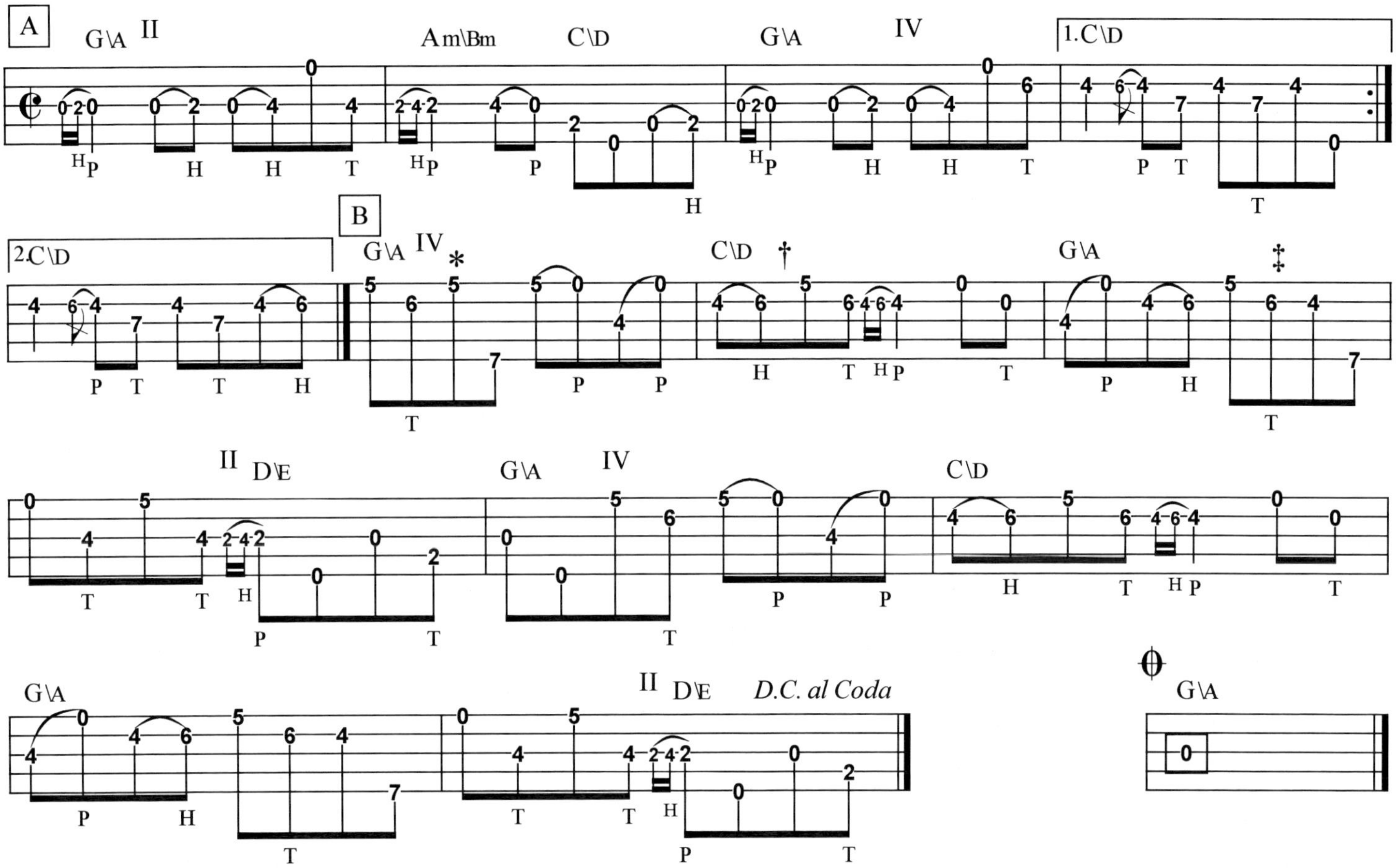

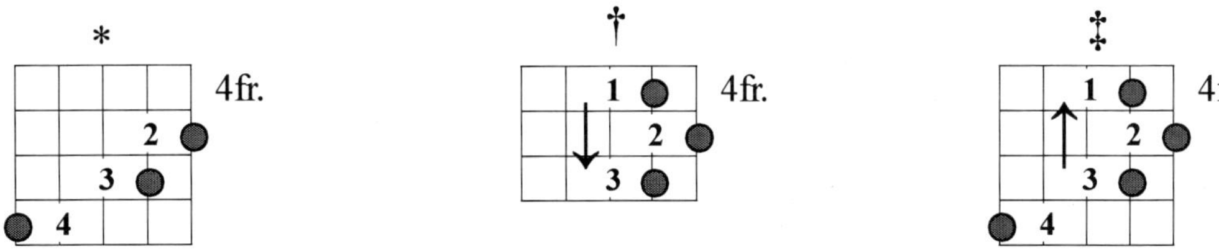

Playing Tips for *St. Kilda Wedding*

***Dual Chord Symbols:** Chord to left of backslash goes with open banjo; chord on right is for capoed banjo or fiddle*

• Part B, measure 3. This passage operates entirely out of fourth position, as shown in Diagram ‡. At the end of beat 2, balance on the 3rd finger at fret 6, string 2, and reach with the 2nd finger to fret 5, string 1. Then use the 2nd finger as a pivot to swing over the 1st and 4th fingers to fret 4, string 2 and fret 7, string 5, respectively (as also shown in the diagram).

82

Dinkie's Reel

Origin: Ireland
Source: Ward MacDonald
Appears on: *Frails & Frolics*

Key: A (G on Banjo)
Mode: Major 3rd & Variable 7th
Tuning: gDGCD (Capo-2)

"Dinkie's Reel" hales from County Donegal in northwestern Ireland; it was popularized by Francie Byrne of Cashel (1904-87), who named it for his friend, Hughie "Dinkie" Dorrian. The tune was introduced to Cape Breton by Irish fiddler Dermot McLaughlin of Derry, who learned it from Byrne. Standard notation for my source version is on *bowingdownhome.ca.*

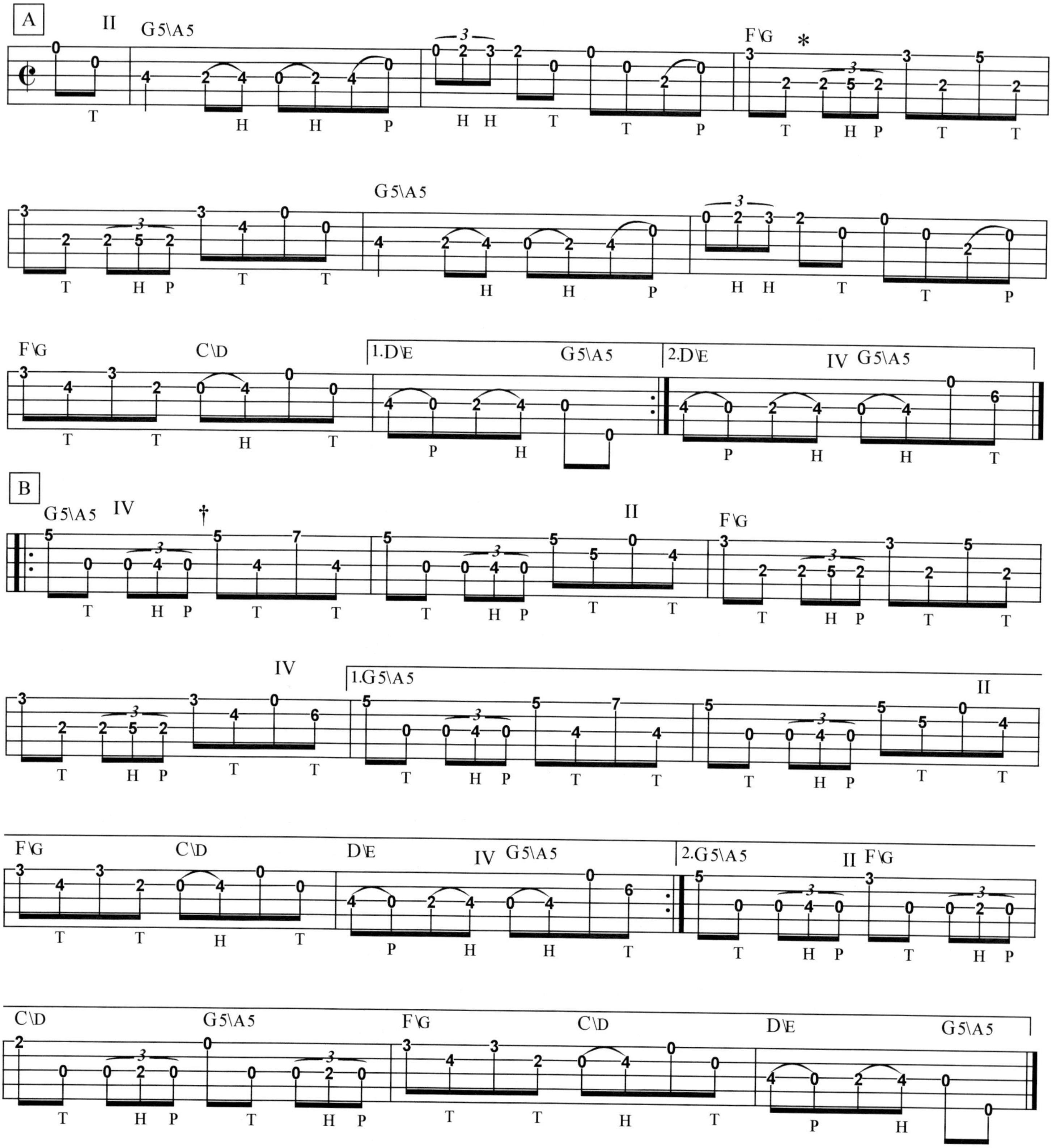

*For *Dinkie's Reel* Fingering Diagrams & Playing Tips, See Facing Page *

Fingering Diagrams for *Dinkie's Reel*

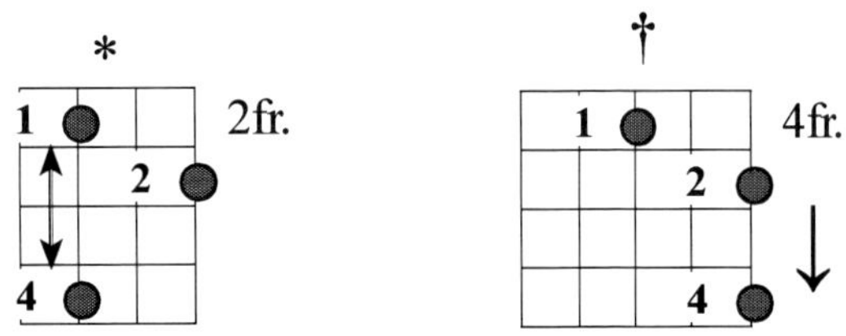

Playing Tips for *Dinkie's Reel*

Dual Chord Symbols: Chord to left of backslash goes with open banjo; chord on right is for capoed banjo or fiddle

• Part B, measures 2-3. On beat 3 of measure 2, make sure to stop fret 5, string 1 with the 2nd finger and use that as a pivot to bring the 1st finger into place at fret 5, string 2. On beat 4, use the time interval provided by the open string to glide down with the 3rd finger to stop fret 4, string 2. Then at the beginning of measure 3, use the 2nd and 1st fingers to catch fret 3, string 1 and fret 2, string 3, respectively.

• Part B measures 5-6 (2nd ending). Keep gliding down string 1 with the 2nd finger from fret 5, to fret 3, to fret 2. Each time that finger lands, use the 1st finger on string 3 to obtain the H-P triplet.

83

Lasses of Glenaladale

Origin: Scotland or Cape Breton
Source: Gus Longaphie
Appears on: *Frails & Frolics*

Key: A (G on Banjo)
Mode: Minor-Like (See Intro)
Tuning: gDGCD (Capo-2)

In the 1770s, John MacDonald, Laird of Glenaladale led the first expedition of Scottish settlers to Prince Edward Island. Although this tune has been recorded and previously published as "Lasses of Glenaodale," the title used here makes more sense given that Glenaladale is a place of significance in the history of Scottish immigration to the Maritimes, while "Glenaodale" does not seem to be an actual place name. The melody is minor-like with minor 3rd and 7th tones, but no 6th tone (A-B-C-D-E-G-A on fiddle; G-A-B♭-C-D-F♮-G on open banjo) Observe that the reel is short-format, and Part B is *not* repeated. Standard notation for my source version is in *Fiddle Music of P.E.I.*

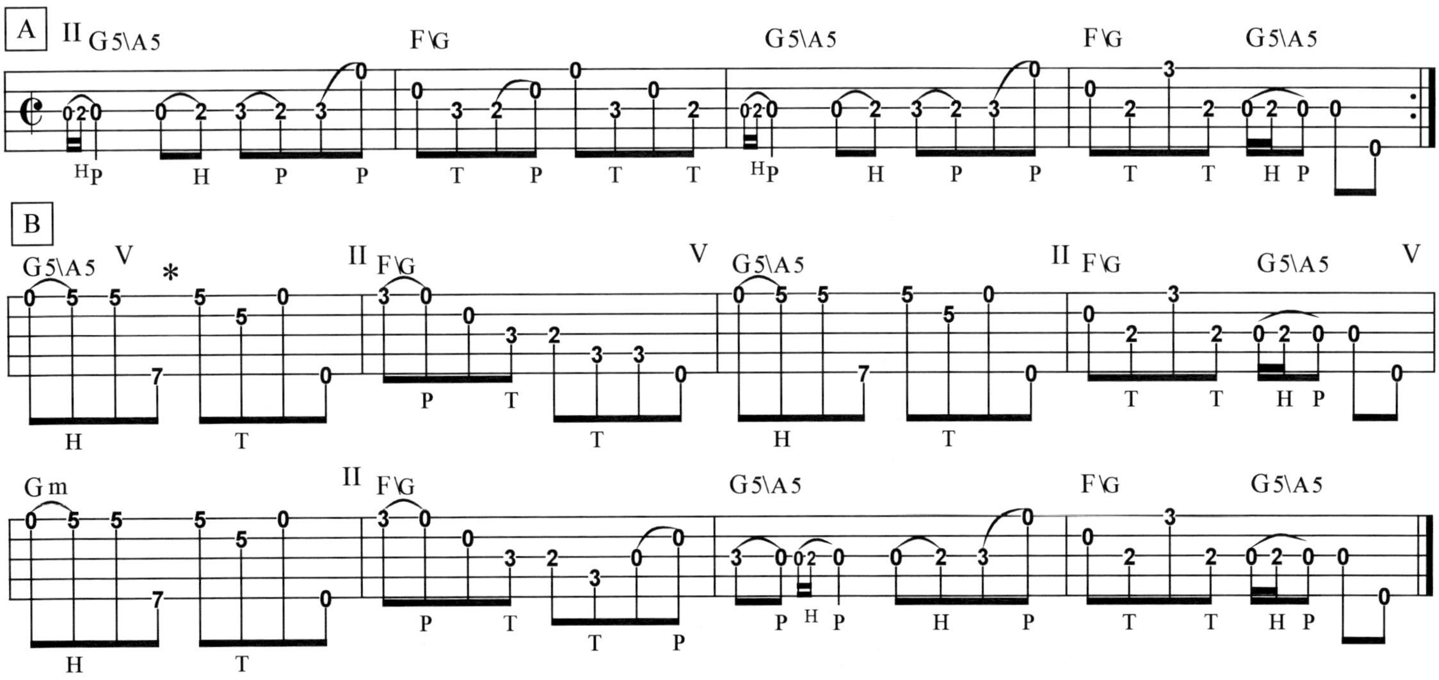

Playing Note for *Lasses of Glenaladale*

Dual Chord Symbols: Chord to left of backslash goes with open banjo; chord on right is for capoed banjo or fiddle

84

Carleton County Breakdown

Composer: Earl Mitton
Source: Leonard McDonald
Appears on: *Frails & Frolics*

Key: A (G on Banjo)
Mode: Major
Tuning: gDGBD (Capo-2)

Earl Mitton (1926-91) was a popular New Brunswick fiddler whose band, The Rhythm Valley Boys played frequently on local radio and television in the middle decades of the last century. He also appeared on the *Don Messer's Jubilee* television show and sometimes filled in as a summer replacement for Messer on radio. Mitton named this tune for a county in the west-central part of the province, and first recorded it in 1958. It has since become extremely popular on P.E.I. and is one of the most widely played tunes there – particularly in culturally Acadian sectors. I had to take the B Part up an octave to make it fit on banjo. Standard notation for my source version is in *Fiddle Music of P.E.I.*

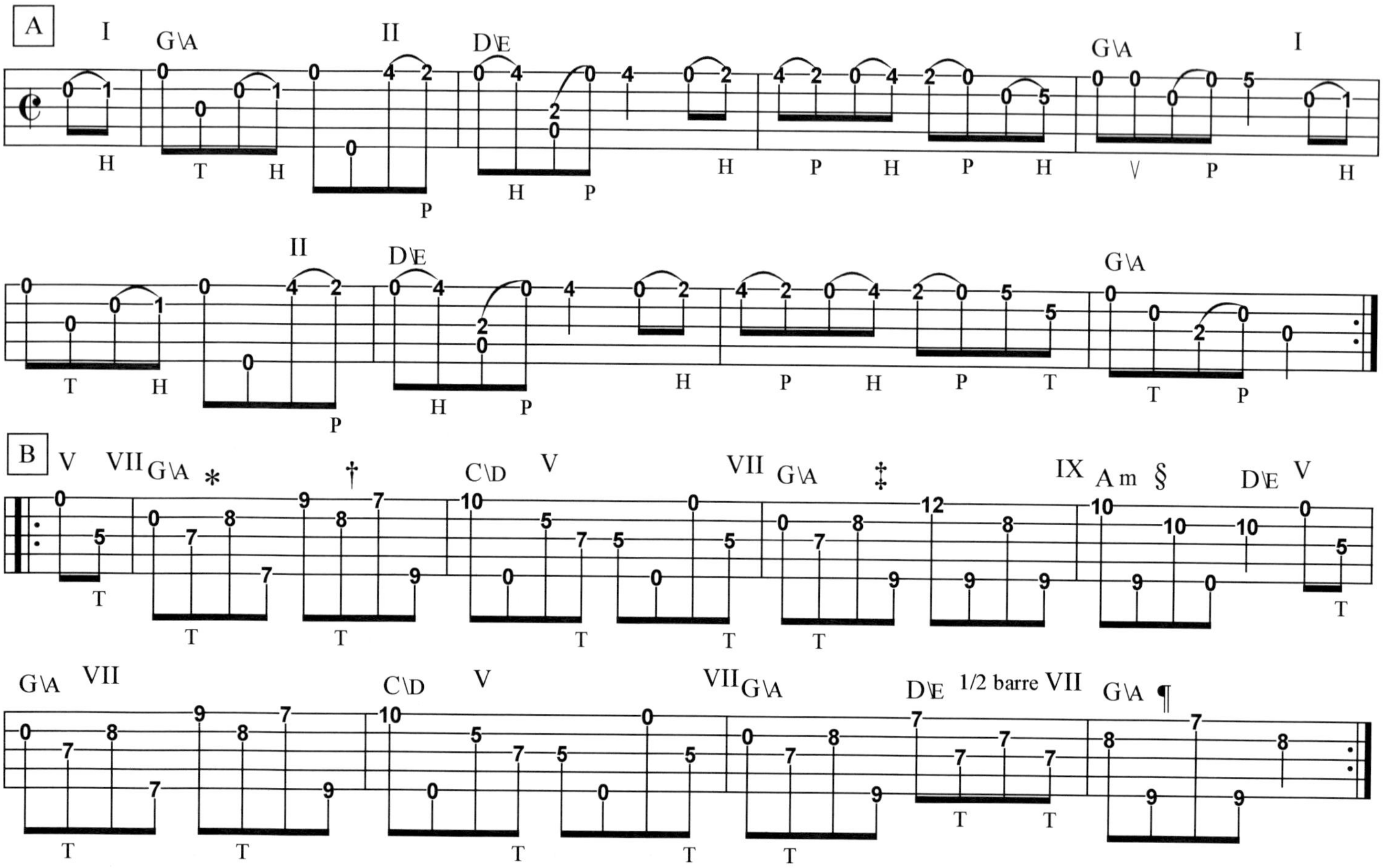

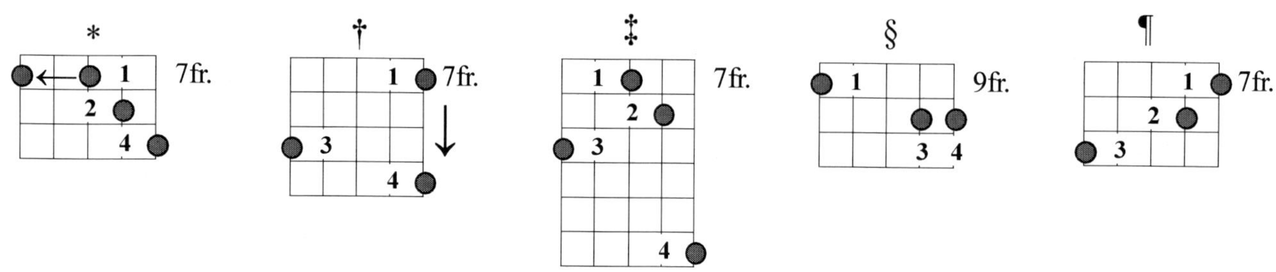

Playing Tips for "Carleton County Breakdown"

Dual Chord Symbols: Chord to left of backslash goes with open banjo; chord on right is for capoed banjo or fiddle.

• Part B, measures 1-2. On beat 4 of measure 1, pivot on the 2nd finger at fret 8, string 2 (Diagram *) and swing the 1st finger to fret 7, string 1. Then use it as a pivot to swing the 3rd and 4th fingers into position as shown in Diagram †.

• Part B, measure 3. At the end of beat 2, release the 1st finger (at fret 7, string 3) and balance on the 3rd finger at fret 9, string 5. Keeping that finger and the 2nd finger (at fret 8, string 2) firmly in place, reach up with the 4th finger to fret 12 (as shown in Diagram ‡). Be sure to release the 4th finger once you no longer need it.

Andy Renwick's Ferret

85

Composer: Gordon Duncan
Source: Paul MacDonald
Appears on: *Island Boy*

Key: A (G on Banjo)
Mode: Dorian Gamut
Tuning: gCGCD *or* gDGCD (Capo-2)

Gordon Duncan (1964-2005) was a noted Highland bagpiper who lived most of his life in Pitlochry, Scotland. He played in both traditional pipe bands and in such popular "folk" bands as Wolftone and the Tannahill Weavers; he was renowned both as a composer and for his innovative approach to the instrument. This tune is his best-known composition and is played by pipers world-wide (and by fiddlers in the Canadian Maritimes). I used a capoed C tuning on the recording because I needed the extra low note for the other tunes in the medley – "Captain Campbell" (p. 163) and "The Cape Breton Wedding Reel (p. 87). Since no notes fall on the fourth string in this setting, it will also work in G-modal tuning. Standard notation for my source version is in *Fiddle Music of P.E.I.*

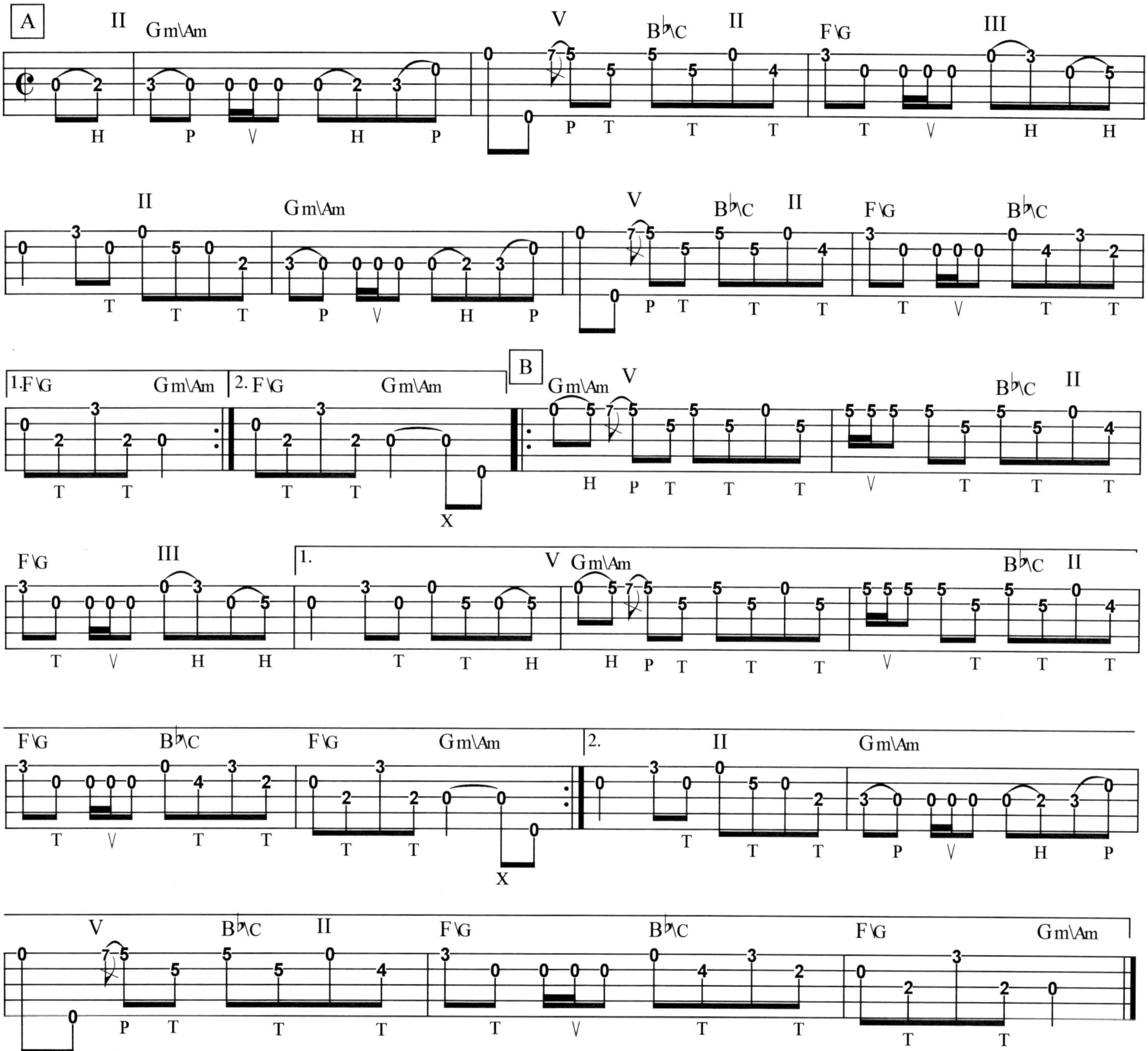

Playing Tips for *Andy Renwick's Ferret*

Dual Chord Symbols: Chord to left of backslash goes with open banjo; chord on right is for capoed banjo or fiddle

• Part A, measures 1, 3, 5, & 7; and several measures in Part B. This piece features ornaments known as "cuts" or birls – appearing as two sixteenth notes plus an eighth beamed together – obtained here by sandwiching an upstroke between two downstrokes (for more on this, see p. 20). Make sure these are fast and even so that you don't break stride.

86

The Prince Edward Island Wedding Reel

Origin: Probably Northeastern P.E.I.
Source: "Old Peter" Chaisson
Appears on: *Frails & Frolics*

Key: A (G on Banjo)
Mode: Major
Tuning: gDGBD (Capo-2)

This tune was once used to accompany a special dance at wedding celebrations in northeastern Kings County, P.E.I. A variant of an old dance called the *Scotch Reel*, it began with two couples standing at opposite ends of the floor – bride with best man and bridesmaid with groom. Over the course of the dance, and after much complicated stepping and maneuvering, bride is united with groom, and bridesmaid joins best man (see also "The Cape Breton Wedding Reel," p. 94). Be aware that I altered the octave range of all three parts. I had to move up Part A an octave for it to fit on banjo, and then moved Part B up an octave to maintain its original relationship with Part A. In the original tune, Part C moves up to a higher octave than Part B; this was impractical on banjo so I created contrast by moving it down an octave. The tune is circular, and I've provided final-sounding ending. Standard notation for my source version is in *Fiddle Music of P.E.I.*

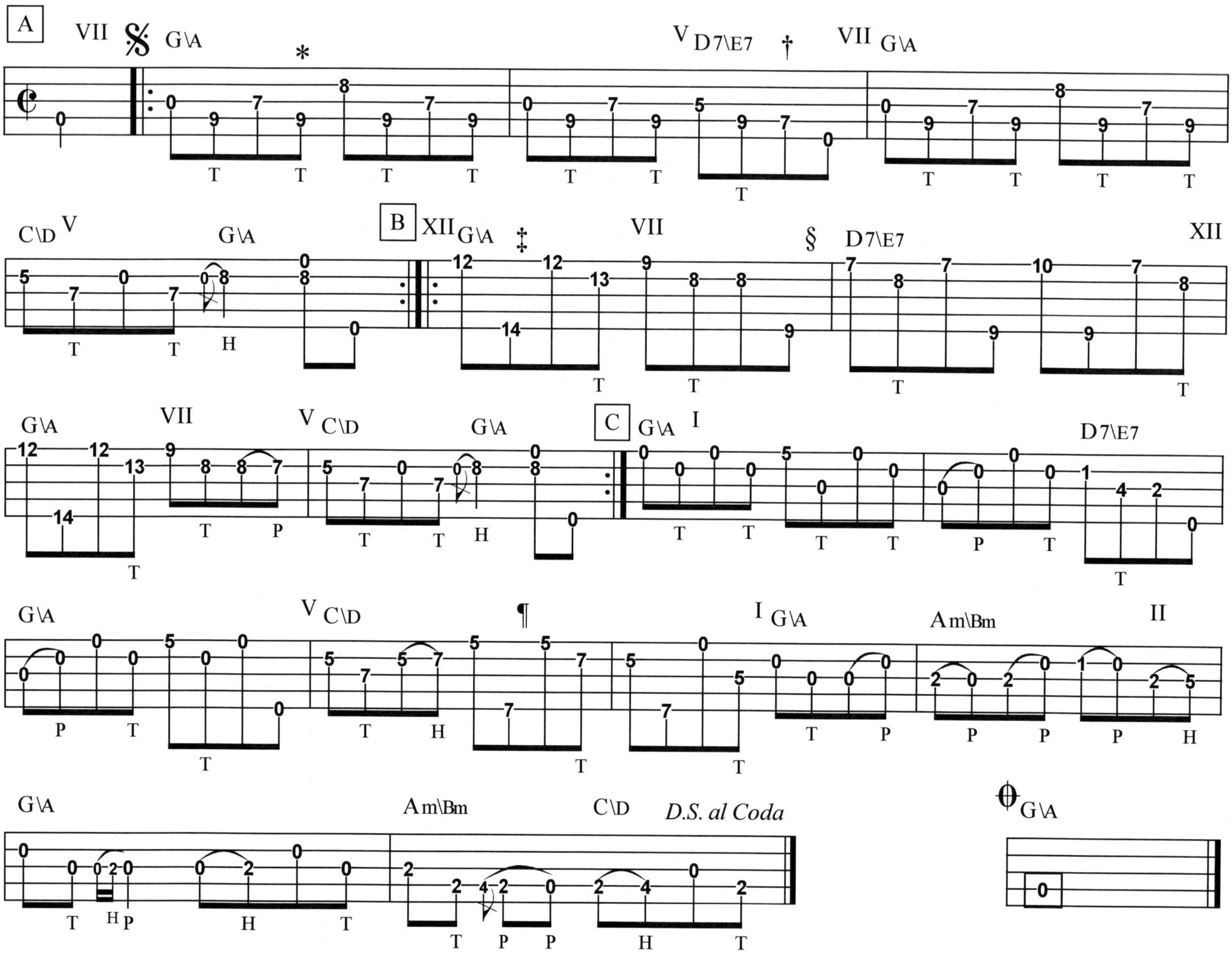

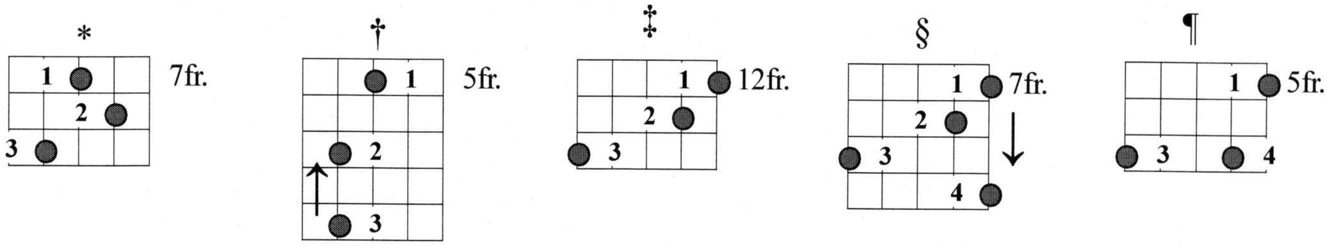

*For *P.E.I. Wedding Reel* Playing Tips See Facing Page*

DUAL CHORD SYMBOLS: Chord to left of backslash goes with open banjo; chord on right is for capoed banjo or fiddle

• Part A, measure 2. At the end of beat 2, balance with the 3rd finger at fret 9, string 4 and – keeping that note sounding – stretch with the 1st finger to fret 5, string 3 as shown in Diagram †.

• Part B, measure 1-2. At the end of beat 2 of measure 1, balance with the 2nd finger on fret 13, string 2. At the beginning of beat 3, glide down string 2 on that finger to fret 8, then use it as a pivot to swing the 4th finger into position on fret 9, string 1. The 3rd finger comes into play at the very end of measure 1; use it to pivot into the shape shown in Diagram §.

87

MacKinnon's Rant

ORIGIN: SCOTLAND
SOURCE: GEORGE MACPHEE
APPEARS ON: *FRAILS & FROLICS*

KEY: A (G ON BANJO)
MODE: SEE INTRO
TUNING: gDGCD (Capo-2)

This melody appears in William Christie's, *A Collection of Strathspeys, Reels, Hornpipes, Waltzes, &c.* (1820); it was recorded in 1937 as "MacKinnon's Rant" by Cape Breton fiddler Alick Gillis, and was printed under that name in *The Traditional Fiddle Music of Cape Breton* (1986). The mode is complex; Part A is diatonic with a variable 3rd and minor 7th (A-B-C/C♯-D-E-F♯-G-A on fiddle; G-A-B♭/B-C-D-E-F♮-G on open banjo). Part B, on the other hand, avoids both the 3rd and 7th tones, which implies Re-Pentatonic (A-B-D-E-G-A on fiddle; G-A-C-D-F♮-G on open banjo). Observe that this is a "short-format" reel, and Part B is *not* repeated. Standard notation for my source version is in *Fiddle Music of P.E.I.*

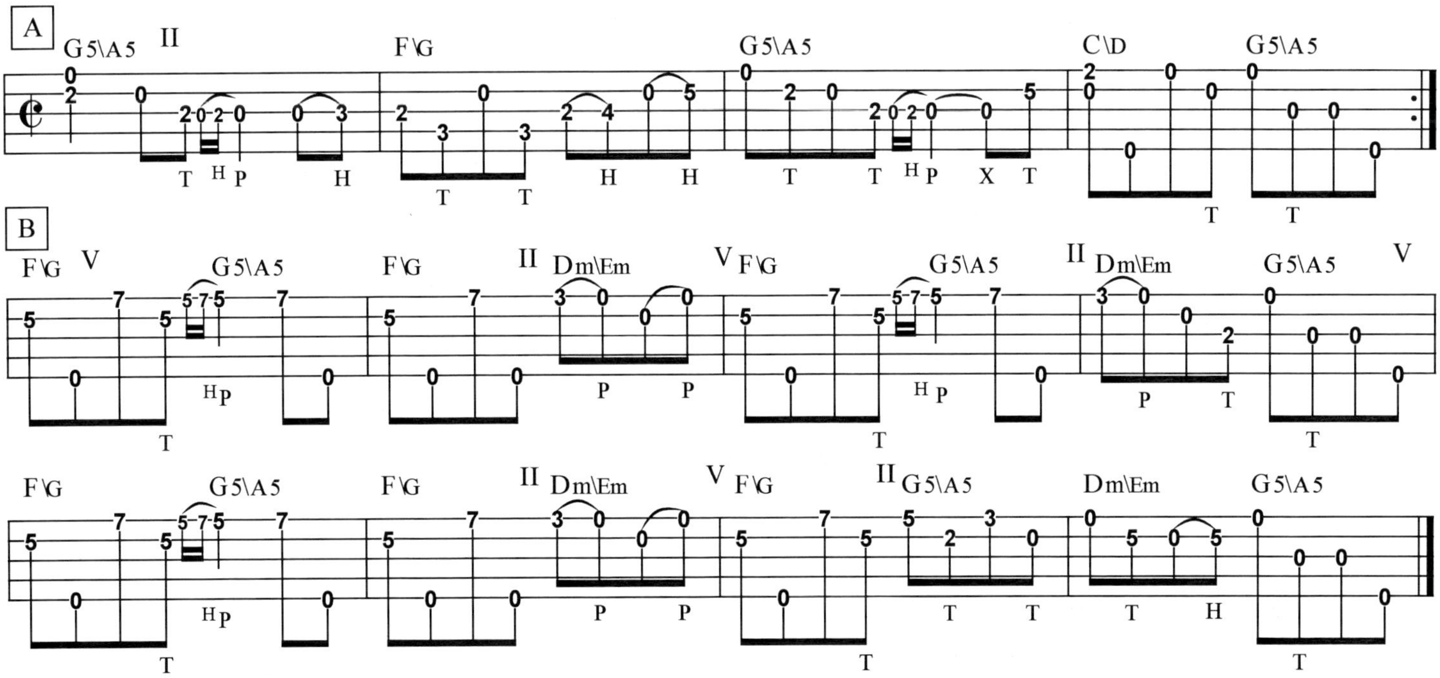

PLAYING TIPS FOR *MACKINNON'S RANT*

DUAL CHORD SYMBOLS: Chord to left of backslash goes with open banjo; chord on right is for capoed banjo or fiddle

• PART B, MEASURE 7. On beat 2, stop fret 7, string 1 and fret 5, string 2 with the 4th and 1st fingers, respectively. On beat 3, glide with both those fingers down to second position, while stretching them out far enough to catch fret 5, string 1 and fret 2, string 2. Then on beat 4, use the 2nd finger to stop fret 3, string 1.

88

Big John McNeil

Composer: Peter Milne
Source: Hector MacAndrew
Appears on: *Devil in the Kitchen; Northern Banjo*

Key: A (G on Banjo)
Mode: Major
Tuning: gDGBD (Capo-2)

Milne (1824-1908) was a mentor of the great fiddler-composer and performer, James Scott Skinner. The tune was first published as simply, "John McNeil" in *Middleton's Selection of Strathspeys, Reels, Etc. [. . .]* (1870); Skinner later included it in *Harp & Claymore.* The "*Big* John" moniker may be traceable to a 1942 recording by Don Messer & His Islanders. The tune is one of the most widely played tunes on Prince Edward Island, and is particularly popular in the western half of the Island where it is highly favored for accompanying step dancers. The tune is notable for having quite a large range, and I had to raise it up an octave to make it fit on banjo. The second ending of Part B is circular; a final-sounding tag ending is included. Standard notation for my source version is in *Fiddle Music of P.E.I.*

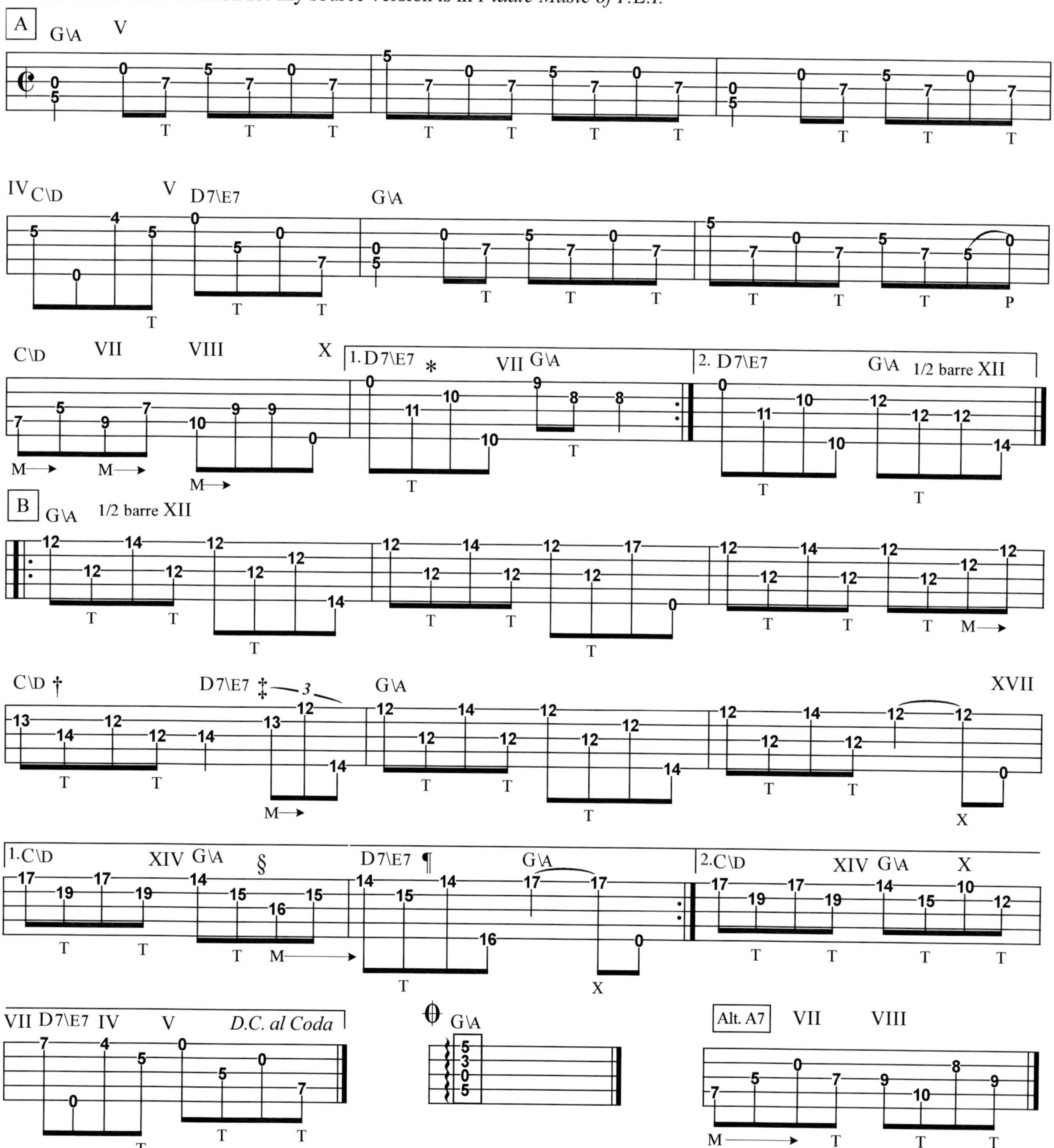

*For *Big John McNeil* Fingering Diagrams & Playing Tips See Facing Page*

Fingering Diagrams for *Big John McNeil*

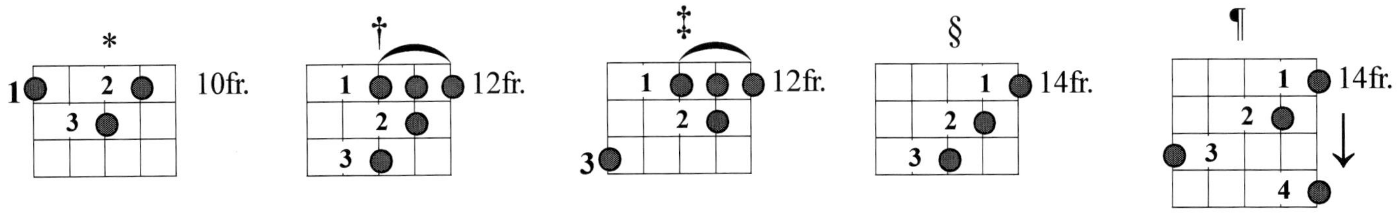

Playing Tips for *Big John McNeil*

Dual Chord Symbols: Chord to left of backslash goes with open banjo; chord on right is for capoed banjo or fiddle

• Part A, measure 8 (both endings). At the end of beat 2 you should be in the fingering configuration suggested by Diagram *. In the first ending, cut short fret 10, string 5 (1st finger) and with the 2nd finger glide down string 2 to fret 8; then use that finger as a pivot to bring the 4th finger into contact with fret 9, string 1. In the second ending, cut short fret 10, string 5 (1st finger again), and scoot up the neck with that finger to grab a 1/2-barre at fret 12. This then puts you in position to play the first phrase of Part B.

• Part B, measure 8 (second ending). The trick here is to glide down the neck with the 1st finger in succession from fret 17 to frets 14, 10, 7, and 4. Each time you establish a new position with the 1st finger, use it as a pivot to bring either the 2nd or 3rd finger into contact with the second string, as applicable.

Playing Tips for *Trip to Windsor* (tab on p. 98)

Dual Chord Symbols: Chord to left of backslash goes with open banjo; chord on right is for capoed banjo or fiddle

• Part B, measure 6. At the end of beat 3, balance on both the 2nd and 3rd fingers at fret 8, string 2 and fret 9, string 5 as shown in Diagram †. Then on beat 4, glide with both fingers up their respective strings to frets 15 and 16 (you'll need to compress the distance between the two fingers a little to reflect shortened fret lengths). Then use the 3rd finger on fret 16 as a pivot to assume the shape shown in Diagram ‡.

• Part B, measure 8 (both endings). At the end of beat 1, balance with the 3rd finger on fret 16, string 3. At the start of beat 2, cut that note short and glide down to fret 14, reaching out with the 1st finger to stop fret 12, string 5.

Playing Tips for *Marquis of Huntly* (tab on p. 99)

Dual Chord Symbols: Chord to left of backslash goes with open banjo; chord on right is for capoed banjo or fiddle

• Part A, measure 4. At the end of beat 1, balance on the 3rd finger at fret 14, string 5 and reach over with the 1st finger to establish a ½-barre on strings 1 and 2 at fret 12, as shown in Diagram ‡. At the end of beat 2, cut the ½-barre short and reach up with the 2nd and 3rd fingers to stop fret 14 and 15 on strings 1 and 2, respectively (as shown in Diagram §). Then on beat 4, balance on the 3rd finger and use it as a pivot to swing the 1st and 4th fingers in place on strings 2 and 3, respectively, as also shown in Diagram §.

• Part A, measure 5. At the end of beat 1, balance on the 2nd finger at fret 14, string 5 and reach up with the 4th finger to grab fret 17, string 1 as shown in Diagram ¶. Hold onto that finger and – halfway through the beat reach across with the 3rd finger to catch fret 16, string 5.

89

Trip to Windsor

Composer: Dan R. MacDonald
Source: Francis MacDonald
Appears on: *Frails & Frolics*

Key: A (G on Banjo)
Mode: Major
Tuning: gDGBD (Capo-2)

Windsor, Ontario – right across the border from Detroit and home to a thriving automobile industry – attracted a substantial population of Cape Breton emigrées. Fiddlers from the home Island were often brought down to play for dances and concerts. Well-known bluegrass fiddler Joe Greene once recorded a suspiciously similar tune entitled "Road to Jenkins." I had to raise the B Part up an octave for it to fit on banjo. I've also included the fancy tag ending I recorded on *Frails & Frolics.* Standard notation for my source version is in *Fiddle Music of P.E.I.*

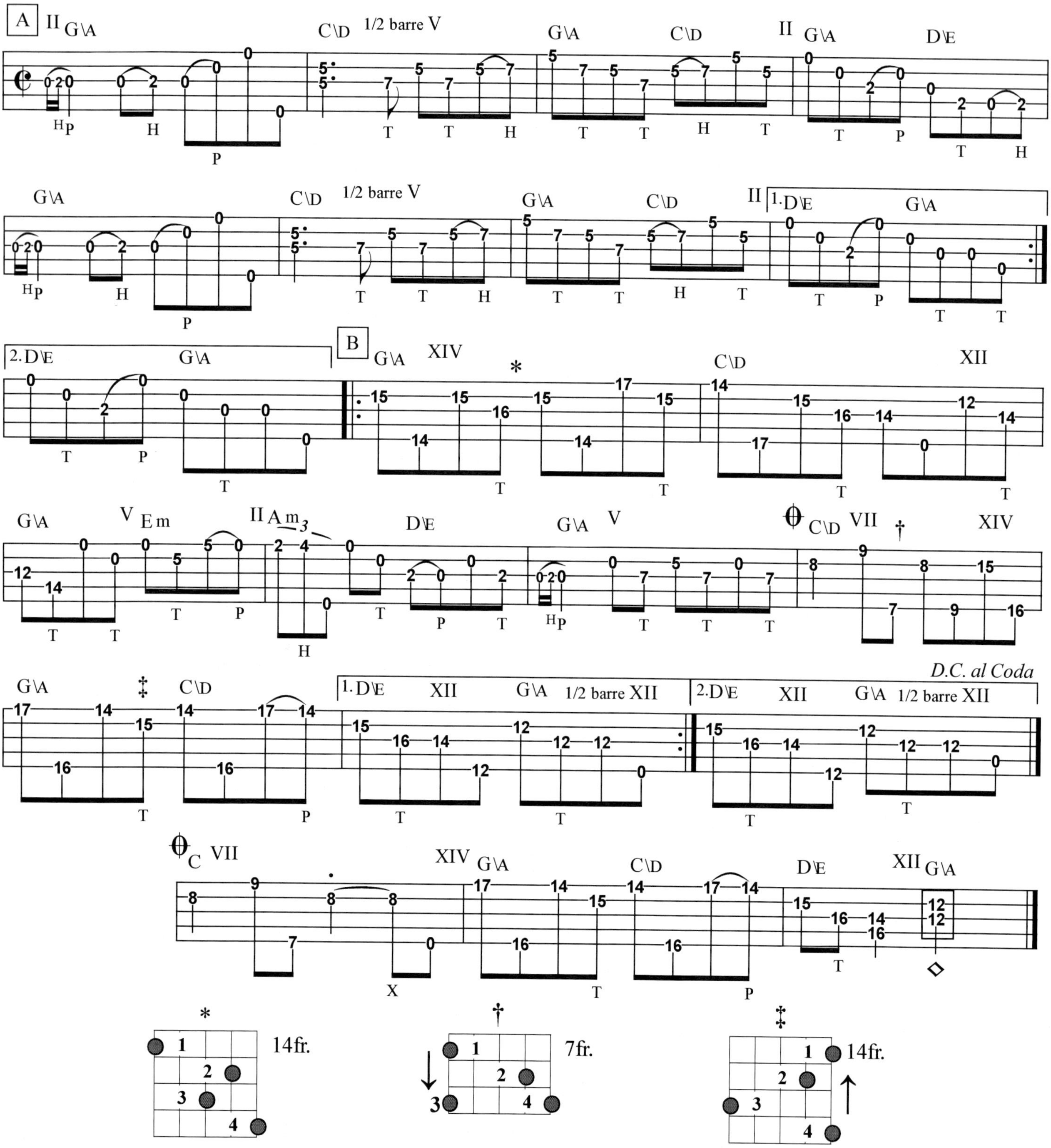

*For *Trip to Windsor* Playing Tips, See Page 97*

90

The Marquis of Huntly

Composer: Peter Milne (1824-1908)
Source: "Old Peter" Chaisson
Appears on: *Frails & Frolics*

Key: A (G on Banjo)
Mode: Major
Tuning: gDGBD (Capo-2)

The aristocratic Gordon family of Huntly were major patrons of Scottish fiddling (a "Marquis" – pronounced *MAR-kwiss* – ranks between Earl and Duke on the scale of British nobility). Composer Milne, a mentor of James Scott Skinner, originally published this tune in *Middleton's Selection of Strathspeys, Reels, Etc.* (1870), a work for which he served as an editor. Buddy MacMaster recorded it in the 1980s on his debut LP, *Judique on the Floor.* I had to raise Part A up an octave to fit it on banjo. Standard notation for my source version is in *Fiddle Music of P.E.I.*

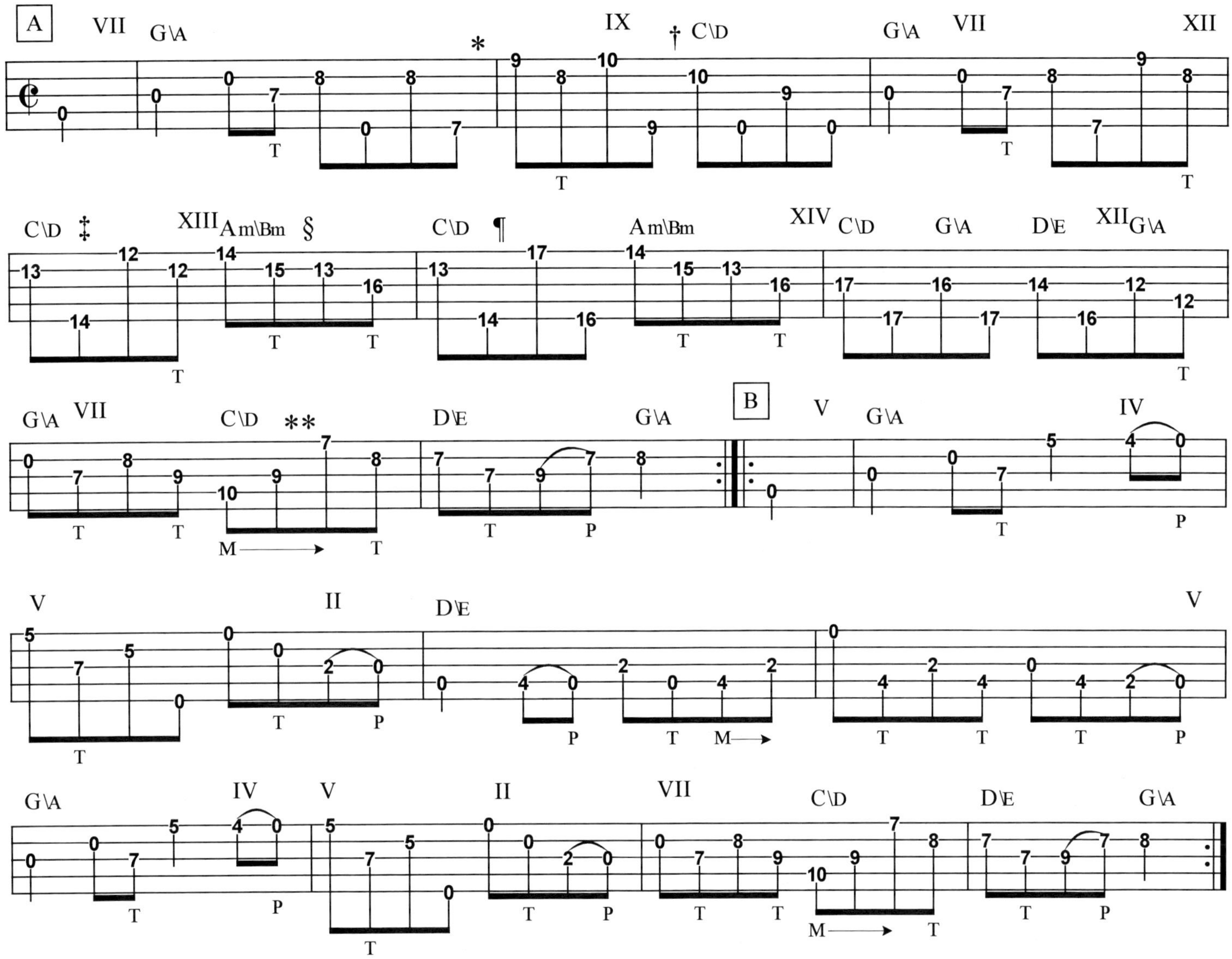

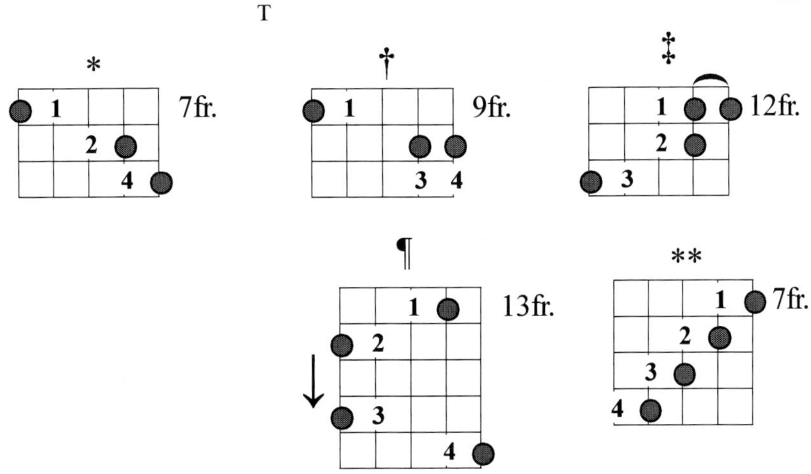

*For *Marquis of Huntly* Playing Tips, See Page 97*

91

Miller's Reel

Composer: Zeke Backus
Sources: Various
Appears on: *Frails & Frolics*

Key: A (G on Banjo)
Mode: Major
Tuning: gDGBD (Capo-2)

"Miller's Reel" is very widely played throughout North America and is closely related to the Irish reel, "The Dawn." It dates back at least to the third quarter of the 19th century, appearing in *Coe's Album of Jigs & Reels* (1876) and *Ryan's Mammoth Collection* – both of which cite as composer Zeke Backus, a member of the prominent mid-19th century troupe, Christy's Minstrels. Don Messer often played this tune on his radio and television programs, but under the title, "Dusty Miller's Reel." I had to raise the A Part up an octave for it to fit on banjo.

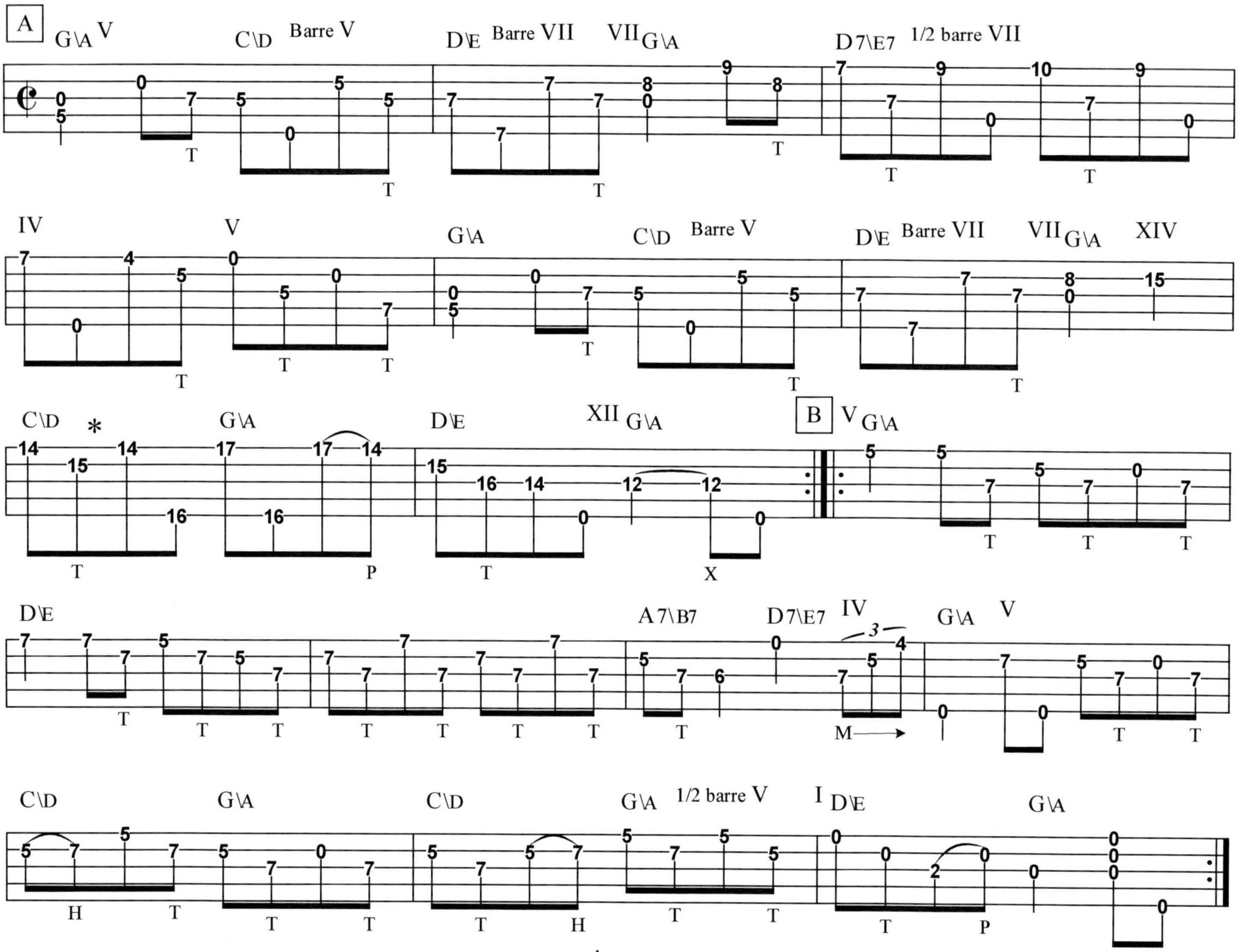

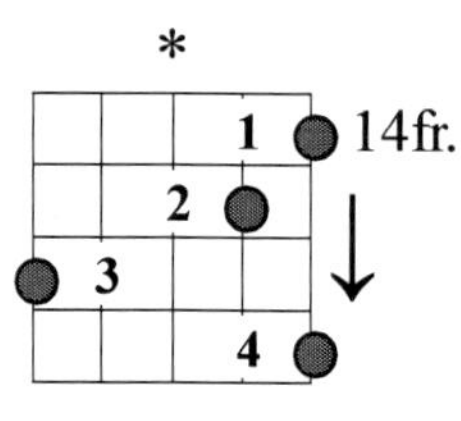

Playing Tips for *Miller's Reel*

Dual Chord Symbols: Chord to left of backslash goes with open banjo; chord on right is for capoed banjo or fiddle

• Part A, measures 6-8. The key here is the 2nd finger. At the end of beat 3 of measure 6, balance on the 2nd finger at fret 8, string 2. On beat 4, glide with that finger all the way up string 2 to fret 15. At the start of measure 7, use the 2nd finger to pivot the 1st and 3rd fingers into position on fret 14, string 1 and fret 16, string 5 as shown in Diagram *. Keep the 2nd finger in place throughout measure 7, so that you can use it again on fret 15 at the start of measure 8.

• Part B, measure 3. On beat 1, stop fret 7 on strings 3 and 2 with the 3rd and 4th fingers, respectively. On beat 2, obtain fret 7, string 1 by collapsing the outer side of your fretting hand and in effect making a ½-barre with the 4th finger.

Chapter 8. *Reels – & Hornpipes – in C, F, & B♭*

THE KEY OF C HAS A RICH TONALITY ON BOTH FIDDLE AND BANJO; it could be said that C is the 5-string banjo's native key: the one where the instrument sounds most resonant and where pitches fall most conveniently. Key-of-C fiddle tunes tend to have a fairly wide range; they often start low and not infrequently rise up to catch the high-C note on the first string of both fiddle and banjo, which is a little higher than normal fiddle-tune range. Tunes in C tend to be a little harder to play on fiddle than those in other common keys.

Playing in the keys of F and B♭ on fiddle – known on Cape Breton and P.E.I. as *playing on the flats* – could present a daunting prospect, but fiddlers in the Maritimes have developed some ingenious fingering shortcuts. For key-of-F tunes they tend to keep the first finger planted firmly on the F-note of fiddle-string 1; for key-of-B♭ tunes they keep that finger planted as a "half-barre" on fiddle-strings 1 & 2 at F and B♭, respectively. The other fingers are then pivoted into place on the various strings as needed – a strategy that is practical because many tunes in these keys have a relatively limited range.

On banjo, I find that most key of F tunes are convenient to play via double-C (gCGCD), a tuning that also brings out the sweet but insistent character of tunes in that key. Alternatively, some F tunes seem to work better and sound better in G modal tuning (gDGCD). For the key of B♭, I find that G modal tuning is usually the best bet.

Most "modal" tunes that you'll encounter in C, F, and B♭ are diatonic with major 3rd and variable 7th tones. For more on modal variation, see Chapter 3.

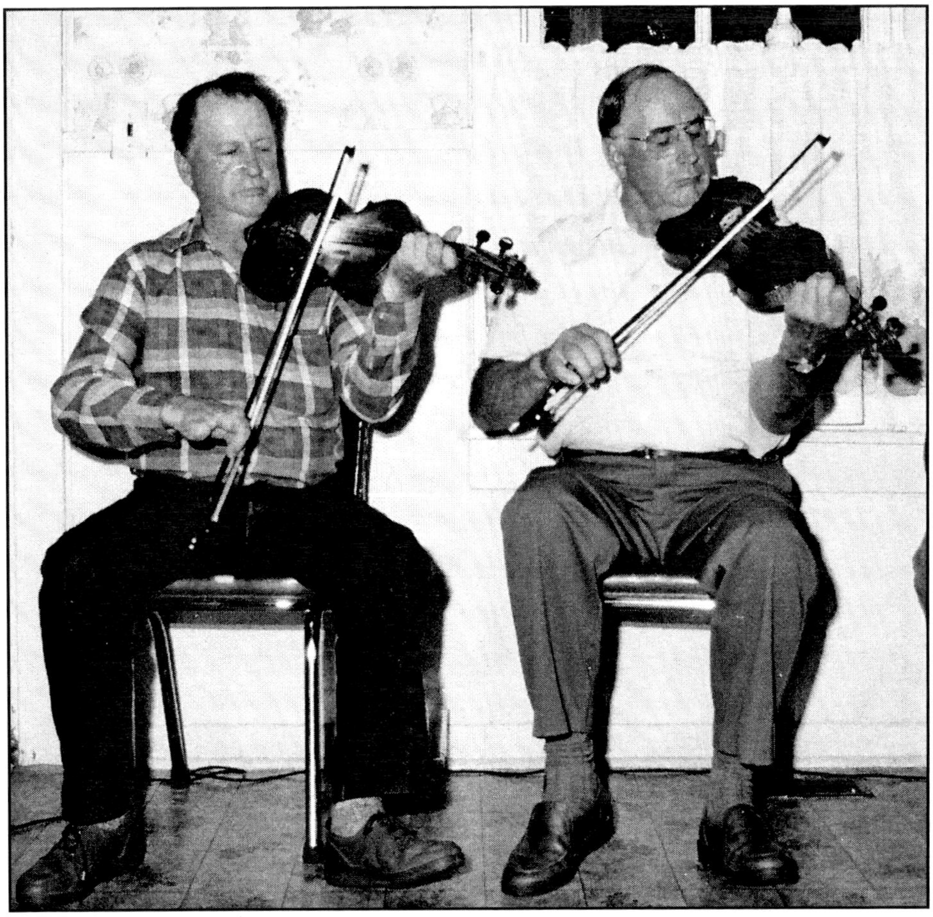

Carl & Jackie Webster at Project Headquarters: Monticello, P.E.I. (1992).
Photo by Earthwatch Team; courtesy Robertson Library, University of P.E.I.

92

The Haggis

ORIGIN SCOTLAND
SOURCE: HECTOR MACANDREW
APPEARS ON: *DEVIL IN THE KITCHEN*

KEY: C
MODE: MAJOR 3RD & VARIABLE 7TH
TUNING: gCGCD

This 18th-century reel is named for a traditional Scottish dish consisting of oatmeal & giblets cooked and served in a sheep's stomach; the dish's globular appearance on the plate is associated by some with the bag of a bagpipes. And indeed, in Fraser's *Airs & Melodies Peculiar to the Highlands* (1815), the tune is described as a pipe reel. "The Haggis" also appears in *Lowe's Collection, Kerr's Merry Melodies,* and *The Skye Collection.* It was recorded by several Cape Breton fiddlers in the 1940s and 50s, including John A. MacDonald (1893-1974), Donald MacLellan (1918-2003), and Winston "Scotty" Fitzgerald. A version by Aberdeen-area fiddler Hector MacAndrew originally caught my fancy, but the setting here was also influenced by the playing of two fiddlers from northeastern Kings County, P.E.I. – George MacPhee and "Young Peter" Chaisson. The tune is circular, concluding on the modal-dominant chord, B♭; and I've included a final-sounding tag ending.

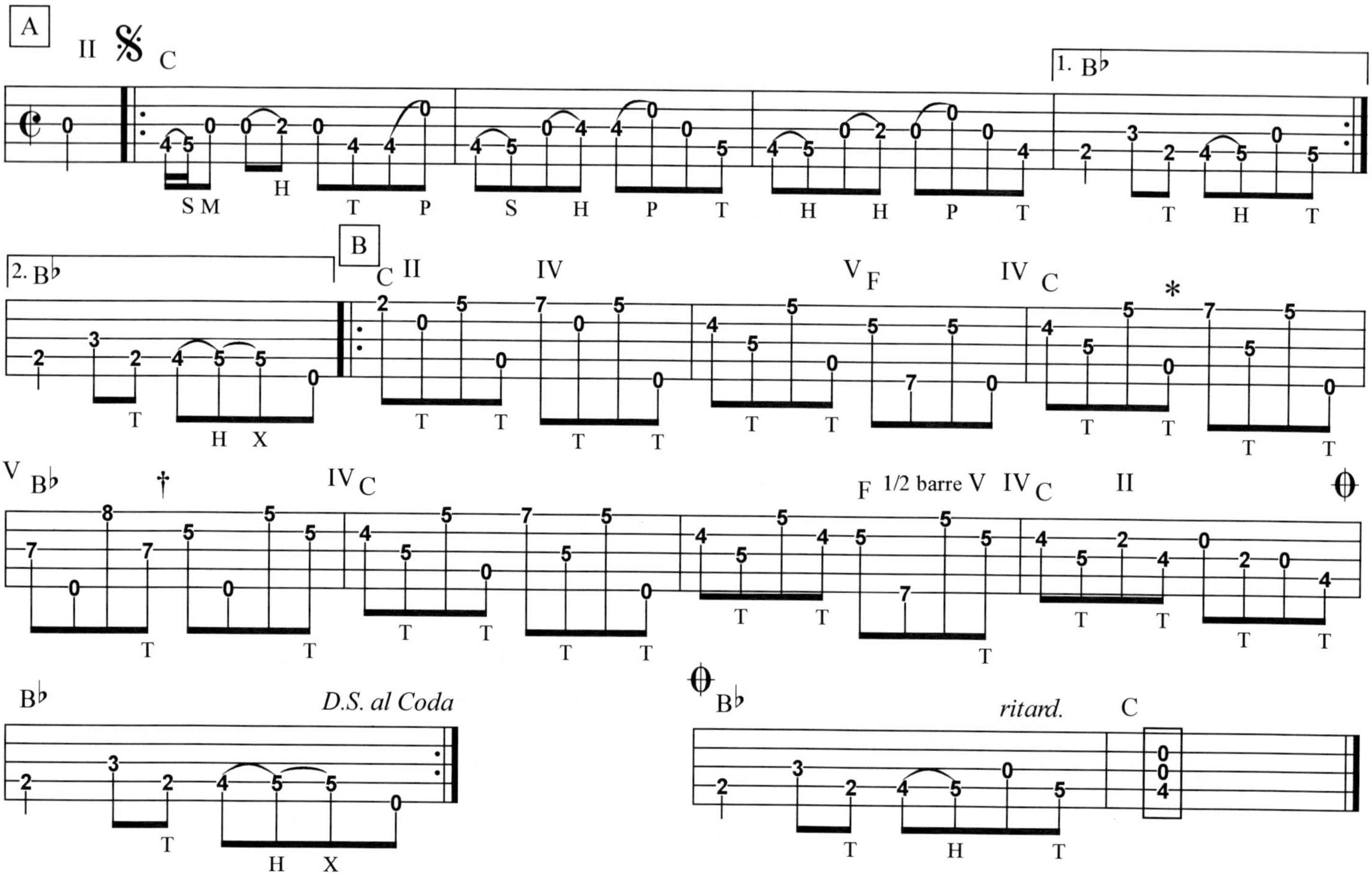

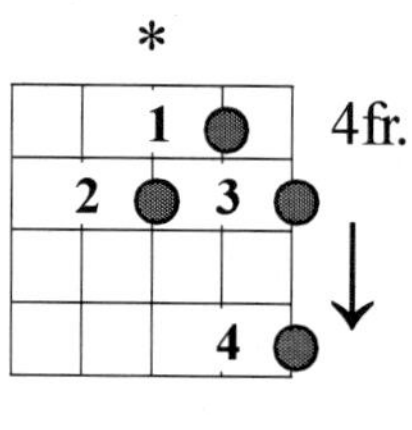

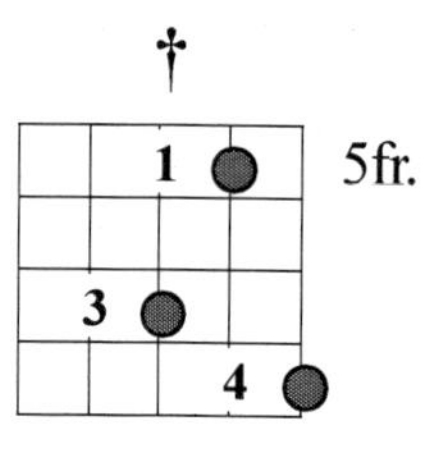

PLAYING TIPS FOR *THE HAGGIS*

- PART A, MEASURE 1. The measure starts on a sixteenth-note slide; the count for the first two beats is: 1-a-&-(a)-2-&. . .
- PART B, MEASURE 1. The double-thumbing in this passage is meant to emulate the sound of a rocking bow. To get the right sound, try to slightly exaggerate your range of motion as you alternate downstrokes and thumb-strokes.

93

The Bonny Lass of Fisherrow

Composer: Daniel Dow (1732-83)
Source: Carl & Jackie Webster
Appears on: *Island Boy*

Key: C
Mode: Major
Tuning: gCGCD

Fisherrow is located on the south bank of the Firth of Forth, roughly ten miles due east of Edinburgh. Dow first published the tune himself in the 1770s; it was later re-published in *The Gow Collection* and several important 19th-century Scottish works, including *Lowe's Collection, Kerr's Merry Melodies,* and *The Athole Collection.* A well-known variant in the key of D called "Bonnie Kate" was popularized via a 1934 recording by iconic Irish fiddler Michael Coleman (1891-1945). Standard notation for my source version is in *Fiddle Music of P.E.I.*

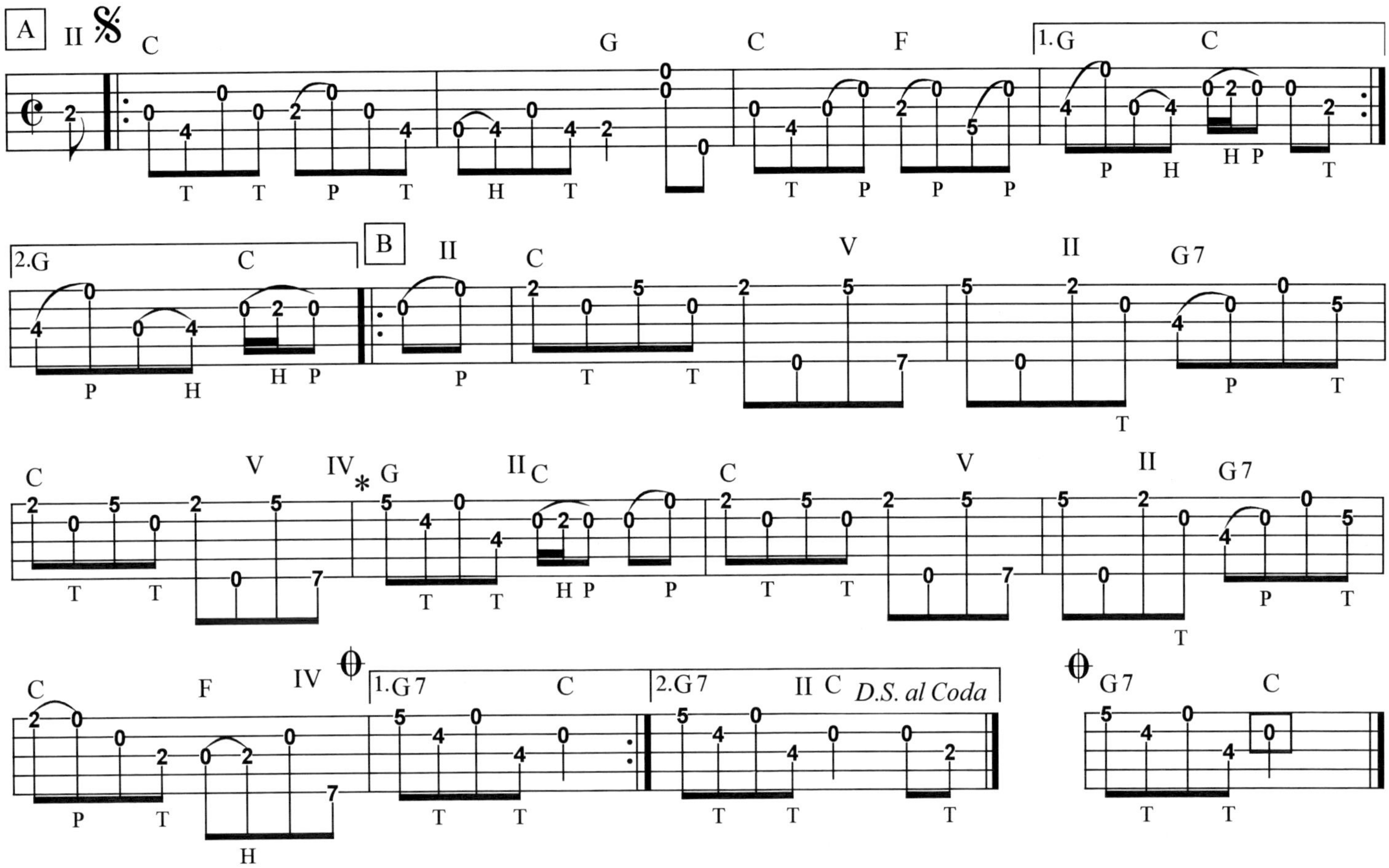

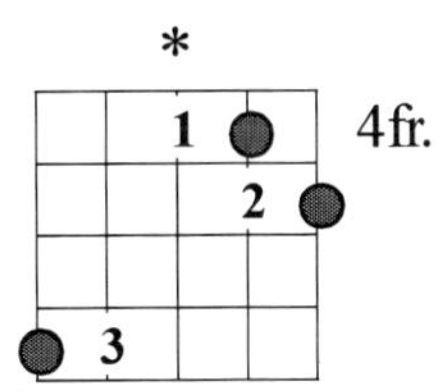

Playing Tips for *The Bonny Lass of Fisherrow*

- Part B, measure 3-4. On beat 4 of measure 3, use the 1st finger to stop fret 5, string 1 and the 3rd finger to stop fret 7, string 5. At the start of measure 4, leave the 3rd finger in place as you stretch up with the 1st and 2nd fingers to press down fret 4, string 2 and fret 5, string 1, respectively as shown in Diagram *. Once the 1st and 2nd fingers are in place, release the 3rd finger.

94

Souris Breakwater

Origin: See Intro
Source: Carl & Jackie Webster
Appears on: *Frails & Frolics*

Key: C
Mode: Major-Like but No 7th Tone
Tuning: gCGCD

I got this truly lively tune from Carl & Jackie Webster of Cardigan in Kings County P.E.I., but I have also heard it played on Cape Breton. The title refers to Souris (pronounced SOO-ree), the largest town in northeastern Kings County. I was convinced that the tune was local or regional, but as I was preparing this book I was alerted to a recording by fiddler Marcus Martin of Macon County, North Carolina (1881-1974) – clearly a very close variant of this melody – that he called "Kiss Me Sweet." This presents a bit of a mystery, but the most likely explanation is that this a very old tune that once spread widely in North America but only survived in a few isolated locales. Standard notation for my source version is available on *bowingdownhome.ca.*

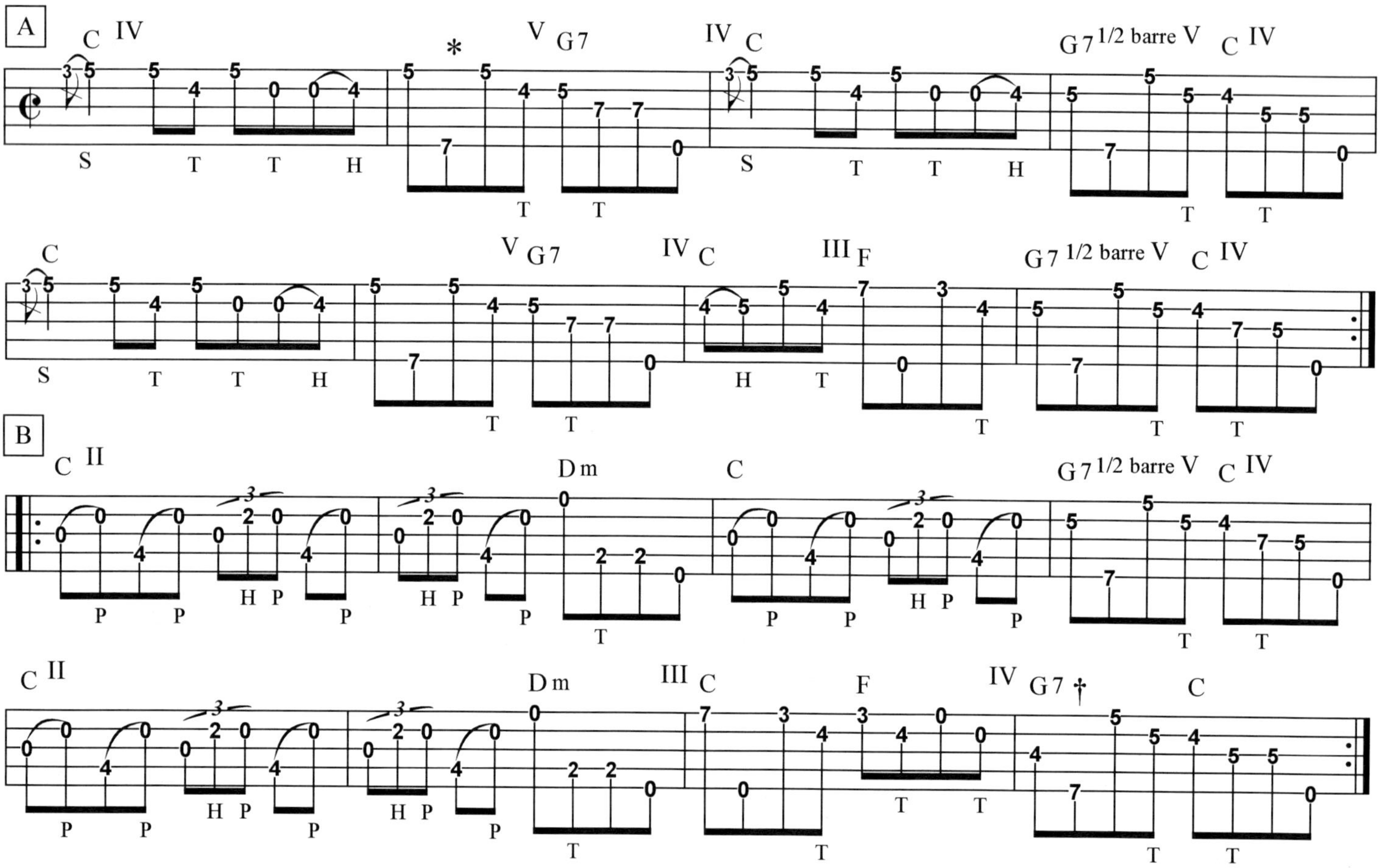

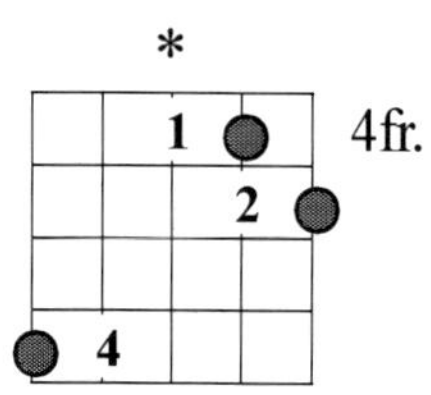

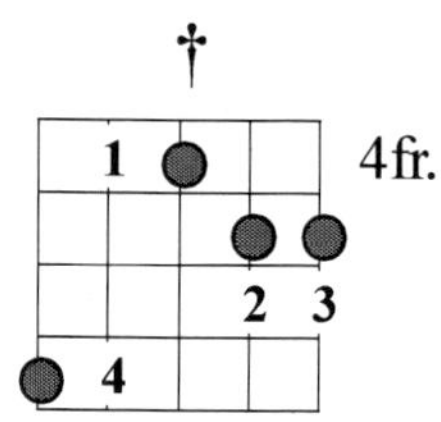

Playing Tips for *Souris Breakwater*

• Part A, measures 7-8. At the end of measure 7, balance with the 2nd finger on fret 4, string 2 and cut the note short. At the start of measure 8, sneak in the 1st finger, glide it up to fret 5, and flatten it into a ½-barre; then pivot the 3rd finger over to fret 7, string 5. On beat 3, unflatten the ½-barre and with the 1st finger glide back down string 2 to fret 4. Finally, use that finger as a pivot to swing the 4th finger into place on fret 7, string 3.

• Part B, measure 8. At the start of the measure, use the 1st and 4th fingers to stop fret 4, string 3 and fret 7, string 5 respectively as shown in Diagram †. On beat 2 , balance on the 4th finger and swing your 2nd and 3rd fingers over to catch fret 5, string 2 and fret 5, string 1, respectively.

95

Jack Webster's Reel

Origin: Local Variant of Scottish Tune
Source: Jack Webster
Appears on: *Frails & Frolics*

Key: C
Mode: Major
Tuning: gCGCD

I found this tune on a home-made tape recording of fiddler Jack Webster, the most prominent dance fiddler of southeastern Kings County, P.E.I. from the 1930s to the 70s (there was no local name for the tune, so it seemed only fitting to name it for him). The melody seems to be a local variant of the 18th-century strathspey, "Rothiemurchus Rant" (p. 167); it is also related to the Irish reel, "Graf Spee," named for a German battleship of the 1930s. The tune is circular, and I've suggested an ending that resolves to the tonic chord. Standard notation for my source version appears on *bowingdownhome.ca.*

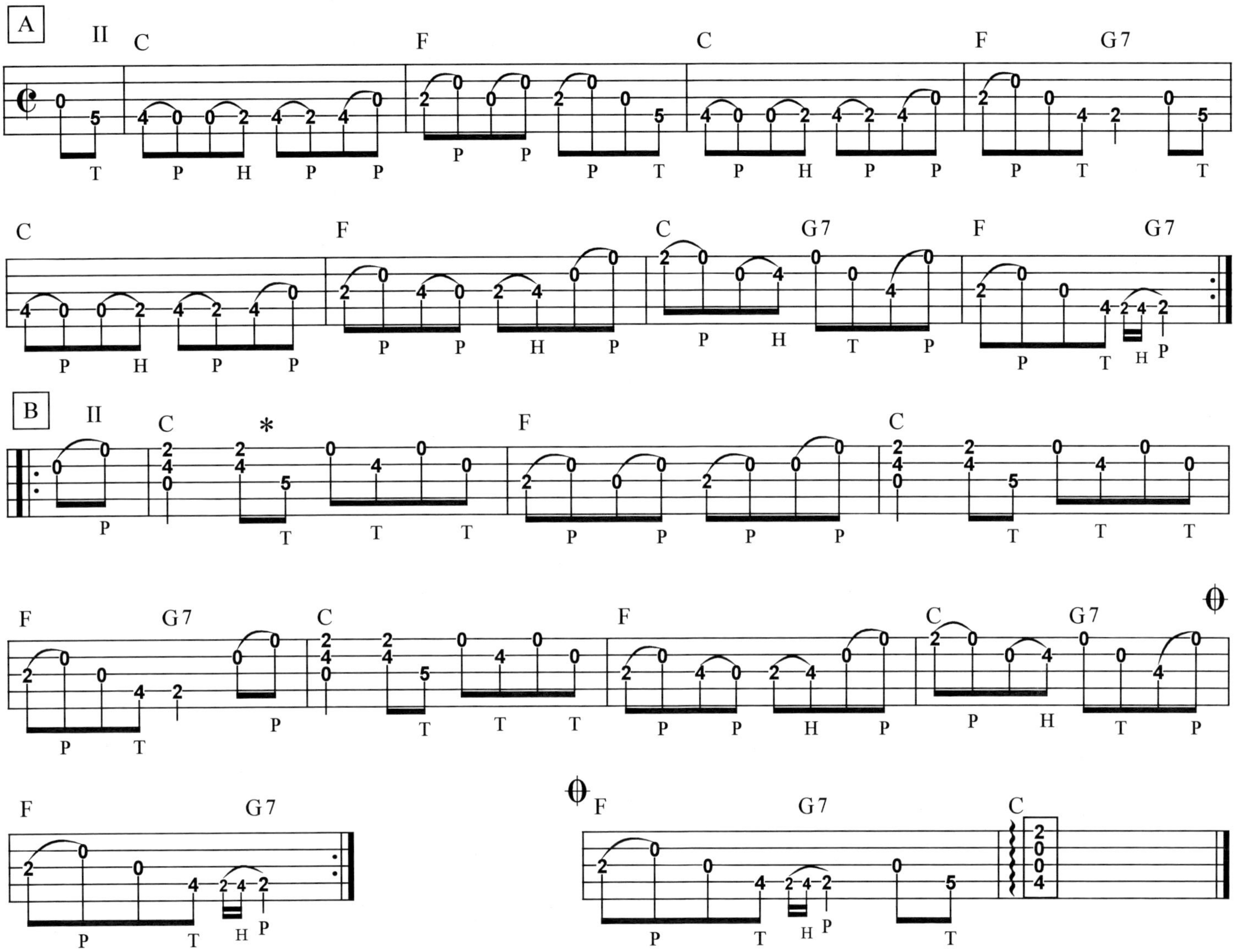

*

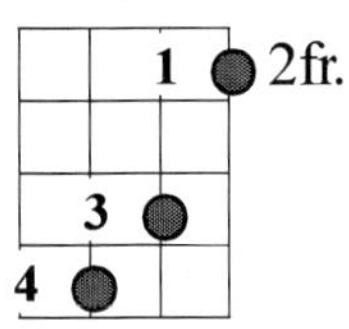

Playing Tips for *Jack Webster's Reel*

- Part A, measure 2. Use the 2nd finger on string 2 for all three alternate-string P's; that frees up either the 3rd or 4th finger to press down fret 5, string 4 midway through beat 4.

96

The Democratic Rage

Origin: Probably New England
Source: Carl & Jackie Webster
Appears on: *Northern Banjo*

Key: B♭
Mode: Major
Tuning: gDGCD

This hornpipe appears in *Ryan's Mammoth Collection* and is probably associated with the New England contradance of the same name created in the aftermath of the American Revolution. It appears as "One of the Boys" in *O'Neill's Music of Ireland* and as "Leddy's Hornpipe" in Cristeson's *Old-Time Fiddlers' Repertory* (1971). Standard notation for my source version is in *Fiddle Music of P.E.I.*

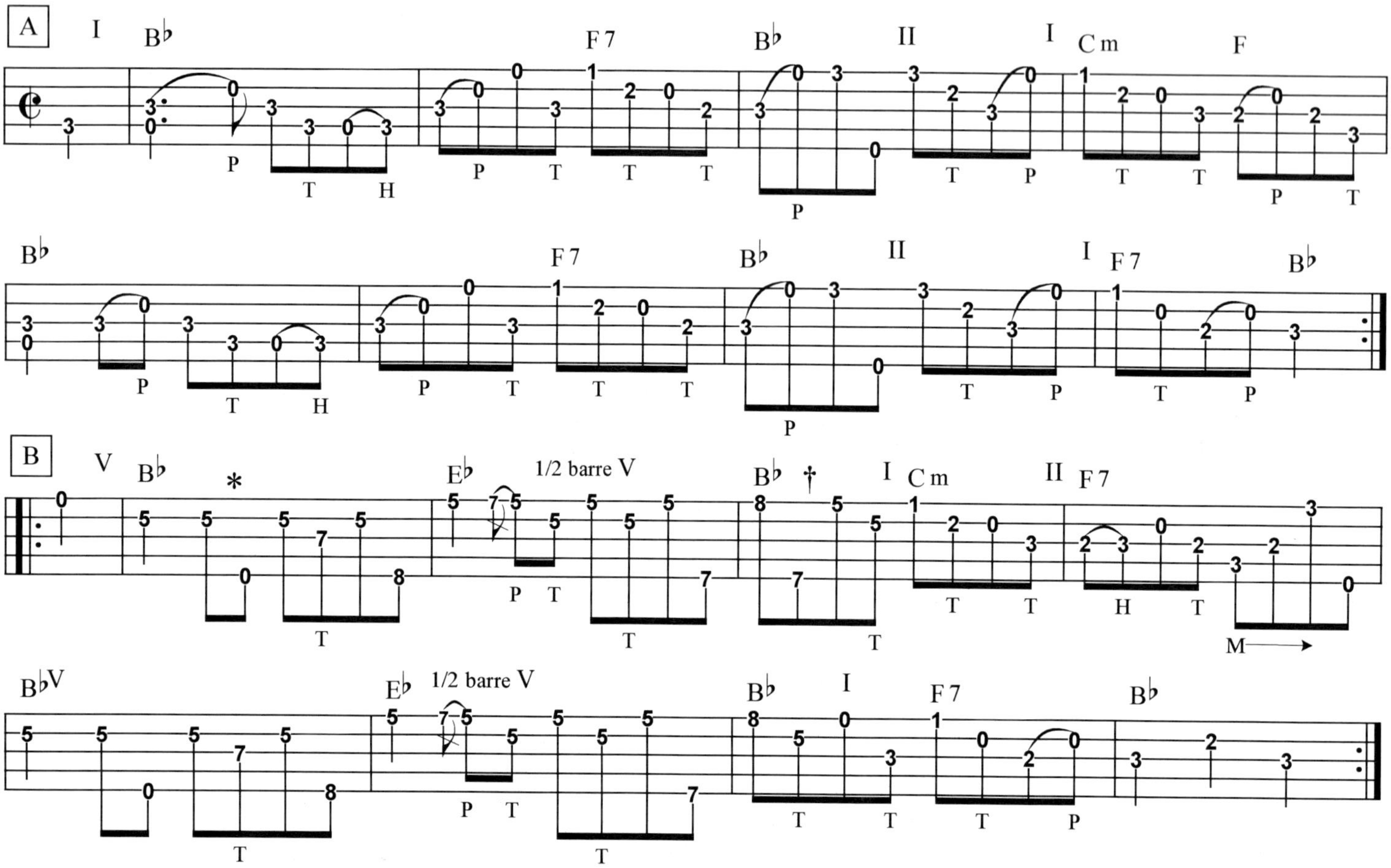

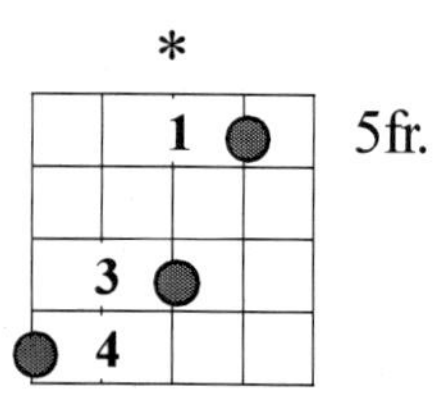

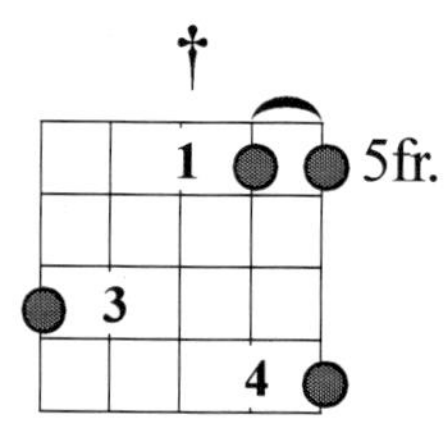

Playing Tips for *The Democratic Rage*

• Part A, measure 1. At the start of the measure, use the 3rd finger to press down fret 3, string 3 and hold it. Use the 1st finger for the alternate-string P; then on beat 3, use the 2nd finger to stop fret 3, string 4.

• Part B, measure 3. At the end of beat 2, balance with the 1st finger on fret 5, string 2 (Diagram †). Cut that note short, then scoot down with the 1st and 2nd fingers to grab fret 1, string 1 and fret 2, string 2 respectively.

• Part B, measure 4. For this three-string arpeggio, observe that you need to skip a string at the start of beat 4. It takes a little extra concentration here to not let the beat falter.

97

Miss Barker's Hornpipe

Origin: Scotland or Ireland
Source: Paul MacDonald
Appears on: *Frails & Frolics*

Key: C
Mode: Variable 7th Tone
Tuning: gCGCD

"Miss Barker" appears in *Ryan's Mammoth Collection*; it can also be traced to earlier books and manuscripts under such titles as "Miss Baker's Hornpipe," "Paddy Miles' Hornpipe," and "Admiral Nelson." The tune was re-popularized in the 1980s via a recording by Cape Breton fiddler Jerry Holland. Holland "improved" the tune by changing one note; in Part A, measure 2 he moved the original E♮ (fret 4, string 4) down to E♭ (fret 3, string 4), thereby transforming a fairly pedestrian major tune into an intriguing modal one. Standard notation for my source version is in *Fiddle Music of P.E.I.*

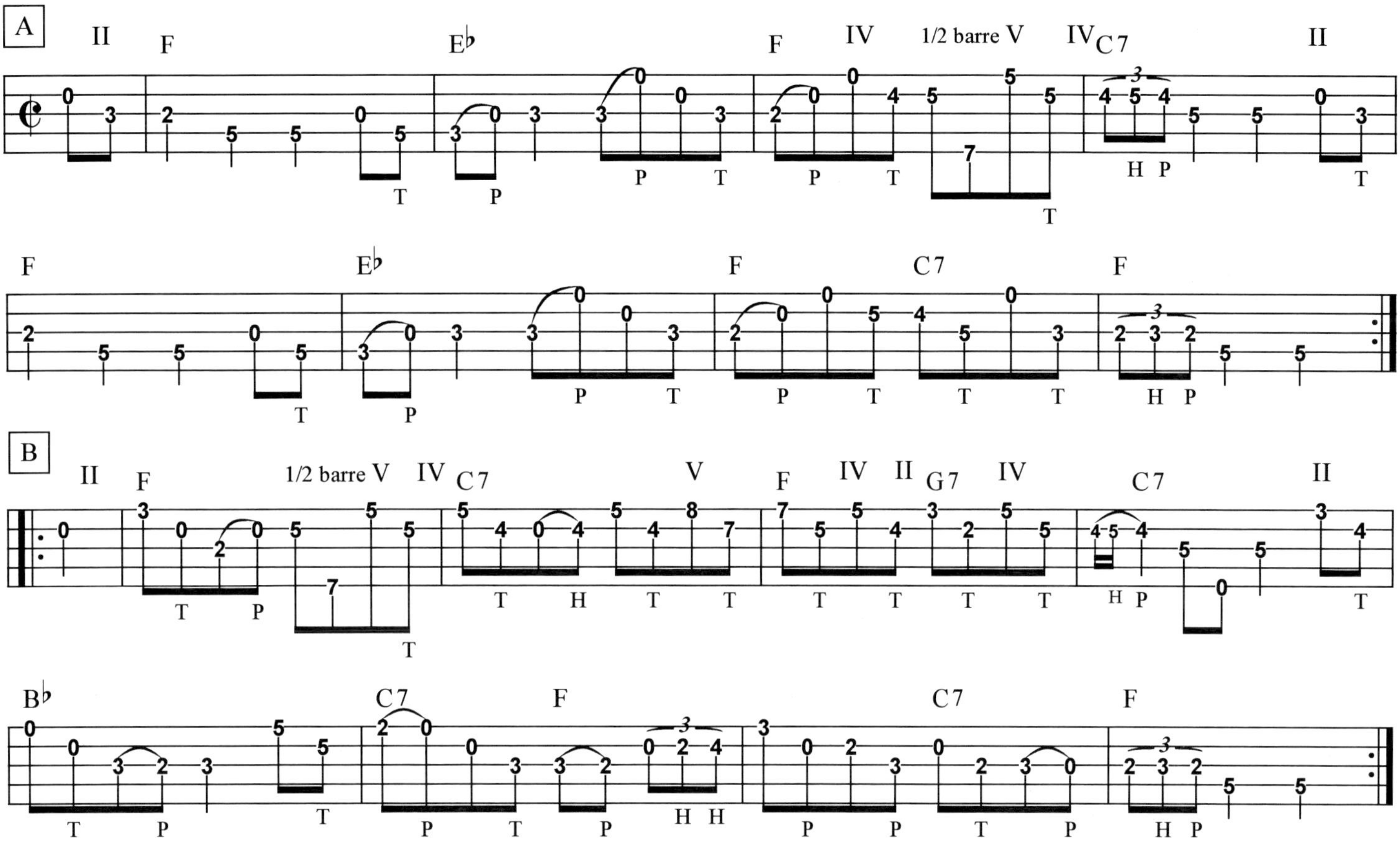

Playing Tips for *Miss Barker's Hornpipe*

• Part A, measure 3. Halfway through beat 2 of measure 3, balance with the 1st finger on fret 4, string 2. At the start of beat 3, glide with that finger up to fret 5, flatten it into a ½-barre, and pivot the 3rd finger over to fret 7, string 5.

• Part A, measures 3-4. At the end of measure 3, balance with the 1st finger on fret 5, string 2, and – at the start of measure 4 – unflatten the ½-barre and glide the arched finger back down string 2 to fret 4.

• Part B, measures 1-2. At the end of measure 1, balance with the 1st finger on fret 5, string 2, and – at the start of measure 2 – unflatten the ½-barre and glide the arched finger down string 2 to fret 4. Then use that finger as a pivot to swing the 2nd finger into place at fret 5, string 1.

98

Koehler's Hornpipe

Origin: Scotland
Source: Paul MacDonald
Appears on: *Island Boy*

Key: C
Mode: Major
Tuning: gCGCD

This tune first appeared – entitled simply, "Hornpipe" and attributed to arranger W.B. Laybourn – in *Köhler's Violin Repository of Dance Music*, published by Ernest Köhler & Sons of Edinburgh (1881). In recent times it caught the fancy of American contradance musicians, who found the Baroque-style harmonic changes in Part B reminiscent of "Pachelbel's Canon" and nicknamed the tune "Pachelbel's Reel." Standard notation for my source version is in *Fiddle Music of P.E.I.*

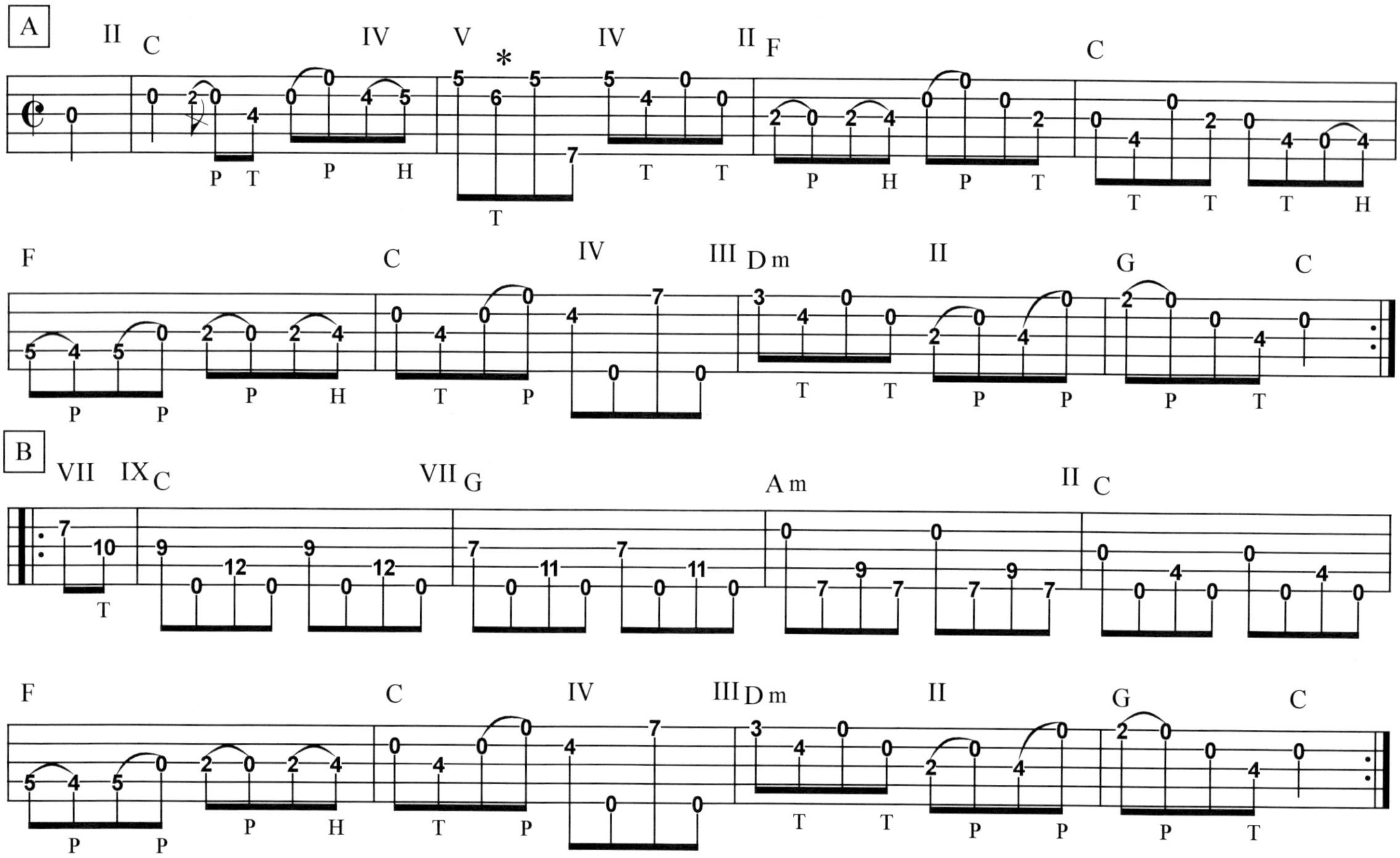

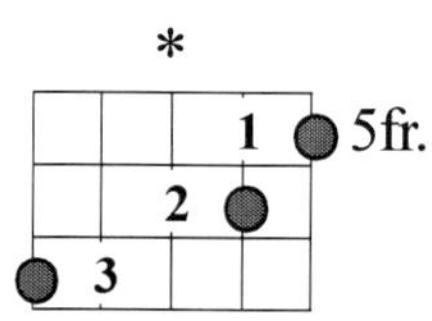

Playing Tips for *Koehler's Hornpipe*

- Part A, measures 1-2. At the end of measure 1, balance with the 2nd finger on fret 5, string 2. At the start of measure 2, glide up with that finger on string 2 to fret 6, and use that as a pivot to get the 1st and 3rd fingers into position on strings 1 and 5, respectively as shown in Diagram *.

- Part A, measure 2. Halfway through beat 2, balance on the 3rd finger at fret 7, string 5 and begin to stretch with the 1st and 2nd fingers towards fourth position. By the start of beat 3, the 1st and 2nd fingers should have landed at fret 4, string 2 and fret 5, string 1 respectively.

- Part B, measures 1-4. This is the section reminiscent of "Pachelbel's Canon." To enhance this effect, the setting has been adjusted to allow for keeping all strings ringing as long as possible (observe that all drone strings in this section should be treated as if they belong to arpeggiated chords).

99

Fisher's Hornpipe (F Setting)

Composer: (Possibly) J. Fishar | **Key:** F
Source: Winston "Scotty" Fitzgerald | **Mode:** Major
Appears on: *Northern Banjo* | **Tuning:** gCGCD

"Fisher's Hornpipe" is one of the most widely played tunes in the Celtic & North American fiddling repertoires. That said, it was a 1950s-era recording of "Fisher's" by Cape Breton fiddle great Winston "Scotty" Fitzgerald that re-popularized it in Atlantic Canada (and ultimately inspired this banjo arrangement). Fitzgerald employed the original key-of-F setting of the tune instead of the much more widely played key-of-D setting, and paired it in medley with "Archie Menzies" (p. 110). The earliest cited publication date for "Fisher's" is 1778, when it appeared in a collection by J. Fishar entitled simply, "Hornpipe #1"; it first appeared as "Fisher's Hornpipe" in John Anderson's, A *Second Selection of the most Approved Highland Strathspeys [&] Country Dances* [. . .] (1791). Its first North American publication was in Rhode Island dancing master John Griffith's, *A Collection of the newest and most fashionable country dances [. . .]* (1794). Some important subsequent appearances include *Kerr's Merry Melodies, Ryan's Mammoth Collection, The Athole Collection,* and *O'Neill's Music of Ireland.* My banjo setting features the fancy tag ending I used on *Northern Banjo*.

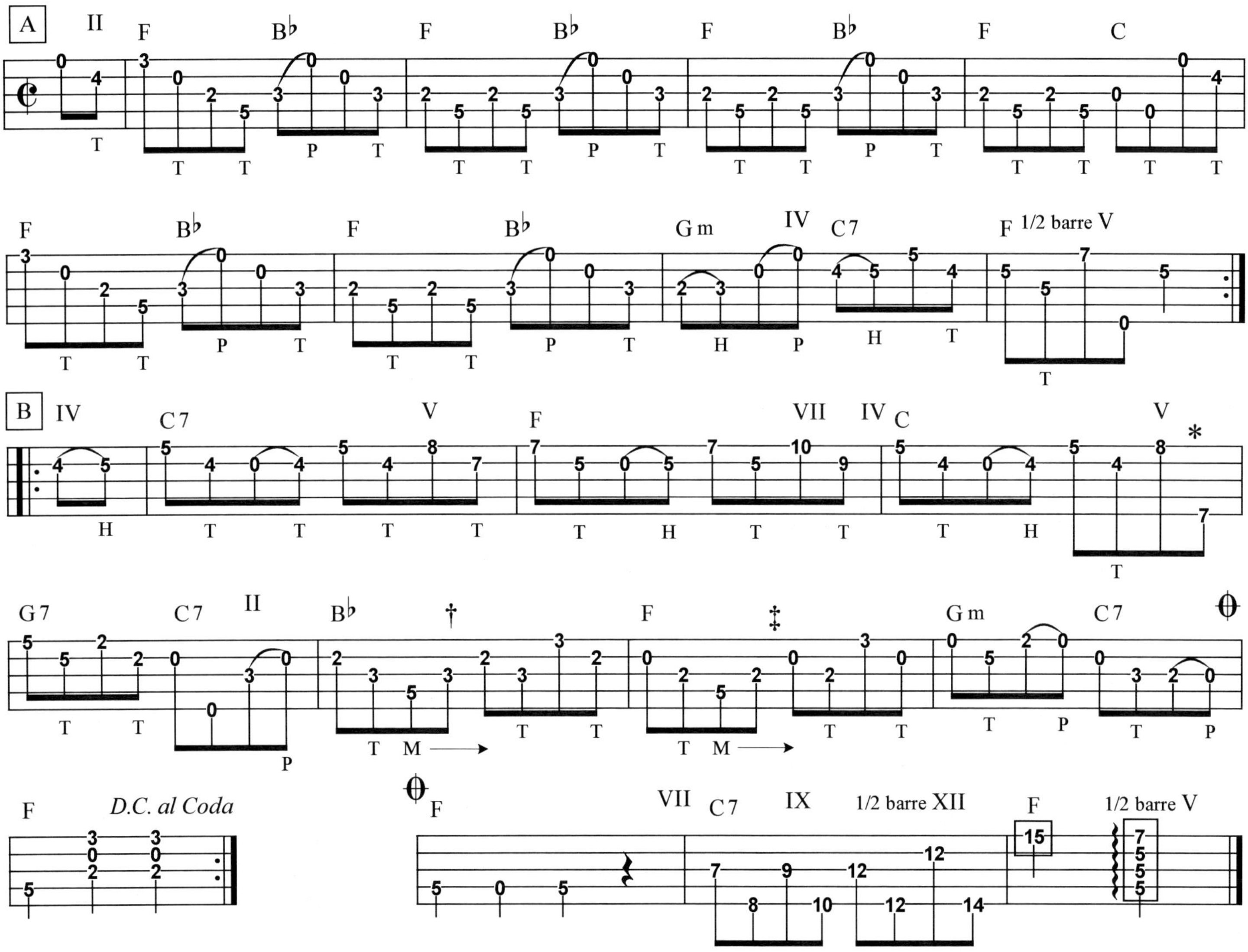

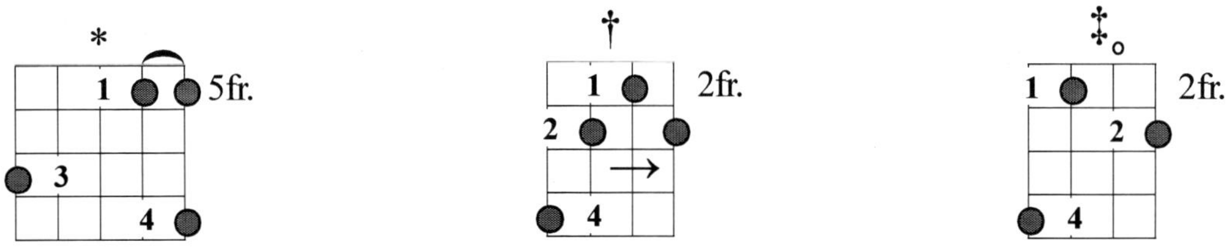

Playing Tips for *Fisher's Hornpipe*

• Part B, measures 3-4. At the end of measure 3, assume a half-barre at fret 5 as indicated in Diagram *. At the start of measure 4, play strings 1 and 2 as indicated; then on beat 2, glide the half-barre all the way down to fret 2.

100

Archie Menzies

Composer: John Lowe (c. 1760-1820)
Source: Winston "Scotty" Fitzgerald
Appears on: *Devil in the Kitchen*

Key: F
Mode: Major
Tuning: gCGCD

The Menzies family originated in Normandy and has resided for centuries in Menzies Castle, Aberfeldy, Scotland (the Scottish pronunciation of the name is "Mingus"). The tune was most likely named for Archibald Menzies (1754-1842), a well-known medical doctor, botanist, and explorer. According to *The Scottish Tune Index*, the tune first appeared in print in *Lowe's Collection, vol. 1* (1844), compiled by the composer's son, Joseph Lowe (1797-1866). The tune's wide contemporary circulation in Atlantic Canada is owed in great part to a popular 1950's recording by renowned Cape Breton fiddler Winston Fitzgerald, who paired it in medley with the Key of F-setting of "Fisher's Hornpipe " (p. 109).

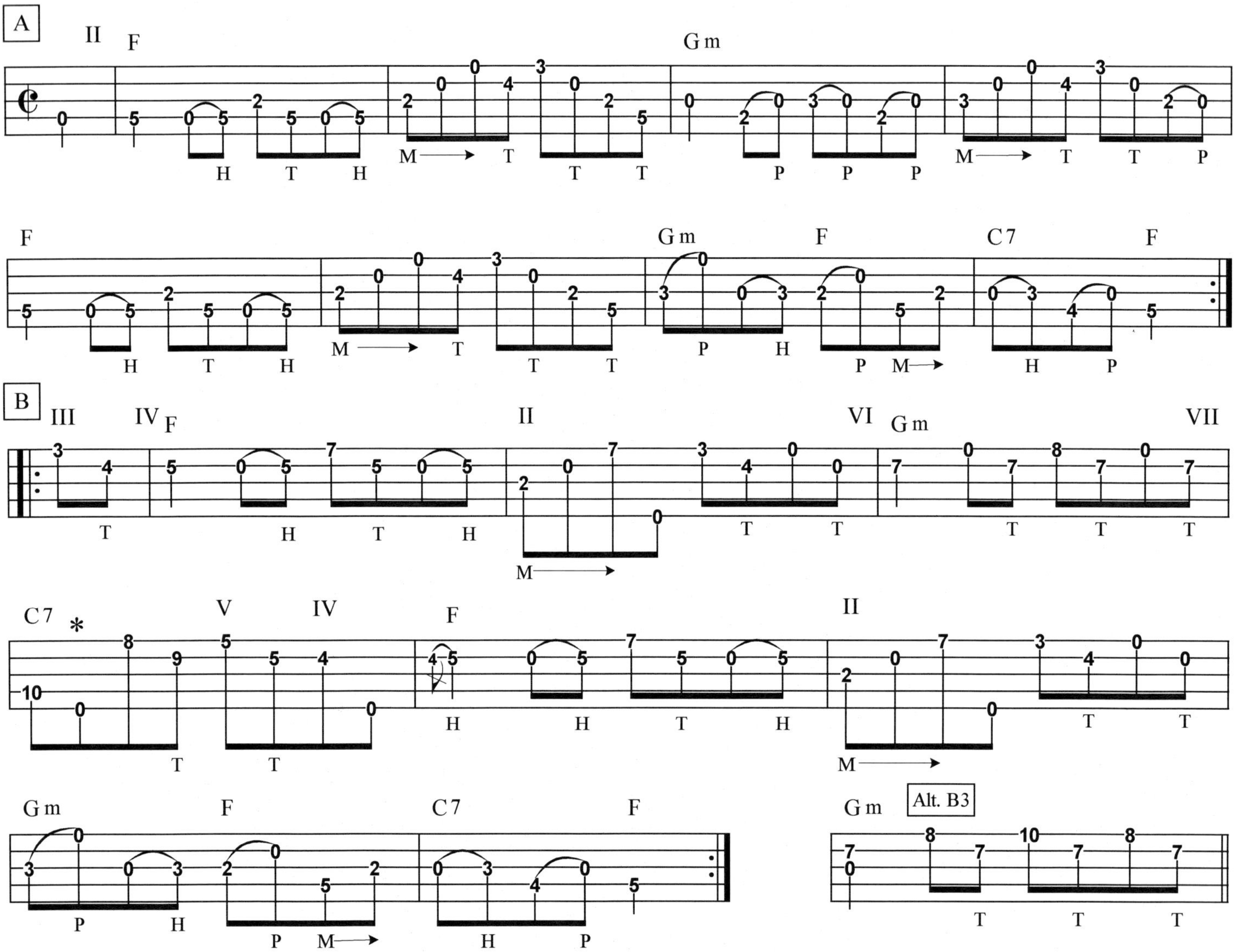

*

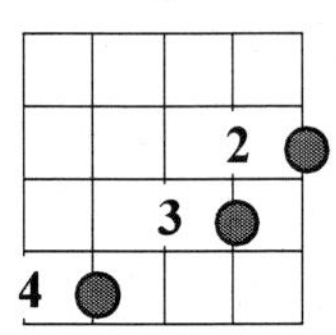

Playing Tips for *Archie Menzies*

• Part B, measures 4. Start the measure in the fingering shape shown in Diagram *, using the 2nd and 3rd fingers on frets 8 and 9 of strings 1 and 2, respectively. On beat 3, glide down string 1 with the 2nd finger to fret 5, pivot on that finger and swing the 1st finger into place on fret 5, string 2. On beat 4, cut that last note short and glide down string 2 with the 1st finger to fret 4.

101

The Braes of Auchtertyre

Origin: Scotland
Source: George MacPhee
Appears on: *Northern Banjo*

Key: C
Mode: Major
Tuning: gCGCD

This tune is named for a village in Scotland, pronounced as follows – *au* as in "awe"; *ch* in the guttural Gaelic style; accent on the first syllable; last syllable rhymes with "hire." It shows up in mid-18th century manuscripts and was subsequently featured in *The Gow Repository, Lowe's Collection, Kerr's Merry Melodies, The Athole Collection* and many other tunebooks. A 1930s recording by Cape Breton fiddler Angus Chisholm popularized the tune in Atlantic Canada. My banjo arrangement was inspired by the playing of Northeastern Kings County fiddler George MacPhee, who nearly always played this tune during his frequent visits to my collecting-project headquarters."The Braes of Auchtertyre" is circular; I've suggested a workable ending that resolves on the tonic. Standard notation for my source version is in *Fiddle Music of P.E.I.*

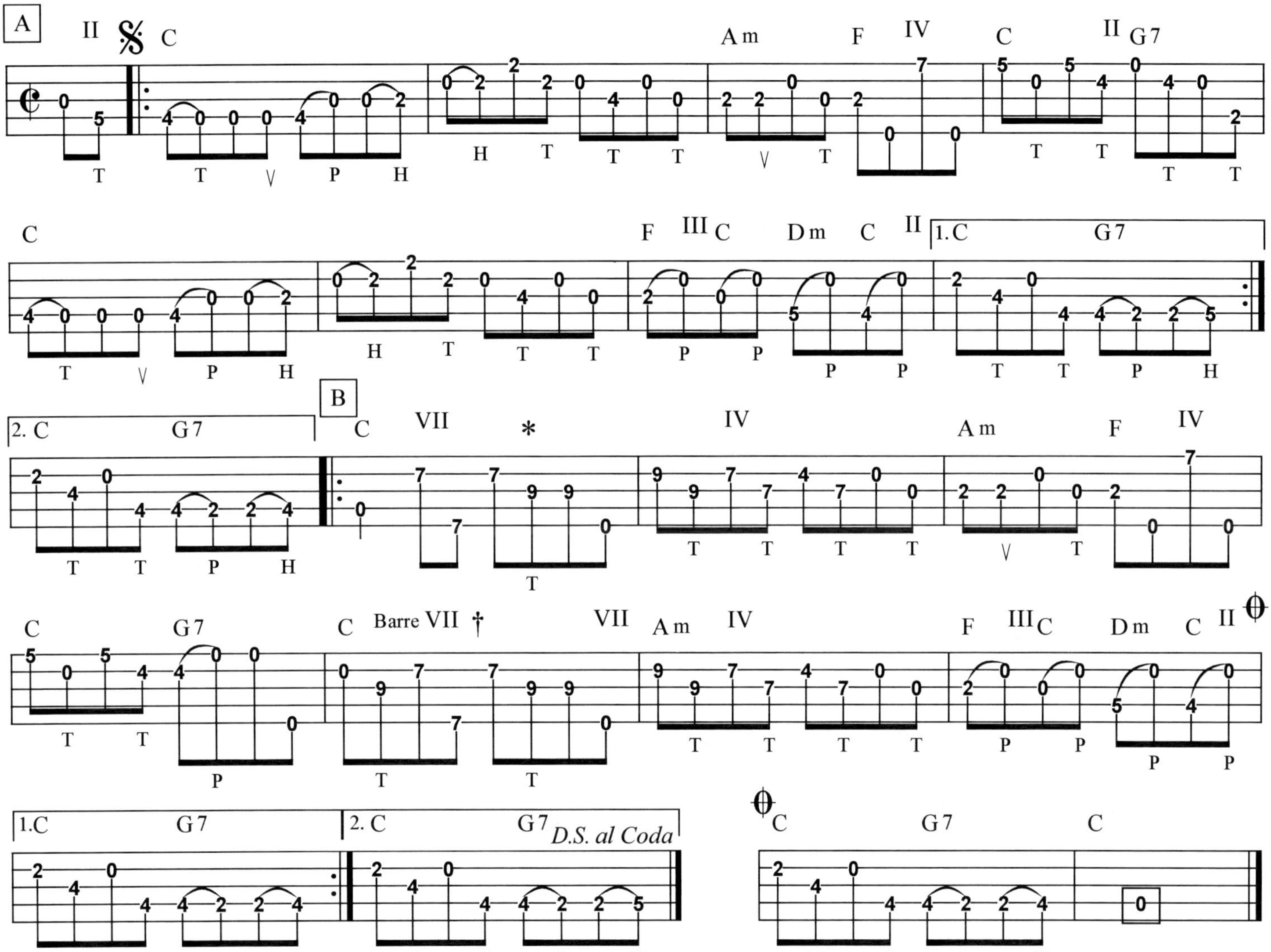

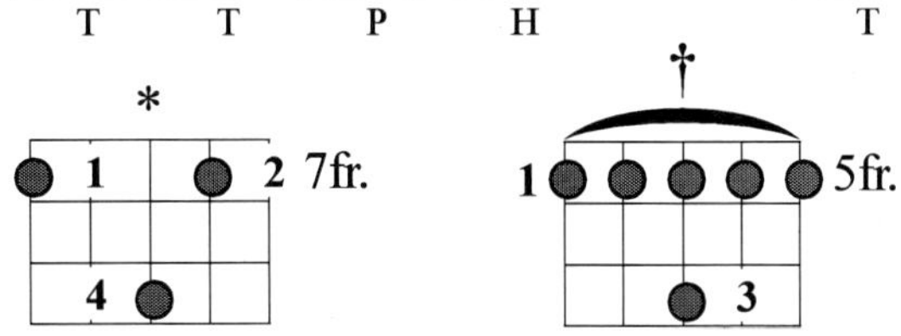

Playing Tips for *Braes of Auchtertyre*

• Part A, measure 7. Halfway through beat 2, use the 1st finger for the alternate-string P on string 2 and keep that finger hovering over string 2. On beat 3, use the 3rd finger to stop fret 5, string 4 and use the 1st finger again for the alternate-string P. Then on beat 4 use the 2nd finger to stop fret 4, string 4 and once again use the 1st finger for the alternate-string P.

• Part B, measures 1-2. On beat 4 of measure 1, leave the 3rd finger in place on fret 9, string 3. On beat 1 of measure 2, add the 4th finger at fret 9, string 2. On beat 2, glide with both fingers down to fret 7. Then on beat 3, leave the 3rd finger in place on fret 7, string 3 and stretch with the 1st finger to catch fret 4, string 2.

102

The Bee's Wing Hornpipe

Composer: James Hill (1811-53)
Source: Iain Powrie (1923-2011)
Appears on: *Devil in the Kitchen*

Key: B♭
Mode: Major
Tuning: gDGCD

James Hill grew up Dundee, Scotland, moved to Newcastle-on-Tyne in northeastern England as a young man and made his musical mark there; the intensely lyrical "Bee's Wing Hornpipe" is one of his best-known compositions. The tune is featured – as "Bees' Wings" – in *Ryan's Mammoth Collection*, and probably moved from there into general North American circulation. I learned it in the late 1980s from Powrie – who added a few *Scotch snaps* (see p. 151) and triplets for flavor – during a week's sojourn at the Stirling Fiddle Academy in Stirling, Scotland.

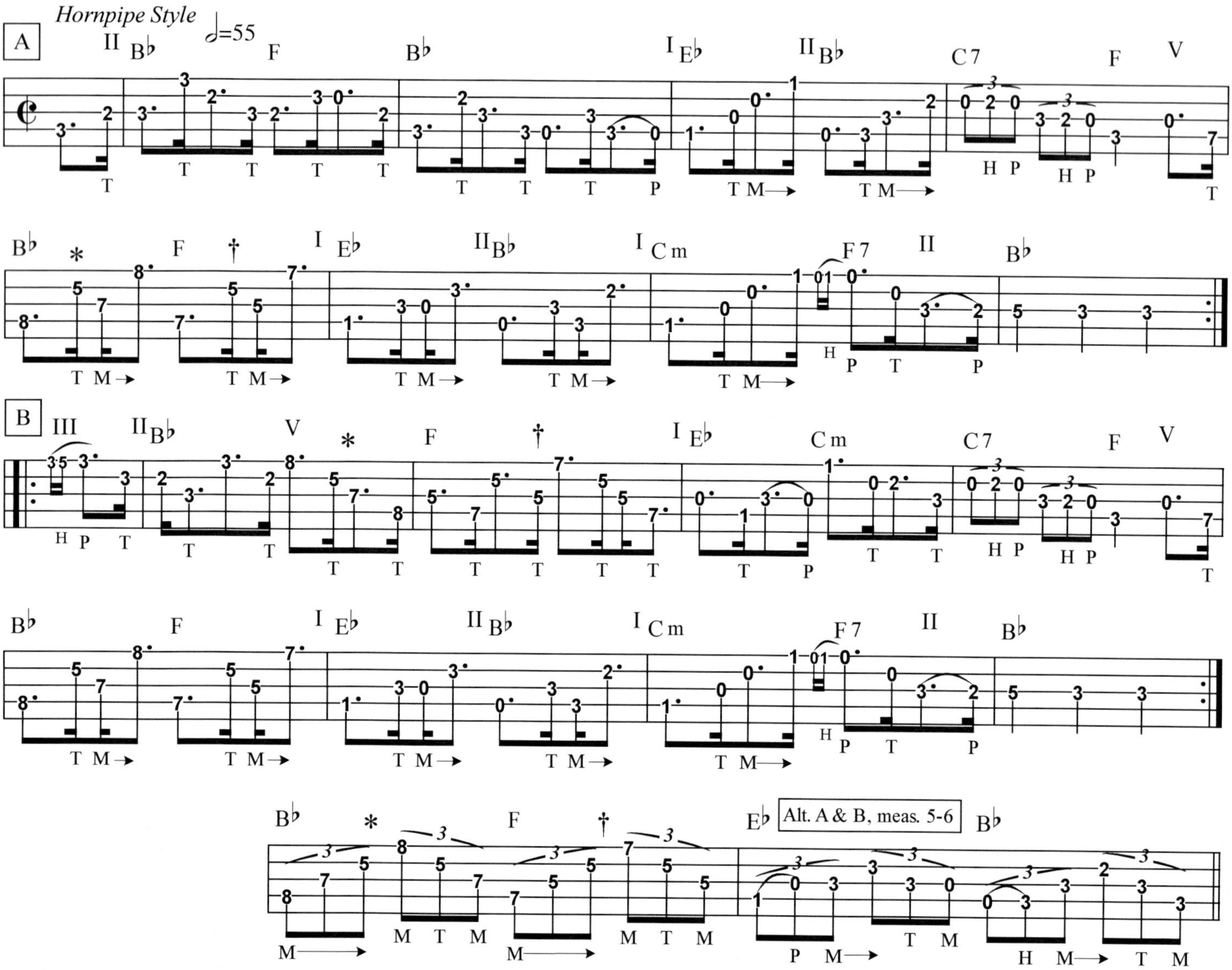

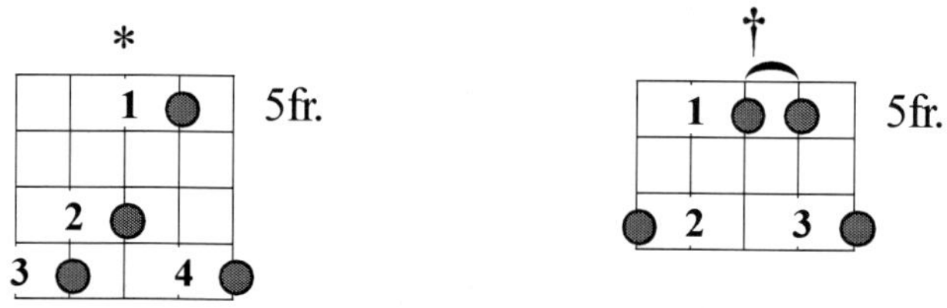

Playing Tips for *Bee's Wing Hornpipe*

• Part A, measures 1-3. To get the right phrasing, the plucking-hand thumb (T) needs to cross over the position of the M/I finger on several upbeats. To accomplish this, rock your hand back and reach the thumb under the former position of the M/I finger. For example, on the first beat of measure 1, play fret 3, string 3 with the M/I finger, then rock back and reach under it to catch fret 3, string 1 with T. Luckily, the relatively slow tempo here makes this approach practical.

• Part B, measure 1. At the end of beat 2, balance with the 1st finger on fret 2, string 2. Glide up with that finger to string 2, fret 5 and use it as a pivot to swing your other fingers into the shape shown in Diagram *.

103

Compliments to Buddy MacMaster

Composer: Jerry Holland
Source: Gus Longaphie
Appears on: *Northern Banjo*

Key: F
Mode: Major
Tuning: gCGCD

Jerry Holland's wonderful tunes always sound as if they were composed at least 200 years ago. He named this one for Cape Breton master fiddler Buddy MacMaster, uncle to well-known fiddle-performer Natalie MacMaster. Standard notation for my source version is in *Fiddle Music of P.E.I.*

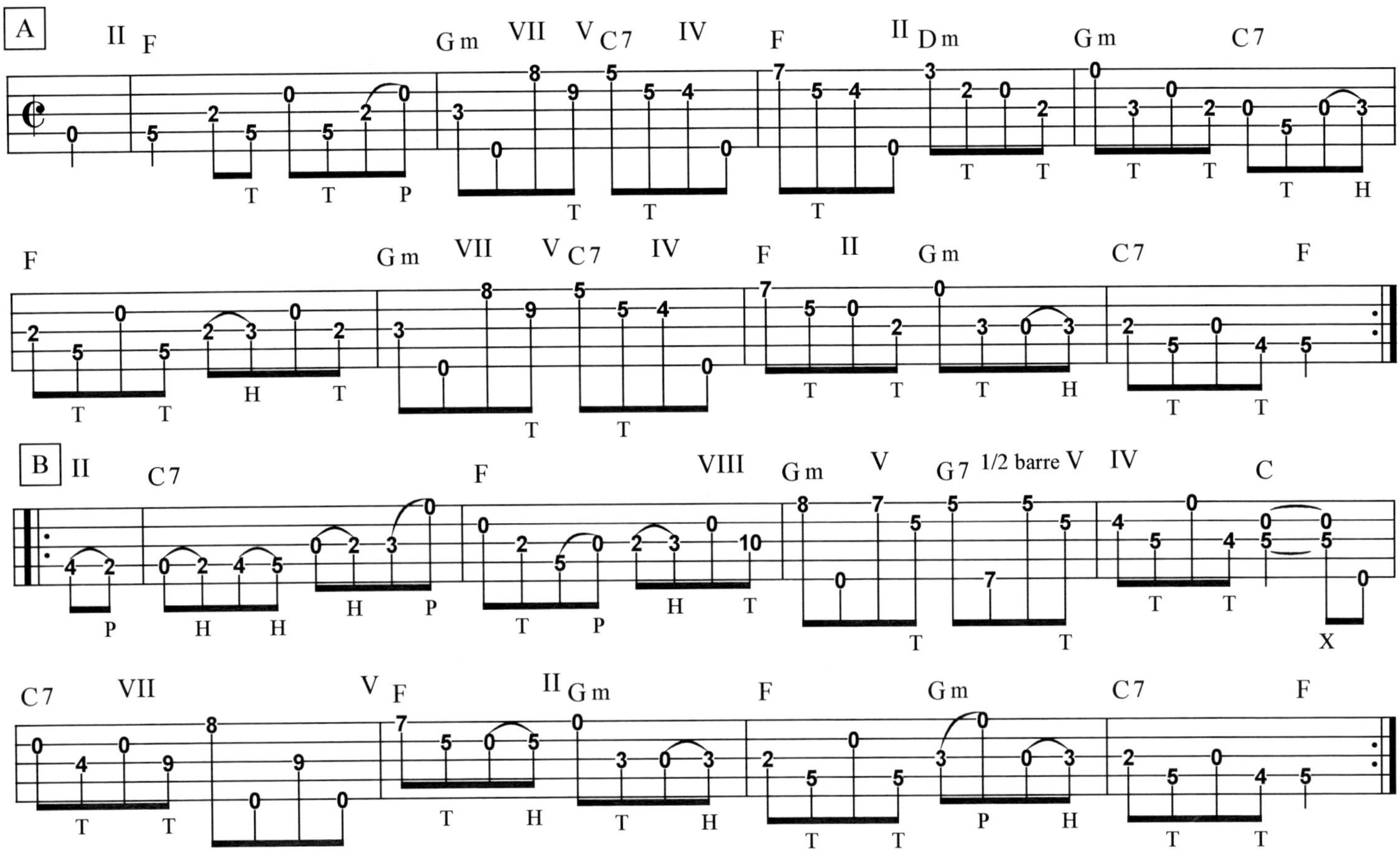

Playing Tips for *Compliments to Buddy MacMaster*

• Part A, measure 2. Once the open 5th-string note has sounded at the end of beat 1, scoot up the neck and use the 2nd and 3rd fingers to grab fret 8, string 1 and fret 9, string 2 respectively. Then glide down on string 1 with the 2nd finger, stop fret 5 and use it as a pivot to swing the 1st finger into place at the same fret on string 2. Finally, on beat 4, glide down with the 1st finger to fret 4, string 2.

• Part B, measures 2-3. On beat 4 of measure 2, use the time interval provided by the open string to scoot way up the neck with the 3rd finger and grab fret 10, string 3. Then at the start of measure 3, use the 1st finger to press down fret 8, string 1. Half a beat later, use the open string to scoot down to fifth position and use the 1st and 4th fingers to stop fret 5, string 2 and fret 7, string 1 respectively.

104

Fred Wilson's Hornpipe

Origin: American
Source: *Ryan's Mammoth Collection*
Appears on: *Frails & Frolics*

Key: F
Mode: Major
Tuning: gDGCD

This tune, which appears in *Ryan's Mammoth Collection,* was named for a popular mid-19th century minstrel show performer, best known for his clog dancing as a member of Bryant's Minstrels and other theatrical companies. In the late 1850s, he published his own tune collection through Oliver Ditson Company of Boston called *Fred Wilson's Clogs*. Canadian fiddlers Don Messer and Graham Townsend both recorded versions of the tune as "Fred Wilson's Clog."

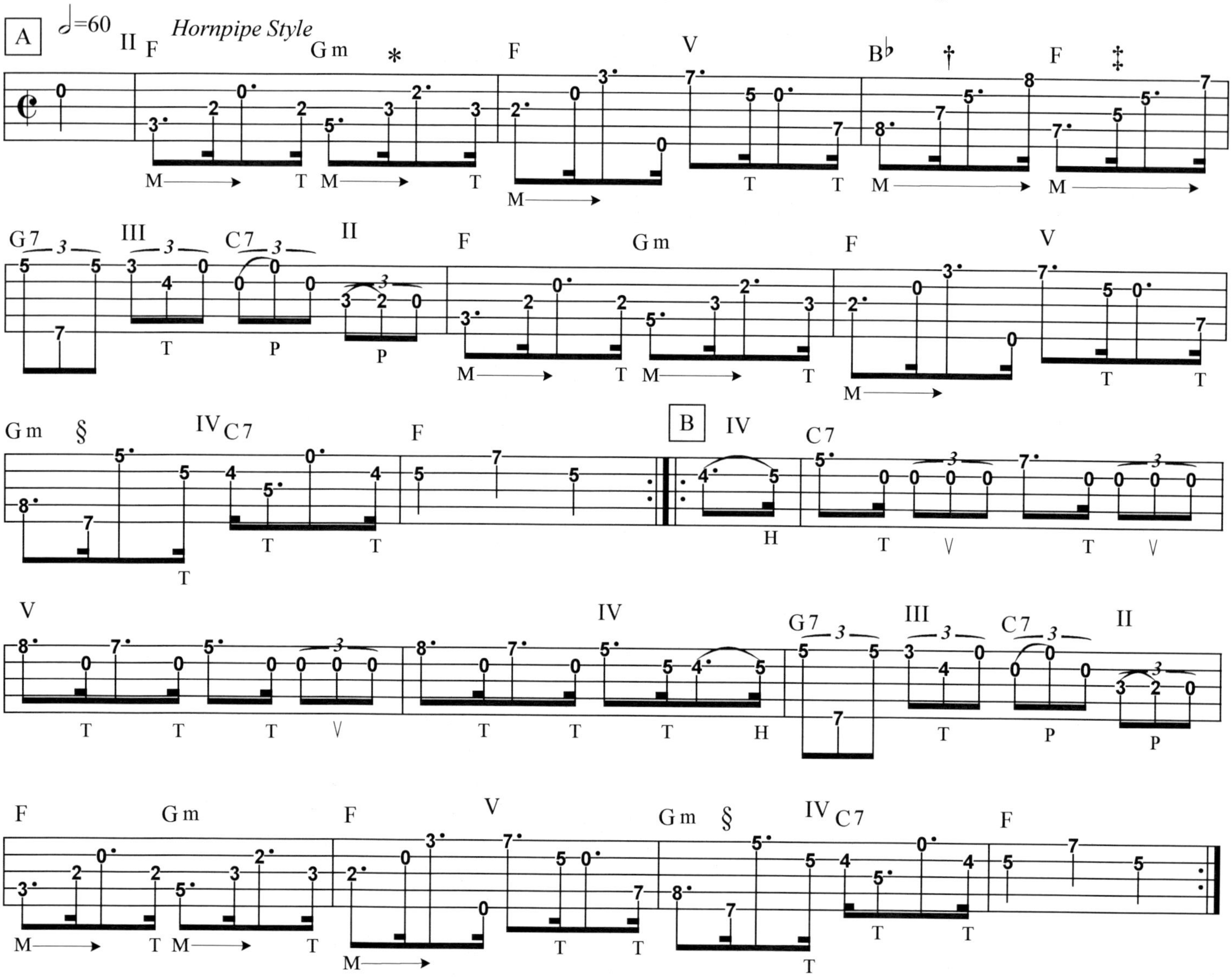

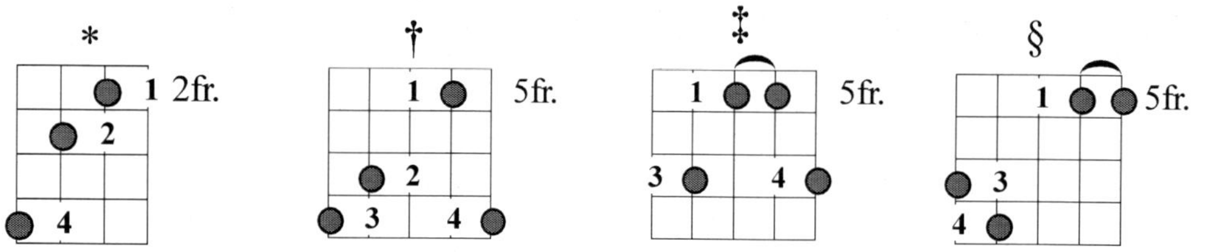

Playing Tips for *Fred Wilson's Hornpipe*

• Part A, measures 2-3. At the end of measure 2, balance on the 3rd finger at fret 7, string 4. At the start of measure 3, glide up on that finger to fret 8, firmly plant it and use it as a pivot to get to the shape shown in Diagram †.

• Part A, measure 4. At the end of beat 1, balance on the 1st finger at fret 5, string 1. At the start of beat 2, glide down string 1 with that finger to fret 3, then use it as a pivot to get the 2nd finger in place on fret 4, string 2.

• Part B, measures 1-2. The middle note of these triplets are upstrokes (see p. 12); make sure that the notes in each triplet are played evenly.

105

Carnie's Canter

Origin: Scotland
Source: Kenny Chaisson
Appears on: *Frails & Frolics*

Key: F
Mode: Major
Tuning: gCGCD

This super-exciting reel appears in James Scott Skinner's *Miller O'Hirn Collection* (1881). In 1936, Dan J. Campbell (1895-1981) became one of the first Cape Breton fiddlers to record it; more recent recordings by Jerry Holland and the Cape Breton Symphony have expanded the tune's circulation. Standard notation for my source version is in *Fiddle Music of P.E.I.*

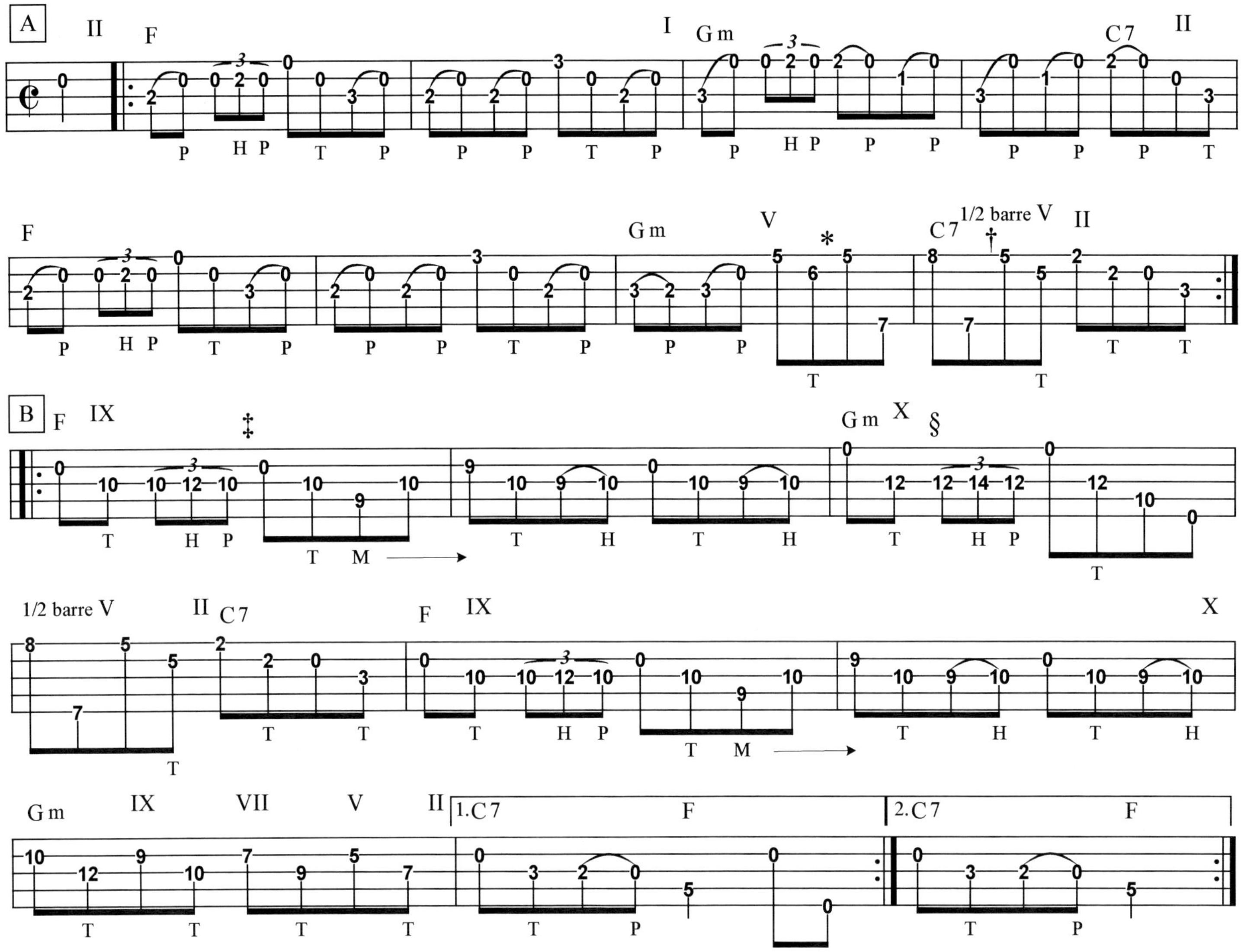

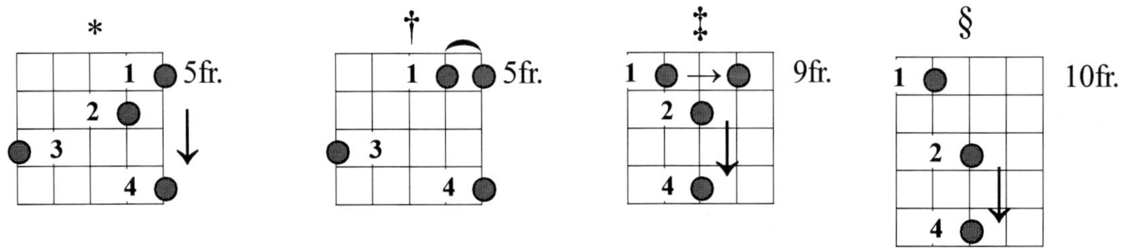

Playing Tips for *Carnie's Canter*

• Part A, measures 7-8. At the end of measure 7, balance with the 3rd finger on fret 7, string 5 and use that as a pivot to swing your fingers into the shape shown in Diagram †.

• Part B, measure 1-2. Use the 2nd finger on fret 10, string 3. Use the 4th finger for the H-P triplet, then on beat 4 swing your 1st finger over to fret 9, string 4. On beat 1 of measure 2, move the 1st finger over from string 4 to the same fret on string 2 (Diagram ‡).

• Part B, measure 3. Use the 2nd finger on fret 12, string 3 and hold it in place. Use the 4th finger for the H-P triplet, then stretch your 1st finger to fret 10, string 4 as shown in Diagram §.

The Banks Hornpipe

Composer: Attributed to "Parazotti"
Source: J.S. Skinner's *Scottish Violinist*
Appears on: *Northern Banjo*

Key: B♭
Mode: Major
Tuning: gDGCD

Now considered a staple in both the Scottish and Cape Breton fiddle repertoires, "The Banks Hornpipe" sounds a lot like classical music but has the structure of a fiddle-tune and a typical hornpipe ending. The tune is often attributed to a 19th-century composer with last name Parazotti, who – according to Alastair Hardie's *The Caledonian Companion* (1981) – was the grandson of an Italian immigrant to Glasgow. It appears in Skinner's *Harp & Claymore* and *The Scottish Violinst*; in *Köhler's Violin Repository* it is entitled "Mrs. Taff, or Banks Hornpipe"; and in *Ryan's Mammoth Collection* a rather meandering variant is called "Souvinir de Venice." It is doubtful that the tune was ever intended for dance accompaniment; instead it is generally played as a show piece with what might be described as a "slow reel" feel. To fit the tune on banjo I had to transpose it to B♭ from its original key of E♭.

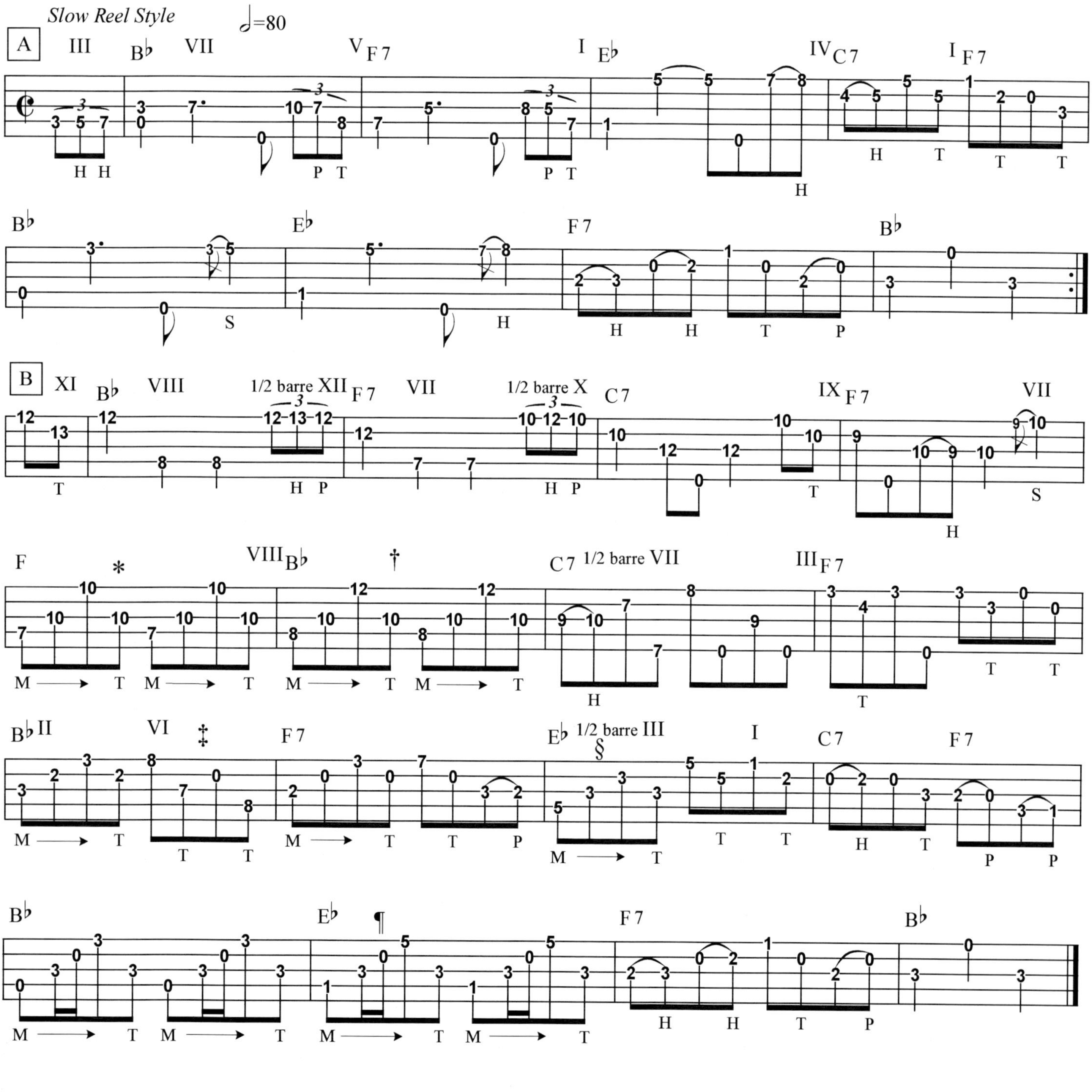

*For *Banks Hornpipe* Fingering Diagrams & Playing Tips, See Facing Page *

Fingering Diagrams for *The Banks Hornpipe*

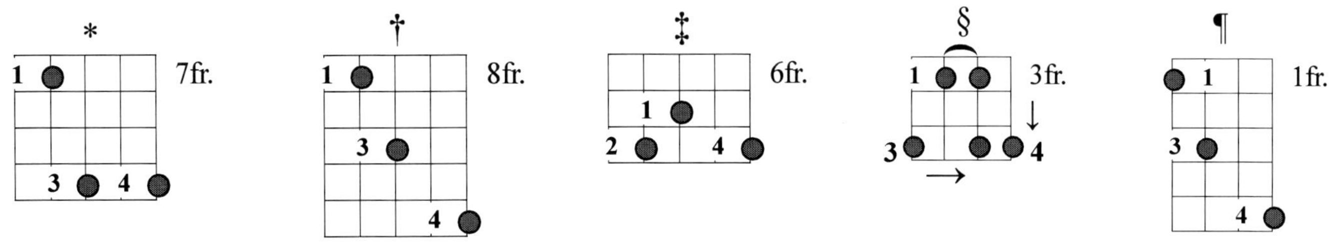

Playing Tips for *The Banks Hornpipe*

• Part B, measures 1-2. Both measures feature what appear to be unnatural stretches. Because of the phrasing, however, you don't have to hold the higher notes down for very long before moving down the neck to the lower ones (just establish the sound, cut the note short and scoot!).

• Part B, measure 11. On beat 1, have a ½-barre on fret 3 and the 3rd finger on fret 5, string 4, as shown in Diagram §. On beat 3, remove the 3rd finger from string 4 and reach over with both 3rd and 4th fingers to stop fret 5 on strings 2 and 1. Then on beat 4, scoot down with the 1st and 2nd fingers to stop fret 1, string 1 and fret 2, string 2 respectively.

• Part B, measures 13-14. The extended arpeggio strokes in this passage are meant to emulate the sound of *spiccato* bowing on the fiddle. Make sure your timing is precise on the eighth and sixteenth notes.

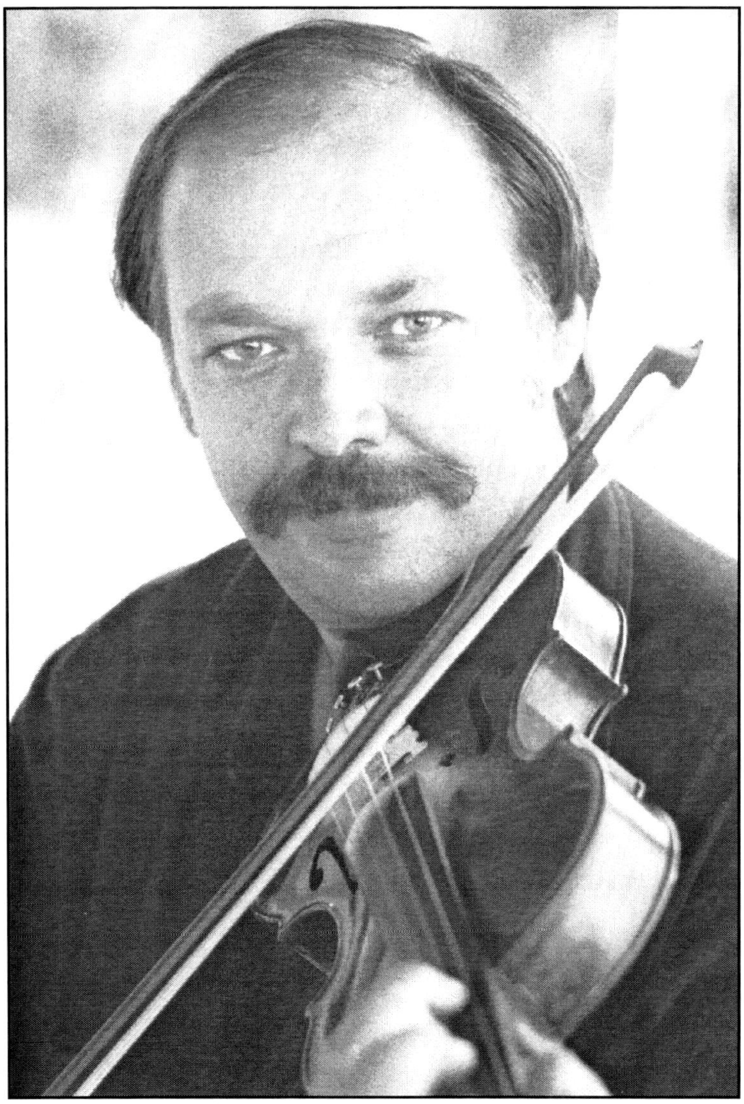

Jerry Holland c. 1985; courtesy Cranford Publications

107

Caber Feidh

Origin: Scotland
Source: Winston "Scotty" Fitzgerald
Appears on: *Northern Banjo*

Key: C
Mode: Major
Tuning: gCGCD

'The Gaelic title of this old Scottish reel translates to "Deer's Antlers." The pronunciation is roughly "KAH-ber Fay" in Gaelic, but I often hear musicians say "KAY-ber Fay" or even "KAY-per Fay." The tune first appeared in mid-18th century manuscripts and was first published in the 1770s; since then it has been printed in numerous tunebooks, including *Lowe's Collection, The Athole Collection, The Skye Collection,* and *Kerr's Merry Melodies.* The extended B' Part – and the Coda that resolves this circular tune – are my original variations inspired by the opening phrases of Part B. Observe that for the most part the Coda reprises Part B', measures 13-16.

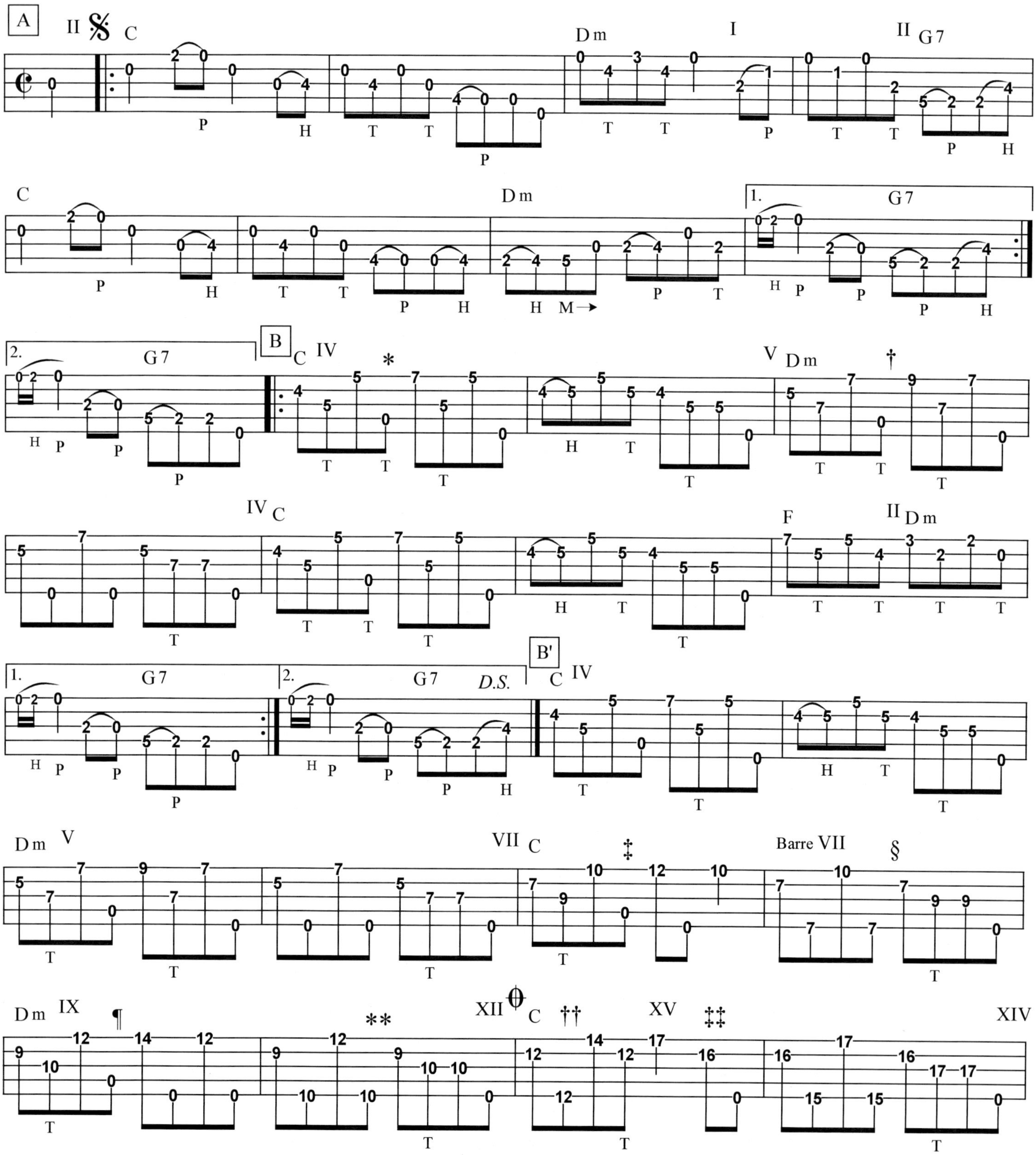

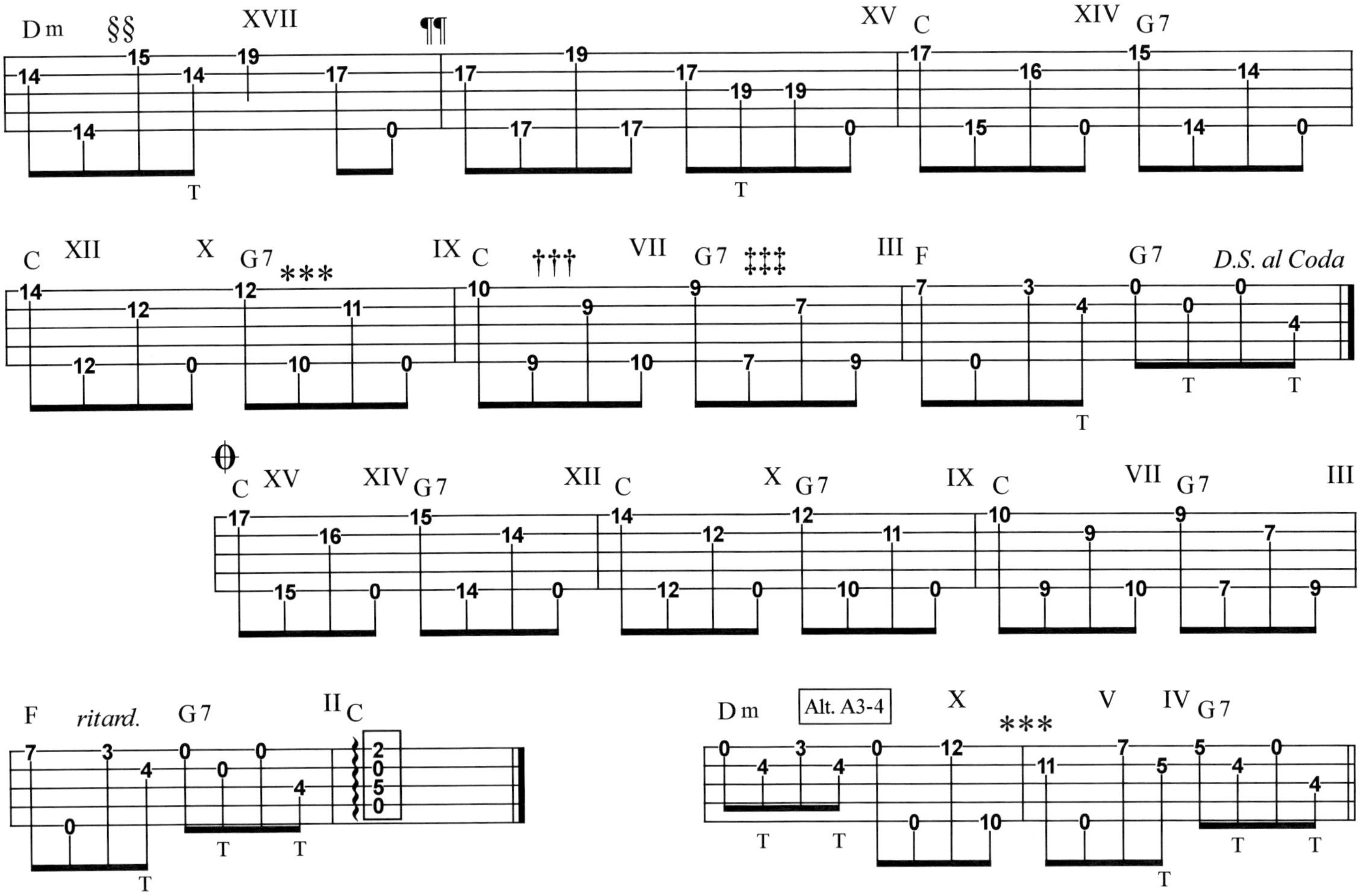

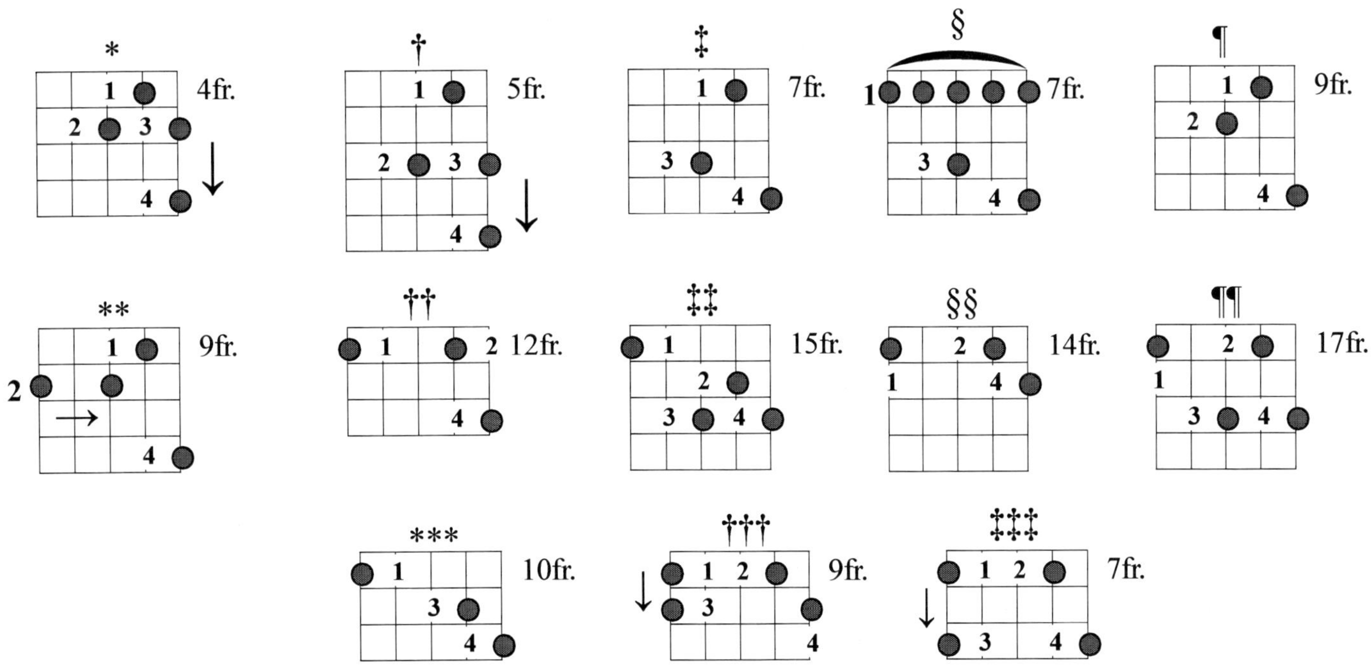

Playing Tips for *Caber Feidh*

• Part B', measures 5-6. On beat 4 of measure 5, balance with the 4th finger on fret 10, string 1. Then on beat 1 of measure 6, use that finger as a pivot to swing into the shape shown in Diagram §.

• Part B' measures 7-8. On beat 4 of measure 7, balance with the 4th finger on fret 12, string 1. Then on beat 1 of measure 8, use that finger as a pivot to swing into the shape shown in Diagram **.

• Part B', measures 13-14 (and Coda measures 1-2). Use the open 5th-string notes in these measures as breathing room to get into position for each successive fingering shape.

108

The High Level Hornpipe

Composer: James Hill (1811-53)
Sources: Ervan Sonier & Toussaint Arsenault
Appears on: *Frails & Frolics*

Key: B♭
Mode: Major
Tuning: gDGCD

Hill composed this tune to commemorate the completion in 1849 of the High Level Bridge over the River Tyne between the cities of Newcastle and Gateshead. A noted composer of lyrical and harmonically complex tunes, Hill was born in Dundee, Scotland but at a fairly young age moved with his family to the Newcastle region of northeastern England. Both Dan R. MacDonald and "Little Jack" MacDonald recorded versions of the tune quite early in the Cape Breton recording era. Standard notation for my source version is in *Fiddle Music of P.E.I.*

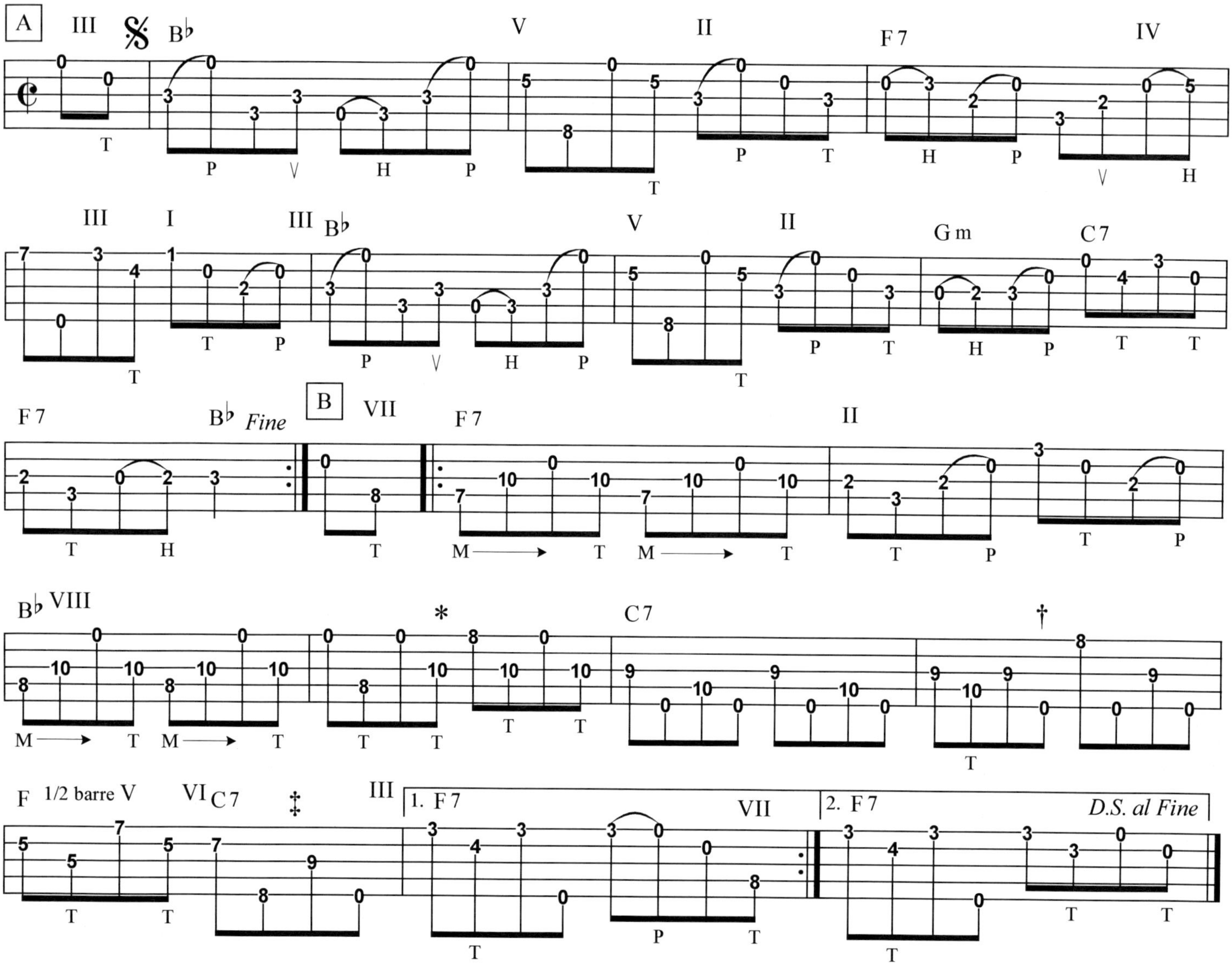

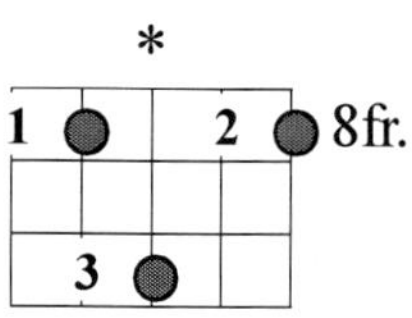

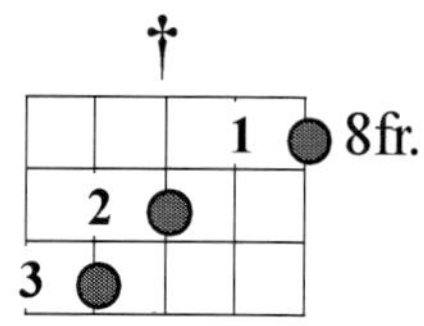

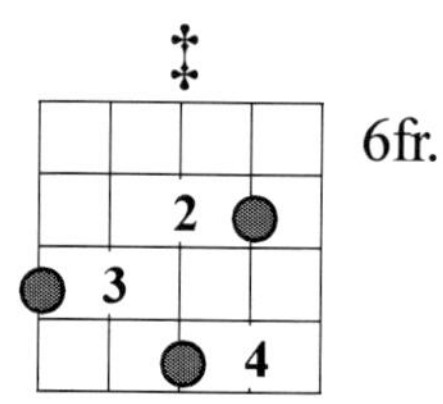

Playing Tips for *High Level Hornpipe*

- Part A, measures 1-2. At the end of measure 1, use the time provided by the open string to skip up the neck and grab fret 5, string 2 and fret 8, string 5 with the 1st and 4th fingers, respectively.

- Part B, measure 3. You'll have to skip over the 2nd string in the two arpeggio maneuvers; this requires particular attention to steady timing.

- Part B, measures 7. At the end of beat 2, cut fret 5, string 2 short. Then scoot up with the 2nd finger to fret 7, string 2 and use that as a pivot to get the 3rd and 4th fingers into position as shown in Diagram ‡.

Chapter 9. *Jigs (Tunes in 6/8 Time)*

THINK OF 6/8-TIME AS HAVING JUST *TWO BEATS* PER MEASURE, with each beat divided into *three* pulses (forget about the "6" part of 6/8). The best way to count time in 6/8 is akin to counting triplets in 4/4 time, namely: 1-&-a, 2-&-a; 1-&-a, 2-&-a. Example J-1 shows the kinds of notes you are likely to encounter in a typical jig or other kind of tune in 6/8 time.

- **Dotted quarter note** (measure 1): each dotted quarter note fills half a measure
- **Quarter-eighth pair** (measure 2): each quarter note occupies two pulses, each eighth note fills just one
- **Three eighth-note group** (measure 3): an eighth note is played on each pulse
- **Quarter-eighth pair followed by three eighth-note group** (measure 4)

Jig Tempos. Jigs are generally played at roughly 120-130 beats per minute (metronome markings: ♩.=120, or ♩.=130).

109

Example J-1: Types of Notes in 6/8 Time

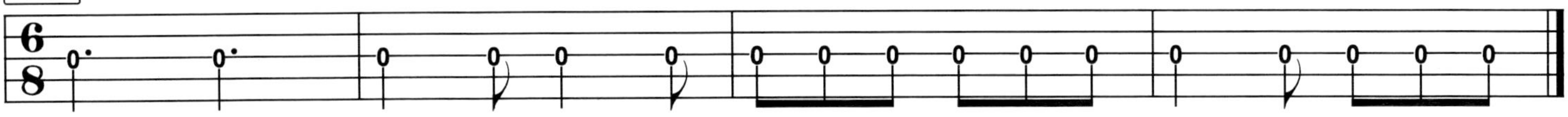

6/8 Time & Clawhammer

Here's how to adapt basic clawhammer techniques to functioning in the 6/8-time universe.

Default Plucking Hand Notation. As was the case for "regular" meters, unless otherwise indicated in the tab use a downstroke on the long strings and a thumb-stroke on the 5th string.

Dotted Quarter Notes. Play all dotted quarters with a downstroke.

Quarter-Eighth Pairs. Quarter-eighth pairs are extremely easy to play in clawhammer via basic techniques. Example J-2 illustrates three common methods: downstroke + drone (measure 1); drop-thumbing (measures 2-3); and downstroke + hammer-on or pull-off (measure 4). Observe that the first note in each pair (the quarter note) is exactly twice as long as the second note (the eighth note). The count in each measure is 1-&-a, 2-&-a; the quarter note is played on the "number-count"; the eighth note is played on the "a-count"; and the "&-count" is skipped. Measure 5 shows a variant of this technique: a quarter-eighth pair with *the eighth note first.* Here the eighth note is played on a number-count; the quarter note is then played on the &-count and held through the a-count.

110

Example J-2: Methods for Obtaining Quarter-Eighth Pairs

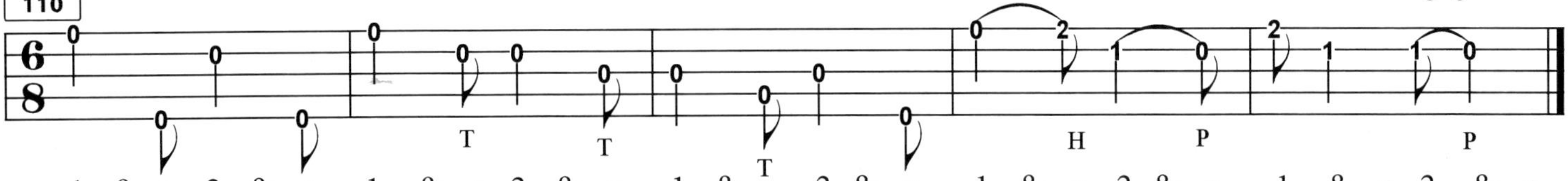

Parallels with Conventional Picking. Most clawhammerists are used to playing notes in a 2:1 rhythm. Pairs of eighth notes in Appalachian fiddle music – and hornpipes – are often played as *swing eighths,* in which the first note of each pair sounds twice as long as the second (Example J-3). As shown in measure 1, swing eighths are often written as dotted pairs (that is, a dotted-eighth note plus a sixteenth). Since a dotted eighth note is actually three times longer than a sixteenth, it would be more accurate to notate swing eighths as triplets with the first two notes tied (measure 2). This rhythm can be expressed more "elegantly" as a quarter note plus a single eighth note under a triplet bracket (measure 3). If you then simply discard the triplet bracket, this notation translates directly to 6/8 time (measure 4).

111

Example J-3: Swing Eighths to Quarter-Eighth Pairs

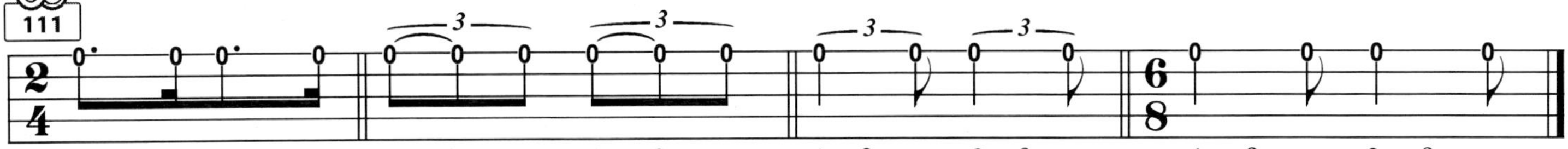

From Quarter-Eighth Pairs to Three Eighth-Note Groups

As illustrated in Example J-4, three-note groups can be obtained by merely inserting a hammer-on or pull-off between the notes of a quarter-eighth pair. The plucking hand still plays the quarter-eighth pair, while the fretting hand provides the middle note. In measure 1, a three-note grouping is obtained by inserting a hammer-on between two downstrokes; in measure 2, a pull-off is inserted between two downstrokes; in measure 3, a pull-off is inserted between the two notes of a drop-thumb pair.

112

Example J-4: From Quarter-Eighths to Three-Note Groups

Tuning: gDGBD

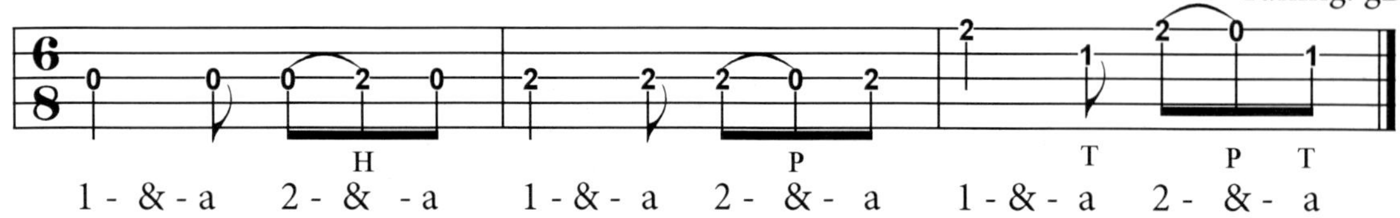

Three Eighth-Note Groups Obtained Entirely via the Plucking-Hand

To obtain three-note groups played exclusively via plucking-hand techniques, get your first two notes with a drop-thumb or downstroke-plus-drone, then get the third note by adding on an additional down-stroke (Example J-5). The count is still 1-&-a, 2-&-a; but this time play a plucking hand note on every count: the number-count, the &-count, and the a-count.

113

Example J-5: Three-Note Groups

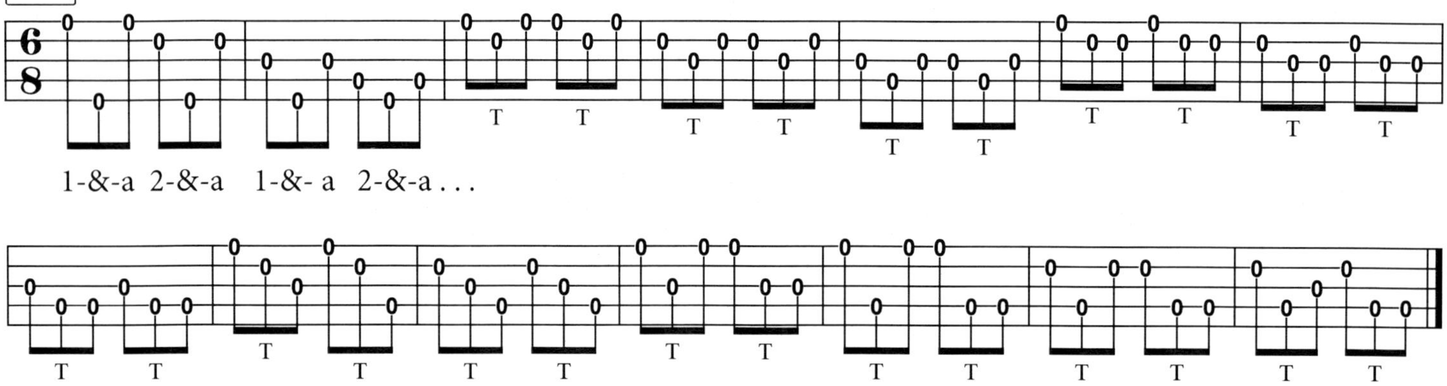

Another Way to Think About Plucking-Hand Generated Three-Note Groups. Think of each three-note group as a double-thumbing maneuver from which the final thumb-note has been dropped, as illustrated in Example J-6 (this would be a good time to review the *Double-Thumbing Exercise* on p. 15). In each measure, the four-note group on the left represents a double-thumbing maneuver; the three-note group on the right is derived from it by leaving off the last thumb-note.

- **Measure 1.** The three-note group is derived by omitting the final drone-note from *regular* double thumbing
- **Measure 2.** The three-note group is derived by omitting the final drop-thumb from *reverse* double thumbing
- **Measure 3.** The three eighth-note group is derived by omitting the final drone from *second downstroke returns to drop-thumb string*
- **Measure 4.** The three eighth-note group is derived by omitting the final drone from *backward roll* type double-thumbing

114

Example J-6: From Double-thumbing Patterns to Three-Note Groups

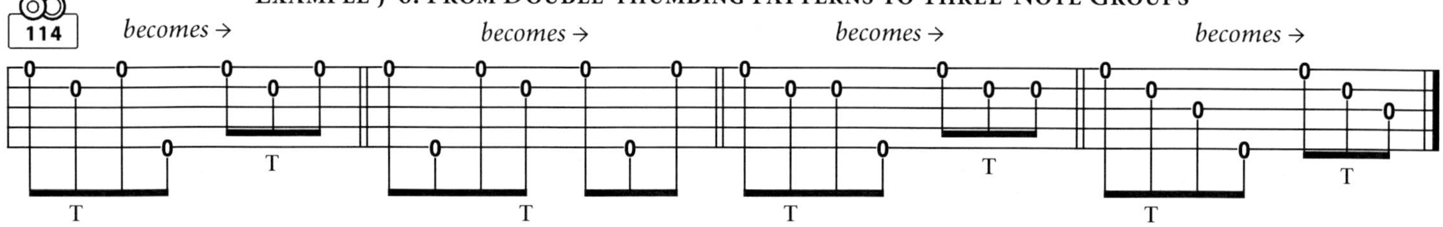

Jig Phrasing

Jigs are dance tunes, and as such you'll always want to lead strongly from upbeat to downbeat, and from weak beat to strong beat. If you have a quarter-eighth pair, the eighth note always leads to the next group of notes or to the downbeat of the next measure. For three-note groups, the last note of each group always leads to the first note of the next group, or to the first note of a quarter-eighth pair. This is illustrated in Example J-7 (and on the companion audio).

115

Example J-7: Jig Phrasing (Excerpt from *Jackson's Jig*)

Tuning: gDGBD

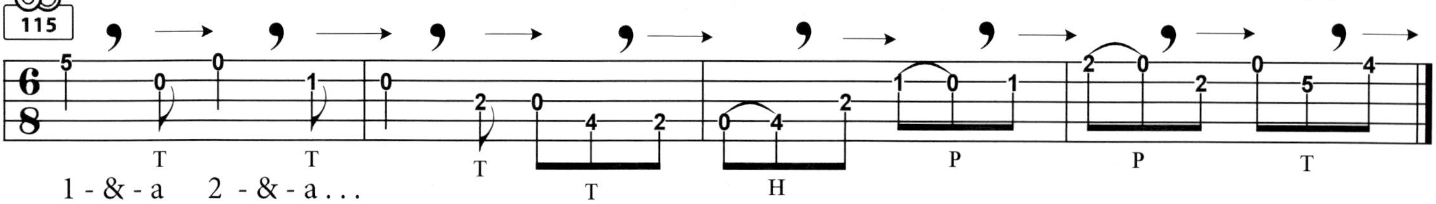

116

West Point Jig

Origin: Prince Edward Island
Source: Johnny Joe Chaisson

Key: D (C on Banjo)
Mode: Major
Tuning: gCGCD (Capo-2)

This lively jig was named for a cape in southwestern Prince County, P.E.I. and is widely played throughout the Island. It features the sing-songy, happy-go-lucky feel that is typical of home-grown Canadian jigs. Standard notation for my source version is in *Fiddle Music of P.E.I.*

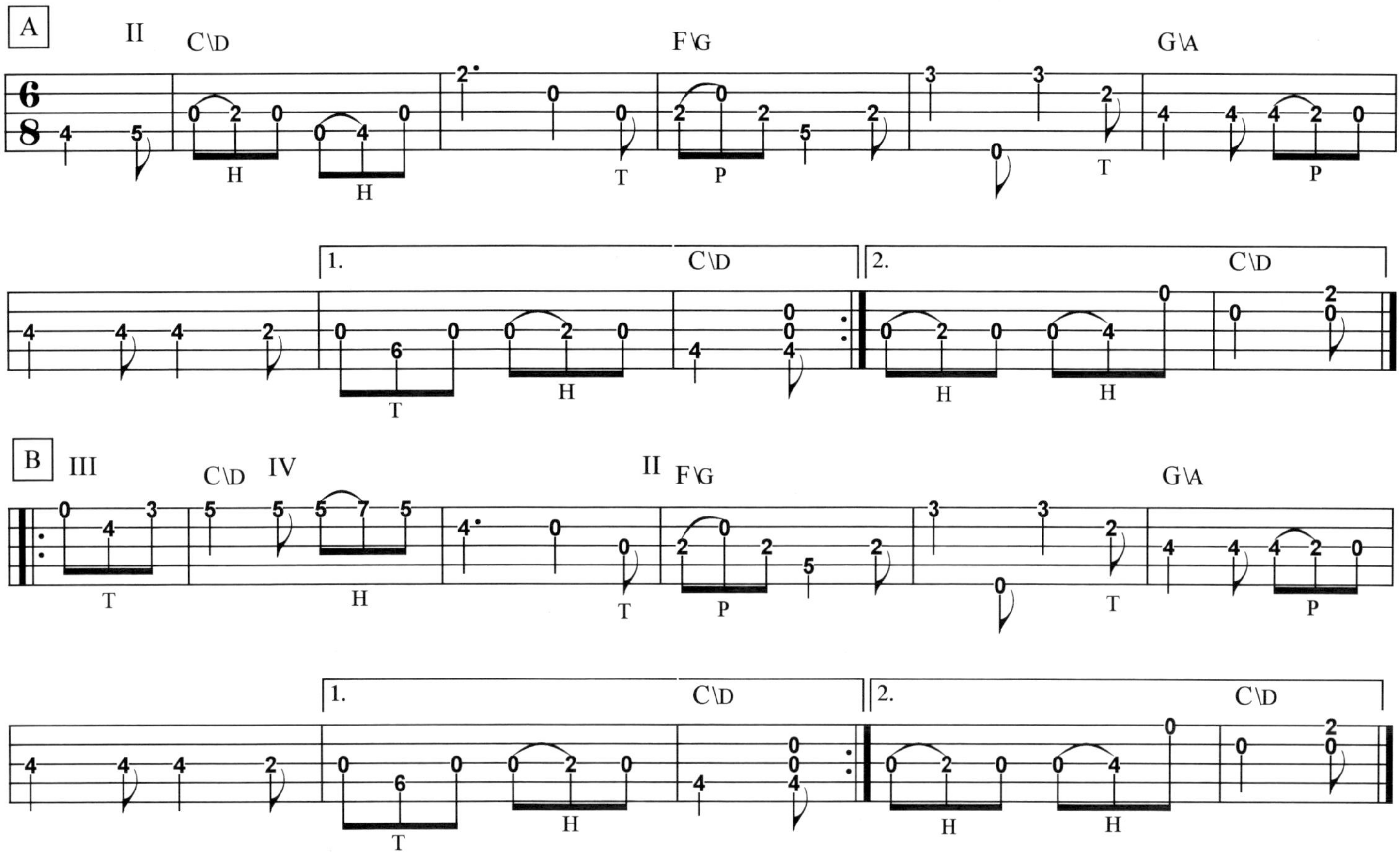

Playing Tips for *West Point Jig*

Dual Chord Symbols: Chord to left of backslash goes with open banjo; chord on right is for capoed banjo or fiddle

• Part B, measure 1. At the start of the measure, stop fret 5, string 1 with the 3rd finger and cut that note short. On the first "a-count," switch to fourth position and stop that same note with the 2nd finger. This puts you in position to use the 4th finger to obtain the following H from fret 5 to fret 7 on string 1.

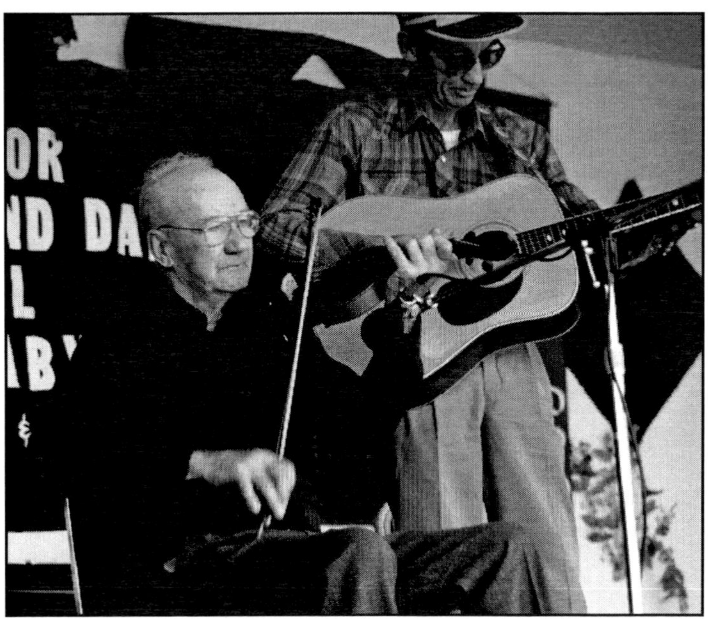

Elmer Robinson (fiddle) & Eldon MacArthur at Richmond Festival: Richmond, P.E.I. (1991). Photo by Earthwatch Team; courtesy Robertson Library, University of P.E.I.

117

Belfast Jig

Origin: Probably Southeastern P.E.I.
Source: Elliott Wight
Appears on: *Island Boy*

Key: D (C on Banjo)
Mode: Major
Tuning: gCGCD (Capo-2)

Named for a district in southeastern Queens County not far from Wight's native Flat River, P.E.I. this lively jig is in all probability a local tune. Standard notation for my source version is in *Fiddle Music of P.E.I.*

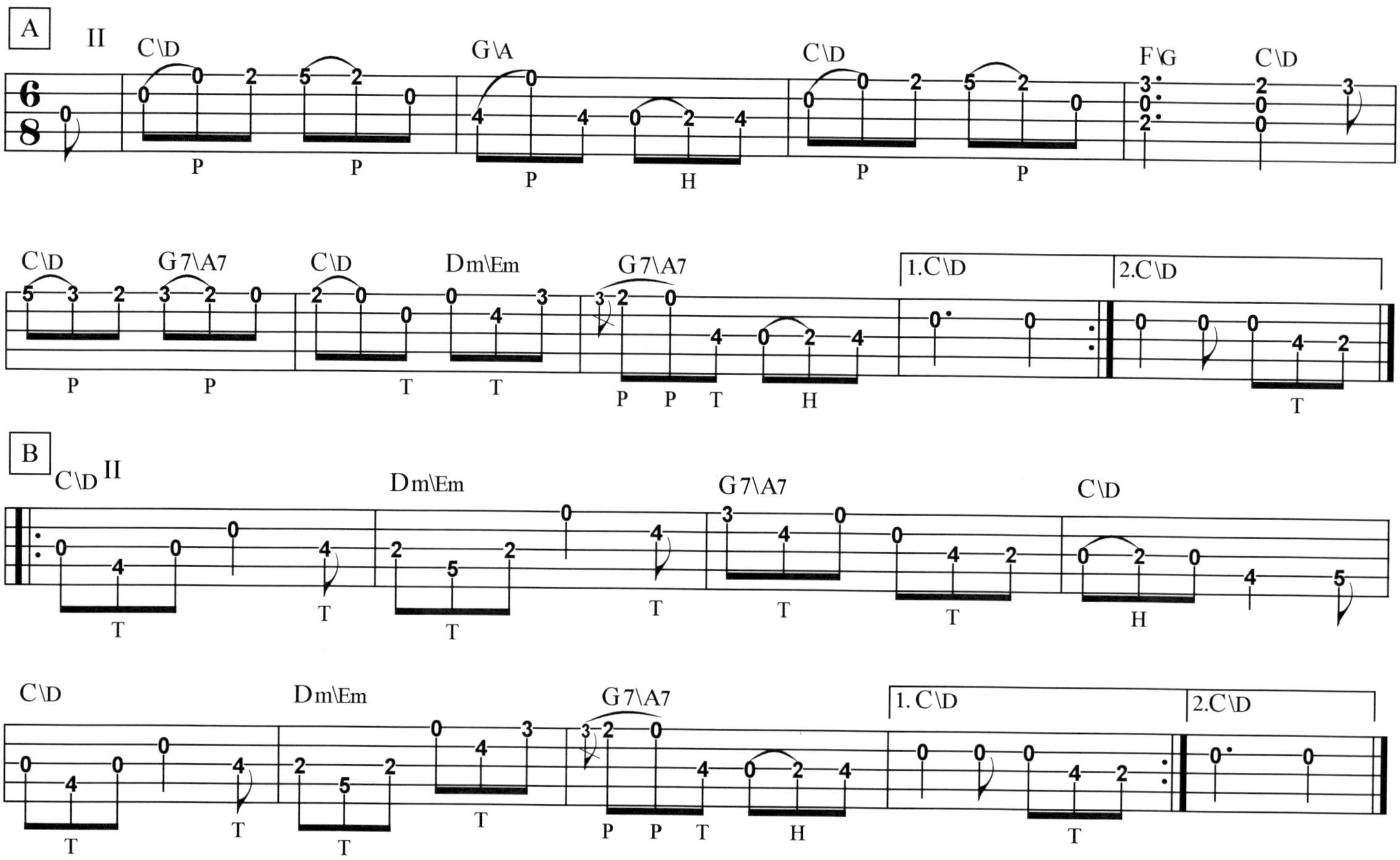

Playing Note for *Belfast Jig*

***Dual Chord Symbols:** Chord to left of backslash goes with open banjo; chord on right is for capoed banjo or fiddle*

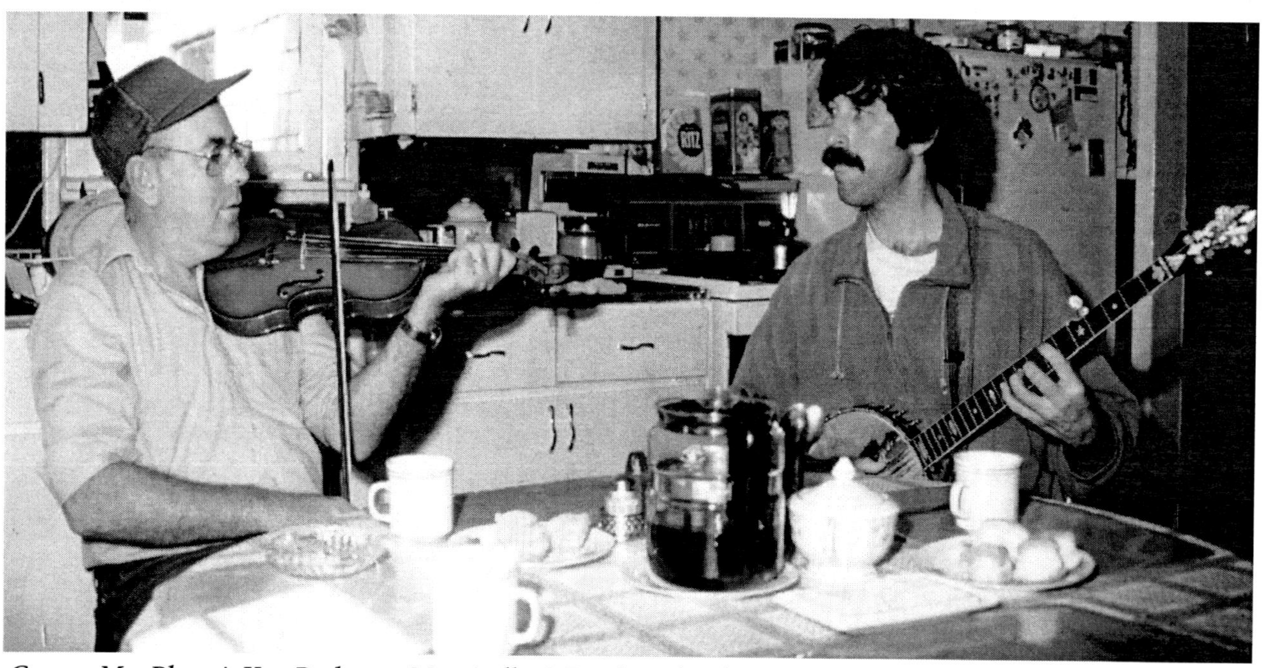

George MacPhee & Ken Perlman: Monticello, P.E.I. (1992). Photo by and © Mike Hird; used by permission

118

Shandon Bells

Origin: Ireland
Source: Allan MacDonald
Appears on: *Northern Banjo*

Key: D (C on Banjo)
Mode: Major
Tuning: gCGCD (Capo-2)

Named for a famous bell-tower in the city of Cork, this tune first appeared in print in *O'Neill's Music of Ireland.* O'Neill's source had no title for the tune, so O'Niell – a native of County Cork – simply invented one that celebrated his home town. He then elected to reprint the tune on the opening page of his next collection, *O'Neill's Dance Music of Ireland.* New Brunswick fiddler Earl Mitton recorded "Shandon Bells" in 1960 on the LP, *Fiddlin' for Fun with Earl Mitton & the Rhythm Valley Boys*. Standard notation for my source version is in *Fiddle Music of P.E.I.*

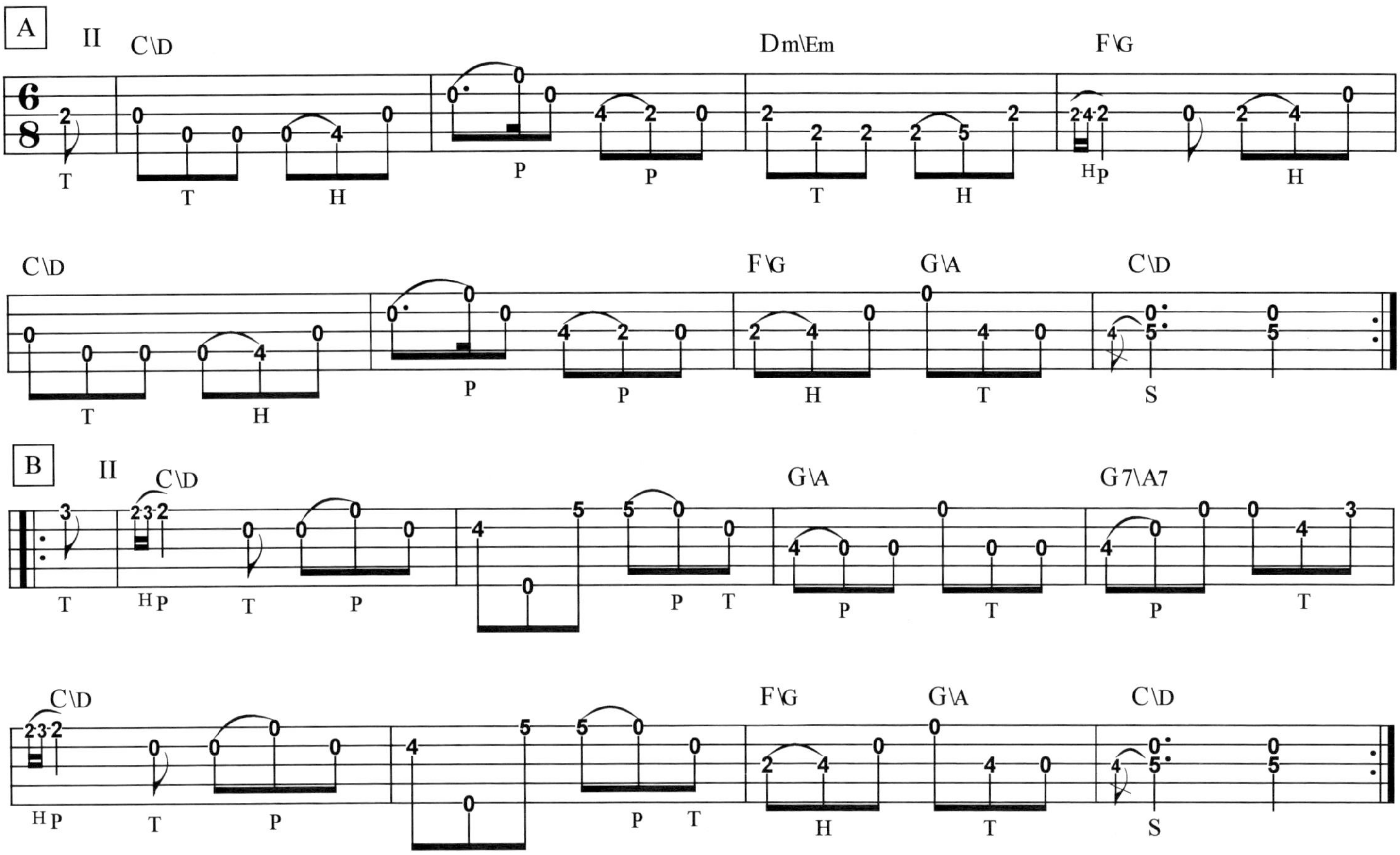

Playing Note for *Shandon Bells*

***Dual Chord Symbols:** Chord to left of backslash goes with open banjo; chord on right is for capoed banjo or fiddle*

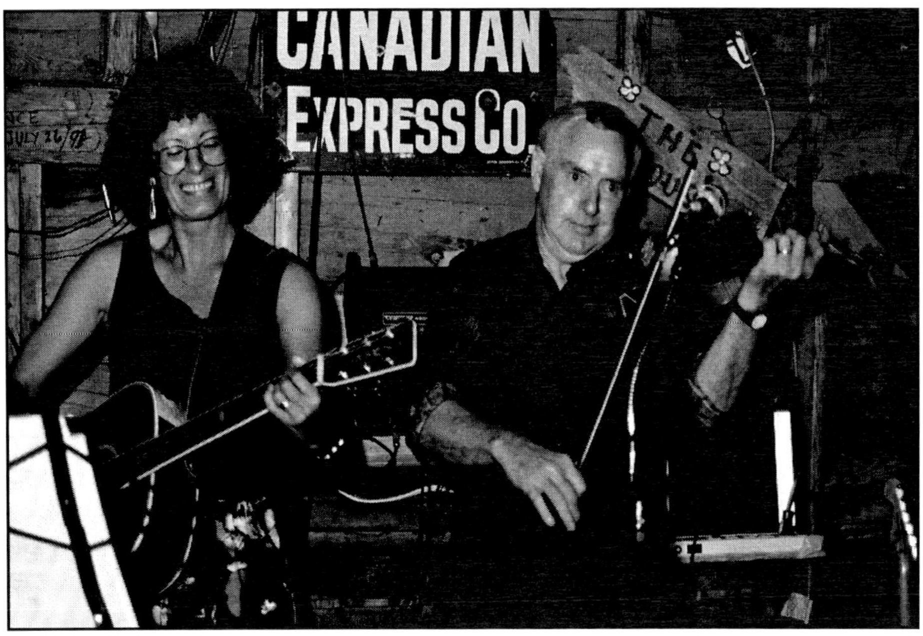

Claire & Leonard McDonald: Kellys Cross, P.E.I. (1992). Photo by Ken Perlman; courtesy Robertson Library, University of P.E.I.

119

The Stool of Repentance

Origin: Scotland
Source: Reuben Smith
Appears on: *Devil in the Kitchen*

Key: A (G on Banjo)
Mode: Major
Tuning: gDGBD (Capo-2)

The title refers, perhaps ironically, to a Scottish Presbyterian custom that remained in force right up to the early 19th century; individuals adjudged to be moral offenders were forced to occupy an elevated seat in church during the service and exhibit themselves for public penance. Interestingly, the tune made its first appearance in print just around the time the custom was waning. "The Stool of Repentance" is featured in *The Gow Collection, Lowe's Collection, Kerr's Merry Melodies, The Skye Collection,* and *The Athole Collection.* Winston Fitzgerald recorded it in the 1950s on his LP, *Canada's Outstanding Scottish Fiddler.* Part B seems to have been "inherited" from an earlier tune appearing in several mid-18th century Scottish manuscript collections that went by a variety of names, such as "Wright's Rant" and "Scots Over the Border." Standard notation for my source version is in *Fiddle Music of P.E.I.*

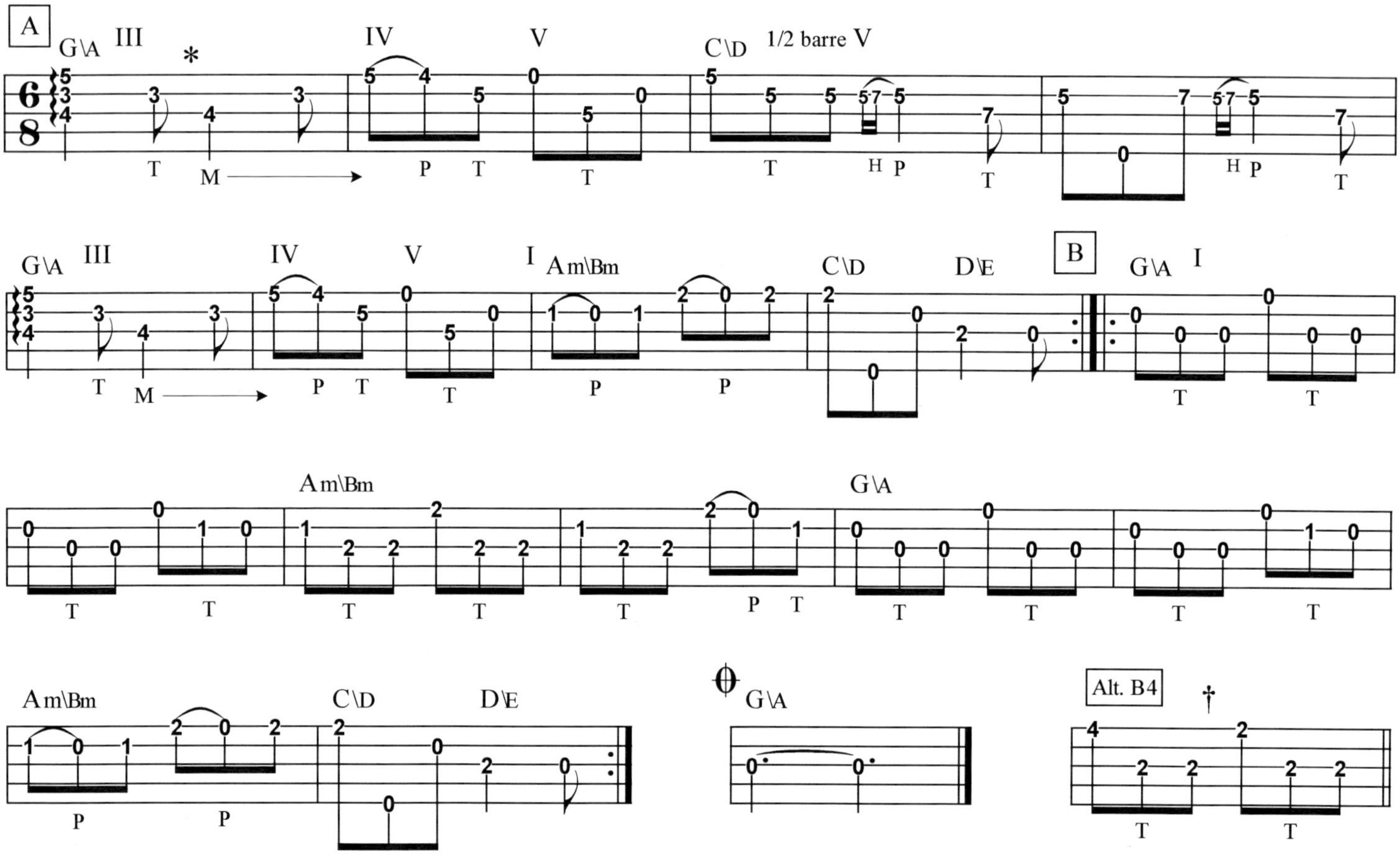

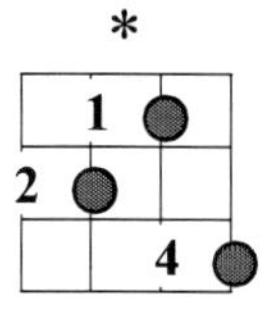

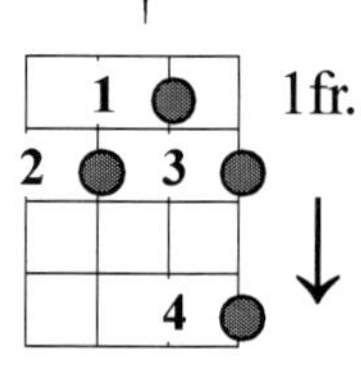

Playing Tips for *Stool of Repentance*

__Dual Chord Symbols:__ Chord to left of backslash goes with open banjo; chord on right is for capoed banjo or fiddle

• Part A, measure 2. At the start of the measure place three fingers on the fretboard at once – the 1st finger at fret 4, string 1, the 2nd finger at fret 5, string 2 and the 3rd finger at fret 5, string 1. The sequence is then as follows: pull-off on string 1 from fret 5 to fret 4; pluck string 2 with T; then on the open string, use the 2nd finger as a pivot and move the 1st finger over to fret 5, string 3.

120

Come Under My Plaidie

Origin: Scotland
Source: "Old Peter" Chaisson
Appears on: *Devil in the Kitchen*

Key: A (G on Banjo)
Mode: See Intro
Tuning: gDGBD (Capo-2)

This tune goes back to the late 18th century. The original Scottish name seems to have been "Johnny McGill," and indeed the tune appears under this moniker in *The Gow Repertory, The Skye Collection,* and *The Athole Collection*; it is dubbed "The Black Rogue" in *O'Neill's Music of Ireland.* The "Come Under My Plaidie" name comes from the title of a Scottish song set to this melody; that name appears in *Kerr's Merry Melodies* and *Ryan's Mammoth Collection*, and is the one most associated with the tune nowadays. The tune is usually played in G; I performed it with the capo on the recording so I could medley it with "Stool of Repentance" (p. 126). The character of the mode is ambiguous. Although the tune seems to be major-like with an A key center (G on open banjo), each part ends on a strong F♯-note (E♮ on open banjo), implying that the tune is minor. To further complicate matters, the note D (C on open banjo) – that is, the 4th *tone* of the major scale and 6th of the minor – is completely missing from both parts. Standard notation for my source version is in *Fiddle Music of P.E.I.*

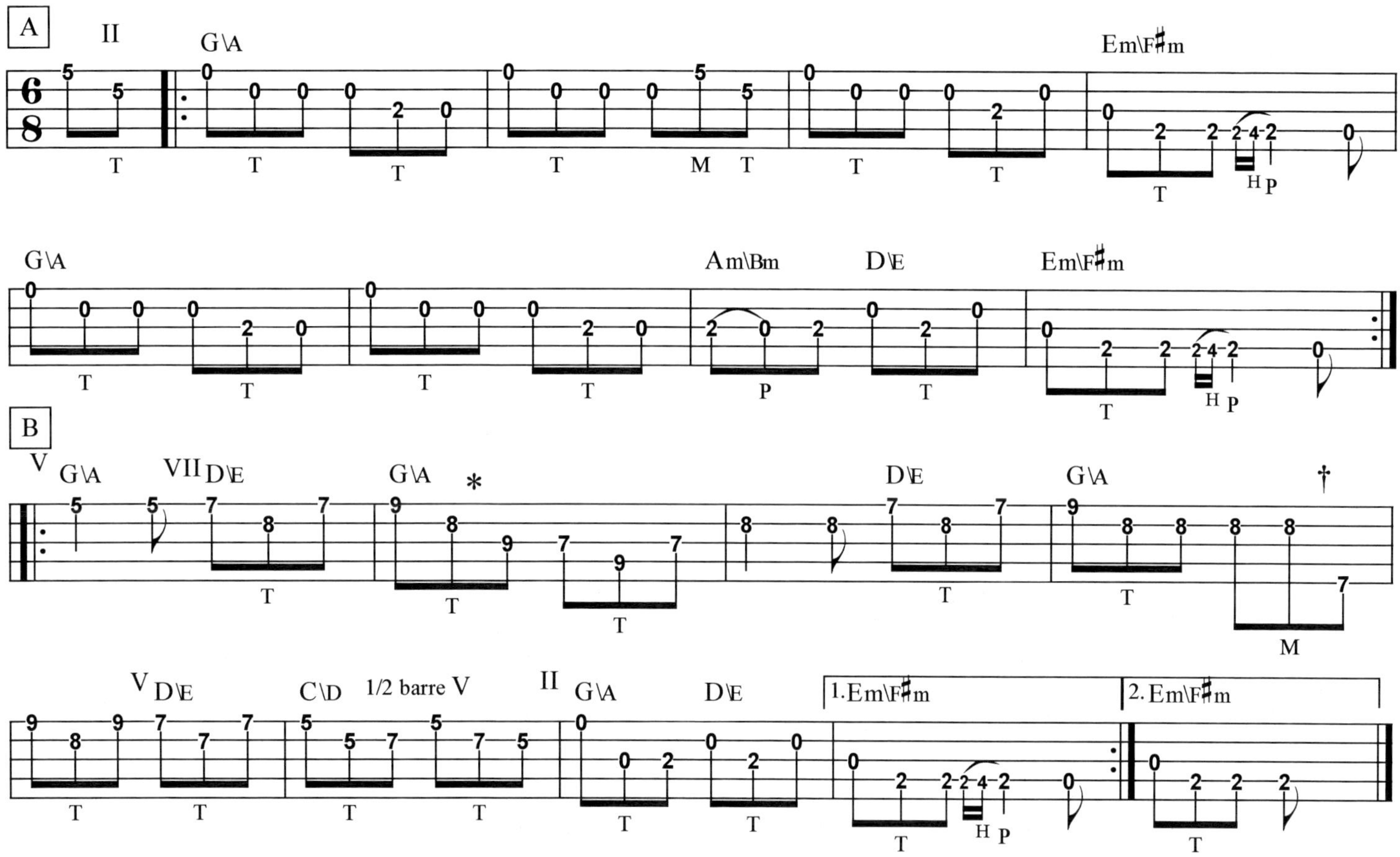

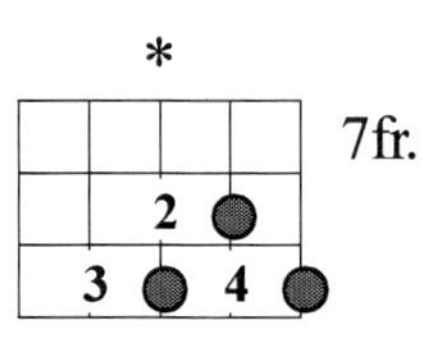

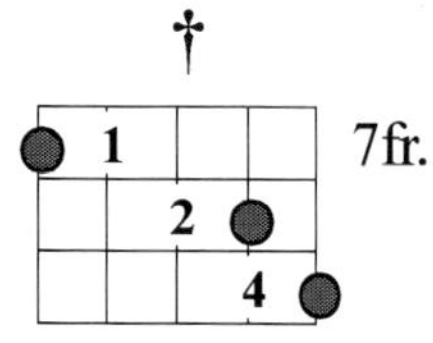

Playing Tips for *Come Under Me Plaidie*

***Dual Chord Symbols:** Chord to left of backslash goes with open banjo; chord on right is for capoed banjo or fiddle*

• Part B, measures 1-2. At the end of measure 1, the 1st and 2nd fingers should be stationed at fret 7, string 1 and fret 8, string 2 respectively. At the beginning of measure 2, use the 2nd finger as a pivot and swing the 3rd and 4th fingers into place on fret 9, string 3 and fret 9, string 1 respectively as shown in Diagram *. Then cut short fret 9, string 3 and reach over with the 1st and 3rd fingers to catch fret 7, string 3 and fret 9, string 4 respectively.

Irishman's Heart to the Ladies

121

ORIGIN: IRELAND
SOURCE: EDDY ARSENAULT
APPEARS ON: *ISLAND BOY*

KEY: A (G ON BANJO)
MODE: MAJOR
TUNING: gDGBD (Capo-2)

"Irishman's Heart to the Ladies" is fairly common in Celtic-music circles around the world. It appears under this title in *Ryan's Mammoth Collection*, and as "Sweet Biddy Daly" in *O'Neill's Music of Ireland.* I patterned my banjo arrangement on Eddy Arsenault's unique approach to the phrasing of the tune. Standard notation for my source version is in *Fiddle Music of P.E.I.*

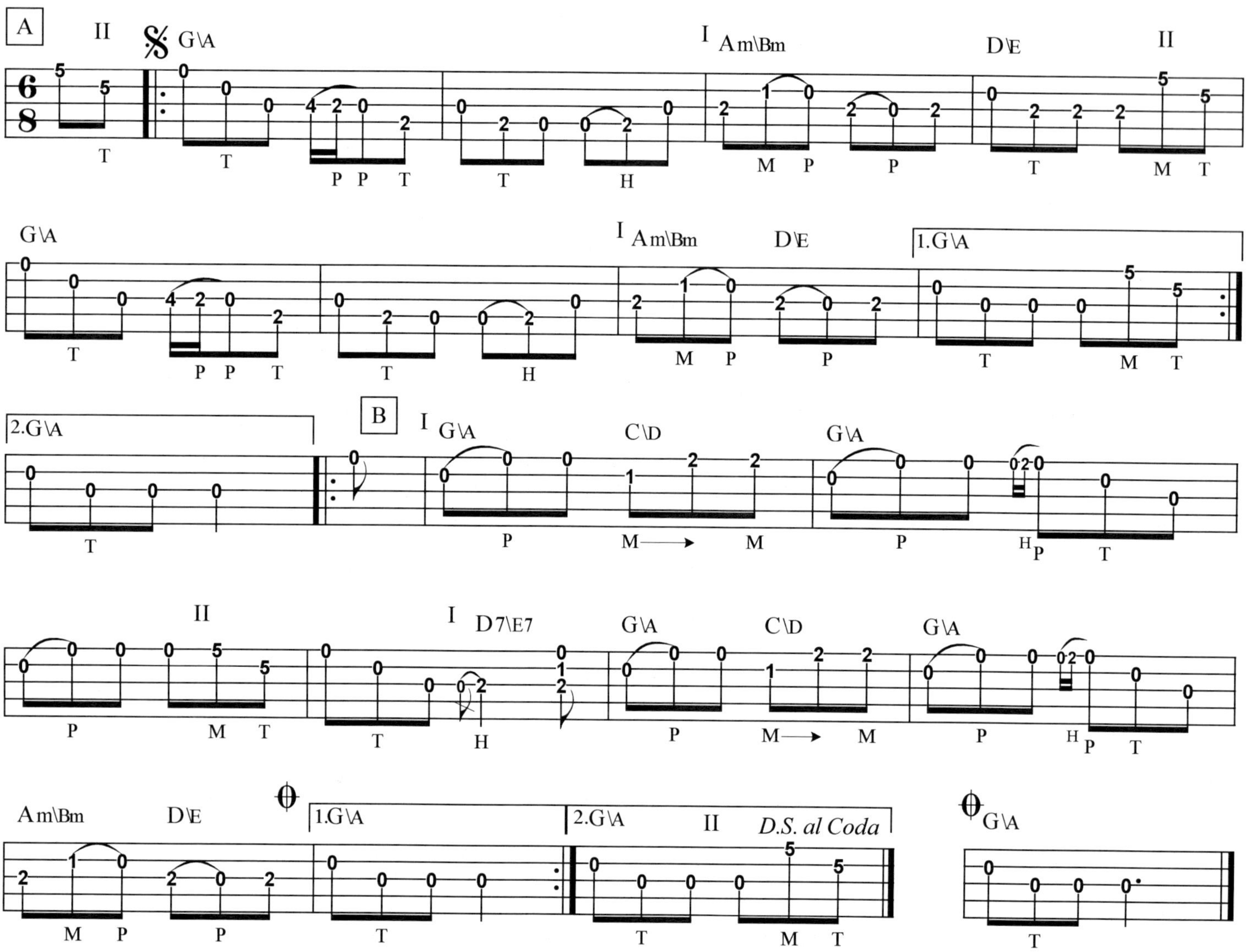

PLAYING NOTE FOR *IRISHMAN'S HEART TO THE LADIES*

***DUAL CHORD SYMBOLS:** Chord to left of backslash goes with open banjo; chord on right is for capoed banjo or fiddle*

122

River Bend Jig

Composer: Dan R. MacDonald
Source: Andrew Jones
Appears on: *Island Boy*

Key: A (G on Banjo)
Mode: See Intro
Tuning: gDGBD (Capo-2)

Dan R. MacDonald was one of the most prolific composers in the Cape Breton idiom. The title commemorates a successful day of fishing at a stream near the composer's home. Recordings of the tune were released in the 1970s on Rounder by Carl MacKenzie and Theresa MacLellan (1927-2020). Most of the tune features the major 3rd and minor 7th of a Mixolydian gamut, but at the start of the Part B second ending, the minor 3rd – C♮ on fiddle, B♭ on open banjo – makes a brief, but dramatic appearance. Standard notation for my source version is in *Fiddle Music of P.E.I.*

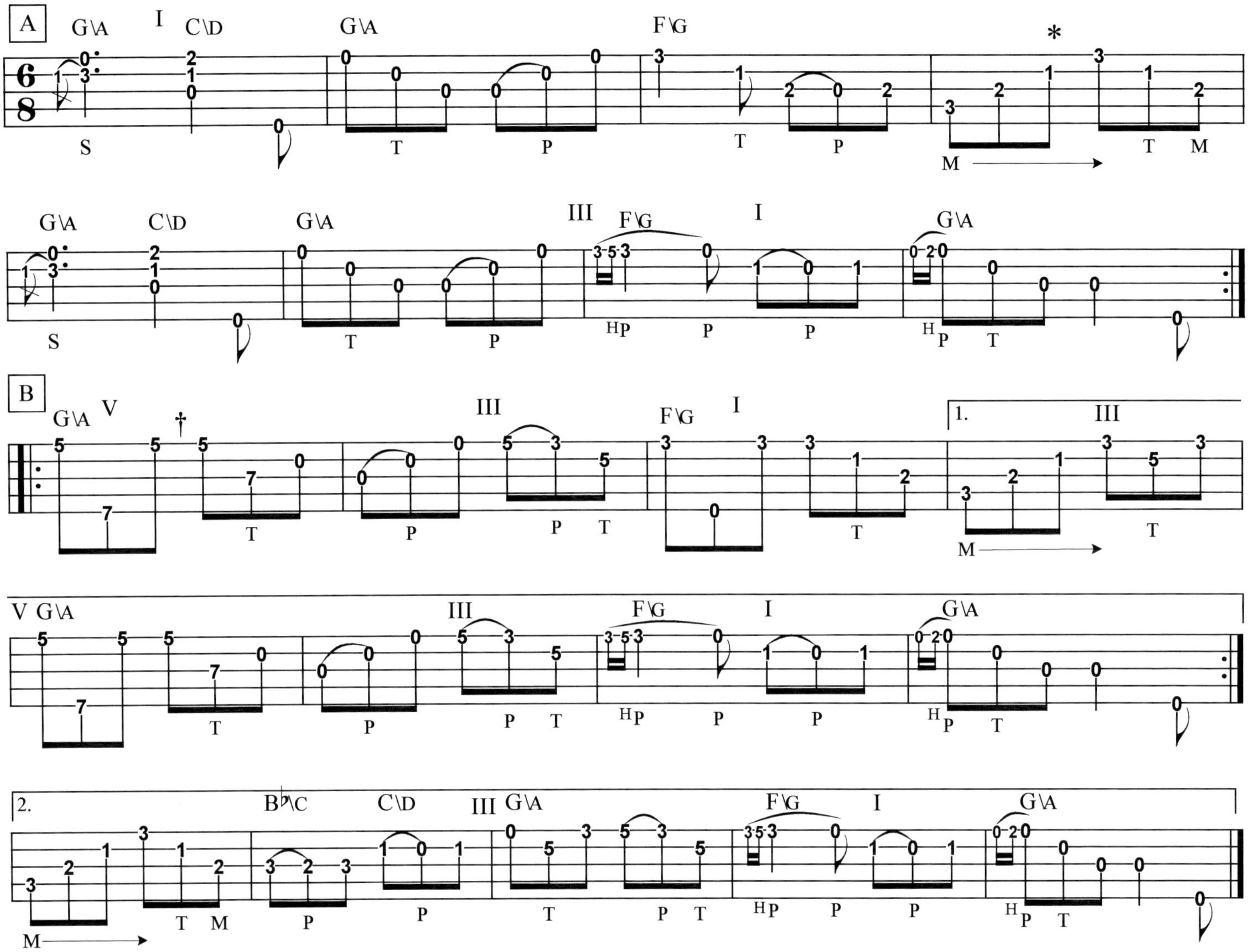

Playing Note for *River Bend Jig*

***Dual Chord Symbols:** Chord to left of backslash goes with open banjo; chord on right is for capoed banjo or fiddle*

Rock Valley Jig

123

Origin: Québec or Ontario
Source: Sidney Baglole
Appears on: *Northern Banjo*

Key: C
Mode: Major
Tuning: gCGCD

Rock Valley Jig was first recorded in 1933 by George Wade & His Cornhuskers, a prominent Canadian band that often included Québecois master fiddler Jean Carignan (Don Messer later credited the Cornhuskers with inspiring him to create his own ensemble, Don Messer & His Islanders). Messer himself recorded the tune on a 78 disk; it was later re-issued on his 1970s LP, *The Good Old Days.* Standard notation for my source version is in *Fiddle Music of P.E.I.*

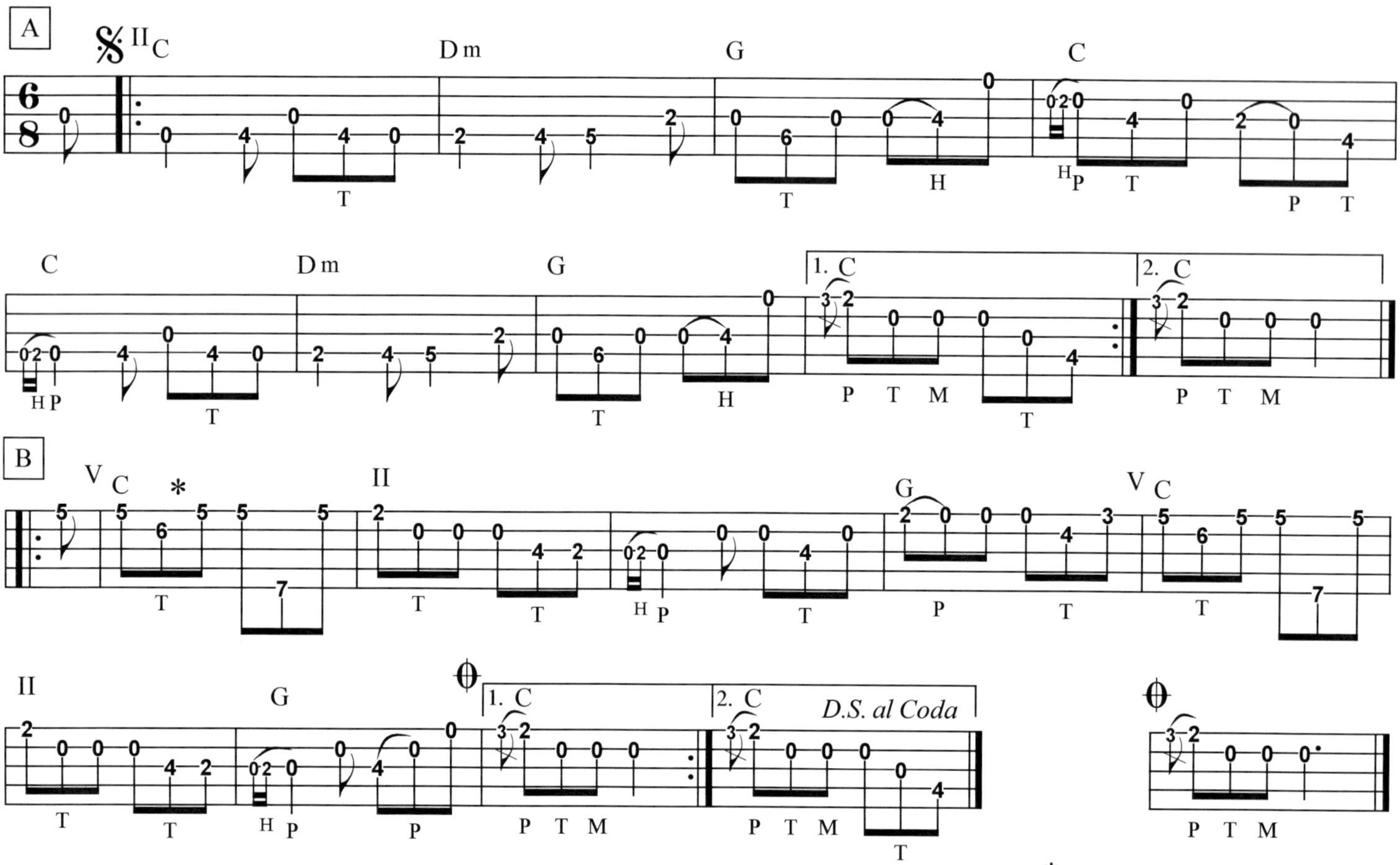

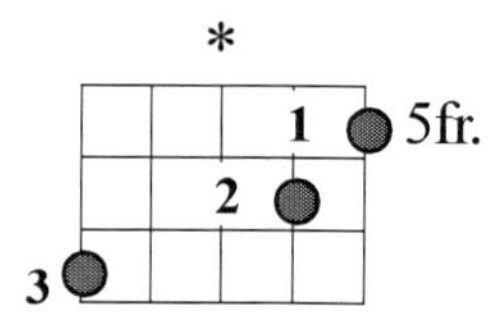

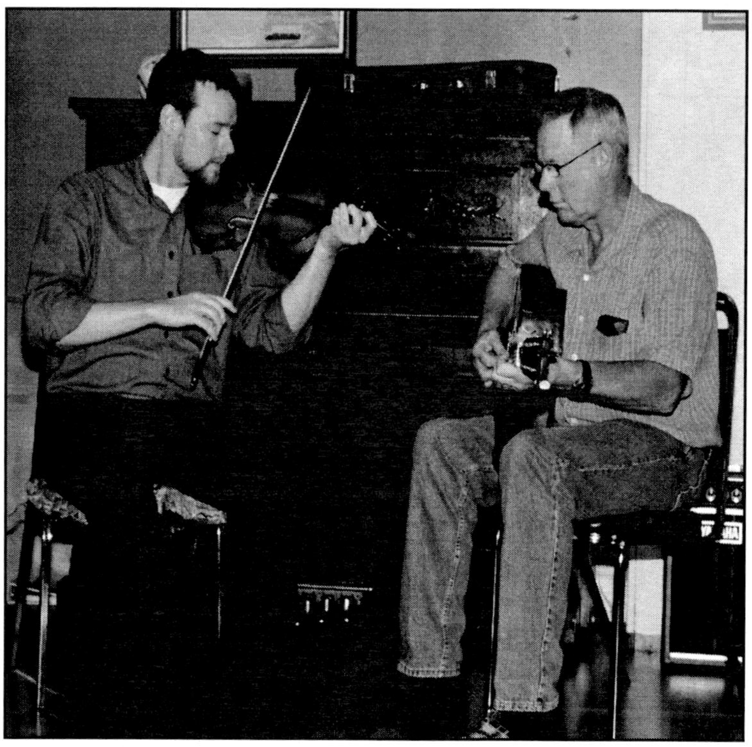

Ward MacDonald (fiddle) & Allan MacDonald: Bangor, P.E.I. (2006). Photo by Ken Perlman; courtesy Robertson Library, University of P.E.I.

124

The Orange & Blue

ORIGIN: SCOTLAND
SOURCE: STEPHEN TOOLE
APPEARS ON: *NORTHERN BANJO*

KEY: D (C ON BANJO)
MODE: MAJOR
TUNING: gCGCD (Capo-2)

Orange and blue were the colors of William of Orange, the Dutch prince who was crowned King of England in the 1690s. The melody has been played in a few different metric formats and in different keys (C is the most common). In *Kerr's Merry Melodies, vol. 2* and *The Skye Collection,* it appears in 6/8 time. In *The Gow Repertory, Lowe's Collection,* and *Kerr's Merry Melodies, vol. 1* it is presented in 4/4 time and classed as a strathspey or Highland schottische. I have also heard it played in cut time as a set tune. Cape Breton fiddlers Johnny Wilmot, Donald Angus Beaton, and Buddy MacMaster recorded the 6/8 version. Two stylistic notes: I follow Toole's practice of playing the high part first; and I inserted moving bass lines in that part to enhance the arrangement. Standard notation for my source version is in *Fiddle Music of P.E.I.*

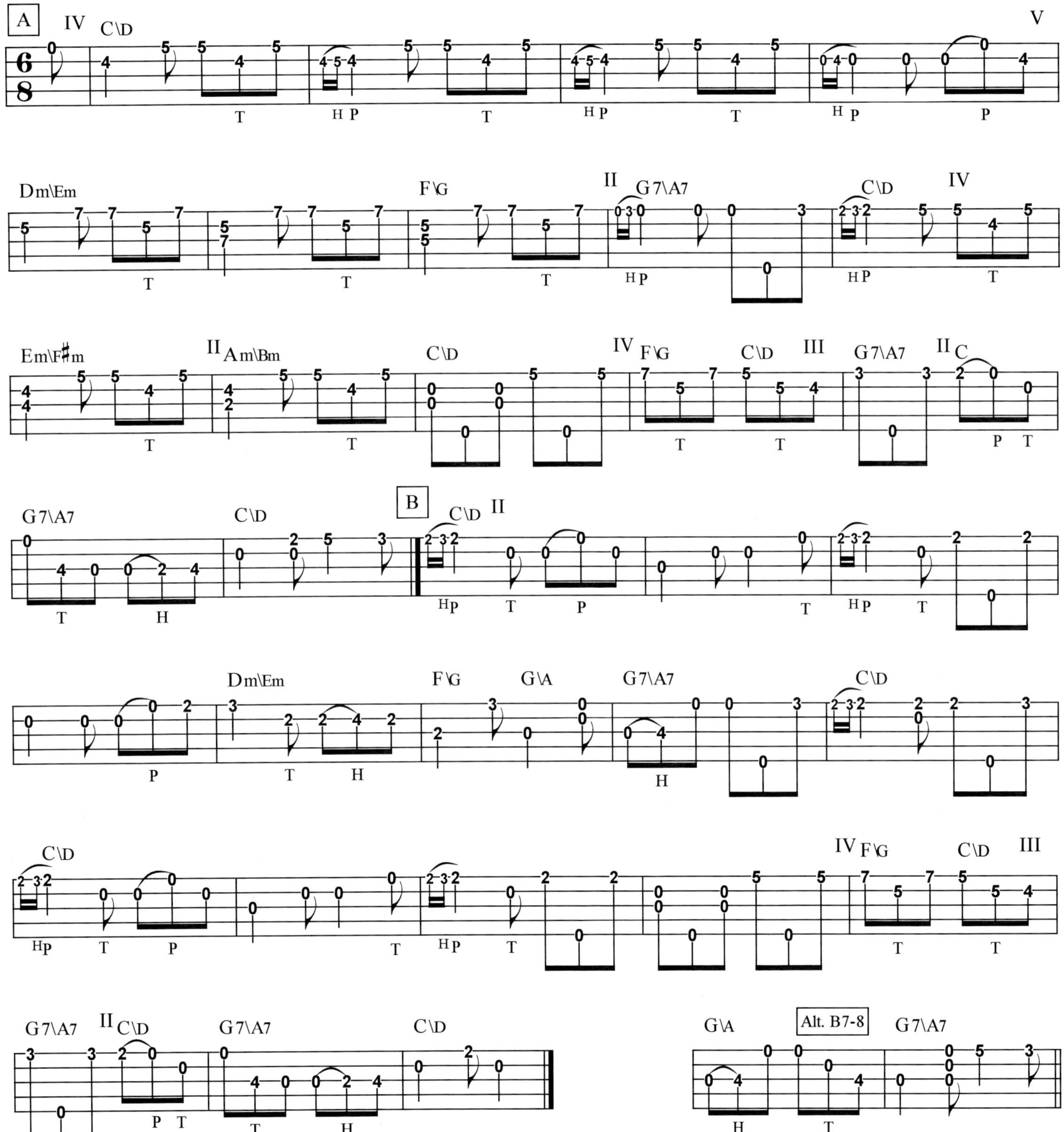

***DUAL CHORD SYMBOLS:** Chord to left of backslash goes with open banjo; chord on right is for capoed banjo or fiddle*

125

Bear River Jig

Composer: See Intro
Sources: Kevin Chaisson
Appears on: *Island Boy*

Key: D (C on Banjo)
Mode: Major
Tuning: gCGCD (Capo-2)

Back in the 90s, Kevin Chaisson played me a tune that had just sprung to mind; he hadn't named it yet but decided on the spot to call it "Bear River Jig" after his home district. And when I recorded the tune on *Island Boy*, Chaisson accompanied me on piano. Recently, he informed me that he no longer claims the tune because of similarities to "Jerry Holland's Jig," an earlier composition by Cape Breton fiddler Howie MacDonald (b. 1965). Comparing the two melodies, the A Parts do indeed appear to have substantial similarities; but the B Parts are quite distinct. Both tunes appear here; judge for yourself! Standard notation for my source version of "Bear River Jig" is in *Fiddle Music of P.E.I.*

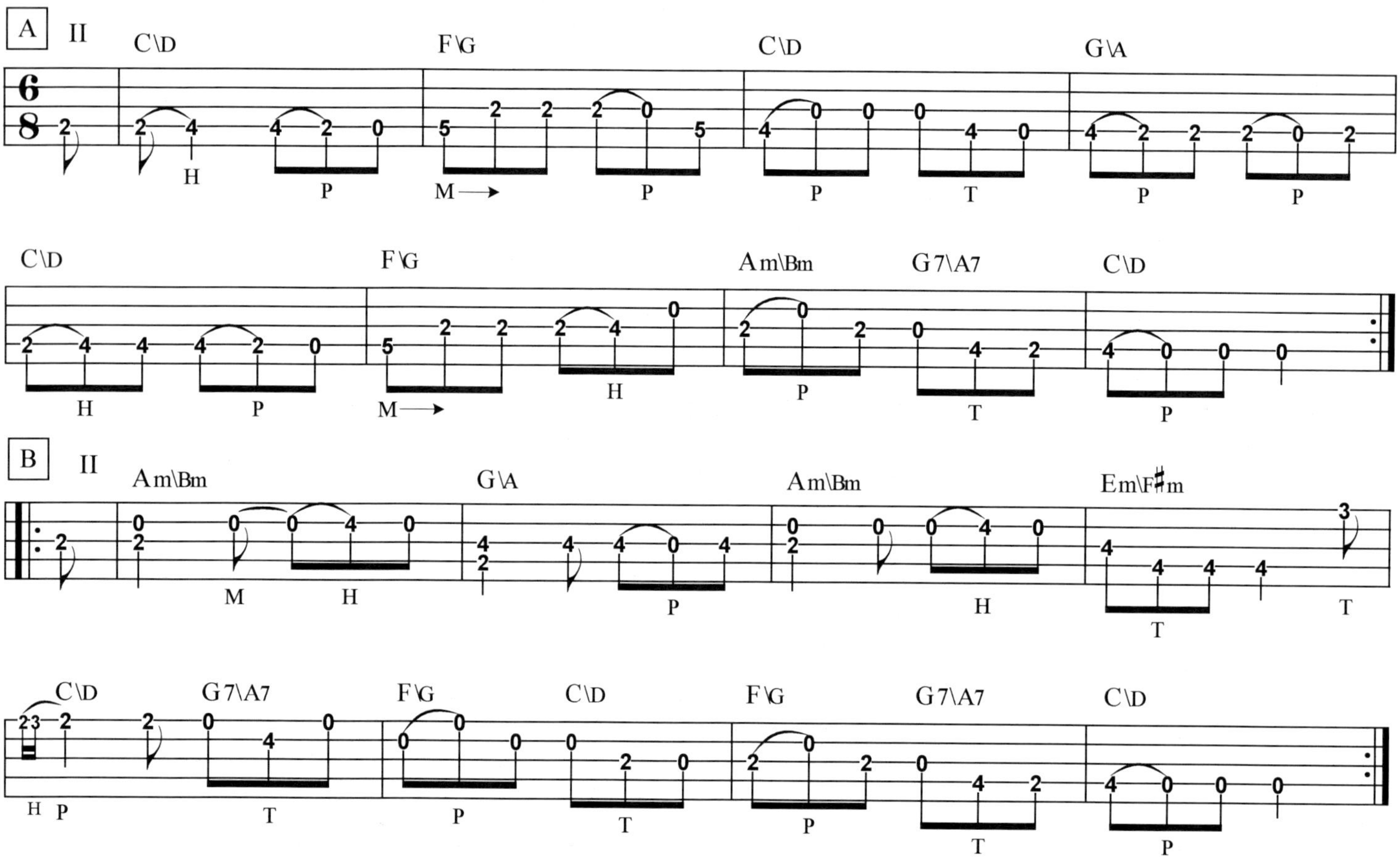

Dual Chord Symbols: Chord to left of backslash goes with open banjo; chord on right is for capoed banjo or fiddle

126

Jerry Holland's Jig

Composer: Howie MacDonald
Source: Howie MacDonald

Key: A (G on Banjo)
Mode: Major
Tuning: gDGBD (Capo-2)

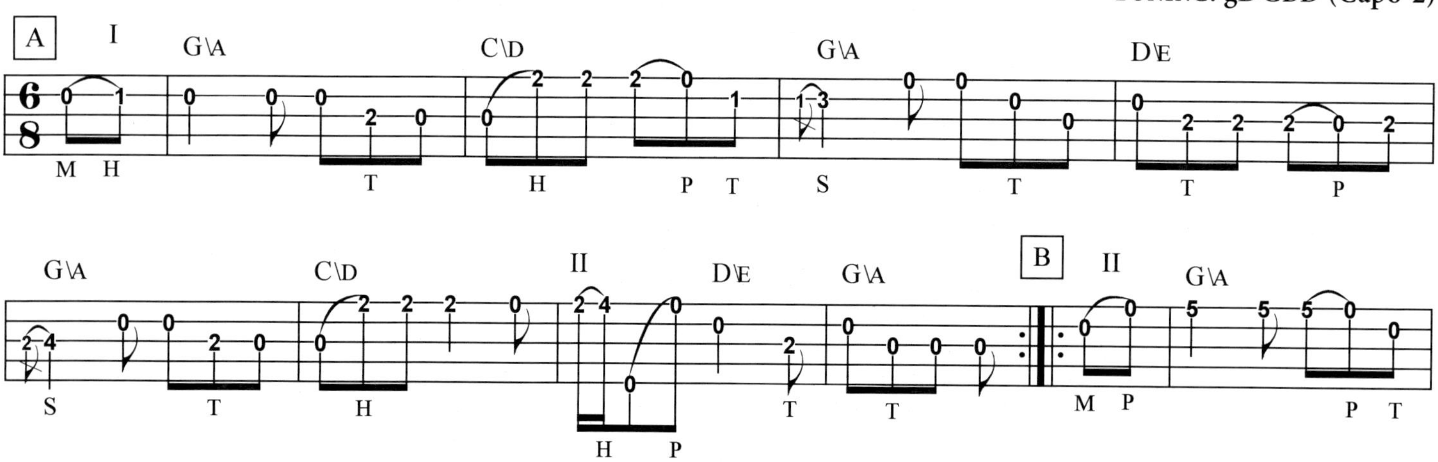

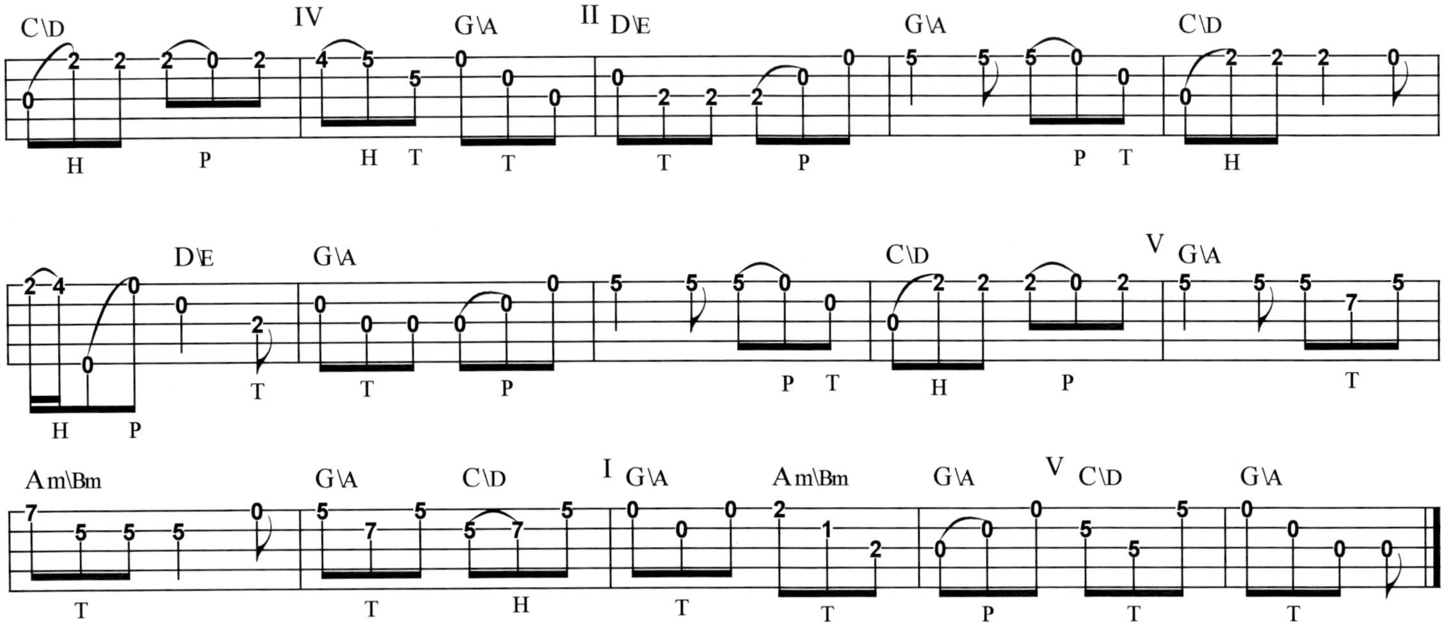

"Jerry Holland's Jig" © 1987 by Howie MacDonald. SOCAN; used by permission

Don't Be Teasing

127

ORIGIN: IRELAND
SOURCE: STERLING BAKER
APPEARS ON: *FRAILS & FROLICS*

KEY: D
MODE: MAJOR
TUNING: gDGBD

"Don't be Teasing" is widely played on PEI; it is of Irish origin and is printed in *O'Neill's Dance Music of Ireland,* but nowadays it does not seem to be widely known in the Irish traditional music scene. I opted to play this key of D tune in open G tuning to sandwich it in a medley between two tunes in the key of G – "Rose of Tennessee" (p. 137) and "Whiskey Jig" (p. 136). Standard notation for my source version is in *Fiddle Music of P.E.I.*

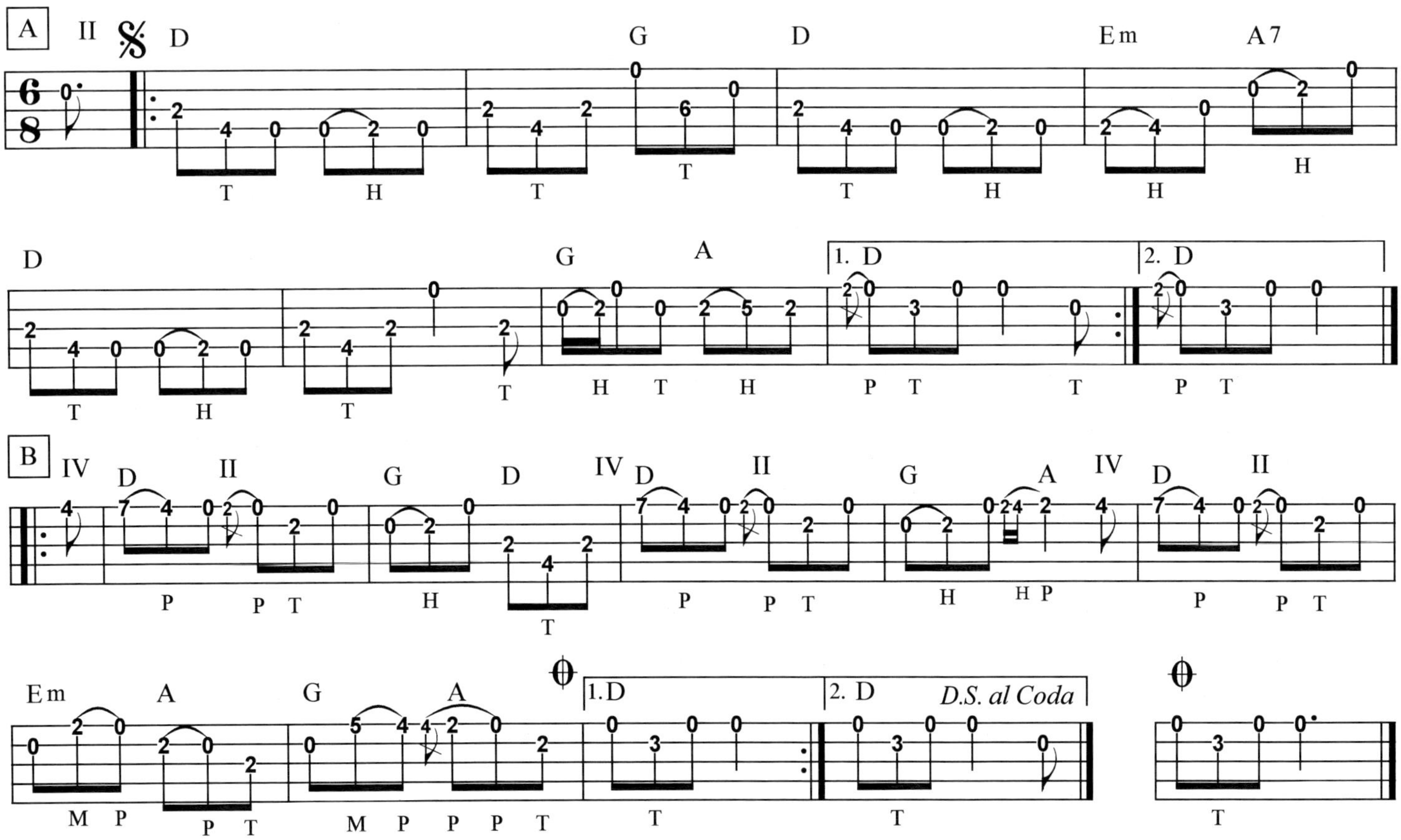

128

The Shores of Lough Gowna

Origin: Ireland
Source: Kevin Chaisson
Appears on: *Frails & Frolics*

Keys: B & D (A & C on Banjo)
Mode: See Intro
Tuning: gCGCD (Capo-2)

Named for a lake not far from the city of Longford in central Ireland, this popular Irish session tune has been recorded many times over the last few decades by traditional Irish musicians. A version of the tune was printed in *O'Neill's Music of Ireland* as "Banks of Lough Gowna." The mode for Part A is close to minor pentatonic – no 2nd at all (C♯ on fiddle; B on open banjo) and just a hint of an Aeolian 6th (G♮ on fiddle; F♮ on open banjo). At the start of Part B, the melody seems to move into a major mode but completely avoids the 7th tone (C♯ on fiddle; B on open banjo). The upshot is that the note C♯ (B♮ on open banjo) is absent throughout. The tune is circular; and I've included a final-sounding ending. Standard notation for my source version is in *Fiddle Music of P.E.I.*

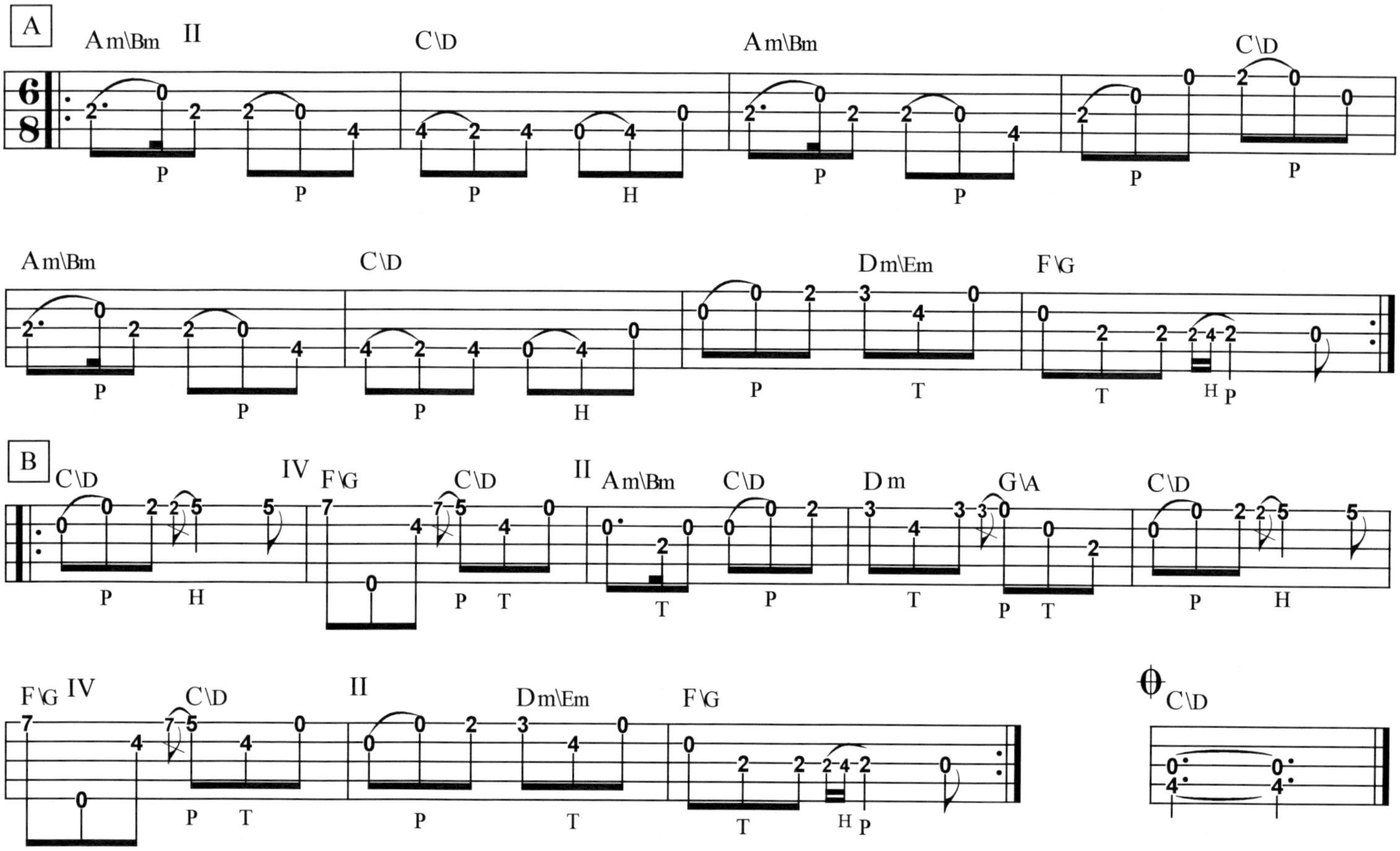

Playing Note for *The Shores of Loughgowna*

***Dual Chord Symbols:** Chord to left of backslash goes with open banjo; chord on right is for capoed banjo or fiddle*

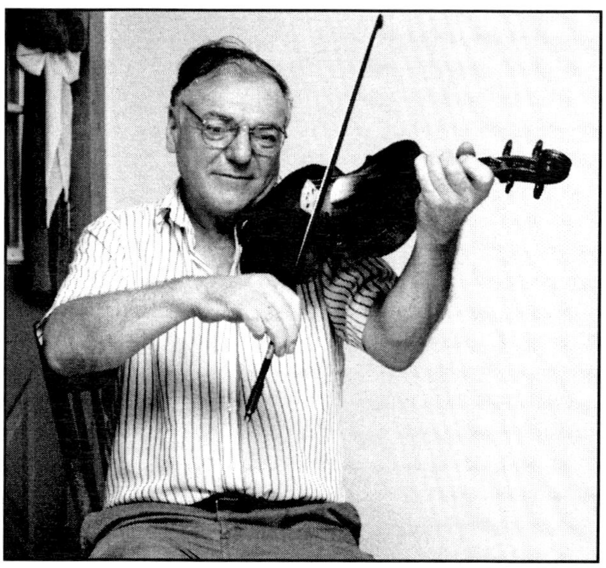

Dennis Pitre: St. Felix, P.E.I. (1996). Photo by Ken Perlman; courtesy Robertson Library, University of P.E.I.

129

Teviot Bridge

Composer: See Intro
Source: Gus Longaphie
Appears on: *Frails & Frolics*

Key: A (G on Banjo)
Mode: Major
Tuning: gCGCD (Capo-2)

In 1795, a bridge was built over the River Teviot near the town of Kelso in southern Scotland. This commemorative tune is attributed to "A. Gives of Kelso" and appears in various 19th-century Scottish tune books including *The Gow Repository, Kerr's Merry Melodies, The Skye Collection* and *The Athole Collection*. Relatively close variants appear as "Pivot Bridge" in *Ryan's Mammoth Collection* and "Boys of Ballinafad" in *O'Neill's Dance Music of Ireland*. Winston Fitzgerald recorded the tune on his LP, *Canada's Outstanding Scottish Fiddler*. I use a capoed C tuning in order to medley "Teviot Bridge" with two tunes for which this tuning was the best choice – "The Bonny Lea Rig" (p. 147) and "The Shores of Lough Gowna" (facing page). Standard notation for my source version is in *Fiddle Music of P.E.I.*

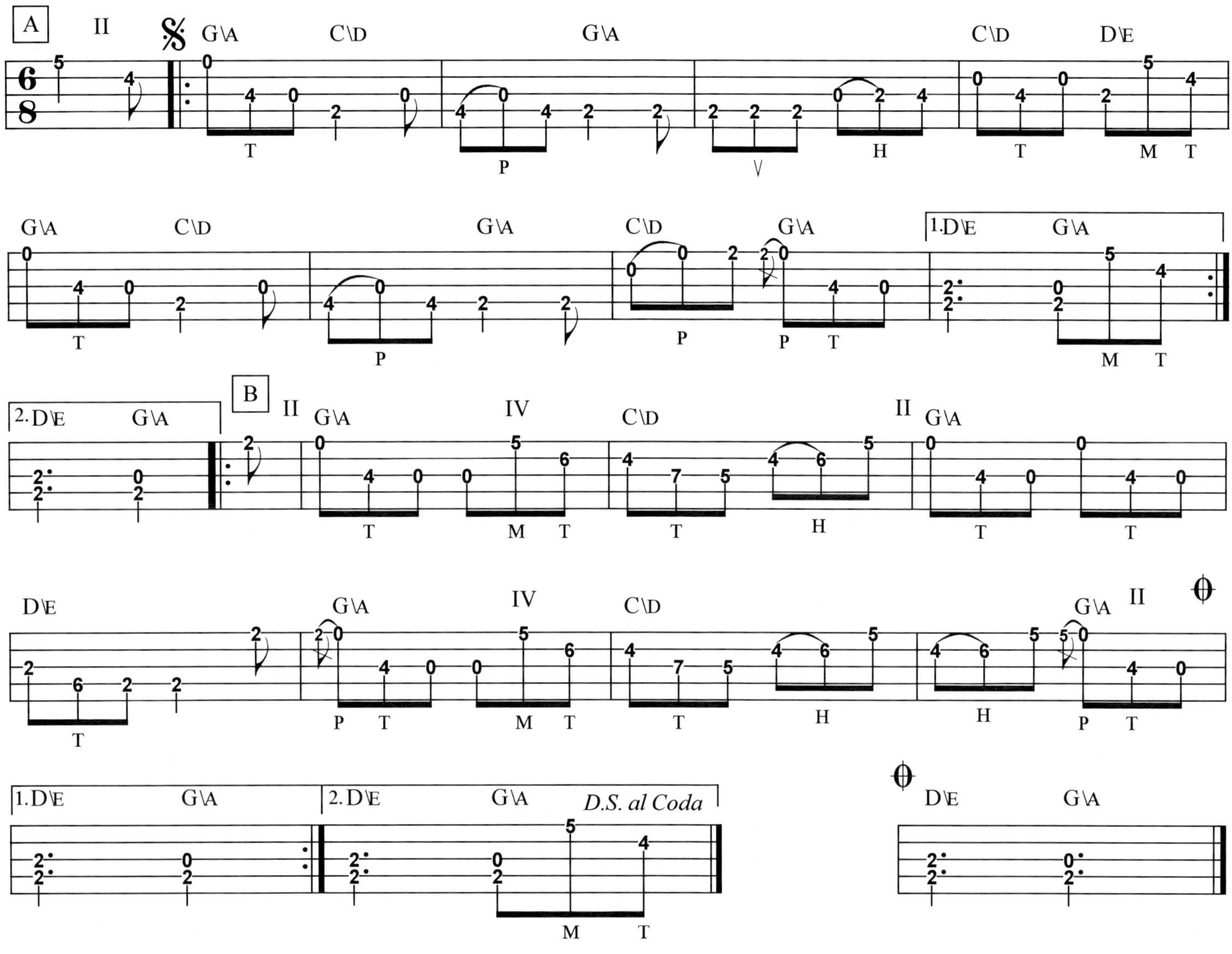

Playing Tips for *Teviot Bridge*

Dual Chord Symbols: Chord to left of backslash goes with open banjo; chord on right is for capoed banjo or fiddle

- Part B, measures 1-2. Towards the end of measure 1, stop fret 5, string 1 and fret 6, string 2 with the 2nd and 3rd fingers, respectively. Balance on the 3rd finger, and – at the beginning of measure 2 – swing the 1st and 4th fingers into place on fret 4, string 2 and fret 7, string 3 respectively. Just before the mid-point, stop fret 5, string 3 with the 2nd finger, and – at the start of the second group of eighth notes – pivot on that finger and swing the 1st and 2nd fingers into position at fret 4, string 2 and fret 5, string 1 respectively. This frees up the 3rd finger to accomplish the subsequent hammer-on from fret 4 to fret 6 on string 2.

130

Whiskey Jig

ORIGIN: HYBRID VARIANT OF IRISH TUNE
SOURCE: STEPHEN TOOLE
APPEARS ON: *FRAILS & FROLICS*

KEY: G
MODE: MAJOR
TUNING: gDGBD

This tune was recorded as "Whiskey Jig" by Donald Angus Beaton (1912-82) and is printed with that appellation in *Traditional Fiddle Music of Cape Breton* (1986). It was previously recorded by Five MacDonald Fiddlers as "Harbour Lights Jig," and by Dan Joe MacInnis (1922-91) as "Marie's Family Jig." Parts B and C derive from "The Irish Jaunting Car," a melody borrowed on the eve of the American Civil War for the Confederate anthem, "The Bonnie Blue Flag." Another variant of "Irish Jaunting Car" – stretched out to cut time and renamed "Coleman's March" – is widely played in the contemporary American old-time music scene. Standard notation for my source version is in *Fiddle Music of P.E.I.*

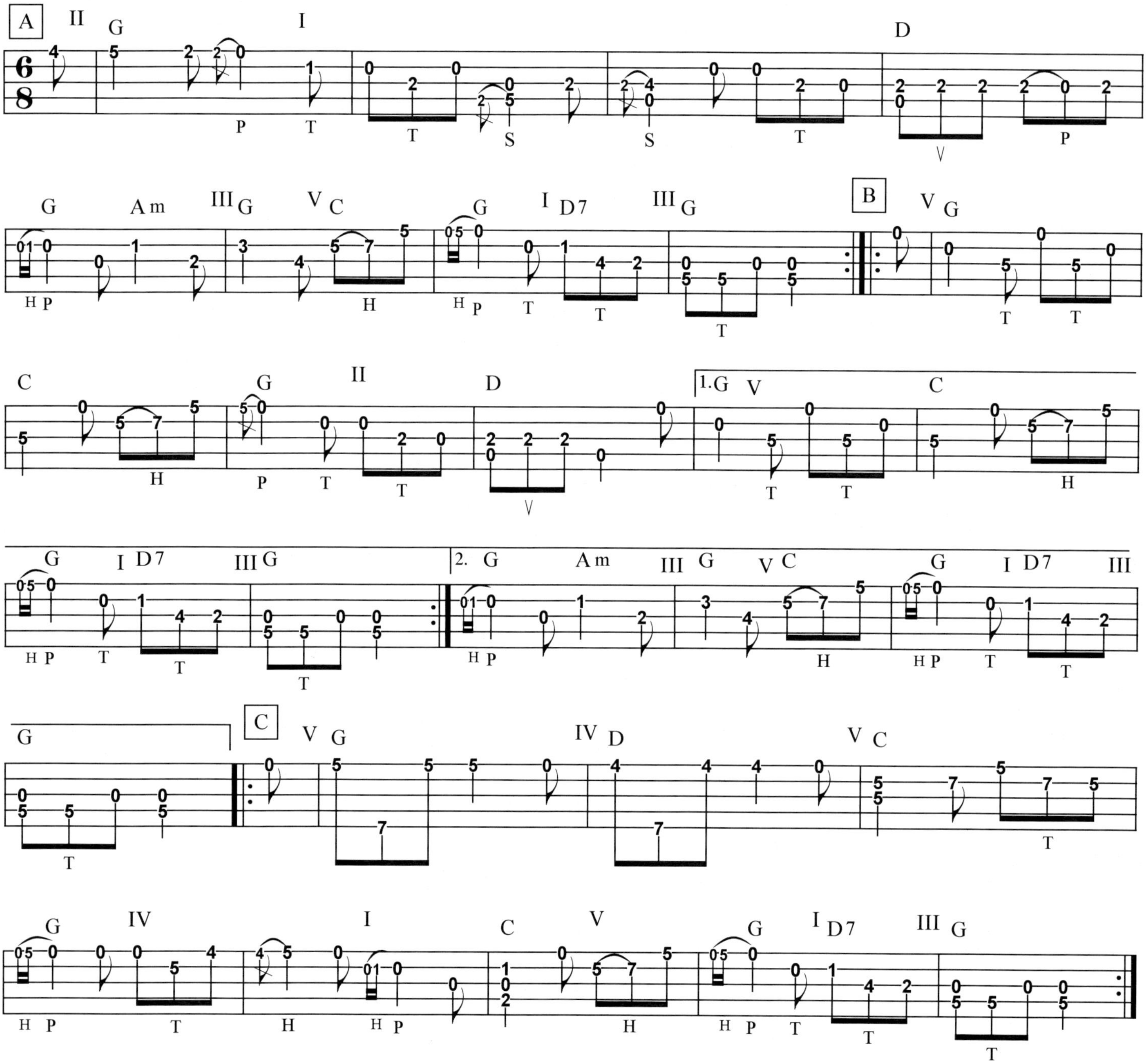

131

The Rose of Tennessee

Origin: Probably Canadian Maritimes
Source: Stephen Toole
Appears on: *Frails & Frolics*

Key: G
Mode: Major
Tuning: gDGBD

"The Rose of Tennessee" represents a style of jig melody that is quite widespread in the Canadian Maritimes and is associated with accompanying the *quadrille* (for more on quadrilles, see Chapter 1). The tune has also been recorded by Cape Breton fiddlers as "Kenloch Jig" and "The Grand Mira." Standard notation for my source version is in *Fiddle Music of P.E.I.*

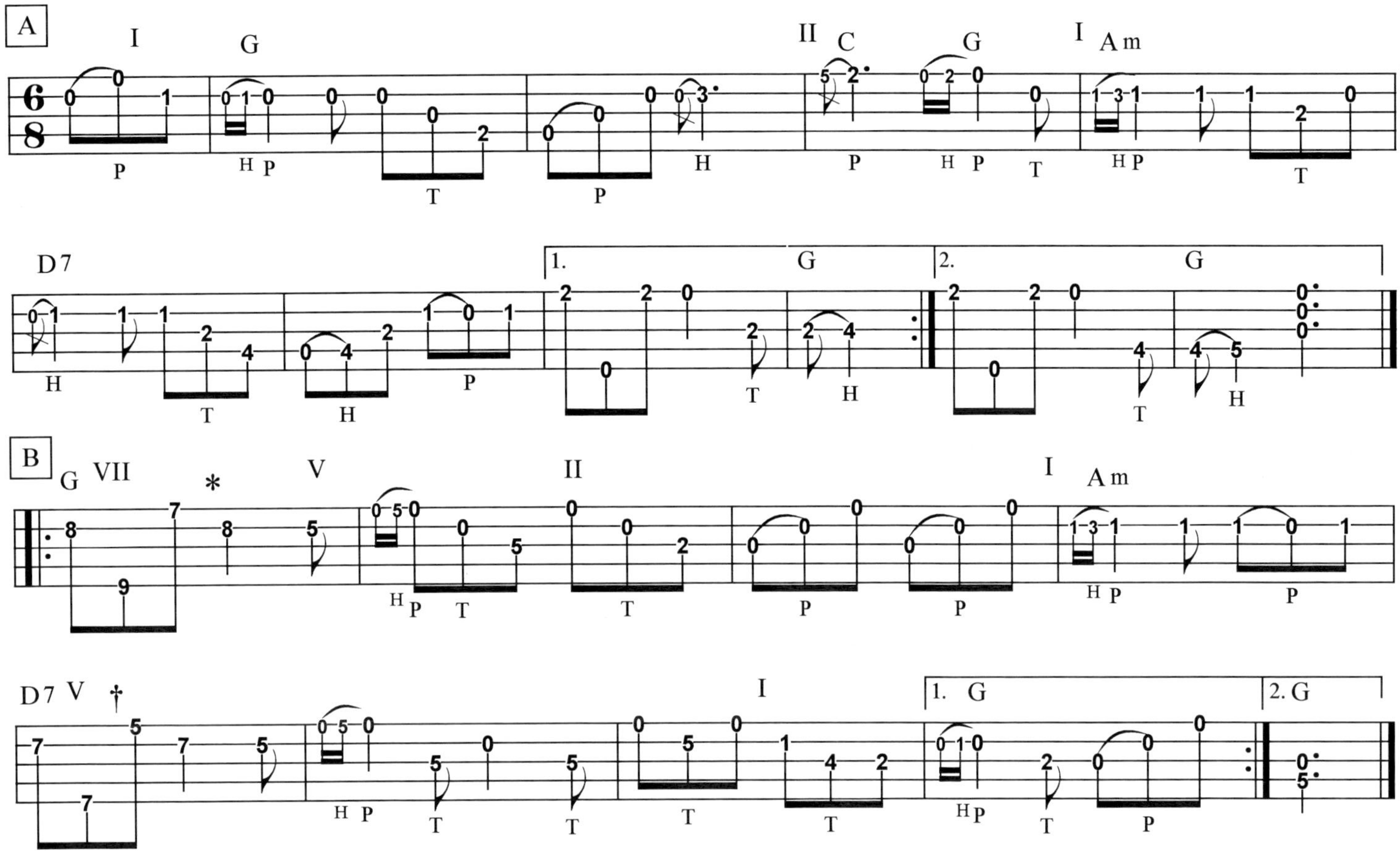

*

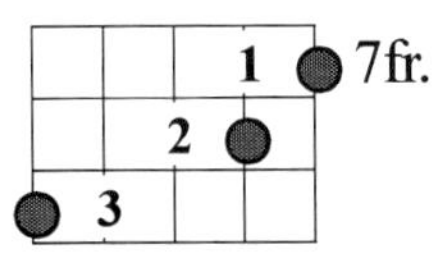

†

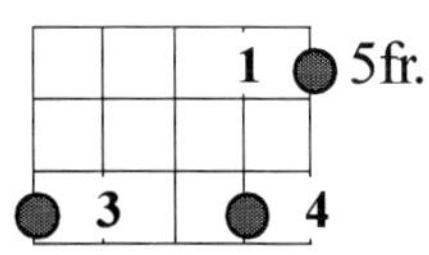

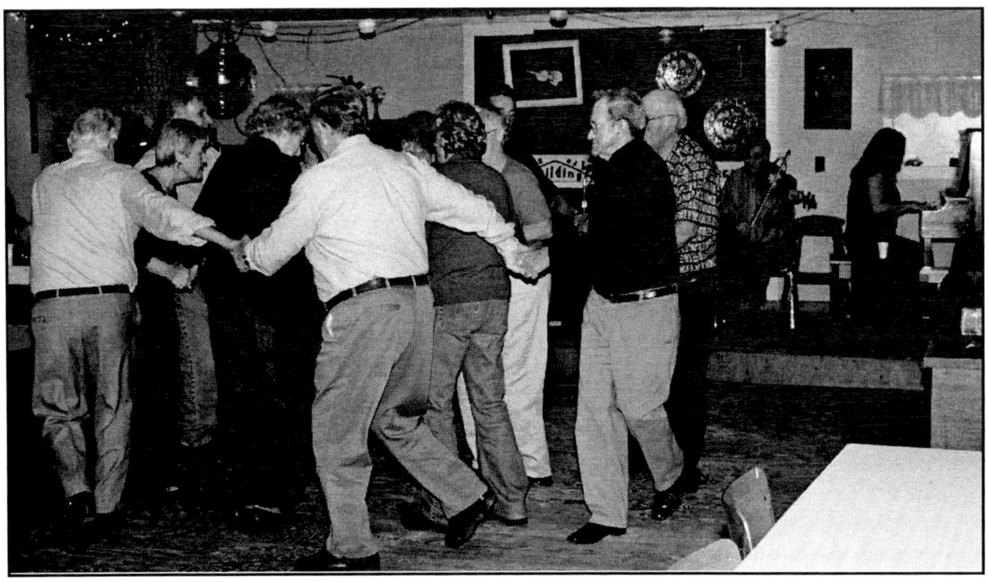

"Ladies in the Center" Quadrille Figure: The Blueberry Warehouse in Goose River, P.E.I. (2006). Photo by Ken Perlman; courtesy Robertson Library, University of P.E.I.

When I Go Out the Door, or Hector MacDonald's Jig

132

Composer: Arthur Sullivan
Source: Hector MacDonald
Appears on: *Frails & Frolics*

Key: C
Mode: Major
Tuning: gCGCD

I got this tune – which fully fits the thematic profile of a homegrown Canadian jig – from a family-made recording of fiddler Hector MacDonald of Bangor, Kings County P.E.I.; I hadn't found a title by the time I recorded the tune on *Frails & Frolics* so I simply named it for him. Imagine my surprise when I subsequently learned that the melody could be traced to the song, "When I Go Out the Door" from the Gilbert & Sullivan play, *Patience, or Bunthorne's Bride*. It's not clear where MacDonald encountered the melody, but keep in mind that the Gilbert & Sullivan opus was popular throughout the English-speaking world; that the capital city, Charlottetown has long had an active theatrical tradition; and that for generations it was the custom in many rural communities on P.E.I. to organize stage plays and musicals for performance on and around St. Patrick's Day. Standard notation for my source version is available on *bowingdownhome.ca*.

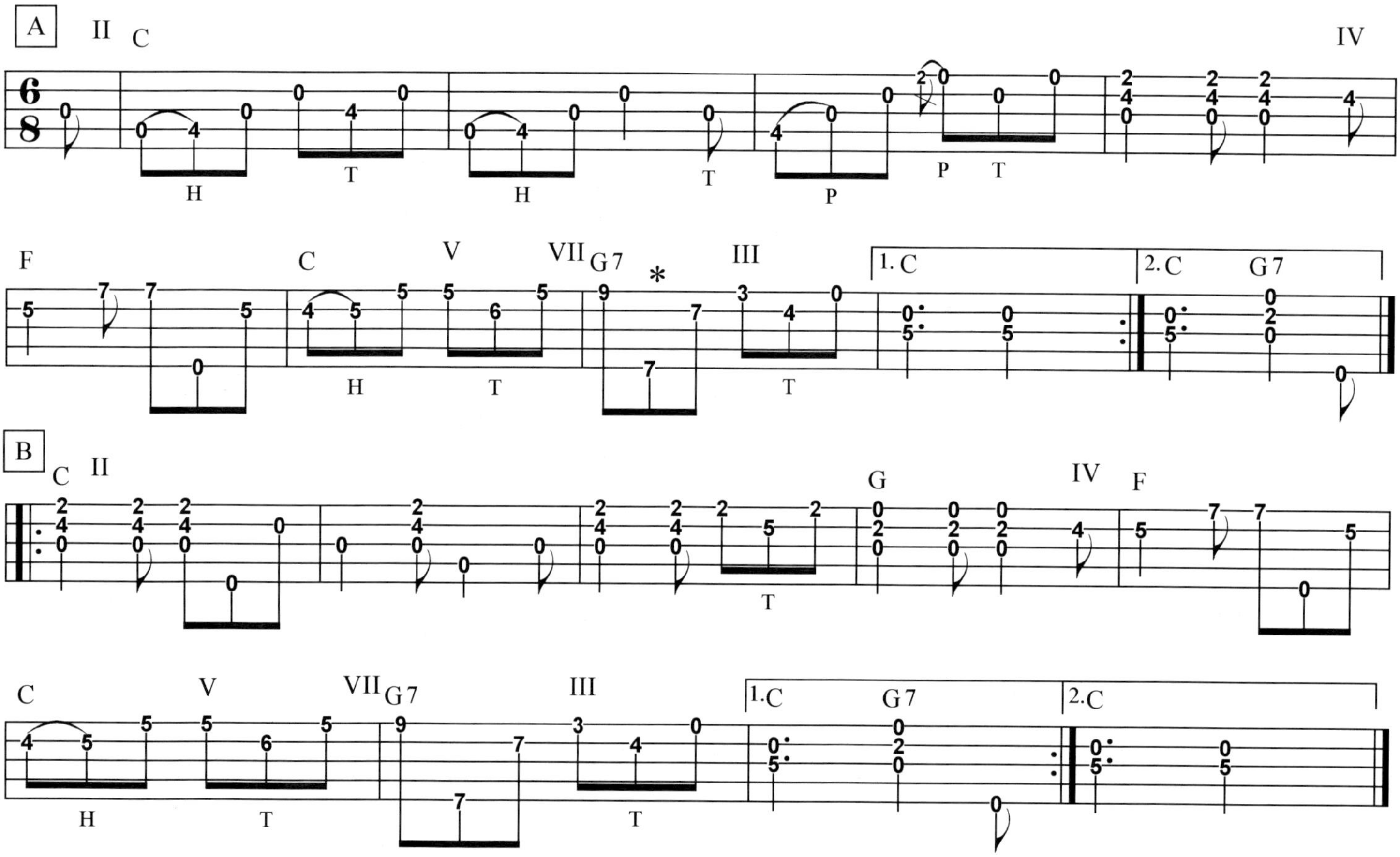

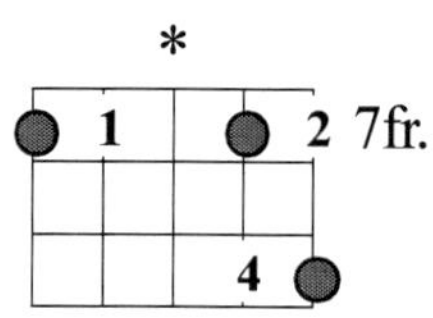

Playing Tips for *When I Go Out the Door*

• Parts A & B, measure 7. Start the measure with your fingers in the configuration shown in Diagram *. Just before the mid-point, cut fret 7, string 2 short (2nd finger) and glide with that finger down to fret 4. Then use it as a pivot to swing the 1st finger into position on fret 3, string 1.

133

Wilfred's Fiddle

Composer: Dan R. MacDonald
Source: Allan MacDonald
Appears on: *Northern Banjo*

Key: E
Mode: Dorian Gamut
Tuning: gDGBD

Dan R. MacDonald named this tune for fiddler-composer Wilfred Gillis of Arisaig, Nova Scotia (1923-2002). Both John Campbell and Carl MacKenzie recorded the tune for Rounder in the 1970s. I altered the descending run in Part B, measures 13-14 to make the transition to the closing phrase a little less abrupt. Standard notation for my source version is in *Fiddle Music of P.E.I.*

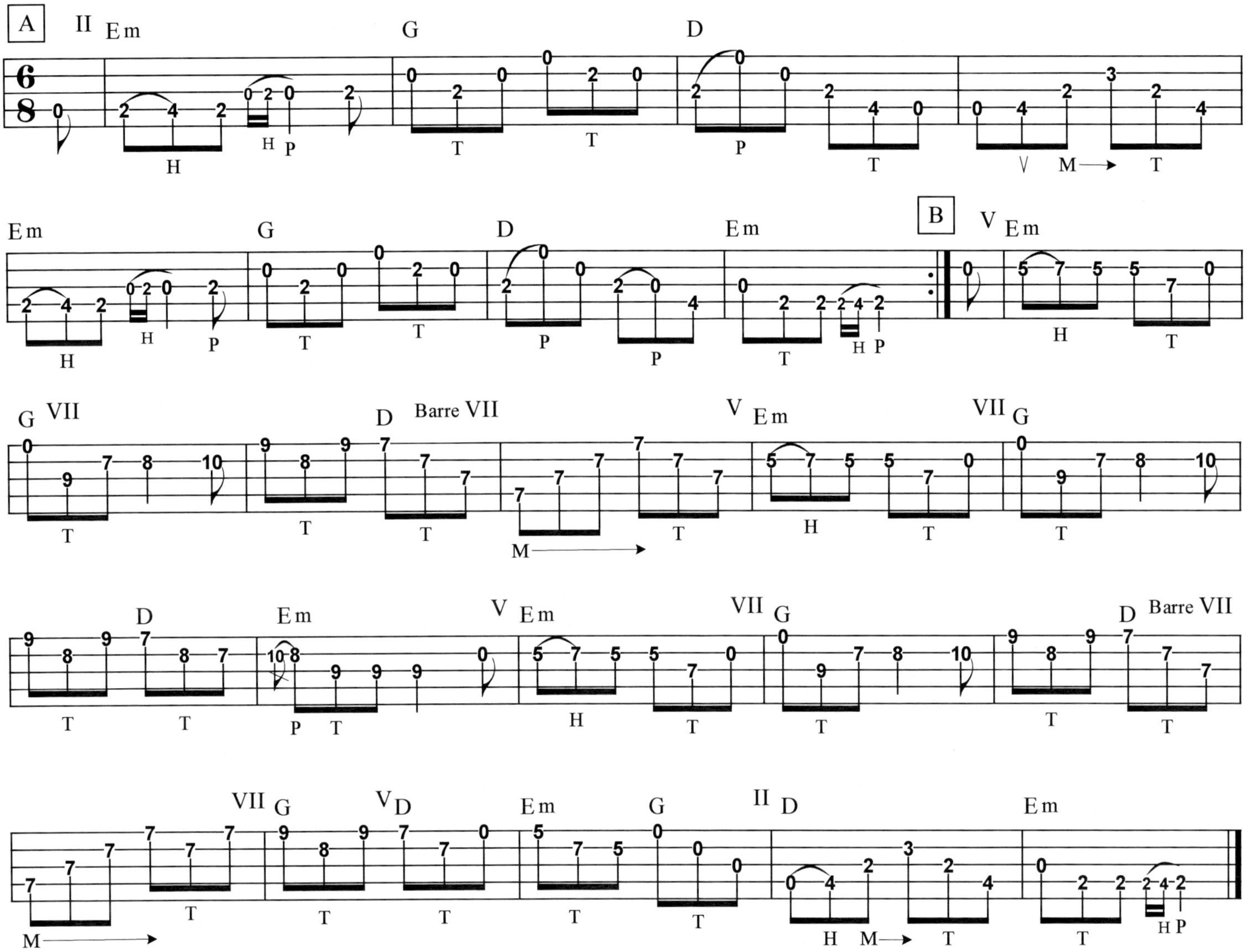

Playing Tips for *Wilfred's Fiddle*

- Part B, measures 3 & 11. At the start of both measures, use the 2nd and 3rd fingers on fret 8, string 2 and fret 9, string 1 respectively. As the midpoint approaches, balance on the 3rd finger and swing the 1st finger into place as a full barre at fret 7.

- Part B, measures 13-14. At the start of measure 13, use the 3rd and 4th fingers on fret 8, string 2 and fret 9, string 1 respectively. At the midpoint, glide both fingers down to fret 7 on their respective strings. At the start of measure 14, keep the 3rd finger on string 2, then move the 1st finger into place on fret 5, string 1.

134

Light & Airy

ORIGIN: SCOTLAND
SOURCE: CARL & JACKIE WEBSTER
APPEARS ON: *NORTHERN BANJO*

KEY: F
MODE: MAJOR
TUNING: gCGCD

One of the earliest print appearances of this very sweet 18th-century Scottish tune with its contemporary-sounding title was in *The Gow Collection*; it subsequently appeared in *Lowe's Collection, Kerr's Merry Melodies* and *Ryan's Mammoth Collection*. Well-known Cape Breton fiddler Angus Chisholm recorded the tune on a 78 rpm disk in 1935. I have frequently heard fiddlers from Cape Breton and P.E.I. medley the tune with "The Munster Lass" (facing page). Note that the order of parts is always as follows: AABB/A'A' BB. The tune is circular; and I've included a final-sounding tag ending. Standard notation for my source version is in *Fiddle Music of P.E.I.*

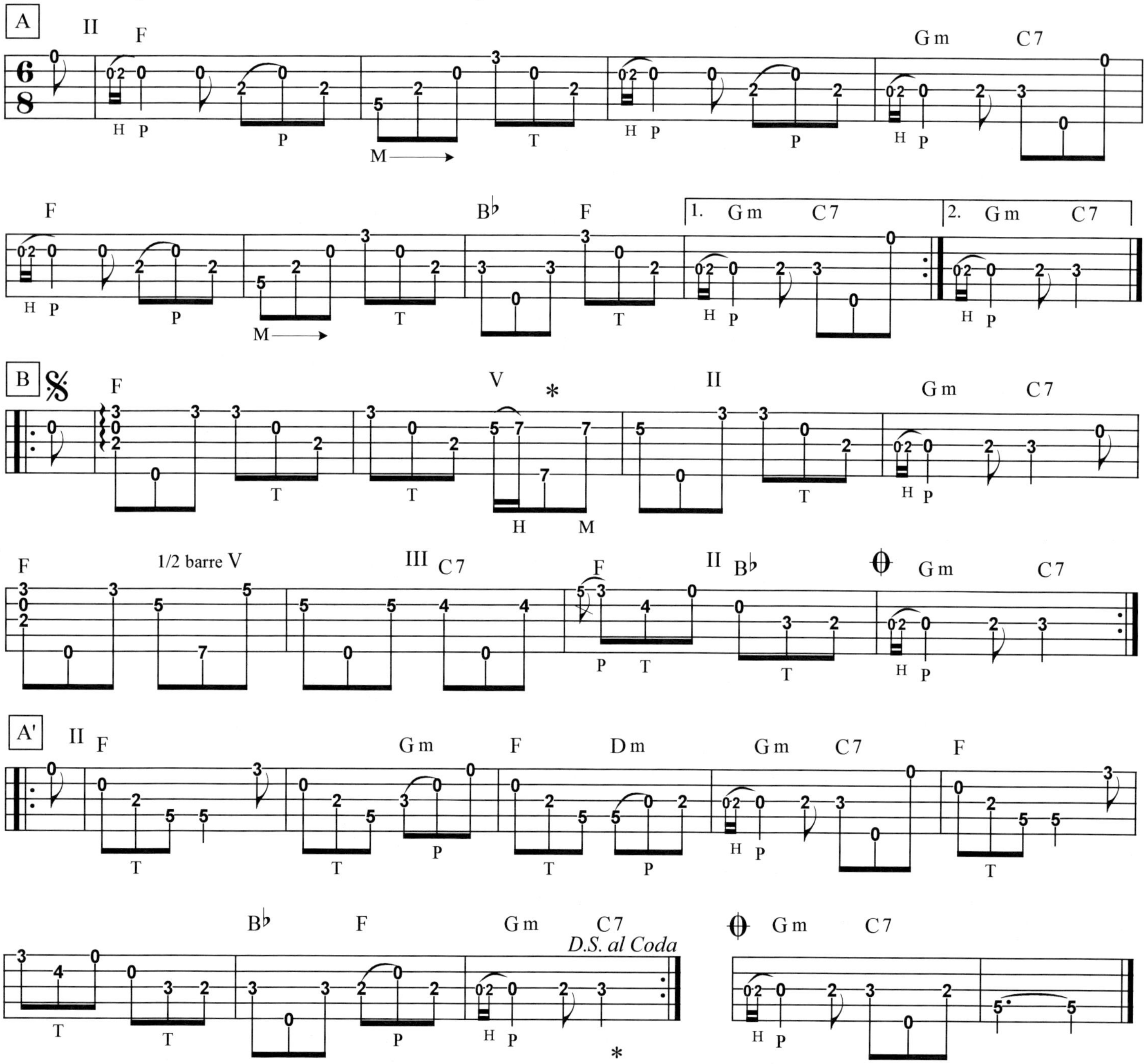

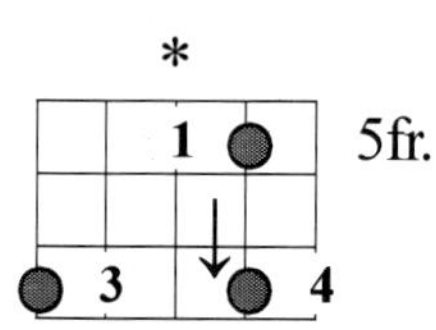

PLAYING TIPS FOR *LIGHT & AIRY*

- Part B, measure 2. Just before the mid-point, cut short the note at fret 2, string 3 and quickly scoot up the neck with the 1st and 3rd fingers to grab fret 5, string 2, and fret 7, string 5 respectively. Then – holding those two fingers in place – use the 4th finger to perform a very quick H on string 2 from fret 5 to fret 7.

135

The Munster Lass

Origin: Ireland
Source: Carl & Jackie Webster
Appears on: *Northern Banjo*

Key: F
Mode: Major
Tuning: gCGCD

"The Munster Lass" first appeared in a 19th-century manuscript collection compiled by James Goodman, a clergyman from Cork, Ireland (1828–1896). It was subsequently printed in *Ryan's Mammoth Collection.* I have frequently heard fiddlers from Cape Breton and Prince Edward Island medley the tune with "Light and Airy" (facing page). The coda represents the tag ending I used for the tune on *Northern Banjo*. Standard notation for my source version is in *Fiddle Music of P.E.I.*

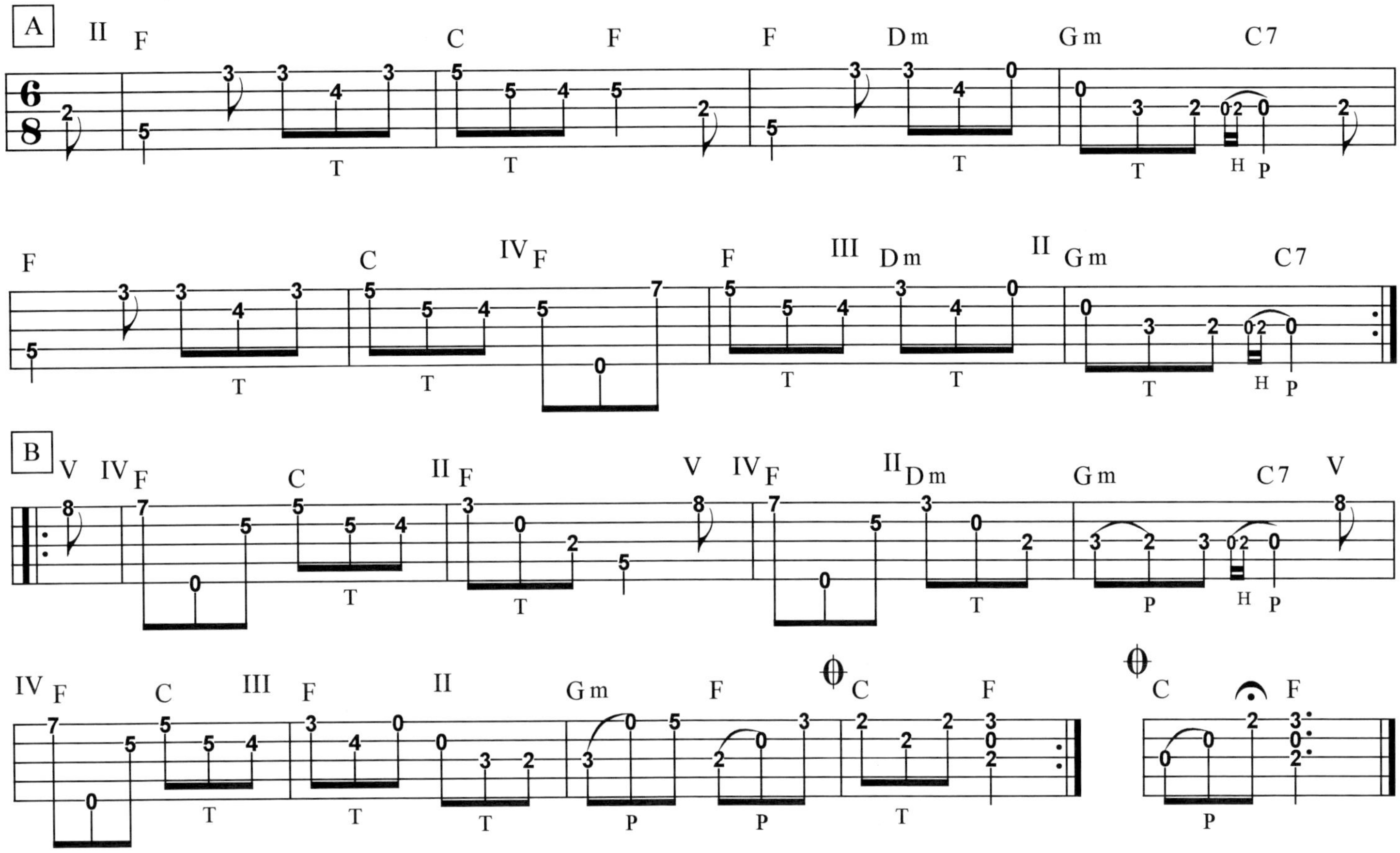

Playing Tips for *The Munster Lass*

• Part B, measures 1-2. Just before the mid-point of measure 1, balance on the 2nd finger at fret 5, string 2. Hold this finger in place and – at the beginning of the second group of eighth notes – and use it as a pivot to swing the 3rd finger onto fret 5, string 1. Towards the end of the measure, cut fret 5 short and glide with the 2nd finger down to fret 4. Then at the beginning of measure 2, cut fret 4 short and scoot down the neck to grab fret 3, string 1 with the 3rd finger.

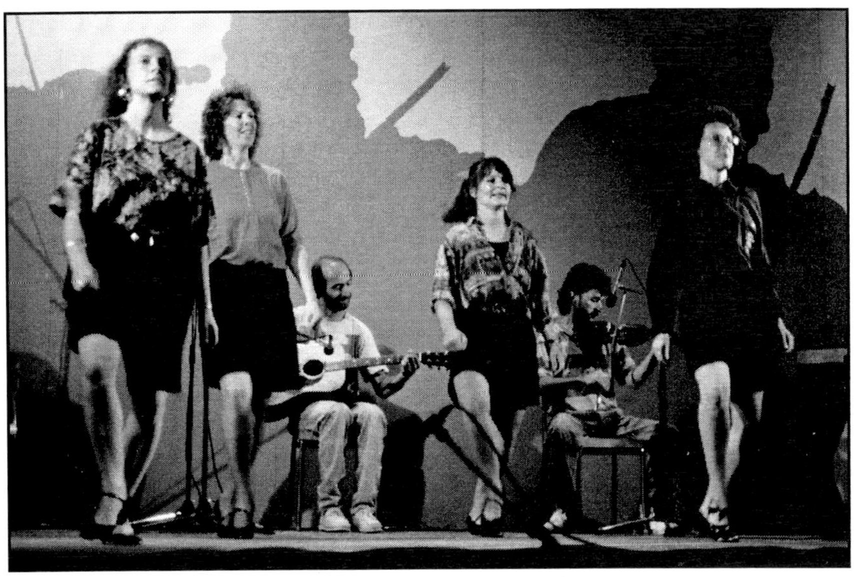

Step Dancing Exhibition: Atlantic Jamboree, Abram-Village, P.E.I. (1992; Fiddler is Peter Arsenault of Mont Carmel). Photo by Ken Perlman; courtesy Robertson Library, University of P.E.I.

136

Royal Circus Jig, or Omer Cheverie's Jig

Origin: Scotland
Source: Omer Cheverie
Appears on: *Frails & Frolics*

Key: F
Mode: Major
Tuning: gCGCD

Named for a circular street, or *circus* in the New Town section of Edinburgh, this lyrical tune appears in *The Gow Collection, vol. 2* (1788). It has been recorded by Cape Breton fiddlers Buddy MacMaster and Jerry Holland; and in 1979 Carl MacKenzie recorded it under the title, "Drury Lane." Not having a title when I recorded the tune on *Frails & Frolics,* I named it for my source fiddler. Standard notation for my source version is available on *bowingdownhome.ca.*

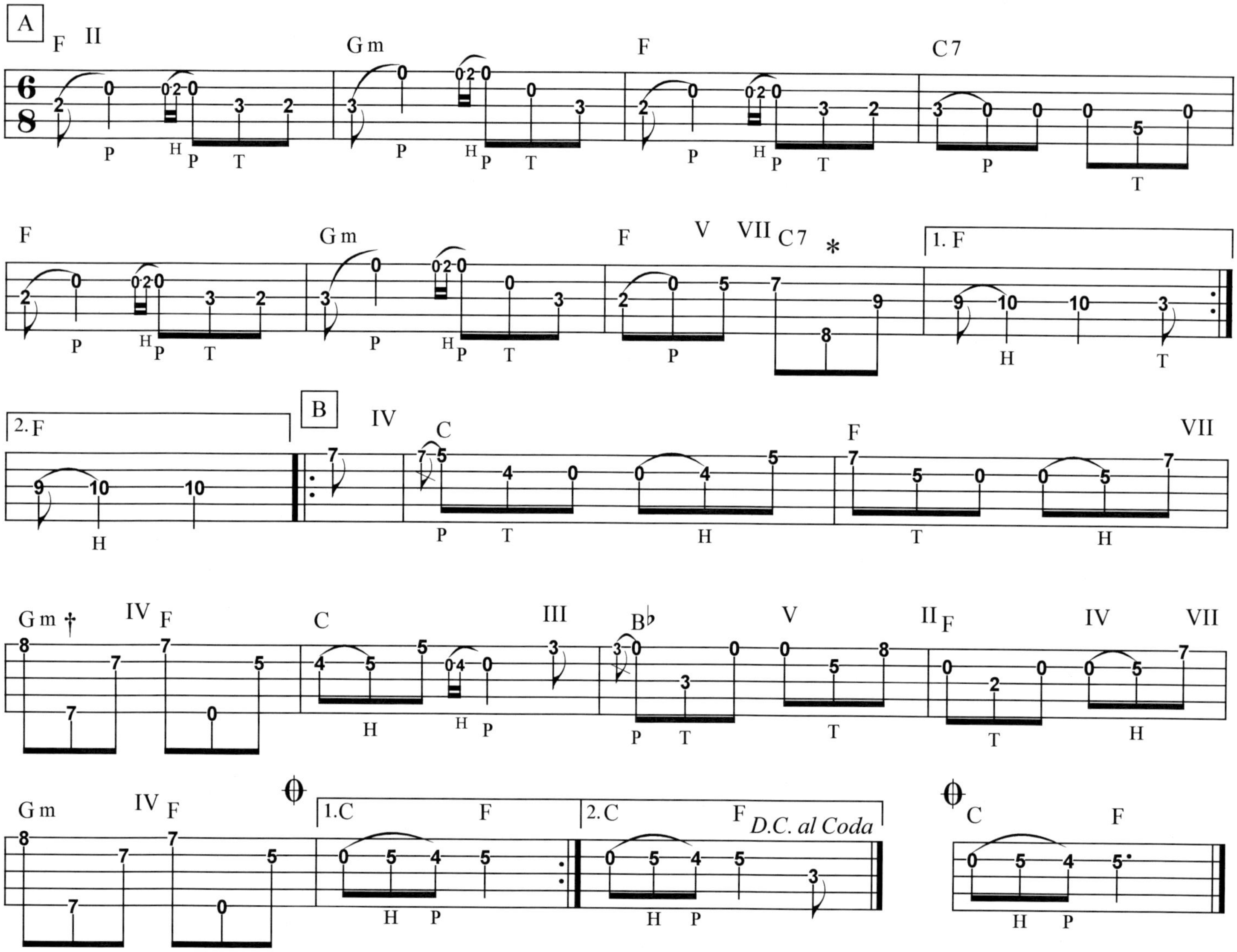

*

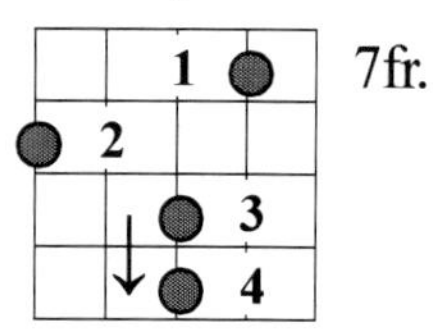

†

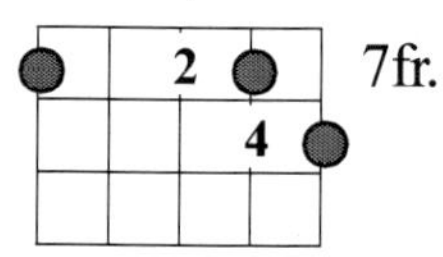

Playing Tips for Royal Circus Jig

- Part A, measure 7. Just before the midpoint, catch fret 5, string 2 with the 1st finger, and – at the start of the second eighth-note group – continue riding up string 2 with that finger to fret 7. Then use the 1st finger as a pivot to swing the 2nd and 3rd fingers into the positions shown in Diagram *.

- Part B, measures 3-4. At the start of measure 3, use your 4th finger on fret 8, string 1 as shown in Diagram †. As the mid-point approaches, use that finger to glide down string 1 to fret 7, then use it as pivot to swing the 2nd finger over to fret 5, string 2. This puts you in position to use the 1st finger on fret 4, string 2 at the start of measure 3.

Fig for a Kiss, or The Old Dutch Churn (6/8 Version)

137

Origin: Variant of Irish Tune
Source: Winston "Scotty" Fitzgerald
Appears on: *Frails & Frolics*

Key: G
Mode: Minor-Like (see Intro)
Tuning: gCGCD

This tune circulated among fiddlers for generations as a *slip jig*, a type of tune characterized by a 9/8 meter (*three* groups of three eighth notes per measure). The melody has appeared as a slip jig under several titles and keys, notably "Fig for a Kiss" in E-modal (*O'Neill's Dance Music of Ireland*), and "The Old Dutch Churn" in G-modal (*Ryan's Mammoth Collection*). Fiddlers in and around the Cape Breton village of Cape North, however, converted the melody into an ordinary jig (they compressed it to fit a 6/8-time format with *two* groups of three eighth notes per measure). Winston Fitzgerald – whose home town White Point is just down the road from Cape North – recorded the 6/8 version on his LP, *It's New!,* referring to it merely as a "Cape North Jig." The mode is characterized by a minor 3rd, minor 7th, and missing 6th (G-A-B♭-C-D-F-G). I elected to use a C tuning in order to create a multi-key medley that opens in F with "Royal Circus Jig" (facing page) and concludes in C with "When I Go Out the Door" (p. 138).

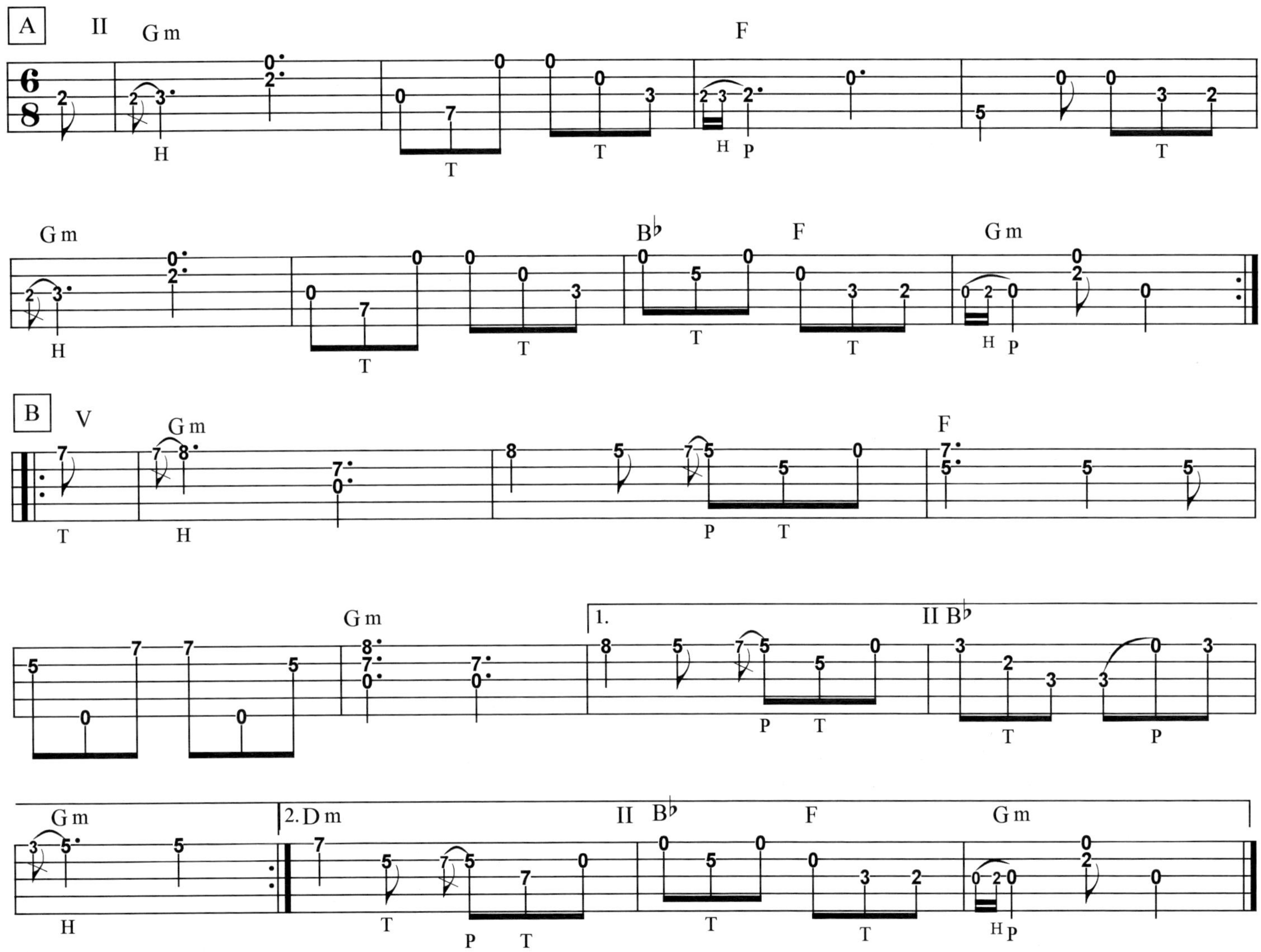

138

Kenmure's On & Awa', Willie

Origin: Scotland
Source: "Old Peter" Chaisson
Appears on: *Northern Banjo*

Key: G
Mode: Major
Tuning: gDGBD

The above title comes from lyrics set to this melody by the great Scottish poet Robert Burns; one of its first publications under this name was in *The Gow Repository*. The tune subsequently appeared – with slight variations in title – in both *Kerr's Merry Melodies* and *Ryan's Mammoth Collection*. Other published titles include "Kenmore lads" (*The Skye Collection* and *The Athole Collection*); "I Will If I Can," (*O'Neill's Dance Music of Ireland*); and "Boys from the West" (*The Roche Collection*). The Cape Breton ensemble, Five MacDonald Fiddlers recorded the tune under the title "Graham's Brook Jig." Standard notation for my source version is in *Fiddle Music of P.E.I.*

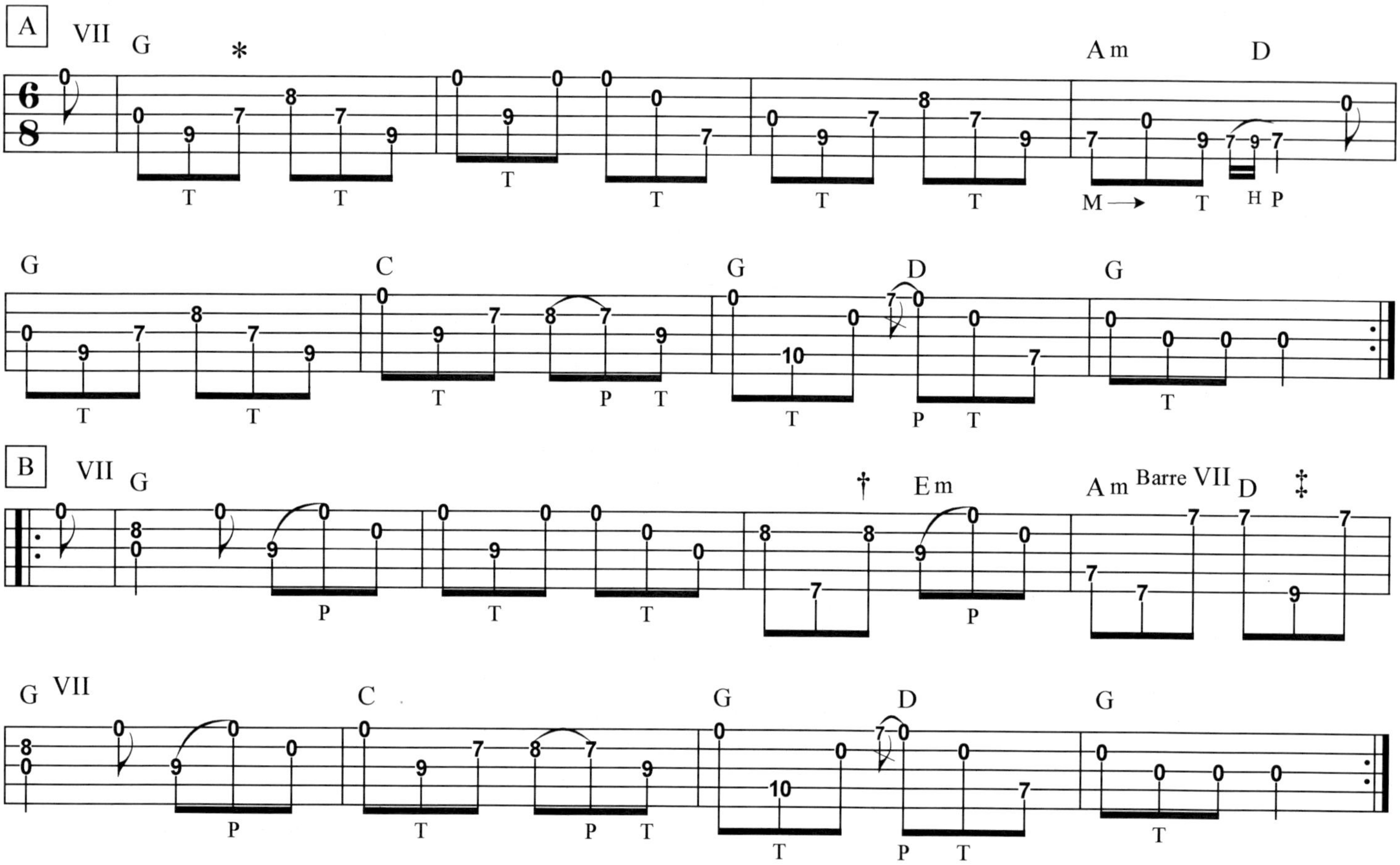

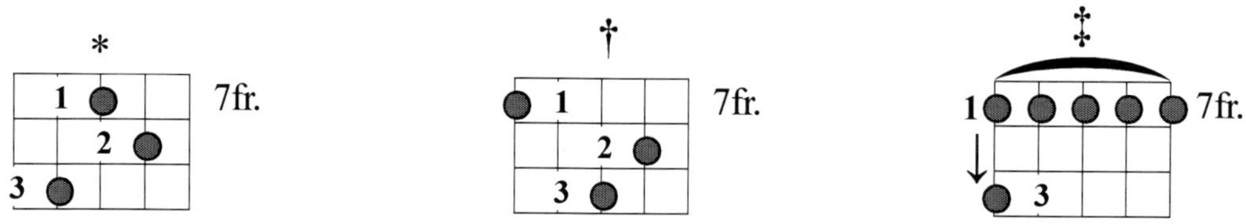

Playing Tips for *Kenmure's On & Awa', Willie*

- Part B, measure 3. Wait until the midpoint to place the 3rd finger on fret 9, string 3 (Diagram †). When you do place that finger, also place the 1st finger on string 1 (at roughly fret 7). Wait for the duration of one eighth note, then use the 1st finger for the indicated alternate-string P.

139

Jackson's Jig

ORIGIN: PROBABLY CAPE BRETON
SOURCE: REUBEN SMITH
APPEARS ON: *NORTHERN BANJO*

KEY: G
MODE: MAJOR
TUNING: gDGBD

"Jackson's Jig" is in the style of melodies once used to accompany the quadrille (for more on quadrilles, see Chapter 1). It has elements in common with "Margaree's Fancy," as recorded in the 1930s by Alick Gillis & the Inverness Serenaders. The ensemble treatment on the *Northern Banjo* cut – featuring banjo with whistle, uillean pipes, and bodhran – was inspired by such Irish groups as Planxty and the Chieftains, who themselves brought to fruition ideas about Irish music ensembles conceived by composer-musicologist Sean O'Riada. The coda represents the fancy tag ending I used on the recording.

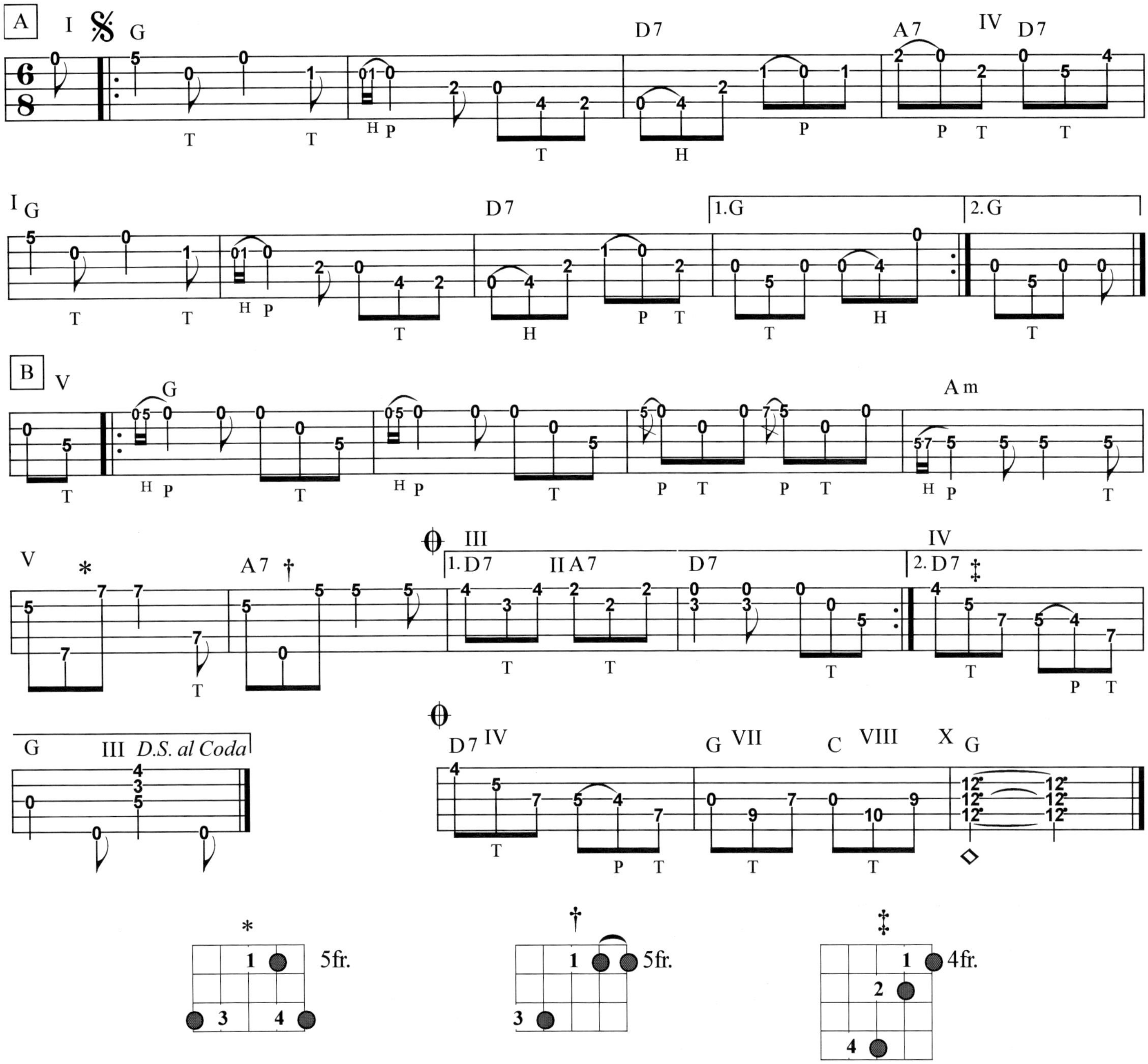

Inverness Jig

140

Origin: Cape Breton
Source: Stephen Toole
Appears on: *Island Boy*

Key: D & A (C & G on Banjo)
Mode: Major
Tuning: gCGCD (Capo-2)

Named for the town of Inverness in Cape Breton, this lively, early 20th-century jig appears in Gordon MacQuarrie's *Cape Breton Collection of Scottish Melodies for the Violin* (1940), where it is attributed to J.D. Kennedy. The Part A melody is in the key of D, but Part B moves to the dominant key, A and does not return (on open banjo, the tune shifts from the key of C to the key of G). To achieve a final-sounding ending you must return to the top and wrap up the tune at the end of Part A. Standard notation for my source version is in *Fiddle Music of P.E.I.*

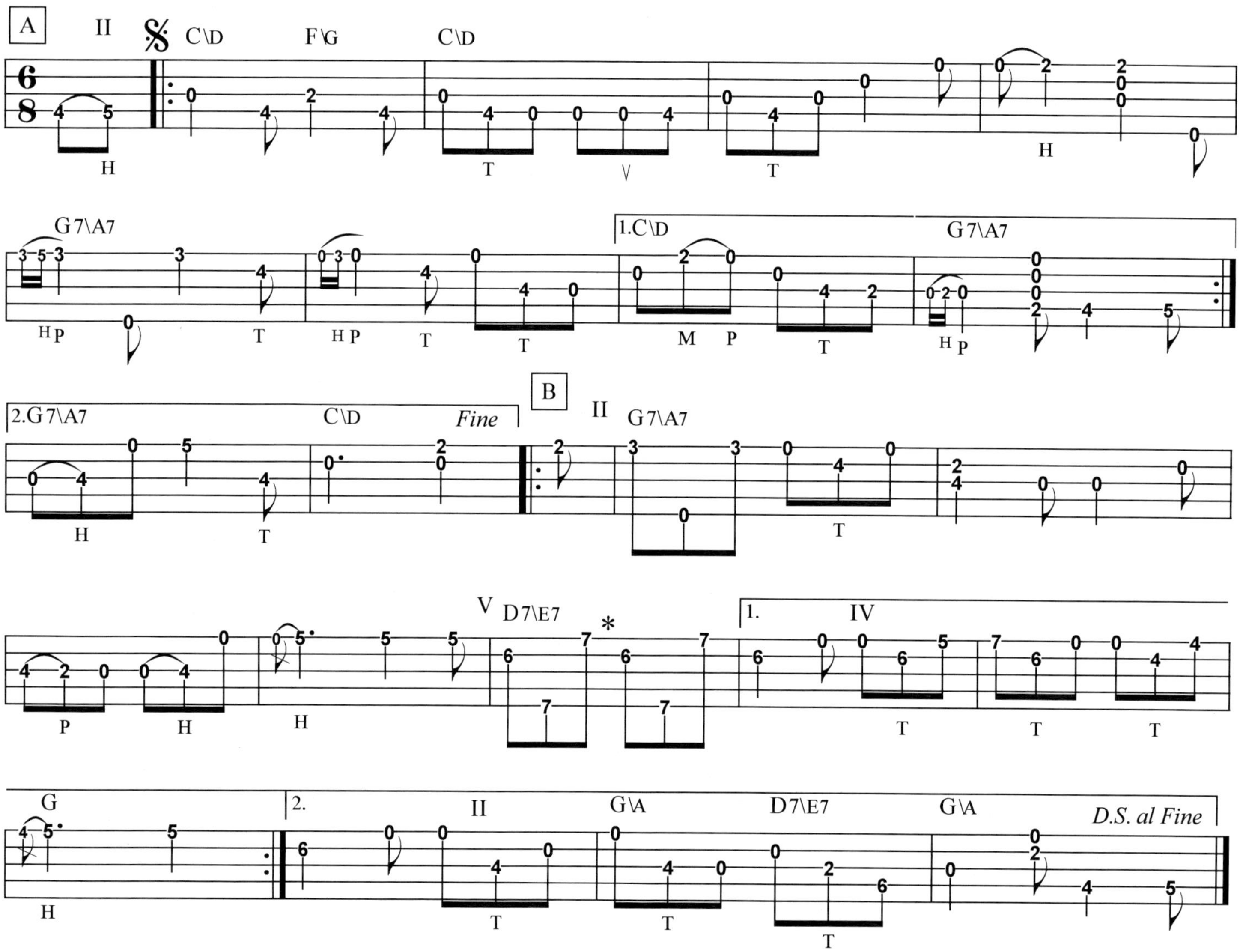

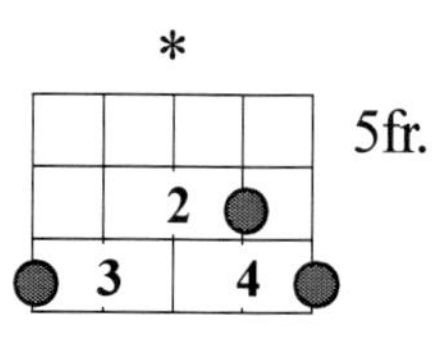

Playing Tips for *Inverness Jig*

Dual Chord Symbols: Chord to left of backslash goes with open banjo; chord on right is for capoed banjo or fiddle

- Part B, measure 6-7 (first ending). At the start of measure 6, your 2nd finger should already be at fret 6, string 2 (Diagram *). Keep it there throughout that measure and the first half the next, using it as a pivot – first to move the 1st finger to fret 5, string 1 – and then to move the 4th finger to fret 7, string 1. Just before the midpoint of measure 7, glide on the 2nd finger down to fret 4 and use it as a pivot to swing the 3rd finger over to fret 4, string 1.

141

The Bonny Lea Rig

Origin: Probably Scots Song Melody
Source: Gus Longaphie
Appears on: *Frails & Frolics*

Key: D (C on Banjo)
Mode: Major
Tuning: gCGCD (Capo-2)

In the Scots language, a *lea rig* is a grassy area such as a knoll or hillock, in the midst of, or alongside a plowed field. Cape Breton master fiddler Buddy MacMaster recorded the tune in the 1980s on his debut LP, *Judique on the Floor.* I had to take both parts up an octave to fit the tune on banjo. Standard notation for my source version is in *Fiddle Music of P.E.I.*

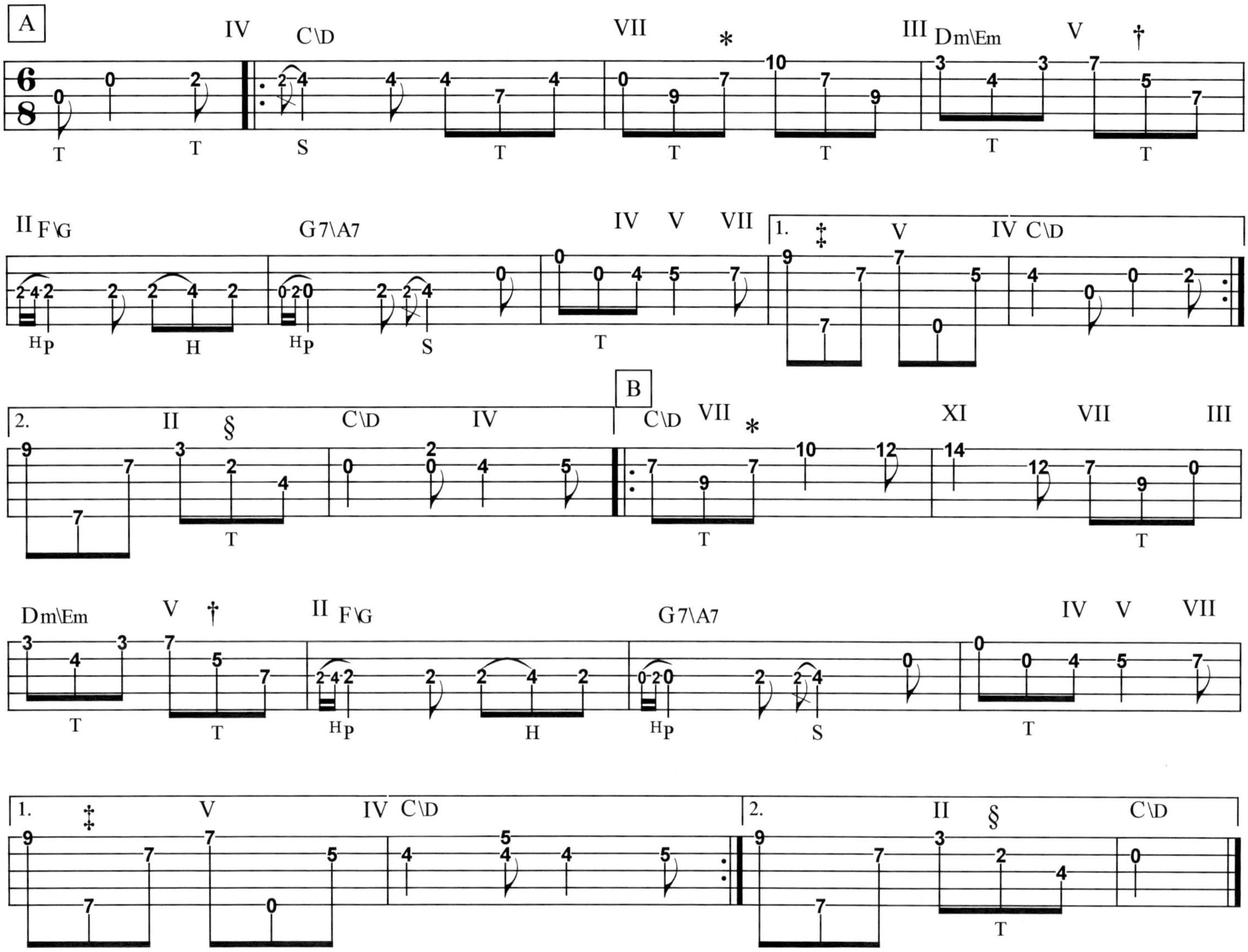

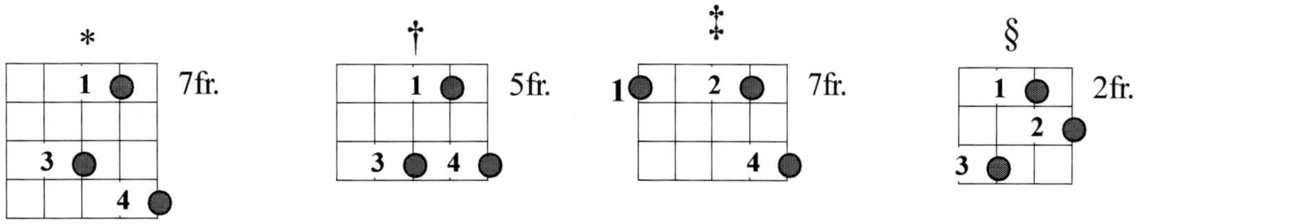

Playing Tips for *The Bonny Lea Rig*

***Dual Chord Symbols:** Chord to left of backslash goes with open banjo; chord on right is for capoed banjo or fiddle*

• Part B, measures 1-2. Start measure 1 in the fingering configuration shown in Diagram *. Then use the 4th finger to ride up string 1 from fret 10, to fret 12 and – at the start of measure 2 – to fret 14. As you approach the midpoint of measure 2, use the 2nd finger on fret 12, string 2; then cut that short and scoot down with the 1st and 3rd fingers to get fret 7, string 2 and fret 9, string 3 respectively.

142

Chorus Jig

Origin: Scotland
Source: Paul MacDonald
Appears on: *Northern Banjo*

Key: D (C on Banjo)
Mode: See Intro
Tuning: gCGCD (Capo-2)

An early print appearance for this four-part tune was in Alexander McLashan's, *A Collection of Scots Measures, Hornpipes, Jigs Etc.* (1781); it was subsequently featured in *The Gow Repertory, Lowe's Collection*, and *The Skye Collection.* A variant converted from 6/8 to reel time (2/2) has long been employed to accompany the well-known New England contradance also known as "Chorus Jig." In the 20th century, musicians from Kilfenora in western Ireland added a fifth part and popularized the tune in the Irish music scene; since then most Irish musicians have referred to the tune as, "The Kilfenora Jig." The mode features a major 3rd and variable 7th (D-E-F♯-G-A-B-C/C♯-D on fiddle; or C-D-E-F-G-A-B♭/B-C on open banjo). The tune is circular; and I've included the special tag ending used on *Northern Banjo*. Standard notation for my source version is in *Fiddle Music of P.E.I.*

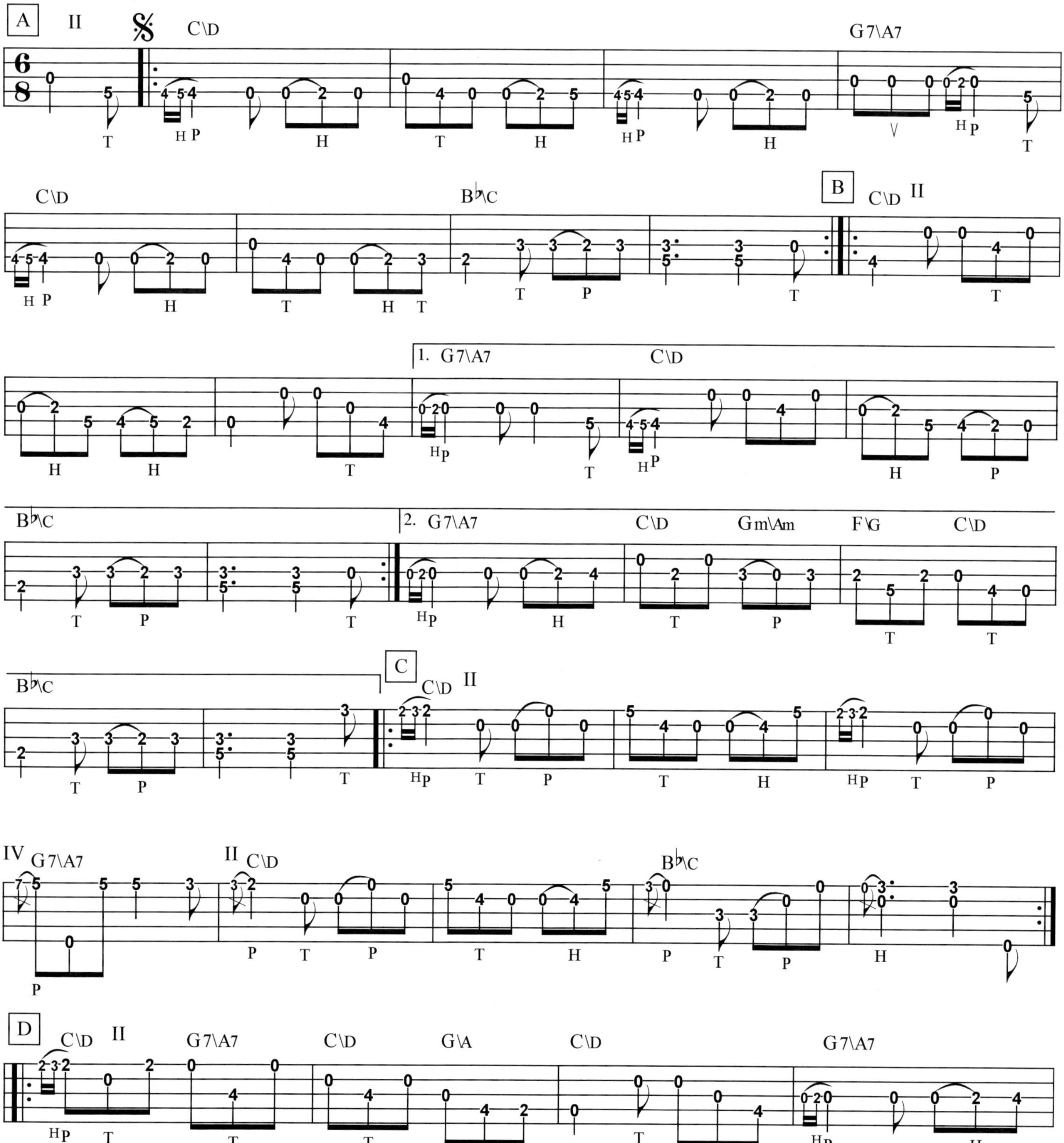

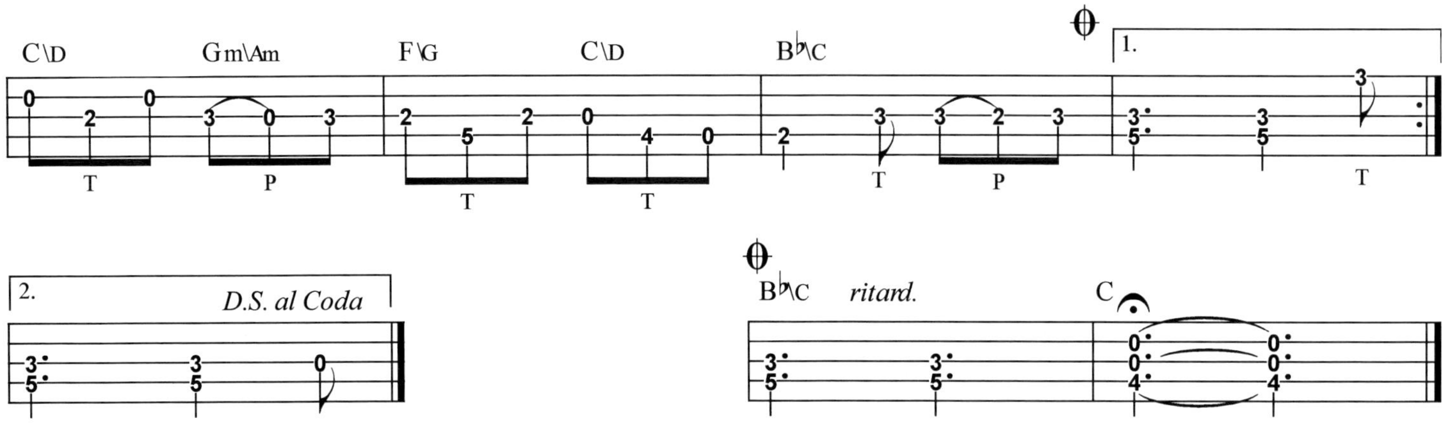

Playing Tips for *Chorus Jig*

Dual Chord Symbols: Chord to left of backslash goes with open banjo; chord on right is for capoed banjo or fiddle

• Note on the Accompaniment. In this tune, the "variable 7th tone is most expressed at the *cadences,* or ends of phrases. Reflecting this feature in the melody, I suggest the major-dominant A chord (G on open banjo) halfway through each part, but the modal-dominant C chord (B♭ on open banjo) at the end of each part.

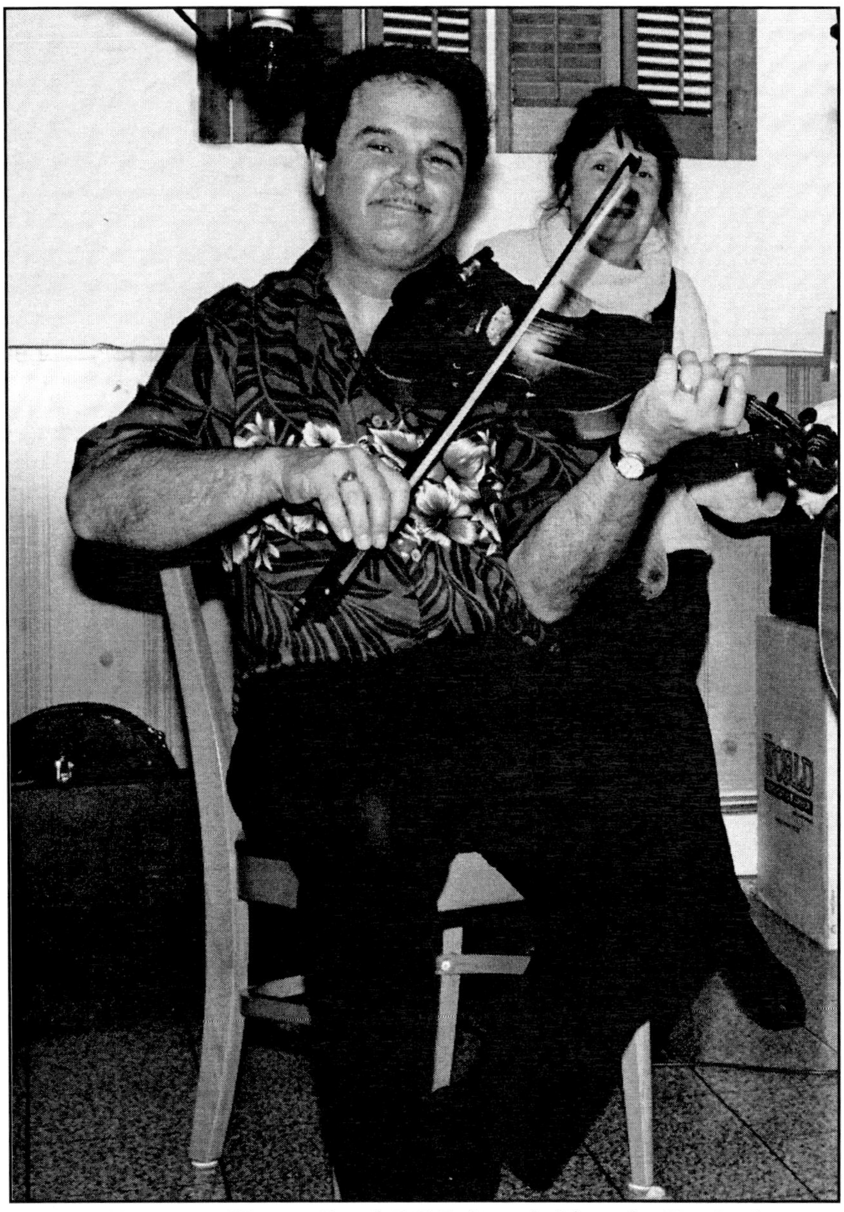

Victor Doucette: Harper Road, P.E.I. (2006). Photo by Ken Perlman; courtesy Robertson Library, University of P.E.I.

Chapter *10. Marches, Strathspeys, Airs, & a Waltz*

STRATHSPEYS, MARCHES, AND AIRS SHARE A COMMON ROLE in the Scottish, Cape Breton, and Prince Edward Island fiddling traditions – namely as opening or transitional tunes in *Scottish sets (*performance medleys). Some tune lineups have become so widespread that they are now known merely by initials: M.S.R. (march-strathspey-reel) or A.S.R. (air-strathspey-reel). The three genres also share other common features in terms of rhythms and phrasing, which are discussed below. But first here are some definitions.

PIPE MARCHES & FIDDLE MARCHES. The most common type of march in the repertoire is the cut-time *pipe-march.* Pipe marches have four repeated eight-measure parts, with a thematic sequence of ABA'B'. Generally, the last or B'-part has a four-measure second ending that recalls the ending of Part A. This tune genre developed as a by-product of the 19th-century Scottish piping-contest milieu, and many four-part marches played today date from that period. Also quite popular is a related sub-genre known as the *fiddle march.* Fiddle marches have just two eight-measure parts; the second or B Part often features a four-measure-long second ending that reprises the ending of the Part A. Observe that tempo markings for cut-time are shown with half notes (𝅗𝅥=) as the primary unit.

STRATHSPEYS (pronounced: struth-SPAYS) originated in the mid-to-late 18th century in the Strath Spey region (Spey River Valley) of northeastern Scotland. They were originally known as *strathspey reels* (reels played in the strathspey style), and – like hornpipes – are essentially slowed-down, rhythmically elaborated adaptations of the reel form. Most strathspeys have two parts, each either four or eight bars in length. Four-bar parts are generally repeated, while eight-bar parts are usually played just once. In the 18th century, a medley consisting of strathspeys followed by reels was the prime accompaniment for a then highly popular dance known as the *Scotch Reel.* Nowadays, this style of medley is used in Atlantic Canada to accompany step dancing (since strathspeys are virtually *expected* to lead on to another tune, most of them have been composed to be circular). Strathspey tempos can vary widely; since most strathspeys are notated in a true 4/4 time, tempo markings are shown with quarter notes (♩=) as the primary unit.

AIRS are intended for listening rather than dancing. A distinctive feature of the genre is that players are not required to keep a steady beat; at their discretion they can allow the melody to "breathe" between phrases.

WALTZES are 3/4-time tunes designed for couples' dancing. Most waltz tunes have two repeated sixteen-bar parts, but just about any measure-format will serve. The genre developed in central Europe during the second half of the 18th century; it was introduced to England in 1812 and by mid-century had spread to Canada and throughout the rest of the British Empire.

RHYTHM & PHRASING FOR STRATHSPEYS & MARCHES

RHYTHM. Since the notation used for marches and strathspeys is made up primarily of dotted pairs, the appearance of both genres on the page is quite similar to that of "hornpipe style" tunes (Example S-1, measure 1). As is the case for hornpipe style, these dotted pairs are not played exactly as written. Although a dotted-eighth note is actually three times as long as a sixteenth, in the Cape Breton and P.E.I. traditions these notes are generally played so that the dotted eighths are only twice as long as the sixteenths, becoming in effect eighth-note triplets with the first two notes tied (measure 2). This rhythm can be expressed more "elegantly" as a quarter note plus a single eighth under a triplet bracket (measure 3). The count, as for triplets, is 1-&-a, 2-&-a, 3-&-a, 4-&-a, etc. Play the dotted eighth on the "number-count" and the sixteenth on the "a-count" (the "&-count" is skipped).

143

EXAMPLE S-1: "DOTTED" PAIRS IN STRATHSPEYS & MARCHES

Tuning: gDGBD

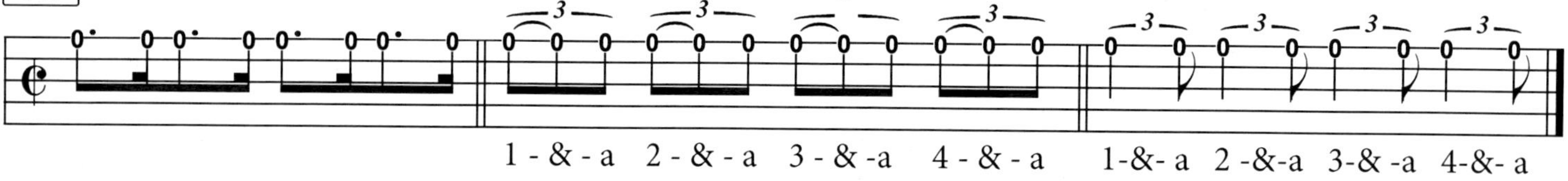

PHRASING FOR DOTTED PAIRS. Each dotted pair in a strathspey or march is usually played so that the second note – that is, the note written as a sixteenth – leads on to the first note of the next dotted pair (or whatever other kind of note occupies the start of the following beat; see Example S-2). If you play your dotted pairs with the sixteenth note connected in phrasing to the preceding dotted eighth, the tune loses its character.

144

Example S-2: "Dotted-Pair" Phrasing

Tuning: gDGBD

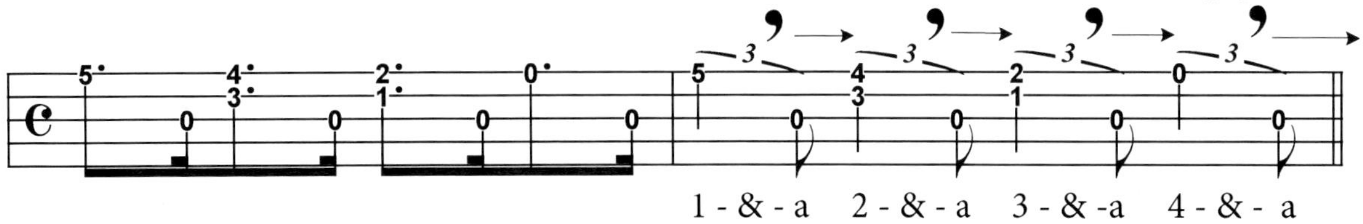

Phrasing for Triplets. Similarly if there are triplets in the strathspey or march, the last note of each triplet leads on to the first note of the next one, (or whatever other kind of note occupies the following beat), as shown in Example S-3.

145

Example S-3: Triplets Phrasing in Marches & Strathspeys

Tuning: gDGBD

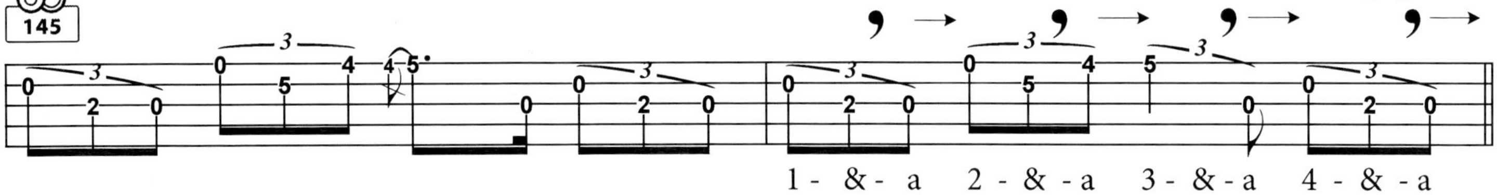

The *Scotch Snap*

One of the most distinctive features of strathspeys and marches is the frequent appearance of a kind of note pair known as the *Scotch snap* (Example S-4). A Scotch snap is essentially a reverse dotted pair, written as a sixteenth-note followed by a dotted eighth-note (measure 1). This implies that the second note should sound three times as long as the first, but in North American fiddling traditions the second note sounds only twice as long as the first. This yields a triplet with the *last* two notes tied (measure 2), or – more "elegantly" – an eighth-quarter combination under a triplet bracket (measure 3). Again, the count is 1-&-a, 2-&-a, etc.; this time play the sixteenth on the number-count, the dotted-eighth on the &-count, and hold that last note through the a-count. Traditionally the last note of the snap is played with something of a sudden, "explosive" character and - if the note is fretted - that note should be cut short (p. 14). To get the idea, try saying the word "bottom" out loud with an over-emphasized first syllable and an explosive, truncated second syllable (BOTT'm).

146

Example S-4: Scotch Snap Rhythm

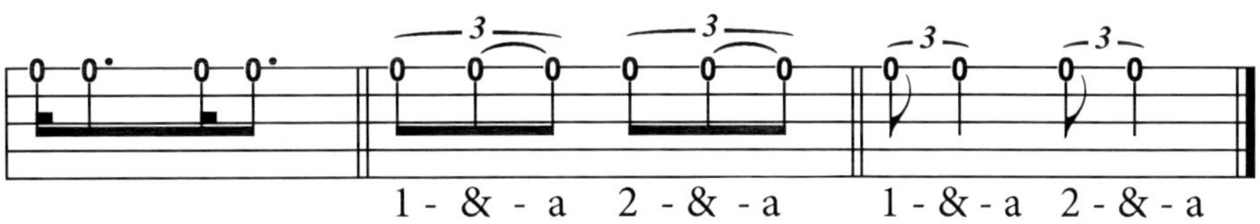

Tuning: gDGBD

Characteristic Strathspey & March Phrases

Characteristic strathspey and pipe-march melodies combine dotted pairs, triplets, sixteenth notes and Scotch snaps into a colorful tapestry. Example S-5 shows Part A, measures 1 and 2 of the strathspey, "The Duke of Gordon's Birthday," presented – for ease of interpretation – an octave lower than in the banjo arrangement on p. 164. In each illustration below, the measure on the left shows how the passage appears on the page, while the measure on the right illustrates how to interpret it in terms of triplet-based counting and proper phrasing. In the audio example, the two examples are played consecutively with no break; observe how the last note in Part A, Measure 1 leads strongly to the first note of Part A, measure 2. Also pay attention to how dotted pairs interact with immediately following Scotch snaps (the second note of the dotted pair leads strongly to the Scotch snap).

Example S-5: Typical Strathspey Phrases (Tuning: gDGBD)

147 Source: *Duke of Gordon's Birthday,* Part A, Measure 1

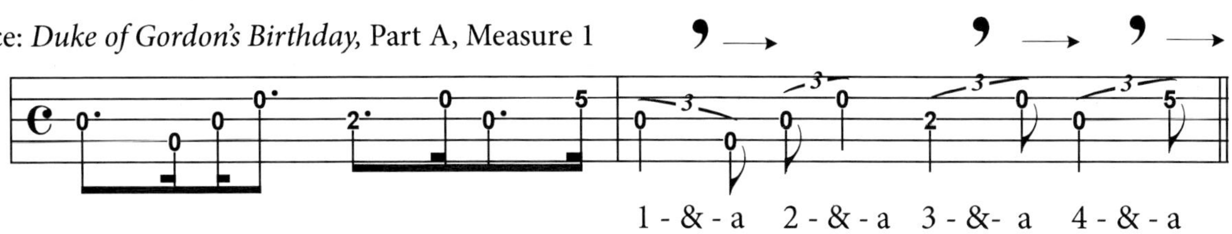

Source: *Duke of Gordon's Birthday,* Part A, Measure 2

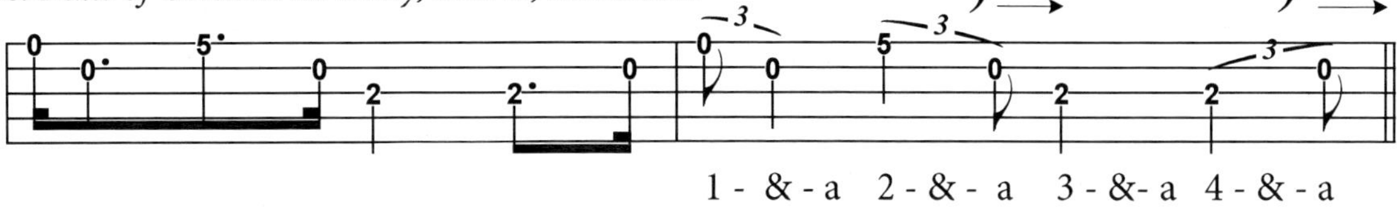

148

The Marchioness of Tullibardine

Pipe March

Origin: Scotland
Source: Omer Cheverie
Appears on: *Frails & Frolics*

Key: A (G on Banjo)
Mode: Mixolydian Gamut
Tuning: gDGCD (Capo-2)

In the ranks of Scottish nobility, the Duke of Gordon's eldest son is called the *Marquis of Tullibardine* [pronounced: MAR-kwess of tull-ee-BAR-din]; his wife is known as the *Marchioness* [mar-shee-a-NESS]. This mid-19th-century four-part Scottish pipe march appears in *The Skye Collection* and in James Scott Skinner's *Harp & Claymore* (1908). Skinner recorded it around the turn of the 20th century, and since then fiddlers have generally performed the tune with a relatively straight reel-like rhythm instead of using the highly "dotted" rhythms often associated with Scottish march style. The first fiddler from the Cape Breton tradition to record the tune was Alick Gillis (1900-74). The Cheverie version departs in some details from previously published and recorded settings; standard notation for his version is available on *bowingdownhome.ca*.

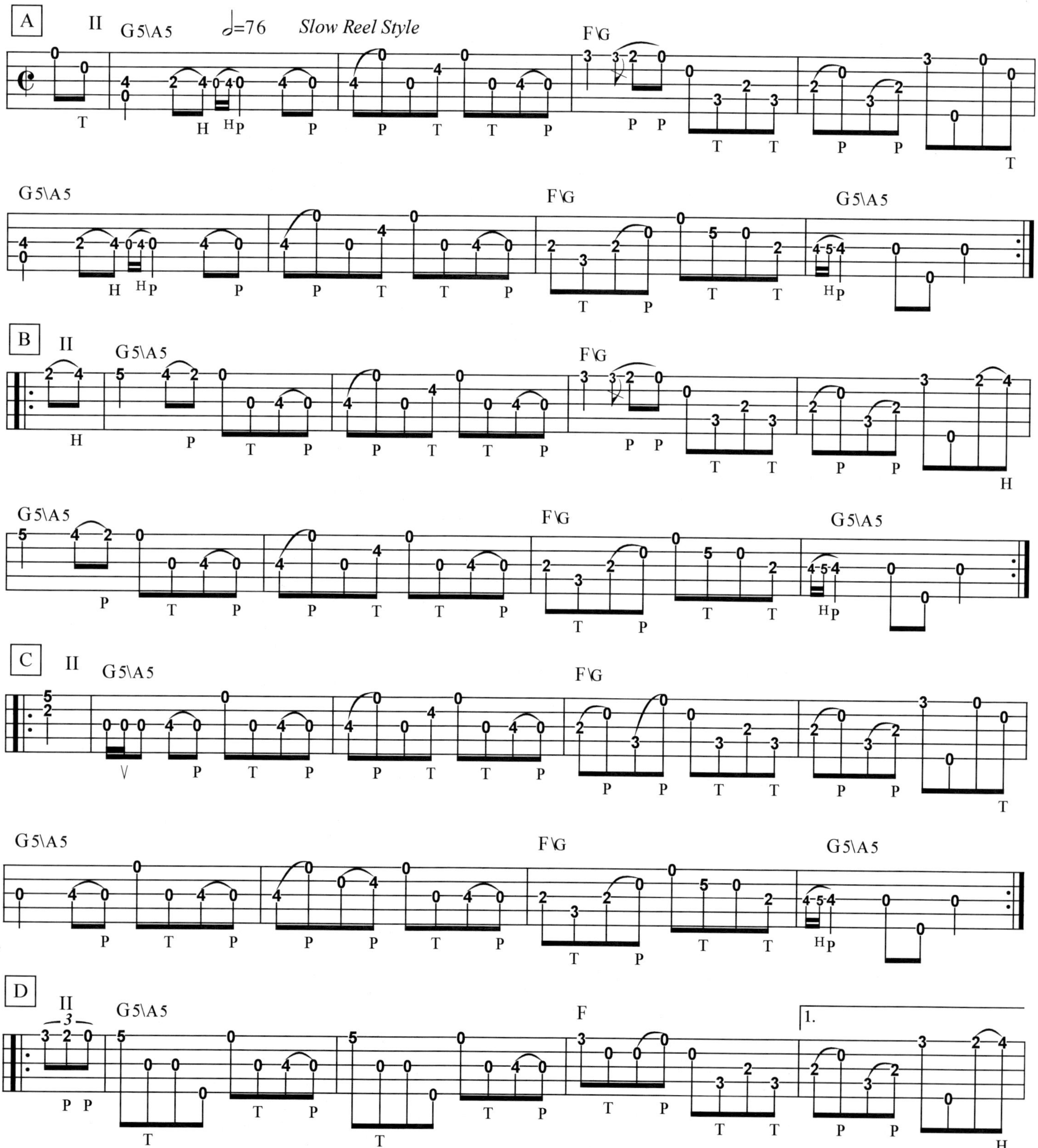

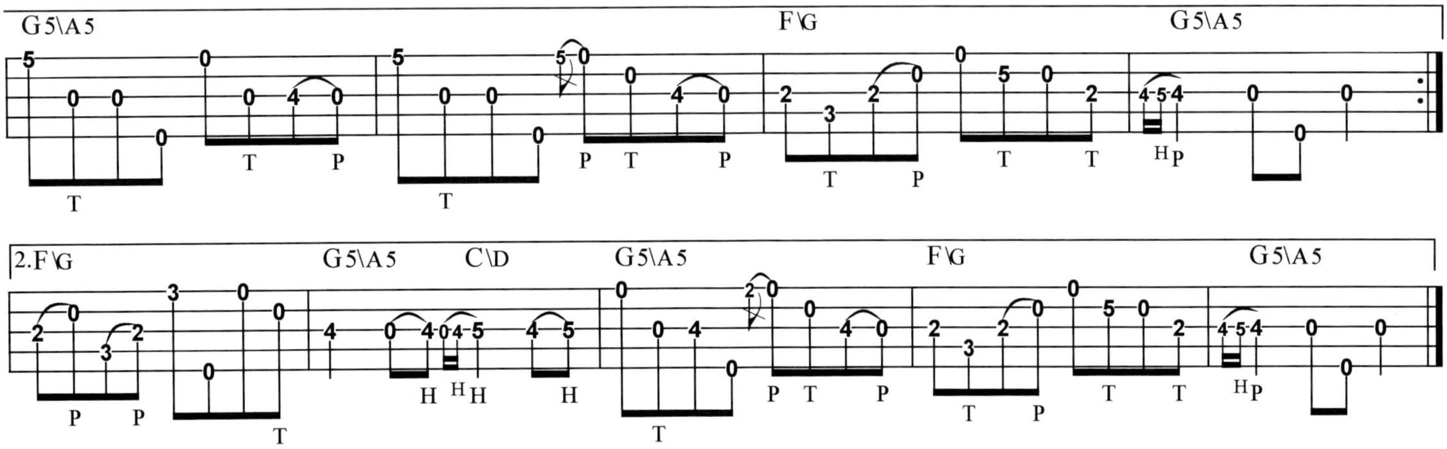

Playing Tips for *Marchioness of Tullibardine*

Dual Chord Symbols: Chord to left of backslash goes with open banjo; chord on right is for capoed banjo or fiddle

• Part A, measure 2 (and several other times in the piece). Midway through beat 2, to get the phrasing right you'll need to perform a thumb-crossover. Here's how: on beat 2, pluck open string 3 with a downstroke. Then rock back your entire hand (rotating it counter-clockwise relative to the banjo head) so that T can cross over the position of string 3 to pluck fret 4, string 2 as shown. Then rock the hand back in time to play open string 1 in the normal manner.

149

Cutting Ferns

Strathspey

Origin: Scotland
Source: Eddy Arsenault

Key: A (G on Banjo)
Mode: Re-Pentatonic
Tuning: gDGCD (Capo-2)

The above title comes from an old Gaelic song set to this melody. Since "Cutting Ferns" is often the first strathspey learned by budding Cape Breton and Prince Edward Island fiddlers, it makes sense to make it the initial strathspey in this chapter. An early appearance of the tune was in *A Collection of Strathspey Reels [. . .],* (Edinburgh, c. 1830) by Duncan MacKercher (1796-1873); it was subsequently printed in *Kerr's Merry Melodies, The Skye Collection,* and *The Athole Collection.* A variant in 6/8 time called "Drummond Castle" is widely played among contemporary Scottish musicians.

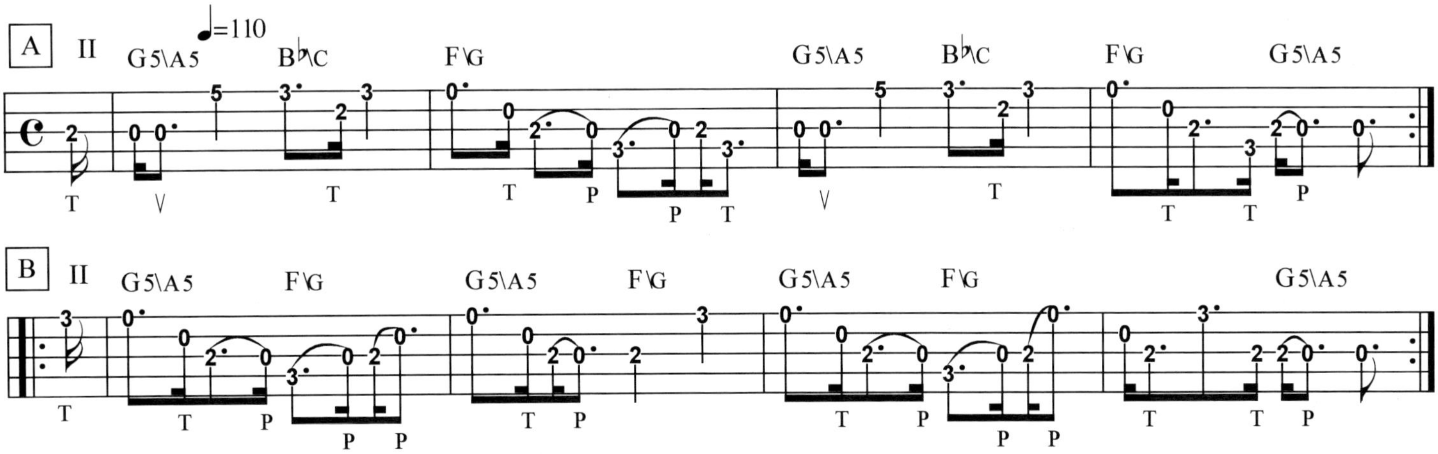

Playing Note for *Cutting Ferns*

Dual Chord Symbols: Chord to left of backslash goes with open banjo; chord on right is for capoed banjo or fiddle

150

Glencoe March

Composer: Dan R. MacDonald
Source: P.E.I. Fiddlers' Society
Appears on: *Devil in the Kitchen*

Key: D (C on Banjo)
Mode: Major
Tuning: gCGCD (Capo-2)

A breathtakingly beautiful mountain-ringed valley, Glencoe is one of the most famous landmarks of Scotland. The site has long been remembered for the infamous *Glencoe Massacre;* in 1692, some 30 members of the MacDonald clan were murdered in their sleep by soldiers commissioned by the Earl of Argyll and commanded by Robert Campbell of Glenlyon (the MacDonalds had frustrated the authorities by refusing to renounce their loyalty to the recently deposed British monarch, James II). One of Dan R. MacDonald's most widely played tunes, this fiddle march has been recorded by Buddy MacMaster and Joe Cormier, and also by the fiddling ensemble known as The Cape Breton Symphony. Standard notation for my source version is in *Fiddle Music of P.E.I.*

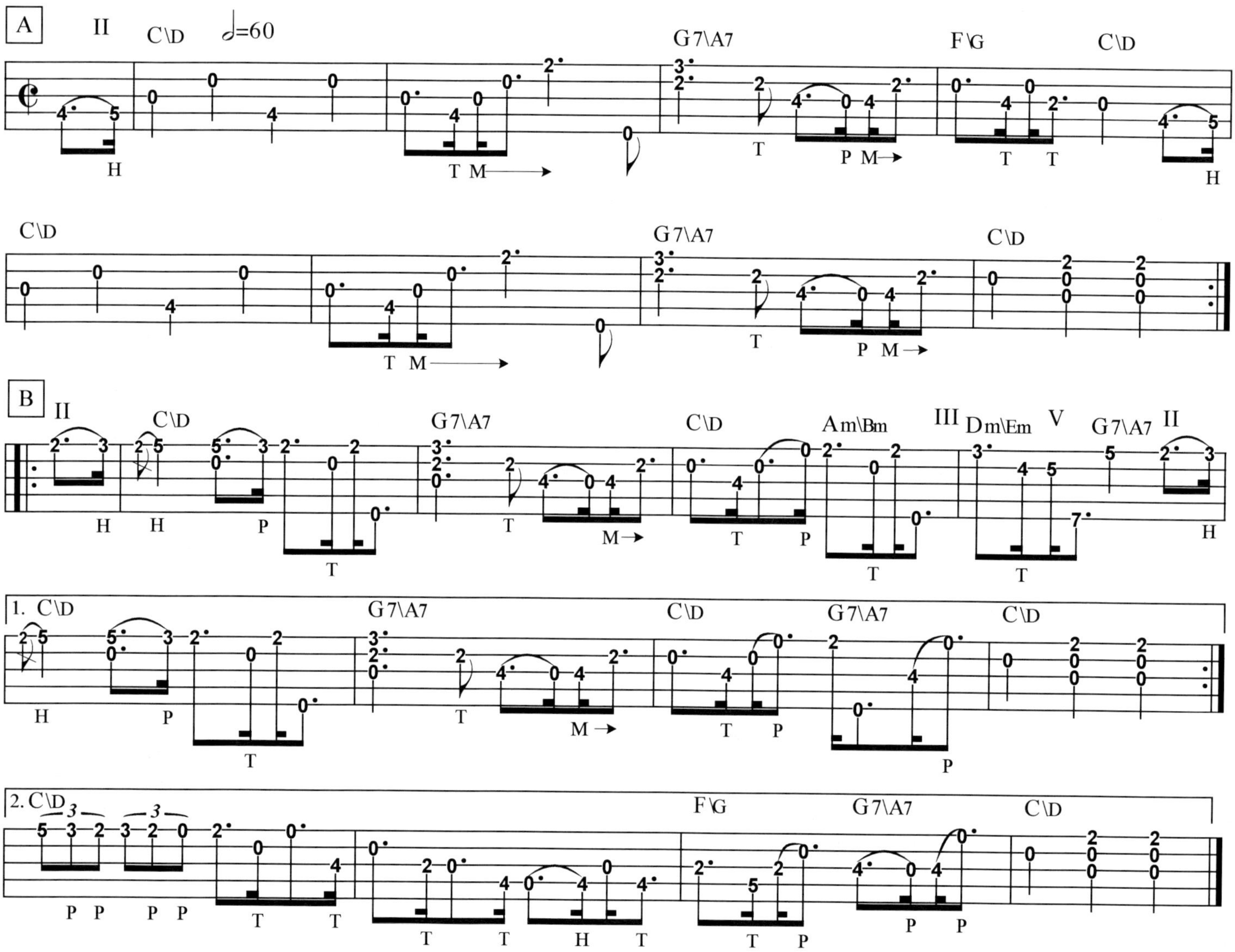

Playing Tips for *Glencoe March*

***Dual Chord Symbols:** Chord to left of backslash goes with open banjo; chord on right is for capoed banjo or fiddle*

- Part B, measure 4. At the end of beat 1, balance with the 2nd finger on fret 4, string 2 and cut that note short just before the start of beat 2. On beat 2, scoot up with the 1st finger to fret 5, string 2 and use that finger as a pivot to swing the 3rd finger over to stop fret 7, string 5.

151

The Iron Man

Strathspey

Composer: James Scott Skinner
Source: Francis MacDonald
Appears on: *Northern Banjo*

Key: A (G on Banjo)
Mode: Major
Tuning: gDGBD (Capo-2)

The "Iron Man" honored here was Skinner's friend and patron, W.M.F. McHardy of Forgue, about 35 miles northwest of Aberdeen, Scotland (Skinner also named another well-known strathspey for McHardy's aristocratic title, "The Laird of Drumblaire"). Skinner himself recorded the tune on a 78-rpm disk in 1922 and published it as sheet music the following year. Winston Fitzgerald recorded the tune on his LP, *Canada's Outstanding Scottish Fiddler*. Standard notation for my source version is in *Fiddle Music of P.E.I.*

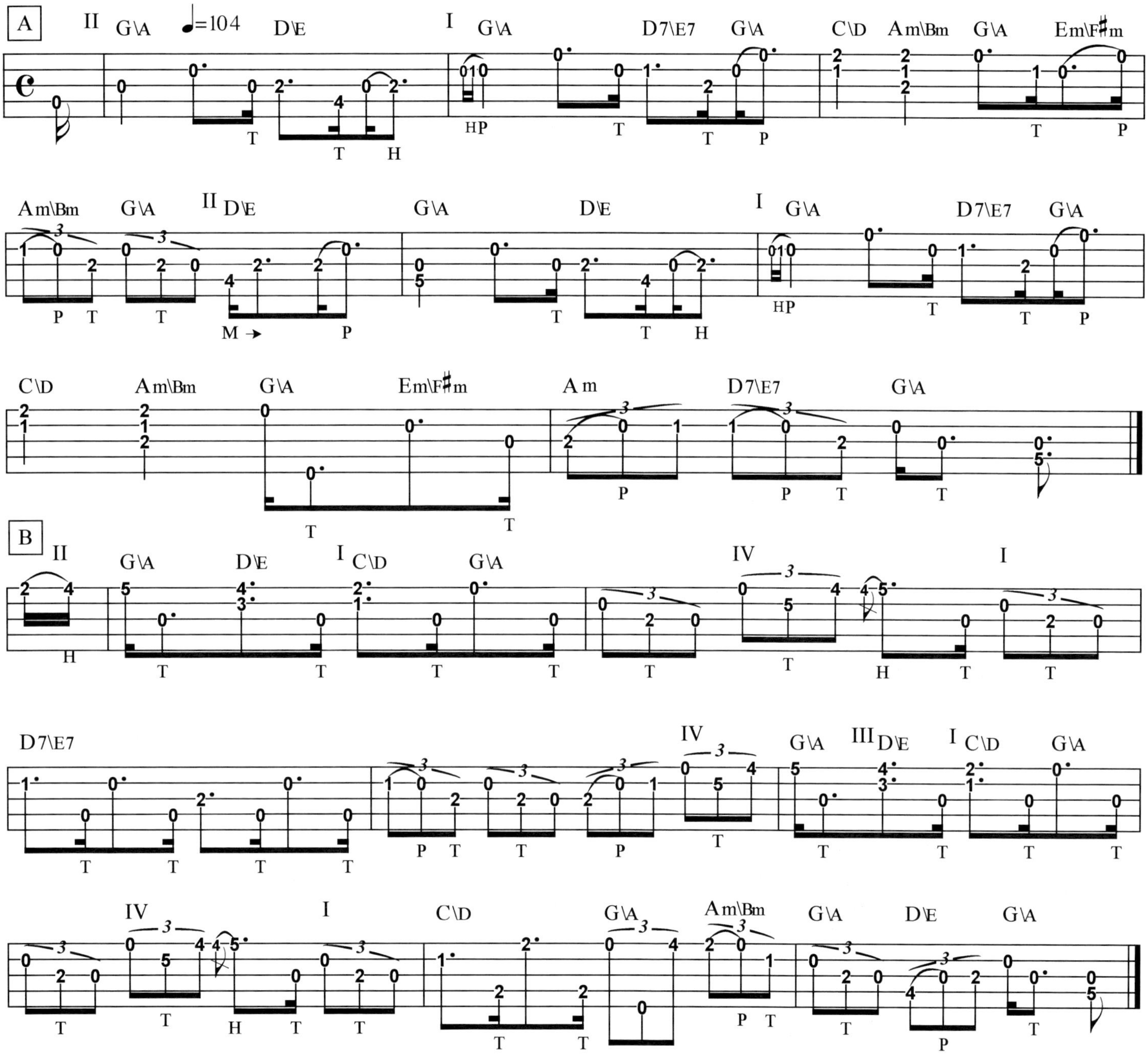

Playing Note for *The Iron Man*

***Dual Chord Symbols:** Chord to left of backslash goes with open banjo; chord on right is for capoed banjo or fiddle*

152

Where the North River Flows

Waltz

Composer: Lillian Frizzell
Source: Elliott Wight
Appears on: *Frails & Frolics*

Key: D (C on Banjo)
Mode: Major
Tuning: gCGCD (Capo-2)

Wight was best known for his lively style of playing jigs and reels, but the last time I recorded him in 2006 I was most struck by a lovely waltz he played. When I inquired about its origin, he mentioned that his neighbor, Lillian Frizzell had composed it. Frizzel (1912-2009) maintained a musical household and often invited local fiddlers in for a good long music session. According to her son Lowell, she was always tinkering on the keyboard coming up with new melodies.

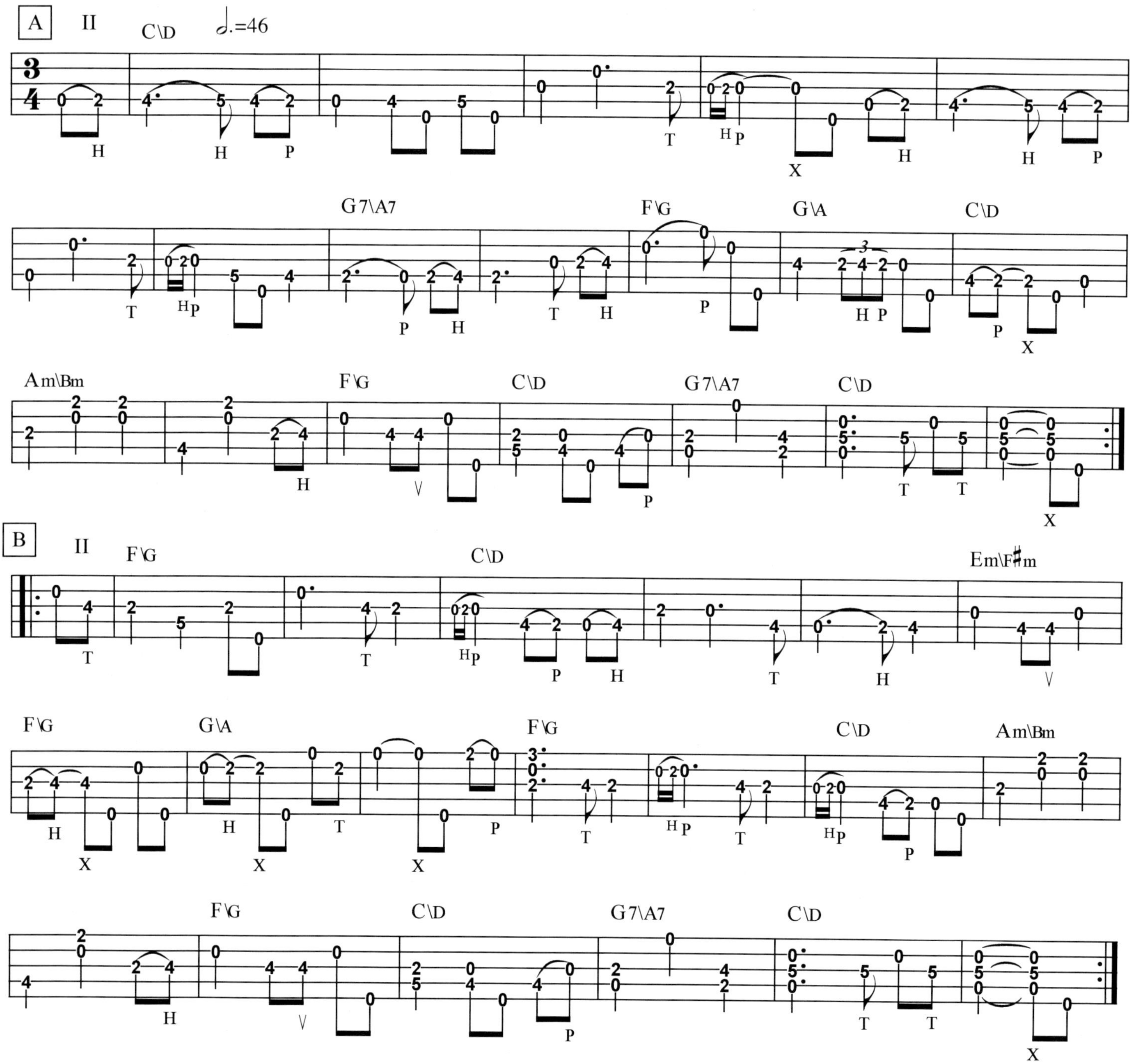

Playing Note for *Where the North River Flows*

__Dual Chord Symbols:__ Chord to left of backslash goes with open banjo; chord on right is for capoed banjo or fiddle

153

Munlochy Bridge

Strathspey

Origin: Scotland
Source: "Old Peter" Chaisson
Appears on: *Devil in the Kitchen*

Key: G
Mode: (Mostly) Major Pentatonic
Tuning: gDGBD

This tune seems to have originated as a song or *puirt-a-beul* (vocalized dance tune with nonsense lyrics), as implied by the alternative title, "I'll Hap Ye in Me Plaidie," that appears in both *Kerr's Merry Melodies* and *The Athole Collection*. The "Munlochy Bridge" name (pronounced mun-LO-chee with a guttural Gaelic-style "ch") – which refers to a village just north of Inverness – seems to derive from the piping world. And in fact, one of the melody's earliest appearances under this title was in *Ross's Collection of Pipe Music* (1869). This tune is circular; on *Devil in the Kitchen* I segue into the reel, "Heather on the Hill" (for a banjo arrangement of "Heather on the Hill," see *Everything Clawhammer*). Standard notation for my source version is in *Fiddle Music of P.E.I.*

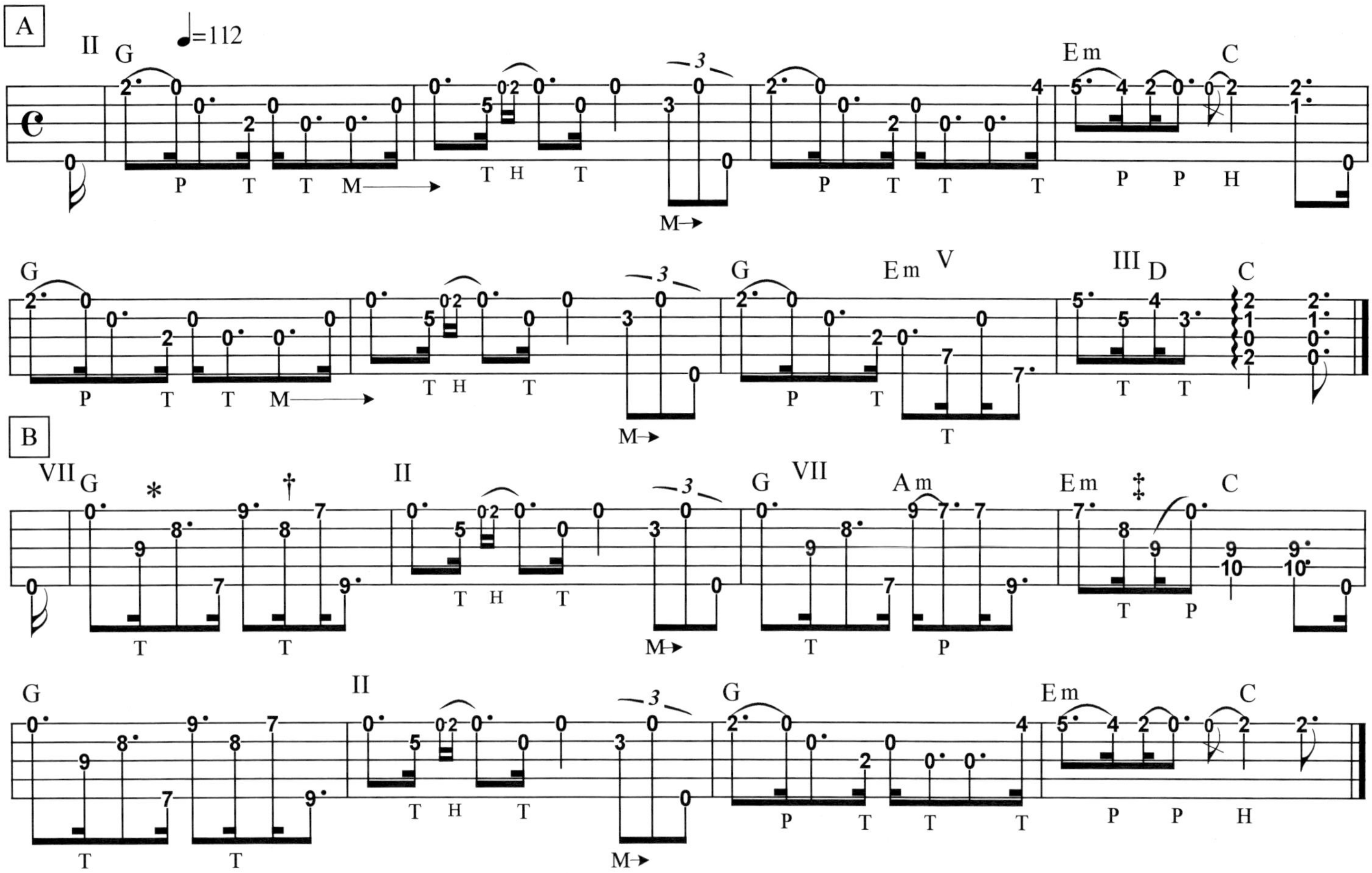

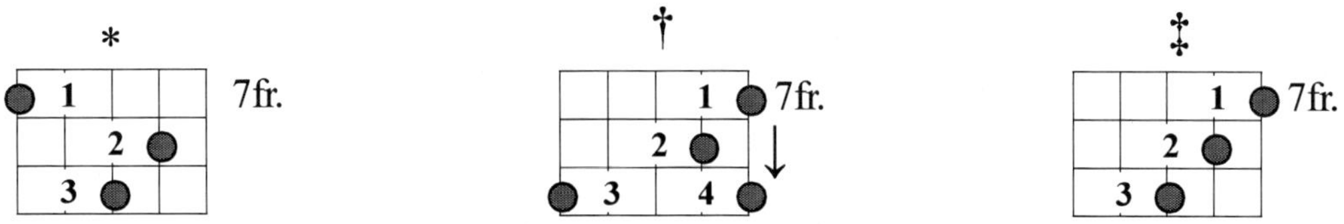

Playing Tips for *Munlochy Bridge*

- Part B, measure 1. When shifting from the shape shown in Diagram * to the one in Diagram †, the key is to pivot on the 2nd finger at fret 8, string 2.

- Part B, measure 3. At the end of beat 2, cut fret 7, string 5 short (1st finger), then quickly move that finger over to fret 7, string 1 to serve as the destination note for the pull-off on that string from fret 9 to fret 7 (the 4th finger is the most convenient one to place on fret 9 for initiating that pull-off).

154

Devil in the Kitchen

Strathspey

Origin: Scotland
Source: John Campbell
Appears on: *Devil in the Kitchen*

Key: A (G on Banjo)
Mode: Mixolydian Gamut
Tuning: gDGBD (Capo-2)

James Scott Skinner arranged and popularized a violin setting for this bagpipes tune, which he attributes to piper William Ross (1823-91). It appears in two of Skinner's collections: *Harp & Claymore* and *The Scottish Violinist*. Little Jack MacDonald (1887-1969) was among the first Cape Breton fiddlers to record the tune. The double-sixteenth + eighth note figures throughout emulate the sound of the Cape Breton *cut* ornament (p. 20). The tune is circular; on the *Devil in the Kitchen* CD – which as you might suspect was named for this tune – I segue into the reel, "The Black Mill" (for a banjo arrangement of "The Black Mill," see *Everything Clawhammer*).

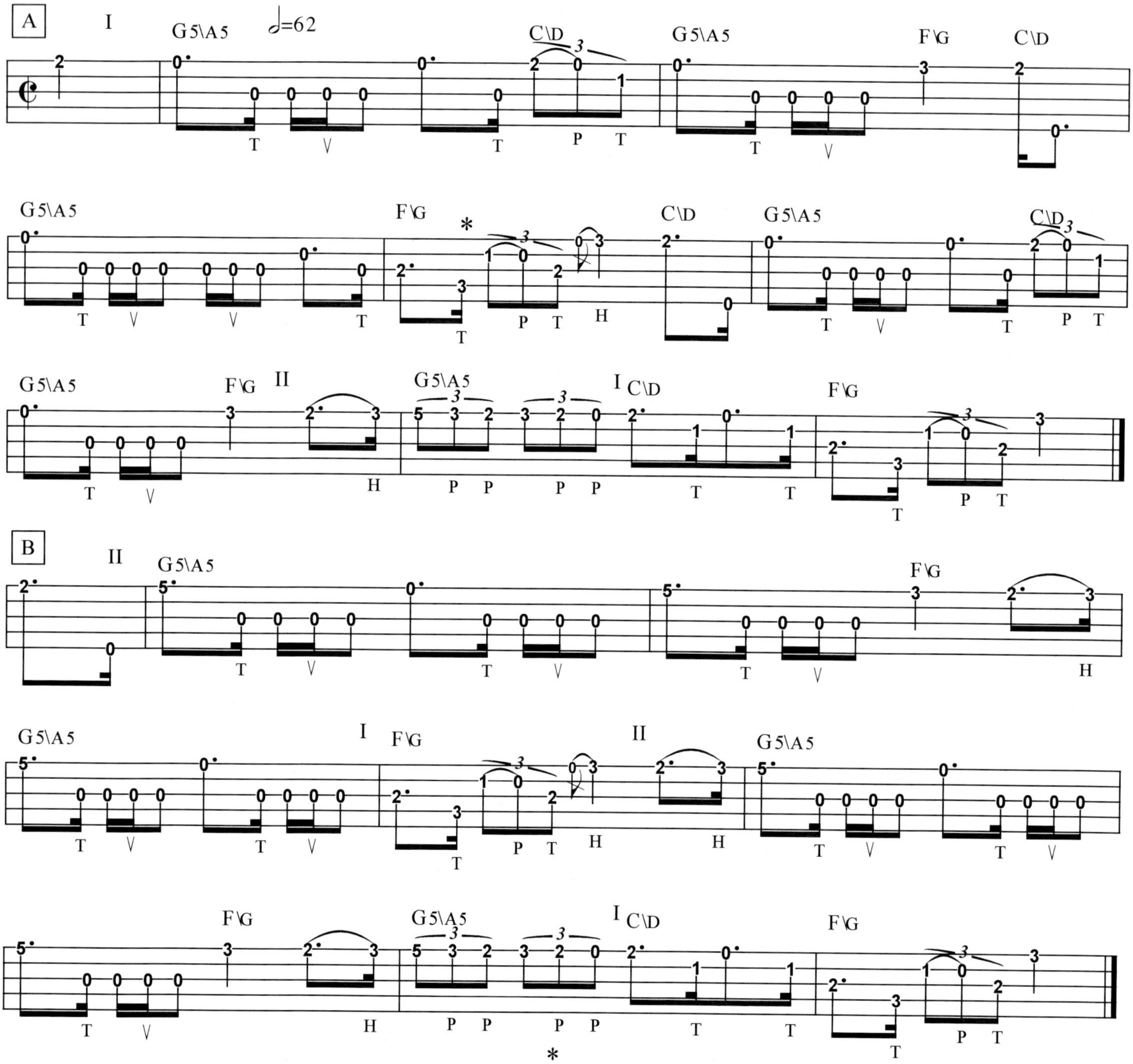

*

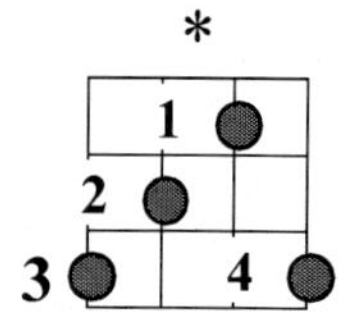

Playing Note for *Devil in the Kitchen*

Dual Chord Symbols: Chord to left of backslash goes with open banjo; chord on right is for capoed banjo or fiddle

The Bonniest Lass in A' the World

155

AIR

ORIGIN SCOTLAND
SOURCE: STERLING BAKER
APPEARS ON: *FRAILS & FROLICS*

KEY: G
MODE: MAJOR
TUNING: gDGBD

One of this very sweet tune's earliest appearances in print was in John Young's, *A Collection of Original Scotch Tunes for the Violin* (1720); it was later featured in numerous 18th-century collections, notably James Oswald's *The Caledonian Pocket Companion* (1740) and Wm. MacGibbon's *A Collection of Scots Tunes [. . .]* (1746). The song, "Hamilla" was set to this melody by Scottish poet Robert Crawfurd; these words and music together appeared for the first time in Wm. Thomson's *Orpheus Caledonius (*1733). Standard notation for my source version is in *Fiddle Music of P.E.I.*

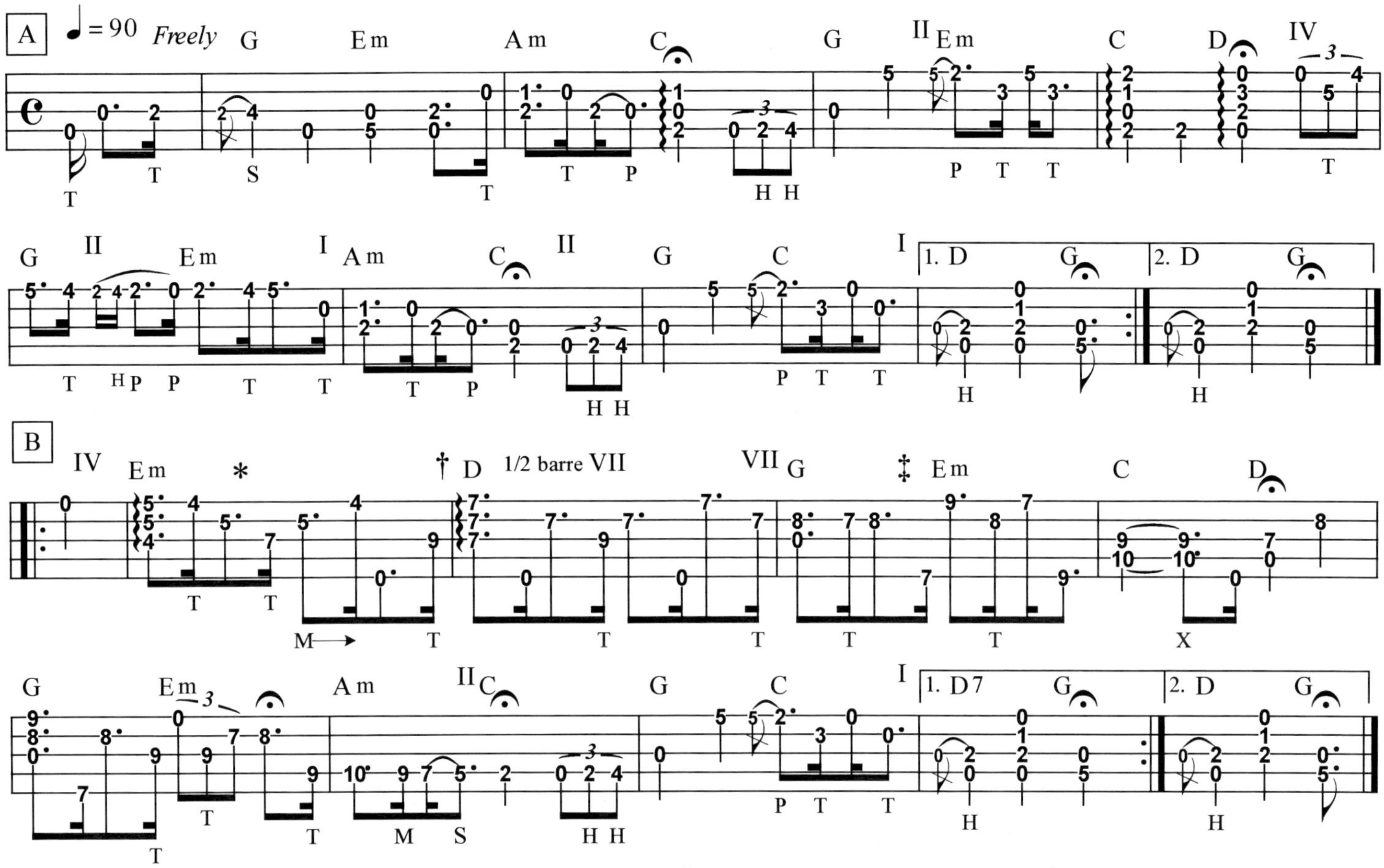

*

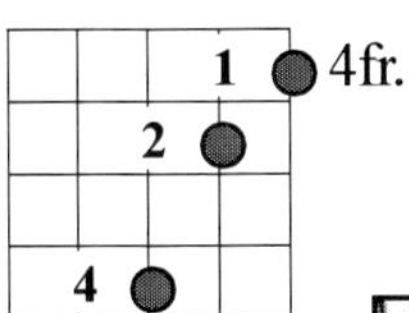

†

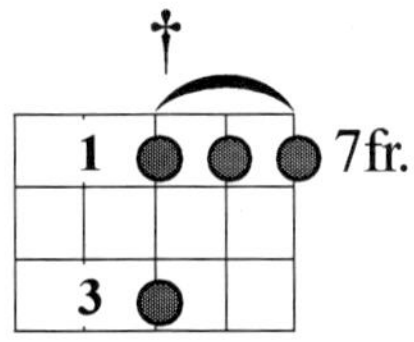

‡

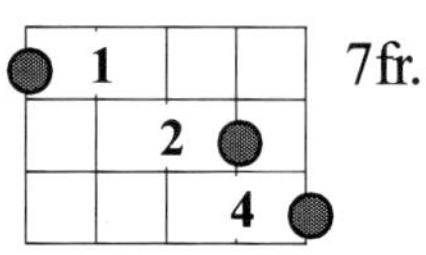

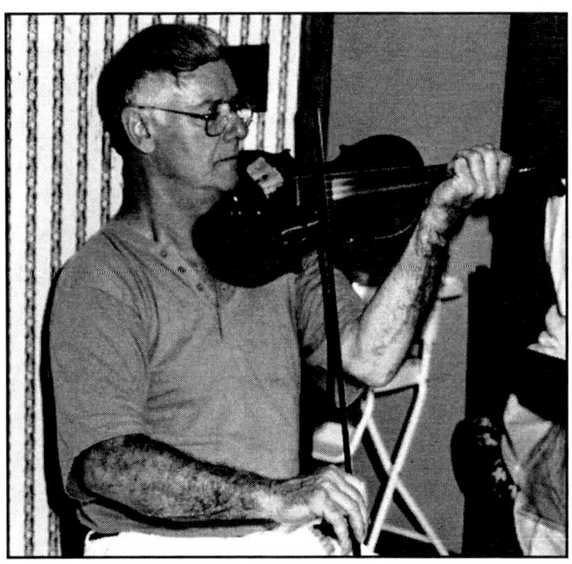

Elliott Wight: North River, P.E.I. (1992). Photo by Ken Perlman; courtesy Robertson Library, University of P.E.I.

156

Miss Maxwell

Strathspey; or Fiddle March

Origin: Scotland
Source: Allan MacDonald
Appears on: *Island Boy*

Key: D (C on Banjo)
Mode: Major
Tuning: gCGCD (Capo-2)

This truly lyrical tune first appeared in William Shepherd's, *A Collection of Strathspeys and Reels [. . .]* (1793). Although the tune was composed as a strathspey, its flowing melody and the long second ending of Part B make it very close in structure and general feel to the fiddle marches that have been composed in the Canadian Maritimes over the last few generations (see, for example, "Glencoe March," p. 154). And indeed, when I first encountered the tune on P.E.I in the early 1990s, fiddlers played it in march style and used it to open the kind of performance set that generally progresses from march to strathspey to reel. Standard notation for my source version is in *Fiddle Music of P.E.I.*

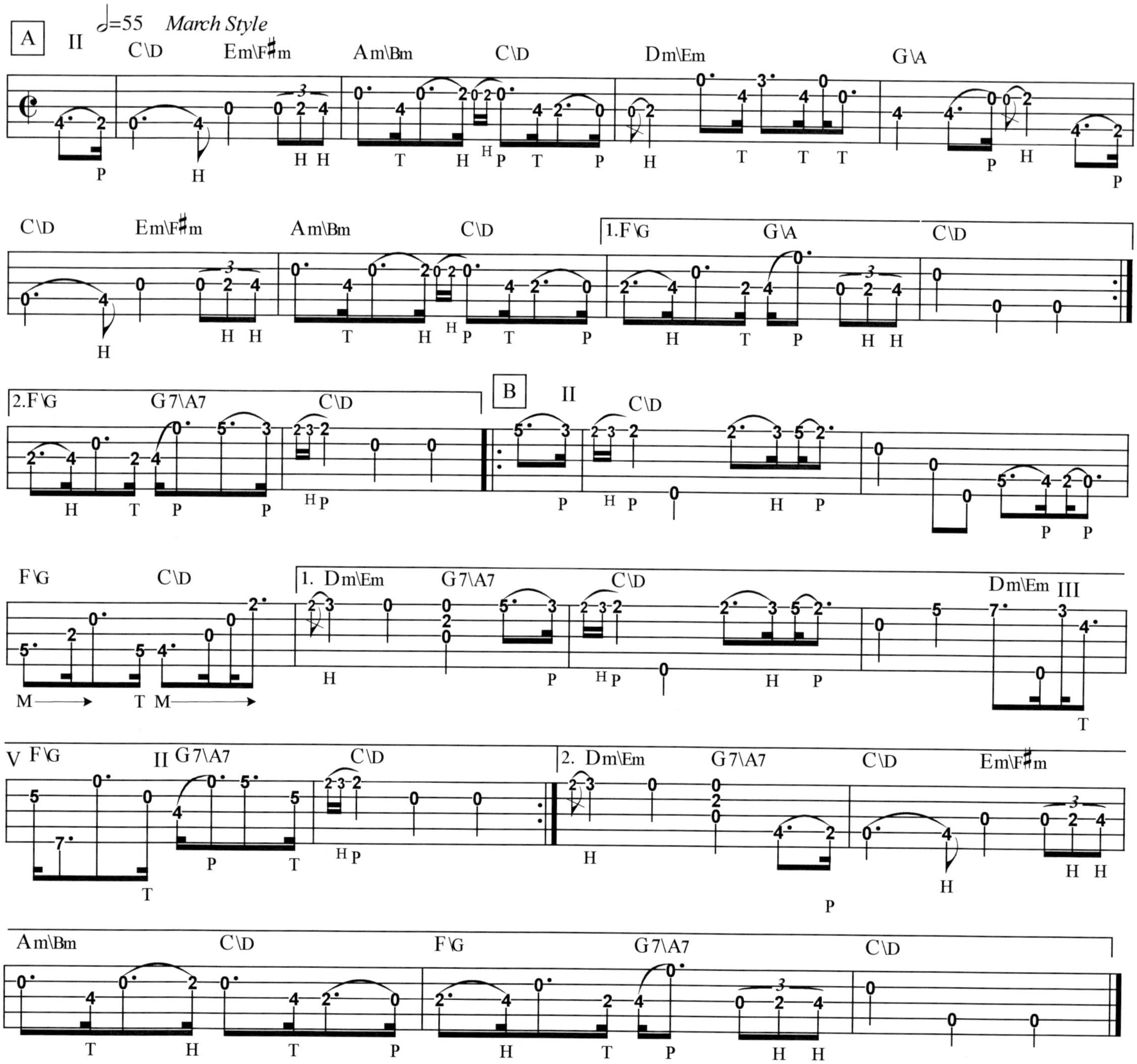

Playing Note for *Miss Maxwell*

***Dual Chord Symbols:** Chord to left of backslash goes with open banjo; chord on right is for capoed banjo or fiddle*

157

Miss Gordon

Strathspey

Origin: William Marshall (1748-1833)
Source: "Young Peter" Chaisson
Appears on: *Island Boy*

Key: D (C on Banjo)
Mode: Major
Tuning: gCGCD (Capo-2)

The Huntly family, Dukes of Gordon – based in Gordon Castle near Fochabers, Scotland – were great patrons of Scottish fiddling. Composer Marshall himself was employed for many years by Alexander, 4th Duke of Gordon (1743–1827) as a court musician. The tune appears in Marshall's *Scottish Airs, Melodies [. . .] for the Violin* (1822). It's a great strathspey, and is still widely played among musicians in both Scotland and the Canadian Maritimes. The tune is circular; the measure labeled "Alt. B8" leads seamlessly to the reel, "Robert Stubbert" (p. 65), which follows it in medley on *Island Boy*. Standard notation for my source version is in *Fiddle Music of P.E.I.*

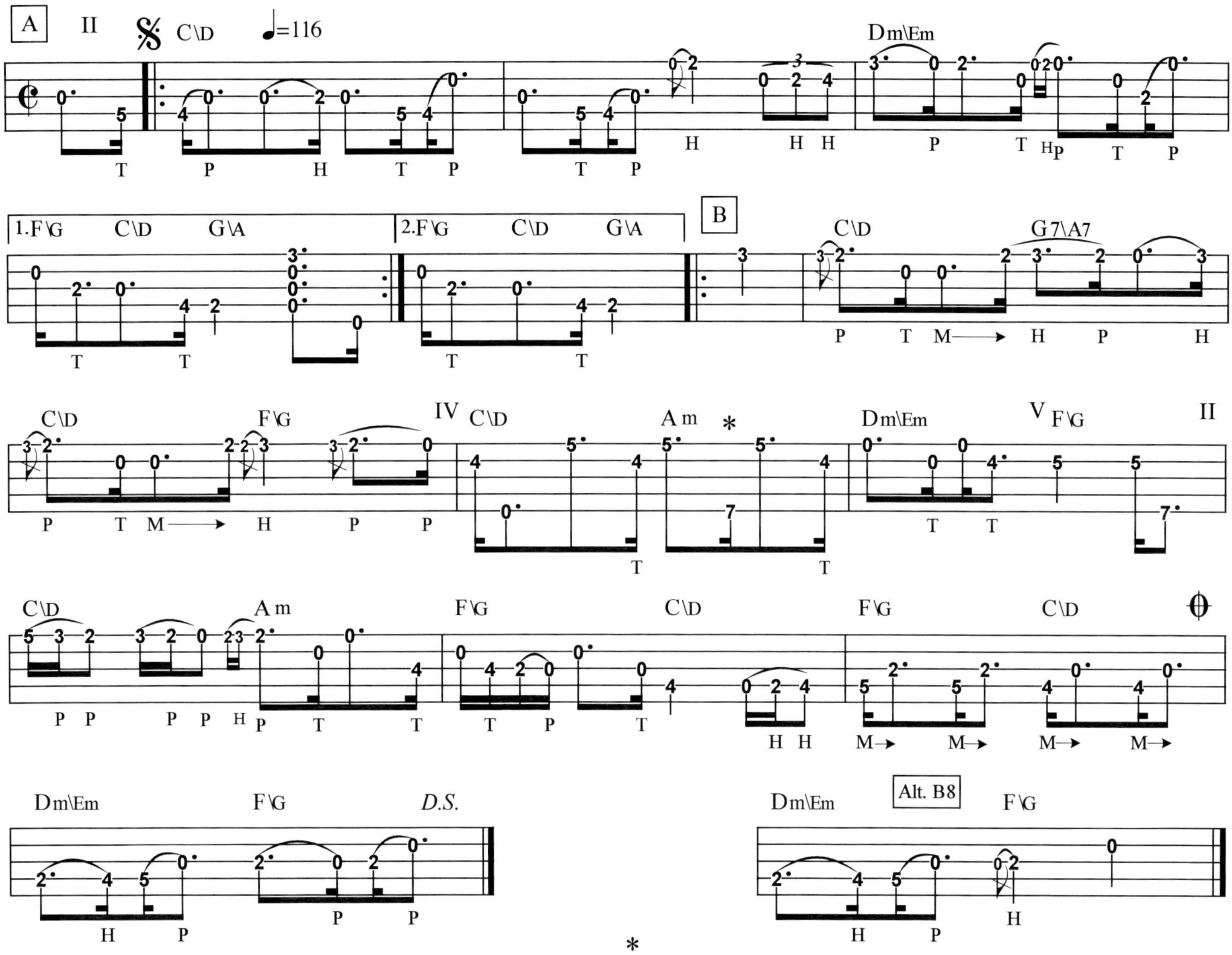

*

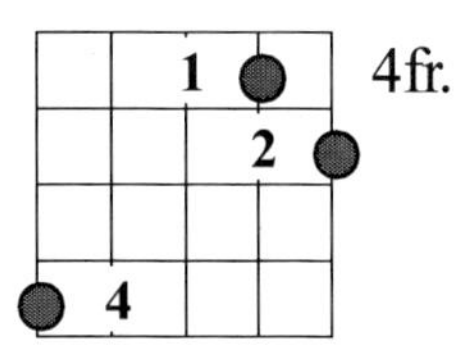

Playing Tips for *Miss Gordon*

__Dual Chord Symbols:__ Chord to left of backslash goes with open banjo; chord on right is for capoed banjo or fiddle

• Part B, measures 4-5. At the end of measure 4, cut short fret 7, string 5, quickly move down the neck to second position and place the 1st, 2nd, and 4th fingers on string 1 simultaneously at frets 5, 3, and 2. Then at the start of measure 5, peel those fingers off one at a time to create the pull-offs in the first double-sixteenth + eighth note figure.

158

Joe MacInnis' March

Composer: Carl MacKenzie
Source: Joe Cormier
Appears on: *Devil in the Kitchen*

Key: A (G on Banjo)
Mode: Dorian Gamut
Tuning: gDGCD (Capo-2)

I recorded this tune on *Devil in the Kitchen* as "Cape Breton Johnny Cope"; I learned its actual provenance and title several years later when I had the honor of working with the composer at a music camp. Named for fiddler Joe MacInnis of Sydney, Nova Scotia (1887-1944), this haunting fiddle march is a truly unforgettable piece of music.

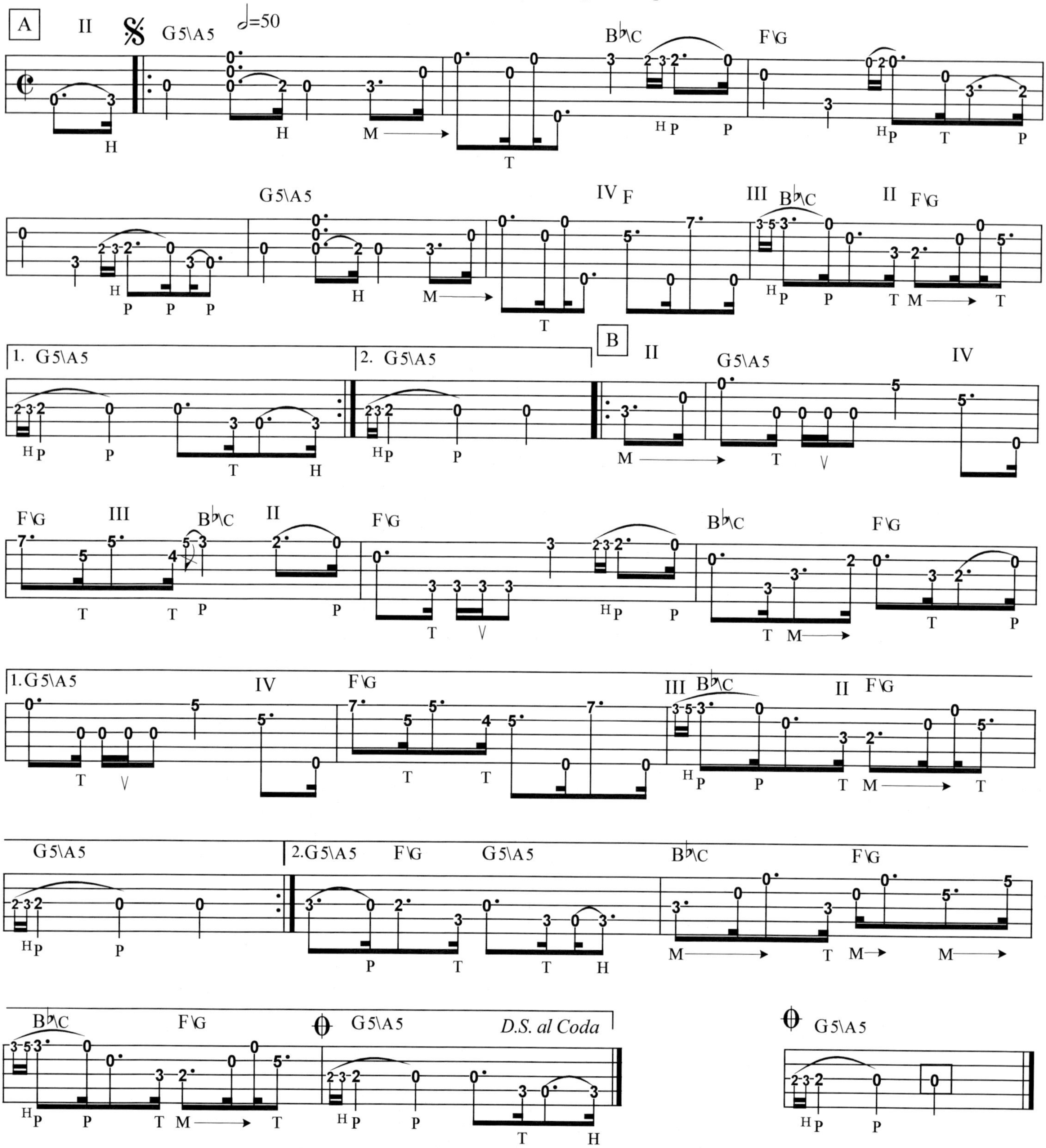

Playing Note for *Joe MacInnis' March*

***Dual Chord Symbols:** Chord to left of backslash goes with open banjo; chord on right is for capoed banjo or fiddle*

159

Captain Campbell

Strathspey

Origin: Scotland
Source: Eddy Arsenault
Appears on: *Island Boy*

Key: A (G on Banjo)
Mode: See Intro
Tuning: gCGCD (Capo-2)

"Captain Campbell" is a 19th-century tune; it appears in *Lowe's Collection, Kerr's Merry Melodies,* and *The Athole Collection.* The mode is close to a Dorian gamut, but avoids the 6th tone of the scale entirely (F♯ on fiddle; E♮ on open banjo). I used a capoed C tuning for this arrangement because I needed the low, open fourth-string note in Part A, measure 2. Standard notation for my source version is in *Fiddle Music of P.E.I.*

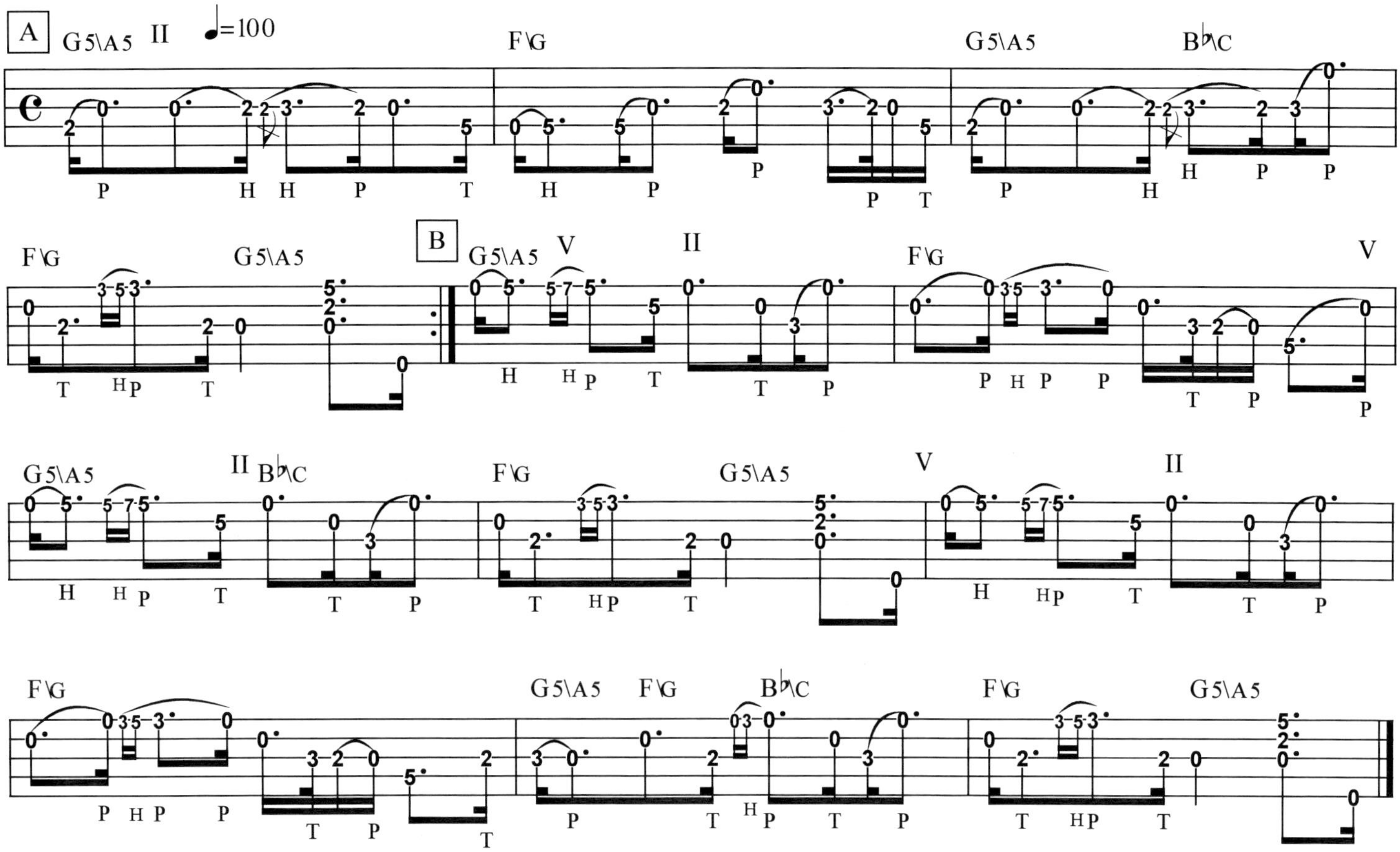

Playing Note for *Captain Campbell*

Dual Chord Symbols: Chord to left of backslash goes with open banjo; chord on right is for capoed banjo or fiddle

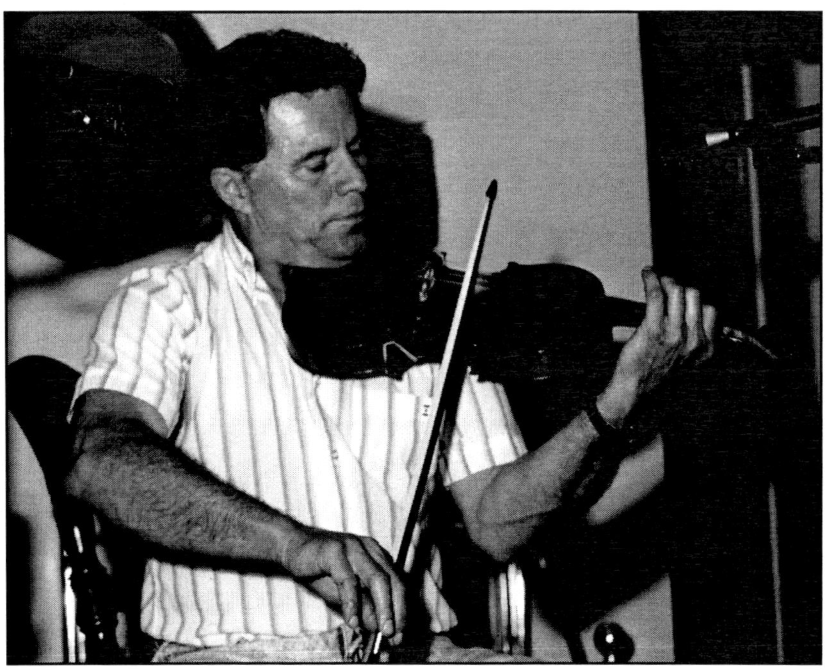

Edward P. Arsenault: Wellington, P.E.I. (1992). Photo by Earthwatch Team; courtesy Robertson Library, University of P.E.I.

160

The Duke of Gordon's Birthday

Strathspey

Composer: William Marshall (1748-1833)
Source: Eddy Arsenault
Appears on: *Island Boy*

Key: G
Mode: See Intro
Tuning: gDGBD

This is one of the most commonly played strathspeys on P.E.I., and one of the few strathspeys there to have acquired a distinctive local character. Composer Marshall was a long-term recipient of Gordon family patronage and dedicated many tunes to the Duke and his family. Certainly among the first places the tune appeared in print was in Marshall's own *Scottish Airs, Melodies [. . .] for the Violin* (1822). It was subsequently printed in numerous other works, including *The Gow Repository, Lowe's Collection, Kerr's Merry Melodies, The Skye Collection,* and *The Athole Collection.* Among the many fiddlers from the Cape Breton orbit who have recorded the tune since the 1920s are Colin Boyd, John A. MacDonald, Joe MacLean, Carl MacKenzie, and Buddy MacMaster. The mode is close to major pentatonic; the 4th tone, C is missing entirely and there is just a hint of the 7th tone, F♯. I had to take Part A up an octave for it to fit on banjo. Standard notation for my source version is in *Fiddle Music of P.E.I.*

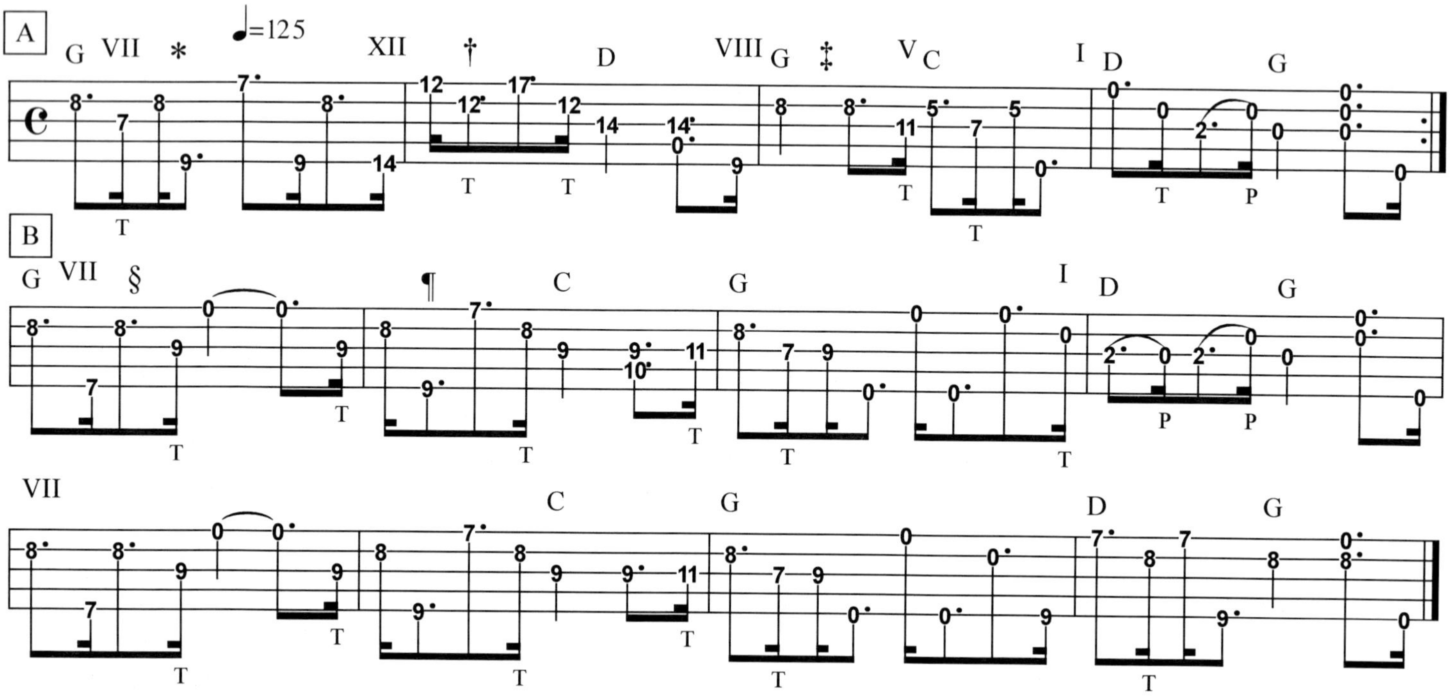

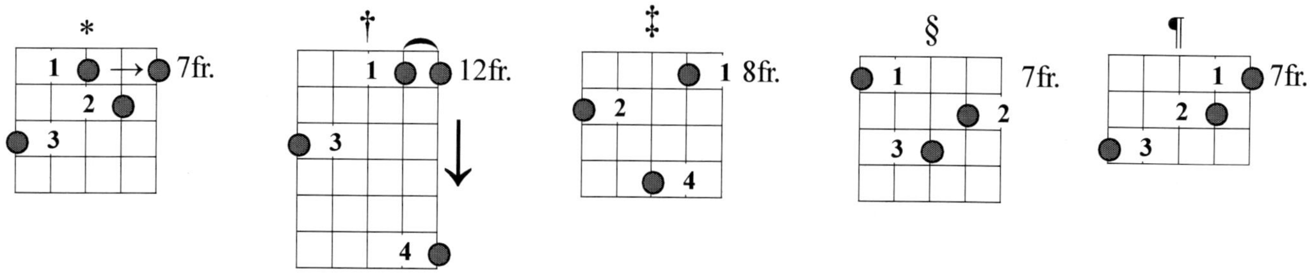

Playing Tips for *The Duke of Gordon's Birthday*

• Part A, measures 1-2. On beat 4 of measure 1, cut short fret 8, string 2 (2nd finger; the 3rd finger should already be in place at fret 9, string 5 as shown in Diagram *). Halfway through that beat, glide up string 5 with the 3rd finger to fret 14 and – at the start of measure 2 – use it as a pivot to swing the 1st finger into a half-barre on fret 12 as shown in Diagram †.

• Part A, measures 2-3. On beat 4 of measure 2, cut short fret 14, string 3 (3rd finger). Halfway through that beat, head down the neck and grab fret 9 with the 2nd finger, then use it as a pivot to position the 1st and 4th fingers as shown in Diagram ‡.

161

Stella's Trip to Kamloops

Fiddle March

Composer: Patricia Chafe
Source: "Young Peter" Chaisson
Appears on: *Devil in the Kitchen; Northern Banjo*

Key: A (G on Banjo)
Mode: Major
Tuning: gDGBD (Capo-2)

"Stella's Trip" is now played by fiddle-music enthusiasts worldwide; it was composed in the 1970s by a young piano player from Glace Bay, Nova Scotia named Pat Chafe, the daughter of well-known fiddler Winnie Chafe. The tune was named for Pat's aunt Stella Chafe, a Nun with the Sisters of Charity, who had just been transferred to teach at a Catholic school in Kamloops, a small city in British Columbia. The composer notes that both the new tune and its name were unveiled to loud acclaim at Stella's going away party: "These days I still tell Stella, it's ironic that so quiet a member of a group of charitable ladies has become famous in her own right, simply through a little tune." Standard notation for my source version is in *Fiddle Music of P.E.I.*

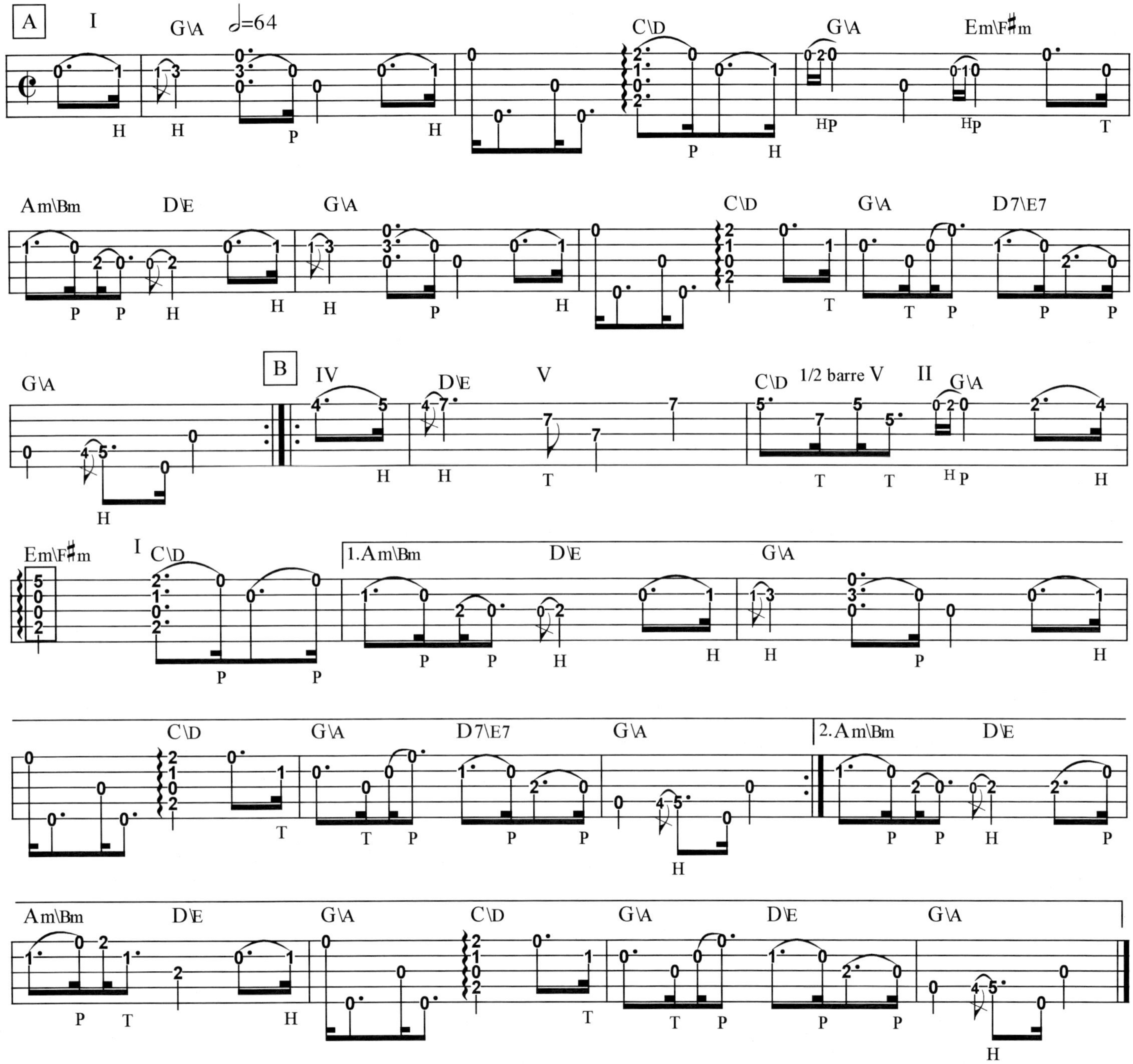

Playing Note for *Stella's Trip to Kamloops*

***Dual Chord Symbols:** Chord to left of backslash goes with open banjo; chord on right is for capoed banjo or fiddle*

162

Dr. Keith, Aberdeen

Strathspey

Composer: James Scott Skinner
Source: Kenny Chaisson
Appears on: *Frails & Frolics*

Key: F
Mode: Major
Tuning: gCGCD

This tune was first published in Skinner's *Miller o'Hirn Collection* (1881); it appeared soon afterward in *The Skye Collection.* Winston "Scotty" Fitzgerald recorded it on his LP, *The Inimitable Winston "Scotty" Fitzgerald.* The tune is circular; on *Frails & Frolics,* the segue is to "Miss Barker's Hornpipe" (p. 107). Standard notation for my source version is in *Fiddle Music of P.E.I.*

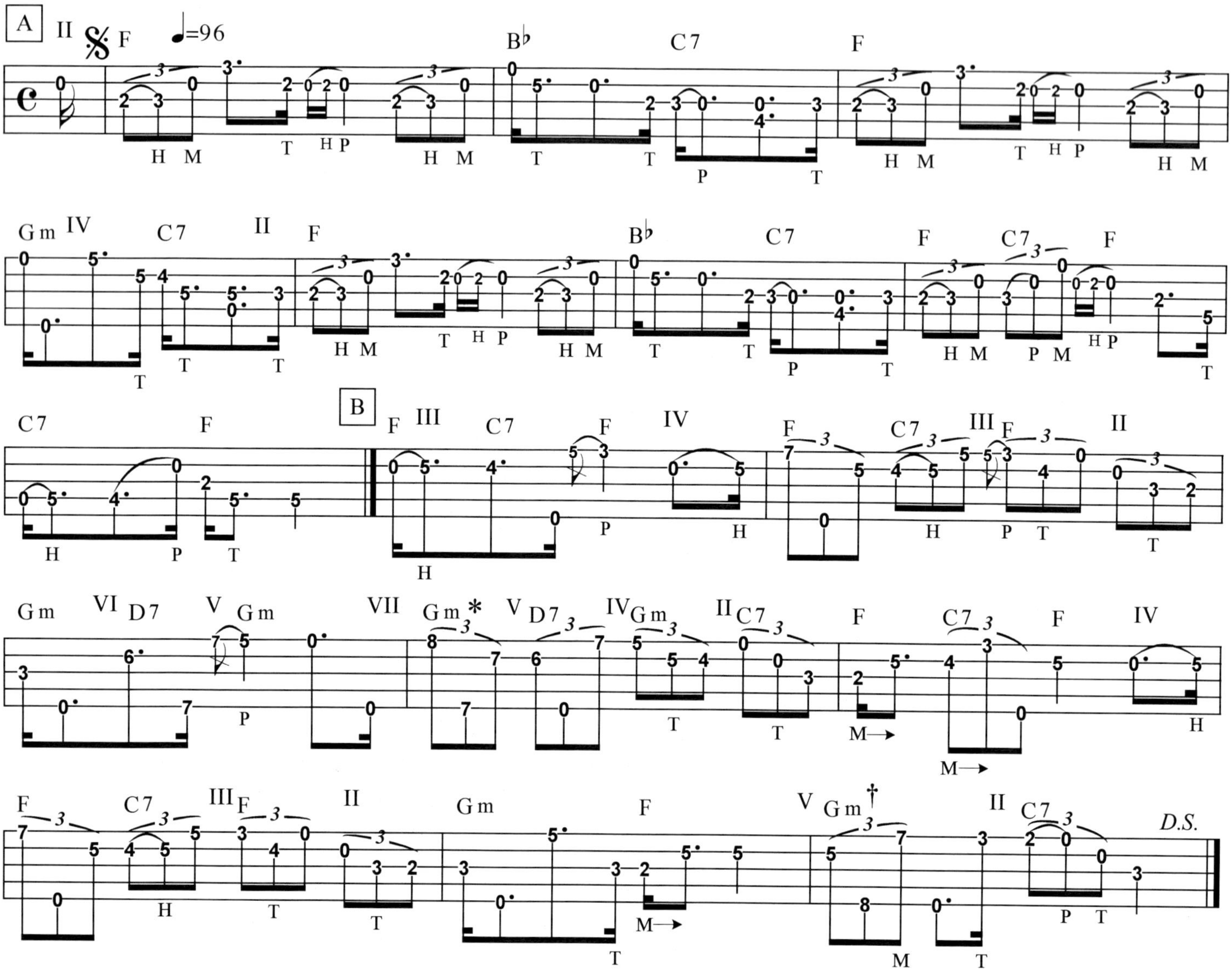

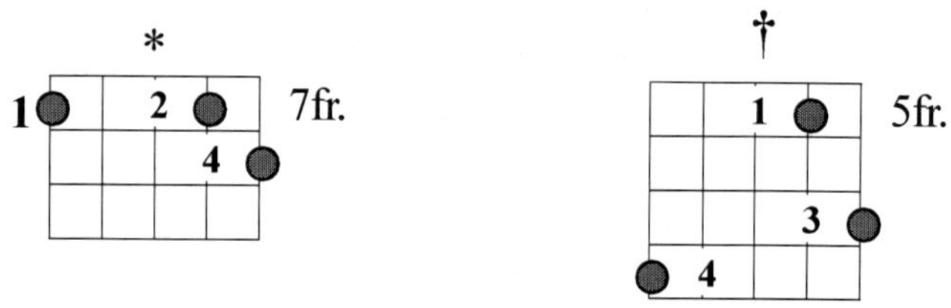

Playing Tips for *Dr. Keith, Aberdeen*

• Part B, measure 4. Start with the shape in Diagram *. On beat 2, glide down string 2 with the 2nd finger to fret 6 and use it as a pivot to bring the and 4th finger into place on fret 7, string 1. Then on beat 3, glide down again on string 2 with the 2nd finger, but this time to fret 5; then use that finger as a pivot to swing the 3rd finger into place at fret 5, string 1.

• Part B, measure 8. At the end of beat 1, obtain the last triplet note with a downstroke. The thumb then leads off on beat 2 with an open 5th-string note. To obtain the following note you need to cross T over to pluck *string 1* (rotate your wrist counterclockwise relative to the banjo head and reach out). Then on beat 3, lead off with a downstroke on string 1.

163

Rothiemurchus Rant

Strathspey

Composer: Robert Bremner (1713-89)
Source: "Young Peter" Chaisson
Appears on: *Island Boy*

Key: C
Mode: Major
Tuning: gCGCD

The village of Rothiemurchus (pronounced: rah-thie-MUR-kuss) lies roughly 35 miles southwest of Inverness, Scotland. Composer Bremner included this four-part strathspey in his book, *A Collection of Scots Reels or Country Dances* (4 Vols., 1757-61). Scottish poet Robbie Burns (1759-96) was much taken with this melody and wrote a set of lyrics to it entitled "Lassie wi' the Lint-White Locks." In the 19th century, the tune appeared in several compendiums, including *The Gow Repository, Lowe's Collection, Kerr's Merry Melodies, The Athole Collection,* and *The Skye Collection.* Cape Breton fiddler Angus Chisholm recorded the tune in the 1930s on a 78-rpm disk. I borrowed the practice of using minor chords to harmonize the openings of Parts B and D from Kevin Chaisson. The tune is circular; on *Island Boy* the segue is to the reel, "Bonnie Lass of Fisherrow" (p. 103). Standard notation for my source version is in *Fiddle Music of P.E.I.*

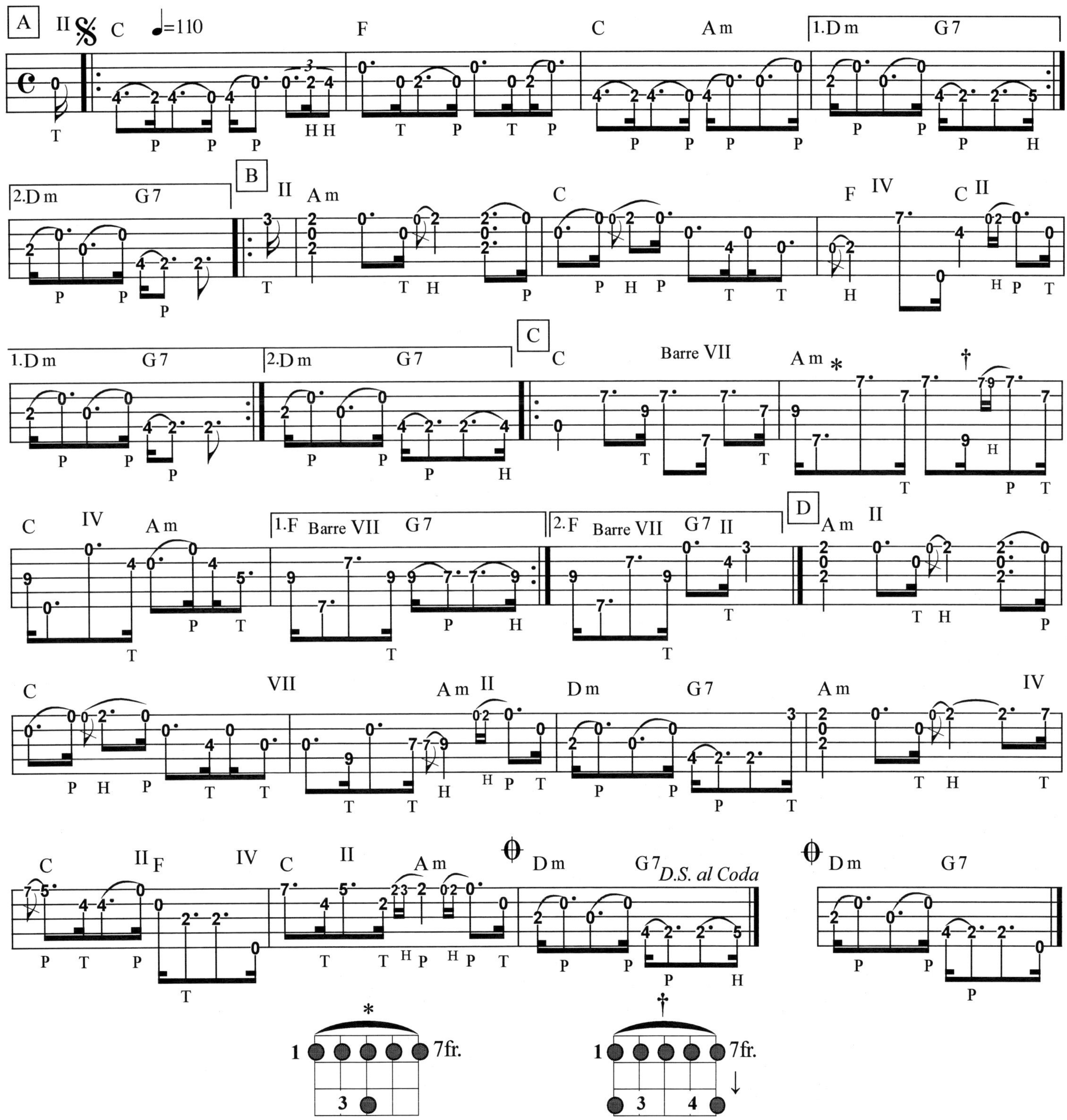

164

The North Side of the Grampians

STRATHSPEY

Origin: Scotland
Source: Hector MacAndrew
Appears on: *Frails & Frolics*

Key: C
Mode: Major
Tuning: gCGCD

The title refers to a mountain range in northwestern Scotland. I fell in love with this tune after hearing it played on a recording by Scottish fiddler Hector MacAndrew; it is often attributed to Capt. Simon Fraser (1773-1852), compiler of the well-known collection, *Airs & Melodies Peculiar to the Highlands* (1816). The tune appears as "The North of the Grampians" in *Lowe's Collection* and *The Skye Collection;* and as "North of the Grampians" in *Kerr's Merry Melodies* and *The Athole Collection.* To enhance my banjo setting, I created octave-up variations for both parts. The tune is circular; on *Frails & Frolics*, the segue is to "Jack Webster's Reel" (p. 105).

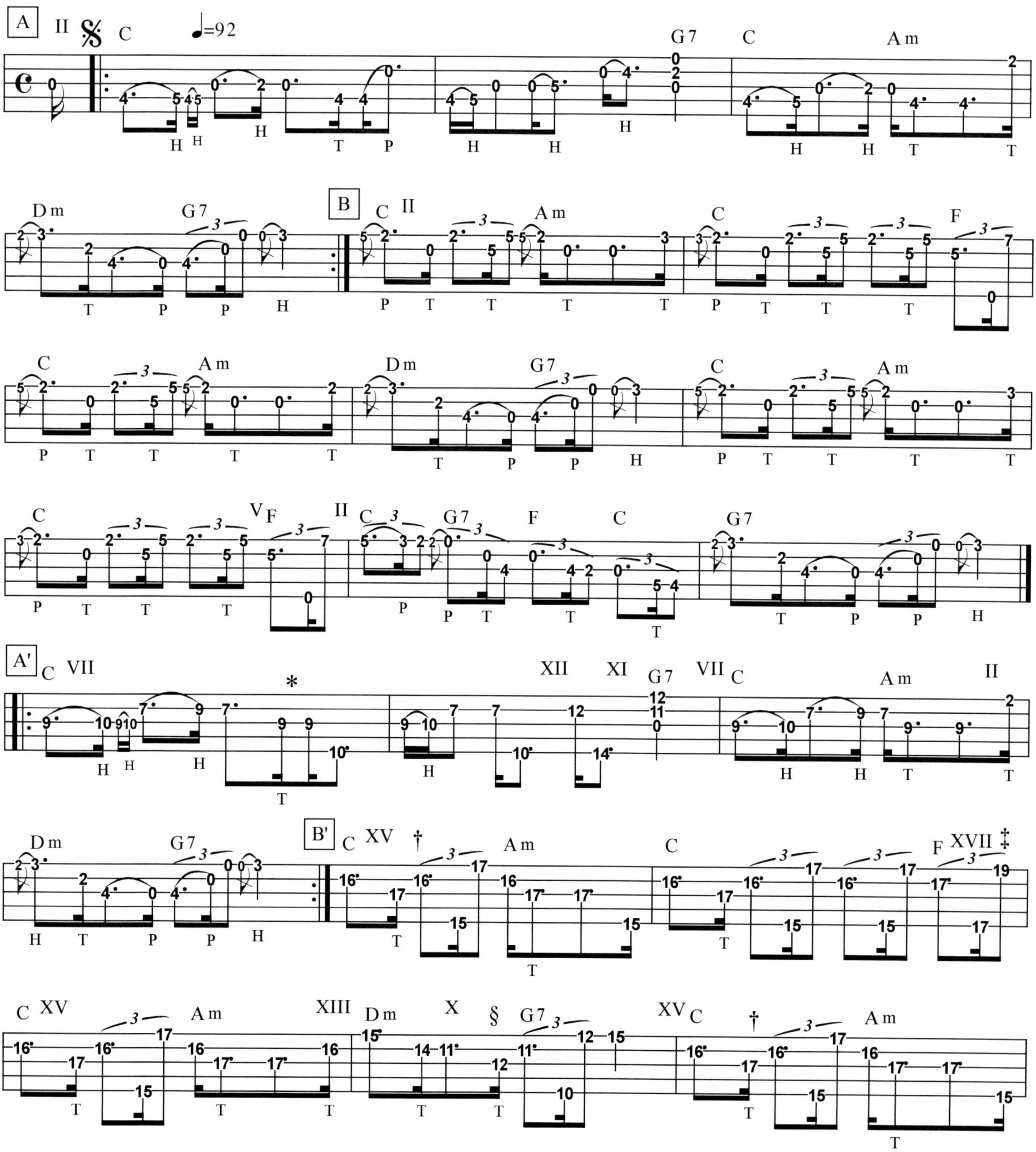

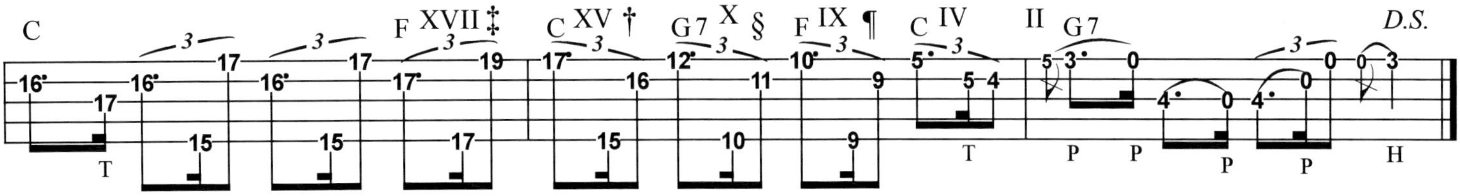

Fingering Diagrams for *North Side of the Grampians*

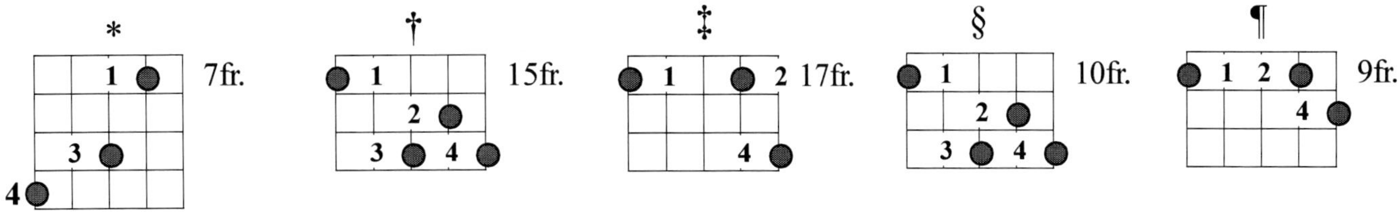

Playing Tips for *North Side of the Grampians*

• Part B', measure 2. To shift from the shape in Diagram † to the one in Diagram ‡ on beat 4, glide up the second string with the 2nd finger from fret 16 to fret 17, and use that finger as a pivot to swing the others into position.

• Part B', measure 3-4. Halfway through beat 4 of measure 3, cut short fret 17, string 3 (3rd finger) and move that finger down to stop fret 16, string 2. On beat 1 of measure 4, use the 3rd finger as a pivot to get the 2nd and 1st fingers in place on fret 15, string 1 and fret 14, string 2 respectively. Then on beat 2 cut fret 14 short and glide with the 2nd finger down to fret 11; then use that finger as a pivot to swing the other three fingers into position as shown in Diagram §.

• Part B', measure 7. As you move through the measure, keep the 1st and 4th fingers in position on strings 5 and 1, respectively and use them both to glide down the neck and act as pivots as you shift among shapes.

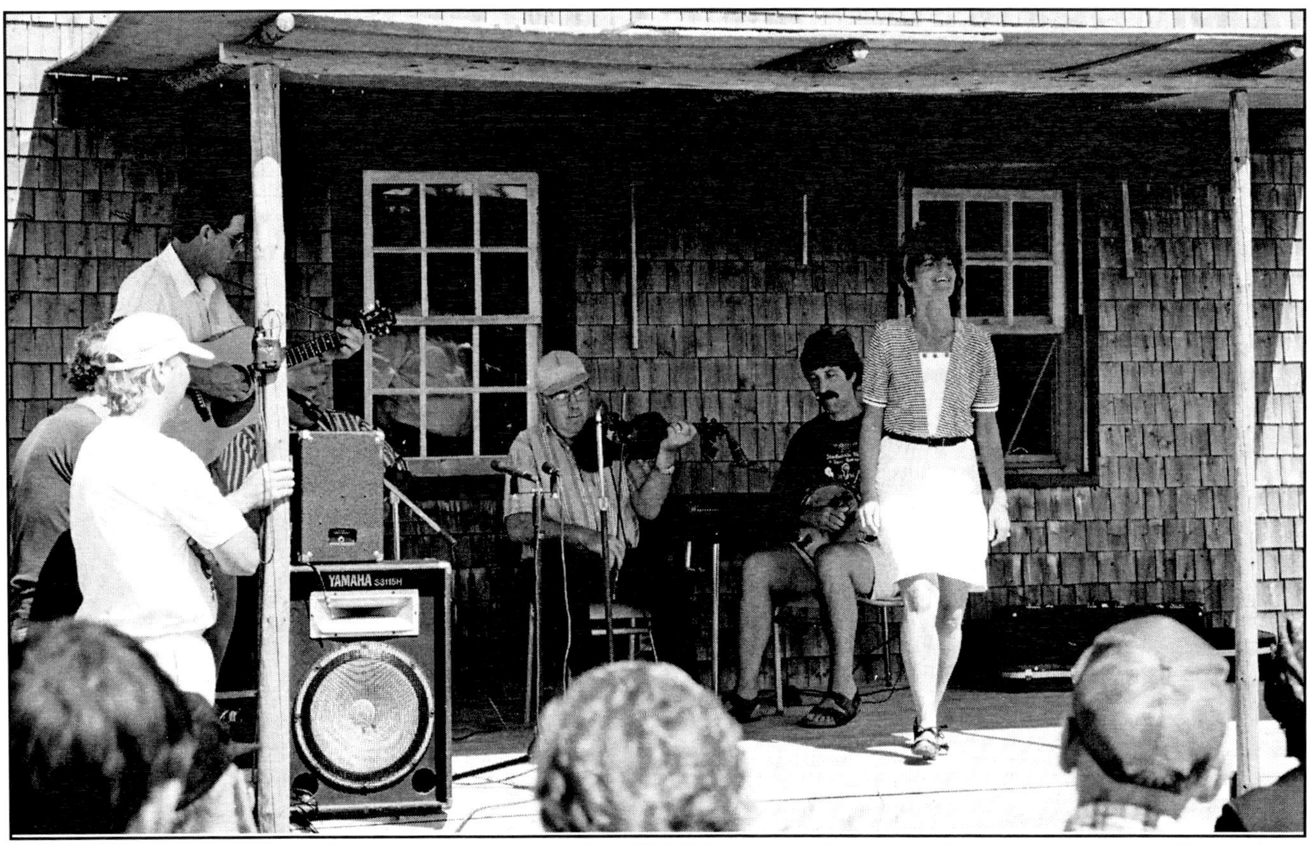

L-R: Alan MacDonald (guitar), George MacPhee (fiddle), Ken Perlman, Marlene MacKinnon Gallant at The Monticello Tea Party: Monticello, P.E.I. (1991). Photo by Earthwatch Team; courtesy Robertson Library, University of P.E.I.

165

Robert Cormack, Aberdeen

Air

Composer: James Henry (1860-1914)
Source: "Young Peter" Chaisson
Appears on: *Northern Banjo*

Key: F
Mode: Major
Tuning: gCGCD

Composer Henry lived in Aberdeenshire, Scotland; he helped found the Aberdeen Strathspey and Reel Society in 1903 and served as its director for the rest of his life. This lyrical air originally appeared in his own publication, *Eight Airs for the Violin* (c. 1895). It was subsequently printed in J. Henderson's, *The Flowers of Scottish Melody* (1935) and recorded by Cape Breton fiddler Carl MacKenzie for Rounder in 1977. It would be logical to assume that Chaisson learned the tune from MacKenzie – either via recording or live performance. Standard notation for my source version is in *Fiddle Music of P.E.I.* To get the right sound, make sure to let the tune "breathe" between phrases as suggested by the notated *fermatas* (p. 15).

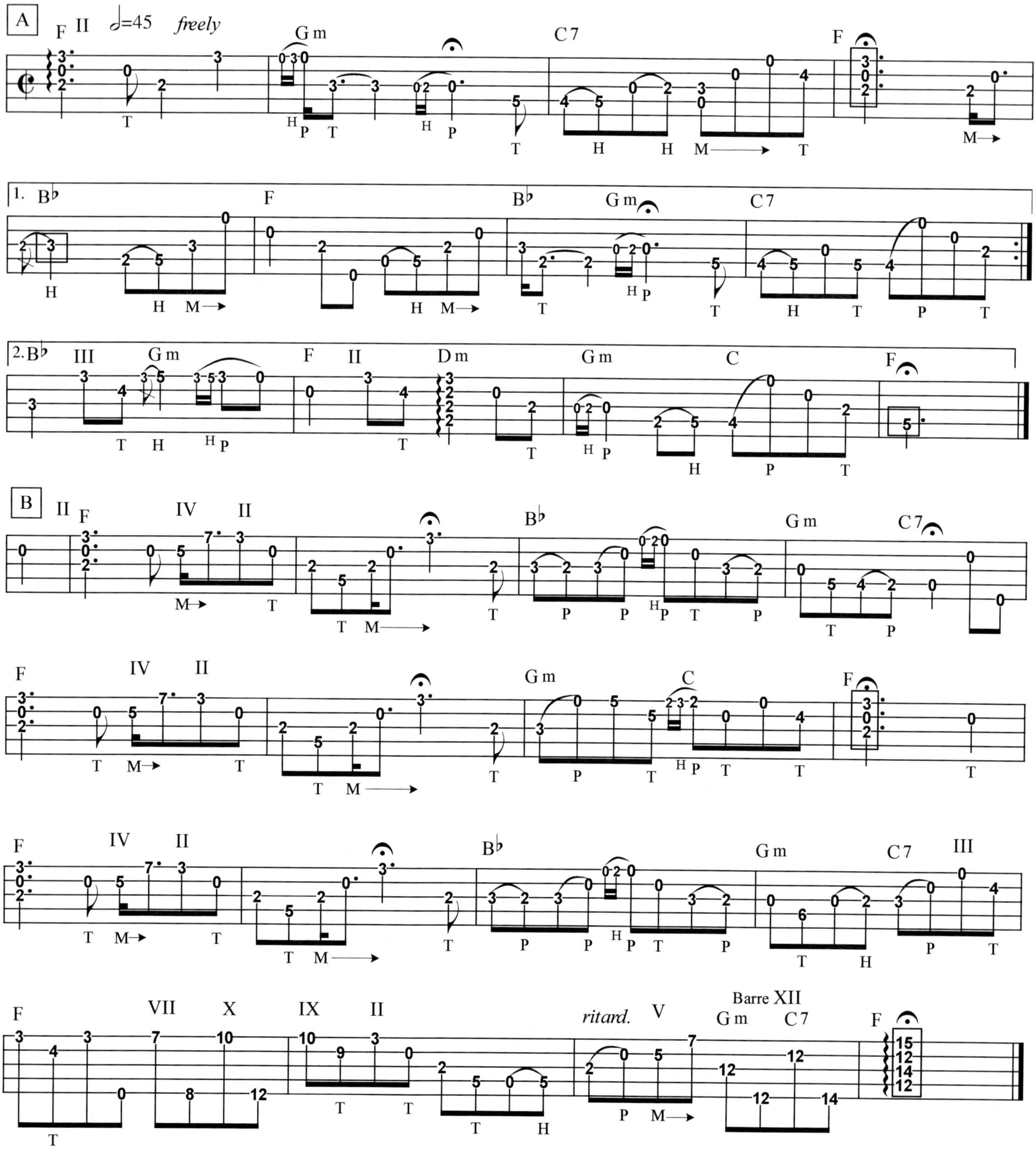

166

Miss Lyall Strathspey, or *Panmure House*

Origin: Scotland
Source: Joe Cormier
Appears on: *Devil in the Kitchen*

Key: A (G on Banjo)
Mode: Dorian Gamut
Tuning: gDGCD (capo-2)

This tune first appears, as "Miss Lyle," in John Hall's, *A Selection of Strathspeys, Reels, Waltzes [. . .]* (1818). In *The Gow Repository* and *Lowe's Collection* it bears the title, "Panmure House." The "Miss Lyall" spelling appears in *The Athole Collection, The Skye Collection,* and *Kerr's Merry Melodies*. In *The Roche Collection* the tune is known as "Faill na mBan Hornpipe." Cape Breton master fiddler Angus Chisholm recorded it on a 78 rpm disk in 1936. I had to take both parts up an octave to fit them on banjo, which required venturing quite far up the neck in Part B.

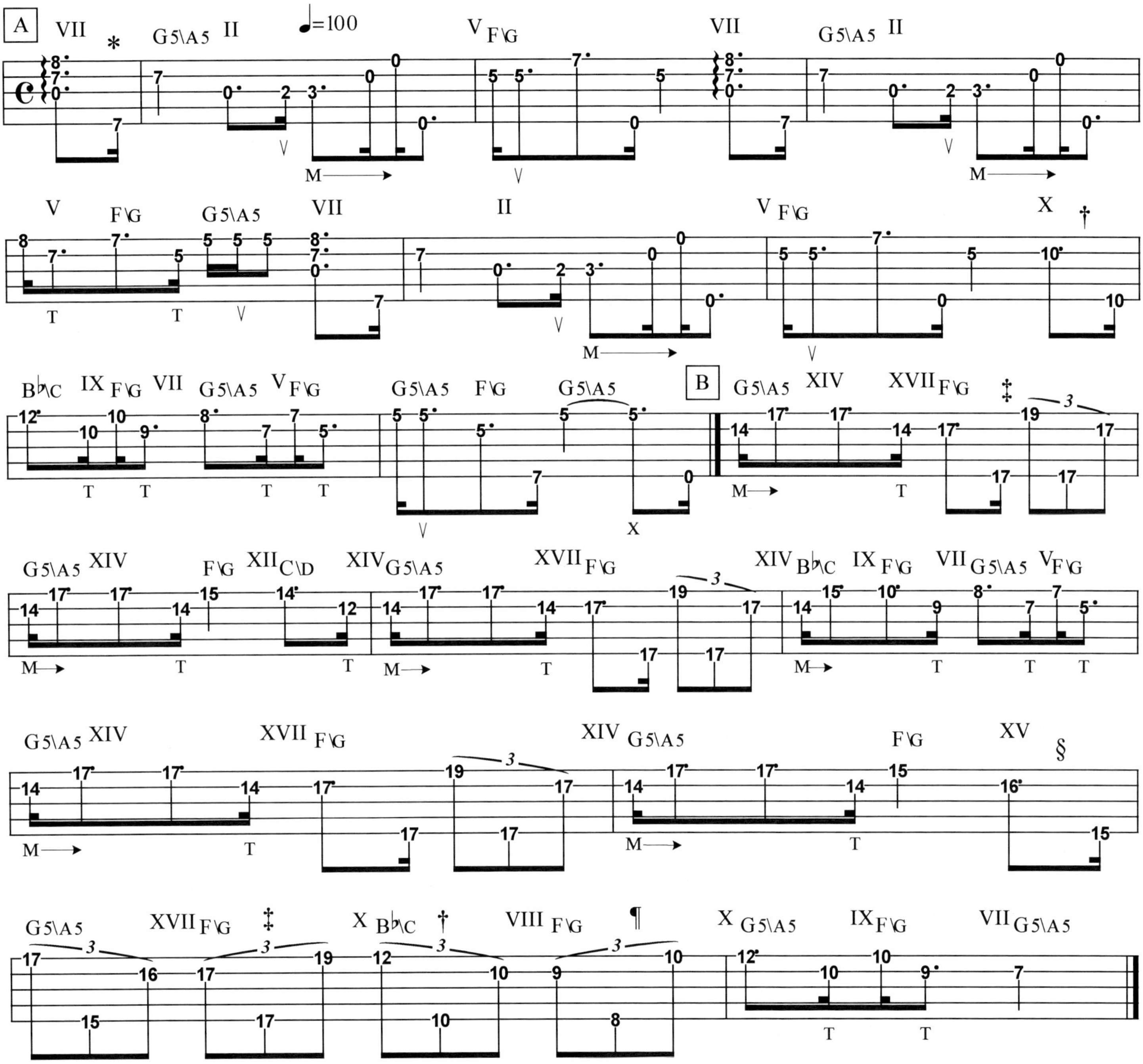

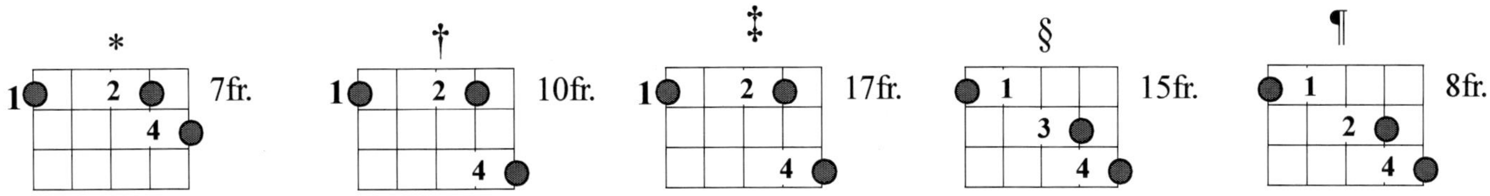

For *Miss Lyall Strathspey* Playing Tips, See Page 173

167

Killiecrankie

Air, or Slow March

Origin: See Intro
Source: George MacPhee
Appears on: *Devil in the Kitchen*

Key: C
Mode: Major
Tuning: gCGCD

The title references the Battle of Killiecrankie (pronounced: kill-ee-CRAN-kee); in 1689 Catholic Highlanders supporting King James II of England soundly defeated a force of Protestant Scots in favor of placing William of Orange on the throne. Although the tune is generally characterized as an air and almost all published collections have the tune in the key of D, fiddlers on Cape Breton and Prince Edward Island have developed a distinctive version in the more resonant key of C that is performed more like a slow march – with a rolling cut-time rhythm replete with dotted eighth-note pairs and Scotch snaps – an approach whose origin has been attributed to master fiddler Angus Chisholm. The melody first shows up in print . . .

Killiecrankie Intro continues, opposite page

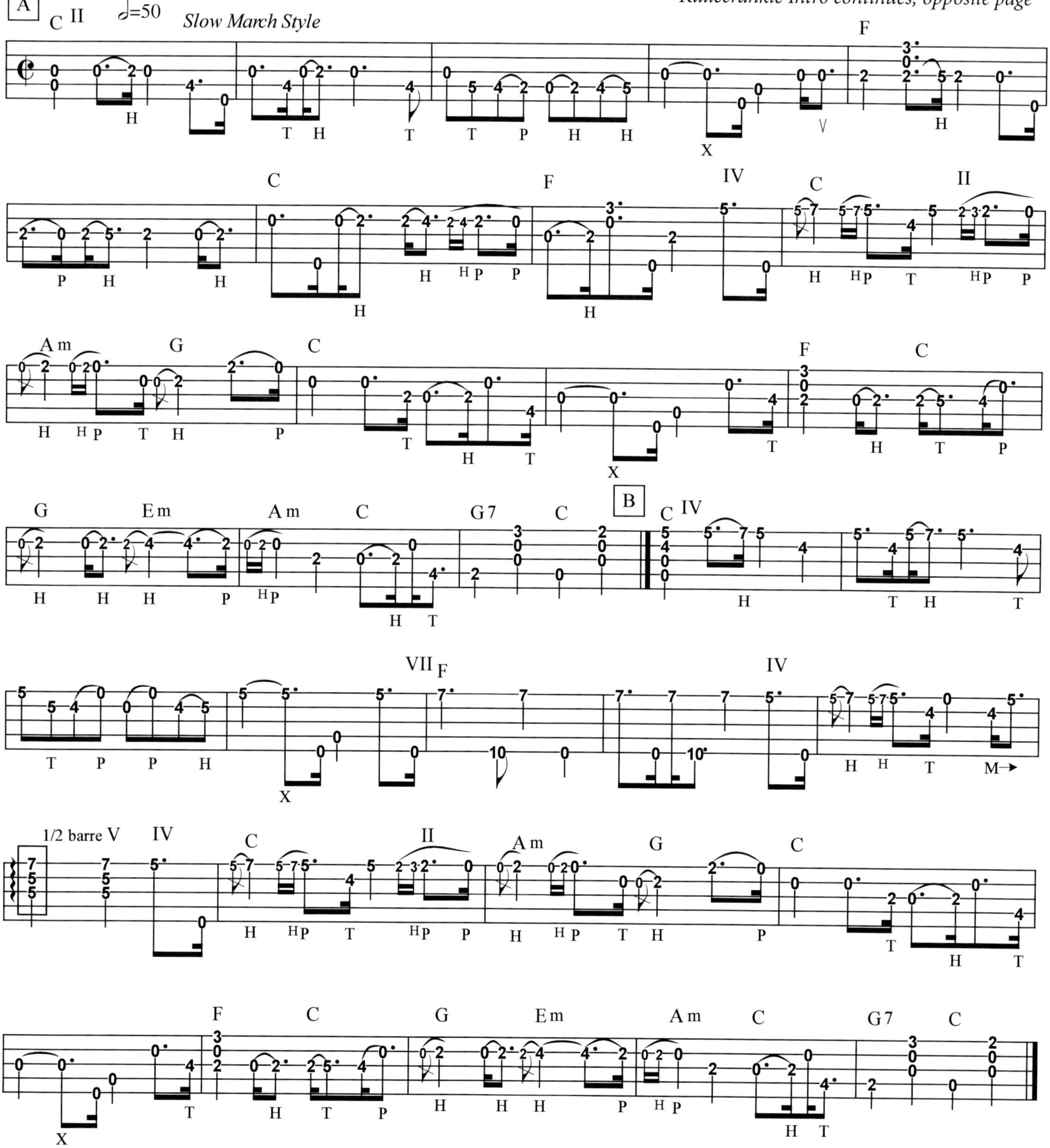

. . . as "Keele Cranke" in Henry Playford's *Collection of Original Scotch Tunes [. . .]* (1700); it then appears in several 18th- and 19th-century collections, notably James Oswald's, *The Caledonian Pocket Companion* (1743), *The Gow Collection,* and *Kerr's Merry Melodies* (each of these collections offers its own unique spelling of the tune name). Ireland has its own origin story for the melody, which is known there as "Planxty Davis" and attributed to blind harper Thomas O'Connellan of Sligo (d. 1698); it appears as "Planxty Davis" in both *O'Neill's Dance Music of Ireland* and *The Roche Collection.* Standard notation for my source version is in *Fiddle Music of P.E.I.*

Playing Tips for *Miss Lyall Strathspey* (tab on p. 171)

***Dual Chord Symbols:** Chord to left of backslash goes with open banjo; chord on right is for capoed banjo or fiddle*

- Part B, measure 1. At the end of beat 2, cut fret 14, string 2, short (1st finger). On beat 3, skip up the neck with the 2nd finger to grab fret 17, string 2; then use it as a pivot to swing the 1st and 4th fingers into place as shown in Diagram ‡.

- Part B, measures 6-7. At the end of measure 6, assume the shape in fifteenth position shown in Diagram §. In measure 7, the fingering shape and position on the neck changes with every beat. Follow the fingering indicated in the diagrams. The trick is to keep the 1st and 4th fingers on strings 5 and 1, respectively throughout and use them both to glide down the neck and act as pivots as you shift among shapes.

Playing Tips for *Miller o' Drone* (tab on p. 174)

***Dual Chord Symbols:** Chord to left of backslash goes with open banjo; chord on right is for capoed banjo or fiddle*

- Part A, measure 7. Coming out of the shape shown in Diagram †, the 2nd and 4th fingers should be at fret 10, string 2, and fret 12, string 1 respectively. At the end of beat 1, cut short both notes, and on beat 2 glide with those fingers directly down the same strings to frets 7 and 9. At the end of beat 2, cut short those last two notes and – on beat 3 – glide with the 4th finger down to fret 5 and use it as a pivot to swing the 1st finger into position on fret 3, string 2.

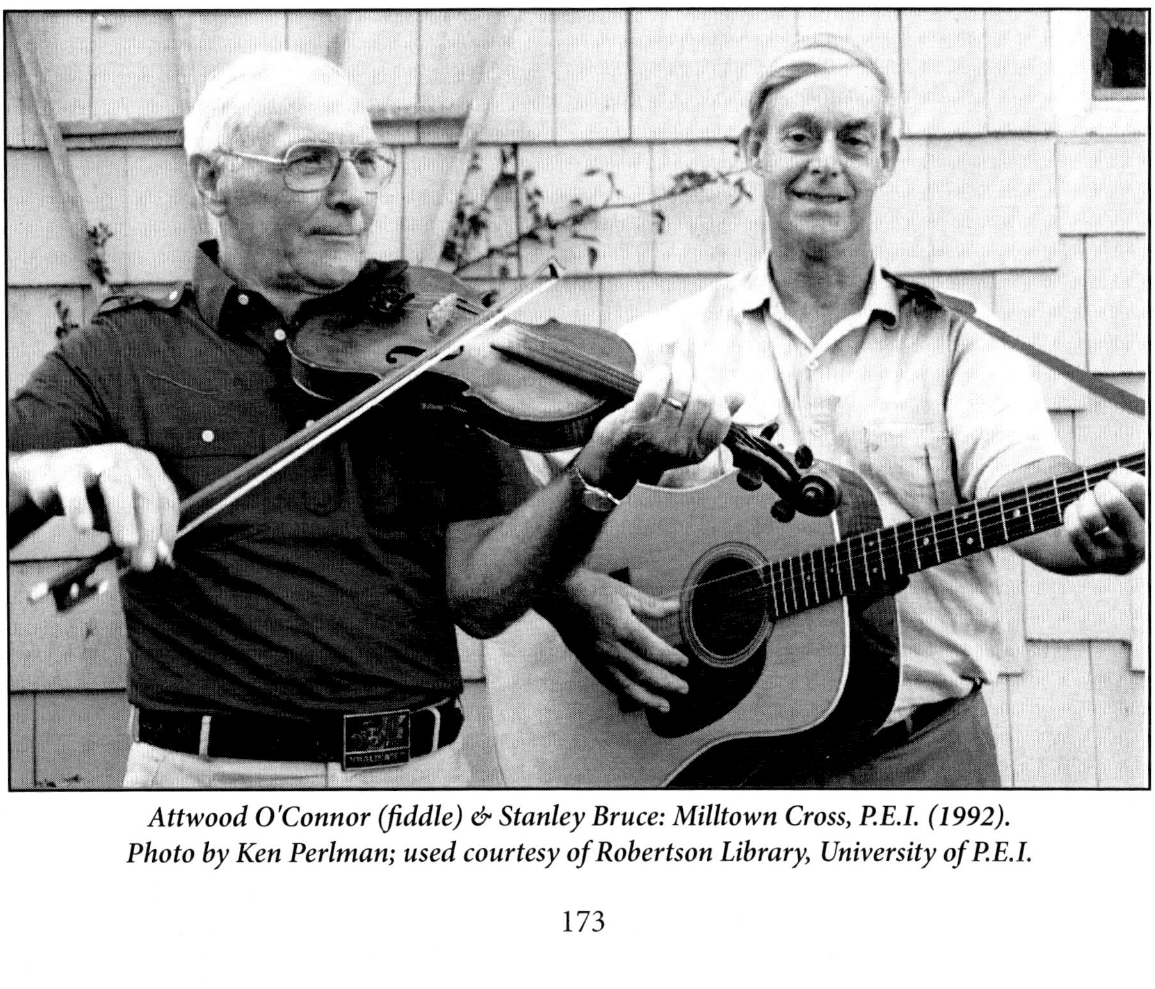

Attwood O'Connor (fiddle) & Stanley Bruce: Milltown Cross, P.E.I. (1992).
Photo by Ken Perlman; used courtesy of Robertson Library, University of P.E.I.

168

The Miller o' Drone

Strathspey

Composer: See Intro
Source: Boston Scottish Fiddle Club
Appears on: *Devil in the Kitchen*

Key: A (G on Banjo)
Mode: Major
Tuning: gDGBD (Capo-2)

Composer credit for this classic Scottish tune is disputed; the three likely candidates are Niel Gow (1727-1807); his son Nathaniel Gow (1763-1831); and John Pringle (b. 1770). It appears in numerous 19th- and early 20th-century Scottish compendiums, including *The Gow Repository, Lowe's Collection, Kerr's Merry Melodies, The Athole Collection,* and James Scott Skinner's *Harp & Claymore*. It has spawned two important variants: the strathspey, "Christy Campbell," – one of the tunes once played on P.E.I. to accompany the Wedding Reel dance (see. p. 94) – and the well-known American tune, "Grey Eagle." Cape Breton fiddler Dan J. Campbell recorded "The Miller o' Drone" on a 78 rpm disk in 1935.

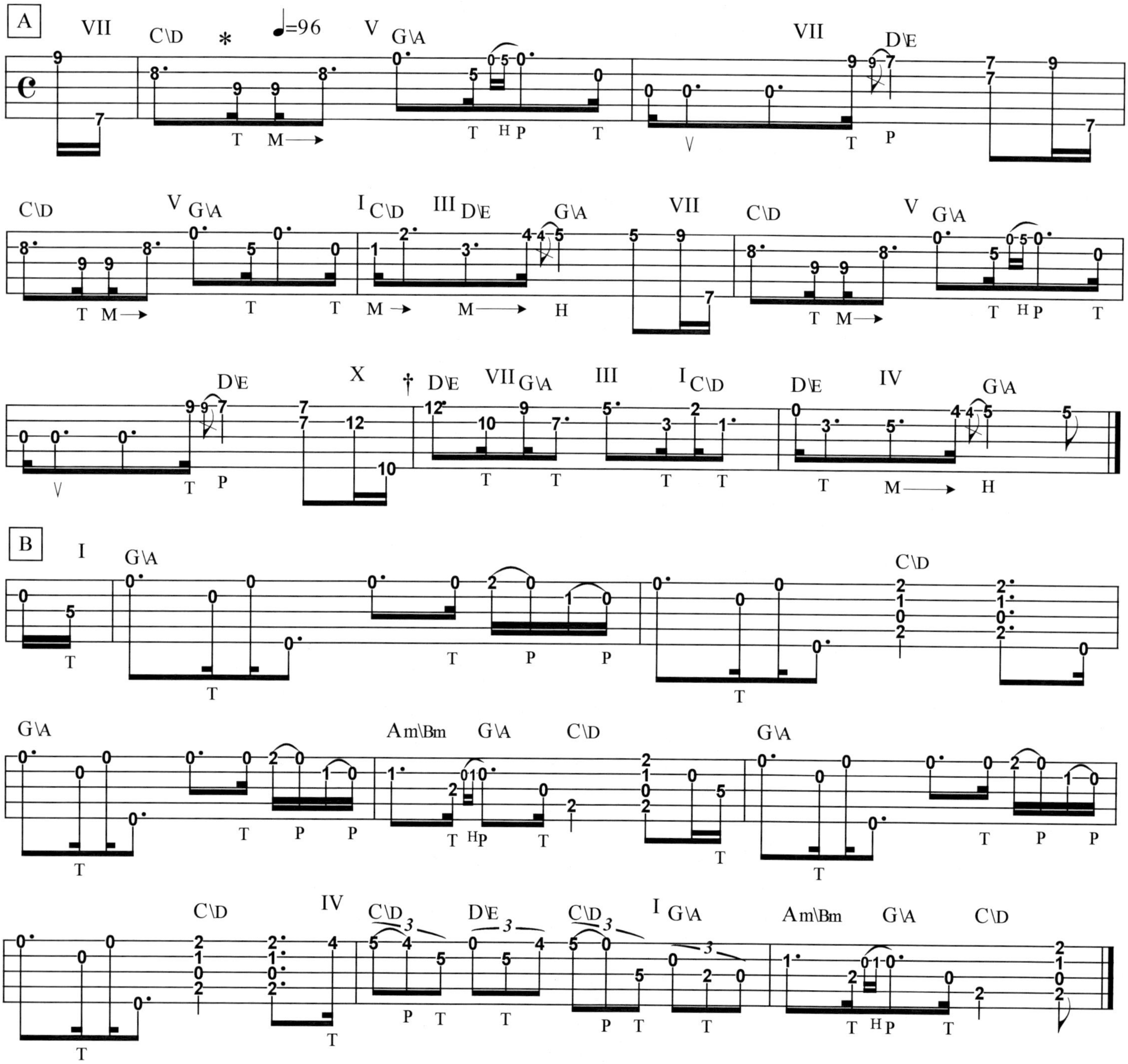

For *Miller o' Drone* Playing Tips, See Page 173

169

Mr. Murray

Strathspey

Composer: William Martin
Source: Elmer Robinson
Appears on: *Frails & Frolics*

Key: A (G on Banjo)
Mode: Major
Tuning: gDGBD (capo-2)

Mr. Murray appears in *The Skye Collection,* which attributes it to Martin. Cape Breton master fiddler Angus Chisholm recorded it on a 78 rpm disk in 1936. I had to take the B Part up an octave for it to fit on banjo. Standard notation for my source version is in *Fiddle Music of P.E.I.*

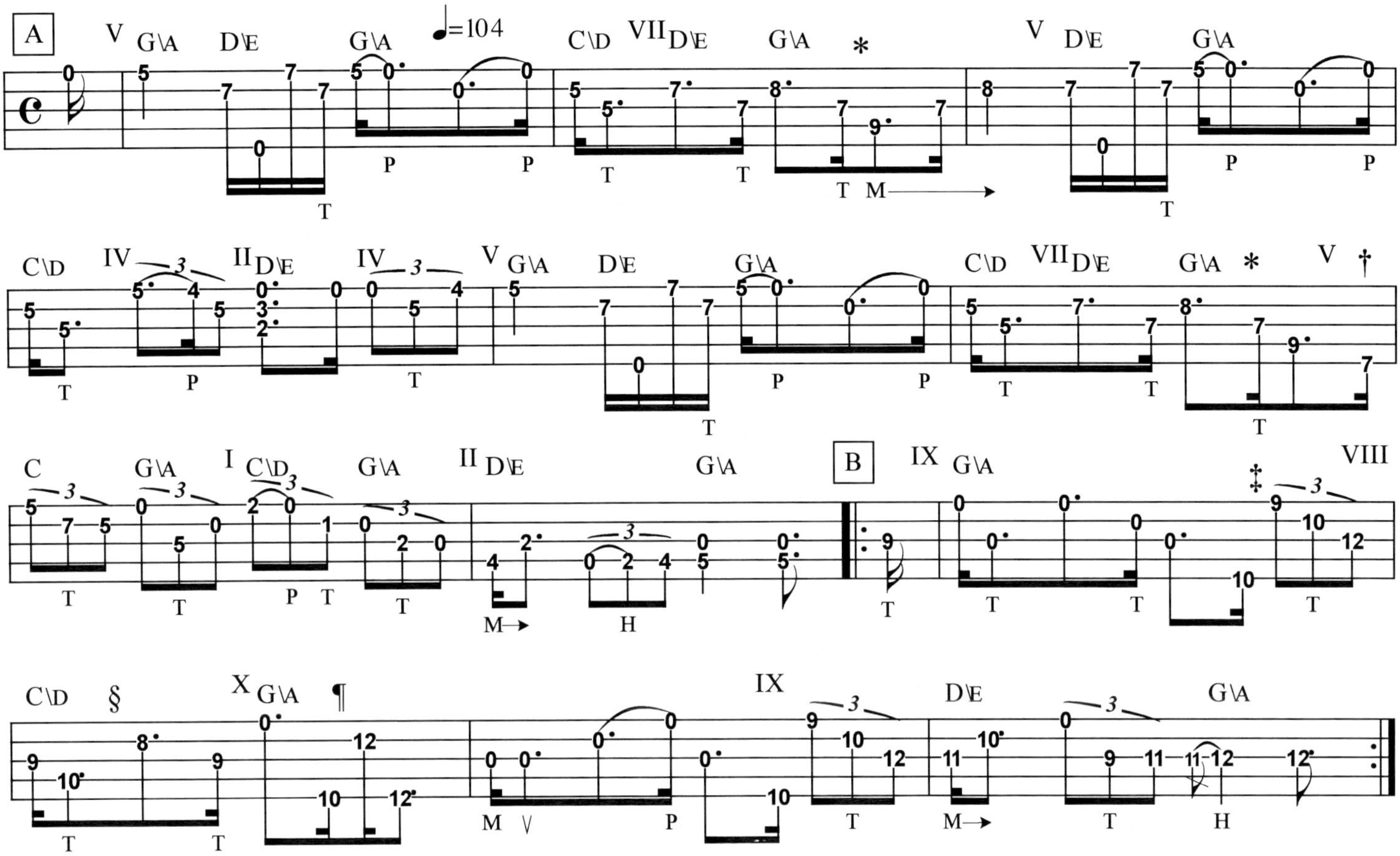

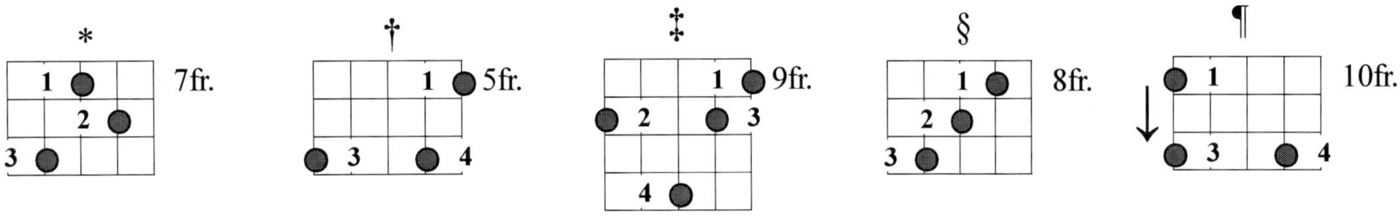

Playing Tips for *Mr. Murray*

***Dual Chord Symbols:** Chord to left of backslash goes with open banjo; chord on right is for capoed banjo or fiddle*

- Part A, measure 6-7. Halfway through beat 4 of measure 6, cut fret 9, string 4 short (3rd finger, see Diagram *), and skip down with that same finger to stop fret 7, string 5. Then use the 3rd finger as a pivot to swing the 1st and 4th fingers into place as shown in Diagram †.

- Part B, measure 1. Halfway through beat 3, stop fret 10, string 5 with the 2nd finger and use it as a pivot to swing the other three fingers into position as shown in Diagram ‡.

- Part B, measure 2. Halfway through beat 3, stop fret 10, string 5 with the 1st finger. Then on beat 4, use that finger as a pivot to swing the 3rd and 4th fingers into position on fret 12 as shown in Diagram ¶. Note: as soon as the 3rd finger reaches fret 12, string 5, you can release fret 10.

Appendix A. Ken Perlman's CD Playlists & Credits

KEY
* = Title updated or corrected in this book
† = Tab appears only in *Everything Clawhammer*
‡ = Tab appears only in *Appalachian Fiddle Tunes for Clawhammer*
§ = Could not locate copyright owner
¶ = Tab not yet published

Devil in the Kitchen

PLAYLIST

1. Professor Blackie (guitar solo)
2. The Bay of Fundy†
3. The Bee's Wing / President Garfield's Hornpipe†
4. Farewell to Killikrankie* /Archie Menzies / The Haggis
5. The Miller of Drone* / Big John MacNeil
6. Cape Breton Johnny Cope* / Miss Lyle* / The Black Mill†
7. MacNab's Hornpipe† / The Plains of Boyle
8. Da Slockit Light / The Smith's a Jolly Fireman / The Bride's Reel (guitar solo)
9. Rakish Paddy†
10. Stella's Trip to Kamloops / Devil in the Kitchen / The High Reel†
11. You Married My Daughter & Yet You Didn't
12. Glencoe March / Lord Gordon
13. The Stool of Repentance / Come Under My Plaidie
14. Munlochy Bridge / Heather on the Hill† / Sheehan's Reel† / Farmer's Reel
15. Coilesfield House / Traditional Strathspey (guitar solo)

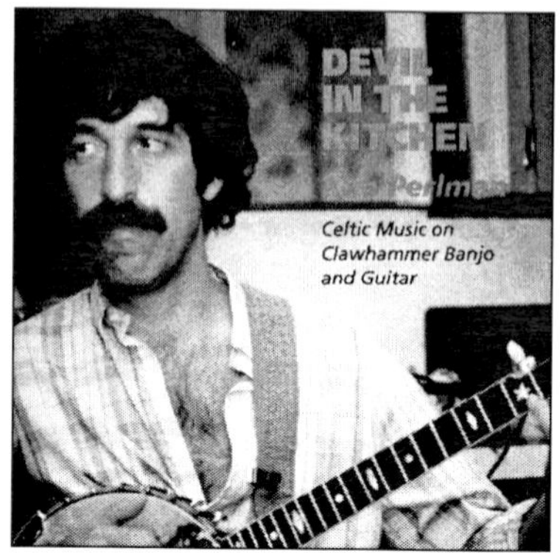

CREDITS
Label: *Marimac*
Date Released: *1993*
Where Recorded: *Crown Point, Indiana*
Recording Engineer: *Larry MacBride*
Accompanist: *Fred Campeau (guitar)*

Island Boy

PLAYLIST

1. Lord MacDonald's Reel / The Princess Reel
2. Miss Maxwell / Miss Gordon / Robert Stubbert
3. The Brae Reel / The Miramichi Fire
4. Belfast Jig / Inverness Jig / Bear River Jig
5. Glenfiddich Strathspey / Homeward Bound (guitar solo)
6. Northside Tune / Over the Briny Ocean†
7. Captain Campbell / The Cape Breton Wedding Reel / Andrew Renwick's Ferret*
8. Upper Denton Hornpipe† / Fiddlin' Phil†
9. Niel Gow's Fiddle / Scourdiness (guitar solo)
10. The Duke of Gordon's Birthday / The Dragger's Reel / The Green Meadow Reel / Paddy on the Turnpike
11. Irishman's Heart to the Ladies / River Bend Jig
12. Rothiemurchus Rant / The Bonny Lass of Fisherrow / Koehler's Hornpipe
13. Joe Kearney's Reel / Darlin' Don't You Meddle Me / Fermoy Lasses
14. Space Available§ / The Dismissal† / Dublin Porter
15. Bishop MacDonald / Glengarry's Dirk / The Bird's Nest (guitar solo)
16. Island Boy / St. Anne's Reel

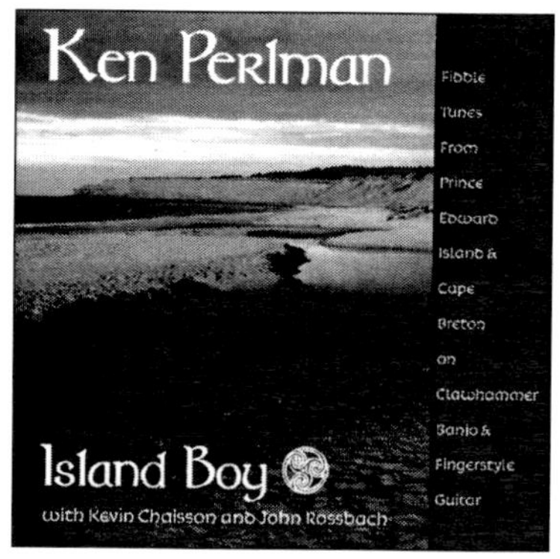

CREDITS
Label: *Wizmak*
Date Released: *1996*
Where Recorded: *Wingdale, New York*
Recording Engineer: *Tom White*
Production Assistance: *John Rossbach, Eric Kilburn, & Pete Sutherland*
Mastering Studio: *9 West Mastering*
Accompanists: *Kevin Chaisson (piano) & John Rossbach (guitar)*

Northern Banjo

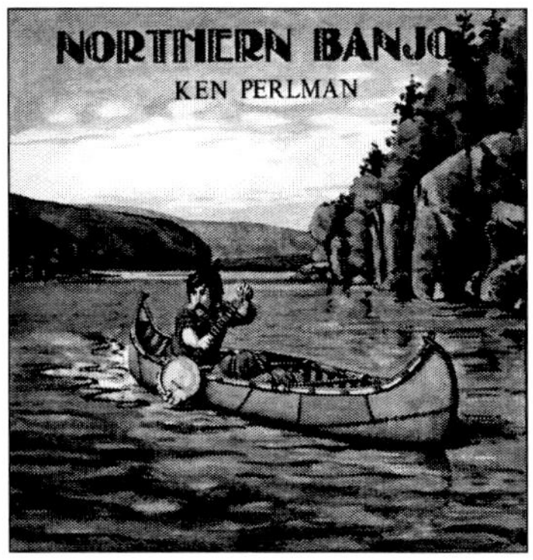

PLAYLIST

1. The Poppy Leaf / Stack of Barley / The East Neuk of Bear River
2. Rock Valley Jig / Light & Airy / The Munster Lass
3. The Banks Hornpipe / The Democratic Rage / Miss Johnson of Pittworth†
4. Robert Cormack, Aberdeen / Compliments to Buddy MacMaster / Fisher's Hornpipe
5. Kenmure's Awa' */ Wilfred's Fiddle / Jackson's Jig
6. Road to Mexico†
7. Niel Gow's Lament for His Second Wife (guitar solo)
8. Lord MacDonald's Reel / The Princess Reel / The Honeymoon
9. The Braes of Auchtertyre / Caber Feidh
10. Lament for James Moray, Abercarney / Dunie Mains / The Chaisson Reel (guitar solo)
11. Shandon Bells / The Orange and Blue / Chorus Jig
12. Stella's Trip to Kamloops / The Iron Man / Angus Campbell / Dillon Brown / Big John MacNeil*
13. The Sweetness of Mary / Mason's Apron (guitar solo)
14. Georgina Campbell* / Little Jack's Reel / Levantine's Barrel

CREDITS

Label: *Copper Creek*
Date Released: *2001*
Where Recorded: *Stratford, Ontario*
Recording Engineer: *Paul Benedict*
Mastering: *Charlie Pilzer, Airshow Studio*
Cover Painting: *John Gould*
Accompanists:
Ken Brown (guitar); Ben Grossman (percussion); Sandy MacIntyre (fiddle); Pat O'Gorman (uillean pipes); Loreto Reed (flute & whistle); John Rossbach (guitar & mandolin); Oliver Schoerer (fiddle); James Stephens (fiddle); Brian Taheny (Irish bouzouki, dobro, & fiddle); David Woodhead (bass)

Frails & Frolics

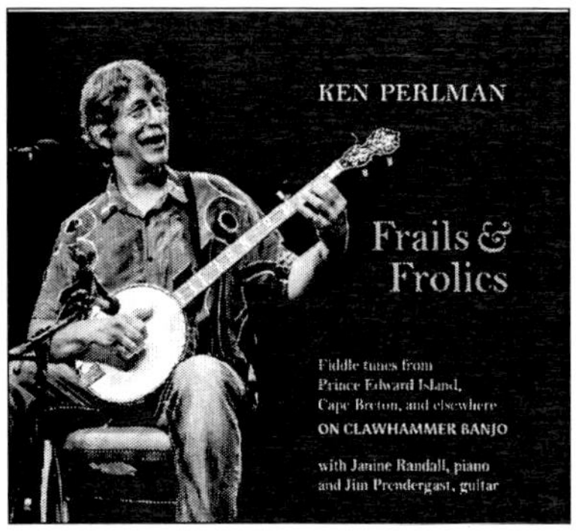

PLAYLIST

1. Londonderry Hornpipe / Jenny Dang the Weaver / Sleepy Maggie
2. Dr. Keith Strathspey / Miss Barker's Hornpipe / Carney's Canter*
3. Omer Cheverie's Jig* / Fig for a Kiss / Hector MacDonald's Jig*
4. Pride of the Ball / MacKinnon's Rant / Lasses of Glenaladale / St. Kilda Wedding
5. Bonniest Lass in A' the World / Emil Gaudet's Reel / Cheticamp Reel
6. Dallas Rag ¶
7. The North Side of the Grampians / Jack Webster's Reel / Souris Breakwater
8. Rose of Tennessee / Don't Be Teasing / Whiskey Jig
9. Carlton County Breakdown* / Miller's Reel / Trip to Windsor
10. Where the North River Flows
11. The Marchioness of Tullibardine / Dinky's Reel* / Little Donald in the Pigpen
12. Hector's New Dance Hall / Hector's Fancy / Durang's Hornpipe
13. Fred Wilson's Hornpipe / High Level Hornpipe
14. Ottawa Valley Reel / Lad O'beirne's / Marie à Pierre
15. The Bonny Lea Rig / Shores of Loughgowna* / Teviot Bridge
16. Tennessee Mountain Fox Chase‡
17. George V's Army† / Mr. Murray Strathspey / The Marquis of Huntley* / Prince Edward Island Wedding Reel

CREDITS

Label: *Redbud*
Date Released: *2017*
Where Recorded: *Mill Pond Studio, (Portsmouth, New Hampshire)*
Recording Engineer: *Jim Prendergast*
Accompanists: *Jim Prendergast (guitar) & Janine Randall (piano)*

Appendix B. Fiddlers' Hall of Fame

* **Eddy Arsenault** (b. 1921-2014; pronounced "AR-se-noe"). From St. Chrysostome in Prince County, P.E.I. Arsenault was the most influential fiddler for decades in the Evangeline Coast region. His playing represented a lively blend of the soaring Cape Breton sound and the syncopated rhythms of Acadian fiddling.

* **Edward P. Arsenault** (b. 1938). Also from the St. Chrysostome area, Arsenault took up the fiddle at the instigation of his wife Marie when he was 32 years old. He ultimately became a sought-after dance fiddler with a lively Acadian style of playing. Also a prolific composer, his tune, "The Acadian Reel" is known all across P.E.I.

* **Louise Gallant Arsenault** (b. 1956). From the Mont Carmel area of Prince County, P.E.I. Arsenault grew up in a large musical family. Fiddling females were a curiosity on P.E.I. during her childhood and her talents were much in demand for community events. In the 1990s she joined the ensemble Barachois, which toured widely on the world folk-festival circuit.

* **Sidney Baglole** (1912-97; pronounced "BAG-lole"). Originally from Southwest Lot 16 in Prince County, P.E.I. Baglole started fiddling at 9 and learned by listening to fiddlers in his family and community. An active dance fiddler for most of his life, he was known both for his powerful, highly rhythmic style and for his treasure trove of old Island tunes.

* **Sterling Baker** (1945-). From the Montague area in Kings County, P.E.I. Baker learned his first tunes from local fiddlers while growing up. He started out as a guitarist and did not take up the fiddle until his mid-twenties. An exceptionally clean and tasteful player, in the late 1980s he became one of the first Island fiddlers to play regularly at commercial "ceilidhs."

* **Wilfred Bernard** (1919-96). From Souris Line Road in Kings County, P.E.I. Bernard started fiddling at about age 10 and learned his tunes both from local fiddlers and from fiddlers on radio such as Lem Jay and Don Messer. His playing was also influenced by recordings of early American country music, to which he was exposed via Canadian radio.

* **The Bear River Chaissons.** The Chaisson (pronounced CHAY-son) family of Bear River in northeastern Kings County, P.E.I. is working on at least its fifth generation of fiddle players. From the 1950s through the 1990s, they were generally acknowledged to be the prime exponents of Cape Breton style fiddling on P.E.I. They were also instrumental in founding both the P.E.I. Fiddlers' Society and the Rollo Bay Scottish Fiddle Festival.

> * **Kenny Chaisson** (b. 1947) has an elaborate yet powerful style and a vast repertoire of tunes. He is also a prolific composer, and some of his tunes have become local standards.
>
> * **Kevin Chaisson** (b. 1950) resisted family pressure to take up the fiddle during his youth and turned to the piano instead, becoming perhaps the strongest and most-in-demand piano accompanist for fiddle music on the Island. In recent years he has become an avid composer; many of his tunes are now widely played on both P.E.I. and Cape Breton.
>
> * **"Young Peter" Chaisson** (1941-2015). A strong player with a stately, ornate, and sensitive style, he had a full grasp of both the Scottish/Cape Breton and older P.E.I. repertoires. He dedicated his last few decades to running a free weekly fiddling school for would-be musicians from his region.
>
> * **"Old Peter" Chaisson** (1929-2010) was a frequent prize winner at local fiddle contests in his youth. His style and repertoire were strongly influenced by Cape Breton players but his intensely lyrical approach to the tunes showed the more rolling bowing attack of the older generation of P.E.I. fiddlers.

* **Johnny Joe Chaisson** (1918-97) came from a prominent fiddling family from Souris (SOO-ree) in northeastern Kings County, P.E.I. He took up the fiddle at about 12 years of age and played extensively for local dances through the 1970s. An "Island fiddler" of the old school, he played the Cape Breton repertoire only sparingly.

***John Campbell** (1929-2010). Campbell grew up in Glenora Falls, NS but lived much of his adult life in Watertown, Mass. A powerful fiddler with a prodigious repertoire, for many years he was a mainstay of the Boston area Cape Breton emigrée community. He recorded a number of LPs for Rounder Records, including *Cape Breton Violin Music* (1976).

* **Omer Cheverie** (1925-2019); pronounced "SHEH-veh-ree"). From the Souris area in Kings County, P.E.I. Cheverie took up the fiddle at age 11, and by 13 he was playing for dances. Although his playing and repertoire was strongly influenced by the Cape Breton sound, it still had plenty of local flavor. He was said to have had thousands of tunes in his memory banks.

* **Angus Chisholm** (1908-79). Chisholm grew up in Margaree Forks, NS but spent much of his adult life in the Boston area. In the 1930s, he recorded numerous 78s for the Celtic label that would become classics in their field and help establish Cape Breton fiddling as a distinct idiom. A frequent visitor to P.E.I., he was often hosted by the Webster family of Cardigan.

* **Joe Cormier** (1927-2016). Originally from Cheticamp, NS Cormier moved to Waltham, Mass. and became a musical mainstay of the local Cape Breton emigrée community. In the late 1940s, he performed regularly at dances in Sydney with Winston "Scotty" Fitzgerald. In 1974 he recorded the LP, *Scottish Violin Music from Cape Breton Island* (Rounder Records).

* **Victor Doucette** (1954- ; pronounced "doo-SETT"). From Harper Road in western Prince County, P.E.I. Doucette is the son of noted West Prince fiddler Joseph Doucette. He took up the fiddle at age 9 but got away from it as a teenager; he returned to the violin in the late 1970s and ultimately developed a powerful, highly rhythmic voice on the instrument.

* **Winston "Scotty" Fitzgerald** (1914-88). Originally from White Point, NS Fitzgerald started fiddling at 8, gradually improved his skills and by the time he was a young adult he was playing extensively for dances and on the radio. When he got out of the Canadian Army in the late 1940s, he took the Sydney dance scene by storm and began creating a series of highly influential recordings. In 1953, he was the first Canadian fiddler to record an LP. He is noted in particular for "mining" repertoire from not-specifically-Scottish tunebooks such as *Ryan's Mammoth Collection.*

* **David Gaudet** (1952-; pronounced "Goody"). From Harper Road in western Prince County, P.E.I. Gaudet grew up in a fiddling family and learned much of his style and repertoire from his uncle Emil Gaudet. A vigorous player with an authentic Acadian sound, his large repertoire includes many tunes that have fallen out of local circulation.

* **Niel Gow** (1727-1807). From Perthshire, Scotland Gow was the most famous Highland fiddler of his day. A frequent recipient of largess from the Dukes of Atholl, he was a prolific composer and publisher of fiddle tunes. He would publish *The Gow Collection*; his son Nathaniel (1763-1831) published *The Gow Repository* and many other fiddle-tune compendiums.

* **Jerry Holland** (1955-2009). Holland grew up in Brockton, Mass.; at a very young age he fell in love with Cape Breton music, developed a reputation as a child prodigy, and at about the age of 20 relocated to Cape Breton – eventually becoming one of the style's best-known players and most prolific composers.

* **Lem Jay** (1880-1960) of Fanningbrook near Mt. Stewart in northeastern Queens County, P.E.I. had the distinction of being the first fiddler to ever play on local radio; from 1925-31 he had his own radio show on station CFCY, Charlottetown. From 1932-58, he conducted annual New Year's Eve broadcasts on CFCY that featured his fiddling.

* **Roland Jay** (1906-98). From Mt. Stewart in north-central Queens County, P.E.I. Jay accompanied his father Lem on piano during his famous New Year's Eve broadcasts. He started fiddling at age 7.

* **Andrew Jones** (1918-?) From Pleasant View in western Prince County, P.E.I. Jones learned to play fiddle at about 12 and was soon playing for local dances. He learned his tunes both from local fiddlers and from fiddle broadcasts emanating from Cape Breton, New Brunswick, and Québec. His highly syncopated bowing style was heavily influenced by Acadian fiddling.

* **Joe Kearney** (1914-1993; pronounced "KAR-nee"). From Sturgeon in southeastern Kings County, P.E.I. Kearney took up the fiddle at age 8 and was soon playing for dances. His tunes came from local fiddlers; he had a powerful bowing arm and was still fiddling vigorously when we recorded him in mid-1992.

* **Ludger LeFort** (c. 1935-). Originally from Cheticamp, NS LeFort moved to Waltham, Mass. and became a musical mainstay of the local Cape Breton emigrée community. He was extremely helpful to me as I began exploring the Cape Breton tradition, and for several years we met regularly for music sessions at his home.

* **Gus Longaphie** (1914-2000; pronounced "LON-ga-fee"). From the Souris area of Kings County, P.E.I. Longaphie started playing fiddle at 8 and was playing at dances by his mid-teens. He started out on local tunes, but switched over to Cape Breton material through the influence of the Bear River Chaissons; he was an extremely vigorous player with a large repertoire.

* **Hector MacAndrew** (1903-1980). From Aberdeenshire, MacAndrew was considered by many to be the foremost Scottish fiddler of the second half of the 20th century. He devoted himself in particular to playing plaintive airs and highly ornamented, dramatic strathspeys; he never considered himself a dance player.

* **Allan MacDonald** (b. 1950) From Bangor in Kings County, P.E.I. MacDonald comes from a prominent fiddling family. His father Hector MacDonald was one of the best-known players of his time. By the time he was 20, Allan and his father were playing regularly for dances at a hall they built on their own property. His son, Ward also became an important local player.

* **Dan R. MacDonald** (1911-76). From South Judique, NS Dan R. released his first recording in 1939. He helped greatly expand the Cape Breton repertoire via two routes: he served as a conduit for older Scottish tunes into the repertoire via his collection of classic Scottish tune books; and he became one of the most prolific composers in the Cape Breton idiom.

* **Francis MacDonald** (b. 1940) From Bangor in Kings County, P.E.I. MacDonald comes from a long line of fiddlers on

both sides of his family. In fact, family lore has it that his fiddling ancestors were on the very first boatload of settlers that landed in Tracadie Bay in the 1790s. For many years he played for a weekly square dance in the village of Tracadie.

* **Hector MacDonald** (c. 1910-82). Hector MacDonald of Bangor in Kings County, P.E.I. was a major fiddler in his region from the 1920s through much of the 1970s. In the 1960s, he and his son Allan built a dance hall on their property that served as a major community gathering place.

* **Hilda MacPhee MacDonald** (1904-2005). Born in Selkirk in northeastern Kings County, P.E.I. MacDonald came from a large fiddling family. Although she was an accomplished player in her youth, she felt that negative community attitudes about female fiddlers kept her from fully developing her art. Fiddler George MacPhee of Monticello is her nephew.

* **Paul MacDonald** (b. 1974). From Charlottetown, P.E.I. MacDonald played only classical violin until age 12, when he was inspired by the Bear River Chaissons to take up fiddling in the Cape Breton style. He quickly became one of the best young players in the Maritimes. He would later move out of the province and put fiddling on the back burner.

* **Ward MacDonald** (b. 1978). From Bangor in Kings County, P.E.I. MacDonald comes from a prominent fiddling family. His father is Allan MacDonald; his grandfathers were Hector MacDonald and another local fiddler, Ward Crane. He has served as head of the Queens County branch of the P.E.I. Fiddlers Society; he also helped organize the Festival of Small Halls.

* **Carl MacKenzie** (1938-2018). From Sydney Forks, NS MacKenzie started playing fiddle at age 9. By the 1970s he was playing for dances all across Cape Breton; he would ultimately record ten LPs, including *Welcome to Your Feet Again* (1977); he would also become a frequent presence at folk festivals and music camps throughout North America.

* **Hugh A. "Buddy" MacMaster** (1924-2014). From the Judique area of Nova Scotia, MacMaster frequently toured to Boston and Toronto; he also became a great favorite at North American folk festivals and music camps. He was renowned as a great dance player with a vast repertoire. His first LP, issued in 1989, was *Judique on the Floor.*

***George MacPhee** (b. 1941) From Monticello in Kings County, P.E.I. MacPhee comes from a long line of fiddlers. He is a strong, elaborate player whose tune versions often show highly original "twists." He was a great friend to our collecting project, and arranged for us to rent a family-owned farmhouse to serve as our headquarters.

* **Leonard McDonald** (1933-?). From Emyvale in Queens County, P.E.I. McDonald started fiddling at age 11. He learned his first tunes from the "jigging" (lilting) of his mother, then fleshed out his repertoire with tunes from local fiddlers and via radio broadcasts by Don Messer and others. He was a very active dance player in his region through the early 1980s.

* **Don Messer** (1909-73). Messer grew up in a musical family in New Brunswick. In 1939, he was hired by CFCY, Charlottetown to create the fiddle-based ensemble, Don Messer & His Islanders. He would dominate fiddle broadcasting on P.E.I. and throughout much of Canada for decades – both on radio, and later via the *Don Messer's Jubilee* television show.

* **Johnny Morrissey** (1913-1994). From Vernon River in southeastern Queens County, P.E.I. Morrissey first heard fiddling at the house of a neighbor: "I'd be walking up to me grandfather's and I'd be passing the house and I'd hear the violin going. I'd just stand out in the yard and listen to the music. It sounded good to me. So that's how I got to be interested in the violin."

* **Attwood O'Connor** (1923-2009). From Milltown Cross in southeastern Kings County, P.E.I. O'Connor came from a large fiddling family. He started fiddling at 7 and began playing for dances in his early teens. In the early 1990s when I first met him, his lively style was still very much in demand at area benefits and celebrations.

* **Elmer Robinson** (1910-2000). From Woodstock in Prince County, P.E.I. Robinson started out on pump organ and piano and didn't take up the fiddle in a serious way until his mid-20s. He developed a very lively style of bowing that owed much to the influence of his Acadian neighbors.

* **James Scott Skinner** (1843-1927). From Aberdeenshire, Scotland Skinner made his living as both dancing master and fiddler. He was a prolific composer and publisher and was among the very first "folk" or "ethnic" fiddlers to record – first on Edison cylinders and later on 78 rpm disks. Both his tune collections and recordings have been extremely influential among several successive generations of Scottish and Cape Breton musicians.

* **Reuben Smith** (1931-2006). From Blooming Point in northeastern Queens County, P.E.I. Smith started fiddling at 12 and was playing for dances by the age of 18. He played a mixture of P.E.I. and Cape Breton tunes in a powerful, straight-ahead style. For many years, he played for weekly square dances in the northeastern Queens County village of Tracadie.

* **Ervan Sonier** (1920-94; pronounced "SONE-yay"). From Summerside in Prince County, P.E.I. Sonier was perhaps the last of a long line of fiddling barbers on the Island. He grew up in a musical family and learned to play by watching the fiddlers

who came to visit his grandfather. He was an influential member of the Prince County Fiddlers' Association.

* **Archie Stewart** (1917-2003). From Milltown Cross in southeastern Kings County, P.E.I. Stewart came from a fiddling family. He started playing as soon as he "could reach the fingerboard," learned his tunes mostly from local fiddlers, and was playing for dances by the age of 12. To me, Archie will always be "the fiddling sage"; he spent a lifetime asking other fiddlers how and why they did things; and he remembered it all!

* **Brenda Stubbert** (b. 1959). From Point Aconi, NS Stubbert grew up in a musical family; her father Robert was renowned in the Cape Breton tradition as an exponent of Irish music; she was one of the few females of her generation to pursue a fiddling career. She recorded seven cassettes and CDs between 1982 and 2011.

* **Stephen Toole** (1927-95). From Green Road in Queens County, P.E.I. Toole came from a fiddling family. He started playing at 10 and was playing for dances at 14. For many years he played at a weekly square dance in Charlottetown. He maintained a wide repertoire, and his playing was replete with understated double stops and sophisticated bowing.

* **Jack Webster** (c. 1900-1975). From Cardigan in southeastern Kings County, P.E.I. Webster was perhaps the most in-demand dance fiddler in his region during his lifetime; it was said that Jack's playing "would lift your feet right off the floor." Well-known Cape Breton fiddler Angus Chisholm often sojourned with Webster's family during his visits to P.E.I.

* **Carl Webster** (1938-2008) & **Jackie Webster** (1932-2013). From Cardigan in Kings County, P.E.I. these sons of Jack Webster played both local and Cape Breton tunes in a lively, "straight-ahead" manner.

* **Elliot Wight** (1935-2013). Originally from Flat River in southeastern Queens County, P.E.I. Wight started playing for dances at 15. He learned his tunes from local fiddlers and also from Don Messer on radio. Later in life he moved to North River near Charlottetown; for many years, he played at a weekly square dance in the Charlottetown area.

Appendix C. About the Companion Audio Selections (& CD Back Stories)

Most of the Audio selections are excerpted from the four CDs described in Appendix A – *Devil in the Kitchen, Island Boy, Northern Banjo,* and *Frails & Frolics*. I felt that it was better to offer heartfelt, up-to-speed treatments of the banjo settings presented here, instead of the moderate-tempo teacherly illustrations that usually go along with instruction books. If you need or prefer a slower version, extremely helpful technology now exists for just such a purpose (I particularly recommend the software known as *Amazing Slowdowner*). Audio illustrations for all music examples and exercises – and for the 20 tunes that did not appear on these four CDs – were recorded at home via a Marantz 16-bit dedicated digital recorder. These 20 tunes were ably accompanied on guitar by Ruth Rappaport of Watertown, Massachusets.

Many of the original fiddle recordings used as models for my banjo settings are available on *www.bowingdownhome.ca*, which is cross-referenced both by *Tunes* and *People.*

CD Back Stories

* ***Devil in the Kitchen*** **(1993).** Marimac proprietor Larry MacBride was renowned in the folk scene for his authentic recordings of roots and contemporary players; his studio was in the basement of his home in Crown Point, Indiana. He brought in guitarist Fred Campeau from the old-time string band, The Volo Bogtrotters to serve as accompanist; Fred quickly learned the chords for each piece on the spot and performed flawlessly. The recording was originally released just as a cassette; soon afterward, CD replication costs suddenly became affordable and it was also released as a CD.

* ***Island Boy*** **(1996).** Tom and Geri White had just started up a Mom & Pop recording company in upstate New York and set up a recording studio in their home. They agreed to fly piano player extraordinaire Kevin Chaisson down from P.E.I. to accompany me, and we recorded most of the banjo tracks in the course of a single weekend. Guitarist John Rossbach later enhanced the overall sound by overdubbing a second accompaniment part on his "Pre-War" Martin Dreadnoughts.

* ***Northern Banjo*** **(2001).** Around the turn of the last century, guitarist Ken Brown came up with the idea of creating a banjo-based ensemble that also involved some of the great acoustic musicians from the Toronto area. Ken and I laid down the basic tracks; all the other instrument combinations were then overdubbed. Putting this project together at Paul Benedict's studio in Stratford, Ontario often felt like creating a musical tapestry.

* ***Frails & Frolics*** **(2017).** This project represents my return to the Cape Breton and P.E.I. fiddle-tune repertoires after 15 years or so in which much of my musical focus was on the duo I had forged with old-time Appalachian-style fiddler, Alan Jabbour. I relied on two great Boston-area accompanists: guitarist Jim Prendergast (who doubled as sound engineer); and piano player Janine Randall. The recording and mixing processes were spread out over a couple of years.

Appendix D: Alphabetical Index of Tunes & Online Audio Playlist

AUDIO TRACKS SOURCES KEY:
* = from *Devil in the Kitchen*
† = from *Island Boy*
‡ = from *Northern Banjo*
§ = from *Frails & Frolics*
^ = recorded by Ken for this volume

Audio Playlist For Musical Examples & Illustrations

Some Alternative Titles

* = This title appeared on one of Ken's CD's but was later updated

Appendix E: Ken Perlman Bibliography & Discography

* In chronological order; starting with most recent *

Books

- *Appalachian Fiddle Tunes for Clawhammer Banjo* (Mel Bay)
- *Couldn't Have a Wedding Without the Fiddler: the Story of Traditional Fiddling on Prince Edward Island* (University of Tennessee Press; Charles Wolfe Series)
- *Everything You Wanted to Know About Clawhammer Banjo* (Mel Bay)
- *The Fiddle Music of P.E.I: Celtic and Acadian Tunes in Living Tradition* (Mel Bay)
- *Advanced Fingerstyle Guitar* (Centerstream; originally *More Fingerstyle Guitar)*
- *Clawhammer Style Banjo* (Centerstream Music)
- *Celtic & New England Fiddle Tunes for Clawhammer Banjo* (Mel Bay; originally *New England and Irish Fiddle Tunes for Clawhammer Banjo*)
- *Fingerstyle Guitar* (Centerstream Music)
- *Melodic Clawhammer Banjo* (Centerstream Music)
- *Fingerpicking Fiddle Tunes for Guitar* (Centerstream Music)

Video & Audio Instruction

- *Ken's Clawhammer Clinics* (video recordings of Ken's online series of banjo workshops)
- *Beginning Clawhammer Banjo / Intermediate Clawhammer Banjo* (Centerstream)
- *Clawhammer Style Banjo* (Centerstream; companion to the book)
- *Fingerstyle Guitar* (Centerstream Music; companion to the book)
- *Melodic Clawhammer Banjo* (Homespun Tapes; six CD audio series)

Recordings

- *Frails & Frolics* (Redbud)
- *You Can't Beat the Classics* (self-released; collaboration with Alan Jabbour & Jim Watson)
- *Southern Summits* (self-released; collaboration with Alan Jabbour)
- *Northern Banjo* (Copper Creek; re-released on Redbud)
- *Island Boy* (Wizmak; re-released on Redbud)
- *Devil in the Kitchen* (Marimac)
- *Live in the U.K.* (Halshaw)
- *Clawhammer Banjo & Fingerstyle Guitar Solos* (Folkways)
- *Melodic Clawhammer Banjo* (Kicking Mule Records; anthology)

Field Recording Anthologies Produced by Ken

- *The Prince Edward Island Style of Fiddling: Fiddlers of Western PEI* (Rounder)
- *The Prince Edward Island Style of Fiddling: Fiddlers of Eastern PEI* (Rounder)
- *The Fiddle Music of P.E.I* (Mel Bay; companion to the book)
- *The Old Time Fiddlers of Prince Edward Island* (Marimac)

Field Recording Website Curated by Ken

- *Bowing Down Home: www.bowingdownhome.ca* (University of Prince Edward Island; devoted to field recordings of traditional Prince Edward Island fiddlers)